REPORT

UPON

THE INVERTEBRATE ANIMALS

OF

VINEYARD SOUND AND ADJACENT WATERS,

WITH AN ACCOUNT OF

THE PHYSICAL FEATURES OF THE REGION.

BY

A. E. VERRILL and S. I. SMITH,

(SHEFFIELD SCIENTIFIC SCHOOL, NEW HAVEN, CONN.)

EXTRACTED FROM THE REPORT OF PROFESSOR S. F. BAIRD, COMMISSIONER OF FISH AND FISHERIES, ON THE CONDITION OF THE SEA-FISHERIES OF THE SOUTH COAST OF NEW ENGLAND IN 1871 AND 1872.

WASHINGTON:
GOVERNMENT PRINTING OFFICE.
1874.

TABLE OF CONTENTS.

[The figures refer to the inside paging of the report.]

VIII.—REPORT UPON THE INVERTEBRATE ANIMALS OF VINEYARD SOUND AND THE ADJACENT WATERS, WITH AN ACCOUNT OF THE PHYSICAL CHARACTERS OF THE REGION.

By A. E. Verrill.

A.—HABITS AND DISTRIBUTION OF THE INVERTEBRATE ANIMALS.

I.—General remarks.

The investigation of the invertebrate life of these waters, undertaken at the request of the United States Commissioner of Fish and Fisheries, was actively carried forward during the entire summer of 1871, and the very extensive collections then made have been studied by Mr. S. I. Smith, Mr. O. Harger, and myself, as thoroughly as possible during the time that has been at our disposal. The work upon the collections is by no means complete, but is sufficiently advanced to serve the immediate purposes of the Fish Commission.

To Mr. Smith I am indebted for the identification of all the Crustacea referred to in this report and the accompanying lists, except the Isopods, which have been determined mostly by Mr. Harger, to whom my thanks are also due for several excellent drawings of those animals. To Professor A. Hyatt I am indebted for the identification of some of the Bryozoa, and for most of the figures of that class. I am also under obligations to Dr. A. S. Packard, Dr. G. H. Horn, and Dr. H. A. Hagen, who have identified the insects inhabiting salt water.

According to the plans adopted these explorations had in view several distinct purposes, all more or less connected with the investigation of the fisheries. The special subjects attended to by this section of the Fish Commission party were chiefly the following:

1st. The exploration of the shores and shallow water for the purpose of making collections of all the marine animals and algæ living between tides, on every different kind of shore, including the numerous burrowing-worms and crustacea, and to ascertain as much as possible concerning their habits, relative abundance, stations, &c.

2d. The extension of similar observations by means of the dredge, trawl, tangles, and other instruments, into all depths down to the deepest waters which were accessible to us, and to make a systematic survey, as complete as possible, of all the smaller bays and harbors within our reach, both to obtain complete collections of the animals and plants and to ascertain the precise character of the bottom, special attention being paid to the localities known to be the feeding-grounds of valuable fishes, and to those animals upon which they are known to feed.

3d. The depth of the water and its temperature, both at the surface and bottom, was to be observed and recorded in as many localities as possible, and especially where dredging was to be done, and lists of the animals and plants from special localities or depths were to be prepared, so as to show the influence of temperature and other physical features upon animal and vegetable life. Many valuable observations of this kind were made.

4th. The life of the surface waters was to be investigated by means of hand-nets and towing-nets, on every possible occasion, and at all hours. Towing-nets of different sizes, made of strong embroidery-canvas, and attached to stout brass rings, were used with excellent results, but very many interesting things were obtained by hand-nets skilfully used. The surface collections are of great interest in themselves, and of special importance practically, as they show the nature of the food of those fishes that feed at or near the surface.

5th. The collections obtained were to be preserved by the best methods: 1st, for the purpose of making a more thorough study of them than could usually be done at the time, and for the purpose of insuring accuracy in their identification and fullness in the special lists for the final reports; and 2d, in order to supply the Smithsonian Institution, Yale College museum, and a number of other public museums, both American and foreign, with sets of the specimens collected. For this last purpose large quantities of duplicates were collected and preserved, and will be distributed at an early day.

6th. Those species of animals which cannot be preserved in good condition for study were to be examined with care and minutely described while living. The colors and appearance of the soft parts of other species were to be described in the same way, and also the eggs and young of all kinds.

7th. It was regarded as of great importance to secure accurate drawings of the living animals, and especially of such as greatly change their form and appearance when preserved, such as worms, naked mollusks, ascidians, polyps, &c. Unfortunately the available funds were not sufficient to enable us to employ a special artist for this purpose during the summer, but this deficiency has been partially remedied by the figures subsequently drawn by Mr. J. H. Emerton, Mr. S. I. Smith, Mr. O. Harger, and the writer.

8th. In all these investigations the relations existing between the fishes and the lower animals which serve as food for them were to be constantly borne in mind, and all information bearing directly upon this subject that could be obtained was to be recorded. To this end large numbers of stomachs from fishes newly caught were examined, and lists of the species found in them were made. Most of those thus ascertained to be their ordinary food were traced to their natural haunts from whence the fishes obtain them.

9th. The parasites of fishes, both external and internal, were to be collected and preserved for future study.

A large collection of such parasites was made, but the internal parasites, which are very numerous, have not yet been studied. The internal parasites were collected chiefly by Dr. Edward Palmer.

The map accompanying the present report serves to show the localities explored, and the extent of the labor in dredging and sounding. The operations during the first six weeks were under the charge of Mr. S. I. Smith, who remained until July 25. He was assisted by Dr. W. G. Farlow, who also investigated the algæ. Professor J. E. Todd, of Tabor, Iowa, then took charge of the work for three weeks, until I was able to join the party, on the 16th of August. During the remainder of the season, until September 20, the operations were under my immediate superintendence; but Professor A. Hyatt, of Boston; Dr. A. S. Packard, of Salem; Dr. Farlow, of Cambridge; and Professor D. C. Eaton, of New Haven, gave very important aid in carrying out our investigations, and our thanks are due to all of these gentlemen for their assistance. Several other naturalists were present, from time to time, and coöperated with our party in various ways.

The dredging operations in the shallow waters of Vineyard Sound and Buzzard's Bay were carried on at first by means of a sail-boat, but during the greater part of the time by means of a steam-launch. The dredgings outside of these waters, and off Martha's Vineyard, were all done by means of a United States revenue-cutter, the steamer Moccasin, under command of Captain J. G. Baker. Our thanks are due to the officers of the Moccasin, who were very courteous, and gave us all the facilities within their power for carrying out our investigations successfully. Without this important assistance we should have remained in complete ignorance of the temperature and peculiar fauna of the deeper waters off this shore, for the localities were too distant to be reached by means of the steam-launch or sail-boats.

The examination of the bottom was done by means of dredges of various sizes, constructed much like those in general use for this purpose; by "rake-dredges" of novel construction, consisting of a heavy A-shaped iron frame, to the arms of which bars of iron armed with long, thin, and sharp teeth, arranged like those of a rake, are bolted, back to back; a rectangular frame of round iron, supporting a deep and fine dredge-net, follows just behind the rake to receive and retain the animals raked from the soft mud or sand by the rake; a trawl-net, with a beam about fourteen feet long, made of stout, iron gas-pipe, and having a net, fine toward the end, about forty feet deep, and provided with numerous pockets; "tangles," consisting of an A-shaped iron frame, to which frayed-out hemp-ropes are attached. The best form has several small chains of galvanized iron attached to the frame by one end, so as to drag over the bottom, and the pieces of frayed-out rope are attached along the sides of the chains.

The ordinary dredges can be used on all kinds of bottom, except where there are rough rocks and ledges, but they generally merely scrape the surface or sink into the bottom but slightly. The rake-dredges are used only on bottoms of soft mud or sand, and are intended to catch burrowing animals of all kinds, which are always numerous on such bottoms. The trawl is adapted for the capture of bottom-fishes, as well as for crabs, lobsters, large shells, and all other animals of considerable size, which creep over or rest upon the bottom. It cannot be used where the bottom is rocky or rough, and does not usually capture many animals of small size, or those that burrow. It is, however, a very important instrument when used in connection with the ordinary dredge, for it will capture those species which are too active to be caught by the dredge, and much greater quantities of the larger species than can be obtained by the dredge alone. The "tangles" are particularly useful on rough, rocky, or ledgy bottoms, where the dredge and trawl cannot be used, but they cannot be depended upon for obtaining all the small species, especially of shells and worms. They capture mainly those kinds of animals which have rough or spiny surfaces, such as star-fishes, sea-urchins, corals, bryozoa, rough crabs, &c., and those kinds which are disposed to cling to foreign objects, such as many of the small crustacea, which are often taken in countless numbers by this means. Star-fishes and sea-urchins are especially adapted to be caught by this instrument, and are often brought up in great quantities. The tangles can be used on all kinds of bottoms, wherever there are any of those kinds of animals which they are adapted to capture.

The localities where dredgings were made by these various instruments were located on Coast Survey charts as accurately as possible, and were sufficiently numerous to give a pretty satisfactory knowledge of the nature of the bottom and its inhabitants throughout the region explored. The total number of casts of the dredges made during the three months devoted to this work was about 400. A large part of these, including all the more important ones, have been located on the map accompanying this report. The more important points where the temperature of the water was observed have also been indicated on the map and the temperatures given, the figures *above* two parallel lines indicating the surface temperature, those *below* such lines indicating the bottom temperature—thus: $\frac{62^\circ}{57^\circ}$.

In prosecuting our explorations we soon found that there are, in the waters of this region, three quite distinct assemblages of animal life, which are dependent upon and limited by definite physical conditions of the waters which they inhabit. The first of these includes all those kinds which inhabit the bottom and shores of Vineyard Sound, Buzzard's Bay, and the other similar bodies of shallow water along this coast from

Cape Cod westward and southward. These shallow waters consist of nearly pure sea-water, which has a relatively high temperature, especially in summer, for it is warmed up both by the direct heat of the sun, acting on the shallow waters spread over broad surfaces of sand, and by water coming directly from the Gulf Stream, and bringing not only its heat, but also its peculiar pelagic animals. The temperature at the surface in August was 66° to 72° Fahrenheit. Owing to this influence of the Gulf Stream these waters never become very cold in winter, for some of the small, shallow harbors never freeze over. The greater part of the animals inhabiting these bays and sounds are southern forms.

The second assemblage is a very peculiar one, which inhabits the estuaries, ponds, lagoons, harbors, and other similar places, where the water is shallow and more or less brackish, and very warm in summer, but cold in the winter. The third group inhabits the shores of the outer islands and headlands and the bottoms in moderately deep water, outside of the bays and sounds. These outer waters are comparatively cold, even in summer, and are no doubt derived from an offshoot of the arctic current, which drifts southward along our shores in deep water and always has a tendency to crowd against and up its submarine slopes, in which it is also aided in many cases by the tides. In August, the temperature of the surface was 62° to 65°, of the bottom 57° to 62° Fahrenheit. The animals inhabiting these cold waters are mostly northern in character and much like those of the coast of Maine and Bay of Fundy. The surface waters in the bays and sounds, although usually somewhat warmer in summer than those outside, differ less in temperature than the bottom waters. Consequently we find less difference in the surface animals. We have therefore found it most convenient to group all the surface animals together, as a special division of those inhabiting the bays and sounds. In each of the groups or assemblages we find that certain kinds are restricted to particular localities, depending upon the character of the bottom or shore. Thus there will be species, or even large groups of species, which inhabit only rocky shores; others which inhabit only sandy shores; others which dwell in the muddy places; and still others that prefer the clean gravelly bottoms where the water is several fathoms deep, &c.

I have found it desirable, therefore, in describing the character of the marine life of this region, to group the animals according to the localities which they inhabit, adopting the three primary divisions given above, but, for greater convenience of reference, placing all the parasitic species together in one group. The subdivisions of these groups will be given under each, in the succeeding pages.

The primary groups will stand as follows:

1. The fauna of the bays and sounds.
2. The fauna of the estuaries and other brackish waters.
3. The fauna of the cold waters of the ocean shores and outer banks and channels.

In describing the animals belonging in these different divisions and subdivisions it has not been found desirable to mention, in this part of the report, all the species found in each, but only those that appear to be the most abundant and important, and especially those that are known to serve as the food of fishes. But in the general systematic list, which accompanies this report, all the species of the region, so far as determined, will be enumerated.

II.—The fauna of the bays and sounds.

In Buzzard's Bay, Vineyard Sound, Nantucket Sound, and Muskeget Channel, (see map,) the water is shallow, being generally less than 8 fathoms deep, and rarely exceeding 14 fathoms, even in the deepest spots. It will be seen by reference to the map, on which soundings have been given and contour lines drawn, representing the zones having depths below 3, 10, 14, and 20 fathoms, respectively, that the greater part of Buzzard's Bay is less than 10 fathoms deep, and that the 3-fathom curve is nearly parallel with the shore lines, and the same is true of the 6-fathom line, which has not been drawn. The 10-fathom curve is very irregular and only extends a short distance within the mouth of the bay; but an irregular area, in which the water exceeds 10 fathoms in depth, the central part over a limited area being about 15 fathoms, is situated to the west of Penikese, Nashawena, and Cuttyhunk Islands; this is inclosed on all sides by shallower water. The 14-fathom curve is situated from four to eight miles farther off and does not enter the bay at all, showing only a very slight curvature in that direction; yet it extends far up Narragansett Bay, and to a considerable distance within the mouth of Vineyard Sound, but, like the 10-fathom line, does not enter Muskeget Channel or Nantucket Sound at any point, and shows scarcely any curvature toward those waters, which are very shallow throughout their whole extent, and much obstructed by banks and broad shoals of moving sands. The 20-fathom line at nearly all points is situated far off shore, and does not conform at all to the outline of the coast. There is, however, an area of water exceeding this depth off Newport, in the mouth of Narragansett Bay.

Vineyard Sound is deeper and much more varied in its depth and in the character of its bottom than Buzzard's Bay or Nantucket Sound, and therefore its fauna is richer in species and the facilities for collecting are much greater. In Vineyard Sound the 3-fathom curve follows the outlines of the shore very closely, and the same is true of the 6-fathom curve, which has not been represented on the map. The 10-fathom line when it enters the mouth of the sound incloses the greater part of its width and is approximately parallel with its shores, but after it passes the narrowest part of the sound, between the northern end of Martha's Vineyard and Wood's Hole, it rapidly narrows and is finally interrupted by shallows and sand-bars after passing Holmes's Hole, but there are beyond this several isolated areas of water exceeding this depth and having their long axes nearly parallel with the central axis of the channel, or rather parallel with the direction of the tidal currents. One of these areas, south of Osterville, Massachusetts, is 15 fathoms deep, but of no great size. These deeper depressions are surrounded by banks and ridges of sand, some of which rise nearly to the surface and form dangerous shoals; the shoals, like the deep channels, have their longer axes parallel with the prevailing tidal currents, but as they are mostly composed of loose moving sands, they are liable to be altered in form and position by severe storms.

These moving sands are generally very barren of life, and form true submarine deserts. Included within and nearly inclosed by the 10-fathom line, there is, between Martha's Vineyard and Naushon Island, a large area of shallower water, which is connected with the shallow water of the shore at the northern end of Martha's Vineyard, off the "West Chop," near Holmes's Hole. In some places this shallow rises nearly to the surface and forms the "middle ground," and other shoals parallel with the current that sets through the channels on either side, and consequently nearly parallel with the shore of Martha's Vineyard. It is evident that this rather extensive bank is due to the action of the tidal current which sweeps around West Chop toward the mouth of the sound, following the direction of the deeper channels, the projecting point at West Chop furnishing a lee in which the movement of the water is retarded and the sediment deposited; but this action is modified by the tidal current which enters the mouth of the sound and flows in the opposite direction, for although this current is somewhat less rapid, its duration is longer, especially that branch of it which flows between the Middle Ground Shoal and Martha's Vineyard, for this flows eastward seven hours and twenty-six minutes, while the opposite current flows westward for only four hours and thirty-four minutes; the effect of the current flowing eastward would, therefore, be to keep this channel from filling up by the sediments carried along by the westward currents. The same effect would be produced in the main channel, outside of this shoal, although the difference in the duration of the flow in the two directions is there less, the eastward flow lasting six hours and fifteen minutes, while the westward tide lasts five hours and forty-five minutes.

Similar causes determine, without doubt, the position of all the other shoals and banks of sand in this region, as well as the existence of the isolated deep areas between them, but in many cases the direction of the wind-waves produced by the more violent storms must betaken into account. The 14-fathom line extends into the mouth of the sound, as far as a point opposite Nashawena Island; and beyond this there are several isolated areas which are of this depth; the most extensive of these is opposite the southern half of Naushon Island and in a line with the main channel at the mouth of the sound. Since the tides are greater in Buzzard's Bay than in Vineyard Sound, and neither the times of low water and high water, nor the relative duration of the ebb and flow are coincident, very powerful currents set through the passages, between the Elizabeth Islands, connecting these two bodies of water. This is most noticeable in the case of Wood's Hole, because there the channel is narrow and shallow, and much obstructed by rocks. These channels are, therefore, excellent collecting grounds for obtaining such animals as prefer rocky bottoms and rapidly flowing waters.

The shores of Vineyard Sound and Buzzard's Bay are quite diversified and present nearly all kind of stations usually found in corresponding latitudes elsewhere, except that ledges of solid rock are of rare occurrence, but there are numerous prominent points where the shore consists of large rocks or boulders, which have been left by the denudation of deposits of glacial drift, forming the cliffs along the shores. Sandy beaches are frequent, and gravelly and stony ones occasionally occur. Muddy shores are less common and usually of no great extent.

In Buzzard's Bay the bottom is generally muddy, except in very shallow water about some of the islands, where patches of rocky bottom occur, and opposite some of the sandy beaches where it is sandy over considerable areas. Tracts of harder bottom, of mud or sand, overgrown with algæ, occasionally occur. In Vineyard Sound the bottom is more varied. It is sandy over large districts, especially where the shoals occur, and in such places there are but few living animals, though the sand is often filled with dead and broken shells, but in other localities the sand is more compact and is inhabited by a peculiar set of animals. Other extensive areas have a bottom of gravel and small stones and broken shells; on such bottoms animal life is abundant, and the entire bottom seems to be covered in some places by several kinds of compound ascidians, which form large masses of various shapes, often as large as a man's head. In still other places, chiefly off rocky points and in the channels between the islands, rocky bottoms occur, but they are usually of small extent. Muddy bottoms are only occasionally met with. They occur in most of the deep areas which are isolated, and sometimes in the deep channels, but are more common in sheltered harbors and coves.

In Nantucket Sound and Muskeget Channel the bottom is almost everywhere composed of sand, and the same is true of an extensive area to the east and northeast of Nantucket Island, where shoals of moving sand are numerous and often of large size, but in the partially sheltered area on the north side of Nantucket, there is more or less mud mixed with the sand.

For greater convenience the following subdivisions have been adopted in describing the animals of the bays and sounds:

1. Rocky shores, between high-water and low-water marks.
2. Sandy and gravelly shores.
3. Muddy shores and flats.
4. Piles of wharves, buoys, &c.

5. Rocky bottoms below low-water mark.
6. Stony, gravelly, and shelly bottoms.
7. Sandy bottoms.
8. Muddy bottoms.
9. Free-swimming and surface animals.
10. Parasitic animals.

It must, however, be constantly borne in mind that very few kinds of animals are strictly confined to any one of these subdivisions, and that the majority are found in two, three, or more of them, and often in equal abundance in several, though each species generally *prefers* one particular kind of locality. In other cases the habits vary at different seasons of the year, or at different hours of the day and night, and such species may be found in different situations according to the times when they are sought. The more common and characteristic species are, however, pretty constant in their habits and may be easily found in their respective stations at almost any time.

Since those animals that inhabit the shores, between tides, are most frequently seen and can be most easily obtained and studied by those who are not professional naturalists, I have entered into more details concerning their habits and appearances than in the case of those obtained only by dredging. Such species as have not been previously named and described in other works will be more fully described in the systematic list, to follow this report, and references will there be given to descriptions of the others.

II.—1. ANIMALS INHABITING THE ROCKY SHORES OF THE BAYS AND SOUNDS.

The principal localities where these animals were studied and collected are at Nobska Point, just east of Wood's Hole; Parker's Point, between Great Harbor and Little Harbor, near Wood's Hole; the neck of land north of Wood's Hole Channel; several localities on Naushon and the adjacent islands; and numerous localities on the shores of Long Island Sound, as at Savin Rock and Light-House Point, near New Haven; Stony Creek; Thimble Islands, &c.

In all these places the rocks, in a zone extending from near low-water mark of ordinary tides to near half tide, are generally covered with an abundance of "rock-weeds," (*Fucus nodosus* and *F. vesiculosus*,) which hang in great olive-brown clusters from the sides of the rocks or lie flat upon their surfaces when left by the tide, but are floated up by means of their abundant air-vessels when the tide rises. Mingled with these are several other algæ, among which the green "sea-cabbage" (*Ulva latissima*) is one of the most abundant. Below this zone of *Fucus* there is a narrow zone which is only exposed during spring-tides; in this the *Ulva* and many other more delicate green and red algæ flourish. Above the Fucus-zone there is another zone of considerable width which is covered for a short time by every tide; and still higher up another zone which is ordinarily only washed by the waves and spray, but is in part occasionally covered by unusually high tides. As the tides do not rise very high in this region these zones are all much narrower and less distinctly marked than on the coast further north, and especially on the coast of Maine and in the Bay of Fundy, but yet they can always be easily recognized and distinguished by their peculiar forms of animal and vegetable life. Pools of sea-water left by the tide frequently occur in each of these zones, among the rocks, and afford excellent opportunities for studying and collecting the animals.

The animals of rocky shores are to be sought for in a variety of ways. A few occur quite exposed, clinging to the rocks or weeds, in defiance of the surf. These are chiefly univalve shells, barnacles, and such animals as grow like plants, firmly attached to solid objects, among these are the bryozoa, hydroids, and sponges. A much larger number seek shelter under the rocks, or on their lower sides, or in crevices and cavities between them; these must be sought by turning over the rocks and exploring the crevices concealed by the *Fucus*, &c. Many other species conceal themselves still more effectually by burrowing in the mud, gravel, and sand beneath and between the rocks; these are often uncovered in turning over the rocks, but must also be sought for by digging with a spade, stout trowel, or some other tool, in the dirt exposed when the rocks are removed. The number of curious species of annelids, holothurians, bivalve-shells, actiniæ, &c., which can be unearthed in this way is always very surprising to the inexperienced in this kind of collecting. Still other kinds can be found by carefully examining the pools and discovering the smaller animals by their motions, or by the shadows that they cast when the sun shines, or by noticing their burrows, or, if time will not admit of a more careful examination, by sweeping a fine hand-net through the weeds along the edges. Many small crustacea, shells, etc., may also be found clinging to the corallines and other algæ growing in such pools, or even among the algæ lying upon the rocks, and especially among masses of detached algæ, thrown up by the waves.

In the uppermost zone the animals are of comparatively few kinds, but these usually occur in great abundance. The most conspicuous is, perhaps, the common "rock-barnacle" or "acorn-shell," *Balanus balanoides*, which adheres firmly to the rocks by its base and can resist the most violent surf, even on the outer ocean shores. When left by the tide these dull white conical shells are not calculated to attract much attention, except on account of their vast numbers, for they sometimes completely whiten the rocks for long distances along the zone in which they flourish best, and even so crowd against each other that they cannot assume their normal form, but become greatly elongated. But when the tide comes in, each one lifts up the double-door which closes the aperture at the summit of the shell and puts out an organ, bearing a cluster of gracefully curved and fringed arms, which t quickly sweeps forward with a grasping motion and then quickly withdraws, as if in search of food, and this motion will be repeated with great regularity for a long time, unless the creature be disturbed, when it instantly withdraws its net and closes its doors. No one who will take the trouble to examine this little animal, when in active operation in one of the tide-pools, can fail to admire its perfect adaptation to its mode of life and the gracefulness of its motions. The movement referred to serves not only to obtain food, which, in the form of microscopic animals, is always abundant in the water, but also to supply fresh currents of water for respiration. This creature is also well worthy of mention here because it serves as food for the tautog, and probably for other fishes that can obtain it at high water.

Two species of small univalve shells (*Littorina*) are always to be found in abundance clinging to the surface of the rocks, or among the seaweeds, or creeping about in the tide-pools. These are often found quite up to high-water mark, but the full-grown ones are more common lower down among the "rock-weeds." One of these (Plate XXIV, fig. 138) is subglobular in form, the spire being depressed and the aperture wide. This is the *Littorina palliata*. It varies much in color; the most common color is dark olive-brown, not unlike that of the *Fucus*, but orange-colored and pale yellow specimens are not uncommon, while others are mottled or banded with yellow or orange and brown. The second species is more elongated and has a more elevated and somewhat pointed spire. This is *Littorina rudis*, and it has many varieties of form, color, and sculpture; one of its varieties is represented on Plate XXIV, fig. 137. Some specimens are smooth, others are covered with revolving lines or furrows; in color it is most frequently dull gray, olive-green, or brown, but it is often prettily banded, checked, or mottled with yellow or orange, or even black, and sometimes with whitish. This species is viviparous. These shells are both vegetarians and feed upon the algæ among which they live. Another allied shell, the *Lacuna vincta*, (Plate XXIV, fig. 139,) is found clinging to the sea-weeds at low-water mark and sometimes in the tide-pools. This is usually pale reddish or purplish brown, or horn-colored, and most commonly is encircled by two or more darker, chestnut-colored bands. This also feeds upon the algæ. Associated with the last, two or three other kinds of small shells are generally found. One of the most abundant of these is the *Bittium nigrum*, (Plate XXIV, fig. 154,) which is, as its name implies, generally black, especially when young, but large specimens are often only dark brown or even yellowish brown below; it occurs in great abundance, clinging to the sea-weeds and eel-grass at and below low-water mark, and is also to be found in the tide-pools and on the under sides of rocks. Associated with the last, and resembling it in form and color as well as in habits, another much less common species occurs, which is remarkable for having its whorls reversed, or coiled to the left, in the direction opposite to that of most other shells. This is the *Triforis nigrocinctus*, (Plate

XXIV, fig. 152.) This species is more at home at the depth of a few fathoms, among algæ. Another still smaller and lighter colored species, which often occurs abundantly in similar situations, both on algæ and under stones, is the *Rissoa aculeus*, (Plate XXIV, fig. 141,) but this generally seeks more sheltered situations. All these shells feed upon the algæ. With them there can usually be found large numbers of several carnivorous species. The most abundant one is a small but pretty shell, having a smooth surface and quite variable in color, though usually reddish or purplish brown, and irregularly mottled or banded with yellowish or whitish, the light-colored spots often taking the form of crescents, and varying much in size and number. This is the *Astyris lunata*, (Plate XXI, fig. 110.) It lives among the algæ, and also among hydroids, and may be found in almost all kinds of localities, both above and below low-water mark. It is usually abundant on the under sides of rocks among hydroids, &c., and can nearly always be found in the tide-pools. Another allied species of larger size, and much less common, the *Anachis avara*, (Plate XXI, fig. 109,) often occurs with it. Clinging to the rocks, or sheltered in the crevices and on their under surfaces, a much larger, dull-white or grayish, roughly-sculptured shell can usually be found in abundance. This is the *Urosalpinx cinerea*, (Plate XXI, fig. 116,) which the oystermen call "the drill," a name very suggestive of its habits, for it gets its living, like many other similar univalve shells, by drilling a round hole, by means of the sharp, flinty teeth that cover its tongue, through the shells of oysters and other bivalves and then sucking out the contents at its leisure. It is usually very abundant on the oyster-beds, and often proves very destructive. Another shell of about the same size, somewhat resembling the last, and having similar habits, is often found associated with it on the more exposed rocky points, as at Nobska Point, the Wepecket Islands, &c. This is, however, a very northern and arctic shell, which extends also around the northern coasts of Europe, and is called *Purpura lapillus*, (Plate XXI, figs. 118 and 119;) it is here near its southernmost limits, for it is not not found in Long Island Sound or farther south; while the former is a southern shell, abundant on the whole southern coast as far as the Gulf of Mexico, and rare north of Cape Cod, except in a few special localities of sheltered and warm waters. The *Purpura* is seldom found living much below low-water mark, and prefers the exposed rocky headlands on the ocean shores, where it flourishes in defiance of the breakers. It lays its eggs in smooth, vase-shaped capsules, attached to the sides or under surfaces of stones by a short stalk, and usually arranged in groups, (Plate XXI, fig. 120.) The eggs of "the drill" are laid in similar places, but the capsules have very short stalks, or are almost sessile, and are compressed, with an ovate outline, and angular ridges pass down their sides. The "limpet," another northern and European shell, having a low conical form, is occasionally found clinging to the rocks at low-water in this region, but is far more common north of

Cape Cod. This shell is the *Acmæa testudinalis*, (Plate XXIV, figs. 159, 159*a*;) it is extremely variable in color, but is most commonly radiated, checked, or tesselated with brown, pale greenish, and white. It grows much larger on the coast of Maine than here. A peculiar narrow form of this shell, (var. *alveus*,) represented by fig. 159*b*, lives on the leaves of eel-grass. Beneath the rocks, and generally attached to their under sides, among hydroids, bryozoa, &c., several species of small, slender, pointed, and generally whitish shells occur, which belong to the genus *Odostomia*. The most common of these are *O. trifida*, (Plate XXIV, fig. 145,) *O. bisuturalis*, (Plate XXIV, fig. 146,) and *O. fusca*, (Plate XXIV, fig. 144,) but other similar species are often to be found. These all have the singular habit of spinning a thread of mucus by means of which they can suspend themselves from any surface. In confinement they will often creep along the surface of the water, using the bottom of the foot as a float, in a manner similar to that of many fresh-water shells. On the under sides of rocks are occasionally found some very beautiful and interesting naked mollusks; but this group of animals is far less abundant in this region than farther north. The largest and finest species observed here is the *Doris bifida*, (Plate XXV, fig. 176,) which grows to be about an inch long. Its body is deep purple, specked with white and bright yellow, and the beautiful wreath of gills is covered with bright golden specks; the ends of the tentacles are also bright yellow. Its eggs are contained in convoluted gelatinous ribbons, which are attached to the under sides of rocks or in crevices. Another rare and curious species, the *Doridella obscura*, (Plate xxv, fig. 173,) is occasionally found on the under side of stones. This is a small, oval, flattened species, of a dark brown or blackish color, with small, white retractile tentacles on the back, but the gills are very small and situated underneath, near the posterior end of the body, in the groove between the mantle and foot. The eggs are inclosed in a delicate gelatinous string, which is coiled up something like a watch-spring, and attached to the under side of stones.

Of bivalve shells several species are common on rocky shores, especially in the crevices and under the rocks. Three kinds of muscles are usually met with. The species which lives at high-water mark, clustering about the small upper pools and in the crevices, and having its shell ribbed with radiating ridges and furrows, is the *Modiola plicatula*, (Plate XXXI, fig. 238.) This species is far more abundant, however, along the borders of estuaries and on salt marshes and muddy shores, always preferring the upper zone, where it is covered for a very short time by the tide. The most common species among the rocks, toward low-water mark, and in the larger pools, is the *Mytilus edulis*, (Plate XXXI, fig. 234,) which is the "common muscle" all along our coast from North Carolina to the Arctic Ocean. It is perfectly identical with the common muscle of Europe, which there forms a very important article of food, and in many places, as on the coast of France, is extensively cultivated for the market. On our coast it is seldom used as food, although quite as good as on the European shores; but it is collected on some parts of our coast in vast quantities to be used for fertilizing the soil. It is most abundant in the shallow waters of bays and estuaries, where the water is a little brackish, but flourishes well in almost all kinds of situations where there is some mud, together with solid objects to which it can attach itself. Along the coasts of Long Island and New Jersey it is taken in almost incredible quantities from the shallow sheltered bays and lagoons that skirt those shores. It grows very rapidly and under favorable conditions becomes full grown in one season. Like all other kinds of true muscles, it has the power of spinning strong threads by means of the groove in its long, slender foot, and, by extending the foot, glues them firmly by one end to rocks, shells, or any other solid substances, while the other end is firmly attached to its body. When they attach their threads to their neighbors they form large clusters. Thus a very firm and secure anchorage is effected, and they are generally able to ride out the most violent storms, though, by the giving way of the rocks or shells to which they are attached, many are always stranded on the beaches after severe storms. They are not confined to the shallow waters, for very large specimens were dredged by me, several years ago, in 40 to 50 fathoms in the deep channels between Eastport, Maine, and Deer Island, where the tide runs with great force; and it has since been dredged by our parties in still deeper water in the same region, showing that it can live and prosper equally well under the most diverse conditions. The specimens from sheltered localities and sandy bottoms are, however, much more delicate in texture and more brilliant in color than those from more exposed situations. Some of the thinner and more delicate specimens, from quiet and pure waters, are translucent and very beautifully colored with brown, olive, green, yellow, and indigo blue, alternating in radiating bands of different widths; while others are nearly uniform pale yellow, or translucent horn-color. Those from the exposed shores are generally thicker, opaque, and plain dull brown, or bluish black, and not unfrequently they are very much distorted. This species breeds early in the spring. I have found immense numbers of the young, about as large as the head of a pin, which had just attached themselves to algæ, hydroids, &c., on the 12th of April. These shells are not destined to remain forever fixed, however, for they not only swim free when first hatched, but even in after life they can, at will, let go their anchor-threads, or "byssus," and creep about by means of their slender "foot," until they find another anchorage that suits them better, and they can even climb up the perpendicular sides of rocks or piles by means of the threads of the "byssus," which they then stretch out and attach, one after another, in the direction they wish to climb, each one being fastened a little higher up than the last. Thus, little by little, the heavy shell is drawn up, much in the manner employed by some spiders when moving or suspending an unusually large victim. This common muscle is not only useful to man directly as food, and as a fertilizer, but it serves as an important article of food for many fishes, both in its young stages and when full grown. The tautog makes many a hearty meal on the full-grown shells, as do several other kinds of fishes, while the "scup" and others devour the young. The common star-fishes feed largely upon muscles, as well as oysters, and they also have many other enemies. A small parasitic crab, *Pinnotheres maculatus*, lives in their shells, between their gills, in the same manner as the common *Pinnotheres ostreum* lives in the oyster. Another larger muscle, sometimes called the "horse-muscle," which is the *Modiola modiolus*, (Plate XXXI, fig. 237,) lives at extreme low-water mark in the crevices between the rocks, and usually nearly buried in the gravel and firmly anchored in its place. Sometimes it occurs in the larger pools, well down toward low-water mark. It is, like the last, a northern species, and extends to the Arctic Ocean and Northern Europe. It is much more abundant on the northern coasts than here, and, although it is almost entirely confined to rocky shores and bottoms, it extends to considerable depths, for we dredged it abundantly in the Bay of Fundy, at various depths, down to 70 fathoms. Like the preceding, it is devoured by the tautog and other fishes. Its thick shell, covered with a glossy, chestnut epidermis, and rudely hairy toward the large end, are points by which it can easily be recognized, and its shape is also peculiar. The common "long clam," *Mya arenaria*, (Plate XXVI, fig. 179) is very often met with buried in the sand and gravel beneath stones and rocks, but it is far more abundant on sandy and muddy shores, and especially in estuaries, and will, therefore, be mentioned with more details in another place.

Another shell, somewhat resembling the "long clam," but never growing so large, and more cylindrical in form though usually much distorted, is occasionally met with under the rocks or in crevices. This is the *Saxicava arctica*, (Plate XXVII, fig. 192.) It is much more abundant farther north, and has a very extensive range, being found on most coasts, at least in the northern hemisphere. On those coasts where limestone exists it has the habit of burrowing into the limestone, after the manner of *Lithodomus* and many other shells. The only localities on our coast where I have observed this habit are at Anticosti Island, in the Gulf of Saint Lawrence, where the soft limestones are abundantly perforated in this way. On the New England coast limestones rarely occur, and they have to be content with such cracks and crannies as they can find ready made; consequently their shells, in growing to fit their places, become very much distorted. This species can also form a byssus, when needed, to hold its shell in position. The siphon-tube is long and much resembles that of *Mya*, (see fig. 179,) but is divided at the end for a short distance, and generally has a reddish color. The "bloody clams," *Scapharca transversa*, (Plate XXX, fig. 228,) and *Argina pexata*, (Plate XXX, fig. 227,) are occasionally met with at low water, under or among rocks, and generally attached by a byssus, but their proper home is in the shallow waters off shore, especially on muddy, shelly, and gravelly bottoms. The fishermen call them "bloody clams," because the gills are red, and when opened they discharge a red fluid like blood. The little shell called *Kellia planulata* (Plate XXX, fig. 226) is also sometimes found under stones at low water. Attached to the sides and surfaces of rocks and ledges along many parts of this coast, young oysters, *Ostræa Virginiana*, often occur in vast numbers, sometimes completely covering and concealing large surfaces of rocks. But these generally live only through one season and are killed by the cold of winter, so that they seldom become more than an inch or an inch and a half in diameter. They come from the spawn of the oysters in the beds along our shores, which, during the breeding season, completely fill the waters with their free-swimming young. They are generally regarded as the young of "native" oysters, but I am unable to find any specific differences between the northern and southern oysters, such differences as do exist being due merely to the circumstances under which they grow, such as the character of the water, abundance or scarcity of food, kind of objects to which they are attached, age, crowded condition, &c. All the forms occur both among the northern and southern ones, for they vary from broad and round to very long and narrow; from very thick to very thin; and in the character of the surface, some being regularly ribbed and scolloped, others nearly smooth, and others very rough and irregular, or scaly, &c. When young and grown under favorable conditions, with plenty of room, the form is generally round at first, then quite regularly oval, with an undulated and scolloped edge and radiating ridges, corresponding to the scollops, and often extending out into spine-like projections on the lower valve. The upper valve is flatter, smooth at first, then with regular lamellæ or scales, scolloped at the edges, showing the stages of growth. Later in life, especially after the first winter, the growth becomes more irregular, and the form less symmetrical; and the irregularity increases with the age. Very old specimens, in crowded beds, usually become very much elongated, being often more than a foot long, and perhaps two inches wide. In the natural order of things this was probably the normal form attained by the adult individuals, for nearly all the oyster-shells composing the ancient Indian shell-heaps along our coast are of this much-elongated kind. Nowadays the oysters seldom have a chance to grow to such a good old age as to take this form, though such are occasionally met with in deep water. The young specimens on the rocks are generally mottled or irregularly radiated with brown. They were not often met with on the shores of Vineyard Sound, for oysters do not flourish well in that sandy region, though there are extensive beds in some parts of Buzzard's Bay, and a few near Holmes's Hole, in a sheltered pond. The oysters prefer quiet waters, somewhat brackish, with a bottom of soft mud containing an abundance of minute living animal and vegetable organisms. In such places they grow very rapidly, and become fat and fine-flavored, if not interfered with by their numerous enemies. I shall have occasion to speak of the oyster again, when discussing the fauna of the estuaries, &c.

Another shell, related to the oyster and like it attached by one valve to some solid object, is common, adhering to the under sides and edges of rocks near low-water mark. This is the *Anomia glabra*, (Plate XXXII, figs. 241, 242,) and it is often called "silver-shell" or "gold-shell" on account of its golden or silvery color and shining luster; and sometimes "jingle-shell" from its metallic sound when rattling about on the beach with pebbles, &c. This shell, however, does not grow firmly to the rock like an oyster, but is attached by a sort of stem or peduncle, which goes out through an opening in the side of the lower valve; this is soft and fleshy at first, but late in life often becomes ossified, or rather calcified, and then forms a solid plug.

Of the lower classes of Mollusca, several Ascidians and Bryozoa occur under and among the rocks. Among the former the *Molgula Manhattensis* (Plate XXXIII, fig. 250) is the most common. This usually has a subglobular form, especially when its tubes are contracted, and is almost always completely covered over with foreign matters of all sorts, such as bits of eel-grass and sea-weeds, grains of sand, &c. When these are removed its color is dark or pale olive-green, and the surface is a little rough. This species is often attached to the underside of rocks, but is still more frequently attached to sea-weeds and eel-grass, and is sometimes so crowded as to form large clusters. Another species, having some resemblance to the last when contracted, is the *Cynthia partita*, (Plate XXXIII, fig. 246,) but besides the great difference in the tubes and apertures, this has a rougher and wrinkled surface and a rusty color. The specimens that grow on the under sides of stones are often much flattened, as in the figure, but it grows more abundantly attached to the piles of wharves and on shelly bottoms in shallow waters, off shore, and in such places assumes its more normal erect position, and a somewhat cylindrical form. Each aperture is marked with four alternating triangles of flake-white and purplish red. This and the preceding are eaten by the tautog. Most of the other ascidians are much more at home on the bottom, off shore, although some of them sometimes occur at low-water on rocks or in pools.

A delicate and elegantly branched bryozoan, the *Bugula turrita*, (Plate XXXIV, figs. 258, 259,) is often found attached to sea-weeds in the pools, and it is also frequently thrown up in large quantities by the waves, after storms. A smaller kind, with slender, ivory-white, and stellate branches, the *Crisia eburnea*, (Plate XXXIV, figs. 260, 261,) also occurs on the sea-weeds in pools. And with this is a coarser species, which forms calcareous crusts and tubercles, having the surface covered with the prominent tips of the tubes; this is the *Cellepora ramulosa*, and like the *Crisia* it is a northern species, which inhabits also the shores of northern Europe. Still other species of bryozoa occur in these situations. One of the most abundant is *Alcyonidium hispidum*, which forms soft gelatinous incrustations around the stems of *Fucus*. On the under sides of the stones several additional kinds occur, the most common of which is the *Escharella variabilis*, (Plate XXXIII, fig. 256,) which forms broad calcareous crusts, often several inches across, and of some thickness, composed of small perforated cells. While living this species is dark-red or brick-red, but it turns green when dried, and then fades to yellow, and finally to white. It is far more abundant on shelly bottoms, off shore, in 3 to 10 fathoms of water, and in such places often covers every stone, pebble, and shell, over wide areas, and in some cases forms rounded coral-like masses two or three inches in diameter and more than an inch thick.

Crustacea in considerable numbers may also be found upon the rocky shores. Of crabs four or five species are common, concealed under the rocks and in crevices. The "green crab," *Carcinus granulatus*, occurs quite frequently well up toward high-water mark, hiding under the loose stones, and nimbly running away when disturbed. It may also be found, at times, in the larger tidal pools. Its bright green color, varied with spots and blotches of yellow, makes this species quite conspicuous. The common "rock-crab," *Cancer irroratus*, is generally common under the large rocks near low-water mark and often lies nearly buried in the sand and gravel beneath them. This species is usually larger than the preceding, often becoming three or four inches across the shell, and though less active it uses its large claws freely and with force. It can be easily distinguished by having nine blunt teeth along each side of the front edge of its shell or carapax, and by its reddish color sprinkled over with darker brownish dots. This crab also occurs in the pools, where the comical combats of the males may sometimes be witnessed. It is not confined to rocky shores, but is common also on sandy shores, as well as on rocky and gravelly bottoms off shore. It is widely diffused along our coast, extending both north and south, and is common even on the coast of Labrador. Like all the other species of crabs this is greedily devoured by many of the larger fishes, such as cod, haddock, tautog, black-bass, and especially by sharks and sting-rays. Two smaller kinds of crabs are also very abundant under the stones, especially where there is some mud. These are dark olive-brown and have the large claws broadly tipped with black. They are often called mud-crabs on account of their fondness for muddy places. One of these, the *Panopeus depressus*, (Plate I, fig. 3,) is decidedly flattened above, and is usually a little smaller than the second, the *Panopeus Sayi*, which is somewhat convex above. They are usually found together and have similar habits. A third small species of the same genus is occasionally met with under stones, but lives rather higher up toward high-water mark, and is comparatively rare. This is the *Panopeus Harrisii.* It can be easily distinguished, for it lacks the black on the ends of the big claws and has a groove along the edge of the front of the carapax, between the eyes. This last species is also found in the salt marshes, and was originally discovered on the marshes of the Charles River, near Boston. All the species of *Panopeus* are southern forms, extending to Florida, or to the gulf-coast of the Southern States, but they are rare north of Cape Cod, and not found at all on the coast of Maine. They contribute largely to the food of the tautog and other fishes. The lobster, *Homarus Americanus*, is sometimes found lurking under large rocks at low-water, but less commonly here than farther north, as, for instance, about the Bay of Fundy. In this region it lives also on sandy and gravelly bottoms, off shore, but in rather shallow water. It is an article of food for many fishes, as well as for man. Active and interesting little "hermit-crabs," *Eupagurus longicarpus*, are generally abundant in the pools near low-water, and concealed in wet places beneath rocks. In the pools they may be seen actively running about, carrying upon their backs the dead shell of some small gastropod, most commonly *Anachis avara* or *Ilyanassa obsoleta*, though all the small spiral shells are used in this way. They are very pugnacious and nearly always ready for a fight when two happen to meet, but they are also great cowards, and very likely each, after the first onset, will instantly retreat into his shell, closing the aperture closely with the large claws. They use their long slender antennæ very efficiently as organs of feeling, and show great wariness in all their actions. The hinder part of the body is soft, with a thin skin, and one-sided in structure, so as to fit into the borrowed shells, while near the end there are appendages which are formed into hook-like organs by which they hold themselves securely in their houses, for these spiral shells serve them both for shields and dwellings. This species also occurs in vast numbers among the eel-grass, both in the estuaries and in the sounds and bays, and is also frequent on nearly all other kinds of bottoms in the sounds. It is a favorite article of food for many of the fishes, for they swallow it shell and all. A much larger species, belonging to the same genus, but having much shorter and thicker claws, (*Eupagurus pollicaris*,) is also found occasionally under the rocks at low-water, but it is much more common on rocky and shelly bottoms in the sounds and bays. Its habits are otherwise similar to the small one, but it occupies much larger shells, such as those of *Lunatia heros*, *Fulgur carica*, &c. This large species is devoured by the sharks and sting-rays.

The Amphipods are also well represented on the rocky shores by a considerable number of species, some of which usually occur in vast numbers. These small crustacea are of great importance in connection with our fisheries, for we have found that they, together with the shrimps, constitute *a very large part of the food of most of our more valu-*

able edible fishes, both of the fresh and salt waters. The Amphipods, though mostly of small size, occur in such immense numbers in their favorite localities that they can nearly always be easily obtained by the fishes that eat them, and no doubt they furnish excellent and nutritious food, for even the smallest of them are by no means despised or overlooked even by large and powerful fishes, that could easily capture larger game. Even the voracious blue-fish will feed upon these small crustacea, where they can be easily obtained, even when menhaden and other fishes are plenty in the same localities. They are also the favorite food of trout, lake white-fish, shad, flounders, scup, &c., as will be seen from the lists of the animals found in the stomachs of fishes. One species, which occurs in countless numbers beneath the masses of decaying sea-weeds, thrown up at high-water mark on all the shores by the waves, is the *Orchestia agilis* SMITH, (Plate IV, fig. 14,) which has received this name in allusion to the extreme agility which it displays in leaping, when disturbed. The common name given to it is "beach-flea," which refers to the same habit. Its color is dark olive-green or brown, and much resembles that of the decaying weeds among which it lives, and upon which it probably feeds. It also constructs burrows in the sand beneath the vegetable debris. It leaps by means of the appendages at the posterior end of the body.

A much larger species, and one of the largest of all the amphipods, is the *Gammarus ornatus*, (Plate IV, fig. 15,) which occurs in great numbers beneath the stones and among the rock-weed near low-water mark. The males are much larger than the females, and sometimes become nearly an inch and a half long. They cannot leap like their cousins that live at high-water mark, but skip actively about on their sides among the stones and gravel, until they reach some shelter, or enter the water, when they swim rapidly in a gyrating manner back downward, or sideways. But although they can swim they are seldom met with away from the shore or much below low-water mark. The zone of *Fucus* is their true home. This species is abundant on all our shores, wherever rocks and *Fucus* occur, from Great Egg Harbor, New Jersey, to Labrador. Its color is generally olive-brown or reddish-brown, much like that of the *Fucus* among which it lives. The only good English name that I have ever heard for these creatures is that of "scuds" given by a small boy, in reference to their rapid and peculiar motions.

Another smaller species, *Gammarus annulatus* SMITH, frequently occurs under stones in similar places, but usually a little higher up. This is a pale species, having darker bands, with red spots on the sides of the abdomen. Still higher up, *G. marinus* often occurs.

With the *Gammarus ornatus* another, much smaller, light slate-colored amphipod is generally to be found. This is the *Melita nitida* SMITH. Its habits appear to be similar to those of the *Gammari*. Another small species, found in the same situations, is the *Mœra levis* SMITH; this is whitish in color, with black eyes.

Two species of the genus *Amphithoë* also live under rocks at low water, but these, like the other species of this genus, construct tubes in which they dwell. The *Amphithoë maculata* (Plate IV, fig. 16) is much the larger, and constructs large, coarse tubes of gravel, bits of sea-weed, &c., and attaches them in clusters to the under sides of stones. They often leave their tubes, however, and may be found free among the weed or under stones. The color is generally dark green, though sometimes reddish, and there is often a series of light spots along the back, and the whole surface is covered with minute blackish specks; the eyes are red. The second species, *Amphithoë valida* SMITH, is much smaller, being generally less than half an inch long. It is usually bright green in color, and has black eyes. It often lives among the bright green fronds of *Ulva latissima*, and its color is nearly that of the *Ulva*.

Another amphipod, resembling a small *Gammarus*, about half an inch long, and light olive-brown or yellowish brown in color, is sometimes found in large numbers swimming actively about in the larger tidal pools, and occasionally darting into the growing sea-weeds for rest or concealment. This is the *Calliopius læviusculus*. It also often occurs in vast numbers swimming at the surface, far from land, not only in the sounds and bays, but out at sea, as for instance in the vicinity of St. George's Bank and in the Gulf of St. Lawrence, where it is equally abundant. It is devoured in large quantities by numerous fishes. The *Hyale littoralis* occurs near high-water, among algæ, and in pools.

The Isopods are also well represented on the rocky shores. One of the most common is the *Sphæroma quadridentata*, (Plate V, fig. 21,) which bears some resemblance, both in form and habits, to the "pill-bugs,' which live upon the land. This species is found in abundance under stones and rocks, or creeping slowly about among the branches and roots of sea-weeds, on their sides and upper surfaces, from low-water mark nearly up to high-water mark. In color it is exceedingly variable, for no two can be found that are alike; but the colors, consisting of irregular blotches and dashes of dark gray, light gray, slate, greenish, and white, are so blended as to imitate very closely the colors of the barnacles and gray surfaces of the rocks where they live, and no doubt they derive considerable protection from their enemies by these imitative colors. When disturbed they curl themselves up in a ball and fall to the bottom.

Another smaller and much more active species, which has a more slender form, is found in vast numbers creeping actively about over the rocks and barnacles, and especially beneath rocks and drift-wood. This is the *Jæra copiosa*. It is also excessively variable in color, but shades of green, gray, and brown predominate, and cause it to imitate very effectively the surfaces of the rocks covered with small green algæ, where it loves to dwell. It is found nearly up to high-water mark, and has a wide range both northward and southward along the coast.

Another very common and much larger isopod is the *Idotea irrorata*, (Plate V, fig. 23,) which grows to be nearly an inch long. Its colors are extremely varied. Often the general color is dark gray, light gray, dull green, or brownish, thickly specked and blotched with darker, but the colors are often brighter and the markings more definite; not unfrequently a band of white, or yellowish, or greenish, runs along the middle of the back, with perhaps another along each lateral border. This species occurs creeping among the "rock-weeds" and other algæ at low water, in the pools, creeping on the under sides of stones, adhering to eel-grass, and also among floating sea-weeds, away from the shore, and in many other situations. Its colors are generally well adapted for its concealment, by imitating, more or less perfectly, the rocks and weeds among which it lives. Even those with bright green markings are thus protected when living on eel-grass or *Ulva;* the dark, obscurely marked ones when on dead eel-grass or dark *Fucus;* the grays and browns when on stones and among barnacles, &c. This protection is not perfect, however, for they often fall victims to hungry fishes of many kinds.

The *Idotea phosphorea* HARGER, is a closely allied species, which grows even larger. It can easily be distinguished by the tail-piece, which is acute in this, but tridentate in the last, and by its rougher surface and more incised lateral borders. Its colors are similar and equally variable, though they are frequently in larger and more definite spots and blotches, and the light spots are often bright yellow. It is, as its name indicates, decidedly phosphorescent. It lives under the same circumstances as the preceding species, but is much less common in this region, though it is abundant in the Bay of Fundy. It often occurs among the crowded stems of *Corallina officinalis* in the larger tide-pools.

Another related species, the *Erichsonia filiformis* HARGER, (Plate VI, fig. 26,) also occurs among the *Corallina* and other algæ in the tide-pools. This is a smaller species than the two preceding, but is somewhat similar in its colors, which are equally variable and equally adapted for its concealment; in this the colors are more commonly various tints of brown, or dull reddish, or light red, which are well adapted to blend with the colors of the *Corallines.* Quite a different looking creature is the *Epelys montosus*, which is occasionally found concealed beneath stones where there is more or less mud. This species also frequents muddy bottoms, and is pretty effectually concealed by its rough-looking back and the coating of mud and dirt that always adheres to it.

Clinging to the hydroids and delicate algæ on the under sides of stones, and in tide-pools, curious slender-bodied crustacea belonging to the genus *Caprella* (similar to fig. 20, Plate V) may often be found in considerable numbers, but they are still more abundant on rocky bottoms off shore. They have the habit of holding on firmly by the posterior legs, and extending the body out at an angle, with the long, rough front legs stretched out in various directions. While in these attitudes and at rest they often closely resemble the branches of the hydroids and algæ among which they live, especially as they also imitate them in colors, for all these species are variable in color, being generally gray, with darker specks, when living among hydroids, but often bright red when living among red algæ. This habit of holding themselves stiffly in such peculiar positions recalls the similar habits of many insects, especially some of the Orthoptera and the larvæ of the geometrid moths, and they also recall the larvæ, just named, by their singular mode of climbing actively about among the branches of the hydroids and algæ, for they bend the slender body into a loop, bring the hind legs up to the front ones, and taking hold with them stretch the body forward again, just like those larvæ, though their legs are long and slender and differ widely in structure. These little creatures are very pugnacious and are always ready to fight each other when they meet, or to repel any intruder similar in size to themselves. Their large claws are well adapted for such purposes.

The marine worms or Annelids are very numerous under the rocks between tides, and concealed beneath the surface of the gravel and mud that accumulates between and beneath the stones and in crevices. Many kinds also live in the pools, lurking among the roots of the algæ, burrowing in the bottom, or building tubes of their own in more exposed situations. Many of these annelids are very beautiful in form and brilliant in color when living, while most of them have curious habits and marvelous structures. Several species are of large size, growing to the length of one or two feet. Some are carnivorous, devouring other worms and any other small creatures that they can kill by their powerful weapons; others are vegetarians; but many are mud-eaters, swallowing the mud and fine sand in great quantities, for the sake of the animal and vegetable organisms that always exist in it, as is the case with clams and most of the bivalve shells, and many other kinds of marine animals.

All these Annelids are greedily devoured by most kinds of marine fishes, whenever they can get at them, and, since many of the annelids leave their burrows in the night to swim at the surface, or do this constantly at the breeding season, they make an important element in the diet of many fishes besides those that constantly root for them in the mud and gravel, like the tautog, scup, haddock, &c. The young of nearly all the annelids also swim free in the water for a considerable time, and in this state are doubtless devoured in immense numbers by all sorts of young and small fishes.

One of the largest and most common Annelids found under rocks, burrowing in the sand and gravel, is the *Nereis virens*, (Plate XI, figs. 47–50.) It lives both at low-water mark and at a considerable distance farther up. It grows to the length of eighteen inches or more, and is also quite stout in its proportions. The color is dull greenish, or bluish green, more or less tinged with red, and the surface reflects bright iridescent hues; the large lamellæ or gills (fig. 50) along the sides are greenish anteriorly, but farther back often become bright red, owing to the numerous blood-vessels that they contain. It is a very active and voracious worm, and has a large, retractile proboscis, armed with two strong, black, hook-like jaws at the end, and many smaller teeth on the sides, (figs. 48, 49.) It feeds on other worms and various kinds of marine animals. It captures its prey by suddenly thrusting out its proboscis and seizing hold with the two terminal jaws; then withdrawing the proboscis, the food is torn and masticated at leisure, the proboscis, when withdrawn, acting somewhat like a gizzard. These large worms are dug out of their burrows and devoured eagerly by the tautog, scup, and other fishes. But at certain times, especially at night, they leave their own burrows and, coming to the surface, swim about like eels or snakes, in vast numbers, and at such times fall an easy prey to many kinds of fishes. This habit appears to be connected with the season of reproduction. They were observed thus swimming at the surface in the daytime, near Newport, in April, 1872, by Messrs. T. M. Prudden and T. H. Russell, and I have often observed them in the evening, later in the season. At Watch Hill, Rhode Island, April 12, I found great numbers of the *males* swimming in the pools among the rocks at low-water, and discharging their milt. This worm also occurs in many other situations, and is abundant in most places along the sandy and muddy shores, both of the sounds and estuaries, burrowing near low-water mark. It occurs all along the coast from New York to the Arctic Ocean, and is also common on the northern coasts of Europe.

With the last, in this region and southward, another similar species, but of smaller size, is usually met with in large numbers. This is the *Nereis limbata*, (Plate XI, fig. 51, male.) It grows to the length of five or six inches, and can easily be distinguished by its slender, sharp, light amber-colored jaws, and by the lateral lamellæ, which are small anteriorly and narrow or ligulate posteriorly. Its color, when full grown, is usually dull brown, or smoky brown or bronze-color anteriorly, with oblique light lines on the sides, and often with a whitish border to each ring, which form narrow, pale bands at the articulations; posteriorly the body and lateral appendages are pale red, and the longitudinal dorsal blood-vessel is conspicuous. The male, of which the anterior part is represented in fig. 51, differs greatly from the female in the structure of the middle region of the body, which is brighter red in color, and has the side appendages more complicated and better adapted for swimming. The females agree with the males very well in the form and structure of the head and anterior part of the body, but the middle region does not become different from the anterior, as in the male. Both sexes are often dug out of their burrows, under stones or in the sand, but in such places there are few males in proportion to the females. The males, however, sometimes occur swimming free at the surface in vast numbers. They swim with an undulating motion, and are quite conspicuous on account of the bright red color of the middle region of their bodies. Mr. S. I. Smith observed them swimming in this way, in the daytime, in August, at Fire Island, on the southern side of Long Island, where they occurred in incredible numbers and were eagerly pursued by the blue-fish, which at such times would not take bait. We often caught them in Vineyard Sound, in the evening, at the surface, with towing-nets. These worms must, therefore, contribute largely to the food of many fishes. It is very common on our sandy shores as far south as South Carolina. A third species, *Nereis pelagica*, (Plate XI, figs. 52–55,) is abundant under stones farther north, but in this region is chiefly found on shelly bottoms, in the deeper waters of the sounds. These three species of *Nereis* are called "clam-worms" by the fishermen. Two large species of worms belonging to the genus *Rhynchobolus* (formerly *Glycera*) are often met with in burrows, in the mud beneath stones. These are pale reddish, deep flesh-colored, or dull purplish red, and rather smooth-looking worms, thickest in the middle, and tapering to both ends. They have a large proboscis, armed at the ends with four black, hook-like jaws, and are remarkable for their rapid spiral gyrations. They belong more properly to the muddy and sandy shores, and will, therefore, be mentioned more particularly in another place. They are represented on Plate X, figs. 43–46. *Ophelia simplex* occurs under stones at half-tide, and below.

The *Marphysa Leidyi* (Plate XII, fig. 64) is a large and handsome worm, occasionally met with under stones at low-water mark, but is more common on shelly bottoms in shallow water off shore. It grows to the length of six inches or more, and its body is flattened, except toward the head, where it becomes much narrowed and nearly cylindrical. It is yellowish or brownish red, and brilliantly iridescent. The branchiæ are bright red, and commence at about the sixteenth segment; the first ones have only one or two branches, but farther back they become beautifully pectinated. There are six unequal caudal cirri, the lower lateral ones longest. It is furnished with powerful jaws, and is carnivorous in its habits.

A small but very active worm, *Podarke obscura* V., (Plate XII, fig. 61,) is often found in large numbers beneath stones. These are dark brown or blackish in color, sometimes with lighter bands. They come out at night and swim at the surface in vast numbers. They are also often met with at the surface among eel-grass, in the daytime, in large numbers. A large and very singular worm, which burrows and constructs tubes in the mud and gravel beneath stones, is the *Cirratulus grandis* V., (Plate XV, figs. 80, 81.) This is usually yellowish brown, dull orange, or ocher-colored, and is remarkable for the numerous long, flexible, reddish or orange cirri that arise all along the sides. Another very large and interesting worm, often associated with the last, both among and under rocks, and on muddy shores, is the *Amphitrite ornata*, (Plate XVI, fig. 82.) This worm constructs rather firm tubes out of the consolidated mud and sand in which it resides, casting cylinders of mud out of the orifice. It grows to be twelve to fifteen inches in length. Its color is flesh-color, reddish, and orange-brown to dark brown, and it has three pairs of large plumose or arborescent gills, which are blood-red. The tentacles are flesh-colored, very numerous, and capable of great extension, even to the length of eight or ten inches, and are kept in constant motion in gathering up the materials with which it constructs its tube. Two species of worms, remarkable for their soft bodies filled with bright red blood, which is not contained in special blood-vessels, are also found under stones where there is mud in which they can burrow. The smaller of these is *Polycirrus eximius*, (Plate XVI, fig. 85.) Its tentacles are very numerous, and are extended in every direction by forcing the blood into them, which can be seen flowing along in the form of irregular drops, distending the tubular tentacles as it passes along. The second species is a much larger and undescribed species, remarkable for its very elongated body and for having very singular branching gills on the sides along the middle region; the first and last of these gills are simple or merely forked, but those in the middle are divided into numerous branches; and in either case each branch is tipped by a cluster of setæ. In allusion to this remarkable feature I have called it *Chætobranchus sanguineus*. Its tentacles are like those of the last species, but longer and more numerous; in full-grown specimens they can be extended twelve to fifteen inches or more. Its color is blood-red anteriorly, but more or less yellowish at the slender posterior part. It is very fragile and it is seldom that a large specimen can be obtained entire. It grows to be twelve to fifteen inches long. This, like the three species last mentioned, feeds upon the minute organisms contained in the mud, which it swallows in large quantities. Two species of *Lumbriconereis* are, also, frequently found burrowing in the mud and sand beneath stones, but they belong more properly to the muddy shores. They are long, slender, reddish, and brilliantly iridescent worms, readily distinguished by having a smooth, blunt-conical head, without tentacles. They are carnivorous and have complicated jaws. The head and anterior part of the body of the larger species (*L. opalina* V.) is represented in Plate XIII, figs. 69, 70. The other (*L.tenuis* V.) is very slender, thread-like, nearly a foot long, and has no eyes.

There are several kinds of highly organized annelids which may be found adhering to the under side of stones or concealing themselves in crevices. Among these are three species, which have the back covered with two rows of large scales. One of these, having twelve pairs of nearly smooth scales, is the *Lepidonotus sublevis* V., (Plate X, fig. 42;) the color is variable, but usually brown or grayish, with darker specks, thus imitating the color of the stones. Another more common species is the *Lepidonotus squamatus*, (Plate X, figs. 40, 41,) which also has twelve pairs of scales, but they are rough, and covered with small rounded or hemispherical tubercles; this is usually dark brown. The third species has sixteen pairs of smooth scales, and belongs to another genus. This is *Harmothoë imbricata;* it varies exceedingly in color, but is usually grayish or brownish, more or less specked, blotched, or striped with blackish; sometimes there is a black stripe along the middle of the back; sometimes the general color is dark reddish. These three species of scaly worms all have a large proboscis with four powerful jaws at the end, and a circle of papillæ, as in figs. 40 and 41; they are carnivorous in their habits and rather sluggish in their movements. When disturbed they curl themselves up into a ball. They are very complicated in their appendages, and the spines and setæ of these appendages are very curious in structure, when examined with a microscope. Notwithstanding their numerous sharp spines they are often devoured by fishes, and they frequently also fall victims to their more powerful companions belonging to the Nereis tribe, and are sometimes destroyed even by the apparently inoffensive Nemerteans. Adhering to the under sides of the rocks and stones there are several kinds of tubes constructed by annelids. One of the most common and abundant kinds of these tube-dwelling worms is the *Sabellaria vulgaris* V., (Plate XVII, figs. 88, 88*a*.) This worm constructs firm and hard tubes out of fine sand and a cement secreted by special glands. These tubes are bent and twisted in various directions and are generally united together into masses or colonies, sometimes forming aggregations of considerable thickness and perhaps several inches or a foot across. The tubes of this worm are also common on the shells of oysters. Another very curious and beautiful worm, the *Scionopsis palmata* V., constructs much larger and coarser tubes out of bits of sea-weeds and shells, sand, small pebbles, and other similar materials; these tubes are long and crooked and attached for their whole length to the under side of rocks. The worm that constructs them has some general resemblance to the *Amphitrite ornata*, but is seldom more than three or four inches long and is usually darker colored, the color being generally reddish brown or dark brown, more or less speckled with white. There are only seventeen fascicles of setæ on each side. The gills are only three in number, viz: an odd median one, much larger than the others, placed just behind the tentacles; and a pair of smaller ones, but similar in form and just back of the first; all three gills have a stalk or peduncle, and branch toward the end in a palmate or digitate manner, each of the divisions again subdividing. The gills can be retracted beneath a sort of collar which arises just behind them; their color is greenish, specked with white. The gills of this worm are very elegant in form, and quite unlike those of any other known species, both in position and form. Therefore it is necessary to establish a new genus for this species. It has been found from Vineyard Sound to New Jersey; both among eel-grass in shallow water, and under stones. The *Nicolea simplex* is a related species, with similar habits.

The crooked, round, calcareous tubes made by *Serpula dianthus* V., are often to be found adhering to the under surfaces and sides of stones near low-water mark, and also in the pools in more exposed situations; sometimes they are even aggregated together into masses. When disturbed the worm suddenly withdraws its beautiful wreath of gills into its tube and closes the aperture closely by means of a curious plug or operculum. This is placed at the end of a rather long pedicle, and is funnel-shaped, the outside longitudinally striated and the edge bordered by about thirty sharp denticles; from the middle of the upper side another smaller, short, funnel-shaped process arises, the edge of which is divided into twelve or thirteen, long, rather slender, rigid processes, which are usually a little curved inward at the top, but may be spread apart in a stellate form. A small, rudimentary, club-shaped operculum exists on the other side. When these tubes are placed in sea-water and left undisturbed for a short time, the occupant will cautiously push out its operculum and display its elegant wreath of branchiæ, which varies much in color in different specimens, but often recalls the varied hues and forms of different kinds of pinks, (*Dianthus*.) The name which I have given to it alludes to this resemblance. Fine specimens of this *Serpula* may often be found, also, in the pools near low-water mark, attached to the upper surfaces or sides of rocks, and in such situation they display their charms to great advantage. The wreath of branchiæ is nearly circular, consisting of two symmetrical parts, each of which is made up of about eighteen pectinate branchiæ; these are covered on their inner surfaces with slender filaments which extend nearly to the ends, but leave the tips naked. Young specimens have fewer branchiæ. In the more common varieties these branchiæ are purple at base, with narrow bands of light red or pale yellowish green; above this they are transversely banded or annulated with purplish brown, alternating with yellowish green, or with purple and white; the pinnæ usually correspond in color to the part from which they arise, but are sometimes all purple. In other specimens the branchiæ are yellowish white, or greenish white, banded with brown. In one variety (*citrina*) they are bright lemon-yellow, or orange-colored, throughout. The operculum, in all the varieties, is usually brownish green above, with the sides purplish brown, lined with whitish near the edge, and with a greenish white band at the base; the pedicle is usually purplish, with two or more bands of white. The body is usually deep greenish yellow, with the back lemon-yellow; the collar is broad with an undulated border, and is pale green, veined with darker green blood-vessels. This species is also often met with in dredging on shelly bottoms.

The *Potamilla oculifera* (Plate XVII, fig. 86) is another beautiful annelid, related somewhat to the *Serpula*, but its tubes are tough and flexible; they are constructed out of fine sand and other foreign matters, glued firmly together with the special secretions of the animal. These tubes are often found attached to the under sides of stones, but, passing around to the sides, open upward by a free extremity; they also frequently occur in sheltered nooks in the tide-pools. The worm, when undisturbed, puts out a beautiful wreath of branchiæ somewhat resembling that of the *Serpula*, but there is no operculum. The branchiæ are always beautifully colored, though the colors are quite variable. In one of the commonest styles of coloration, the branchiæ are surrounded at base with reddish brown; above this with a ring of white; next by a band of reddish brown; then for the terminal half the color is yellowish gray, with indistinct blotches of brown; on the outer sides of the branchiæ there are one to three dark red eyes. There are ten or more branchiæ in each half of the wreath, and they are longer on one side than on the other.

Another related species, the *Sabella microphthalma* V., also occasionally occurs in the pools and on the under sides of stones, constructing tubes very much like those of the last species. This is a much shorter and stouter worm, with the branchial wreath relatively much larger and nearly half as long as the body. The branchiæ are pale yellowish, greenish, or flesh-color, with numerous transverse bands of darker green extending to the pinnæ; on the outer side of the branchiæ there are numerous minute eye-like spots of dark brown, arranged in two rows on each. The body is usually dull olive-green. The *Fabricia Leidyi* V., is another member of this group of worms, but is of very minute size. It constructs delicate, flexible tubes, free toward the end, which usually stands upright. Its tubes may be found in the pools and on the under side of stones. The worm itself is very small, slender, and when undisturbed protrudes a wreath, composed of six branchiæ, to a considerable distance above the mouth of the tube. The branchiæ have five to seven pinnæ on each side, the lowest much the longest, so that when expanded they all reach nearly to one level. At the base of the branchiæ there are two pulsating vesicles, alternating in their beats; and just back of these there are two minute brown eye-specks; two similar eyes exist at the posterior end. Eleven segments of the body bear fascicles of setæ. Color yellowish white, the blood-vessels red.

Two or more species of the minute but beautiful worms belonging to the genus *Spirorbis* are found attached to the fronds of sea-weeds, to shells, stones, &c., especially in the pools. These are related to the *Serpula*, and like it form solid calcareous tubes, but these are always coiled up in a close spiral, and the coil is attached by one side. The little worms put out an elegant wreath of branchiæ, and are furnished with an operculum. Another very interesting and beautifully colored worm, sometimes found under and among the stones, where there is mud, is the *Cistenides Gouldii* V., (Plate XVII, figs. 87, 87*a*.) This constructs very remarkable, conical, free tubes, of grains of sand arranged in a single layer, like miniature masonry, and bound together by a water-proof cement. This worm belongs more properly to the muddy and sandy shores and will be mentioned again.

Under stones and decaying sea-weeds, near high-water mark, two or more kinds of small slender worms are usually found in great numbers; these differ widely from all those before mentioned, and are more nearly related to the common earth-worms of the garden. One of these is white, slender, and about an inch long, tapering to both ends. This is *Halodillus littoralis* V., apparently forming a new genus allied to *Enchytræus*. Another is of about the same size, but rather longer and more slender, and light red in color. It has a moniliform intestine, with a red blood-vessel attached to it above and below. It belongs apparently to the genus *Clitellio*, (*C. irroratus* V.)

In addition to all these setigerous *Annelids* which have been enumerated, there are quite a number of worms to be found on the rocky shores which are destitute of all these external appendages, and have the surface of the body smooth and ciliated. There are two tribes of such worms: in one of them the body is much elongated, and either roundish, or flattened, and usually very changeable in form and capable of great extension and contraction. These are known as *Nemerteans*; most of them have a proboscis which they can dart out to a great length. In the other group, known as *Planarians*, the body is broad, short, and depressed, and often quite flat, and their internal structure is quite different.

One of the largest of the Nemerteans, the *Meckelia ingens*, (Plate XIX, figs. 96, 96*a*,) is met with under stones where there is sand, but it belongs properly to the sandy shores. It is an enormous, smooth, flat worm, yellowish, flesh-colored, or whitish, and sometimes grows to be ten or twelve feet long and over an inch wide. The *Meckelia rosea* also occurs occasionally in similar places. This is similar in form, but is smaller, less flattened, and decidedly red in color. It is often covered by adhering sand. Another species, belonging to the Nemerteans, is often found in great abundance under stones from mid-tide to near high-water mark. Many of them are often found coiled together in large clusters. This is the *Nemertes socialis*; it is very slender or filiform, and often five or six inches long when extended. Its color is dark ash-brown or blackish, a little lighter beneath, and it has three or four eyes in a longitudinal group on each side of the head. Another larger species, apparently belonging to the genus *Cerebratulus*, but not sufficiently studied while living, is also abundant under stones. It is much stouter and is usually dark olive-green, brownish-green, or greenish-black in color, but a little lighter below and at the borders of the head. Several other small Nemerteans occur under similar circumstances. In the pools, creeping over and among the algæ and hydroids, a yellowish or light orange-colored species, one or two inches long, is often met with. This species secretes an unusual amount of mucus, which is, perhaps, connected with its climbing habits, and I have on this account named it *Polinia glutinosa* V., (Plate XIX, fig. 97.) It varies in the number of its eyes, according to its age, but they are always grouped in oblique clusters as in the figure.

The color is sometimess bright orange anteriorly, but lighter posteriorly, with a faint dusky or greenish line along the middle.

Another species, closely resembling the last in form, color, and size, is quite common under stones, and especially in dead tubes of *Serpula*, near low-water mark. This is the *Cosmocephala ochracea* V., (Plate XIX, figs. 95, 95*a*;) it has numerous eyes on the sides of the head, three or four on each side forming an anterior row parallel with the margin; the others forming two parallel oblique groups, usually with two or three eyes in each, farther back. On the lower side of the head there is, on each side, an obliquely transverse groove. The color is usually dull yellowish-white or grayish; the anterior part is often tinged with orange and the posterior with ash-gray; there is generally a distinct paler median line, most distinct anteriorly. It grows to be two or three inches long, when extended.

Of the Planarians several species are also found creeping over the under side of stones and in the tide-pools. One of the most abundant is *Procerodes frequens*, which is a very small but lively species, found creeping on the under side of stones near high-water. It is usually about an eighth of an inch long, dark brown or blackish above and gray below, and it has two reniform eyes. The *Monocelis agilis* is still smaller, elliptical, with only one median eye; its color is dark brown or blackish. By some writers this genus is placed among the Nemerteans. Two larger species of this group are also occasionally found on the under side of stones. One of these, the *Planocera nebulosa*, (Plate XIX, fig. 100,) is usually about half an inch wide and three-fourths long, but may become nearly circular, or may extend into a long elliptical form. It is flat and thin, with flexuous edges. Its color is olive-green above, with a lighter median stripe behind, and yellowish green below. The tentacles on the back are whitish and retractile.

The *Stylochopsis littoralis* V., (Plate XIX, fig. 99,) is also frequently found on the under side of stones. It is remakable for having a cluster of eyes on each tentacle, other clusters in front of them, and two or more rows of eye-spots around the margin, especially in front. Its color is variable, but usually greenish, greenish yellow, or brownish yellow, often reticulated with flesh-color; there is generally a pale median streak posteriorly. The eggs were laid July 12th in large clusters, composed of many small white eggs closely crowded together, side by side, and attached to the surface of the glass jar in which they were kept.

There are also representatives of the "round worms," or Nematodes, to be found beneath the stones and among the roots of algæ, hydroids, &c. The commonest of these is, perhaps, the *Pontonema marinum* (Plate XVIII, fig. 94.) This is a small, very slender, smooth, white, round worm, tapering to both ends, and very active in its movements, constantly coiling itself into a spiral and again uncoiling itself. Its head is furnished with about six minute cirri; in the male the tail is short, narrow, nearly straight, but one-sided, rapidly tapering. and subacute; in the female the body is much longer, and the tail is long, slightly tapered, straight, and obtuse. The *Pontonema vacillatum* also occurs in similar places in abundance. In this species the male has a short, obtuse, incurved tail; the female a straight, tapering, narrow, obtuse one. Both species are oviparous, and the female genital orifice is near the middle of the body. These worms are from a quarter to half an inch or more in length. Their complete history is not known; they are closely allied to many of the parasitic worms, and it is possible that in some stages of their development these are also parasites.

Of the Radiates there are also numerous species to be found on these rocky shores.

Although the purple "sea-urchin," *Arbacia punctulata*, and the green "sea-urchin," *Strongylocentrotus Dröbachiensis*, (Plate XXXV, fig. 268,) are sometimes met with, their occurrence is irregular and uncertain at low-water in this region. The former occurs in abundance on rocky and shelly bottoms in the sounds; while the latter occurs chiefly on similar bottoms in the cold area, and at low-water on the outer rocky shores, and still more abundantly farther north.

The green star-fish, *Asterias arenicola*, (Plate XXXV, fig. 269,) is found in large numbers at low-water among the rocks at certain times, but at other times is seldom met with, though a few young specimens can almost always be found by careful search beneath the stones. The adults were very abundant on the shore at Parker's Point, in the latter part of June; but by the middle of July very few could be found there. Their habit of coming up to the shore may be connected with their reproductive season. They are always abundant on shelly bottoms in the bays and sounds, especially where there are beds of muscles or oysters, upon which they feed. They often prove exceedingly destructive of oysters planted in waters that are not too brackish for their comfort. They manage to eat oysters that are far too large for them to swallow whole, by grasping the shell with their numerous adhesive feet, and then, after bending their five flexible rays around the shell so as partly to inclose it, they protrude the lobes and folds of their enormous saccular stomach from the distended mouth, and surrounding the oyster-shell more or less completely with the everted stomach they proceed to digest the contents at leisure, and when the meal is finished they quietly withdraw the stomach and stow it away in its proper place. In this way a large "school" of star-fishes will, in a short time, destroy all the oysters on beds many acres in extent, unless their operation be interfered with by the watchful owners. In one instance, within a few years, at Westport, Connecticut, they thus destroyed about 2,000 bushels of oysters, occupying beds about 20 acres in extent, in a few weeks, during the absence of the proprietor.

In order to stop their operations it is necessary to dredge over the oyster-grounds and destroy all the star-fishes thus brought up, by leaving them on shore above high-water mark; for if simply torn in pieces and thrown overboard, as is sometimes done, each ray has the power of reproducing all the lost parts, so that each fragment may, after a time, become a perfect star-fish.

The color of this species is generally dark green or brownish green, with the madreporic plate bright orange; the males are more inclined to brown, and sometimes have a reddish tint. It is found all along the coast from Massachusetts Bay to Florida.

The eggs of this species, like those of most other star-fishes, produce peculiar larvæ, entirely unlike the parents, and provided with vibrating cilia by means of which they swim about in the water, or at the surface, for a considerable time. The young star-fish develops within the larva and gradually absorbs the substance of the larva into its own organization.

The development of this and our other common species has been very fully described and illustrated by Mr. A. Agassiz.

Of the Hydroids many species occur in the pools, or attached to the lower sides of overhanging rocks, or of stones that have an open space beneath them, or growing upon the *Fucus* and other sea-weeds at low-water mark. The most abundant of all is the *Sertularia pumila*, (Plate XXXVII, fig. 279,) which grows in small tufts of delicate branches on the stems and fronds of all the larger sea-weeds, and on the sides and lower surfaces of stones. Another beautiful species, the *Obelia commissuralis*, (Plate XXXVII, fig. 281,) occurs at low-water mark and in tide-pools, attached to stones and sea-weeds. It is very delicate and much branched, and sometimes grows five or six inches high, though usually smaller. At certain times it produces small medusæ in its urn-shaped reproductive capsules; these are discharged and swim free for some time, having sixteen tentacles when they become free. Several other species of this genus also occur attached to the sea-weeds at low-water. The most common of these is *O. diaphana*, which grows about an inch high, attached to the stems of *Fucus*. The *Campanularia flexuosa* is another similar hydroid, remarkable for its large reproductive capsules, in which medusæ are developed that never become free. This species occurs in the pools at low-water, on weeds and stones, and also on the lower sides of overhanging rocks or the timbers of wharves. It is much more abundant farther north, as at Eastport, Maine, where it grows in profusion on the timbers of the wharves, hanging down from their lower sides, collapsed and dripping, while the tide is low. The *Pennaria tiarella* (Plate XXXVII, figs. 277, 278) is a very conspicuous and beautiful species on account of its much-divided black branches and numerous bright red flower-like hydroids. It occurs occasionally in the pools, and just below low-water mark, attached to stones, corallines, &c., but is more common in somewhat deeper water on rocky and shelly bottoms. The "file-fish" feeds on this species, and probably on other allied hydroids, for its stomach was found full of the stems and branches, cut up in fine pieces. Its broad, sharp-edged jaws are admirably adapted for browsing on hydroids, but yet this may not be its principal food, for our observations were very few on this fish, owing to its rarity. One of the most interesting of the hydroids, found in the rocky pools at low-water, or in other shaded places, is the *Hybocodon prolifer*, (Plate XXXVIII, fig. 282.) This is one of the largest and most beautiful of the tubularians, and is very conspicuous on account of its deep orange-red color. It is by no means common, and grows only in those pools where the water is pure and cool, or under the shade of overhanging rocks. It usually grows singly or in groups of two or three clustered together. The delicate hydrarium of *Bougainvillia superciliaris* (Plate XXXVII, fig. 276) is also occasionally met with in the larger tide-pools near low-water mark, and the small, free medusæ, which are produced by budding from the hydrarium, are frequently found swimming in the waters in spring. The *Clava leptostyla* is a beautiful and apparently soft and tender species, but it grows in clusters on the fronds of *Fucus* at low-water mark, on the most exposed shores, and withstands the most powerful surf, unharmed. The colonies are bright light red in color and consist of numerous hydroids arising from creeping stolon-like tubes, which interlace to form the base of the colony. Each of the hydroids consists of a cylindrical stem, slender at base and about a quarter of an inch high, at the end of which there is a thicker, club-shaped or fusiform "head," covered with about fifteen to thirty, long, slender tentacles, but the form both of the heads and tentacles is constantly changing, owing to their contractions. The small medusa-buds are grouped in clusters below the tentacles and do not become free. This species is also to be found in the pools and on the under sides of large stones close to low-water mark.

The *Hydractinia polyclina* is often met with covering the dead shells inhabited by the hermit-crabs, whether in the pools or in deeper water off shore, with a soft, velvet-like, reddish coating, which is made up of hundreds of hydroids united together by their bases into a rather firm, continuous layer, covered with conical points. This basal layer sometimes not only entirely covers the shell, but extends out considerably beyond the borders of the aperture, so as to increase the capacity of the interior. This is no doubt a great gain to the crab, because he will not be so soon compelled to exchange his shell for a larger one. Each colony of these hydroids is either male or female; the sexes differ in depth of color, the male colonies being palest. But in each colony there are also many sterile individuals, who have to do the eating and digesting for the whole community, while the sexual individuals attend to the reproduction of the race. Farther north, as at Nahant, Massachusetts, this species often incrusts broad surfaces of the rocks in the pools, but I have not observed it growing in this way south of Cape Cod; yet in one instance we dredged it growing on a rock.

The *Halecium gracile* V. is frequently found growing in profusion on the under side of stones, in tide-pools, and attached to oysters, dead shells, &c., in shallow waters, both of the sounds and estuaries. It forms rather dense, pale, flexible tufts, three or four inches high, with very numerous slender branches.

Of Polyps there are several species belonging to the actinians, or "sea-anemones," and one species of genuine coral, (*Astrangia*,) but the latter is seldom found at low-water, though common in shallow water, on rocky bottoms. The most common of the actinians is the "fringed sea-anemone," *Metridium marginatum*. This may almost always be found on the under sides of large stones that have sufficient space beneath, in sheltered crevices near low-water mark, and adhering to the rocks along the borders of the larger tide-pools, where they are shaded and protected by the overhanging sea-weeds. In full expansion this species has a very graceful form. From the expanded base the body rises in the form of a tall, smooth column, sometimes cylindrical, sometimes tapering slightly to the middle, and then enlarging to the summit. Toward the top the column is surrounded by a circular thickened fold, above which the character of the surface suddenly changes, the skin becoming thinner and translucent, so that the internal radiating partitions are visible through it. This part expands upward and outward to the margin, which is folded into numerous deep undulations or frills, and everywhere covered with very numerous, fine, short, crowded tentacles. The tentacles also cover the upper side of the disk, half way to the mouth, but are larger and less crowded in proportion to the distance from the margin. The mouth is oval and the lips divided into numerous folds. The largest specimens are sometimes five or six inches high and three or four inches across the disk. The colors are extremely variable. Most frequently the sides of the body are yellowish brown or orange-brown, but it may be of any shade from white, flesh-color, pink, salmon, chestnut, orange, yellow, light brown, to dark umber-brown; or it may be mottled and streaked with two or more of these colors. The upper part of the body and tentacles are translucent, and have lighter colors, generally either white, pink, flesh-color, or pale salmon; the tentacles are also frequently banded with flake-white, and often have dark tips. This species, when much irritated, throws out from minute loop-holes along the sides large numbers of long, slender, white threads, which are covered with microscopic stinging-organs, powerful enough to defend them from the attacks of fishes and other enemies; but they do not penetrate the human skin.

Another species, the "white-armed anemone," *Sagartia leucolena*, (Plate XXXVIII, fig. 284,) is also common at low-water, especially on the under side of large stones, and sometimes nearly buried in sand and gravel. This is more elongated and slender than the last, and has a smaller, simple and plain disk, with the tentacles much longer and more slender, and crowded together near the margin; the surface of the body is smooth and uniform, without any thickened fold. The color is usually pale salmon or flesh-color, and the skin is translucent, so as to show the internal lamellæ; the tentacles are paler and more translucent, and usually whitish, but sometimes pale salmon. The tentacles, in full expansion, are over an inch long. A second elongated species of *Sagartia* (*S. modesta*) occurs buried up to its tentacles in the gravel and sand among rocks. This species is quite rare, and has a much thicker and firmer skin, which is nearly opaque and dull yellowish in color; the tentacles are shorter, with dark greenish markings at the base.

The *Halocampa producta* (Plate XXXVIII, fig. 285) also occurs under the same circumstances with the last, though it may also be found on sandy shores, slightly attached to a shell or pebble, perhaps a foot beneath the surface, but in expansion it stretches its body so as to expand its tentacles at the surface, above its burrow, into which it quickly withdraws when disturbed. This species is remarkable for the great length and slenderness of its body in full extension; for having only twenty tentacles, with swollen tips; and for the rows of suckers along the sides, to which it fastens grains of sand, &c. It has no distinct disk at the base, which is bulbous and adapted for burrowing Its color is whitish, flesh-color, or pale salmon, with the suckers whitish. The tentacles usually have darker brown tips, but sometimes the tips are flake-white. In full expansion the length of large specimens is about a foot, and the diameter about a third of an inch, but in contraction the body becomes much shorter and more swollen.

The *Astrangia Danæ*, which is the only true coral yet discovered on the coast of New England, is occasionally found on the under side of overhanging rocks, or in pools where it is seldom or never left dry. The coral forms incrusting patches, usually two or three inches across, and less than half an inch thick, composed of numerous crowded corallets, having stellate cells about an eighth of an inch in diameter. The living animals are white, and in expansion rise high above the cells and expand a circle of long, slender, minutely warted tentacles, which have enlarged tips. These coral-polyps, when expanded, resemble clusters of small, white sea-anemones, and like them they will seize their prey with their tentacles and transfer it to their mouths. They feed readily, in confinement, upon fragments of mollusca or crustacea.

Several species of sponges also occur in the rocky pools and on the under sides of stones. The most conspicuous one is a bright red species, which forms irregular crusts, and rises up in the middle into many small, irregular, lobe-like branches. Another species forms broad, thin incrustations, of a sulphur-yellow color, on the under side of stones. These species have not been identified. A small, urn-shaped or oval species, with a large aperture at the summit, surrounded by a circle of slender, projecting spicula, occurs in the pools, and is probably the same as the *Grantia ciliata* of Europe.

In addition to the numerous species already enumerated, most of which belong to groups that are essentially marine animals, there are a few species of marine insects that are frequently met with under stones, or among the small green algæ. Among these a small lead-colored insect belonging to the family of "spring-tails," *Anurida maritima*, is the most abundant. With it a spider, *Bdella*, and several species of mites (*Trombidium*) are often found. Several specimens of a "false scorpion," *Chernes oblongus*, were also found by Mr. Smith near low-water mark under stones. In the pools and on the rocks, among the green confervæ and other sea-weeds, the active green larvæ of a two-winged fly, *Chironomus oceanicus*, is often found in abundance. This larva we have detected in the stomach of the "tom-cod," mixed with small crustacea.

List of species inhabiting the rocky shores of the sounds and bays.

In the following list the species living in these situations are brought together systematically, whether mentioned in the preceding pages or not. The lists are not to be regarded as complete, but include most of the species ordinarily met with. The references are to the pages of this report, where remarks upon the species may be found:

ARTICULATA.

Insects.

	Page.		Page.
Chironomus oceanicus	331	Bdella marina....	331
Anurida maritima..........	331	Trombidium, several species	331
Chernes oblongus	331		

Crustacea.

	Page.		Page.
Cancer irroratus	312	Mœra levis	315
Panopeus depressus	312	Melita nitida..............	314
P. Sayi....................	312	Amphithoë maculata.......	315
P. Harrisii	313	A. valida..................	315
Carcinus granulatus........	312	Caprella, sp...............	316
Eupagurus pollicaris	313	Sphæroma quadridentata ..	315
E. longicarpus	313	Idotea irrorata	316
Homarus Americanus.......	313	I. phosphorea	316
Orchestia agilis	314	Erichsonia filiformis.......	316
Hyale littoralis............	315	Epelys montosus	
Calliopius læviusculus......	315	Jæra copiosa	315
Gammarus ornatus.........	314	Balanus balanoides........	304
G. annulatus...............	314	Numerous small Entomostraca.	
G. Marinus.................	314		

Annelids, (Chætopods.)

Oligochæta.

Nemerteans.

Planarians.

Nematodes.

MOLLUSCA.

Gastropods, (Univalves.)

Lamellibranchs, (*Bivalves.*)

Ascidians.

Bryozoa, (*or Polyzoa.*)

RADIATA.

Echinoderms.

Acalephs.

	Page.		Page.
Obelia commissuralis	327	Halecium gracile	328
O. pyriformis	390	Sertularia argentea	408
O. diaphana	327	S. pumila	327
O. geniculata	407	Bougainvillia superciliaris	328
Clytia Johnstoni	408	Margelis Carolinensis	
Orthopyxis caliculata	408	Clava leptostyla	328
Platypyxis cylindrica	408	Pennaria tiarella	327
Campanularia volubilis	408	Hybocodon prolifer	328
C. flexuosa	327	Hydractinia polyclina	328
Lafoëa calcarata	408		

Polyps.

	Page.		Page.
Metridium marginatum	329	Halocampa producta	330
Sagartia leucolena	329	Astrangia Danæ	329
S. modesta	330		

PROTOZOA.

Sponges.

	Page.		Page.
Grantia ciliata	330	Tedania, sp	330
Leucosolenia botryoides (?)	391	Renieria, sp	330
Halichondria, sp	330		

II.—2. FAUNA OF THE SANDY SHORES OF THE BAYS AND SOUNDS.

These sandy shores vary considerably in character according to their situations and composition. In the more exposed positions the beaches of fine loose sand differ but little in character from those that prevail so extensively on the ocean shores, from Cape Cod to North Florida. In more sheltered situations there is generally more or less mud mixed with the sand, which often forms shores with a very gentle slope, running down to broad flats, bare at low-water; such flats of sandy mud are the favorite homes of large numbers of burrowing creatures; but even on the exposed beaches of loose siliceous sand, which are completely torn up and remodeled by every storm, there are still to be found many kinds of animals perfectly adapted to such conditions, finding there their proper homes. In other cases there is more or less gravel and pebbles mixed with the sand, which, under some conditions of exposure, produce a firm and compact deposit, admirably adapted to the tastes and habits of certain tube-dwelling and burrowing creatures. In other places, especially in sandy coves or other sheltered situations, the sandy flats are partly covered by tufts and patches of eel-grass, and there are many animals that find congenial resorts on such flats. Then there will sometimes be pools or rivulets of sea-water on the sandy flats, in which certain creatures often spend the short time while thus imprisoned by the tide.

The special localities where the sand-dwelling species of this region were chiefly studied, are the beaches on Naushon and adjacent islands; Nobska Beach and several other beaches near Wood's Hole; the extensive sand-beach between Falmouth and Waquoit; the beach at Menemsha Bight, on Martha's Vineyard; several beaches on the shores of Buzzard's Bay; the beaches at South End, Savin Rock, and other localities near New Haven; the beaches on Great South Bay, Long Island; the beaches at the mouth of Great Egg Harbor, New Jersey, &c., besides the outer beaches at various other points.

Along the upper part of the sand-beaches there is generally an almost continuous belt of dead sea-weeds, broken shells, fragments of crabs, lobsters, and various other débris cast up by the waves. Although many of the dead shells, &c., which occur in this way, belong really to the sandy shores near low-water, others have come, perhaps, from deeper water and other kinds of bottom. Therefore, although such rubbish-heaps may afford good collecting grounds for those who frequent the shores after storms, it would be useless to enumerate the species that more or less frequently occur in them. Beneath such masses of decaying materials many insects and crustacea occur, together with certain genuine worms. Part of these are truly marine forms, and are never found away from the sea-shores, but many, especially of the insects, are in no sense marine, being found anywhere in the interior where decaying matters abound. The two-winged flies (*Diptera*,) of many kinds, are especially abundant, and their larvæ occur in immense numbers in the decaying sea-weed. Some of these flies are, however, true marine species, and live in the larval state in situations where they are submerged for a considerable time by the tide. I have often dug such larvæ from the sand near low-water mark, and have also dredged them at the depth of four or five fathoms off shore. During unusually high tides immense quantities of the fly-larvæ will be carried away by the encroachment of the waters, and thus become food for fishes of many kinds, and especially for the young ones, which frequent the shallow waters along the shores. There are also many species of beetles (*Coleoptera*) which frequent these places, and several of them are genuine marine insects, living both in the larval and adult conditions in burrows between tides. Among these are two or three species of *Bledius*, belonging to the *Staphylinidæ;* several tiger-beetles (*Cicindela*,) and representatives of other families. The "tiger-beetles" are very active, carnivorous insects and frequent the dry sands just above high-water mark; when disturbed they rise quickly and fly away to the distance of several yards before alighting. They are so wary that it is difficult to catch them without a net. Most of the species reflect bright, metallic, bronzy or green colors, and many of them have the elytra more or less marked with white. Mr. S. I. Smith found the larva of our largest species (*C. generosa*) at Fire Island, living in holes in the sand below high-water mark, associated with the species of *Talorchestia*.

Beneath the decaying sea-weeds on the sandy shores immense numbers of the lively little crustacean, *Orchestia agilis*, (p. 314, Plate IV, fig. 14,) may always be found. Two other related species, of larger size and paler colors, but having the same habit of leaping, though not in such a high degree, occur among the weeds, or burrowing in the sand, or beneath drift-wood, &c., a little below high-water mark. In fact the sand is sometimes completely filled with their holes, of various sizes. Both these species are stout in form, and become about an inch long when mature. One of them, *Talorchestia longicornis*, can be easily distinguished by its very long antennæ ; the other, *T. megalophthalma*, by its shorter antennæ and very large eyes. Both these species are pale grayish, and imitate the color of the sand very perfectly. When driven from their burrows by unusually high tides or storms they are capable of swimming actively in the water. They make dainty morsels for fishes and many shore birds, as well as for certain crabs, especially *Ocypoda arenaria*.

On sandy beaches near high-water mark, especially where the sand is rather compact and somewhat sheltered, one of the "fiddler-crabs," *Gelasimus pugilator*, is frequently found in great numbers, either running actively about over the sand, or peering cautiously from their holes, which are often thickly scattered over considerable areas. These holes are mostly from half an inch to an inch in diameter, and a foot or more in depth, the upper part nearly perpendicular, becoming horizontal below, with a chamber at the end. Mr. Smith, by lying perfectly still for some time on the sand, succeeded in witnessing their mode of digging. In doing this they drag up pellets of moist sand, which they carry under the three anterior ambulatory legs that are on the rear side, climbing out of their burrows by means of the legs of the side in front, aided by the posterior leg of the other side. After arriving at the mouth of their burrows and taking a cautious survey of the landscape, they run quickly to the distance, often of four or five feet from the burrow before dropping their load, using the same legs as before and carrying the dirt in the same manner. They then take another careful survey of the surroundings, run nimbly back to the hole, and after again turning their pedunculated eyes in every direction, suddenly disappear, soon to reappear with another load. They work in this way both in the night and in the brightest sunshine, whenever the tide is out and the weather is suitable. In coming out or going into their burrows either side may go in advance, but the male more commonly comes out with the large claw forward. According to Mr. Smith's observations this species is a vegetarian, feeding upon the minute algæ which grow upon the moist sand. In feeding the males use only the small claw with which they pick up the bits of algæ very daintily; the females use indifferently either of their small claws for this purpose. They always swallow more or less sand with their food. Mr. Smith also saw these crabs engaged in scraping up the surface of the sand where covered with their favorite algæ, which they formed into pellets and carried into their holes, in the same way that they bring sand out, doubtless storing it until needed for food, for he often found large quantities stored in the terminal chamber. Mr. T. M. Prudden has since ascertained that one of the other species of "fiddlers" on our shores (*G. minax*) is also a vegetarian and feeds upon similar algæ, which grow on the muddy salt-marshes.

The *Ocypoda arenaria* is a crab allied to the "fiddlers" and similar in some of its habits. It is a southern species, ranging as far as Brazil, and adult specimens have not yet been observed on the coast of New England, but Mr. Smith has observed the young in abundance at Fire Island, and we have the young from Block Island; it occurs at Great Egg Harbor, New Jersey, of larger size, and therefore it may be looked for on the beaches of Nantucket and Martha's Vineyard. This crab lives on the beaches at, and even far above, high-water mark. It digs large holes like the fiddlers, often in the loose dry sand, back from the shore, yet when disturbed it will sometimes take to the water in order to escape. though it soon returns to the shore. In digging its holes, according to Mr. Smith's observations, it works in the same way as the "fiddler-crabs," except that it is quicker in its motions, and often, instead of carrying the pellets of sand to a distance from the hole, it throws it away with a sudden and powerful jerk, scattering the sand in every direction, It is even more cautious in its movements, and is always on the alert, even the slightest movement on the part of one who is watching them is sure to send them all into their holes instantly. In color this species imitates the sand very perfectly, especially while young, when they are irregularly mottled and speckled with lighter and darker shades of gray. They also have the habit of crouching down closely upon or into the sand, when suddenly frightened, and aided by their colors will often thus escape observation. At other times they will trust to their speed and scamper over the sand with such swiftness that they are not easily captured. This crab is carnivorous in its habits and, according to Mr. Smith's observations, it lives largely upon the "beach-fleas" (*Talorchestia*) which inhabit the same localities. It will lie in wait and suddenly spring upon them, very much as a cat catches mice. It also feeds upon dead fishes and other animals that are thrown on the shore by the waves.

Another inhabitant of the upper part of the sand-beaches, just below high-water mark, is the *Scyphacella arenicola* SMITH, which has, as yet, been found only on the coast of New Jersey, but probably occurs farther north. It is a small, sand-colored Isopod crustacean, which has no near relatives, so far as known, except in New Zealand. It burrows in the sand, making a little conical mound around the mouth of the holes.

The only Annelid observed high up on the sand-beaches is the slender, white *Halodrillus littoralis*, referred to on page 324, which lives under the decaying sea-weeds in great numbers.

On the lower parts of the sand-beaches, toward low-water mark, and especially on the broad flats, which are barely uncovered by the lowest tides, a much larger number of species occurs.

Among the Crustacea of these sandy shores we frequently find the common *Cancer irroratus*, (p. 312,) which is very cosmopolitan in its habits. Occasionally we meet with a specimen of *Carcinus granulatus*, but this is not its favorite abode; but the "lady-crab" or "sand-crab," *Platyonichus ocellatus*, (Plate I, fig. 4,) is perfectly at home among the loose sands at low-water mark, even on the most exposed beaches. This species is also abundant on sandy-bottoms off shore, and as it is furnished with swimming organs on its posterior legs, it can swim rapidly in the water and was taken at the surface in Vineyard Sound in several instances, and some of the specimens thus taken were of full size. When living at low-water mark on the sand-beaches it generally buries itself up to its eyes and antennæ in the sand, watching for prey, or on the lookout for enemies. If disturbed it quickly glides backward and downward into the sand and disappears instantly. This power of quickly burrowing deeply into the sand it possesses in common with all the other marine animals, of every class, which inhabit the exposed beaches of loose sand, for upon this habit their very existence depends during storms. By burying themselves sufficiently deep they are beyond the reach of the breakers. The means of effecting this rapid burrowing are very diverse in the different classes. Thus one of the fishes (*Ophidium marginatum*), which lives in these places, has a long acute tail and by its peculiar undulatory motions can instantly bury itself tail-first in the sand. Others have acute heads and go in head-first.

The "lady-crab" is predacious in its habits, feeding upon various smaller creatures, but like most of the crabs it is also fond of dead fishes or any other dead animals. In some localities they are so abundant that a dead fish or shark will in a short time be completely covered with them, but if a person should approach they will all suddenly slip off backwards and quickly disappear in every direction beneath the sand; after a short time, if everything be quiet, immense numbers of eyes and antennæ will be gradually and cautiously protruded from beneath the sand, and after their owners have satisfied themselves that all is well, the army of crabs will soon appear above the sand again and continue their operations. The color of this crab is quite bright and does not imitate the sand, probably owing to its mode of 'concealment. The ground-color is white, but the back is covered with annular spots formed by specks of red and purple. It is devoured in great numbers by many of the larger fishes.

Another curious burrowing creature, living under the same circumstances as the last, is the *Hippa talpoida*, (Pate II, fig. 5.) But this species burrows like a mole, head-first, instead of backward. It can also swim quite actively and is sometimes found swimming about in the pools left on the flats at low-water. It is occasionally dug out of the sand at low-water mark, and is often thrown up by the waves, on sand-beaches, but it seems to live in shallow water on sandy bottoms in great numbers, for in seining on one of the sand-beaches near Wood's Hole for small fishes, a large quantity of this species was taken. Its color is yellowish white, tinged with purple on the back. It is one of the favorite articles of food of many fishes. Mr. Smith found the young abundant at Fire Island, near high-water, burrowing in the sand. This species is still more abundant farther south.

The curious long-legged "spider-crab," *Libinia canaliculata*, is frequently met with at or just below low-water mark on sandy shores, but its proper home is on muddy bottoms.

Creeping, or rapidly running, over the bottom in shallow water, or in the tide-pools on the flats, the smaller "hermit-crab," *Eupagurus longicarpus*, (p. 313,) may almost always be observed ensconced in some dead univalve shell, most commonly that of *Ilyanassa obsoleta*. This species is still more abundant among eel-grass, and on muddy shores.

The common "sand-shrimp," *Crangon vulgaris*, (Plate III, fig. 10,) always occurs in great numbers on the sandy flats and in the tide-pools and rivulets, as well as on the sandy bottoms in deeper water off shore. This species is more or less specked irregularly with gray, and imitates the color of the sand very closely. When resting quietly on the bottom, or when it buries itself partially and sometimes almost entirely, except the eyes and long slender antennæ, it cannot easily be distinguished by its enemies, and, therefore, gains great protection by its colors. When left by the tide it buries itself to a considerable depth in moist sand. It needs all its powers of concealment, however, for it is eagerly hunted and captured by nearly all the larger fishes which frequent the same waters, and it constitutes the principal food of many of them, such as the weak-fish, king-fish, white perch, blue-fish, flounders, striped bass, &c. Fortunately it is a very prolific species and is abundant along the entire coast, from North Carolina to Labrador, wherever sandy shores occur. The young swim free for a considerable time after hatching, and were taken at the surface in the evening, in large numbers. The common prawn, *Palæmonetes vulgaris*, (Plate II, fig. 9,) often occurs, associated with the *Crangon*, but it is much more abundant among the eel-grass, and especially in the estuaries where it has its proper home. As this is one of the most abundant species and of great importance as an article of fish-food, it will be mentioned again, with more details, in connection with the fauna of the estuaries.

Several species of smaller crustacea also burrow in the sand at low-water mark. One of the most remarkable of these is an Amphipod, the *Lepidactylis dytiscus*, which by its external form reminds one of *Hippa*, with which it agrees in habits, for it burrows in the sand like a mole.

It is also occasionally found under stones in sandy places. Its color is pale yellowish white. The *Unciola irrorata* (Plate IV, fig. 19) often lives in tubes in the sand in abundance, but is by no means confined to such localities, for it occurs on all kinds of bottoms and at all depths down to at least 430 fathoms (off St. George's Bank,) and is abundant all along the coast, from New Jersey to Labrador. It is particularly abundant on shelly and rocky bottoms, and although it habitually lives in tubes, it does not always construct its own tube, but is ready and willing to take possession of any empty worm-tube into which it can get, and having once taken possession it seems to be perfectly at home, for it remains near the end of the tube protruding its stout claw-like antennæ, and looking out for its prey, in the most independent manner. It will also frequently leave its tube and swim actively about for a time, and then return to its former tube, or hunt up a new one. It seems, however, to be capable of constructing a tube for itself, when it cannot find suitable ones ready-made. Its color is somewhat variable, but it is generally irregularly specked with red and flake-white, and the antennæ are banded with red. It contributes very largely to the food of many fishes, such as scup, pollock, striped bass, &c.

On the moist sand-flats curious crooked trails made by the *Idotea cæca* (Plate V, fig. 22) may generally be seen. This little Isopod burrows like a mole just beneath the surface of the sand, raising it up into a little ridge as it goes along, and making a little mound at the end of the burrow, where the creature can usually be found. This species is whitish, irregularly specked with dark gray, so as to imitate the color of the sand very perfectly. It is also capable of swimming quite rapidly. The *Idotea Tuftsii* is another allied species, having the same habits and living in similar places, but it is much more rare in this region. It has also been dredged on sandy bottoms off shore. It is a smaller species and darker colored, with dark brown markings. The *Idotea irrorata* (p. 316, Plate V, fig. 23) also occurs on sandy shores wherever there is eel-grass, among which it loves to dwell.

The well known "horseshoe-crab" or "king-crab," *Limulus Polyphemus*, is also an inhabitant of sandy shores, just below low-water mark, but it is more abundant on muddy bottoms and in estuaries, where it burrows just beneath the surface and feeds upon various small animals. At the breeding season, however, it comes up on the sandy shores to deposit the eggs, near high-water mark. According to the statements of Rev. S. Lockwood, (in American Naturalist, vol. iv, p. 257,) the spawning is done at the time of high tides, during May, June, and July; they come up in pairs, the males, which are smallest, riding on the backs of the females and holding themselves in that position by the short feet, provided with nippers, which are peculiar to the males. The female excavates a depression in the sand and deposits the eggs in it, and the male casts the milt over them, when they again return to deeper water, leaving the eggs to be buried by the action of the waves.

In aquaria, under favorable circumstances, the eggs hatch in about six weeks, but in their natural conditions they probably hatch sooner than this; under unfavorable conditions the hatching may be delayed for a whole year. The eggs are very numerous. In addition to the interesting observations of Mr. Lockwood, Dr. A. S. Packard has since given more detailed accounts of the development of the embryos and young of *Limulus* in the proceedings of the American Association for the Advancement of Science, 1870, p. 247, and in the Memoirs of the Boston Society of Natural History, vol. ii, p. 155, 1872.

Annelids are quite numerous on the sandy shores where the conditions are favorable. It is evident that these soft-bodied creatures would be quickly destroyed by the force of the waves and the agitation of the sand, were they not provided with suitable means for protecting themselves. This is effected mainly in two ways: the sand-dwelling species either have the power of burrowing deeply into the sand with great rapidity, or else they construct long durable tubes, which descend deeply into the sand and afford a safe retreat. Many of the active burrowing species also construct tubes, but they usually have but little coherence and are not very permanent, nor do they appear to be much relied on by the owners. There is, however, great diversity both in the structure and composition of the tubes of different species, and in the modes by which the rapid burrowing is effected.

The large green *Nereis* (*N. virens*, p. 317) is found on the sandy shores in places that are somewhat sheltered, especially if there be an admixture of mud or gravel with the sand to give it firmness and solidity. This species burrows deeply beneath the surface and lines the interior of its large irregular burrows with an abundant mucus-like secretion, which gives smoothness and some coherency to the walls, but does not form a solid tube. With this, and in greater numbers, the smaller species, *Nereis limbata*, (p. 318,) is also found, and its habits appear to be essentially the same. Both this and the preceding can burrow rapidly, but much less so than some other worms, and consequently they are not well adapted to live on exposed beaches of moving sands, but prefer coves and harbors. The two large species of *Rhynchobolus* are much better adapted for rapid burrowing. Their heads are very small and acute, and destitute of all appendages, except four minute tentacles at the end; the body is long, smooth, and tapers gradually to both ends, and the muscular system is very powerful, and so arranged as to enable these worms to coil themselves up into the shape of an open spiral, like a corkscrew, and then to rapidly rotate themselves on the axis of the spiral. When the sharp head is inserted into the loose mud or sand and the body is thus rotated, it penetrates with great rapidity and disappears almost instantly. Both these species are found on sandy as well as on muddy shores and flats near low-water mark, and also in deeper water. The one usually most abundant is *R. dibranchiatus*, (Plate X, figs. 43, 44;) this is readily distinguished by having a simple gill both on the upper and lower sides of the lateral appendages. The other, *R. Americanus*, (Plate X, figs. 45, 46,) has gills that are more or less branched on the upper side of the appendages, as shown in fig. 46, but none on the lower side; the appendages are also longer, especially posteriorly, and differently shaped. The proboscis is remarkably long and large, and when fully protruded it shows four large, black, sharp, fang-like jaws or hooks. Both these worms are destitute of true blood-vessels, such as most of the allied worms possess, but have the general cavity of the body filled, between the various organs, with bright red blood, which shows through the skin, giving a more or less red or purple color to the whole body and proboscis.

The two species of *Lumbriconereis* already referred to (p. 320,) occur in similar localities, and are usually associated with the two preceding species, but they are less rapid burrowers and require for their safety localities where the sand is compact and mixed more or less with mud, or where it is somewhat sheltered from the force of the waves. In sandy coves, and especially on the flats of sandy mud, close to low-water mark, the smaller species, *L. tenuis*, is generally very abundant, penetrating the sand, beneath the surface, in every direction. It is often a foot or more in length when extended, and not much larger than coarse thread or small twine, and bright red in color. When the sand in these localities is turned up with a spade, their drawn-out, red, thread-like bodies can usually be seen in large numbers, but they are so fragile that it is difficult to obtain an entire specimen. The head is obtusely conical, a little flattened, smooth, pale red, and iridescent, without eyes. The other species, *L. opalina* V., (Plate XIII, fig. 69,) is much larger, growing to the length of eighteen inches or more, and about .10 to .12 of an inch in diameter. Its color is dark bronze, or reddish brown, or pale red, the surface reflecting the most brilliant opal-like colors. It is easily distinguished from the *L. tenuis* by its four eyes in a row across the back part of the head. Both these species, when removed from their burrows, coil themselves in a long spiral. They burrow readily and deeply, but not so rapidly as many other worms, and do not seem to have permanent tubes. Another worm, found in similar places and readily mistaken for *L. tenuis* on account of its long, slender, almost thread-like body and red color, is the *Notomastus filiformis* V.; but in this species the head is very acute, the lateral appendages and setæ are very different, and the color is paler red, with bands or rings of bright red. This species has, moreover, a smooth, subglobular proboscis, without jaws, while the former has a powerful set of complicated jaws, without a distinct proboscis, and they are widely different in internal anatomy. The latter feeds upon the organic matter contained in the mud that it swallows, while the species of *Lumbriconereis* are carnivorous, feeding upon other worms, &c. A second and much larger species of *Notomastus* occurs in similar places, though apparently preferring a greater proportion of mud. This species, *N. luridus* V., grows to be about ten inches long and .10 in diameter. Its color is a dark purplish or lurid brown, specked with white, and sometimes inclined to red. Its head is very acute, and it has a smooth, swollen, dark blood-red proboscis. It is a rapid burrower, penetrating deeply into the fine mud and sand. The *Maldane elongata* V. is another worm allied to the last, and usually associated with it, but this species constructs rather firm, round tubes out of the fine sand and mud, which are very long and descend deeply into the soil, and are often .20 to .25 of an inch in diameter. This worm is six or eight inches long, with a round body of nearly uniform diameter, which looks as if obliquely truncated at both ends, but the obliquely-placed upper surface of the head is bordered by a slight ridge or fold on each side and behind. The color is dark umber-brown, or reddish brown, the swollen part of each ring often lighter grayish or yellowish brown, but usually bright red, owing to the blood-vessels showing through. The intestine is large and filled with sand. Another worm, belonging to the same family with the last and, like it, constructing long, round tubes of agglutinated sand, is the *Clymenella torquata*, (Plate XIV, figs. 71, 72, 73,) but this species often lives where the sand is more free from mud, or even in nearly pure, siliceous sand, and sometimes considerably above low-water mark, though it is also found in deep water. It generally constructs its long and nearly straight tubes very neatly, of fine white sand, without mud. It loves, however, to dwell in sheltered spots, in coves, or in the lee of rocks and ledges, and is also partial to those spots on the sandy shores where eel-grass grows, building its tubes among the roots. It is a rather handsomely colored species, being usually pale red, with bright red bands around the swollen parts of the rings, but it is sometimes brownish red or dull brown. It can always be recognized by the peculiar collar on the fifth ring, and by the peculiar funnel-shaped caudal appendage, surrounded by small papillæ, and preceded by three segments or rings that are destitute of setæ.

The large and singular worm, *Anthostoma robustum* V., (Plate XIV fig. 76,) lives like the last, with which it often occurs, in nearly pure sand, where it is somewhat sheltered from the violence of the waves, but is also fond of places where there is more or less gravel mixed with the sand. It sometimes occurs some distance above low-water mark, and constructs a large, thick, somewhat firm tube by consolidating and cementing the sand around its burrow. These tubes descend nearly perpendicularly to a great depth, and can usually be distinguished by a slightly elevated mound of dirt around the opening, which is usually different in color from the surrounding sand; and sometimes there are recently-ejected cylindrical masses of such earth on the summit of the little hillocks. The worm itself, when full grown, is fifteen inches or more in length, and nearly half an inch in diameter. The head is very acute and the front part of the body is firm and muscular, with very small lateral appendages, and fascicles of setæ in four rows; but back of the twenty-fourth body-segment an appendage develops below the lower fascicles of setæ, and farther back becomes broad, foliaceous, and divided into several lobes; back of the twenty-eighth segment the branchiæ appear in a row on each side of the back, and soon become long and ligulate; at the same time other ligulate appendages develop from the upper lateral appendages, which become dorsal, and these, with the gills, form four rows of processes along the back, outside of which are the elongated setæ and other appendages. The posterior part of the body is more slender and much more delicate than the anterior part, and so fragile that an entire specimen can rarely be obtained, and those that are obtained, when in confinement very soon detach fragment after fragment, until only the anterior part is left. In their natural habitations they would undoubtedly be able to reproduce their lost parts, like many other annelids. The color of this worm is ocher-yellow, tinged with orange, or dark orange; there are usually two rows of dark-brown spots along the back; the branchiæ are blood-red; and posteriorly there is a brownish red median dorsal line. The proboscis is very singular, for it is divided into several long, flat, digitate processes, separate nearly to the base, and somewhat enlarged at the end.

Another species of this genus, of smaller size, *A. fragile* V., often occurs in the sandy flats in great numbers, its small holes sometimes completely filling the sand over considerable areas and extending nearly up to half-tide mark. This species grows to the length of four inches or more, with a diameter of about .10. Its head is even more acute than in the last species, with a very slender, translucent apex. The body has the same form, but is more slender. The processes above and below the fascicles of setæ begin to appear at the fourteenth segment, and the setæ begin to be decidedly elongated at the fifteenth. The dorsal branchiæ begin on the sixteenth segment, and become long and ligulate at the twentieth. The color is yellowish orange to orange-brown; the dorsal surface, posteriorly, and the branchiæ are red. The body posteriorly is very slender and extremely fragile. The last or caudal segment is smooth, oblong, with two long filiform cirri at the end. The proboscis is large and broad, consisting of numerous, often convoluted, lobes or folds, united by a thinner membrane or broad web.

The *Aricia ornata* V. is another related species, living in similar places with the last and having similar habits. The head is acute in this species, but the dorsal branchiæ and lateral appendages commence much nearer the head, and the side appendages are developed into crest-like, transverse series of papillæ, which cover the lateral and ventral surfaces of the body anteriorly.

Two species of *Spio* also occur in similar situations inhabiting small round tubes or holes made in the sand near low-water, often occuring in great numbers in certain spots. They prefer localities that are not exposed to the full force of the storms. One of these, *S. setosa* V. (Plate XIV, fig. 77,) is remarkable for the length of the setæ in the dorsal bundles; the two large tentacles (of which only one is drawn in the figure) are usually folded backward between the red dorsal branchiæ, which form a row along the back on each side. The other, *S. robusta* V., is a stouter species, which has much shorter setæ in the dorsal fascicles; the middle lobe of the head is emarginate in front and the lateral lobes are convex. Both species have four small eyes on the top of the head, those of the posterior pair nearest together. In similar places, and often associated with the two preceding species, another allied worm often occurs in great abundance, completely filling the sand, in its chosen abodes, with its round vertical holes, and throwing out cylinders of mud. It is so gregarious that in certain spots hundreds may be found within a square foot, but yet a few yards away, on the same kind of ground, none whatever may be found. This is *Scolecolepis viridis* V. This species, like the two preceeding, has a pair of large tentacles on the back part of the head, which are usually recurved over the back between the rows of ligulate branchiæ, and four eyes on the top of the head; the central lobe of the head is slightly bilobed in front, the lateral ones convex; the branchiæ are long, slender, ligulate, meeting over the back, and exist only on about one hundred segments, or on about the anterior third part of the body. The body is rather slender, depressed, and about three inches long when full grown. The color is usually dark green, or olive-green, but sometimes light green, or tinged with reddish anteriorly; the branchiæ are bright red; the large tentacles are light green, usually with a row of black dots, and often crossed by narrow flake-white lines or rings. This species has been found abundantly on Naushon Island, and other localities in that region; at New Haven; and at Somer's Point and Beesley's Point, New Jersey. With the last species at Great Egg Harbor, New Jersey, another more slender species of the same genus occurred, *Scolecolepis tenuis* V. This was three or four inches long and very slender; the body was pale green; the tentacles longer and more slender than in the last, whitish, with a red central line; the branchiæ red, often tinged with green, shorter than in the last. The head is relatively broad, with the central lobe rounded in front. The branchiæ are confined to the anterior part of the body. The setæ in the upper fascicles are much longer than in the last species, those of the three anterior segments longer than the others and forming fan-shaped fascicles, directed upward and somewhat forward.

Another singular Annelid, belonging to the same tribe and having nearly the same habits, is represented in Plate XIV, fig. 78, this has been found by Mr. A. Agassiz burrowing in sandy mud at about half-tide, both at Naushon Island and at Nahant, Massachusetts, and he has also described its development and metamorphoses, but I have not met with the adult myself in this region, although the young were frequently taken in the towing-nets in the evening. Mr. Agassiz regards it as perhaps identical with *Polydora ciliatum* of Europe. It occurred in large colonies, closely crowded together, building upright tubes in the mud. The presence of a large group of peculiar stout setæ on each side of the fifth segment will distinguish this from all the preceding species. The young of this, like those of most of the annelids, swim free at the surface for some time, and are often taken in great numbers in the towing-nets.

The *Nerine agilis* V., is still another representative of the group to which the last five species belong, and like them it has two long and large tentacles on its head, but it is a far more active and hardy species than any of them, and much better adapted for rapid burrowing. It accordingly lives on exposed beaches even where the sand is loose, and can also maintain itself on the exposed sandy beaches of the outer ocean-shores, exposed to the full force of the surf, its extremely quick burrowing affording it the means of protecting itself against the action of the sea. It lives in small round holes near low-water mark; unlike the related species, already mentioned, it has a very sharp conical head. The two large tentacles are about half an inch long, and originate close together on the upper side of the back of the head, and are usually recurved over the back when the worm is swimming in the water, as it is capable of doing, but when it is wriggling about on the sand they are twisted about in all directions and variously coiled; and when in their holes the tentacles are protruded from the opening. The eyes are four, small, black, placed close together in front of the base of the tentacles. The upper lobe of the lateral appendages is large and foliaceous and connected with the branchiæ along the anterior part of the body, but partially free farther back. The body is two or three inches long and rather slender; the color is reddish or brownish anteriorly, greenish white on the sides, except on the anterior third; the branchiæ, which extend the whole length of the body, are light red; tentacles greenish white.

One of the largest and most beautiful Annelids of this region is the *Diopatra cuprea*, (Plate XIII, figs. 67 and 68.) This species grows to be more than a foot long, with the body depressed and often nearly half an inch broad. It constructs a very curious permanent tube in which it dwells very securely. The part of these tubes beneath the surface of the sand is composed of a tough parchment-like material, and often descends obliquely to the depth of two or three feet or more; the upper end of the tube projects two or three inches from the surface of the sand or mud, and is thickly covered with bits of eel-grass and sea-weeds, fragments of shells, and other similar things, all of which are firmly attached to the tube, but project externally in all directions, giving this part of the tube a very rough and ragged appearance externally, but it is very smooth within, and often it has an opening half an inch in diameter, or large enough so that the worm can turn around, end for end, inside of it. When undisturbed the occupant thrusts its head and the anterior part of the body out of the tube to the distance of several inches in search of food, or materials to add to its tube, exposing the curious bright red gills, which are shaped something like miniature fir trees. The central stem is long and tapering, with a blood-vessel winding spirally up to its summit, and another winding in the opposite direction down to its base; the basal part is naked, but above this slender branches are given off, forming spirals all along the stem and gradually decreasing in length to the tip; each of the branches contains two slender blood-vessels. These branchiæ commence at the fifth segment and do not extend to the end of the body, the last ones being much smaller, with few branches. The first four setigerous segments have an acute, conical, papilliform ventral cirrus at the base of the lateral appendages; on the fifth and following segments these become low, broad, rounded, whitish tubercles, with longitudinal wrinkles or grooves, and with a dark spot in the middle; these appear to contain the glands which secrete the cement used in constructing the lining of the tube, for when attaching any additional object at the end, after adjusting it in the desired position the worm constantly rubs this part of the lower surface backward and forward over the edge of the tube and the object to be cemented to it, until a perfect adherence is effected, and a smooth coating of firm mucus is deposited, and this operation is repeated for every piece added to the tube. It is very interesting to watch these worms, when in confinement in an aquarium, while engaged in constructing their tubes. By placing bits of bright colored shells, tinsel, cloth, or even pieces of bright colored feathers, near the tubes, they can be induced to use them, and thus some very curious looking tubes will be produced; but they evidently prefer the more rough and homely materials to which they are accustomed, when they can be had. The iridescent, opaline colors of this species are usually very brilliant and beautiful, especially on the back, head, and bases of the antennæ. The general color of the body is reddish brown, or deep brown, thickly specked with gray; the antennæ are paler brown; the lateral appendages yellowish brown, finely specked with white and dark brown; the gills usually blood-red, but varying from light red to dark brown. There are two, small, black eyes between the bases of the odd median and upper lateral antennæ. This species is often quite abundant on the sand-flats near low-water mark, especially where there is more or less mud mixed with the sand, but it is still more abundant in the shallow or moderately deep waters off shore, on muddy and shelly bottoms. It is difficult, however, to obtain entire specimens with the dredge, for it usually merely cuts off the upper end of the tube, while the occupant retreats below; occasionally the head of the worm is cut off in this way. On the shore, also, it is not easy to obtain entire specimens unless the tubes be cautiously approached and the retreat of the worm prevented by a sudden and deep thrust of the spade below it, so as to cut off the tube. This species is carnivorous and has a very powerful set of black jaws, which are unequal on the two sides of the mouth, (fig. 68.)

The *Marphysa Leidyi* (p. 319, Plate XII, fig. 64) is allied to the preceding species, and has somewhat similar habits, but does not construct such perfect tubes. It is occasionally dug out of the sand at low-water, but is much more common in deeper water.

The *Staurocephalus pallidus* V. is also an inhabitant of these sandy shores, burrowing in the sand at low-water. It is a slender species, about two inches long and one-tenth broad. It is peculiar in having four long, slender antennæ or tentacles on the front of the head, arranged in a cross-like manner, to which the generic name alludes. There are also four, small, dark red eyes on the upper side of the head. The color is pale yellowish, the red blood-vessels showing through anteriorly. This worm is allied to the two preceding, and to *Lumbriconereis*, and like them it is predacious in its habits and has a very complicated set of jaws, consisting of numerous sharp, fang-like pieces of various shapes, arranged in several rows on both sides.

The *Sthenelais picta* V. is another curious Annelid, which is sometimes found burrowing in the sand at low-water mark, but it also occurs on shelly and muddy bottoms in deep water. It has a long, slender body, six inches or more in length, and the back is covered with two rows of thin, smooth scales, which are very numerous. The head is usually brownish, with a whitish spot on each side; there is generally a dark brown band along the back; the scales are translucent, and vary in their color-markings, but more commonly there is a border of dark brown or blackish along the inner edge, which is usually connected with a similar border along the anterior edge, or with an anterior angular spot, and often with a dark border along the posterior edge, leaving more or less of the central part of each scale white and translucent.

The *Nephthys picta* (Plate XII, fig. 57) is also sometimes found burrowing in sandy mud at low-water mark, but it is much more frequent in the deeper waters of the sounds. It can be distinguished at once from all the other species of *Nephthys* found in this region by its greater slenderness, and by having the body whitish and variously marked or mottled on the back, toward the head, with dark brown; it sometimes has a dark brown median dorsal-line. The shape of the head and position of the tentacles are also peculiar.

In sheltered situations, where there is some mud with the sand, the *Cirratulus grandis* V., (p. 319, Plate XV, figs. 80, 81,) is often met with burrowing beneath the surface. In similar places, and also in nearly pure, compact sand, and in sand mixed with gravel, the large tubes of *Amphitrite ornata* (p. 320, Plate XVI, fig. 82) are often to be seen; these show a round opening, a quarter of an inch or more in diameter, surrounded by a slightly raised mound of sand, often different in color from that of the surface, and sometimes there are cylinders of such sand around the opening. These tubes are scarcely to be distinguished from those of *Anthostoma robustum*, described above, and are found in similar places. But the worms are very unlike in appearance and structure.

Several species of slender, greenish worms, belonging to the genera, *Phyllodoce*, *Eumidia*, *Eulalia*, and *Eteone*, are occasionally dug out of the sand. In all these the head is well-developed and provided with four *antennæ* at the end, and in the three last with an odd median one on its upper side, and they all have two well-developed eyes, and oval or lanceolate, leaf-like branchiæ along the sides of the back. They are very active species, and most of them belong properly to the shelly and rocky bottoms in deeper water, where they are often very abundant. In sheltered coves, where there is mud with the sand, *Cistenides Gouldii* V., (p. 323, Plate XVII, figs. 87, 87*a*,) often occurs, but it is more partial to the muddy shores. On various dead shells, as well as on certain living ones, and on the back of *Limulus*, &c., the masses of hard, sandy tubes, built and occupied by the *Sabellaria vulgaris* V., (p. 321, Plate XVII, figs. 88, 88*a*,) often occur.

Of the Nemerteans the largest and most conspicuous is the *Meckelia ingens* (p. 324, Plate XIX, figs. 96, 96*a*.) This species lives in the clear sand, near low-water mark, as well as in places that are more or less muddy, and notwithstanding its softness and fragility, by its means of burrowing rapidly, it can maintain itself even on exposed shores, where the sands are loose and constantly moved by the waves. The young, several inches or even a foot in length, are quite common, but the full-grown ones are only occasionally met with. The largest that I have found were at least 15 feet long, when extended, and over an inch broad, being quite flat; but they could contract to two or three feet in length, and then became nearly cylindrical and about three-quarters of an inch in diameter; the body was largest anteriorly, tapering very gradually to the posterior end, which was flat and thin, terminated by a central, small, slender, acute, contractile process one-quarter of an inch or less in length. The proboscis of the largest one, when protruded, was fifteen inches long, and about one-fifth of an inch in diameter where thickest. This proboscis, which is forcibly protruded from a terminal opening in the head, appears to be an organ of locomotion, at least to a certain extent, for when it penetrates the loose sand in any direction it makes an opening into which the head can be thrust, and then, by enlarging the opening, it can easily penetrate. But the proboscis is probably used, also, as an instrument for exploring the sand in various directions, either in search of food or to test its hardness or fitness for burrowing, thus economizing time and labor. At any rate, the ways in which this remarkable instrument is used by these worms, when kept in confinement with sand, suggest both these uses. But the proboscis is by no means the principal organ of locomotion, for the head itself is used for this purpose, urged forward by the undulatory movements of the muscular body, and aided by the constantly changing bulbous expansions, both of the head and body, which both crowd the sand aside, making the burrow larger, and furnish points of resistance toward which the parts behind can be drawn, or against which the head and anterior parts can push in continuing the burrow. The head, moreover, is extremely changeable in form, at one time being spear-shaped, with a pointed tip and thin edges, and constricted at the neck; in the next minute broadly rounded; then perhaps truncate or even deeply emarginate at the end ; then gradually losing its distinctness and blending its outlines continuously with those of the body; or perhaps shrinking down to a small oval form, not more than one-third as wide as the body just back of it. All these and many other changes can often be witnessed within a very few minutes, and are so effected as greatly to aid the creature in burrowing This worm can also leave the bottom and swim rapidly in the water, the body being usually kept up edgewise and impelled forward by the undulations of the body, which thus become horizontal. When swimming in this way the motion reminds one of the swimming of a snake or an eel. In addition to the terminal pore, for the proboscis, there is a deep lateral slit or fossa on each side of the head, and a large ventral orifice beneath. The latter is very changeable in form, changing from elliptical, long oval, oblong, or hour glass-shape, to circular in rapid succession. There are no eyes. Along each side of the greater part or the length of the body, the voluminous, transversely-banded lateral organs can be imperfectly distinguished through the translucent integument, as well as the median cavity, in which a dark pulsating tube can sometimes be seen. The lateral organs commence at about the anterior fourth in small specimens, but in the larger ones relatively nearer the head, for in the largest they originate only six or eight inches back of it. The portion in front of the lateral organs is thicker and more cylindrical than the rest of the body.

The color of the largest specimens is generally light red or flesh-color, with the lateral edges and central band translucent grayish white, the lateral organs showing through as dull yellowish transverse branches, with diverticula between them; head yellowish. But one large specimen was dull brownish yellow; others are yellowish white, with the lateral organs deep chestnut-brown, crossed by white lines. The small specimens are generally paler, usually pale flesh-color or yellowish white and often milk-white. Some of the diversity in color may be due to sexual differences. This species has also been dredged on sandy and shelly bottoms in six to eight fathoms in the sounds.

Dr. Leidy has also described another similar species, from Great Egg Harbor, under the name of *Meckelia lactea*, which I have not been able to distinguish, unless it be what I have regarded as the light-colored young of *M. ingens;* the white color seems to have been the principal character by which it was distinguished from the latter.

The *Meckelia rosea* is, however, a very distinct species, but it lives in similar places and is often associated with the *M. ingens*. It has very similar habits, but does not grow to a very large size. The largest specimens observed are only six or eight inches long, and about a fifth of an inch broad. The body is also more cylindrical, the flattened part being relatively thicker and narrower, and not thin at the edges; in contraction it becomes nearly cylindrical. The lateral fossæ of the head are long and deep; the ventral opening is relatively much smaller than in *M. ingens* and usually round. The proboscis is very long, slender; color, light purplish red or rose-color. The integument is rather firm and secretes a tenacious mucus to which a thin coating of sand often adheres when the worms are taken from their burrows. This species seems to construct an imperfect tube by slightly cementing the sand with its mucus. All these species of *Meckelia* when caught and when kept in confinement generally break off portions from the posterior part of the body, one after another, until nothing but the head and a lot of short segments remain. Under favorable conditions they would doubtless be able to restore the lost parts, for other Nemerteans, having the same habit, are known to do so, and in some cases even the small fragments from the central parts have been known to again become entire worms. Various fishes feed upon these *Meckeliæ*, and it is probable that the habit of dismembering, or rather disarticulating themselves, may serve an important purpose, by enabling them to escape, in part at least, when seized by fishes or crabs, for if even half the body should be lost the remaining half would be much better than nothing, for it could soon restore either a head or a tail.

Another Nemertean, which lives in sand at low water, is the *Tetrastemma arenicola* V., (Plate XIX, fig. 98.) This is slender, subcylindrical, and four or five inches long when extended. The head is versatile in form, usually lanceolate or subconical, and has four eyes on the upper side. There is a deep fossa on each side of the head. The ventra opening, which is behind the lateral fossæ, is small, triangular. The color is deep flesh-color or light purplish.

The *Balanoglossus aurantiacus* is a very remarkable worm, related to the Nemerteans, which lives in the clear, siliceous sand near low-water mark. It is gregarious in its habits and occurs abundantly in certain spots, although not to be found in other similar places near by. It makes tubes or holes in the sand, twelve or fourteen inches deep, and lined with a thick and smooth layer of mucus. It throws out of the orifice peculiar elliptical coils of sand, by which the nature of the occupant may be known. This species was found by our party on the shore of Naushon Island, but Mr. A. Agassiz has found it abundantly at Newport, and on the beach just beyond Nobska Light, and also at Beverly, Massachusetts. Dr. Packard informs me that he has collected it at Beaufort, North Carolina, and I have received specimens found at Fort Macon, from Dr. Yarrow. The specimens first discovered were found at Charleston, South Carolina, by Dr. William Stimpson, twenty years ago, but they were only briefly and imperfectly described by Mr. Girard, at that time, under the name of *Stimpsonia aurantiaca.* Mr. A. Agassiz has recently described and illustrated this worm, very fully, under the new name, *B. Kowalevskii*, in the Memoirs of the American Academy of Arts and Sciences, vol. ix, p. 421, and he has also given an account of its remarkable development and metamorphoses, proving that the larva is a free-swimming form, long known as *Tornaria*, and generally supposed to be the larva of a star-fish. This worm, when full grown, attains a length of six inches or more and a diameter of about a quarter of an inch. The body is elongated, tapering gradually, with a long, slender posterior portion. The body is somewhat flattened dorsally throughout most of its length. At the anterior end it is furnished with a broad thickened collar, in which large numbers of mucus-secreting glands are situated; the anterior border of the collar is undulated, and from within the concavity, on the dorsal side arises a large muscular proboscis, which has a distinct peduncle, or narrower basal stem, above which it swells out into a somewhat flattened, long, pyriform, or elongated and subconical form, the shape constantly changing during life. The proboscis is somewhat wrinkled longitudinally, and more strongly horizontally, being furnished with muscles running in both these directions, and its surface contains mucus-secreting glands. According to Mr. Agassiz the cavity of the proboscis is not connected with the alimentary canal, but opens externally by a pore at the end, and by a narrow slit on the ventral side near the base, in advance of the mouth. The mouth is large and situated at the base of the proboscis on the ventral side. For some distance along each side of the back, behind the collar, is a row of complex gills; these are remarkable on account of their structure and position; they are formed from diverticula of the œsophagus and finally communicate with a row of external orifices situated along each side of the median dorsal-vessel. The gills are supported by a system of solid supports, constituting a sort of internal skeleton; the base of the proboscis is also connected with a firm internal frame-work. The color of this species is somewhat variable; in young specimens the body was brownish yellow with lighter mottlings, the collar red, and the proboscis white; in large specimens the proboscis is pale reddish yellow, the collar darker colored, the body purplish or brownish, the sides mottled with greenish and whitish, owing to the lateral organs or liver showing through. The proboscis of this worm, according to the observations of Mr. Agassiz, is the principal organ of locomotion, but the collar also aids in the movements. The proboscis appears to be used much as certain bivalve mollusks, such as *Solen*, *Petricola*, &c., use their foot in burrowing; the end being contracted to a point, is thrust forward into the sand; water being then forced into it, by the muscles farther back, the end expands into a bulb, enlarging the hole and giving a point of resistance toward which the rest of the body can be drawn; the front part of the proboscis being again contracted and the water expelled, the point can be again thrust forward and the movements repeated.

Two species of Sipunculoid worms are also found living in the sand at low-water. The largest and most common of these is the *Phascolosoma Gouldii*, (Plate XVIII, fig. 93.) This species grows to the length of a foot or more, and is often nearly half an inch in diameter, though more commonly about a quarter of an inch. The body is round and constantly changing in size and shape, owing to its contractions and expansions; the surface is smoothish, but longitudinally lined with muscular fibers anteriorly, and transversely wrinkled posteriorly. The integument is firm and parchment-like. The mouth is surrounded by numerous short tentacles, which are partially connected together by a thin web, and crowded together in several circles. The color is yellowish white, grayish white, or yellowish brown. It burrows deeply in the sand and gravel, using its body for this purpose very much as the *Balanoglossus*, just described, uses its proboscis.

Another much smaller species of the same genus occurs in sand at low-water, and has similar habits, but it appears to be rather uncommon and has not been satisfactorily identified.

Comparatively few species of Mollusks naturally inhabit sandy shores, though the shells of many species may be found on the beaches. On the more exposed beaches of loose siliceous sand none but those which have the power of burrowing quickly and deeply beneath the surface can exist. We find, however, that quite a number of our species, both of gastropods and bivalves, possess this power in a high degree and do habitually live on the exposed beaches of loose sand.

Among the Gastropods one of the largest and most conspicuous is the *Lunatia heros*, (Plate XXIII, figs. 133–136.) This species occurs all along our coast, from the Gulf of St. Lawrence to Cape Hatteras or beyond, wherever sandy shores and pure waters are to be found, and it even seems to prefer the outer ocean beaches, where the waves break with full force, for it is abundant and of very large size on the outer beaches of the coast of New Jersey. When in motion (Fig. 134) the white soft parts are protruded from the shell to a remarkable extent and spread out broadly on all sides, so as to nearly conceal the shell; the foot is large, flat, and broadly expanded, with thin edges, and by means of it the animal is able to burrow, like a mole, beneath the surface of the sand, both for protection and in search of the bivalve shells upon which it preys. The foot when well expanded is concave below and lubricated by a very abundant secretion of mucus, and therefore, when extended beneath the surface of the moist sand, it acts like a great sucker, holding the animal in place pretty firmly by the atmospheric pressure, thus serving as a sort of anchor in the sand. But nevertheless large numbers of these mollusks are uncovered, overturned, and thrown high up on the beaches by the storms, especially in winter and early spring. This species, like many others of its tribe, drills round holes through the sides of various bivalve shells by means of the small flinty teeth on its lingual ribbon, which acts like a rasp, and having thus made an opening it inserts its proboscis and sucks out the contents. All sorts of burrowing bivalves in this way fall victims to this and the following species, nor do they confine themselves to bivalves, for they will also drill any unfortunate gastropods that they may happen to meet, not even sparing their own young.

A variety of this species (var. *triseriata*, Plate XXIII, figs. 135, 136) has three revolving rows of chestnut or purplish spots, and has been regarded by most writers as a distinct species, and sometimes as the young; but both the plain and spotted shells occur of all sizes, from the the youngest to the oldest, and they are nearly always found together. In some cases, however, a shell that has the spots well defined until half grown, afterwards loses its spots and becomes perfectly plain, showing that the difference is only a variation in the color, but each style varies considerably in form.

Another allied shell, growing nearly as large and generally much more abundant, except on the outer beaches, is the *Neverita duplicata*, (Plate XXIII, fig. 130.) This species has the same habits as the preceding and in this region they are often found together; but this is a more southern species, extending to the Gulf of Mexico and even to Texas, but it is not very common north of Cape Cod and does not extend to the eastern coast of Maine and Bay of Fundy.

The curious egg-cases of this and the last species are often met with on the sandy and muddy flats at low-water. They consist of a broad, thin ribbon of sand, coiled up into a circle and shaped something like a saucer, but without a bottom; the ribbon is composed of innumerable little cells, each containing one or more eggs and surrounded with grains of fine sand cemented together by mucus. The cells can easily be seen by holding one of these ribbons up to the light and looking through it. The peculiar form of these egg-masses is due to the fact that they are molded into shape by being pressed against the body of the shell when they are being extruded, and while they are still soft and gelatinous; they thus take the form and spiral curvature of that part of the shell, and when laid in the sand the fine grains at once adhere to and become imbedded in the tenacious mucus, which soon hardens.

The *Tritia trivittata* (Plate XXI, fig. 112) is also frequently found on sandy shores and flats. When left by the tide it creeps along the surface of the sand, leaving long crooked trails, and sometimes burrows beneath the surface, and when burrowing it moves with the aperture downward and the spire pointing obliquely upward, but when at rest in its burrow it reverses its position and rests with the spire downward and the aperture toward the surface.

The *Ilyanassa obsoleta* (Plate XXI, fig. 113) is also generally to be found in considerable numbers creeping over the flats, and making trails and burrows like the last, but this species has its proper home on the muddy shores and in estuaries, and will, therefore, be mentioned again.

At certain times, especially in the spring, multitudes of the young shells of *Bittium nigrum* (p. 305, Plate XXIV, fig. 154) are found creeping on the surface of the moist sand in sheltered places, at low-water, and generally associated with large numbers of the *Astyris lunata*, (p. 306, Plate XXII, fig. 110.) But this is not the proper habitat of either of these species; the reason of this habit is not obvious, unless they may have been accidentally transported to such places. They may be found, however, on the eel-grass growing on sandy shores. The *Lacuna vincta* (p. 305, Plate XXIV, fig. 139) also frequently occurs on eel-grass and sea-weeds in such places.

The *Crepidula fornicata* (Plate XXIII, figs. 129, 129*a*) and *C. unguiformis* (Plate XXIII, fig. 127) occur on shells inhabited by the hermit crabs as well as on the living shells of *oysters*, *Pecten*, *Limulus*, &c; and the smaller and darker species, *C. convexa*, (Plate XXIII, fig. 128) occurs both on the eel-grass, and on the shells of *Ilyanassa obsoleta*, especially when occupied by the small hermit-crabs. Occasionally specimens of *Fulgur carica* (Plate XXII, fig. 124) and of *Sycotypus canaliculatus* are found crawling on sandy flats or in the tide pools, especially during the spawning season, but they do not ordinarily live in such situations, but in deeper water and on harder bottoms off shore. The curious egg-cases of these two species are almost always to be found thrown up by the waves on sandy beaches. They consist of a series of disk-shaped, subcircular, or reniform, yellowish capsules, parchment-like in texture, united by one edge to a stout stem of the same kind of material, often a foot and a half or two feet in length. The largest capsules, about an inch in diameter, are in the middle, the size decreasing toward each end. On the outer border is a small circular or oval spot, of thinner material, which the young ones break through when they are ready to leave the capsules, each of which, when perfect, contains twenty to thirty, or more, eggs or young shells, according to the season.

Dr. Elliott Coues, who has observed *F. carica* forming its cases at Fort Macon, North Carolina, states that the females bury themselves a few inches below the surface of the sand on the flats that are uncovered at low-water, and remain stationary during the process. The string of capsules is gradually thrust upward, as fast as formed, and finally protrudes from the surface of the sand, and when completed lies exposed on its surface. The string begins as a simple shred, two or three inches long, without well-formed cases; the first cases are small and imperfect in shape, but they rapidly increase in size and soon become perfect, the largest being in the middle; the series ends more abruptly than it begun, with a few smaller and less perfect capsules. The number of capsules varies considerably, but there are usually seventy-five to one hundred or more. At Fort Macon Dr. Coues observed this species spawning in May, but at New Haven they spawn as early as March and April. It is probable that the period of spawning extends over several months. Mr. Sanderson Smith thinks that they also spawn in autumn, on Long Island. It is not known how long a time each female requires for the formation of her string of capsules. There are two forms of these capsules, about equally abundant in this region. In one the sides of the capsules are nearly smooth, but the edge is thick or truncate along most of the circumference, and crossed by numerous sharp transverse ridges or partitions, dividing it into facets. Dr. Coues states that these belong to *F. carica*. An examination of the young shells, ready to leave the capsules, confirms this. The other kind has larger and thinner capsules, with a thin, sharp outer edge, while the sides have radiating ridges or raised lines. Sometimes the sides are unlike, one being smooth and more or less concave, the other convex and crossed by ten or twelve radiating, elevated ridges, extending to the edge. This kind was attributed to *F. carica* by Dr. G. H. Perkins, and formerly by Mr. Sanderson Smith, but a more careful examination of the young shells, within the capsules, shows that they belong to *S. canaliculata*.

Among the sand-dwelling bivalve shells we find quite a number of species that burrow rapidly and deeply, some of them living in permanent holes or perpendicular burrows, into which they can quickly descend for safety, and others burrowing in the sand in all directions, without permanent holes.

The "razor-shell," *Ensatella Americana*, (Plate XXVI, fig. 182, and Plate XXXII, fig. 245,) is a common inhabitant of sand-flats and sand-bars, where the water is pure, generally living near low-water mark or below, but sometimes found considerably above low-water mark, as on the sand-bar at Savin Rock. This curious mollusk constructs a deep, nearly round, somewhat permanent burrow, which descends nearly perpendicularly into the sand to the depth of two or three feet. These holes can generally be recognized, by their large size and somewhat elliptical form, when the tide is out. Sometimes they are very abundant in certain spots and not found elsewhere in the neighborhood. They sometimes come to the top of the burrow, when left by the tide, and project an inch or two of the end of the shell above the surface of the sand; at such times, if cautiously approached, many can easily be secured by pulling them out with a sudden jerk, but if the sand be jarred the whole colony will usually take the alarm and instantly disappear. When thus warned it is generally useless to attempt to dig them out, for they quickly descend beyond the reach of the spade. They will often hold themselves so firmly in their holes by means of the expanded end of the long muscular foot, that the body may be drawn entirely out of the shell before they will let go. When not visible at the orifice they can often be secured by cutting off their retreat with a sudden oblique thrust of the spade below them. They are obliged to come up to the upper part of the burrow on account of the shortness of their siphons, or breathing-tubes, which can be protruded only about an inch in specimens of the ordinary size, and as they depend upon one of these to bring them both food and oxygen, and on the other (dorsal) one to carry off the waste water and excretions, it is essential for their happiness that the orifices of these tubes should be at or near the opening of the burrow most of the time. In this respect the common "long clam," *Mya arenaria*, (fig. 179,) and many others that have very long and extensile tubes have a great advantage. But the "razor-shell" makes up for this disadvantage by its much greater activity. Its foot, or locomotive organ, (see fig. 182,) is long and very muscular and projects directly forward from the anterior end of the shell; at the end it is obliquely beveled and pointed, and it is capable of being expanded at the end into a large bulb, or even into a broad disk, when it wishes to hold itself firmly and securely in its burrow. In excavating its burrows it contracts the end of the foot to a point and then thrusts it beneath the surface of the sand; then, by forcing water into the terminal portion, it expands it into a swollen, bulbous form, and thus crowds the sand aside and enlarges the burrow; then, by using the bulb as a hold-fast, the shell can be drawn forward by the contraction of the foot; the latter is then contracted into a pointed form and the same operations are repeated. The burrow thus started soon becomes deep enough so that the shell will maintain an upright position, when the work becomes much easier and the burrow rapidly increases in depth. The "razor-shell," like all other bivalves, depends upon the minute infusoria and other organic particles, animal and vegetable, brought in by the current of water that supplies the gills with oxygen. It is preyed upon by several fishes that seem to be able to root it out of the sand, or perhaps seize it when at the surface. In this region its principal enemies are the tautog and skates. The latter appear to eat only the *foot*, for in their stomachs there are sometimes many specimens of this organ, but no shells or other parts.

The common "long clam," *Mya arenaria*, (p. 309, Plate XXVI, fig. 179,) is also found on sandy shores from low-water nearly up to high-water mark, but it prefers localities where there is more or less gravel or mud with the sand, so as to render it compact, and it has a decided preference for sheltered localities, and especially abounds on the shores of estuaries where there is a mixture of sand, mud, and gravel. It will, therefore, be more particularly mentioned among the estuary species. Yet it is often found even on the outer ocean-beaches, in favorable localities, but not in the loose sands. It lives in permanent burrows, and on account of its extremely long siphon-tubes, which can be stretched out to the length of a foot or more, it is always buried at a considerable depth beneath the sand. The specimens of this shell that live on the outer sandy beaches are much thinner, whiter, and more regular in form than those found in the estuaries; they are often quite delicate in texture, and covered, even when full grown, with a thin, yellowish epidermis, and look so unlike the homely, rough, and mud-colored specimens usually sold in the markets, that they might readily be mistaken for another species.

The "sea-clam" or "surf-clam," *Mactra solidissima*, (Plate XXVIII, fig. 202,) is a large species which belongs properly to the sandy shores, and is seldom found elsewhere. It is common both in the sounds and on the outer ocean-beaches, but is not very often found above low-water of ordinary tides unless thrown up by the waves. Its proper home is on sandy bottoms in shallow water, just beyond low-water mark and down to the depth of four or five fathoms. It occurs all along our coast, wherever there are sandy shores, from North Carolina to Labrador. Its shells are extremely abundant and of very large size on the outer sand-beaches of New Jersey and the southern side of Long Island. This species grows very large, some of the shells being more than six inches long and four or five broad; and there is great variation in the form of the shell, some being oval, others more oblong or elliptical, and others nearly triangular; some are very swollen, others quite compressed; but all the intermediate grades occur. The siphon-tubes are quite short and the creature does not usually burrow very deeply, nor does it seem to construct any permanent burrows. But it has a very large muscular, compressed foot, with which it can quickly burrow beneath the surface of the sand. Nevertheless large numbers are always thrown on the beaches by violent storms, and once there they are very soon devoured by crows, gulls, and other large birds that frequent the shores. This species is not very largely used as food, and is seldom seen in our markets; partly because it cannot usually be so easily obtained in large quantities as the common "long clam" and "round clam," and partly because it is generally inferior to those species as an article of food, for the meat is usually tougher, especially in the largest specimens. But moderate-sized and young "surf-clams" are by no means ill-flavored or tough, and are quite equal in quality to any of the other clams, either "long" or "round," that are ordinarily sold in the markets.

The *Siliqua costata*, (Plate XXXII, fig. 244,) *Lyonsia hyalina*, (Plate XXVII, fig. 194,) and *Lævicardium Mortoni*, (Plate XXIX, fig. 208,) are usually to be found on sandy shores and beaches, often in considerable numbers, but they do not naturally live above low-water mark, and, when found higher up, have probably been carried there by the action of the waves. Their proper homes are on sandy bottoms, in shallow water off shore. They are all rapidly burrowing species, and can live, for a time at least, in the loose sand above low-water mark.

The *Angulus tener* (Plate XXVI, fig. 180, animal, and Plate XXX, fig. 223, shell) is a species that is partial to sandy bottoms and sandy shores, though it is also often found in soft mud. It frequently occurs living at low-water mark, but is more abundant in deeper water. It is a rapid burrower, and has remarkably long, slender, white siphons, which are entirely separate, from the base, and very flexible. On account of the length of these tubes it can remain buried to a considerable depth beneath the surface of the sand, merely projecting the tubes upward to the surface. It is, nevertheless, like other bivalves, often rooted out of its burrows and devoured by many fishes, especially, in this region, by the "scup" and flounders. This species is found all along the coast, from the Gulf of Saint Lawrence to South Carolina.

The *Macoma fusca* (Plate XXX, fig. 222) is a related species, also furnished with similar, very long, slender, separate tubes, and is, therefore, able to live deeply buried beneath the surface. This species is much more abundant than the preceding, between tides, but it most abounds on shores that are more or less muddy, and in estuaries. But when living on the sandy shores, and where the water is pure, it becomes much smoother and more delicate, and is often of a beautiful pink-color and much larger than the specimen figured. When living in the muddy estuaries it generally has a rough or eroded surface, more or less irregular form, and a dull white or muddy color, often stained with black, resembling in color the *Mya arenaria*, with which it is sometimes associated. It is dug up and eaten by the tautog and other fishes.

The pretty little *Tottenia gemma* (Plate XXX, fig. 220) is a species peculiar to sandy shores, both above and below low-water mark; and it often occurs in immense numbers on the sandy flats laid bare by the tides, buried just beneath the surface of the sand. Owing to its small size it is, however, liable to be overlooked, unless particularly sought for. It is an active species and burrows quickly. It is peculiar in being viviparous, as was first observed by Mr. G. H. Perkins, who found, in January, from thirty to thirty-six, well-formed young shells, of nearly uniform size, in each of the old ones. This shell has a lustrous, concentrically grooved surface; the color is yellowish white or rosy, with the beaks and posterior end usually purple or amethyst-color. It occurs all along the coast from Labrador to South Carolina. The common "round clam" or "quahog-clam," *Venus mercenaria*, (Plate XXVI, fig. 184, animal,) is also common on sandy shores, living chiefly on the sandy and muddy flats, just beyond low-water mark, but is often found on the portion laid bare at low-water of spring-tides. It also inhabits the estuaries, where it most abounds. It burrows a short distance below the surface, but is often found crawling at the surface, with the shell partly exposed. It has short siphon-tubes, united from the base to near the ends, and a large, muscular foot, with a broad, thin edge, by means of which it can easily burrow beneath the sand when necessary. The lobes of the mantle are separate all around the front and ventral edge of the shell, and their edges are thin, white, and folded into delicate frills, some of which, near the siphon-tubes, are elongated and more prominent. Owing to the broad opening in the mantle, the foot can be protruded from any part of the ventral side, and has an extensive sweep, forward and backward. The foot and mantle edges are white; the tubes are yellowish or brownish orange toward the end, more or less mottled and streaked with dark brown, and sometimes with opaque white.

This species is taken in large quantities for food, and may almost always be seen of various sizes in our markets. The small or moderate-sized ones are generally preferred to the full-grown clams. Most of those sold come from the muddy estuaries, in shallow water, and are fished up chiefly by means of long tongs and rakes, such as are often used for obtaining oysters. Sometimes they are dredged, and occasionally they can be obtained by hand at or just below low-water mark. These estuary specimens usually have rough, thick, dull-white, or mud-stained shells, but those from the sandy shores outside have thinner and more delicate shells, often with high, thin ribs, especially when young; and in some varieties the shell is handsomely marked with angular or zig-zag lines or streaks of red or brown, (var. *notata.*) These varieties often appear so different from the ordinary estuary shells that many writers have described them as distinct species, but intermediate styles also occur. This species is very abundant along the coast from Cape Cod to Florida; north of Cape Cod it is comparatively rare and local. It does not occur on the coast of Maine or in the Bay of Fundy, except in a few special localities, in small, sheltered bays, where the water is shallow and warm, as at Quahog Bay, near Portland; but in the southern parts of the Gulf of Saint Lawrence, as about Prince Edward's Island and the opposite coast of Nova Scotia, where the water is shallow and much warmer than on the coast of Maine, this species again occurs in some abundance, associated, in the same waters, with the oyster and many other southern species that are also absent from the northern coasts of New England, and constituting a genuine southern colony, surrounded on all sides, both north and south, by the boreal fauna.

The curious and delicate shell called *Solenomya velum* (Plate XXIX, fig. 210) is occasionally found burrowing in the pure, fine, siliceous sand near low-water mark, about two inches below the surface, but its proper home is in shallow water, beyond low-water mark, and it is, perhaps most abundant where there is mud mixed with sand, and it also lives in soft mud. Its shell is glossy and of a beautiful brown color, and is very thin, flexible, and almost parchment-like in texture, especially at the edges. It is a very active species, and has a very curious foot, which is protruded from the front end of the shell, and can be used in burrowing, very much as the "razor-shell," described above, uses its foot; but the *Solenomya* makes use of its foot in another way, for it can swim quite rapidly through the water, leaving the bottom entirely, by means of the same organ. The foot can be expanded into a concave disk or umbrella-like form at the end, and, by suddenly protruding the foot and expanding it at the same time, a backward motion is obtained by the reaction against the water; or, by suddenly withdrawing the foot and allowing it to remain expanded during most of the stroke, a forward motion is obtained. It is a singular sight to see this shell swim swiftly many times around a vessel of water, at the surface, until, finally, becoming exhausted by its violent exertions, it sinks to the bottom for rest.

The common "scollop," *Pecten irradians*, (Plate XXXII, fig. 243,) is also frequently found living on sandy shores and flats, or in the pools, but it belongs more properly to the sheltered waters of the ponds and estuaries, where it lives among the eel-grass. It will, therefore, be mentioned again in that connection.

The "common muscle," *Mytilus edulis*, (p. 307,) is frequently found in large patches on sandy flats, fastened together by the threads of byssus. Some of the most beautifully colored varieties, (fig. 234,) with radiating bands of blue and yellow, are often found in such places, but the species is much more abundant and larger in other situations, especially in the shallow and sheltered waters of the bays, where there is more or less mud.

Ascidians are almost entirely wanting on the sandy shores, but *Molgula Manhattensis* (p. 311, Plate XXXIII, fig. 250) is sometimes found even on sandy shores, attached to eel-grass.

Of Bryozoa only two species are usually met with, and even these do not have their true stations on the sandy shores. The delicate and gracefully branched *Bugula turrita* (p. 311, Plate XXXIV, figs. 258, 259) is occasionally found growing attached to the eel-grass, which often grows in the sandy tide-pools, or at extreme low-water. It also occurs in great abundance among the masses of sea-weeds thrown up by the waves on the sandy beaches. Such specimens are often large and luxuriant, in some cases being more than a foot in length ; these are derived from the bottom in deeper water, off shore.

The *Escharella variabilis* (p. 312, Plate XXXIII, fig. 256) is often found encrusting dead shells of various kinds, especially such as are inhabited by the larger "hermit-crabs." It is also cast up in abundance, on some beaches, from deeper water.

The Radiates are not numerous on sandy shores, yet several interesting species may be found. Among the Echinoderms we find four species of holothurians, one sea-urchin, one star-fish, and one ophiuran.

The most common holothurian is the *Leptosynapta Girardii*, (Plate XXXV, figs. 265, 266.) This is a long, slender, very delicate and fragile species, which burrows deeply in the sand or gravel near low-water mark. The holes are round and go down almost perpendicularly; they are usually not more than a quarter of an inch in diameter. The creature is not quick in its motions, and can usually be found in the upper part of its burrow when the tide is out. The skin is thin and quite translucent, so that the white muscular bands that run lengthwise of the body, on the inside, can be easily seen, as well as the large intestine, which is always quite full of sand and gives a dark appearance to the body. The tentacles are almost always in motion, and are used in burrowing as well as for other purposes. The skin is filled with minute perforated oval plates, to each of which there is attached, by the shank, a beautiful little anchor, (fig. 266,) quite invisible to the naked eye. The flukes of these anchors project from the skin and give it a rough feeling when touched; they afford the means of adhesion to various foreign substances, having a rough surface, and are doubtless useful to them when going up and down in the burrows. When kept in confinement this species will generally soon commence to constrict its body, at various points, by powerful muscular contractions, which often go so far as to break the body in two, and after a few hours there will usually be nothing left but a mass of fragments.

Another related species, *L. roseola* V., also occurs in similar places and has nearly the same habits, but this species is of a light rosy color, caused by numerous minute round or oval specks of light red pigment scattered through the skin. The anchors are similar but much more slender, with the shank much longer in proportion. The perforated plates are also much smaller in proportion to the length of the anchors.

The *Caudina arenata* is much more rare in this region. It lives at extreme low-water mark, or just below, buried in the sand. Its skin is thicker and firmer than that of the preceding species, and its body is shorter and stouter, while the posterior part narrows to a long slender caudal portion. Its skin is filled with immense numbers of small, round, wheel-like plates, with an uneven or undulated border, perforated near the rim with ten to twelve roundish openings, and usually having four quadrant-shaped openings in the middle; or they may be regarded as having a large round opening in the middle, divided by cross-bars into four parts. This species appears to be rare in this region, and was met with only by Professor H. E. Webster, at Wood's Hole, but it is quite abundant in some parts of Massachusetts Bay, as at Chelsea Beach and some of the islands in Boston Harbor. These and all other holothurians are devoured by fishes.

The *Thyone Briareus* is a large purple species, often four or five inches long and one inch or more in diameter. It is thickly covered over its whole surface with prominent papillæ, by which it may easily be distinguished from any other found in this region. It is more common in the shallow waters off shore, on shelly bottoms.

The "sand-dollar," *Echinarachnius parma*, (Plate XXXV, fig. 267,) is the only sea-urchin that is commonly met with on sandy shores in this region, and this is not often found living on the shore, except at extreme low water of spring-tides, when it may sometimes be found on flats or bars of fine siliceous sand in great numbers, buried just beneath the surface, or even partially exposed. It creeps along beneath the sand with a slow gliding motion, by means of the myriads of minute extensile suckers with which it is furnished. It is far more abundant on sandy bottoms at various depths off shore. It has a very wide range, for it is found all the way from New Jersey to Labrador, and also on the North Pacific coast; and in depth it ranges from low-water mark to 430 fathoms, off Saint George's Bank, where it was dredged by Messrs. Smith and Harger. When living its color is usually a rich purplish brown, but it soon turns green when taken from the water. It gives a dark green or blackish color to alcohol, which stains very injuriously any other specimens put in with it. The fishermen on the coast of Maine and New Brunswick sometimes prepare an indelible marking-ink from these "sand-dollars," by rubbing off the spines and skin and, after pulverizing, making the mass into a thin paste with water. A number of fishes have been found to swallow this unpromising creature for food, and the flounders consume large numbers of them.

The common green star-fish, *Asterias arenicola*, (p. 326, Plate XXXV, fig. 269,) is sometimes met with on sandy shores, but is much less abundant than on rocky shores. The curious "brittle star-fish," *Ophiura olivacea*, is sometimes found among the eel-grass on sandy shores, especially in tide-pools, in sheltered localities. It may be recognized by its nearly circular, disk-like body, about three-quarters of an inch in diameter, with five round, rather slender, tapering, stiff-looking arms, about three inches long. The color is bright green, much like that of the eel-grass among which it lives. When at home in the water it moves about over the sand quite rapidly by means of its arms. When taken from the water it does not usually break itself up into numerous fragments, as readily as most of its related species do. It is rather southern in its distribution, and Vineyard Sound is perhaps its northern limit. It extends southward at least to North Carolina.

Of acalephs there are no species known to me that properly belong to the sandy shores, but *Hydractinia polyclina* (p. 328) is often found on the shells carried about by the hermit-crabs, in such situations, and there are species of *Obelia* and other hydroids that sometimes grow on the eel-grass in the tide-pools, but they are much more frequent in other situations.

Among the Polyps we find several species proper to sandy shores and specially adapted to this mode of life. One of the most interesting of these is the *Halocampa producta*, (p. 330, Plate XXXVIII, fig. 285,) which has already been described. This often occurs in the sand at low-water mark, and makes round holes about a foot deep, which can sometimes be recognized by small cracks radiating from the hole when the tide leaves them uncovered.

The *Sagartia modesta* (p. 330) is also found buried in the sand at low-water, especially where there is also some gravel with the sand. The *Sagartia leucolena* (p. 329, Plate XXXVIII, fig. 284) is sometimes found in similar situations, but belongs properly to the rocky shores.

The *Paractis rapiformis* is a species that is still little known. It lives buried deeply in the sand at and below low-water mark. It appears to be common on the coast of North Carolina, at Fort Macon, where it is often thrown up by storms, and it has also been found at Great Egg Harbor and near New Haven light. The body is three or four inches long when extended, and an inch or more in diameter, and is very changeable in form. The surface is nearly smooth, slightly sulcated lengthwise, and the color is usually pink, or pale flesh-color, translucent. The tentacles are numerous, short, tapering, pale greenish olive, with a dark band around the base, connected with a dark line radiating from the mouth. Toward the upper part of the body the surface is somewhat wrinkled and is capable of attaching grains of sand to itself. When thrown up by the waves it contracts into a globular or pyriform shape and "somewhat resembles a boiled onion or turnip."

List of the species ordinarily inhabiting the sandy shores.

ARTICULATA.

Insects.

	Page.		Page.
Muscidæ, (larvæ)	335	Geopinus incrassatus	335
Cicindela generosa (larva)	336	Phytosus littoralis	335
C. dorsalis	335	Bledius cordatus	335
C. hirticollis	335	B. pallipennis	335
C. albohirta	335	Heterocera undatus	335

Crustacea.

	Page.		Page.
Ocypoda arenaria	337	Orchestia agilis	346
Gelasimus pugilator	336	Talorchestia longicornis	336
Cancer irroratus	338	T. megalophthalma	336
Carcinus granulatus	312	Lepidactylis dytiscus	339
Platyonichus ocellatus	338	Unciola irrorata	340
Libinia canaliculata	339	Idotea irrorata	340
Hippa talpoida	338	I. cæca	340
Eupagurus pollicaris	313	I. Tuftsii	340
E. longicarpus	339	Scyphacella arenicola	337
Crangon vulgaris	339	Limulus Polyphemus	340
Palæmonetes vulgaris	339		

Annelids, (Chætopods.)

	Page.		Page.
Sthenelais picta	348	Polydora ciliatum	345
Nephthys picta	348	Diopatra cuprea	346
Eteone, sp.	349	Marphysa Leidyi	347
Nereis virens	341	Lumbriconereis opalina	342
N. limbata	341	L. tenuis	342
Cirratulus grandis	348	Staurocephalus pallidus	348
Scolecolepis viridis	345	Rhynchobolus Americanus	342
S. tenuis	345	R. dibranchiatus	341

Bryozoa and Ascidians.

	Page.		Page.
Molgula Manhattensis......	361	Bugula turrita............	361
Escharella variabilis........	361		

RADIATA.

Echinoderms.

	Page.		Page.
Thyone Briareus...........	362	Echinarachnius parma.....	362
Caudina arenata...........	362	Asterias arenicola.........	363
Leptosynapta Girardii......	361	Ophiura olivacea..........	363
L. roseola.................	362		

Polyps.

	Page.		Page.
Halocampa producta	363	Sagartia leucolena	363
Sagartia modesta..........	363	Paractis rapiformis........	363

II. 3.—FAUNA OF THE MUDDY SHORES OF THE BAYS AND SOUNDS.

The muddy shores in this region grade almost insensibly into the sandy shores; and shores that are entirely of mud, without any admixture of fine sand, rarely occur except in the estuaries and lagoons. Therefore we find, as might have been anticipated, that it is difficult to draw a very definite line between the animals living upon the sandy shores and those living upon the muddy shores and flats. Many of the species seem, also, to be equally at home, whether living in mud or sand, and many others prefer a mixture, although capable of living in either. But if we were to compare the animals living in pure sand with those living in clear mud, the two lists would be quite different, although a considerable number would be common to both lists. Moreover, the eel-grass grows in considerable quantities both upon sandy and muddy shores, in certain localities, and a large number of species which inhabit the eel-grass will, therefore, be found in both lists.

In discussing the species found on sandy shores, in the preceding pages, references have constantly been made to other stations inhabited by many of the species, and especially in the case of those that are common to the sandy and muddy shores. Therefore it will not be necessary to repeat the facts in this connection, but the species will be enumerated in the list at the end of this section.

A considerable number of species have their place in this list chiefly because they occur on beds of oysters planted on muddy shores, at and just below low-water mark. Without these artificial stations some of them would hardly be found on such shores, or at least but rarely. It is evident that the shells of oysters, when in large quantities, supply, to a certain extent, conditions similar to those of rocky shores, and consequently it is natural that certain rocky-shore species should be found in such situations. Only the more common and most important of these have been introduced into the list, however, for to include all the species to be found among oysters would uselessly extend the catalogue.

Among the Crustacea we find a considerable number of species which have their proper homes on the muddy shores. Of the true crabs there are at least eleven species that constantly occur in these situations, but several of them, viz., *Cancer irroratus*, (p. 312,) *Panopeus depressus*, (p. 312,) *P. Sayi*, (p. 312,) and *Carcinus granulatus*, (p. 312,) are found in greater numbers elsewhere, and depend largely upon the oyster-beds for their safety on these shores. The *Carcinus granulatus*, however, often resorts to the holes and cavernous places under the peaty banks of the shores, or along the small ditches and streams cutting through the peaty marshes near the shore. The marsh "fiddler-crab," *Gelasimus pugnax*, is usually very abundant in the peaty banks and along the ditches and streams at and just above high-water mark, where it excavates great numbers of deep holes, often completely riddling the soil. This species is, however, more at home along the borders of the estuaries and lagoons and will be described more fully in that connection, as well as the *Sesarma reticulata*, which often occurs with it in both situations.

The "oyster-crab," *Pinnotheres ostreum*, (Plate I, fig. 2, male,) is found wherever oysters occur. The female lives, at least when mature, within the shell of the oyster, in the gill cavity, and is well known to most consumers of oysters. The males (fig. 2) are seldom seen, and rarely, if ever, occur in the oyster. We found them, on several occasions, swimming actively at the surface of the water in the middle of Vineyard Sound. They are quite unlike the females in appearance, being smaller, with a firmer shell, and they differ widely in color, for the carapax is dark brown above, with a central dorsal stripe and two conspicuous spots of whitish, as indicated in the figure; the lower side and legs are whitish. The female has the carapax thin and translucent, whitish, tinged with pink. The *Pinnixa cylindrica* (Plate I, fig. 1) is a related species which is occasionally met with on muddy shores. It lives in the tubes of certain large *Annelids* in company with the rightful owner. The specimens hitherto met with in this region were either found free, or dug out of the mud, and it is uncertain with what worm they associate, though it is most likely to be the *Nereis virens*, but on the coast of South Carolina it lives, according to Dr. Stimpson, in the tubes of *Arenicola cristata* STIMPSON. It has been found in the stomach of the ocellated flounder.

The common edible-crab or "blue-crab," *Callinectes hastatus*, is a common inhabitant of muddy shores, especially in sheltered coves and bays. It is a very active species and can swim rapidly; it is therefore often seen swimming at or near the surface. The full-grown individuals generally keep away from the shores, in shallow water, frequenting muddy bottoms, especially among the eel-grass, and are also found in large numbers in the somewhat brackish waters of estuaries and the mouths of rivers. The young specimens of all sizes, up to two or three inches in breadth, are, however, very frequent along the muddy shores, hiding in the grass and weeds or under the peaty banks at high-water, and retreating as the tide goes down; when disturbed they swim away quickly into deeper water. They also have the habit of pushing themselves backward into and beneath the mud for concealment. They are predacious in their habits, feeding upon small fishes and various other animal food. They are very pugnacious and have remarkable strength in their claws, which they use with great dexterity. When they have recently shed their shells they are caught in great numbers for the markets, and these "soft-shelled crabs" are much esteemed by many. Those with hard shells are also sold in our markets, but are not valued so highly. This crab can easily be distinguished from all the other species found in this region by the sharp spine on each side of the carapax.

The common "spider-crab," *Libinia canaliculata*, (p. 339,) is very common on muddy shores and flats. It hides beneath the surface of the mud and decaying weeds or among the eel-grass, and is very sluggish in its motions. Its whole surface is covered with hairs which entangle particles of mud and dirt of various kinds; and sometimes hydroids, algæ, and even barnacles grow upon its shell, contributing to its more ready concealment. The males are much larger than the females, and have long and stout claws. They often spread a foot or more across the extended legs. The females have much smaller and shorter legs and comparatively weak claws.

Another similar species, *Libinia dubia*, is also found on muddy shores and has nearly the same habits. It has a much longer rostrum, more deeply divided at the end.

The two common species of "hermit-crabs" are both found on muddy shores, especially among eel-grass, but the larger one, *Eupagurus pollicaris*, (p. 313,) is comparatively rare. The small one, *E. longicarpus*, (p. 313,) is very common and usually occupies the dead shells of *Ilyanassa obsoleta*, though many may be found in other species of shells.

The *Gebia affinis* (Plate II, fig. 7) is a crustacean somewhat resembling a young lobster three or four inches in length. It lives on muddy shores and digs deep burrows near low-water mark, in the tenacious mud or clay, especially where there are decaying sea-weeds buried beneath the surface. The burrows are roundish, half an inch to an inch in diameter, very smooth within, and go down obliquely for the distance of one or two feet, and then run off laterally or downward, in almost any direction, to the depth of two or three feet, and are usually quite crooked and winding. We have found them most abundant on the shore of Great Egg Harbor, New Jersey, near Beesley's Point, but they also occur at New Haven and Wood's Hole, &c. This species is quite active; it swims rapidly and jumps back energetically. It is eagerly devoured by such fishes as are able to capture it. When living the colors are quite elegant. Along the back there is a broad band of mottled, reddish brown, which is contracted on the next to the last segment; each side of this band the mottlings are fewer, and the surface somewhat hairy. The last segment and the appendages of the preceding one are thickly specked with reddish brown; their edges are fringed with gray hairs. The *Calianassa Stimpsoni* SMITH, (Plate II, fig. 8, large claw,) is also a burrowing species, but its habits are at present little known, owing to its rarity. It has been found in the stomach of fishes, and is probably more common farther south.

The *Squilla empusa* is a very interesting creature, whose habits are still imperfectly known. It is often thrown on the beaches by the waves, and probably it usually burrows in the mud below low-water mark, but in certain localities it has been found burrowing at or near low-water mark of spring-tides, forming large, irregular holes. The very curious, free-swimming young (Plate VIII, fig. 36) were often taken in the towing-nets. Large specimens are eight or ten inches long and about two broad. The body is not so stout built as that of the lobster, and the carapax or shell is much smaller and softer, while the abdomen is much larger and longer in proportion. The legs and all the other organs are quite unlike those of the lobster, and the last joint of the great claw, instead of forming a pair of pincers with the next, is armed with a row of six sharp, curved spines, which shut into corresponding sockets, arranged in a groove in the next joint, which also bears smaller spines. By means of this singular organ they can hold their prey securely, and can give a severe wound to the human hand, if handled incautiously. It also uses the stout caudal appendages, which are armed with spines, very effectively. The colors of this species are quite vivid, considering its mud-dwelling habits. The body is usually pale green or yellowish green, each segment bordered posteriorly with darker green and edged with bright yellow; the tail is tinged with rose and mottled with yellow and blackish; the outer caudal lamellæ have the base and spines white, the last joint yellow, margined with black; the inner ones are black, pale at base; the eyes are bright emerald-green; the inner antennæ are dark, with a yellow band at the base of each joint; and the flagellum is annulated with black and white.

The common shrimp, *Crangon vulgaris*, (p. 339, Plate III, fig. 10,) is frequent on muddy shores, where it has a darker color than when living on sandy shores. The common prawn, *Palæmonetes vulgaris*, (p. 339, Plate II, fig. 9,) is also common in such situations, especially where there is eel-grass, among which it finds its favorite resorts, but it is still more abundant in the estuaries. Another shrimp, the *Virbius zostericola* SMITH, also occurs among the eel-grass, in similar places. It is usually greenish in color.

Two other species of shrimp-like crustacea, belonging to the genus *Mysis*, are also found on muddy shores, especially among eel-grass.

The *Mysis stenolepis* SMITH, (Plate III, fig. 12, female,) is often very abundant in such situations. The small young ones have been taken in May, and the half-grown ones later in the season. In the early spring the adult females, with eggs, occur in great numbers among the eel-grass, in estuaries and ponds. Mr. Vinal N. Edwards caught a large number in a small pond at Wood's Hole, April 1. No males were found at this time with the females; the only adult males observed were taken in autumn. Possibly the males do not survive the winter. The adult females have not been observed in summer, and they probably die after hatching their young in the spring. The whole body is translucent; each segment of the body has a stellate black spot; and there is more or less blackish pigment on the caudal lamellæ, telson, antennal scales, and inner flagellum and peduncle of the antennulæ. This species contributes largely to the food of many fishes. The other species, *M. Americana* SMITH, also lives among eel-grass, as well as in deeper water off shore among algæ. This has been found in large numbers in the stomachs of the shad and the spotted flounder.

Of Amphipods there are comparatively few species. The *Unciola irrorata* (p. 340, Plate IV, fig. 19) is pretty common here, as elsewhere. The *Amphithoë valida* SMITH (p. 315,) is often met with among eel-grass. Another species, *A. compta* SMITH, also occurs in the same places. It differs from the preceding in many characters, but may easily be distinguished by its red eyes. A third species of the genus, *A. longimana* SMITH, is also found among eel-grass. It has black eyes. The *Corophium cylindricum* and *Gammarus mucronatus* occur among eel-grass and algæ, often in great numbers.

Of Isopods there are several species. The *Idotea irrorata* (p. 316, Plate V, fig. 23) is common wherever eel-grass is found. The *Erichsonia attenuata* HARGER, (Plate VI, fig. 27,) is also found clinging to eel-grass in muddy situations. The *Epelys trilobus* (Plate VI, fig. 28) is found creeping about over the bottom or among and beneath the decaying vegetable matter and mud usually to be found in sheltered situations. It is usually so covered up with adhering dirt as readily to escape observation. The *Epelys montosus* also occurs in similar situations.

Whenever lumber or drift-wood has been left for some time on the muddy shores it is found to be more or less eaten by the *Limnoria lignorum*, (Plate VI, fig. 25.) This small isopod gnaws its galleries in the wood to a depth of about half an inch from the surface, and after a time these galleries become so numerous that the superficial layer will be completely honey-combed, and it will then scale off and another layer will be attacked. This little creature often does great damage to the piles of wharves and other kinds of submerged wood-work in this region, and will be mentioned again in discussing the animals inhabiting piles, &c.

The "horse-shoe crab," *Limulus Polyphemus*, (p. 340,) is also common on muddy shores, burrowing beneath the surface, at or just below low-water mark.

Many of the Annelids found on muddy shores occur also on sandy shores, especially where there is a mixture of mud with the sand, and consequently they have been mentioned in the preceding pages. Among these are *Nereis virens* (p. 317, Plate XI, figs. 47–50) and *N. limbata*, (p. 318, Plate XI, fig. 51,) both of which are common on muddy shores; also *Diopatra cuprea*, (p. 320, Plate XIII, figs. 67 and 68;) *Lumbriconereis opalina*, (p. 342, Plate XIII, figs. 69, 70;) *L. tenuis*, (p. 342;) *Maldane elongata*, (p. 343;) *Notomastus luridus*, (p. 342;) *Notomastus filiformis*, (p. 342;) *Cirratulus grandis*, (p. 319, Plate XV, figs. 80, 81;) *Cistenides Gouldii*, (p. 323, Plate XVII, figs. 87, 87*a*;) all of which are found both in mud and sand, but prefer, perhaps, a mixture of the two. *Rhynchobolus Americanus* (p. 342, Plate X, figs. 45, 46) and *R. dibranchiatus* (p. 341, Plate X, figs. 43, 44) are also found in mud, though perhaps more common in fine sand, or sandy mud.

The "blood-drop," *Polycirrus eximius*, (p. 320, Plate XVI, fig. 85) is however, a species that belongs properly to muddy localities, and it delights in the softest and stickiest mud of the shores, near low-water mark. The larger blood-drop, *Chætobranchus sanguineus*, (p. 320,) is also found in similar situations, and the soft mud, filled with decaying vegetable matter, seems to be its most congenial home.

Of Mollusks there are comparatively few species that are peculiar to muddy shores, but there are many that live almost equally well in such localities and on shores or bottoms of other kinds.

Among the Gastropods, the proper mud-dwelling species are few. The *Ilyanassa obsoleta* (p. 354, Plate XXI, fig. 113) is the most abundant, for it occurs everywhere over the mud-flats in great numbers, and, in cold weather, often crowds in large numbers into the pools left on the flats. The *Nassa vibex* (Plate XXI, fig. 114) has nearly the same habits, but is comparatively rare. It is more frequently found among the eel-grass, and is more common farther south.

The *Eupleura caudata* (Plate XXI, fig. 117) is usually found rather sparingly in this region, but in one locality, at Waquoit, it occurred in considerable numbers in the small streams and ditches in the muddy marshes near the shore. It occurs occasionally at low-water, but is more often met with on muddy and shelly bottoms in the shallow water of the bays and sounds, and is much more common farther south. The *Crepidula convexa* (p. 355, Plate XXIII, fig. 128) is very common on the shells of *Ilyanassa obsoleta*, especially when they are inhabited by "hermit-crabs." It is also frequently found on the eel-grass, where, in August, it often deposits its bright yellow eggs inclosed in small, gelatinous masses, which are grouped in clusters.

The *Bulla solitaria* (Plate XXV, fig. 161) is a species restricted to muddy shores and bottoms, in sheltered situations, and is found also in muddy ponds and estuaries. The color of the animal of this species is quite peculiar, and when it is fully extended it has a singular appearance. The general color is usually orange-brown, and it is thickly speckled with darker brown. This shell is devoured in large numbers by the flounders, and doubtless by other fishes.

A number of species which habitually live clinging to eel-grass are to be found in the localities where this plant flourishes, either in the pools or at low-water mark, but they are not peculiar to or characteristic of muddy shores. Among these the most common are *Astyris lunata*, (p. 306;) *Bittium nigrum*, (p. 305;) *Triforis nigrocinctus*, (p. 305;) and *Lacuna vincta*, (p. 305.) The *Littorina irrorata* is occasionally found in sheltered situations, but this region is north of its true range, and such specimens as are found may have been introduced from farther south with oysters. It is very abundant on the southern coast. The *Urosalpinx cinerea* (p. 306) occurs wherever there are beds of oysters, upon which it feeds.

Most of the bivalve shells to be found on muddy shores have already been enumerated as living also on the sheltered sandy shores, and the majority of them flourish equally on both kinds of shores, and on those of a mixed or intermediate character. Among these are *Mya arenaria*, (p. 309;) *Macoma fusca*, (p. 358;) *Angulus tener*, (p. 358;) *Venus mercenaria*, (p. 359;) *Argina pexata*, (p. 309;) *Mytilus edulis*, (p. 307;) *Pecten irradians*, (p. 361.) There are, however, other species that are almost peculiar to muddy shores, and are highly characteristic of them. The *Pholas truncata* (Plate XXVII, fig. 200) excavates deep holes in deposits of tenacious clay at all elevations between tides, and is still more frequently found living in holes in the borders of peat-bogs, or marsh deposits, which have been encroached upon by the sea. In such places they sometimes occur nearly up to the ordinary high-water mark. Their holes are round and nearly perpendicular, and increase in size from the orifice downward. They vary in depth according to the size of the shell; the deeper ones are often a foot or a foot and a half in depth and often an inch in diameter. The shell remains near the bottom and stretches out its long siphon tubes, which are united together quite to the end, until the tips reach the external orifice of the burrow These tubes are generally yellowish white except at the end, where they are blackish or brownish; the orifices and papillæ are also variously marked with purplish brown or dark brown. The dark coloration of the end of the siphon tubes is doubtless for purposes of protection from predacious fishes, crabs, &c. Its foot is short and stout, obliquely truncated, and bevelled at the end. The *Petricola pholadiformis* (Plate XXVII, fig. 199) is generally associated with the preceding species and is more abundant. Its habits are nearly the same, but it does not make its burrows so deep; it is more active in its motions, and can easily climb up to the upper part of its hole by means of its long, thin, white foot, which is tongue-shaped and very extensible and flexible. The siphon-tubes are long and slender, tapering, and united for about a quarter of their length, beyond which they are separate and divergent. They are yellowish white, more or less spotted, especially toward the end, with orange, brownish, or blackish, which, in large specimens, forms streaks near the ends or even becomes confluent, making the tips very dark colored. The branchial orifice is surrounded by a circle of numerous bipinnate papillæ, which usually alternate with smaller and more simple ones ; the papillæ of the dorsal tube are similar, but more simple.

The *Tagelus gibbus* (Plate XXVI, fig. 181, animal; Plate XXX, fig. 217, shell) is another inhabitant of muddy shores, which burrows deeply into the mud. This species is confined, on the shores, chiefly to the zone near low-water mark, but probably lives also in shallow water beyond the reach of the tides. In this species the foot is large and muscular, thick, tongue-shaped, and has a very wide range of motion, for the mantle is open along the whole length of the ventral edge of the shell. The tubes are separate, from the base, and are round, white, and capable of very great extension, for a specimen of ordinary size, kept in confinement, extended the tubes to the length of nine inches. These tubes are translucent, and at the end have small rounded lobes around the aperture, each lobe being furnished at its base, inside, with a small, orange, eye-like spot, which is probably an imperfect visual organ, and with two others on the inside lower down. The branchial tube has six of these lobes and ocelli ; the dorsal one has eight. On each tube there is a row of small, white, slender, obtuse papillæ, corresponding to each terminal lobe, and running along the whole length of the tubes. The color of the animal is white throughout. This bivalve makes deep burrows in the tenacious mud, each of which has two orifices, not far apart, for the two tubes. By this peculiarity their burrows may be at once recognized, whenever seen.

The *Mulinia lateralis* (Plate XXVI, fig. 185, B, animal) is occasionally found living at extreme low-water mark, on muddy flats, but its true home is on the soft muddy bottoms in shallow water, where t is often excessively abundant. In this species the foot is relatively large and muscular, more or less pointed at the end, and capable of assuming many different forms and positions ; it has a wide sweep in its motions and can be thrust forward or backward. The siphon-tubes are united nearly to the end, but the separation is indicated by a groove between them for nearly half the length. The branchial tube is the largest, and its orifice is surrounded by a circle of twelve to twenty-four, slender, elongated, simple papillæ, each of which usually has a small, black, eye-like spot at its base ; a little below this terminal circle there is another, composed of smaller, very short, blunt papillæ. The dorsal tube also has a subterminal circle of similar papillæ, above which the tip forms a retractile cone, with the small, simple orifice at the tip. The animal is yellowish white, the tubes generally pale yellow. This species burrows just beneath the surface of the mud, and it is eaten in large numbers by the scup and other fishes.

The *Cumingia tellinoides* (Plate XXX, fig. 221) and *Kellia planulata* (Plate XXX, fig. 226) are sometimes found living in the mud at low-water, but are rare in such situations. They are more common at the depth of a few fathoms on muddy and shelly bottoms.

The ribbed muscle, *Modiola plicatula*, (p. 307, Plate XXXI, fig. 238, is very abundant near and even above high-water mark, along the muddy borders of the marshes and banks and among the roots of grass. The *Modiola hamatus* is occasionally met with, especially on oyster-beds, adhering to the shells, where it is sometimes very abundant. It has probably been introduced with the oysters, from the South, where it is common. It somewhat resembles the preceding species, but it is shorter, broader, with strong radiating ribs, many of which are forked. Its color is yellow or yellowish brown.

The common "scollop," *Pecten irradians*, (p. 361, Plate XXXII, fig. 243,) occurs among the eel-grass on muddy shores in great abundance, in many localities, especially in sheltered places. The young shells may be found during the whole summer, but the adult specimens come up to the shallow waters and shores in great numbers in the autumn. This species is very active and can rise from the bottom and swim through the water with great rapidity by opening and energetically closing its valves, thus expelling the water from the gill-cavity, the reaction sending the shell backward. It often remains up among the leaves of the eel-grass, resting upon them, where they are matted together, but if alarmed the creature suddenly swims away in the manner described, and takes to the bottom. It is very watchful and quickly perceives its enemies. The thickened outer edge of the mantle, both above and below, is fringed with rows of numerous tapering papillæ or tentacles, the inner ones largest, and among the bases of these there is a row of very bright silvery or bluish eyes, thirty to forty or more to each valve the number increasing with the size of the shell; a short distance within the outer fringe of tentacles there is a raised yellow or orange ridge, which bears another series of smaller papillæ, and the space between these and the outer ones is radiately striated. The central muscle which closes the valves of this shell is large and powerful. This is the portion which is sold in our markets in large quantities, and is highly esteemed by many as an article of food. Its decided sweetish taste is, however, objectionable to some persons. To some, also, it proves actually injurious, sometimes producing nausea and even worse symptoms. After storms this shell is sometimes found thrown upon the beaches in immense quantities.

The oyster, *Ostræa Virginiana*, (p. 310,) is often planted upon the muddy shores at and below low-water mark, in many parts of Long Island Sound and elsewhere, but for this purpose the muddy estuaries are preferred, where the water is more brackish and the bottom less disturbed by the storms. The mud, however, should not be too deep, and ought to have a solid substratum, a few inches beneath.

The Ascidians are generally uncommon on muddy shores, but wherever the eel-grass flourishes, and especially in sheltered situations, the *Molgula Manhattensis* (p. 311, Plate XXXIII, fig. 250) is usually to be found adhering to it. The *Botryllus Gouldii* (Plate XXXIII, figs. 252, 253) is also frequently found growing upon the eel-grass in such situations, as well as upon the piles of wharves, bottoms of boats, &c. This species was found in great profusion upon the eel-grass in Little Harbor, at Wood's Hole, and in Waquoit Pond. In both these localities the water is nearly pure and but slightly, if at all, brackish. But it has also been found by Professor D. C. Eaton on the piles at Brooklyn, New York, where the water is more brackish. This species when young forms thin, soft, circular or oval incrustations covered with stellate clusters of the minute animals, (fig. 253,) which are imbedded in it; each of these has a small circular orifice toward the outer end, opening into the gill cavity, and another orifice opening into a larger cavity in the center of the cluster, which is common to all those in the cluster; and it has a central external orifice, through which the waste water from the gills, the fæces, and the eggs are discharged. These young colonies begin to appear in June and grow very rapidly, new individuals being formed by buds that originate from the first ones in rapid succession, so that in two or three weeks the small colonies will increase from a quarter of an inch in breadth up to three or four inches, if they be situated on a flat surface and have room to spread. If upon the stem or leaf of the eel-grass they will extend entirely around it, and perhaps several inches along its length, if not opposed by other colonies. At the same time the crusts increase very much in thickness. Thus by the end of the summer, the eel-grass, algæ, stems of hydroids, &c., often become completely covered up by the luxuriant growth of this curious compound animal. The colors of this species are extremely variable and often very elegant, and it is seldom that two colonies can be found with precisely the same pattern of color. Growing upon the same leaf of eel-grass, many different colonies may often be found, each showing a different arrangement of the colors.

In one of the most common varieties the general color of the common tissue between the stellate clusters is dull olive-green, thickly specked with small flake-white spots, which are formed by the enlarged terminal portion of stolon-like processes, which bud out from the perfect individuals composing the clusters, and are arranged somewhat in circles around the clusters; the lower portion of these stolons is usually yellow or orange, and the outer part deep purple, tipped with flake-white. The individual animals, or zoöids, composing the stellate clusters, are deep purple, with the branchial orifice yellowish white, surrounded by a circle of orange; a short flake-white longitudinal line runs along the middle of the upper side, interrupted by the branchial opening, but this line is often represented only by two white spots; other flake-white spots are usually irregularly scattered over the outer end.

In another variety the deep purple zoöids have a circle of flake-white around the branchial orifice, a short white bar or spot beyond it on the outer end, a white spot on the middle between the orifices, and another white spot on the inner end near the anal orifice; the stolons colored as in the preceding.

In another common variety (var. *bicolor*) the colors are similar except that the outer half of each zoöid is almost entirely covered with flake-white, sometimes tinged with orange, while the proximal half is deep purple. Another has the purple zoöids spotted and blotched with flake-white over the whole surface; sometimes the specks are so fine and numerous as to give a uniform silvery or frosted appearance, (var. *farinacea.*)

One peculiar variety (*annulata*) has a small circle of white around the the branchial opening, surrounded by another large circle of flake-white, which incloses nearly the outer half of the zoöid. The variety *atrox* has the zoöids covered to a considerable extent with flake-white, so arranged on each as to present the appearance of a skull; the two eyes being formed by deep purple spots.

The variety *variegata* is pale yellowish olive or orange-brown; the zoöids have a white ring around the branchial orifice, inclosed by a brown ring, which is often interrupted; and the latter is surrounded more or less completely by flake-white, there is usually also a median bar of flake-white; the inner portion is deep purple, more or less mottled with white, and there is a white spot at the inner end. In the variety *albida* nearly the whole upper surface of the zoöids is flake-white.

In another very beautiful and distinct variety (var. *stella*) the common tissue is translucent, pale olive, with white-tipped stolons; the zoöids are brown or purple, marked on the upper side with two parallel longitudinal bars of flake-white, which are separated by a narrow dark line, all of which radiate from the center of the cluster, thus producing the appearance of a many-rayed star, with the rays alternately white and dark; the white bars are sometimes interrupted near the inner ends, and small specks of flake-white are sometimes scattered over the outer end. In this form there are often ten to fifteen zoöids in each cluster, and they appear longer and less swollen than in the other varieties, owing, perhaps, to the optical effect of the radiating lines. This is the most distinctly marked variety that was observed, and was at first thought to be a distinct species.

The Radiates are not abundant on muddy shores. The *Thyone Briareus* (p. 362) is sometimes found on such shores, in sheltered situations, among eel-grass. The common star-fish, *Asterias arenicola*, (p. 326, Plate XXXV, fig. 269,) is often altogether too abundant on muddy shores, on the oyster-beds, where it commits great havoc.

The *Hydractinia polyclina* (p. 328) is often found on the shells occupied by "hermit-crabs." Several species of *Obelia* grow upon the eel-grass, where the water is sufficiently clear. The *Halecium gracile* V. (p. 328,) is frequently found attached to the shells of oysters, and to other solid objects.

List of species commonly found on the muddy shores of the bays and sounds.

ARTICULATA.

Crustacea.

	Page.		Page.
Gelasimus pugnax	367	Mysis stenolepis	370
Sesarma reticulata	367	M. Americana	370
Pinnixa cylindrica	367	Squilla empusa	369
Pinnotheres ostreum	367	Gammarus mucronatus	370
Cancer irroratus	367	Amphithoë valida	370
Panopeus depressus	367	A. compta	370
P. Sayi	367	A. longimana	370
Callinectes hastatus	367	Unciola irrorata	370
Carcinus granulatus	367	Corophium cylindricum	370
Libinia canaliculata	368	Idotea irrorata	370
L. dubia	368	Erichsonia attenuata	370
Eupagurus longicarpus	368	Epelys trilobus	370
E. pollicaris	368	E. montosus	370
Callianassa Stimpsoni	369	Limnoria lignorum	370
Gebia affinis	368	Limulus Polyphemus	370
Virbius zostericola	369	Numerous small Entomostraca, of many genera.	
Crangon vulgaris	369		
Palæmonetes vulgaris	369		

Annelids, (Chætopods.)

	Page.		Page.
Nereis virens	371	Cistenides Gouldii	371
N. limbata	371	Amphitrite ornata	320
Diopatra cuprea	371	Rhynchobolus Americanus	371
Lumbriconereis opalina	371	R. dibranchiatus	371
L. tenuis	371	Cirratulus grandis	371
Maldane elongata	371	Polycirrus eximius	371
Notomastus luridus	371	Chætobranchus sanguineus	371
N. filiformis	371		

MOLLUSCA.

Gastropods.

	Page.		Page.
Ilyanassa obsoleta	371	Littorina irrorata	372
Nassa vibex	371	Lacuna vincta	372
Eupleura caudata	371	Bittium nigrum	372
Urosalpinx cinerea	372	Triforis nigrocinctus	372
Astyris lunata	372	Bulla solitaria	371
Crepidula convexa	371		

Lamellibranchs.

Ascidians.

RADIATA.

Echinoderms.

Acalephs.

II. 4.—ANIMALS INHABITING THE PILES AND TIMBERS OF WHARVES AND BRIDGES, BOTTOMS OF VESSELS, BUOYS, AND OTHER SUBMERGED WOOD-WORK.

In these situations a large number of species may be found, but the majority of them are not peculiar to such stations. There are, however, quite a number of species that are nearly always found under these circumstances, and others are directly dependent for their very existence upon submerged wood. Some of these, like the *Teredo*, for example, are of so great importance, owing to the injuries which they do to valuable property, that it seems desirable to make a special division for the animals ordinarily found in connection with wood-work of various kinds, whether injurious or not.

On the piles of wharves and bridges various kinds of sea-weeds often grow in abundance, each species having a particular zone to which it is limited; but as these plants require light, they are found almost exclusively upon the outer rows of piles and timber, and are most abundant on the outer side of the piles and on the southern exposures, where they get the most sunlight. These algæ afford congenial homes to a considerable number of animals, most of which occur also among algæ on the rocky shores and in tide-pools. Beneath the wharves, where the piles are constantly shaded, very few algæ, and those only of the smallest and simplest kinds, such as Ocillatoriæ and Diatoms, are to be found. But in these shaded situations many animals, such as Tubularians and other Hydroids, some Ascidians, Bryozoa, &c., delight to dwell. Many of these adherent animals also live in abundance on the outermost piles of the wharves, at or just below low-water mark, where they are more or less exposed to the sunlight.

The animals that are found among or attached to the seaweeds growing on the piles are, for the most part, identical with those that are to be found in similar situations among the algæ on rocks and in rocky tide-pools.

Among those that are nearly or quite peculiar to submerged wood-work are several species of "ship-worms," (*Teredo* of several species, and the *Xylotrya fimbriata*,) which are bivalve mollusks; the wood-eating *Limnoria;* several species of barnacles, which belong to the Crustacea; some of the tubularians, and other hydroids, &c.

Of the salt-water Insects two species have been observed on the piles of wharves. One of these is a small, slender, green larva, with a dark, firm head, and sharp jaws. It is the larva of a small, two-winged fly, probably identical with the *Chironomus oceanicus* of Packard.

On the piles of a wharf at Menemsha, Dr. Edward Palmer found, in October, a very interesting insect-larva. It lived in a stout tube composed of grains of sand firmly cemented together, and attached by its whole length to the piles; the single specimen is broken at both ends. The tube is flattened, and consists of a central, subcylindrical, tapering portion, or proper tube, which is covered on all sides with a single layer of small grains of sand, neatly arranged; along each side of this, and partly covering its upper surface, and to fill the angle between it and the surface to which it was attached, larger grains of sand are cemented. The preserved portion of the tube is about three-quarters of an inch long and nearly one-quarter wide, at the larger end, but not more than half as wide at the small end. The larva is about a third of an inch long, rather stout, and has a pair of long, sharp, curved jaws, and three pairs of rather long, hairy legs. It belongs to the Phryganidæ, among the Neuroptera, and somewhat resembles some of the well-known larvæ of the caddis-flies, common in fresh water, which make tubes or cases of various kinds. Dr. Hagen, who has examined this specimen, refers it to the genus *Molanna*, of which three North American species are known, but only in the adult state. All the larvæ of this genus, known in Europe, live in fresh water, and no other species of the Phryganidæ has been observed in sea-water, although some live in water that is slightly brackish.

Of Crustacea the most important species is the *Limnoria lignorum*, (p. 370, Plate VI, fig. 25.) This little creature is grayish in color, and covered with minute hairs. It has the habit of eating burrows for itself into solid wood to the depth of about half an inch. These burrows are nearly round, and of all sizes up to about a sixteenth of an inch in diameter, and they go into the wood at all angles and are usually more or less crooked. They are often so numerous as to reduce the wood to mere series of thin partitions between the holes. In this state the wood rapidly decays, or is washed away by the waves, and every new surface exposed is immediately attacked, so that layer after layer is rapidly removed, and the timber thus wastes away and is entirely destroyed in a few years. It destroys soft woods more rapidly than hard ones, but all kinds are attacked except teak. It works chiefly in the softer parts of the wood, between the hard, annual layers, and avoids the knots and lines of hard fiber connected with them, as well as rusted portions around nails that have been driven in, and, consequently, as the timbers waste away under its attacks, these harder portions stand out in bold relief. Where abundant it will destroy soft timber at the rate of half an inch or more every year, thus diminishing the effective diameter of piles about an inch annually. Generally, however, the amount is probably not more than half this, but even at that rate, the largest timbers will soon be destroyed, especially when, as often happens, the *Teredos* are aiding in this work of destruction. It lives in a pretty narrow zone, extending a short distance above and below low-water mark. It occurs all along our shores, from Long Island Sound to Nova Scotia. In the Bay of Fundy it often does great damage to the timbers and other wood-work used in constructing the brush fish-weirs, as well as to the wharves, &c. At Wood's Hole it was formerly found to be very destructive to the piles of the wharves. The piles of the new Government wharves have been protected by broad bands of tin-plate, covering the zone which it chiefly affects. North of Cape Cod, where the tides are much greater, this zone is broader, and this remedy is not so easily applied. It does great damage, also, to ship-timber floating in the docks, and great losses are sometimes caused in this way. Complaints of such ravages in the navy-yard at Portsmouth, New Hampshire, have been made, and they also occur at the Charlestown navy-yard, and in the piles of the wharves at Boston. Probably the wharves and other submerged wood-work in all our sea-ports, from New York northward, are more or less injured by this creature, and, if it could be accurately estimated, the damage would be found surprisingly great.

Unlike the *Teredo*, this creature is a vegetarian, and eats the wood which it excavates, so that its boring operations provide it with both food and shelter. The burrows are made by means of its stout mandibles or jaws. It is capable of swimming quite rapidly, and can leap backward suddenly by means of its tail. It can creep both forward and backward. Its legs are short and better adapted for moving up and down in its burrow than elsewhere, and its body is rounded, with parallel sides, and well adapted to its mode of life. When disturbed it will roll itself into a ball. The female carries seven to nine eggs or young in the incubatory pouch at one time.

The destructive habits of this species were first brought prominently to notice, in 1811, by the celebrated Robert Stephenson, who found it rapidly destroying the wood-work at the Bell Rock light-house, erected by him on the coast of Scotland. Since that time it has been investigated and its ravages have been described by numerous European writers. It is very destructive on the coasts of Great Britain, where it is known as the "gribble."

The remedies used to check its ravages are chiefly copper or other metallic sheathing; driving broad-headed iron nails, close together, into the part of the piles subject to their attacks; and applying coal-tar, creosote, or verdigris-paint, once a year or oftener.

Another singular crustacean, common on the piles at Wood's Hole, is the *Tanais filum*. This is a very slender, whitish species, almost thread-like in form, but has the first pair of legs much thickened, with very peculiar, stout claws, ovate in form; the rest of the anterior legs are very slender. The antennæ are short and thick, the inner ones directed forward; the outer ones more slender, and curved outward and backward. This species lives among the adhering ascidians and hydroids on the piles, and has also been found in deeper water, in the Bay of Fundy. Its habits are little known, but some of the allied species have been accused of boring in wood.

Two species of barnacles are very common on the piles of the wharves. The common barnacle of the rocky shores, *Balanus balanoides*, (p. 305,) is also common on the piles of wharves and bridges, between tides, and also on the bottoms of vessels, &c. It never grows very large, although it may become so crowded together as to form a continuous crust. It is easily distinguished from the other species by its membranous base, which never forms a solid plate, like that of the other species. The "ivory-barnacle," *Balanus eburneus*, is also common on all kinds of submerged wood-work, whether fixed or floating. It is usually abundant on the piles and timbers of wharves, buoys, oyster-stakes, bottoms of vessels, &c. It is chiefly found below low-water mark if on fixed objects, and is even more common in the brackish waters of estuaries than in the purer waters outside, and it is capable of living even in pure fresh water, for Professor Jeffreys Wyman has sent me specimens collected, by himself, about sixty-five miles up the Saint John's River, in Florida, where the water is not at all brackish. This species is sometimes found adhering to the carapax of crabs, the shell of *Limulus*, and various mollusks. It is easily distinguished from most species on account of its low, broad form and its smooth white exterior. It has a shelly base. The *B. crenatus*, common on shells and stones in deep water, also occurs on vessels. Other species are often found on the bottoms of vessels that have come from warmer latitudes. Some of them are of large size. One of the most frequent of these is *Balanus tintinabulum*.

Several species of "goose-barnacles," *Lepas*, are frequently found alive on the bottoms of vessels, and especially such as have recently arrived from the West Indies and other foreign countries. These resemble, in general appearance, *L. fascicularis*, (Plate VII, fig. 33,) which is a common indigenous species, usually found adhering to floating sea-weeds and other small objects in early summer, in large numbers. It is doubtful whether any of those found on the bottoms of vessels can be regarded as true natives of this region. The most common of them is *L. anatifera;* the valves of its shell are bordered with orange. The other common species are *L. anserifera* and *L. pectinata*. Species of the curious genus, *Conchoderma*, also occur on the bottoms of vessels.

Among the Crustacea that commonly occur among the ascidians, hydroids, and algæ on the piles of wharves, are *Panopeus Sayi*, (p. 312,) *P. depressus*, (p. 312, Plate I, fig. 3,) *Gammarus ornatus*, (p. 314, Plate IV, fig. 15,) *Amphithoë compta* S., (p. 370,) *Corophium cylindricum*, (p. 370,) *Melita nitida*, (p. 314,) *Caprella*, sp., (p. 316,) and various small Entomostraca. *Jæra copiosa* (p. 315) often occurs abundantly near high-water mark, on old piles and timber, living in the crevices and cracks, or under loosened bark.

Of Annelids very few if any species occur that are peculiar to these situations. The *Potamilla oculifera* (p. 322, Plate XVII, fig. 86) is quite common on the piles of wharves where the water is pure. *P. microphthalma* V. (p. 323) also occurs under the same circumstances, and also on the piles in harbors, where the water is brackish.

The *Lepræa rubra* V. was found living in tubes among the ascidians on the piles of the wharves. This is a Terebelloid worm, somewhat resembling the *Amphitrite ornata*, (Plate XVI, fig. 82,) but is much smaller, and there are fascicles of setæ on all the segments. There are three pairs of arborescently divided branchiæ, which are pedunculated, the last pair being quite small. The body is bright red, the tentacles pale flesh-color.

The *Nicolea simplex* V. (p. 321,) was also found with the last in large numbers, but mostly of small size. Both males and females of *Nereis limbata* (p. 318, Plate XI, fig. 51, male) were often found among the barnacles and ascidians on the piles of the wharves at Wood's Hole, but the males were the most abundant, while the reverse was the case with those dug out of the sand and gravel on the shores.

Numerous other Annelids were occasionally met with among the ascidians and algæ. Among these were *Polycirrus eximius*, (p. 320, Plate XVI, fig. 85;) *Podarke obscura* V., (p. 319, Plate XII, fig. 61;) a *Phyllodoce*, &c. Two Nemerteans were also common; one of these was an olive-green species, with a light dorsal stripe, belonging probably to the genus *Cerebratulus*, but it was not carefully studied; the second was *Polinia glutinosa*, (p. 324, Plate XIX, fig 97.)

Of Gastropod mollusks quite a number of species occur on the piles of wharves, and some of them in great abundance, especially the smaller kinds which live among the hydroids and confervæ. The most abundant species is generally the *Astyris lunata*, (p. 306, Plate XXI, fig. 110,) which generally occurs among the small algæ and especially on the Tubularians, in countless numbers; *Anachis avara* (p. 306, Plate XXI, fig. 109) is often found in considerable number; *Bittium nigrum* (p. 305, Plate XXIV, fig. 154) and *Triforis nigrocinctus* (p. 305, Plate XXIV, fig, 152) are usually common and the former often is very abundant; *Cerithiopsis Greenii* (Plate XXIV, fig. 153) sometimes occurs, but is rare; *Ilyanassa obsoleta* (p. 354, Plate XXI, fig. 113) and *Tritia trivittata* (p. 354, Plate XXI, fig. 112) are common, especially the former; *Urosalpinx cinerea* (p. 306, Plate XXI, fig. 116) is generally to be found at or below low-water mark on the piles and buoys; *Bela plicata* (Plate XXI, fig. 107) is sometimes met with, but is not common; *Odostomia bisuturalis* (p. 307, Plate XXIV, fig. 146) and other species of the genus are often found near low-water mark on the piles, especially where they are somewhat decayed. *Littorina palliata* (p. 305, Plate XXIV, fig. 138) and *L. rudis* (p. 305, Plate XXIV, fig. 137) nearly always occur near high-water mark, on the piles, where there are algæ. In the harbors, where the water is brackish, and less frequently in the purer waters, the *Alexia myosotis* (Plate XXV, fig. 168) may be found on timbers and piles near high-water mark, and sometimes, also, *Skenea planorbis*, (Plate XXIV, fig. 142,) *Littorinella minuta*, (Plate XXIV, fig. 140,) and *Rissoa aculeus*, (p. 306, Plate XXIV, fig. 141.) Among and feeding upon the Tubularians growing on the piles at and just below low-water mark, the beautiful *Æolidia pilata* (Plate XXV, fig. 174) may often be found, especially in the harbors where the water is more or less brackish.

Another related species, apparently the *Cavolina gymnota*, was found by Professor Todd, on an old wreck in the Wood's Hole passage, but it differs in several points from any form that has been described. The branchiæ were arranged in six transverse simple rows, on each side, those of the second and third longest; in the anterior rows there were four to six branchiæ, the lower ones much shorter than the upper ones. In life the branchiæ were dark green or blackish.

Several other Gastropods are occasionally met with in these situations, but the species above named are about all that ordinarily occur.

Among the Lamellibranchs, or "bivalve-shells," we find the *Teredo* tribe, nearly all of which are peculiar to submerged wood-work, either fixed or floating, and most of them are capable of doing great damage, both to ships and to the timber and piles of wharves and bridges, or other similar structures. Although popularly known as the "shipworm," these creatures are not at all related to the worms, but are true mollusks, quite nearly allied, in many respects, to the common "longclam" (*Mya*) and to the *Pholas*. Like those shells the *Teredo* excavates its holes or burrows merely for its own protection, and not for food; but the *Teredo* selects wood in which to form its holes, and when these have been excavated it lines them with a tube of shelly material. The holes are very small at the surface of the wood, where they were formed by the young *Teredos* but they gradually grow larger as they go deeper and deeper into the wood, until they sometimes become ten inches or more in length and a quarter of an inch in diameter, but the size is generally not more than half these dimensions. The holes penetrate the wood at first perpendicularly or obliquely, but if they enter the side of the timbers or planks across the grain, the burrows generally turn horizontally in the direction of the grain a short distance beneath the surface, unless prevented by some obstruction, or by the presence of other *Teredo* tubes, for they never cross the tubes of their companions or interfere with each other in any way, and there is always a thin layer or partition of wood left between the adjacent tubes. It is, however, not necessary that they should follow the grain of the wood, for they can and do penetrate it in every direction, and sometimes not more than half the tubes run in the direction of the grain, and they are often very crooked or even tortuous. They rapidly form their burrows in all kinds of our native woods, from the softest pine to the hardest oak, and although they usually turn aside and go around hard knots, they are also able to penetrate through even the hardest knots in oak and other hard woods. The Teredos grow very rapidly, apparently attaining maturity in one season, and therefore, when abundant, they may greatly damage or completely destroy small timber in the course of four or five months, and even the largest piles may be destroyed by them in the course of two or three years.

The most abundant species in this region is the *Teredo navalis* (cuts 1 and 2; Plate XXVI, fig. 183, animal; Plate XXVII, fig. 186, shell.)

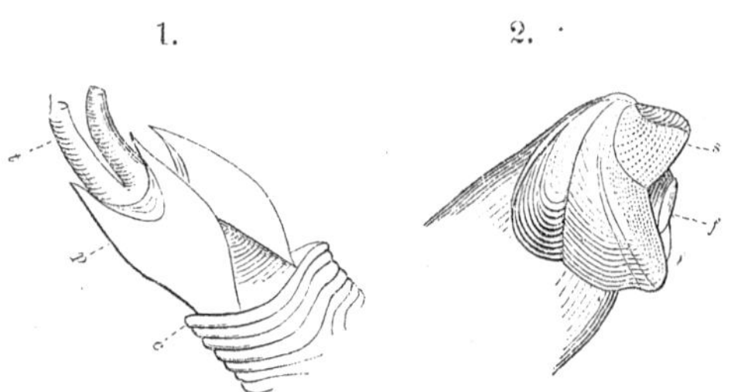

EXPLANATION OF THE CUTS.

Fig. 1. Posterior or outer end of a living *Teredo navalis*, removed from its burrow; *c*, the muscular collar by which it adheres to the shelly lining of its burrow; *p*, the shelly "pallets" which close the aperture when the animal withdraws; *t*, the two retractile siphon-tubes which project from the hole when the animal is active.

Fig. 2. Anterior end and shell of the same; *s*, the front part of the shell; *f*, the foot or boring organ.

This is the same species that has attracted so much attention in Europe, during nearly two centuries, on account of the great damage that it has done, especially on the coast of Holland. Nevertheless no full description of the animal of this species has yet been published, nor any satisfactory figures of the soft parts.

When removed from its tube (see Plate XXVI, fig. 183) the animal is found to have a very long, slender, smooth, soft, whitish body, tapering somewhat toward the outer or posterior end, (fig. 1,) which has a muscular, circularly wrinkled collar, (*c*,) by which the animal is, when living, attached to the inside of the shelly lining of its tube. To the inside of this collar two shelly plates, known as the "pallets," (*p*,) are attached by their slender basal prolongations; their outer portions are broad and flat, and more or less emarginate or two-horned at the end. These are so connected with the muscles that when the animal withdraws its tubes into its hole the free ends of these pallets are made to fold together and close the opening, thus serving as an operculum to protect the soft tubes against enemies of all kinds. Between the bases of the pallets arise the siphonal tubes, (*t*,) which are soft and retractile, united together for half their length or more, but separate and divergent beyond; they are nearly equal, but the ventral or branchial tube is perhaps a little larger than the other, and is fringed with a few small papillæ at the end; the tubes are white or yellowish, sometimes specked with reddish-brown. At the anterior end of the body and farthest from the external opening of the hole, is seen the small, but elegantly sculptured, white bivalve shell, (cut 2, *s;* and Plate XXVI, fig. 183, *s*.) The shell covers the mouth and palpi, liver, foot, and other important organs. The foot (*f*) is a short, stout, muscular organ, broadly truncate or rounded at the end, and appears to be the organ by means of which the excavation of the burrow is effected. The shell is covered by a delicate epidermis, and probably does not assist in rasping off the wood, as many have supposed. The gills are long and narrow, inclosed mostly in the naked part of the body, and are reddish brown in color. The *Teredos* obtain their microscopic food in the same manner as other bivalve mollusks, viz., by means of a current of water constantly drawn into the branchial tube by the action of vibrating cilia within; the infusoria and other minute organisms are thus carried along to the mouth at the other end, while the gills are supplied with oxygen by the same current; the return current passing out of the dorsal tube removes the waste water from the gills, together with the fæces and excretions of the animal, and also the particles of wood which have been removed by the excavating process. As the animal grows larger the burrows are deepened, the lining of shelly matter increases in length and thickness, the shell itself and the pallets increase in size, and the terminal tubes grow longer. But as the orifices of the terminal tubes must necessarily be kept at the external opening of the burrow, the muscular collar at the base of the tubes constantly recedes from the entrance, and with it the pallets; at the same time imbricated layers of shelly matter are usually deposited in the upper end of the shelly tube, which are supposed to aid the pallets in closing the aperture when the tubes are withdrawn. When the animal has completed its growth, or when it has encountered the tubes of its companions and cannot pass them, or when it approaches the exterior of a thin piece of wood and cannot turn aside, it forms a rounded or cup-shaped layer of shelly matter, continuous with the lining of the tubes, and closing up the burrow in front of its shell; sometimes it retreats and forms a second partition of the same kind.

This species produces its young in May and probably through the greater part or all of the summer. The eggs are exceedingly numerous, probably amounting to millions, and they are retained in the gill-cavity, where they are fertilized and undergo the first stages of their development. The embryos pass through several curious phases during their growth. In one of the early stages they are covered with fine vibrating cilia, by means of which they can swim like ciliated infusoria; later they lose these cilia and develop a rudimentary bivalve shell, which is at first heart-shaped, and the mantle begins to appear and larger retractile cilia develop upon its edge, which serve as organs for swimming; but at this period the shell is large enough to cover the whole body when contracted. In this stage they swim actively about in the water; later the cilia become larger, a long, narrow, ligulate foot is developed, by means of which they can creep about and attach themselves temporarily to solid objects; the shells become rounder, a pair of eyes and organs of hearing are developed; after this the little animal begins to elongate, the locomotive cilia are lost, the eyes disappear, and the mature form is gradually assumed. These young *Teredos*, when they finally locate upon the surface of wood-work and begin to make their burrows, are not larger than the head of a pin, and consequently their holes are at first very minute, but owing to their rapid growth the holes quickly become larger and deeper.

This species is very abundant along the southern coast of New England, from New York to Cape Cod, wherever submerged wood-work, sunken wrecks, timber buoys, or floating pieces of drift-wood occur. It also infests the bottoms of vessels not protected by sheathing. It is not confined to pure sea-water, but occurs in the piles and timbers of our wharves in harbors that are quite brackish. I have found it abundant in the piles of Long Wharf in New Haven Harbor, where the water is not only quite brackish, but also muddy and contaminated with sewerage and other impurities. At Wood's Hole it was found to be very abundant in the cedar buoys that had been taken up from various localities and placed on the wharves to dry and be cleaned. Captain B. J. Edwards informed me that formerly, when the buoys were not taken up, they would not usually last more than two years, owing chiefly to the attacks of this *Teredo*, but under the present system there are two sets of buoys, which are alternately taken up and put down every six months. After a set has been taken up and allowed to dry thoroughly they are scraped to remove the barnacles, &c., and then receive a thorough coat of verdigris paint, each time, before they are put down. With this treatment they will last ten or twelve years, but they are more or less perforated and injured every year, until finally they become worthless. Inasmuch as the *Teredos* produce their young all through the summer, and they develop to a very large size in one season, it is evident that the best time to take up the buoys would be in midsummer, before the early crop of young have grown large, and leaving too little time for the later crop to become large, in the buoys thus put down, before winter, when most of them would probably be killed by the cold weather. In this way the damage might be materially diminished, if not inconsistent with the other duties of the officers of the vessels employed in this service. There are, as yet, no means of estimating the extent of the damage done to our wharves, shipping, &c., by this and the various other species of *Teredo* found on our coast, but judging from their abundance along the whole coast, it is much greater than is generally supposed.

The *Teredo navalis* is also abundant on the coast of Europe, from the Mediterranean and Black Seas to Christiania, and the coasts of Great Britain. Its habits have been quite thoroughly investigated by several Dutch naturalists, owing to the great damage that it has done on their coast, at times even threatening a general inundation of the country by destroying the wood-work of the dikes. This *Teredo* occupies a zone of considerable breadth, for it often lives considerably above low-water mark and extends several feet below it, even to the depth of fourteen feet, according to some writers.

The best remedies in common use to resist or prevent its attacks are copper-sheathing, used chiefly on vessels; broad-headed nails, closely driven, used for piles and timbers; creosote and coal-tar, frequently applied. The various poisonous substances that have been applied to timber for this purpose, however useful they may be in other respects, have little or no effect on the *Teredo*, for it does not depend upon the wood for its food, and even protects its body externally with a layer of shell, lining its holes. The only remedies that are likely to succeed are those calculated to prevent the lodgment and entrance of the young ones beneath the surface. Even creosote, thoroughly applied under pressure at the rate of 10 pounds per square foot, has been found insufficient to prevent their attacks, for piles thus treated at Christiania were found by Mr. Jeffreys to be filled with the *Teredo* within two years after they were put down.

Several other species of *Teredo* also occur on this coast. The *Teredo megotara* (Plate XXVII, fig. 188) has been found in floating pine wood at Newport, Rhode Island, and in cedar buoys, &c., at New Bedford, Massachusetts; as well as in Massachusetts Bay, at Provincetown and other places; it is also found as far south as South Carolina at least. This species sometimes grows to a large size, forming tubes at least eighteen inches long. It sometimes occurs, also, in the piles of wharves in this region. The *Teredo Thomsoni* (Plate XXVII, fig. 187) has been found in great numbers in the marine railway and also in cedar buoys at New Bedford. It has also been found at Provincetown in a whaling-ship that had cruised in the West Indies.

The *Xylotrya fimbriata* (Plate XXVII, fig. 189) is very similar to the common *Teredo*, except that it has long, oar-shaped pallets, with slender stalks; the blade is flattened on the inside and convex externally, and consists of ten to twelve, or more, funnel-shaped segments which set one into another; their margins project at the sides, making the edges of the blade appear serrated. This species appears to be indigenous on this coast. It has been found living in a sunken wreck in Long Island Sound, near New Haven, and I have also taken it from the oak timbers of a vessel, the Peterhoff, employed in the blockading service, during the late war, on the coast of the Southern States. It grows to a rather large size, often forming holes a foot or more in length and a quarter of an inch in diameter, though usually smaller. The pallets are sometimes half an inch long.

Among the kinds of bivalve shells that do not bore in wood, there are but few species that commonly inhabit piles of wharves. The most frequent of these is the common muscle, *Mytilus edulis*, (p. 307, Plate XXXI, fig. 234,) which sometimes adheres in large clusters. The common oyster, *Ostræa Virginiana*, (p. 310,) often attaches itself to the piles, but in such situations seldom survives the winter.

Ascidians often occur in large quantities attached to the piles, at and just below low-water mark, and also on the under side of floating timber. They often completely cover large surfaces and spread over the barnacles, hydroids, and algæ, which have previously located. They grow very rapidly, attaining their full size during a few weeks in midsummer.

The most abundant species are usually *Molgula Manhattensis* (p. 311, Plate XXXIII, fig. 250) and *Cynthia partita*, (p. 311, Plate XXXIII, fig. 246.) At Wood's Hole, on the piles of the Government wharf, in August and September, the *Perophora viridis* V. was exceedingly abundant, creeping over and covering up the other ascidians as well as the barnacles, hydroids, and algæ. This is a compound or "social" Ascidian, in which stolon-like tubular processes come out from the basal portion of the first individuals and run in every direction over the surfaces of objects to which they are attached, producing buds at intervals, which rapidly develop into little Ascidians like the old ones, and give out other stolons in their turn; thus they will very soon cover large surfaces, though each individual Ascidian is quite small. The body is compressed, broad oval, or more or less rounded in outline, with a terminal branchial, and lateral anal orifice, both slightly raised on short and broad tubes. The body is attached to the stolons by a short narrow pedicle, and is usually not more than an eighth of an inch high. The color is bright green or yellowish green, and the integument is soft and translucent.

On the piles of the same wharf, and associated with the last, was another compound Ascidian, *Amarœcium constellatum;* this forms solid gelatinous masses, with a smooth, convex surface, usually less than an inch in diameter and about half an inch high, but often larger. The zoöids, or individual animals, are quite small, long, and slender, and entirely imbedded in the gelatinous mass that unites them together. They are arranged in circular, oval, or stellate groups, with a common cloacal orifice in the center of each cluster. The masses are usually pale orange-red, varying to yellowish and pale flesh-color. The stomach of each individual is bright orange-red; the branchial sac is flesh-color, pale yellow, or orange; the tubes and upper part of the mantle bright orange or lemon-yellow.

The *Botryllus Gouldii* (p. 375, Plate XXXIII, figs. 252, 253) also frequently occurs on the piles of the wharves, creeping over the stems of Tubularians, the surfaces of other ascidians, fronds of algæ, or on the surface of the wood itself. It also frequently forms broad, soft incrustations on the bottoms of boats, floating timber, &c.

The Bryozoa are also usually quite abundant on the piles and timbers of wharves, &c.

The *Bugula turrita* (p. 311, Plate XXXIV, figs. 258, 259) is one of the most common as well as one of the most elegant of these. It occurs attached to the adhering sea-weeds, &c., forming delicate white plumes.

The *Escharella variabilis* (p. 311, Plate XXXIII, fig. 256) usually forms firm, coral-like incrustations, but when attached to hydroids and sea-weeds it spreads out into foliaceous or lichen-like, rigid, calcareous fronds, which are dull red while living.

On the piles at Wood's Hole the *Bugula flabellata* was also very abundant. This forms elegant circular or fan-shaped fronds, consisting of numerous repeatedly forked, flat, and rather narrow branches, on which the cells are arranged in about three longitudinal rows. This species, like others of the genus, bears very singular structures, known as avicularia, which, under the microscope, have the form and appearance of the stout, hooked beaks of certain birds, such as the hawk, owl, parrot, &c. These beaks are attached by flexible stems, and are provided internally with powerful muscles by means of which they are constantly opened and closed, and can bite with considerable force. In this species these are attached to the sides of the cells, along the edges of the branches. Their office seems to be to defend the colony against small parasites, and dirt of all kinds, which, unless thus removed, would soon cover up the cells and destroy the animals. In addition to these, various less conspicuous species often occur in abundance, especially *Vesicularia gracilis; V. dichotoma* V.; and *V. cuscuta.*

Of Radiata there are but few species in such localities, with the exception of the Hydroids, which are usually very abundant.

The green star-fish, *Asterias arenicola*, (p. 326, Plate XXXV, fig. 269,) may occasionally occur adhering to the piles just below low-water mark, but it does not have this habit to such an extent as does the *A. vulgaris*, north of Cape Cod, for the latter is almost always to be seen in abundance on the piles of the wharves of the northern seaports, as at Portland, Eastport, &c., and less abundantly at Boston.

One of the most beautiful, as well as one of the most abundant, of the Hydroids that occur on the piles of wharves, and on the under side of floating timber, is the *Parypha crocea*, (Plate XXXVI, fig. 274.) This species grows in great luxuriance upon the piles, especially in those harbors where the water is somewhat brackish. It forms large clusters of branching stems, often six inches or more in height, each of which is surmounted by a beautiful, flower-like, drooping head of a pink or bright red color. These heads are often broken off, or even voluntarily cast off, when the animals are unhealthy, but new ones are soon reproduced, and, therefore, this does not seem to be a very serious accident, though certainly a very inconvenient one, for the mouth, stomach, tentacles, and most other organs are all lost when these "heads" drop off. This species does not produce free-swimming medusæ, but the buds, corresponding to those that develop into free medusæ in many other cases, in this remain attached to the heads in drooping clusters, looking like loose clusters of light red grapes, in miniature.

The buds produced by the hydroid-heads of one colony are either all males or females, and, while attached to the hydroid-heads, eggs or spermules are developed within them; the eggs are fertilized and develop into young hydroids, which, when finally expelled, are provided with a circle of slender tentacles, and need only to attach themselves to some solid substance by the basal end of the body to become fixed, tubularian hydroids, similar to the old ones in many respects, though still very small and simple in structure. These young tubularians swim and crawl about for a time, and after attaching themselves they rapidly grow larger and produce stolons from the base, from which buds arise that develop into forms like the first one; other buds are produced from the sides of the stems, which also become like the others, and in this way the large clusters of tubularians are rapidly formed.

Several species of Campanularians are also to be found attached to the piles and timbers of wharves and bridges. At Wood's Hole the most abundant species was *Obelia pyriformis*, which grew in great profusion on the piles just below low-water mark. It is a delicate and much branched species, with elongated, pear-shaped, reproductive capsules, and is beautifully phosphorescent. On the hull of an old wreck in Wood's Hole passage, where the tide flows with great force, the *Obelia flabellata* was found in abundance, though it does not appear to have been noticed on this side of the Atlantic before. It has very elongated, slender, simple, but crooked stems, with numerous, alternate, short, forking, fan-shaped branches; these generally fork close to their origin, the divisions diverging in opposite directions. The hydroid calicles (hydrothecæ) are small, cup-shaped, or broad bell-shaped, with a smooth rim, and they are borne on slender pedicles that are of various lengths, but mostly short and composed of only four to six rings. The reproductive capsules (gonothecæ) are urn-shaped, with a short, narrow neck; they are borne on short pedicles, of few rings, arising from the axils of the branches. Some of the specimens were eight or ten inches long.

On the piles of Long Wharf, at New Haven, the *Obelia gelatinosa* of Europe was found growing in great luxuriance in September. The water at this locality was quite brackish, but it will probably be found, also, in pure sea-water, for on the coast of Europe it is common both in brackish and pure ocean-water. It is probable that this species has not been observed before on our coast, for although the name occurs in several local lists, these refer, according to Mr. A. Agassiz, to other species, and he does not include the present species in his Catalogue of North American Acalephæ. It is a large species, growing to the length of ten or twelve inches, and branches widely and very profusely. It differs from most of our other species in having a thick, compound stem, composed of many united tubes. The smaller branches are, however, profusely divided, and the branchlets are simple, very slender, white, and translucent, their delicacy contrasting strongly with the stout, dark-colored stems. The larger branches mostly arise in pairs, close together, but immediately diverge; the small branches and branchlets are alternate. The hydrothecæ are very small, deeply bell-shaped, the rim divided into ten or twelve teeth, which are squarish in form, and slightly emarginate at the end; their pedicles vary in length, and are often rather long and slender, especially the terminal ones. The gonothecæ are elongated, urn-shaped, with a narrow, short, tubular neck. I also found this species in April, growing on oysters, at Great Egg Harbor, New Jersey.

Several other species of *Obelia* occur in similar situations, together with various related genera.

The *Sertularia pumila*, (p. 327, Plate XXXVII, fig. 279) often occurs attached to the *Fucus* and other sea-weeds growing on the piles.

The *Halecium gracile* V., (p. 328,) often grows on the piles in great abundance, especially where the water is somewhat brackish, and it sometimes also occurs in great profusion on floating drift-wood.

Of Actinians the most frequent species is the *Sagartia leucolena*, (p. 329, Plate XXXVIII, fig. 284,) which can almost always be found among the adhering barnacles and ascidians; not unfrequently it attaches itself within a dead barnacle, and, in fact, seems quite partial to such a location.

The *Metridium marginatum* (p. 329) also frequently occurs on the piles, but is much less frequent, and generally of smaller size than it is farther north, as about Boston and on the coast of Maine.

Several sponges occur frequently on the piles of the wharves, but they have not been well determined. Among them the *Grantia ciliata*, or a closely allied species, is very common, and also another of the same group, which is tubular and branched, (*Leucosolenia botryoides* ?).

The common, red branching sponge (p. 330) is frequent, and also a slender branching species of *Chalina*, near *C. oculata*. Two or more species of *Tedania*, forming irregular, massive, pale-yellow sponges of a brittle texture, are common.

List of species commonly found on piles and timbers of wharves and bridges on buoys, bottoms of vessels, and other submerged wood-work.

ARTICULATA.

Insects.

	Page.		Page.
Chironomus oceanicus	379	Molanna, sp	379

Crustacea.

	Page.		Page
Panopeus Sayi	382	Jæra copiosa	382
P. depressus	382	Tanais filum	381
Hyale littoralis	315	Balanus eburneus	381
Gammarus ornatus	382	B. crenatus	381
Melita nitida	382	B. balanoides	381
Amphithoë compta	382	B. tintinabulum	381
Corophium cylindricum	382	Lepas anserifera	382
Caprella, sp	316	L. anatifera	382
Limnoria lignorum	379	L. pectinata	382
Idotea irrorata	316	Conchoderma virgata	382
I. phosphorea	316	C. aurita	382

Annelids.

	Page.		Page.
Lepidonotus squamatus	320	Nicolea simplex	382
Harmothoë imbricata	321	Lepræa rubra	382
Eulalia, sp	349	Polycirrus eximius	382
Eumidia, sp	349	Potamilla oculifera	382
Podarke obscura	382	Sabella micropthalma	382
Autolytus cornutus	397	Euchone, sp	416
Nereis limbata	382	Serpula dianthus	322
Sabellaria vulgaris	321	Spirorbis spirillum	323

Nemerteans.

	Page.		Page.
Polinia glutinosa	382	Cerebratulus, (?) sp	382
Nemertes socialis	324		

MOLLUSCA.

Gastropods.

	Page.		Page.
Bela plicata	383	Astyris lunata	383
Urosalpinx cinerea	383	Anachis avara	383
Tritia trivittata	383	Littorinella minuta	383
Ilyanassa obsoleta	383	Rissoa aculeus	383

PROTOZOA.

Porifera, (*Sponges.*)

II. 5.—ANIMALS INHABITING THE ROCKY BOTTOMS OF THE BAYS AND SOUNDS.

In this region the proportion of rocky bottom is relatively quite small, and mostly to be found only in quite shallow water. Therefore the animal life is very similar to that of the rocky shores and tide-pools, near low-water mark.

In Vineyard Sound and vicinity the rocky bottoms examined were chiefly at the following localities, as indicated on the accompanying chart, viz.: 1st. An area south of Parker's Point and occupying a part of the bottom of the passage between Parker's Point and Nonamesset Island, on both sides of the channel, and extending somewhat south of a line drawn from Nobska Point to the southeastern end of Nonamesset Island. The dredgings made in this area are, 9, *a*, *b*, *c*, *d*; 2, *a*, *b*; 3, *a*, *b*, *c*; 4, *a*, *b*; 5, *c*, *d*, *e*; 8, *a*, *b*; 18, *a*, *b*. 2d. An area south and southwest of Nobska Point; dredgings, 21, *b*, *e*; 22, *a*; and others not recorded were made on this patch. 3d. In the Wood's Hole passage, between the north end of Nonamesset Island and the opposite shores, there are numerous rocky patches, and the tides flow with great force; dredgings, 14, *a*, *b*, *c*, *d*, *e*, *f*, *g*; 16, *a*, *b*; 17, *c*, *d*, *e*; 15, *a*, *b*; and many others were made on this bottom. 4th. A small area between Uncatena Island and Long Neck; dredgings, 11, *e*, *f*, and 71, *c*, were on this patch. 5th. A small area, south of the Wepecket Islands, where the dredging, 73, *d*, was made. 6th. A region of rocks and sand off West Chop, north of Martha's Vineyard; in the dredgings made here, 37, *c*, *d*, *e*, some very fine hydroids and ascidians were obtained. 7th. In Quick's Hole, the passage between Nashawena and Pasque Islands, a rocky bottom, with abundant ascidians, hydroids, and sponges, was found, where dredgings 77, *a* and *c*, were made.

In addition to these localities numerous dredgings were made on rocky bottoms off Gay Head and Devil's Bridge, and also between Martha's Vineyard and No Man's Land, but these properly belong to the cold outer region.

In the vicinity of New Haven, rocky bottoms, generally of small extent, are found off the light-house, and off South End and Branford Point, also among the Thimble Islands. All these localities have been examined by me in numerous dredging excursions made during the past eight years. Nevertheless the fauna of the rocky bottoms of this region is probably more imperfectly known than that of other kinds of bottom. This is mainly owing to the difficulties encountered in dredging upon rough rocks.

Rocky bottoms are very favorable for many kinds of Crustacea, both for those that swim free and conceal themselves among the sea-weeds that grow on rocks in shallow water, and for those that take refuge beneath the rocks. Consequently rocky bottoms are the favorite feeding-grounds for certain kinds of fish, especially tautog, striped bass, black bass, cunners, &c., in this region.

The common crab, *Cancer irroratus*, (p. 312,) *Panopeus Sayi*, (p. 312,) *P. depressus*, (p. 312,) the larger hermit-crab, *Eupagurus pollicaris*, (p. 313,) and the smaller hermit, *E. longicarpus*, (p. 313,) are common species on the rocky bottoms. A small species of spider-crab, *Pelia mutica*, occasionally occurs. The *Cancer borealis* has hitherto been a rare species, and little is known concerning its habits or distribution; it appears to frequent rocky bottoms chiefly, but most of the specimens obtained in this region were found thrown up by the waves on the shores of Cuttyhunk Island, No Man's Land, and near Gay Head.

The lobster, *Homarus Americanus*, frequents rocky bottoms, concealing itself under and among the rocks while watching for its prey, but it is much less abundant in this region than on the coast of Maine and in the Bay of Fundy, and does not usually grow to so large a size as in the northern waters. It also occurs on the sandy and gravelly bottoms of Vineyard Sound, where most of those sent to the markets from this region are obtained. The young, free-swimming larvæ of the lobster, in the stages represented in Plate IX, figs. 38, 39, were often taken at the surface in great abundance, during June and July, in the towing-nets. The young lobsters were also found swimming actively at the surface by Mr. S. I. Smith, even after they had acquired the true lobster-like form and structure, and were nearly three-quarters of an inch long. In this stage they swim and act much like shrimp. While young, therefore, the lobster must be devoured in immense numbers by many kinds of fishes, and even when of considerable size they are still preyed upon by the tautog and black bass, and especially by sharks, skates, and rays, and doubtless by other fishes. We found the lobsters very abundant off Menemsha on a sandy and weedy bottom in shallow water. At this place over one hundred were taken at a single haul, by the trawl. The lobsters caught for the market are nearly all caught in "lobster-pots," baited with refuse fish of various kinds.

In addition to the common shrimp, *Crangon vulgaris*, (p. 339, Plate III, fig. 10,) another quite different species (*Hippolyte pusiola*) was often met with on the rocky bottoms. This is a smaller species, about an inch long, of a pale gray, salmon, or flesh-color, often specked with red; there is usually a white stripe along the middle of the back, and sometimes transverse bands of red or white; the antennæ are annulated with flesh-color and light red, and the legs are sometimes specked with brown, and often annulated with brown, or with gray and white. It differs from all the other American species in having a short, acute rostrum, scarcely projecting beyond the eyes, with three or four sharp teeth on its upper edge and none below. In form and general appearance it somewhat resembles the *Virbius* represented in Plate III, fig. 11, but is stouter and quite different in color. It is a northern species, extending to Greenland and Northern Europe, and is more common on the coast of Maine, where it is usually associated with several other larger species of the same genus, all of which are remarkable for their brilliant colors, the various shades of red usually predominating. Their bright colors are no doubt directly connected with their habit of living among the bright red algæ, so abundant in the shallow waters on rocky bottoms.

A beautiful little shrimp-like Crustacean, *Mysis Americana* SMITH, sometimes occurs in immense numbers among the algæ growing on the rocks just below low-water mark, especially in spring. This is an important species, as it is one of the principal kinds of food for the shad and other fishes. The full grown specimens are only about an inch long. It is almost transparent, whitish, with conspicuous black eyes; there is a row of more or less conspicuous, dark stellate spots along the body, both above and below, and similar specks often occur on the tail; a spot of dark brown or blackish often occurs on each side of the carapax. The intestine shows through as a greenish or brownish line.

Another small, shrimp-like species belonging to an interesting new genus, the *Heteromysis formosa* SMITH, often occurred in small colonies, sometimes hid away in the dead shell of some large bivalve or gastropod. The females of this species are of a beautiful light rose color, but the males have the pale color and translucency common to most of the species of *Mysis*.

Numerous Amphipods also occur, most of which are also found in the pools or under stones at low water, and have, consequently, been mentioned on former pages. One of the most curious Amphipods was a small species, found living among the large compound ascidians, which is probably *Cerapus tubularis* SAY. This species constructs a little, slender, free tube, which it inhabits and carries about upon its back when it travels, very much as the larvæ of caddis-flies, common in fresh waters, carry about their tubes. One species of barnacle, the *Balanus crenatus*, was abundant, often completely covering small stones and shells. This has not been met with, as yet, at low-water, although it occurs on the bottoms of vessels.

Of Annelids a large number inhabit rocky bottoms, but as most of them live beneath the rocks, or in tubes attached to rocks and stones, it is difficult to obtain an accurate knowledge of them. Many of the species seem, however, to be found also in pools and beneath the stones on rocky shores, and have already been mentioned.

Perhaps the most characteristic Annelids of rocky bottoms are the scaly worms, of which three species are common in this region, viz.:

Lepidonotus squamatus, (p. 320, Plate X, figs. 40, 41;) *L. sublevis* V., (p. 320, Plate X, fig. 42;) and *Harmothoë imbricata*, all of which cling close to the rough surfaces of the stones, or hide away in the cracks and crevices, or conceal themselves in the interstices between the ascidians, barnacles, roots of algæ, or in the cavities of sponges, &c. Several long, slender, and active species, belonging to the genera *Phyllodoce*, *Eulalia*, *Eumidia*, and *Eteone*, are of frequent occurrence; most of them are bright green or yellowish green in color, and all have small, leaf-like branchiæ along the sides.

The *Nereis pelagica* (p. 319, Plate XI, figs. 52–55) is very common, living beneath the stones, and especially in the interstices between the lobes of a large, sand-covered, compound ascidian, *Amarœcium pellucidum*, in company with the species of *Phyllodoce*, &c., just named. This species of *Nereis* is remarkable for its brilliant iridescence. It is a northern species, extending to the Arctic Ocean and northern coast of Europe. It is very abundant on the coast of Maine, under stones at low-water mark.

Associated with the preceding species among the sandy compound ascidians, occurring both on rocky and gravelly bottoms, were large numbers of the *Lumbriconereis opalina*, (p. 320, Plate XIII, figs. 69, 70,) conspicuous on account of the brilliant iridescent colors. Several other Annelids also occurred among these ascidians. The *Cirrinereis fragilis*, which is a small and delicate species, furnished with conspicuous eyes, and related to the large *Cirratulus*, occurs beneath the stones. The singular *Naraganseta coralii* occurs burrowing in the coral, *Astrangia Danæ*, and in this respect is similar in its habits to the allied genus *Dodecacerea*, which excavates its galleries in the solid shells of *Cyprina Islandica*, *Pecten tenuicostatus*, &c., in the Bay of Fundy. The *Sabellaria vulgaris*, (p. 321, Plate XVII, figs. 88, 88*a*;) *Nicolea simplex*, (p. 321;) *Scionopsis palmata*, (p. 321;) *Potamilla oculifera*, (p. 322,) Plate XVII, fig. 86;) *Sabella microphthalma*, (p. 323;) *Serpula dianthus*, (p 322;) and *Fabricia Leidyi*, (p. 323,) all occur in tubes attached to the rocks and stones.

A species of *Spirorbis*, which forms a small, white, calcareous shell, coiled up in an open spiral, is commonly attached to the algæ and hydroids. The *Autolytus cornutus* (Plate XIII, figs. 65, 66) constructs cylindrical tubes, which are attached to sea-weeds and the branches of hydroids. This is a small flesh-colored species, with conspicuous brown eyes; the ends of the body are often tinged with green, and the dark, greenish intestine shows through as a median line. The males and females are widely different in appearance and structure, and there are also asexual individuals (fig. 65) very different from both. The asexual ones construct the tubes referred to, but do not remain in them constantly, for they are also often taken swimming at the surface. The males and females are also taken at the surface, especially in the evening, but they also occur creeping over and among the hydroids. This worm is particularly interesting on account of its remarkable mode of reproduction, for, like several other marine annelids, it presents the phenomena of alternate generation. Its history has been well given by Mr. A. Agassiz.* The very numerous eggs of the female (fig. 66, *e*) are at first contained in the general cavity of the body, between the intestine and the outer wall, along the whole length of the body; afterwards they pass into a pouch on the lower side of the body, extending from the twelfth to about the twenty-sixth segment; in the pouch they hatch into young worms, and soon after the sac bursts and they escape into the water. The females apparently die after discharging the young. The eggs do not develop into males and females, but into the asexual or neuter individuals, (fig. 65,) which differ widely from the others in form and in the eyes and other appendages of the head, as well as in the internal anatomy and lateral appendages. After these neuter individuals become nearly full-grown, having forty to forty-five segments, a median dorsal swelling arises at about the thirteenth or fourteenth segment, most commonly on the thirteenth, and soon after two others arise from the sides of the same segment and develop rapidly; these swellings finally become the three front tentacles of a new head, (*a*, *a*, *a*, fig. 65;) soon a pair of eyes appears on the upper side of the segment, than a pair of tentacular cirri; then the second pair of eyes; then other appendages of the head, until finally a complete head is formed, having the structure belonging to the head of a male or female, as the case may be. As the new head, with its appendages, becomes more completely organized, the segments posterior to it, which are to become the body of the new individual, become more highly developed, and the lateral appendages more complicated, those back of the fifth in the male, or the sixth in the female, acquire dorsal fascicles of long setæ, and the dorsal cirris becomes longer; at the same time some additional segments are developed; and the ova in the female, or spermatazoa in the male, are formed. Finally the new sexual individual, thus formed out of the posterior segments of the original neuter, breaks its connection and swims off by itself, and becomes a perfectly developed male or female. The head of the female is represented in fig. 66; a male individual is represented as developing from an asexual individual in fig. 65. The male can be easily distinguished from the female by the pair of large antennæ, which are forked in the male, but simple in the female. Farther details concerning this curious mode of reproduction may be found in the memoir of Mr. Agassiz, together with numerous excellent illustrations, in addition to those here copied.

Associated with the preceding species a few specimens were found which probably belong to another species of *Autolytus*. These were quite slender, light-red in color, with paler annulations, but only the asexual individuals were observed. Another species of larger size also occurs among the hydroids, near New Haven, which belongs to *Autolytus* or

* On Alternate Generation in Annelids, and the Embryology of Autolytus cornutus; Boston Journal of Natural History, Vol. VII, p. 384, 1863.

some closely allied genus, but of this only the asexual form has occurred, and it has not yet been carefully studied. This becomes nearly an inch long and quite slender. The body is white, with about fifty annulations of bright purplish red between the segments, but sometimes a red ring is absent, leaving wider white bands; the lateral appendages are simple, and each has a dot of red on the anterior side; the head is orange, with four dark red eyes.

Of Mollusks there are but few species among the higher groups which do not also occur on the rocky shores at low-water, but of the Ascidians and Bryozoa we find numerous additional species. The Gastropods are represented by the large *Fulgur carica* (p. 355, Plate XXII, fig. 124) and *Sycotypus canaliculatus*, (p. 355;) also by the "drill," *Urosalpinx cinerea*, (p. 306, Plate XXI, fig. 116,) which is usually abundant in shallow water; *Astyris lunata* (p. 106, Plate XXI, fig. 110) is abundant on the hydroids and algæ; *A. zonalis*, (Plate XXI, fig. 111,) which is an allied species, of larger size and with plainer colors, is sometimes met with, but is rare in this region. It takes its name from two narrow spiral zones of white that usually surround the whorls. The *Crucibulum striatum* (Plate XVIII, figs. 125, 126) is often met with clinging firmly to the rocks and stones.

The *Leptochiton apiculatus* (Plate XXV, fig. 167) is one of the most characteristic and common species on rocky and gravelly bottoms; this also adheres firmly to the stones and dead shells, and its grayish or dirty whitish shell, often more or less stained, blends its color with that of its surroundings in a way that might deceive the fishes themselves. The back is covered with a series of movable plates, so that when removed the animal can curl itself into a ball, like a "pill-bug," (*Oniscus*,) or like an armadillo, a habit that it shares in common with the scaly annelids, *Lepidonotus* and *Harmothoë*, which live in the same places with it. The flexibility of the shell also enables the chitons to adapt themselves more closely to the uneven surfaces of the rocks than they otherwise could. More rarely the *Leptochiton ruber* (Plate XXV, fig. 166) is met with, though farther north, as in the Bay of Fundy, this is a very common species, while the *apiculatus* is quite unknown there, being decidedly southern in its range. The *ruber* is, as its name implies, a red species, and its colors are usually bright and beautifully varied with lighter and darker. Its bright color would seem at first a fatal gift, calculated to attract the attention of passing fishes, which are always fond of such food, but when we examine its habits more closely we find that it lives almost exclusively on and among rocks that are incrusted by the curious stony algæ, known as "nullipores," (*Lithothamnion polymorphum*,) which are red in color, but of various shades, and often completely cover the rocks with irregular red incrustations, over large areas in shallow water, especially on the coasts farther north, so that this shell and a larger species, (*C. marmoreus*,) usually associated with it, are admirably adapted by their colors for living and concealing themselves on such bottoms, while many other species, frequenting the same localities, have a similar coloration, though belonging to very different groups. As examples we may mention the beautifully variegated star-fish, *Ophiopholis aculeata*, (Plate XXXV, fig. 270,) rare in this region, but very abundant in the Bay of Fundy; *Crangon boreas*, common on the same bottoms in the Bay of Fundy; several species of shrimp belonging to the genera *Hippolyte*, *Pandalus*, &c. The bright red colors of all these animals would certainly be very fatal to them were there no red algæ among which they could conceal themselves and thus escape, to a considerable extent, from the voracious fishes, which are nearly always ready to pounce upon them whenever they expose themselves. One or two handsome species of *Æolis* (similar to fig. 174) were taken, but for lack of opportunity they were not identified while living, and these soft and delicate creatures cannot be preserved in alcohol so as to be identified afterwards with certainty. The handsome little *Doto coronata* (Plate XXV, fig. 170) occurs occasionally on the hydroids, upon the animals of which it feeds. This species is generally less than half an inch in length. The body is pale yellowish, or salmon-color, or rosy, specked with pink, light red, or dark red, which often forms a median dorsal line toward the head; the curious papillose branchiæ along the back are pale orange, the lateral and terminal papillæ being tipped with bright purplish red, dark red, or carmine, with a ring of flake-white below the tip; the head and tentacles are pale and translucent. The eggs are laid upon the hydroids, in long, flattened, and convoluted gelatinous strings, at various times during the early summer.

Another curious and beautifully colored naked mollusk, the *Polycera Lessonii*, also occurs occasionally on rocky bottoms, among hydroids and bryozoa. In this species the body is pale flesh-color, or sometimes pale orange, and thickly covered with bright, deep green specks, giving the whole surface a green color; along the back is a median line of tubercles or papillæ, and there are two other rows on each side, which extend as far as the gills or a little beyond; all these tubercles are tipped with bright sulphur-yellow, except that the last ones of the lateral rows, posterior to the gills, are usually tipped with flake-white, but these have two or three irregular, lateral lobes, which are tipped with yellow; other smaller, yellow tubercles are scattered over the back, sides, head, and tail; the tentacles are also bright yellow, but sometimes specked with green and yellow, with yellow tips. The gills are three in number, in a cluster on the middle line of the back, posteriorly; each one is bipinnate and delicately plumose; they are colored similar to the back, generally more or less specked with bright yellow, and often with flake-white; the tips are usually bright yellow.

Another small but singular species, which also occurs among the hydroids, as well as among dead shells, is the *Doridella obscura*, (Plate XXV, fig. 173;) in this the colors are not conspicuous, but seem rather intended for its concealment. The back is sometimes light, yellowish brown, finely mottled with white, and specked with darker brown; dorsal tentacles white and retractile; lower surface white or light yellowish, a three-lobed yellowish or brownish internal organ showing through in the middle of the foot. Other specimens are very dark-brown or almost black above, finely mottled with whitish. The anterior angles of the head are prolonged into tentacle-like organs or palpi. The gills are situated beneath, in the groove between the edge of the foot and the mantle, on the left side, and near the posterior end of the foot; they consist of a tuft of slender filaments.

Of Lamellibranchs certain species occur on rocky bottoms, which attach themselves firmly to the rocks, either by the side of one valve, like the oyster, *Ostræa Virginiana*, (p. 310,) and the *Anomia glabra*, (p. 311, Plate XXXII, figs. 241, 242;) or by threads of byssus, which they spin and use as cables for anchoring themselves, like the common muscle, *Mytilus edulis*, (p. 307, Plate XXXI, fig. 234,) the "horse-muscle," *Modiola modiolus*, (p. 309, Plate XXXI, fig. 237,) the *Argina pexata*, (Plate XXX, fig. 227,) and *Scapharca transversa*, (Plate XXX, fig. 228,) all of which are common in this region; but certain other species occur, which burrow beneath the stones, like the *Saxicava arctica* (p. 309, Plate XXVII, fig. 192) and *Mya arenaria* (p. 463, Plate XXVI, fig. 179,) and several other less common species.

The Ascidians are usually very abundant on the rocks and stones at all depths. The *Cynthia partita* (p. 311, Plate XXXIII, fig. 246,) is very common, often forming large, rough clusters, much overgrown with hydroids, bryozoa, and algæ. The specimens mostly belong to the erect variety, and in form are quite unlike the one figured. The body is more or less cylindrical, oblong, or urn-shaped, about twice as high as broad when expanded, and with a wide base; the branchial orifice is largest, and situated at the summit of a broad, terminal tube, swollen at base; the anal orifice is smaller, on a short lateral or subterminal tube. Both orifices are usually squarish, and open widely, but, when fully expanded, they sometimes become nearly circular; they are often surrounded at the edge with a narrow circle of red, and each tube has eight longitudinal stripes of white, narrowing downward to a point at the base of the tubes, and alternating with purplish brown ones, which are usually specked with flake-white. The exterior of the test is more or less rough and wrinkled, and generally yellowish or rusty, often tinged with deep purplish brown on the upper parts or throughout. The tubes are usually roughened by small, wart-like papillæ. Unpromising as this species looks, it is devoured by the tautog. The *Molgula Manhattensis* (p. 311, Plate XXXIII, fig. 250) is generally associated with the former. The *Perophora viridis* (p. 388) is often very abundant, creeping over and covering up the two preceding, as well as other ascidians, algæ, hydroids, &c. The most conspicuous species, however, are the massive compound ascidians, which sometimes completely cover the bottom. One of the most abundant of these is the *Amaræcium pel-*

lucidum, which forms large, hemispherical or irregular masses, often six or eight inches, or even more, in diameter, with the surface more or less completely covered by adhering sand. These masses consist of a large number of lobes or basal branches, which come out from a common base as elongated, stolon-like processes, and enlarge upward to the end, which is obtusely rounded, and variable in size, but usually from a quarter to half an inch, while the length may be from one to six inches; these lobes often coalesce, more or less completely, at the upper surface, which is sometimes naked and smooth, translucent, and of a gelatinous appearance. Each of these lobes contains a central cloacal orifice, around which a colony of minute ascidians, or zoöids, are grouped, in a manner analogous to the arrangement in *Botryllus*, already described, (p. 389,) but in the present case the zoöids are very long and slender; the lower end of each, containing the ovaries, with the heart at its extremity, extends down toward the base of the lobe in which they are contained to various distances, varying according to the age and state of development of each zoöid, but the full-grown ones are often nearly an inch long. Each zoöid has its own branchial orifice opening at the surface, as in *Botryllus*, while all the anal tubes discharge the refuse water, fæces, and eggs into the common cloacal ducts.

The *Amarœcium stellatum* is another related species, which is nearly as abundant as the last, and likewise grows to a very large size. It forms large, smooth, irregular plates, or crest-like lobes and masses, which are attached by one edge to the stones and gravel. These plates are sometimes one to two feet long, six inches high, and about an inch thick, and, owing to their smooth surface and whitish color, look something like great slices of salt-pork, and in fact it is often called "sea-pork" by the fishermen. Other specimens will be four or five inches high, and only one or two inches broad at the base, and perhaps half an inch in thickness, and the summit often divides into broad, flat, blunt lobes; various other shapes also occur, some of them very irregular. The larger specimens of this species are generally of a pale-bluish or sea-green color by reflected light when first taken from the water, but pale salmon or flesh-color by transmitted light. The zoöids are much elongated and arranged in more or less regular circular groups over the whole surface, with a small cloacal orifice in the center of each circle. If kept in water, when they grow sickly the zoöids will be forced partially or wholly out of their cavities by the contraction of the tissues around them—a peculiarity seen also in other species of this genus. These zoöids have the branchial tube prominently six-lobed, and of a bright orange-color, this color also extending over the upper or outer end of the body, between the tubes, and more or less over the branchial sac, which is pale yellow or whitish below. The stomach is longitudinally sulcated, with bright orange-red ribs or glands; intestine bright orange or yellow.

This species is devoured by sharks, skates, and the tautog, although it would seem difficult for them to digest it, or get much nutriment from it. The supply is certainly sufficiently abundant.

A third species of this genus, and much more beautiful than either of the preceding, is also common on rocky bottoms. This is the *Amarœcium constellatum* V. (p. 388,) which has already been described as occurring on the piles of the wharves. In deeper water, attached to rocks, it grows to a larger size, forming thick, hemispherical or cake-shaped masses or crusts, sometimes becoming somewhat mushroom-like by the upper parts growing out beyond the central attached portion, which then becomes a short and broad peduncle. It can be easily distinguished from the last on account of its brighter colors, the general color inclining to orange, and by the more irregular and complicated clusters of zoöids. It is less abundant than either of the two preceding.

Two other species of compound Ascidians are also abundant in this region, as well as farther north. These belong to the genus *Leptoclinum;* they form thin, irregular, often broad, white, or salmon-colored incrustations over the surfaces of the rocks, shells, and other ascidians; these crusts are of a firm, coriaceous or gritty texture, and have a finely granulous surface. Under the microscope they are seen to be filled with small, nearly globular particles of carbonate of lime, from which points project in every direction. The zoöids are very minute and are scattered over the surface in large and scarcely distinct groups, which have, however, a common cloacal orifice in the middle, but the several cloacal tubes or channels leading to each central orifice are long, with many crooked branches, reminding one of miniature rivers, and the zoöids are arranged along these ducts and their branches. One of these species, the *Leptoclinum albidum*, is easily distinguished by its chalky white color; the other, *L. luteolum*, is buff or salmon-color. It is possible that the last may even prove to be only a colored variety of the former, but the very numerous specimens that I have collected and examined, in the living state, both in the Bay of Fundy and Vineyard Sound, do no not warrant their union. In these localities both forms are about equally common, but near New Haven the *L. luteolum* has not yet been met with, though the other is not uncommon.

The Bryozoa are very abundant on rocky bottoms at all depths. Some of these incrust the rocks directly, like the *Escharella variabilis*, (p. 312, Plate XXXIII, fig. 256;) *Alcyonidium hirsutum; Escharipora punctata*, &c.; but even these seem to prefer other locations, and by far the greater number occur attached to algæ, hydroids, ascidians, and dead shells. A large part of the species occur also in rocky pools at low-water mark, or attached to the *Fuci* and other sea-weeds between tides, or to the under sides of stones laid bare by low tides, and have, consequently, been previously mentioned. Others which have not yet been detected on the shore will doubtless be found there by more thorough search.

The *Alcyonidium ramosum* (Plate XXXIV, fig. 257) is one of the most conspicuous species, and is often very abundant, attached to rocks in shallow water. In such situations we have often found arborescently branched specimens, twelve to fifteen inches high, with smooth, cylindrical branches about a third of an inch in diameter.

The *Alcyonidium hispidum* (p. 312) does not appear to have been recorded as from our coast, by previous writers, but it is one of our most common species, and may almost always be found incrusting the stems of *Fucus* at low-water mark, as well as the under surfaces of rocks; below low-water mark it is less abundant, generally incrusting *Phyllophora*, and other stout, palmate algæ. It is easily distinguished by the slender, acute, reddish spines, of horn-like texture, which surround each of the cells. It forms soft crusts of moderate thickness, gradually extending over the surface of the sea-weeds to which it becomes attached.

The *A. hirsutum* has also been hitherto overlooked on our coast, but is common, living under the same circumstances as the last, and sometimes associated with it, both above and below low-water mark. I have found it in the greatest abundance in some of the large, rocky tide-pools on the outermost of the Thimble Islands, east of New Haven. It was there growing chiefly upon *Phyllophora membranifolia*, in some cases entirely covering and concealing the plant, from the base of the stem to the tips of the fronds. It also often grows on the "Irish moss," *Chondrus crispus*, on rocky bottoms in shallow water. It forms rather thin, soft crusts, which have small, soft papillæ scattered over the surface; from the summit of each of these papillæa zoöid protrudes, when they expand, and displays an elegant little wreath of tentacles, much as in *A. ramosum*, (see fig. 257.) The *A. parasiticum* is also a species hitherto neglected on our coasts. It forms thin crusts on algæ and hydroids, which generally become coated with a layer of fine sand or dirt. I have not observed it at low-water, but have found it at the depth of a few fathoms on rocky bottoms in Vineyard Sound.

The *Vesicularia dichotoma* V. is a very common species, both on rocky shores, in pools and on the under side of stones; and in shallow water on rocky and shelly bottoms. It is also capable of living in brackish water, and is frequent on the oyster-beds. It usually forms cæspitose clusters of many crowded, slender, white stems, each of which is repeatedly forked, branching in a somewhat arborescent manner. There is a little crowded cluster of small, dark-colored, oval or pear-shaped cells just below each fork, the cells being sessile and arranged in two somewhat spiral rows in each cluster. It generally grows about an inch high, but sometimes two or three inches. When expanded each of the zoöids protrudes from its cell-like body a delicate wreath of eight slender tentacles.

The *Vesicularia cuscuta* is a delicate, creeping species, which resembles, in miniature, the "dodder-plant," (*Cuscuta*,) and creeps over other bryozoa and hydroids, very much as the dodder creeps over other plants. The stem is very delicate, filiform, jointed, and at intervals gives off two very slender, opposite branches, which diverge at right angles, and in their turn branch at intervals in the same way. The cells are small and oval or elliptical, mostly arranged in clusters at or near the branchings of the stems, but some are often scattered on the branches; they are attached by a narrow base. It occurs both at low-water in pools and in shallow water among rocks. The *V. armata* is also a creeping species, but the cells are terminated by four conical prominences, each of which bears a slender spine when perfect. This also occurs both between tides and in shallow water, on hydroids and bryozoa.

With these species of *Vesicularia*, and often attached to them and creeping over them, as well as on other kinds of bryozoa, hydroids, and algæ, a very curious little species often occurs, in which the cells are small, campanulate, and raised on slender pedicels, which rise from slender, white, creeping stems. This is the *Pedicellina Americana*. The zoöids, when expanded, display a wreath of twelve or more tentacles; in contraction and when young they are often clavate.

The *Ætea anguinea* has not been recorded as from our coast, but is very common on rocky and shelly bottoms, creeping over various hydroids, algæ, ascidians, broyozoa, &c.; it also frequently occurs on floating eel-grass and algæ, in company with many hydroids. It consists of delicate, white, creeping, calcareous stolons, from which arise elongated, slender, clavate, white, rigid, erect cells, with the aperture at the end; the narrower, pedicel-like portion of the cell is surrounded by fine, circular, punctate striæ.

The *Eucrate chelata* is also a slender, creeping species, and has somewhat similar habits, but is much less common, and has been met with only in the deeper parts of Vineyard Sound on ascidians and hydroids. In this species each cell arises from the back of the preceding one, near the end, and bends upward and forward obliquely, the cell expanding from a narrow, pedicel-like, basal portion to a more or less oval upper part, with the aperture oblique and subterminal. This, also, is a new addition to the fauna of our coast, although, like the last, long well known on the coast of Europe.

The *Diastopora patina* grows attached to algæ and eel-grass; it forms little circular disks, with tubular cells arising from the upper surface, those in the middle being longest.

The *Tubulipora flabellaris* frequently occurs attached to various kinds of slender-branched algæ, such as *Ahnfeltia plicata*, &c. It forms small, blunt-lobed, coral-like masses, composed of long, crooked, tubular cells, united by a porous mass at base. Toward the borders of the lobes the cells are crowded and polygonal. In the central parts they are more cylindrical and form groups or radiating rows. Associated with the preceding on the algæ, *Crisia eburnea*, (p. 311;) *Mollia hyalina*, (Plate XXXIV, fig. 264;) *Cellepora ramulosa*, (p. 312;) and other species occur. The *Membranipora pilvsa* (Plate XXXIV, figs. 262, 263) is frequent on rocky bottoms, growing chiefly upon *Phyllophora* and other algæ. It may be known by the oval cells, bordered by erect, bristle-like processes, of which the one at the proximal end of the cell is much longer than the rest.

Another species, *M. lineata*, is also common, incrusting rocks and shells in broad, thin, radiating patches. In this the cells are oblong, crowded, and separated only by the linear margins. In the most common variety there are eight or ten slender spinules on each side of the cells, which bend over so as to meet or interlock across the open cells. The cells are much smaller as well as narrower than those of the preceding species.

Of Echinoderms only a few species occur in this region, on rocky bottoms, which causes this fauna to contrast very strongly with that of the rocky bottoms farther north, as in the Bay of Fundy or on the coast of Maine, where numerous other fine species of star-fishes and several additional Holothurians are common. The common green sea-urchin, *Strongylocentrotus Dröbachiensis*, (Plate XXXV, fig. 268,) so very abundant farther north, and especially in the Bay of Fundy, where it occurs in abundance at low-water mark, and on rocky bottoms at all depths down to 110 fathoms, and off St. George's Bank even down to 450 fathoms, is comparatively rare in this region and chiefly confined to the outside colder waters, as off Gay Head and No Man's Land, where it was quite common. But a few specimens were dredged at several localities in Vineyard Sound. The largest occured on the rocky bottoms off West Chop, and off Menemsha. It has been found occasionally in Long Island Sound, as off New Haven and Stratford, Connecticut, but is there quite rare and small. It feeds partly on diatoms and other small algæ, &c., which it cuts from the rocks with the sharp points of its teeth, but it is also fond of dead fishes, which are soon devoured, bones and all, by it in the Bay of Fundy. In return it is swallowed whole in large quantities by the wolf-fish and by other large fishes. The purple sea-urchin, *Arbacia punctulata*, is much more abundant in Vineyard Sound and similar waters, in this region. This is a southern species which is here near its northern limit. It is easily distinguished by its rather stout, unusually long, purple spines; by its ambulacral pores in two simple rows; by the upper surface of the shell being partly destitute of spines; and by the anal region, at the summit of the shell, which is formed of only four rather large plates. It occurred of large size, associated with the preceding species, off West Chop and Holmes's Hole; it was quite abundant in the passage at Wood's Hole, especially on shelly and gravelly bottoms north of Naushawena Island, and it was met with at many other localities.

The common green star-fish, *Asterias arenicola*, (p. 326, Plate XXXV, fig. 269,) is very common on all the rocky bottoms in this region. A smaller and more beautiful northern star-fish was occasionally met with in Wood's Hole passage and several other localities on rocky or gravelly bottoms. This was the *Cribrella sanguinolenta;* it is much more common north of Cape Cod, and is abundant in the Bay of Fundy and northward to Greenland; it is also found on the northern coasts of Europe. It has not been found much south of Vineyard Sound on this coast. It can easily be distinguished by its five round, tapering rays, covered with small spinules, and by having only two rows of locomotive suckers in the grooves on the under side of the rays, instead of four rows, as in the common star-fishes belonging to the genus *Asterias.* Its color is quite variable. It is often orange, or purple, or rose-color, or cream-color, and sometimes mottled with red and purple, &c. Unlike the preceding, and most other species of our star-fishes, this does not have free-swimming young. Its eggs are deposited around the mouth, and retained by the mother until they develop into little star-fishes capable of taking care of themselves.

The Hydroids are very numerous on rocky bottoms. A few species, like *Hydractinia polyclina* (p. 328) and the *Thamnocnida tenella,* attach themselves directly to the rocks, but the greater number adhere to ascidians, algæ, or to other hydroids. Many of the species are also to be found on the rocky shores in tide-pools, and have already been mentioned. Among those not yet detected at low water is a delicate species of *Plumularia,* with slender, alternately pinnate branches, which was found growing upon rocks in company with *Hydractinia.* The *Thamnocnida tenella* is a Tubularian which grows in clusters, two or three inches high, consisting of long, slender, somewhat branched stems, which are more or less crooked, and usually irregularly and distantly annulated, with beautiful pink heads at the top. The general appearance is like that of the *Parypha,* (Plate XXXVI, fig. 274.) The *Obelia dichotoma* was found growing upon ascidians (*Cynthia partita,* &c.) in 8 or 10 fathoms, among rocks. It is a well-known European species, but has not hitherto been established as an inhabitant of our coast. It has dark, horn-colored, slender stems, with pretty long and rather erect, slender, alternate branches, which branch again in the same way. The hydroid cells are deeply campanulate, with the margin slightly sinuous or scolloped, the slight notches corresponding with faint angular ridges which run down on the upper parts of the cells, giving the upper half a slightly polygonal form. In this respect this species closely resembles the *Obelia commisuralis.* The reproducsive capsules are elongated, urn-shaped, with a narrow, raised, sub-conical neck.

The *Obelia geniculata* is often very abundant on the fronds of *Laminaria* and other algæ having flat fronds. Its creeping tubular stolons often thickly cover the surface with a complete net-work; from these the erect stems rise to the height of about an inch. This species may be known by the prominent geniculation at the origin of the hydroid pedicels. The *Obelia fusiformis* has a similar mode of growth, but is much less common. Its hydroid cells are comparatively small and their pedicels very short.

Several very delicate and beautiful creeping hydroids, belonging to the Campanularians, also occur attached to larger hydroids, and the algæ. Among these are *Clytia Johnstoni*, having comparatively large, bell-shaped cups, with a notched rim, each borne on a long, slender, generally simple pedicel, ringed at each end, and arising from the creeping stems. The reproductive capsules are urn-shaped and annulated. The *C. intermedia* is quite similar in its growth, but has smaller and deeper cups, with smaller notches around the rim. The *Orthopyxis caliculata* grows in the same manner; it has beautiful little bell-shaped or cup-shaped cells, with an even rim, each borne on a long, slender, annulated pedicel with one of the rings, just below the cup, very prominent. Its reproductive capsules are large, oblong, smooth, and obtuse at the end. The *Platypyxis cylindrica* has small, very deep, somewhat cylindrical cups, with the rim divided into sharp teeth or notches; each one is borne on a small, slender pedicel, generally less than an eighth of an inch high, feebly annulated at each end. The reproductive capsules are elongated, compressed, flaring slightly at the end. The *Campanularia volubilis*, is also a very small, but elegant species; it has deep cylindrical cups, which have a regularly scolloped rim, the scollops being small and evenly rounded. The pedicels are very slender, and are annulated *spirally* throughout their whole length, so as to appear as if twisted; just below the cup there is one prominent rounded annulation, or bead, the whole resembling in miniature the stem of certain wine-glasses and glass vases. The reproductive capsules are vase-shaped, attached by short pedicels, and have the neck elongated and gradually narrowed to the end, which flares slightly.

The *Lafoëa calcarata* is also a small creeping hydroid, belonging to another family. It has curved tubular cells. It nearly always grows on *Sertularia cornicina*, which is a small species, resembling *S. pumila*, (Plate XXXVII, fig. 279.) The *Sertularia argentea* (Plate XXXVII, fig. 280) is a large, profusely branched species, often growing to the length of a foot or more. It is very abundant in this region. *S. cupressina* is closely related, but much less common. The *Hydrallmania falcata* is also a large species very common on these bottoms. It can be easily distinguished by the spiral arrangement of its branches and the unilateral arrangement of its jug-shaped cells along the branches.

The *Eudendrium ramosum* and *E. dispar* are not uncommon on rocky bottoms, and are both beautiful species, somewhat resembling the *Pennaria*, (Plate XXXVII, fig. 277.)

The species of Polyps are the same as those found on rocky shores at low-water mark. The coral, *Astrangia Danæ*, (p. 329,) is much more common than on the shores, and grows larger, some of the specimens becoming four or five inches across, and rising up in the middle into lobes or irregular branches, sometimes nearly two inches high, making very elegant specimens.

Numerous sponges also occur, but they have not yet been carefully studied. One of the most abundant is a species of *Chalina*, which grows up in clusters of slender, soft, smooth branches, five or six inches high, and from a quarter to half an inch in diameter, of a pale yellowish or buff-color while living. It makes very delicate, white, and beautiful specimens when the animal matter has been thoroughly washed out and the sponge dried in the sun, which can be best done by hanging them up in a reversed position, owing to the flexibility of the branches when wet. This species is closely related to the *Chalina oculata*, which also occurs in this region, in the outside cold waters, as off Gay Head, and is abundant farther north and on the coast of Europe; but the present species is much more delicate, with more slender and rounder branches, and it seems to be a southern form, for it is common all along our coast as far, at least, as North Carolina.

The common, irregularly branched, red sponge is found in abundance, and also several light yellow, irregular, soft, massive species of *Tedania*, and the firm, massive, sulphur-yellow *Cliona sulphurea*.

List of species ordinarily found on the rocky bottoms of the bays and sounds.

ARTICULATA.

Insects.

	Page.		Page.
Chironomus halophilus	415	Pallene, sp	421

Crustacea.

	Page.		Page.
Cancer irroratus	395	Mœra levis	315
C. borealis	395	Autonoë, sp	415
Panopeus depressus	395	Amphithoë maculata	315
P. Sayi	395	A. longimana	370
Pelia mutica	395	Unciola irrorata	340
Eupagurus pollicaris	395	Cerapus tubularis (?)	396
E. longicarpus	395	Caprella geometrica	316
Homarus Americanus	395	Caprella, sp	316
Crangon vulgaris	395	Idotea phosphorea	316
Hippolyte pusiola	395	Erichsonia filiformis	316
Mysis Americana	396	Balanus crenatus	396
Heteromysis formosa	396	Numerous small Entomostraca.	
Lepidactylis dytiscus	339		

Annelids.

	Page.		Page.
Lepidonotus squamatus.....	397	Ophelia simplex..........	319
L. sublevis	397	Cirrhinereis fragilis	397
Harmothoë imbricata.......	397	Naraganseta coralii........	397
Phyllodoce, sp.............	397	Sabellaria vulgaris........	397
Eulalia, sp	397	Nicolea simplex...........	397
Eumidia, sp	397	Scionopsis palmata........	397
Autolytus cornutus	397	Polycirrus eximius	320
Autolytus, sp.............	398	Potamilla oculifera........	397
Nereis pelagica	397	Sabella microphthalma	397
Podarke obscura...........	319	Fabricia Leidyi	397
Marphysa Leidyi...........	319	Serpula dianthus..........	397
Lumbriconereis opalina.....	397	Spirorbis, sp.............	397

Nemerteans.

	Page.		Page.
Cosmocephala ochracea.....	325	Cerebratulus ? sp..........	324
Polinia glutinosa..........	324		

MOLLUSCA.

Gastropods.

	Page.		Page.
Fulgur carica	399	Triforis nigrocinctus.......	305
Sycotypus canaliculatus....	399	Crucibulum striatum.......	399
Tritia trivittata	354	Crepidula fornicata........	355
Urosalpinx cinerea	399	C. unguiformis............	355
Astyris lunata	399	Leptochiton apiculatus	399
A. zonalis	399	L. ruber..................	399
Anachis avara	306	Doto coronata	400
Lacuna vincta	305	Polycera Lessonii..........	400
Bittium nigrum	305	Æolis, sp.................	400
Cerithiopsis Greenii	383	Doridella obscura	400
C. Emersonii..............	417		

Lamellibranchs.

	Page.		Page.
Mya arenaria	401	Mytilus edulis.............	401
Saxicava arctica	401	Modiola modiolus..........	401
Argina pexata	401	Anomia glabra............	401
Scapharca transversa......	401	Ostræa Virginiana	401

Ascidians.

Bryozoa.

RADIATA.

Echinoderms.

Acalephs.

Polyps.

PROTOZOA.

Sponges.

Foraminifera.

6. FAUNA OF THE GRAVELLY AND SHELLY BOTTOMS OF THE BAYS AND SOUNDS.

Bottoms composed of gravel or pebbles, often with small stones, and generally with a considerable proportion of dead and usually broken shells, were of frequent occurence in Vineyard Sound, and a few such localities were found in Buzzard's Bay. Similar bottoms of small extent have also been examined in Long Island Sound, near New Haven. These bottoms are generally the most productive and agreeable for the dredger, for they are the favorite abodes of large numbers of animals of all classes, and the contents of the dredge are often so clean that they require little if any washing in the sieves. They vary much, however, in character, some of them consisting mostly of gravel, with pebbles and perhaps small scattered boulders; others consist largely of broken shells, especially those of *Mactra solidissima* and *Crepidula fornicata*, mixed with more or less gravel, sand, and mud. Others are so completely overgrown with the various large compound ascidians described above, that they might well be called "ascidian bottoms." In many places, however, there are patches of mud or sand, scattered here and there over a bottom which is mostly of gravel and shells, so that the dredge will often bring up more or less mud or sand, with some of the animals peculiar to such patches, mixed with those peculiar to the gravelly bottoms, thus augmenting the number and variety of animals. In other cases more or less mud and sand may be mixed with the gravel throughout, or the bottom may be in process of changing from mud or sand to gravel, or the contrary, owing to frequent changes in the directions of the currents, produced chiefly by the action of storms upon the shoals and bars of sand. Hence it is often difficult to distinguish with certainty the animals properly inhabiting the gravelly and shelly bottoms from those that pertain to the muddy and sandy bottoms, but for our present purposes it is not necessary to make a very sharp distinction between the different lists, for many species are common to all, and the areas of the different kinds of bottom are generally small in this region, and evidently may change their character from time to time.

After a single storm the character of the bottom, in some localities, was found to be greatly altered over wide areas, sometimes several miles in extent, at depths of two to ten fathoms, and the animal life at the bottom was always found to have changed very quickly, when the physical character of the bottom had been modified. The most frequent cause of change was the accumulation of immense quantities of dead seaweeds and eel-grass over bottoms that, a few days before, had been perfectly free from it. Such accumulations must either kill the majority of the animals inhabiting gravelly, sandy, or rocky bottoms, or else cause them to migrate. In all probability the majority of them perish, at such times, beneath the accumulations. In other cases one or two storms sufficed to change gravelly and shelly bottoms to sandy ones, causing, undoubtedly, great destruction of life and a great change in its character over particular areas. These changes in the character of the deposits accumulating on the bottom, attended with extermination of life and changes in its character in particular localities, illustrate on a small scale similar phenomena that have constantly occurred on a grander scale in the history of the past life of the globe, during all the geological ages, from the first commencement of life. Practically it was found quite difficult to find, in this region, large areas of gravelly and shelly bottoms, without some admixture with mud or sand, and it very seldom happened that a continuous series of dredgings could be made on such bottoms without encountering patches of mud and sand. Therefore the accompanying list of species undoubtedly contains many that belong rather to muddy or sandy bottoms than to those now under discussion, for species have not been excluded unless well known, from many observations, to be peculiar, or nearly so, to mud or sand and rarely met with on true hard bottoms.

The following are the principal localities where this kind of bottom was explored in Vineyard Sound and vicinity, but those belonging to the outside cold area are not included:

First. An extensive area extending from off Nobska Point eastward, nearly parallel with the shore, with some interruptions of sandy bottom, as far as Suconesset Shoal, mostly in three to eight fathoms of water; on this bottom were the dredgings of line 6, *a*, *b*, *c*, *d*, *e*, *f*; 21, *a*, *b*, *c*, *d*; 22, *a*, *b*, *c*, *d*; 23, *a*, *b*, *e*, *f*; 25, *b*, *c*, *d*; 26, *a*, *b*, *c*, *d*, *e*; 34, *a*, *b*, *c*, *d*, *e*, *f*; 35, *a*, *b*, *c*, *d*, *e*.

Second. Another similar region nearly parallel with the southeastern shores of Naushon and Nonamesset Island and extending out into mid-channel; dredgings on line 5, *a*, *b*; 7, *b*, *c*, *d*; 8, *c*, *d*, *e*, *f*, *g*; 42, *a*, *b*; 43, *a*, *b*, *c*, *d*, *e*, were made on the shallower portion of this ground, mostly in three to eight fathoms; 38, *a*, *b*, *c*; 39, *a*, *b*; 40, *a*, *b*, *c*, *d*; 41, *b*; 44, *a*, *b*, *c*, *d*, *e*; 46, *e*, were made in the deeper parts of the channel, in eight to fifteen fathoms.

Third. Several areas, in the deeper waters of the sound, north and northeast of Holme's Hole, and doubtless continuous with the last area; dredgings, at line 28, *a*, *b*, *c*, *d*, *e*, *f*; 29, *a*, *b*, *c*; 31, *a*, *b*, *c*, *d*, *e*; 32, *a*, *b*, *c*; 33, *a*, *b*, *c*, *d*, were made on these bottoms.

Fourth. A narrow strip of clean gravelly bottom, swept by the strong currents passing around West Chop, and situated between the "Middle Ground" Shoals and Martha's Vineyard, and extending around to East Chop, with an interruption of rocky bottom just opposite West Chop; dredgings on line 37, *a*, *b*, *c*, *d*, *g*, *h*; 47, *a*, and 48, *a*, *b*, *c*, *d*, were made on this area.

Fifth. In the channel, at the entrance to Great Harbor, off Nonamesset Island, and partially extending into the harbor, there is more or less gravelly and shelly bottom, frequently alternating with rocks and often composed chiefly of dead shells, (mainly *Crepidula fornicata.*) This place is swept by the powerful tidal currents running through Wood's Hole Passage; dredgings at line 3, *d*, *e*; 5, *e*, *f*, *g*; 13, *a*, *b*; 18, *a*, *b*, *c*, *d*; 19, *a*; 20, *a*, *b*, and many others not indicated on the chart, were made here.

Sixth. Another area at the other end of Wood's Hole Passage, north of Hadley Harbor, and extending out into Buzzard's Bay a short distance; some parts of this region had a smooth hard bottom of fine gravel and sand, or coarse sand; in other places it was more or less stony; dredgings on line 10, *e*, *f*; 11, *a*, *b*, *c*, *d*, *e*, *g*; 12, *b*, *c*; 70, *a*, *b*, *c*, *d*; 71, *a*, *b*, were on these gravelly bottoms.

Seventh. A shallow region off Cataumet Harbor, in Buzzard's Bay; the bottom here was hard gravel and shells, much overgrown with algæ; dredgings at line 65, *a*, *b*, and others not indicated, were made here.

Eighth. At Quick's Hole, in the channel between Nashawena and Pasque Islands, good gravelly bottom was found; dredgings at line 45, *a*, *b*; 76, *a*, *b*, *c*; 77, *c*, *d*, *e*, *f*, were on this area.

Similar bottoms of small extent were also met with in other places. There are also gravelly bottoms in the southwestern part of Vineyard Sound, near its mouth, as off Menemsha, but as these are inhabited by the more northern species of animals, they will be grouped with those of the outside waters.

The animals of gravelly and shelly bottoms may be burrowing or tube-dwelling species, like many annelids, amphipods, bivalve-shells, &c.; they may be species that adhere directly to the shells and pebbles, like certain hydroids, bryozoa, bivalve-shells, and the numerous ascidians; the latter are quite as numerous here as upon the rocky bottoms, and for the most part of the same species; they may be species that hide among the shells and pebbles or between the ascidians, &c., like many of the larger annelids, some of the crabs, and other crustacea, &c.; they may be species that live among or attached to the hydroids, bryozoa, ascidians, and algæ which grow upon the shells and pebbles; such are many of the small crustacea, some annelids, many small gastropod shells, and most of the more delicate bryozoa and hydroids; or they may be larger kinds that creep or swim about over the bottom, in search of food, such as the lobster, the larger crabs, hermit-crabs, large gastropod mollusks, star-fishes, sea-urchins, holothurians, &c. Owing to the great abundance of animal life on bottoms of this character they are the favorite feeding-grounds of many kinds of fishes, such as the tautog, scup, black bass, haddock, and cod, together with many others that are less valuable. Most of the "banks" and "fishing-grounds" resorted to by the line fishermen have either gravelly and shelly or else rocky bottoms, and those banks most frequented by fishes are almost always found to be rich dredging-grounds. The gravelly banks in this region are, in winter and spring, fishing-grounds for cod and haddock, but these fishes retreat to colder waters in the summer.

Among the Crustacea the most abundant and important species are the lobster, *Homarus Americanus*, (p. 395,) the common shrimp, *Crangon vulgaris*, (p. 339, Plate III, fig. 10,) the common rock-crab, *Cancer irroratus*, (p. 312,) *Panopeus Sayi*, (p. 312,) *P. depressus*, (p. 312, Plate I, fig. 3,) the larger hermit-crab, *Eupagurus pollicaris*, (p. 313,) the smaller hermit-crab, *E. longicarpus* (p. 313,) the *Heteromysis formosa*, (p. 396,) *Mysis Americana*, (p. 396,) *Unicola irrorata*, (p. 340, Plate IV fig. 19,) *Amphithoë maculata*, (p. 315, Plate IV. fig. 16,) *Corophium cylindricum*, (p. 370,) which lives among the hydroids, and a species of *Autonoë*, which lives in the crevices among the lobes of the sandy ascidians (*Amarœcium pellucidum*) in large numbers. The barnacle, *Balanus crenatus*, (p. 396,) is very abundant.

One of the most interesting of the Crustacea met with was the *Heterocrypta granulata*, which occurred off Falmouth and near Suconesset light-ship. This is one of the triangular crabs in which the carapax is smooth; the chelipeds are long and triangular. It is a southern species, occurring on the Florida coast, and is new to our fauna.

Another triangular crab, the *Pelia mutica*, also occurs on these bottoms, but this has a rough carapax, and resembles a small specimen of the common spider-crabs, *Libinia*.

Clinging to and creeping over the hydroids and ascidians a singular long-legged Pycnogonid is often met with on shelly bottoms. This is the *Phoxichilidium maxillare*, (Plate VII, fig. 35.) It is most frequently deep purple in color, but gray and brown specimens are often met with.

The larvæ of a fly, *Chironomus halophilus*, was dredged in five fathoms.

The Annelids are quite numerous, and the majority of them are the same as those found on the rocky bottoms, for the same species inhabit the interstices of the massive ascidians, found equally on both kinds of bottom, and the same tube-dwelling species can attach themselves to stones and shells just as well as to rocks. Most of the additional species are burrowing kinds, and some of them probably inhabited patches of mud or sand. Among the more interesting species are *Nephthys bucera*, (Plate XII, fig. 58;) *Anthostoma acutum* V., a new species; *Scolecolepis cirrata*, new to the American coast; *Scalibregma brevicauda* V., a very interesting new species; *Cirratulus tenuis* V., a new species; *Ampharete setosa* V., also a new species; *Serpula dianthus* V., (p. 322.) Several rare or undescribed species were also met with that have not yet been fully identified. Among these were a peculiar species of *Nereis*; a large *Anthostoma*; a young *Polydora*; an apparently undescribed species of *Samytha*; a species of *Euchone*, perhaps identical with *E. elegans* V.; the calcareous tubes of a small worm, perhaps a *Vermilia*, which have two carina on the upper side.

Two species of Sipunculoids occurred, one of which is probably undescribed. The other is the *Phascolosoma cæmentarium*, (Plate XVIII, fig. 92,) a species very common on all the northern coasts of New England in deep water. This worm takes possession of a dead shell of some small Gastropod, like the hermit-crabs, but as the aperture is always too large for the passage of its body, it fills up the space around it with a very hard and durable cement, composed of mud and sand united together by a secretion from the animal, leaving only a small, round opening, through which the worm can extend the anterior part of its body to the distance of one or two inches, and into which it can entirely withdraw at will. It thus lives permanently in its borrowed shell, dragging it about wherever it wishes to go, by the powerful contractions of its body, which can be extended in all directions and is very changeable in form. When fully extended the forward or retractile part is long and slender, and furnished close to the end with a circle of small, slender tentacles, which surround the mouth; there is a band of minute spinules just back of the tentacles; the anal orifice is at the base of the retractile part; the region posterior to this has a firmer and more granulous skin, and is furnished toward the posterior end with a broad band of scattered, blackish, acute, recurved spinules, more or less triangular in form, which evidently aid it in retaining its position in the shell. As it grows too large for its habitation, instead of changing it for a larger shell, as the hermit-crabs do, it gradually extends its tube outward beyond the aperture by adding new materials to it. Some of the fishes often suddenly cut short this labor by swallowing the worm, shell and all.

In July the common squids, *Loligo Pealii*, (Plate XX, figs. 102-105,) were taken in considerable numbers by means of the trawl, on gravelly and shelly bottoms off Falmouth, and with them large quantities of the eggs contained in large bunches or groups of long, gelatinous capsules. They were apparently spawning at that time.

Although the Gastropod mollusks are seldom very numerous at any particular spot on these bottoms, yet a pretty large number of species occur, and they are quite generally diffused. Many of them have already been enumerated as occurring on rocky bottoms. The *Fulgur carica*, (p. 355, Plate XX, fig. 124,) and the *Sycotypus canaliculatus*, (p. 355,) are found chiefly on these bottoms, and are often very abundant. Over a barrel of living specimens were obtained on a single excursion. The *Lunatia heros*, (p. 354, Plate XXIII, figs. 133–136,) though generally found on the sandy bottoms, also occurred in great numbers and of very large size on some of the gravelly bottoms. The pretty little *Natica pusilla* (Plate XXIII, fig. 132) is often common on these bottoms; it is usually delicately painted with brown.

The *Crepidula fornicata* (p. 355, Plate XXIII, figs. 129, 129*a*) was one of the most abundant species, often occurring adhering to each other in great clusters, the lowest ones in the group adhering in turn to dead bivalve shells, pebbles, shells of living *Fulgur* and *Sycotypus*, and still more frequently to these shells when dead and occupied by the larger hermit-crabs, (*Eupagurus pollicaris.*) The dead shells of this *Crepidula* were often found in great accumulations, covering considerable areas of bottom, and with but little admixture, either with other shells or with sand and gravel.

The *Crepidula unguiformis*, (p. 355, Plate XXIII, fig. 127,) though very common, did not occur in such great quantities. *Crucibulum striatum* (p. 399, Plate XXIII, figs. 125, 126) is also common, adhering to various dead shells.

The *Vermetus radicula* (Plate XXIV, fig. 157) is a very curious shell, looking, when full grown, very much like the tube of an Annelid, such as *Serpula* or *Protula*, but the inhabitant is a genuine Gastropod, and has a thin, spiral, horny operculum, for closing the aperture when it withdraws. When young this shell often forms a very regular, closely coiled, spiral shell, looking like that of a *Turritella*, and sometimes does not become irregular until the spire is more than an inch long, but sooner or later it goes off on a tangent and becomes irregular and crooked. Sometimes several of these shells interlock irregularly and thus form large clusters.

The curious and minute *Cæcum pulchellum* (Plate XXIV, fig. 158) is occasionally met with in considerable numbers, though very liable to be overlooked owing to its very small size. *Cæcum costatum* V. is of less frequent occurrence, and easily distinguished by the prominent ridges or ribs that run lengthwise of the shell.

Wherever algæ occur in abundance on these bottoms, the *Bittium nigrum* (p. 305, XXIV, fig. 154) is found in immense numbers, and it is generally associated with *Lacuna vincta* (p. 305, Plate XXIV, fig. 139) and with a few specimens of *Triforis nigrocinctus*, (p. 305, Plate XXIV, fig. 152,) *Cerithiopsis Greenii*, (Plate XXIV, fig. 153,) *Astyris lunata*, (Plate XXI, fig. 110,) *Anachis avara*, (Plate XXI, fig. 109,) &c. On the shelly bottoms *Cerithiopsis terebralis* and *C. Emersonii* ofter occur, but they are not usually common. On similar bottoms, sometimes adhering to

Pecten and other shells, we often met with the various species of *Odostomia*, among which *O. seminuda* (Plate XXIV, fig. 148,) was much the most common; but *O. producta*, (Plate XXIV, fig. 143,) *O. impressa*, (Plate XXIV, fig. 147,) and *O. trifida*, (Plate XXIV, fig. 145,) occurred in shallow water; and also *Turbonilla elegans*, (Plate XXIV, fig. 155,) which is a very handsome, glossy, brown shell; and *T. interrupta*, which is a similar shell, but more slender, with less convex whorls. The *Eulima oleacea* (Plate XXIV, fig. 149) is a very elegant, white, polished, and shining shell, and generally rare, but in two instances we found several of them adhering to the skin of the large Holothurian, *Thyone Briareus*, upon which it seemed to live as a quasi parasite or "commensal."

On shelly and muddy bottoms we occasionally found *Scalaria lineata*, (Plate XXI, fig. 123,) and *S. multistriata*, (Plate XXI, fig. 122,) both of which are rare and elegant shells. The *Pleurotoma bicarinatum* (Plate XXI, fig. 106) occurred rarely.

The bivalve shells are also quite numerous on these bottoms. Among them the *Mactra solidissima* (p. 358, Plate XXVIII, fig. 203) is most conspicuous on account of its great size and frequent occurrence; its dead shells were often very abundantly scattered over the bottom, and were generally incrusted with numerous bryozoa and hydroids. The *Gouldia mactracea* (Plate XXIX, figs. 206, 207) was quite common in many localities in a living state, while the dead shells were generally diffused. Among the other species that are common or abundant are *Scapharca transversa*, (Plate XXX, fig. 228,) *Clidiophora trilineata*, (Plate XXVII, fig. 193,) *Nucula proxima*, (Plate XXX, fig. 230,) *Mytilus edulis*, (Plate XXXI, fig. 234,) *Modiola modiolus*, (Plate XXXI, fig. 237,) *Crenella glandula*, (Plate XXXI, fig. 233,) *Pecten irradians*, (Plate XXXII, fig. 243,) *Anomia glabra*, (Plate XXXII, figs. 241, 242.) The *Modiolaria nigra* (Plate XXXI, fig. 236) occurred only in few localities in the deep water of the middle of the Sound, associated with the common muscle. The *Cumingia tellinoides* (Plate XXX, fig. 221) was found living occasionally, but its dead shells were quite common. The same is true of *Corbula contracta*, (Plate XXVII, fig. 191,) which was perhaps a little more commonly found living than the last. The *Cyclas dentata* (Plate XXIX) fig. 211,) is a handsomely sculptured, pure white shell, which we met with only a few times in the living state, though dead valves often occurred. The same remarks will apply to *Coclodesma Leanum*, (Plate XXVII, fig. 198,) of which the shells were much more common. The *Kellia planulata* (p. 310,) and *Montacuta elevata* also occasionally occur on shelly bottoms, but were seldom obtained alive. The *Cyclocardia borealis* (Plate XXIX, fig. 216) and *C. Novangliæ* (Plate XXIX, fig. 215) were quite common in the deeper waters.

The *Gastranella tumida* V., (Plate XXVII, fig. 190) is a small and rare shell, recently discovered, and has, as yet, been found only on a shelly bottom among hydroids, near New Haven, in 4 or 5 fathoms. The *Angulus modestatus* V. (Plate XXX, fig. 224) is a species recently described from specimens dredged by us in Vineyard Sound. It is often handsomely banded with light red and pale yellow. It is still a rare species, but has been dredged also near New Haven.

The Ascidians, with the exception of one or two additional species seldom met with, are the same as those of the rocky bottoms, and they often occur in immense quantities, especially the massive sandy ones, *Amarœcium pellucidum*, (p. 401,) and the "sea-pork," *A. stellatum*, (p. 402,) which together often almost entirely cover the bottom over areas many acres in extent. They furnish excellent hiding-places in the openings and crevices between their lobes for numerous Crustacea and Annelids, many of which can be easily secured by putting the masses of these ascidians into buckets of water and leaving them until the water begins to get stale, when they will come out of their retreats in large numbers and seek the surface or edges of the water for oxygen. Or they may be pulled apart directly and the various creatures secured at once.

The *Molgula arenata* (Plate XXXIII, fig. 251) is a nearly globular, but often somewhat flattened species, which covers itself over with closely adherent grains of sand or gravel. It is most common on sandy bottoms but is found also on gravelly ones.

The *Ciona tenella* is an elongated, erect species, attached at base to rocks, dead shells, &c. It is remarkable for the transparency, whiteness, and softness of its integument, and for the bright orange ocelli around its orifices. It is rare in this region, but very common in the Bay of Fundy.

The Bryozoa are very abundant, especially on the shelly bottoms. Some of them grow on algæ, hydroids, ascidians, &c.; and many form incrustations on the dead shells and pebbles. The two most abundant and prominent species are *Bugula turrita* (p. 311, Plate XXXIV, figs. 258, 259) and *Escharella variabilis*, (p. 312, Plate XXXIII, fig. 256.) The former grows attached to the various sea-weeds in great quantities, forming delicate white plumes, often six inches to a foot in length. The latter mostly forms calcareous incrustations over the surfaces of dead shells and pebbles, thin at first, but eventually becoming thickened by the formation of layer over layer, until the crust may become half an inch to an inch in thickness, with a tabulated and vesicular structure in the interior. The masses thus formed often closely resemble genuine corals, especially some of the ancient fossil forms, and they often occur in great quantities. When living the color is dull red, but when recently dried they have a yellowish-green color, which easily bleaches out, however, by exposure to the sun and air. *Vesicularia dichotoma*, (p. 404,) *Alcyonidium ramosum*, (p. 404, Plate XXXIV, fig. 257,) and *Crisia eburnea* (p. 311, Plate XXXIV, figs. 260, 261) are usually abundant. Most of the remaining species have also been mentioned in the previous pages as inhabitants of rocky bottoms, or else among the shore species.

Among the species not previously mentioned are *Cellepora scabra*, which forms branching, coral-like masses on the slender red algæ; a species of *Lepralia*, found with the last, and also on shells, which is allied to *L. Pallasiana* of Europe; *Mollia hyalina*, which forms circular disks, with irregular, more or less oblique cells; and *Membranipora tenuis*, which is common on the pebbles, often covering their whole surface with a delicate lace-like incrustation, made up of very small, crowded, oval or oblong cells, which have the inner part of the front partly closed over, but with an irregular, mostly three-lobed aperture toward the outer end, which is bordered by small, irregular spinules.

The *Vesicularia fusca* was also found in a few instances, in deep water. It had not been previously known on the American coast. Good specimens of the *Caberea Ellisii* were also dredged in the deeper parts of Vineyard Sound, attached to ascidians.

Of Echinoderms the number of species is not large. The common green star-fish, *Asterias arenicola* (Plate XXXV, fig. 269) is very common; the *Cribrella sanguinolenta*, (p. 407,) is comparatively rare; and the green sea-urchin, *S. Dröbachiensis*, (p. 406,) is quite infrequent. The purple sea-urchin, *Arbacia punctulata*, (p. 326,) is, however, quite common in many localities. The largest and finest specimens were taken off Holmes' Hole, but it was quite abundant, though of moderate size, in Great Harbor and Wood's Hole passage. The *Thyone Briareus* (p. 362) is not uncommon in shallow water, especially among weeds; it has already been mentioned, (p. 418,) as carrying *Eulima oleacea* attached to its skin.

Another Holothurian, the *Pentamera pulchella*, seems to be quite common, judging by the numerous specimens thrown on Nobska beach by the storms, and preserved for us by Mr. Vinal N. Edwards, during the past winter, but it was dredged only in one locality, off Holmes' Hole, by Messrs. T. M. Prudden and T. H. Russell. It is a southern species, not previously known north of the Carolina coasts. It is easily distinguished from the preceding species by its light color, and by having the locomotive-suckers arranged in five broad and very distinct longitudinal bands, with naked spaces between them.

A very delicate little Ophiurian, the *Amphipholis elegans*, was occasionally met with on the shelly bottoms. This is a northern species, much more common in the Bay of Fundy, where it is found from low-water mark to 80 fathoms, and it is found also on the northern coasts of Europe. It has a nearly circular disk, covered with smooth scales, regularly arranged, and each of the scales, on the sides of the slender rays, bears three short, blunt spines. Its color is usually light gray or whitish, frequently more or less marked with dark gray or brown.

The Hydroids are numerous on these bottoms, and mostly of the same species that have been mentioned as occuring on rocky bottoms.

The Polyps are few and essentially the same as those on the rocky bottoms. The only additional species was a small, slender, undescribed species of *Edwardsia*, *E. lineata* V., living in the interstices among ascidians and the tubes of *Sabella* and *Potamilla*.

Sponges also occur in considerable numbers. Among them the most conspicuous is the *Cliona sulphurea*, a bright sulphur-yellow species, growing into hemispherical or irregular, massive forms, of firm texture, the surface covered with scattered, low, wart-like, soft prominences, about an eighth of an inch in diameter, which contract when the sponge is dried, leaving shallow pits. The sponge commences as a boring species, on various dead shells, and as it grows it penetrates the shells in every direction, forming irregular holes and galleries, which continue to grow larger as more and more of the substance of the shell is absorbed, until the shells are reduced to a completely honey-combed, brittle mass, or a mere skeleton; finally the sponge begins to protrude from the surface, and grows up into mammilliform masses, or small, rounded crusts, which continue to grow and spread in every direction, until finally they may form masses six or eight inches in diameter, with the base spreading over and enveloping various dead shells, pebbles, and the coral, *Astrangia Danæ*, though it often happens that living specimens of the latter grow upon the sponge. Owing to the remarkable boring habits of this and other allied sponges, they are very important in the economy of the sea, for they are the principal agents in the disintegration and decay of the shells that accumulate over the bottoms, thus performing the same function in the sea that fungi and insects perform on the land—the removal of dead organisms that otherwise would accumulate in vast quantities. In this work they are aided, in most regions, either by certain boring Annelids, (*Dodecacerea*, &c.,) or by various boring mollusks, (*Lithodomus*, *Pholas*, *Gastrochæna*, &c.,) but the greater part of this work seems to be effected by the sponges.

Numerous species of Foraminifera were obtained on these and also on the rocky bottoms, but they have not yet been studied. The most common kind occurs attached by one side to dead shells, algæ, &c. It consists of several chambers arranged in a spiral manner, and to the naked eye resembles a minute depressed spiral shell.

List of species inhabiting gravelly and shelly bottoms of the bays and sounds.

ARTICULATA.

Insects.

	Page.		Page.
Chironomus halophilus.....	415	Muscidæ, larva	335

Pycnogonids.

	Page.		Page.
Phoxichilidium maxillare.	415	Pallene, sp.................	409

Crustacea.

	Page.		Page.
Cancer irroratus	415	Lepidactylis dytiscus	339
Panopeus depressus	415	Mœra levis	315
P. Sayi	415	Autonoë, sp	415
Pelia mutica	415	Amphithoë maculata	415
Heterocrypta granulata	415	Unciola irrorata	415
Eupagurus pollicaris	415	Corophium cylindricum	415
E. longicarpus	415	Caprella, sp	316
Homarus Americanus	415	Idotea phosphorea	316
Crangon vulgaris	415	Erichsonia filiformis	316
Hippolyte pusiola	395	Epelys trilobus	370
Mysis Americana	415	Balanus crenatus	415
Heteromysis formosa	415	Numerous Entomostraca.	

Annelids.

	Page.		Page.
Lepidonotus squamatus	320	Polydora, sp	416
L. sublevis	320	Scalibregma brevicauda	416
Harmothoë imbricata	321	Cirratulus tenuis	416
Sthenelais picta	348	C. grandis	319
Nephthys picta	348	Cirrhinereis fragilis	397
N. bucera	416	Naraganseta coralii	397
Phyllodoce, sp	349	Dodecacerea, sp	397
Eulalia, sp	349	Clymenella torquata	343
Eulalia, sp	349	Sabellaria vulgaris	349
Eumidia, sp	349	Cistenides Gouldii	349
Eteone, sp	349	Ampharete setosa	416
Autolytus cornutus	397	Samytha, sp	416
A., sp., banded	398	Amphitrite ornata	320
Nereis pelagica	319	Nicolea simplex	321
N. limbata	318	Polycirrus eximius	320
Nereis, sp	416	Potamilla oculifera	322
Diopatra cuprea	346	Sabella microphthalma	323
Marphysa Leidyi	319	Euchone, sp	416
Lumbriconereis opalina	320	Fabricia Leidyi	323
L. tenuis	320	Serpula dianthus	416
Anthostoma acutum	416	Vermilia, sp	416
Anthostoma, sp	416	Spirorbis spirillum	323
Scolecolepis cirrata	416		

Sipunculoids.

	Page.		Page.
Phascolosoma cæmentarium	416	Phascolosoma, sp	416

Nemerteans.

MOLLUSCA.

Cephalopods.

Gastropods.

Lamellibranchs.

	Page.		Page.
Nucula proxima	418	Modiolaria nigra	418
Argina pexata	309	Crenella glandula	418
Scapharca transversa	418	Pecten irradians	418
Mytilus edulis	418	Anomia glabra	418
Modiola modiolus	418	Ostræa Virginiana	310

Ascidians.

	Page.		Page.
Ciona tenella	419	Leptoclinum albidum	403
Cynthia partita	311	L. luteolum	403
Molgula Manhattensis	311	Amarœcium stellatum	419
M. arenata	419	A. pellucidum	419
Perophora viridis	388	A. constellatum	403

Bryozoa.

	Page.		Page.
Alcyonidium ramosum	419	Bugula turrita	419
A. hirsutum	404	B. flabellata	389
A. parasiticum	404	Membranipora pilosa	406
Vesicularia dichotoma	419	M. tenuis	420
V. cuscuta	404	M. lineata	406
V. gracilis	389	Escharella variabilis	419
V. armata	405	Escharipora punctata (?)	403
V. (Avenella) fusca	420	Lepralia, sp.	420
Tubulipora flabellaris	405	Mollia hyalina	420
Crisia eburnea	419	Discopora coccinea (?)	333
Ætea anguinea	405	Cellepora ramulosa	312
Eucratea chelata	405	C. scabra	419
Caberea Ellisii	420	Pedicellina Americana	405

RADIATA.

Echinoderms.

	Page.		Page.
Pentamera pulchella	420	Arbacia punctulata	420
Thyone Briareus	420	Asterias arenicola	420
Strongylocentrotus Dröbachiensis	420	Cribrella sanguinolenta	420
		Amphipholis elegans	420

Acalephs.

	Page.		Page.
Campanularia volubilis	408	Clytia Johnstoni	408
Platypyxis cylindrica	408	Obelia fusiformis	407
Orthopyxis caliculata	408	O. geniculata	407

	Page.		Page.
O. dichotoma	407	Halecium gracile	328
O. commissuralis	327	Eudendrium dispar	408
Lafoëa calcarata	408	Pennaria tiarella	327
Sertularia argentea	408	Thamnocnida tenella	407
S. cupressina	408	Hydractinia polyclina	328
Hydrallmania falcata	408		

Polyps.

	Page.		Page.
Sagartia modesta	330	Edwardsia lineata	421
Metridium marginatum	329	Astrangia Danæ	421

PROTOZOA.

Sponges.

	Page.		Page.
Grantia ciliata	330	Cliona sulphurea	421
Chalina, sp.	409	Halichondria, sp.	330
C. oculata	409	Tedania, sp.	409

Foraminifera.

	Page.
Numerous species	421

II. 7.—FAUNA OF THE SANDY BOTTOMS OF THE BAYS AND SOUNDS.

The sandy bottoms in Vineyard Sound are chiefly found in shallow water, either along the shores or on the banks and shoals. In Buzzard's Bay they were met with only in few places, near the shore, and have no great extent. To the eastward of Vineyard Sound, throughout the greater part of Nantucket Sound, Muskeget Channel, and the waters south and southeast of Nantucket and Cape Cod, the bottom is generally sandy, sometimes passing into gravelly and shelly.

The true sandy bottoms are not favorable to many kinds of animals, and where the sands are constantly changing, as on most of the shoals in this region, the bottom is sometimes almost barren of life, though certain burrowing species may occur.

The following are some of the special localities where dredgings were made on sandy bottoms: In Buzzard's Bay, at line 11, *d*, *e*, *f*; 64, *a*, *b*; 66, *a*, *b*; 67, *a*, *b*; 68, *a*, *b*; 71, *a*, *b*, *d*; 73, *a*, *b*, *c*, *e*, *f*. In Vineyard Sound, at line 14, *g*, *h*; 25, *a*, *b*; 27, *a*, *b*; 30, *a*, *b*; 37, *h*, *i*; 43, *a*, *b*; 46, *c*, *d*; 47, *d*, *e*; 48, *a*, *b*. A large portion of the species occurring on these bottoms have been mentioned before either as inhabitants of the sandy shores at low water, or as living upon gravelly and shelly bottoms. With the exception of a few species living attached to scattered shells or stones, nearly all the species are such as are adapted to burrowing beneath the surface of the sand, though many of them may also occur creeping on its surface.

The most abundant and characteristic species of Crustacea are the lobster, *Homarus Americanus*, (p. 313,) the common shrimp, *Crangon vulgaris*, (p. 339, Plate III, fig. 10,) the "lady-crab," *Platyonichus ocellatus*, (p. 338, Plate I, fig. 4,) the larger hermit-crab, *Eupagurus pollicaris*, (p. 313,) the smaller hermit-crab, *Eupagurus longicarpus*, (p. 313,) *Anthura brunnea*, *Conilera concharum*, *Unciola irrorata*, (p. 340, Plate IV, fig. 19.)

Of Annelids a considerable number of burrowing species occur, and also a few tube-dwelling species, which attach their tubes to dead shells; among these last are *Sabellaria vulgaris* (p. 321, Plate XVII, figs. 88, 88*a*,) and *Serpula dianthus*, (p. 322.)

The Gastropods are not numerous, and but few are peculiar to sandy bottoms; the majority found have their proper homes on shelly or muddy bottoms and live in much smaller numbers in sandy places; others enumerated in the following list inhabit the patches of eel-grass and algæ that are often scattered over the sandy bottoms in shallow water. A few species, however, have their proper homes on the sandy bottoms. Among the most important of these are *Lunatia heros*, (p. 353, Plate XXIII, figs. 133–136,) *Neverita duplicata*, (p. 354, Plate XXIII, fig. 130,) *Natica pusilla*, (p. 354, Plate XXIII, fig. 132,) *Cylichna oryza*, (Plate XXV, fig. 164,) *Utriculus canaliculatus*, (Plate XXV, fig. 160.)

The bivalve shells are more numerous, and most of them are species that burrow beneath the surface. The most common and characteristic species are *Ensatella Americana*, (p. 356, Plate XXVI, fig. 182, and Plate XXXII, fig. 245,) *Siliqua costata*, (p. 358, Plate XXXII, fig. 244,) *Mactra solidissima*, (p. 358, Plate XXVIII, fig. 202,) *Angulus tener*, (p. 358, Plate XXVI, fig. 180, and Plate XXX, 223, shell;) *Tottenia gemma*, (p. 359, Plate XXX, fig. 220,) *Lyonsia hyalina*, (p. 358, Plate XXVII, fig. 194.) In certain localities, where eel-grass grows, the scollop, *Pecten irradians*, (p. 361, Plate XXXII, fig. 243,) occurs in considerable abundance. The common muscle, *Mytilus edulis*, (Plate XXI, fig. 234,) occasionally occurs in patches or beds. *Lævicardium Mortoni* (p. 358, Plate XXIX, fig. 208) is sometimes abundant in sheltered localities. The *Ceronia arctata* appears to be abundant in some places, as it is sometimes thrown on the sandy beaches in large numbers, but it was seldom dredged. The *Thracia Conradi* lives on sandy bottoms, buried six inches or more beneath the surface, but is seldom obtained alive. The dead shells were occasionally dredged in Vineyard Sound.

Very few Ascidians occur. The most frequent one is *Molgula arenata*, (p. 419, Plate XXXIII, fig. 251,) which lives free in the sand and covers itself with a coating of closely adherent grains of sand. Another species, *M. pellucida*, is occasionally met with; this also lives free in the sand, but does not attach the sand to itself. It has a clean translucent integument, a round body, and two tubes which are large and swollen at their bases. Where eel-grass or algæ afford opportunities for its attachment, the *M. Manhattensis* (p. 311, Plate XXXIII, fig. 250) generally occurs.

The Bryozoa are not numerous, unless where dead shells are scattered over the sand for their attachment, when many of the same species that inhabit shelly bottoms may occur. The only species that are frequent on the true sandy bottoms are *Bugula turrita*, (Plate XXXIV, figs. 258, 259,) which occurs attached to eel-grass, &c., and *Escharella variabilis*, (p. 311, Plate XXXIII, fig. 256,) which incrusts dead shells or other solid objects; with the last, *Membranipora lineata*, (p. 406,) and several other species may sometimes be found.

Several species of Echinoderms inhabit the sandy bottoms. The most abundant one is the "sand-dollar," *Echinarachnius parma*, (p. 362, Plate XXXV, fig. 267,) which occurs in immense numbers on nearly all sandy bottoms, except on the most exposed shoals. Another related species, *Melitta testudinaria*, was dredged two or three times in Vineyard Sound, but the specimens were dead and broken. It is a very abundant species south of Cape Hatteras, and may be distinguished by having five large oblong perforations near the edge.

At least three species of Holothurians live upon the sandy bottoms. The most common one is the *Thyone Briareus*, (p. 362,) conspicuous on account of its large size and dark purplish-brown color, as well as for the numerous long papillæ that cover its body. It was found on a sandy bottom off Waquoit, with the *Eulima oleacea* (Plate XXIV, fig. 149) adhering to its surface, just as they occurred together on shelly bottoms, (see p. 418.) The *Pentamera pulchella*, (p. 420,) also inhabits sandy bottoms, in shallow water. During the past winter Mr. Vinal N. Edwards collected numerous specimens of this and the preceding species on Nobsca beach, after storms. They doubtless live in the sand, in shallow water, a short distance off the beach. In similar situations the *Caudina arenata*, (p. 362,) occasionally occurs, but it is apparently rare in this region. It has a thick, yellowish white, harsh skin, without suckers, and its body tapers off into a slender caudal portion. The common star-fish, *Asterias arenicola*, (p. 326, Plate XXXV, fig. 269,) is not uncommon on sandy bottoms, though more abundant in rocky and shelly localities. The *Ophiura olivacea* (p. 363) lives among the patches of eel-grass in shallow water on the sandy bottoms, and travels over the surface of the sand quite rapidly by means of its slender, flexible rays.

Of Hydroids very few species ordinarily inhabit sandy bottoms, and the only one that is usually met with is *Hydractinia polyclina*, (p. 328,) which lives on the shells occupied by hermit-crabs. Others occasionally grow on the eel-grass or on dead shells.

The *Cliona sulphurea*, (p. 421,) is the only large sponge that is commonly met with on sandy bottoms, but another bright yellow siliceous sponge, forming smooth, firm, crest-like lobes and plates, occurred on Edgartown beach.

List of species inhabiting the sandy bottoms of the bays and sounds.

ARTICULATA.

Crustacea.

	Page.		Page.
Cancer irroratus	312	Lepidactylis dytiscus	339
Carcinus granulatus	312	Unciola irrorata	426
Platyonichus ocellatus	436	Idotea cæca	340
Hippa talpoida	338	Epelys trilobus	370
Eupagurus pollicaris	426	Conilera concharum	426
E. longicarpus	426	Anthura brunnea	426
Homarus Americanus	426	Limulus Polyphemus	340
Crangon vulgaris	426		

Annelids.

	Page.		Page.
Sthenelais picta	348	A. acutum	416
Nephthys picta	348	Scolecolepis cirrata	416
Eteone, sp	349	Polydora, sp	416
Neresis pelagica	319	Clymenella torquata	343
Lumbriconereis opalina	320	Sabellaria vulgaris	426
Rhynchobolus dibranchiatus	341	Cistenides Gouldii	323
R. Americanus	342	Amphitrite ornata	320
Anthostoma robustum	343	Serpula dianthus	426

Nemerteans.

	Page.		Page.
Meckelia ingens	349	M. rosea	350

Sipunculoids.

	Page.		Page.
Phascolosoma Gouldii	353	P. cæmentarium	416

MOLLUSCA.

Gastropods.

	Page.		Page.
Fulgur carica	355	Odostomia seminuda	417
Sycotypus canaliculatus	355	Turbonilla interrupta	418
Eupleura caudata	371	Bittium nigrum	305
Urosalpinx cinerea	306	Triforis nigrocinctus	305
Tritia trivittata	354	Cerithiopsis Greenii	417
Ilyanassa obsoleta	354	C. terebralis	417
Anachis avara	306	C. Emersonii	417
Astyris lunata	306	Cæcum pulchellum	417

Polyps.

PROTOZOA.

Sponges.

Foraminifera.

II. 8.—FAUNA OF THE MUDDY BOTTOMS OF THE BAYS AND SOUNDS.

The muddy bottoms are inhabited by a considerable number of species, which find their true homes in such localities. Most of these are either burrowing or tube-dwelling kinds. A few creep or swim about over the surface or conceal themselves in the superficial layer of mud and vegetable *débris.*

The character of the mud itself is quite various, and the different kinds are often inhabited by different groups of animals. The mud may be very thick, heavy, and tenacious, consisting chiefly of clay; such mud is usually inhabited by few species of animals. It may consist of finely comminuted sand, mixed with more or less clay; such bottoms are more favorable to animal life. In other places it consists partly of one of the preceding kinds intimately mixed with large quantities of decaying vegetable *débris,* derived chiefly from eel-grass and algæ; such mud, unless too fetid, is often full of animal life. In some cases, especially in well-sheltered localities, where the water is tolerably pure, the mud may contain large quantities of living and dead microscopic organisms, both animal and vegetable, and these may even constitute more than one-half of the bulk of the mud, which, in such cases, is peculiarly soft and flocculent; such mud is extremely favorable to many kinds of animals that feed on the microscopic organisms, especially the bivalve shells, Holothurians, and many Annelids, and the "menhaden" among fishes. The last variety of bottom, when it has a substratum of sand or gravel a few inches below the surface, is the most favorable kind for *oysters,* which grow very rapidly and become very fat in such places.

In Vineyard Sound and Nantucket Sound muddy bottoms are not common, and are mostly of small extent, situated in coves, harbors, or in places where the tides form eddies around projecting points of land, or in the lee of shoals.

In Buzzard's Bay the bottom is muddy over the greater part of its area, except a region of sandy and shelly bottom in the central part.

In Long Island Sound the bottom is generally muddy throughout its length and breadth, though small areas of rocks, gravel, and sand occur at various places.

The special localities, indicated on the chart, where dredgings were made on muddy bettoms, not including the outside dredgings, are as follows: In Buzzard's Bay, at line 67, *b;* 68, *a, b, c:* 74, *a, b;* 75, *a, b, c, d, e, f;* in Hadley Harbor, at 10, *a, b, c, d;* in Great Harbor, at 17, *b, c;* 19, *b;* in Robinson's Hole, at 78, *a, b, c;* in Vineyard Sound, at 47, *b, c.* Numerous other dredgings were made on muddy bottoms in this region that are not indicated on the chart.

In Long Island Sound numerous dredgings have been made by the writer, with Mr. S. I. Smith and others, during eight years. These extend from a few miles west of the entrance of New Haven Harbor to the Thimble Islands and Faulkner's Island on the east; and from the Connecticut shore nearly across the sound. The greater part of these dredgings were on muddy bottoms, and generally in 3 to 8 fathoms of water.

The following are some of the most common and important of the Crustacea living on these muddy bottoms: the spider-crab, *Libinia canaliculata,* (p. 368,) *L. dubia,* (p. 368,) *Panopeus depressus,* (p. 312, Plate I, fig. 3,) *P. Sayi,* (p. 312,) the "blue-crab," *Callinectes hastatus,* (p. 367,) *Mysis Americana,* (p. 396,) *Ptilocheirus pinguis,* (p. 431,) *Unciola irrorata,* (p. 340, Plate IV, fig. 19,) *Limulus Polyphemus,* (p. 340.) Numerous tube-dwelling Amphipods, including several species of *Ampelisca* and genera belonging to the *Lysianassinæ* occur, some of them in great numbers, and also additional species of crabs and shrimps. All these are of special importance, because they furnish great quantities of food for the fishes frequenting muddy bottoms.

Of Annelids numerous burrowing and tube-dwelling kinds are to be found, some of them in great abundance. One of the most abundant and conspicuous species is *Nephthys ingens,* (Plate XII, figs. 59, 60.) This worm burrows in mud of all kinds, even in that which is so filled with decaying vegetable *débris* as to be very fetid. It grows to the length of more than six inches, with a diameter of a quarter of an inch or more, though most of the specimens are about half this size. The body is whitish, with a red median blood-vessel, but the lateral appendages are dark and the setæ nearly black. It is very active, and wriggles about energetically by undulating its body laterally, to the right and left; this motion enables it to burrow quickly, or to swim quite rapidly. When captured it is very apt to break off the posterior part of its body, but can reproduce it.

The *Diopatra cuprea* (p. 346, Plate XIII, figs. 67, 68) is often abundant where the mud is somewhat firm; the dredge often brings up large quantities of the projecting ends of its large tubes, but the occupant usually escapes by retreating below the surface. The two species of *Rhynchobolus* are also quite common, but *R. dibranchiatus* (p. 341, Plate X, figs. 43, 44) is generally the most abundant. The curious *Travisia carnea* V. is seldom met with, and, like *Brada setosa* V., appears to be rare in this region. The *Trophonia affinis* (Plate XIV, fig. 75) is more common, though found chiefly in the deeper waters, and more frequently in the cold waters outside, as off Cuttyhunk Island and off Block Island. *Ampharete setosa* V. has been found only in Long Island Sound, near New Haven. The *Melinna cristata* is a northern and European species; it was found in the deeper part of Vineyard Sound, inhabiting flexible tubes covered with fine mud. *Euchone elegans* V. (Plate XVI, fig. 84) was found in the deeper parts of Vineyard Sound, living in small tubes of mud; it was much more abundant in the deeper waters outside. The *Meckelia ingens* (p. 349, Plate XIX, figs. 96, 96*a*) occasionally occurs on muddy bottoms, though more common on sandy ones.

Of Gastropod mollusks a comparatively small number of species occur that are characteristic of these bottoms. There are several species that occur on eel-grass, when it grows on the muddy bottoms, which are not included in the following list. They have been mentioned when speaking of the fauna of muddy and sandy shores.

Among the species of special interest were *Mangilia cerina*, which is a rare and little-known species; *Bela plicata* (p. 383, Plate XXI, fig. 107); *Turbonilla elegans*, (p. 418, Plate XXIV, fig. 155), which was recently described from specimens obtained in Vineyard Sound by us; *T. interrupta*, (p. 418;) two species of *Scalaria*, (p. 418;) *Cylichna oryza*, (Plate XXV, fig. 164;) *Amphisphyra pellucida*, (Plate XXV, fig. 162;) and *Utriculus canaliculatus*, (Plate XXV, fig. 160).

The bivalve shells are much more numerous and are mostly burrowing kinds. Among the most abundant are *Mulinia lateralis*, (p. 373, Plate XXVI, fig. 184 B,) which occurs in immense quantities, especially in soft sticky mud; *Clidiophora trilineata*, (Plate XXVII, fig. 193;) *Tellina tenta* (Plate XXX, fig. 225,) which is often very abundant in soft mud, in sheltered places, as in Hadley Harbor; *Callista convexa*, (Plate XXX, fig. 219;) *Nucula proxima*, (Plate XXX, fig. 230;) *Yoldia limatula*, (Plate XXX, 232;) *Astarte castanea*, (Plate XXIX, fig. 204;) and *Mytilus edulis*, (p. 307.)

The last-named shell, which is the common muscle, occurs in patches, "beds," or "banks," often of great extent. One of these muscle-beds, in which the animals were living, was found extending quite across the mouth of Cuttyhunk Harbor, at line 75, *f*, on the chart; another at Quick's Hole, at line 76, *c*, and 45, *a*, *b*; others at 77, *d*, *e*, *f*; 46, *b*, *c*, *d*. In several instances large beds of dead muscles were found, with few living ones, and in all these cases there were on them large numbers of star-fishes, either *Asterias arenicola*, in case of those in Vineyard Sound; or *Asterias vulgaris* on those in the deeper and colder waters near the entrance of the Sound and off Gay Head; and sometimes both kinds, at intermediate localities. These star-fishes had no doubt devoured the muscles. Among the localities of this kind are, 47, *a*, *b*, *c*, *d*; 53, *b*, *c*; 56, *b*, *c*, *d*; 55, *a*, *b*, *c*; 63, *a*, *b*; 58, *d*; 54, *b*. As this species of muscle grows to full size, under favorable circumstances, in one year, it is probable that these muscle-beds vary greatly in size and position in different years. They afford habitations for various kinds of animals that belong properly on shelly or stony bottoms, such as *Arbacia punctulata* (p. 326,) *Cribrella sanguinolenta*, (p. 407,) and various shells, ascidians, hydroids, &c. The *Modiolaria nigra* (Plate XXXI, fig. 236) was found in small numbers, but of good size, associated with the common muscle, in the deeper part of Vineyard Sound.

The oyster does not usually occur on true muddy bottoms in this region, unless placed there by human agency, but unless attacked by the star-fishes or other enemies they will flourish well in such localities. Beds of oysters on muddy bottoms always afford lodgment for large numbers of animals that belong properly to the shelly and rocky bottoms; these have mostly been omitted from the following list.

Among the shells of peculiar interest that live in the mud are the species of *Pholas*. The largest and finest species, *P. costata*, has been found living in New Bedford Harbor, according to Dr. Gould. It lived buried in the mud two or three feet below the surface, and the specimens were dug out by the harbor-dredging machines. This is a southern species, found quite commonly on the coasts of South Carolina and Florida, and in the Gulf of Mexico. With the last, *P. truncata* (p. 372, Plate XXVII, fig. 200) was also obtained, but this is quite common in mud and peat-banks, above low-water mark. Of both the preceding species we dredged dead shells at Wood's Hole and in Great Harbor, and with them we found fragments of another, *Zirphæa crispata*, which is a northern and European species. It is seldom that living adult specimens of such deep-burrowing shells can be obtained by the ordinary dredge, and they are rarely thrown up by the waves.

Ascidians are not often found on the muddy bottoms, and most of those that do occur adhere to the shells of oysters, muscles, &c., or to eel-grass. Hydroids and Bryozoa are likewise nearly wanting on true muddy bottoms, though a few may occur on the eel-grass and oysters.

Of Echinoderms there are but few species. The *Thyone Briareus* (p. 362) sometimes occurs where there is growing eel-grass. The common star-fish, *Asterias arenicola*, (p. 326,) has been mentioned above as inhabiting muscle-beds and oyster-beds. The *Amphipholis abdita* V. is a singular Ophiuran, with a small body and very long, slender, flexible, greenish arms, having three spines on each side arm-plate. The arms are sometimes six inches long. The creature buries itself deeply beneath the surface of the soft mud, and projects one or more of the long arms partially above the surface of the mud. On this account it is seldom dredged entire; the projecting arms are usually cut off by the dredge, and the animal escapes; and as it has the power of restoring lost arms, this is only a temporary inconvenience. The same thing probably happens when a voracious fish seizes one of the arms.

List of species inhabiting muddy bottoms of the bays and sounds.

ARTICULATA.

Crustacea.

	Page.		Page.
Pinnotheres ostreum	367	Squilla empusa	369
P. maculatus	459	Lysianassinæ, several species	431
Cancer irroratus	312	Phoxus Kroyeri	
Panopeus depressus	431	Melita nitida	314
P. Sayi	431	Ampelisca, two species	431
Carcinus granulatus	312	Ptilocheirus pinguis	431
Callinectes hastatus	431	Amphithoë compta	370
Libinia canaliculata	431	Corophium cylindricum	415
L. dubia	431	Unciola irrorata	431
Eupagurus pollicaris	313	Epelys trilobus	370
E. longicarpus	313	E. montosus	370
Callianassa Stimpsoni	369	Limulus Polyphemus	431
Crangon vulgaris	339	Numerous Entomostraca	
Mysis Americana	431		

Annelids.

	Page.		Page.
Nephthys ingens	431	Travisia carnea	431
Phyllodoce, sp	349	Trophonia affinis	432
Eulalia, sp	349	Brada setosa	431
Nereis pelagica	319	Cistenides Gouldii	323
Diopatra cuprea	431	Ampharete setosa	432
Marphysa Leidyi	319	Melinna cristata	432
Lumbriconereis opalina	320	Polycirrus eximius	320
Rhynchobolus Americanus	342	Chætobranchus sanguineus	320
R. dibranchiatus	431	Euchone elegans	432

Nemerteans.

	Page.		Page.
Meckelia ingens	432	Cosmocephala ochracea	325
Cerebratulus,* sp	324		

Sipunculoids.

	Page.
Phascolosoma cæmentarium	416

Nematodes.

	Page.		Page.
Pontonema marinum	325	P. vacillatum	326

MOLLUSCA.

Gastropods.

	Page.		Page.
Mangilia cerina	432	Crepidula fornicata	355
Bela plicata	432	C. convexa	355
Tritia trivittata	354	C. unguiformis	355
Ilyanassa obsoleta	354	Scalaria lineata	432
Eupleura caudata	371	S. multistriata	432
Odostomia seminuda	417	Utriculus canaliculatus	432
O. fusca	307	Bulla solitaria	371
Turbonilla interrupta	432	Amphisphyra pellucida	432
T. elegans	432	Cylichna oryza	432

Lamellibranchs.

	Page.		Page.
Pholas costata	433	Cardium pinnulatum	423
P. truncata	433	Kellia planulata	310
Mya arenaria	309	Montacuta elevata	418
Clidiophora trilineata	432	Solenomya velum	360
Lyonsia hyalina	358	Astarte castanea	432
Periploma papyracea	429	Cyclocardia borealis	418
Mulinia lateralis	432	C. Novangliæ	418
Tagelus gibbus	373	Nucula proxima	432
T. divisus		Yoldia limatula	432
Cumingia tellinoides	418	Argina pexata	309
Macoma fusca	359	Mytilus edulis	432
Angulus tener	358	Modiolaria nigra	433
Tellina tenta	432	Crenella glandula	418
Callista convexa	432	Anomia glabra	311
Venus mercenaria	359	Ostræa Virginiana	433
Petricola pholadiformis	372		

Ascidians.

	Page.		Page.
Molgula Manhattensis	311	Cynthia partita	311

RADIATA.

Echinoderms.

	Page.		Page.
Thyone Briareus	433	Amphipholis abdita	433
Asterias arenicola	433		

II. 9.—FREE-SWIMMING AND SURFACE ANIMALS.

Under this head I have included all the animals found swimming free, whether in the bays and sounds, or in the colder region outside. Nor have I, in this case, attempted to separate those of the estuaries and other brackish waters, although such a distinction might be useful had we sufficient data to make it even tolerably complete. But hitherto very little surface-collecting has been done in waters that are really brackish; and, moreover, since every tide must bring in myriads of free-swimming creatures with the waters from outside, it will always be difficult to distinguish between those that are thus transported and those that properly belong to the brackish waters. A distinction between the free-swimming animals of the bays or sounds and those of the open coast has not been made, partly on account of the constant intermixture of the waters and their inhabitants by the tides, and partly because the observations that were made do not indicate any marked difference in the life or in the average temperature of the surface waters, though the waters of the shallow bays become more highly heated by the direct heat of the sun in summer. The waters of the open coast are evidently more or less warmed by the Gulf Stream, and in fact numerous species of animals that properly belong to the fauna of the Gulf Stream are constantly brought into Vineyard and Nantucket Sounds by the currents, showing conclusively that a portion of the Gulf Stream water must also take the same course.

In Vineyard Sound, during August and the first part of September, the temperature of the surface water in the middle of the day was generally from 68° to 71° Fahrenheit; September 9, off Tarpaulin Cove, the surface temperature was 66°; off to the west of Gay Head, in mid-channel, it was 67° Fahrenheit; but farther out, off No Man's Land, on the same day, it was 62°, (bottom, in 18 fathoms, 62½°;) a short distance west of No Man's Land it was 63°, (bottom, in 11 fathoms, 59°;) about sixteen miles off Newport, at the 29-fathom locality, it was 62° on September 14, (at the bottom 59°;) off Cuttyhunk, in 25 fathoms, it was 64° at the surface on September 13, (bottom 62½°.) According to the record made by Captain B. J. Edwards, during the past winter, from observations taken at 9 a. m. every morning, at the end of the Government wharf at Wood's Hole, (where the temperature must be nearly identical with that of Vineyard Sound,) the average temperature of the surface water was 31° Fahrenheit, from December 27 to February 28. The average temperature for that hour during January was 31.42°; the lowest was 29° on January 29, with the wind N. W.; the highest was 38° on January 17, with the wind S. W.; on the 18th, 19th, and 22d it was 35°. The average for February was 30.75°; the coldest was 29°, on February 24 and 25; the highest 33°, on February 8, 17, and 19. The temperature at the bottom (at the depth of nine feet) was also taken, but rarely differed more than one degree from that of the surface, being sometimes a little lower and sometimes higher than that of the surface, but generally the same. The higher temperatures usually occurred with, or following, southerly or southeasterly winds, (from the direction of the Gulf Stream,) while the lowest ones generally accompanied or followed northerly winds. The tides must obviously also have some effect in modifying the temperature.

It must not be inferred from the preceding remarks that a distinct or constant current flows into these waters from the region of the Gulf Stream, for the facts do not warrant such a belief, nor is there any difficulty in explaining the phenomena in another way. All that is necessary to account for the higher temperatures of this region, and the frequent occurrence of Gulf Stream animals, is to suppose that when southerly or southeasterly winds blow continuously for a considerable time they cause a superficial flow or drift of warmer water from the Gulf Stream region toward these shores, which may also be aided by the tides; such a surface-drift will gradually lose its distinctness as it approaches the coast and mingles more and more with the cooler waters beneath, but the animals borne along by it will still serve to show its direction and origin, even after its temperature becomes identical with that of the adjacent waters. Such surface currents would necessarily be intermittent in character and variable in direction and extent, as well as in duration and temperature. They would also be more frequent in summer than in winter, according with the prevalent direction of the winds. So far as known to me all the facts are in harmony with this view. Accordingly the waters of Vineyard Sound are quite cold in winter, and only occasionally receive a little heat from the Gulf Stream region, and that, probably, largely through the medium of the air itself; but in summer these waters are very warm, for they not only receive frequent accessions of warm water from the Gulf Stream, but they are also favorably situated to be rapidly warmed by the direct heat of the sun.

The fauna of the surface in this region is very rich and varied, especially in summer. In winter, life is also abundant in the surface waters, but very different in character from that found in summer. Had collections been made in spring and autumn, still other groups of animals would doubtless have been found. Our knowledge of the surface animals of Vineyard Sound, in winter, is wholly based on a series of surface-dredgings made by Mr. Vinal N. Edwards in January, February, and March of the past winter. A separate list of the species contained in these collections, so far as identified, has been prepared to follow the general list. The most noticeable feature of the winter collections is the entire absence of the larval forms of crabs, shrimps, lobsters, star-fishes, sea-urchins, annelids, &c., which so abound in the same waters in summer. On the other hand there is a great abundance of Entomostraca, *Sagitta*, several northern Amphipods, species of *Mysis*, &c., together with eggs and young of certain fishes.

In the general list of surface species only those that have been actually observed are introduced, but it must be remembered that the greater part of the crustacea, annelids, mollusks, and echinoderms are well known to have free-swimming young, or larval forms, and that the list might easily be doubled by the introduction of such species, on theoretical grounds; but, by omitting them, the list serves to indicate how much yet remains to be done in this direction. There are large numbers of common species of which neither the young nor the eggs are known, and there are many others of which the eggs, or young, or both, are known, but the time required for the hatching of the eggs and the development of the young is not known. The dates given in the lists refer only to the time of actual capture of the species, and it must not be inferred that at other seasons of the year any of the species so designated are not to be found; for, doubtless, many of those that swim free when adult may be found all the year round. And possibly some species may breed during every month of the year. But the breeding season of most species is probably of short duration, and therefore the larvæ and young may occur only at particular seasons.

Mr. A. Agassiz has made a very large collection of the surface animals in Vineyard Sound, Buzzard's Bay, and off Newport, and to his labors we owe the knowledge of a large proportion of the jelly-fishes. He has also described the larvæ and young of several Annelids and Nemerteans, and has described and beautifully illustrated the larvæ and young of the common star-fishes, (*Asterias*,) and the green sea-urchin, (*Strongylocentrotus Dröbachiensis*.) The *Salpa Cabotti* (Plate XXXIII, figs. 254, 255) was also well described and illustrated by him; and also other species, but a large part of the collection has not yet been elaborated.

Our surface collections were made both in the day and evening, at various hours, chiefly by means of towing-nets and hand-nets. The evening or night hours are generally more productive than the day-time in this kind of collecting, but we were unable, owing to lack of time and superabundance of other specimens, to do as much night-collecting as we desired.

Among the Crustacea there are a considerable number of species that swim at the surface when adult, and others till nearly half-grown, but the majority are free-swimmers only when quite young, or even only when in the zoëa and megalops stages, through which they seem, from Mr. S. I. Smith's observations on several of our species, to pass in a short time. The males of the common oyster-crab, *Pinnotheres ostreum*, (p. 367, Plate I, fig. 2,) were often caught in the day-time swimming at the surface in the middle of Vineyard Sound. The lady-crab, *Platyonichus ocellatus*, (p. 338,) of full size, was also occasionally caught swimming actively at the surface. The "blue-crab," or common edible crab, *Callinectes hastatus*, is well known to be an active swimmer, when adult, but most of those seen at the surface were young. The larvæ of *Cancer irroratus*, (p. 312, Plate VIII, figs. 37, 37*a*,) and of *Platyonichus* in the zoëa and megalops stages, were taken in vast numbers, especially in bright sunshine, together with similar larvæ of many other species. The larvæ and young of the lobster (Plate IX, figs. 38, 39) were also abundant in mid-summer. The numerous specimens obtained have enabled Mr. S. I. Smith to describe the interesting metamorphoses of our lobster, which were entirely unknown before. The young swim actively at the surface, like a shrimp, until more than half an inch long. The larvæ and young of the various species of shrimps are also abundant. The curious larvæ of *Squilla empusa* (Plate VIII, fig. 36) were often met with.

Several species of Amphipods are also common at the surface. The most abundant were *Calliopius læviusculus*, of which Mr. V. N. Edwards also took numerous large specimens in February and March; *Gammarus natator*, which was usually common, and occurred in immense numbers August 10 and on several other occasions; and a *Hyperia*, which infests several species of large jelly-fishes, and also swims free at will. The *Phronima* is a related genus, but is very remarkable for its extreme transparency, which renders it almost invisible in water. *Idotea irrorata* (p. 316, Plate V, fig. 23) and *I. robusta*, Plate V, fig. 24) were very common among masses of floating eel-grass and sea-weeds, and the latter was also very often found swimming entirely free.

A species of *Sapphirina* (Plate VII, fig. 33) was found in great numbers among *Salpæ*, off Gay Head, on several occasions, early in September. This is one of the most brilliant creatures inhabiting the sea. It reflects the most gorgeous colors, blue, red, purple, and green, like fire-opal, although when seen in some positions, by transmitted light, it is colorless and almost transparent. Under the microscope, when living, it is a splendid object, whether seen by transmitted or reflected light, the colors constantly changing, as it is turned in different positions. When seen beneath the surface of the sea, in large numbers, the appearance is very singular, for each one as it turns in the right position reflects a bright gleam of light, of some brilliant color, and then immediately becomes invisible, and these scintillations come from different directions and various depths, many of them being much farther beneath the surface than any less brilliant object could be seen. In some cases one or more were found in the branchial cavity of *Salpæ*, but whether this is normal or accidental was not determined.

The species of *Argulus* are parasitic on the exterior of fishes, but we found at least three species swimming free at the surface. It is, therefore, probable that they are able to leave their hosts for a time, and thus to migrate from one fish to another. The species of *Caligus* are also parasites on fishes, to which they firmly adhere, but the half-grown young of one species was taken at the surface in the towing-nets.

Numerous species of Annelids, in the larval and young stages, were taken at the surface, but many of them have not yet been identified, for owing to the great changes they undergo, this is often impossible, unless the specimens can be raised, or at least connected with the adults by a large series of specimens. For a few this has been done. Several species also swim at the surface in the adult state, especially in the evening. With some this seems to be a habit peculiar to the breeding season, and sometimes only the males are met with.

Among the species most frequently taken in the adult state at the surface, are *Nereis virens*, (Plate XI, figs. 47–50,) chiefly males; *Nereis limbata*, (Plate XI, fig. 51,) mostly males, which occurred both in the evening and day-time; *Nectonereis megalops*, (Plate XII, figs. 62, 63,) which was quite common in the evening; *Autolytus cornutus*, (Plate XIII, figs. 65, 66,) the males, females, and asexual forms; *Podarke obscura*, (Plate XII, fig. 61,) which was extremely abundant in the evening; and several other species. The *Sagitta elegans* was taken at Wood's Hole, July 1, and off Gay Head, among *Salpæ*, September 8. It is a very small and delicate species, and so transparent as to be nearly invisible in water. A larger and stouter species of *Sagitta* was taken in large numbers at Wood's Hole, by Mr. V. N. Edwards, January 30, Febuary 10, and February 27, and at Savin Rock, near New Haven, May 5. This species has a longer caudal portion, with a small terminal fin; some of the specimens were nearly an inch long and many contained in the cavity of the body, posteriorly, a parasitic nematode worm, about half as long as the body. This parasite is round, not very slender; the head has three prominent angles; tail with a small, acute, terminal mucro.

Many of the Mollusca swim free by means of vibrating cilia, for a short time in the larval stages of growth, but as such larvæ are very minute and the period often quite short, these young are not often taken in the nets.

The Cephalopods of this region are all free-swimming species, from the time when they leave the eggs through life, though they may rest upon the bottom when depositing their spawn. Numerous specimens of the "squid," *Loligo Pealii*, (Plate XX, figs. 102–104, embryos and young,) were thus taken by the trawl in July, together with large clusters of their eggs. Later in the season the free-swimming young of this species, from a quarter of an inch to an inch in length, (fig. 105,) were often taken at the surface and were also found in the stomach of the red jelly-fish, *Cyanea arctica*, in considerable numbers. The adults were frequently taken during the whole summer in the pounds. Some of these were over a foot in length, but most of them were not more than five or six inches long. The color when living is very changeable, owing to the alternate contractions of the color-vesicles or spots, but the spots of different colors are much crowded, especially on the back, and the red and brown predominate, so as to give a general reddish or purplish brown color, and this is usually the color of preserved specimens. The clusters of gelatinous egg-capsules of this species were found in great abundance off Falmouth, on a shelly and weedy bottom, as already mentioned, (p. 416;) and near New Haven light-house large clusters, apparently of the same species, were found by Professer Todd, earlier in the season, (June 19.) Some of these masses were six or eight inches in diameter, consisting of hundreds of capsules, like fig. 102, each of which is usually three or four inches long and contains numerous eggs. These last contained embryos in different stages of development, two of which are represented in Plate XX, figs. 103, 104. Even at this early period some of the pigment vesicles are already developed in the mantle and arms, and during life, if examined under the microscope, these orange and purple vesicles may be seen to rapidly contract and expand and change colors, as in the adult, only the phenomena may be more clearly seen, owing to the greater transparency of the skin in the embryos. They are, therefore, beautiful objects to observe under the microscope. At this stage of development the eyes were brown. In these embryos the yolk is finally absorbed through the mouth, which corresponds, therefore, in this respect, to an "umbilicus." The more advanced of these embryos (fig. 103) were capable of swimming about, when removed from the eggs, by means of the jets of water from the siphon.

Another species, *Loligo pallida* V., (Plate XX, figs. 101, 101*a*,) occurs abundantly, in autumn, in the western part of Long Island Sound, from whence Robert Benner, esq., has sent me numerous specimens. This is a pale, translucent, gelatinous-looking species, with much fewer spots than usual, even on the back, and is nearly white beneath. It is a stout species, commonly five or six inches long, exclusive of the arms, but grows considerably larger than that. It is often taken in the seines in large numbers with menhaden, upon which it probably feeds. These squids are eagerly devoured, even when full grown, by many of the larger fishes, such as blue-fish, black-bass, striped-bass, &c. When young they are preyed upon by a still larger variety of fishes, as well as by the jelly-fishes, &c.

Another species of "squid," *Ommastrephes illecebrosa*, has been recorded from Greenport, Long Island, by Mr. Sanderson Smith, but I have not met with it myself, south of Cape Cod. It is common in Massachusetts Bay and very abundant in the Bay of Fundy. Messrs. S. I. Smith and Oscar Harger observed it at Provincetown, Massachusetts, among the wharves, in large numbers, July 28, engaged in capturing and devouring the young mackerel, which were swimming about in "schools," and at that time were about four or five inches long. In attacking the mackerel they would suddenly dart backward among the fish with the velocity of an arrow, and as suddenly turn obliquely to the right or left and seize a fish, which was almost instantly killed by a bite in the back of the neck with the sharp beaks. The bite was always made in the same place, cutting out a triangular piece of flesh, and was deep enough to penetrate to the spinal cord. The attacks were not always successful, and were sometimes repeated a dozen times before one of these active and wary fishes could be caught. Sometimes after making several unsuccessful attempts one of the squids would suddenly drop to the bottom, and, resting upon the sand, would change its color to that of the sand so perfectly as to be almost invisible. In this way it would wait until the fishes came back, and when they were swimming close to or over the ambuscade, the squid, by a sudden dart, would be pretty sure to secure a fish. Ordinarily when swimming they were thickly spotted with red and brown, but when darting among the mackerel they appeared translucent and pale. The mackerel, however, seemed to have learned that the shallow water is the safest for them and would hug the shore as closely as possible, so that in pursuing them many of the squids became stranded and perished by hundreds, for when they once touch the shore they begin to pump water from their siphons with great energy, and this usually forces them farther and farther up the beach. At such times they often discharge their ink in large quantities. The attacks on the young mackerel were observed mostly at or near high-water, for at other times the mackerel were seldom seen, though the squids were seen swimming about at all hours; and these attacks were observed both in the day and evening. But it is probable, from various observations, that this and the other species of squids are partially nocturnal in their habits, or at least are more active in the night than in the day. Those that are caught in the pounds and weirs mostly enter in the night, and evidently when swimming along the shores in "schools." They are often found in the morning stranded on the beaches in immense numbers, especially when there is a full moon, and it is thought by many of the fishermen that this is because, like many other nocturnal animals, they have the habit of turning toward and gazing at a bright light, and since they swim backwards they get ashore on the beaches opposite the position of the moon. This habit is also sometimes taken advantage of by the fishermen who capture them for bait for cod-fish; they go out in dark nights with torches in their boats and by advancing slowly toward a beach drive them ashore. They are also sometimes taken on lines, adhering to the bait used for fishes.

The specimens observed catching young mackerel were mostly eight or ten inches long, and some of them were still larger. The length of time required for these squids to become full grown is unknown, as well as the duration of their lives, but as several distinct sizes were taken in the pounds, and those of each school were of about the same size, it is probable that they are several years in attaining their full size. A specimen, recently caught at Eastport, Maine, was pale bluish white, with green, blue, and yellow iridescence on the sides and lower surface; the whole body was more or less thickly covered with small, unequal, circular, orange-brown and dark brown spots, having crenulate margins; these spots are continually changing in size from mere points, when they are nearly black, to spots 0.04 to 0.06 of an inch in diameter, when they are pale orange-brown, becoming lighter colored as they expand. On the lower side the spots are more scattered, but the intervals are generally less than the diameter of the spots. On the upper side the spots are much crowded and lie in different planes, with the edges often overlapping, and thus increasing the variety of the tints. Along the middle of the back the ground-color is pale flesh-color, with a median dorsal band, along which the spots are tinged with green, in fine specks. Above each eye there is a broad lunate spot of light purplish red, with smaller brown spots. The upper surface of the head is deeply colored by the brown spots, which are here larger, darker, and more crowded than elsewhere, and situated in several strata. The arms and fins are colored like the body, except that the spots appear to be smaller. The suckers are pure white. The eyes are dark blue-black, surrounded by an iridescent border, and in this genus the eyes are provided with distinct lids. In this respect, *Ommastrephes* differs from *Loligo*, for in the species of the latter genus, the integument is continued directly over the eye, the part covering the eye being transparent.

Most of the higher Gastropods inclose their eggs in capsules, which they attach to stones, algæ, or shells, and within these the eggs hatch and the young have a well formed shell before they eat their way out of the capsules, and when free they crawl about by means of the "foot," like the adult. But in the lower orders of Gastropods most of the young, when first hatched, are furnished with vibrating cilia and swim free, by this means, for a short time. These larvæ are very different from the adults, and in case of the naked mollusks (Nudibranchs) the larvæ are furnished with a beautiful, little, glossy, spiral shell, which they afterwards lose.

The Pteropods swim free in all stages. The young and adults swim by means of two wing-like appendages, developed on each side of the neck, which may be compared to the anterior lateral lobes of the foot, seen in Æolis, (fig. 174,) and many other Gastropods, if we suppose these to become enormously enlarged, while the rest of the foot remains in a rudimentary or undeveloped condition, often serving merely for the attachment of the operculum.

The *Styliola vitrea* (Plate XXV, fig. 178) was taken in the day-time at the surface, September 8, among *Salpæ*, off Gay Head. Its shell is a thin, white, transparent, glassy cone, about a third of an inch long, and slightly curved toward the tip. The animal is also white. The *Spirialis Gouldii* has a delicate, white, transparent, spiral shell, when adult having seven whorls, which turn to the left. The shell is marked by very fine revolving lines, visible only under the microscope. This species is seldom met with at the surface in the day-time, but is often abundant in the early evening. According to the observations of Mr. A. Agassiz, in confinement they rarely left the bottom of the jars during the day, merely rising a few inches and then falling again to the bottom. After dark they became very active, swimming actively near the surface of the water. "During the day they often remain suspended for hours in the water simply by spreading their wing-like appendages, and then suddenly drop to the bottom on folding them." Mr. Agassiz captured the specimens upon which his observations were made, at Nahant, Massachusetts, during the summer of 1869, and judging from the figures in Binney's Gould they were probably specimens, not quite adult, of this species. He has also taken adult specimens at Newport. Mr. S. I. Smith captured full grown specimens in the edge of the Gulf Stream, off St. George's Bank, and we have specimens taken from the stomach of mackerel, caught twenty miles south of No Man's Land.

The *Cavolina tidentata* (Plate XXV, fig. 177) is a beautiful and curious species, with a singularly shaped, amber-colored, translucent shell, much larger than that of either of the preceding species. We did not observe it living in these waters, but the shells were twice dredged off Martha's Vineyard, and one of them was perfectly fresh and glossy, as if just dead. It is a southern species which comes north in the Gulf Stream, but it had not been found previously on the coast of New England. Another Gulf Stream species, the *Diacria trispinosa*, is occasionally found at Nantucket, according to Dr. Stimpson, but whether it has been observed there alive is uncertain; eight or nine other species were taken in the Gulf Stream, off St. George's Bank, by Messrs. Smith and Harger in 1872, all of which may, perhaps, occasionally occur about Martha's Vineyard and Nantucket.

Another very interesting and beautiful Pteropod, the *Clione papilionacea*, was taken in considerable numbers at Watch Hill, Rhode Island, April 13, by Professor D. C. Eaton and myself. They were swimming at midday near the surface, associated with *Pleurobrachia rhododactyla*, and appeared to be common at that time. Mr. Vinal N. Edwards obtained two specimens in Vineyard Sound, April 30. This differs from those named above, in being destitute of a shell, as well as in many other characters. The body is stout, somewhat fusiform, tapering gradually to the pointed posterior end; in the largest specimens the length was about 1.5 inches. The head is rounded, with two small conical processes in front, on the upper side. Six tentacle-like organs, or "arms," bearing minute suckers, can be protruded. The wings or fins are large and broad oval in outline.

The body and wings are pale, transparent bluish, with opalescent hues; the mouth and parts around it, the "arms," and part of the head, and some of the internal organs, are tinged with orange; the posterior part of the body is bright reddish orange, for nearly half an inch. Some of the internal organs are orange-brown and olive-brown, and show through the transparent integuments as dark patches. This species has seldom been observed on our coast. Dekay, in 1843, mentioned its occurrence in a single instance, off New York. In 1869, it was taken in considerable numbers at Portland, Maine, by Mr. C. B.

Fuller. It may, nevertheless, occur annually in winter, and yet be seldom observed; for very few naturalists go out to collect marine animals in winter and early spring.

The bivalve shells mostly produce minute young, or larvæ, which are at first provided with vibrating cilia and swim free for several days, as is well known to be the case with the oysters, clams, muscles, *Teredo*, &c. But a few species, like the *Tottenia gemma*, (p. 359,) produce well developed young, furnished at birth with a well formed shell.

The common fixed Ascidians, both simple and compound, mostly produce eggs that hatch into tadpole-shaped young, which swim about for a short time by the undulatory motions of the tail, but finally become fixed by the head-end, and losing, or rather absorbing, the tail-portion, rapidly develop into the ordinary forms of the ascidians. This process, although often very rapid, is a very interesting and complicated one

In *Molgula Manhattensis* there is, according to the observations of Dr. Theodore A. Tellkampf, an alternation of generations. He states that the minute yellow ova were discharged July 18, invested in a viscid yellowish substance, which become attached to the exterior of many specimens. In a few days the "viscid substance" had changed its appearance and became contractile; the ova became larger, round, and of different sizes; "after two or three days the largest protruded somewhat above the surface of the common envelope, and presented a circular or oval aggregation, like that of the *Mammaria* found a year ago;" on the 11th day, the round ova had increased in size, with a central round or oval orifice through which the motion of the ciliæ of the branchial meshes were visible. "The orifice had approached on the 1st of August more or less to one apex; in some specimens, which were now oval, it was terminal." In this stage he names it *Mammaria Manhattensis*, regarding the *Mammaria* as a "nurse;" within each of the *Mammariæ*, at the end opposite the branchial orifice, there was seen a mass of cells, which ultimately developed into a tadpole-shaped larva, similar to that of other ascidians. He observes that the *Mammariæ* increase after the discharge of the larvæ, and that gemmation takes place within the common envelope.* These observations, if correct, are very interesting and important, but they need farther confirmation. The development of the larvæ from the *Mammariæ* into *Molgula* was not traced; neither did he witness the *actual discharge* of the ova, which produced the *Mammariæ*, from the *Molgula*. They may possibly have no relation with one another.

Several kinds of Ascidians, however, swim free in the water during their entire life. The most common Ascidian of this kind is the *Salpa Cabotti*, (Plate XXXIII, figs. 254, 255.) This, like the other species, exists under two different forms; or, in other words, it is one of those animals having alternations of generations. The sexual individuals (fig. 255) are united together into long chains by processes (*c*) from the sides

* Annals of the Lyceum of Natural History of New York, Vol. 10, p. 83, 1872.

of the branchial sac; these chains are often a foot or even a foot and a half long, and contain two rows of individuals, which are united together in such a way that they stand obliquely to the axis of the chain, the branchial openings being all on the upper side of the chain as it floats in the water, while the posterior openings are all on the lower side of the chain, close to the edge. Each individual is connected both with its mate on the right or left side, and to those immediately in front and behind on the same side. The succeeding individuals in the chain overlap considerably. The chains do not appear to break up spontaneously, but when broken apart by accident the individuals are capable of living separately for several days. The chains, when entire, swim about quite rapidly by means of the streams of water passing out of all the cloacal orifices in one direction. The individuals composing the chains, when full grown, are about three quarters of an inch long. They are transparent and white, or pale rose, often with the edges of the mantle and the nucleus bright Prussian blue, and with delicate reticulations of the same blue over the surface of the mantle. Each of the individuals in the chains is hermaphrodite, and each produces a single egg, which develops into an embryo before it is discharged, and finally when it grows to maturity produces an asexual individual, which is always solitary, (Plate XXXIII, fig. 254.) These are larger than those in the chains and are quite different in form, but the color is the same. These when mature produce, by a budding process in their interior, a series of minute individuals united together along a tube into a small chain, (s, fig. 254,) which may be seen coiled up around the nucleus. The chain consists of three sections, those individuals in the section first formed being largest and nearly equal in size; those in the next much smaller; while new ones are just forming at the other end; as the chain grows longer, and the component individuals larger, it projects more and more, and finally the end protrudes from an opening in the tunic, and the little chain becomes detached and is discharged into the sea. These chains consist of twenty to thirty pairs of individual zoöids. This operation is frequently repeated during the summer, and these chains of all sizes, from those just liberated up to the full-grown ones, may be taken at the same time. They appear to grow very rapidly. Thus by autumn these *Salpæ* became exceedingly abundant, at times completely filling the water for miles in every direction, from the surface to the depth of several fathoms, and are so crowded that a bucket of water dipped up at random will often contain several quarts of *Salpæ*. They were found in wonderful abundance on September 8, off Gay Head and throughout the outer part of Vineyard Sound, and on several other occasions were nearly as abundant.

Two species of *Appendicularia* and a species of *Doliolum* were also found in these waters by Mr. A. Agassiz, but we did not observe them. These are also free-swimming Ascidians, related to *Salpa*, but very different in form.

Among the Echinoderms there are no species that swim at the surface when adult, but most of them produce eggs which hatch into very remarkable larvæ, entirely unlike their parents in form and structure, and these swim free in the water, often for a considerable period, by means of vibrating cilia.

The young star-fish or sea-urchin develops gradually within the body of the larva, on the water-tubes, and as it grows larger it gradually absorbs the substance of the larva into its own body. The development of the larvæ of *Asterias vulgaris* (*A. pallida* AG.) and *A. arenicola* (*A. berylinus* AG.) has been described by Mr. A. Agassiz, from the time previous to hatching from the eggs till they become young star-fishes, with the essential characters of the adults. He has also described the young of the common green sea-urchin (under the name of *Toxopneustes Dröbachiensis*) in the same way. The *Cribrella saguinolenta*, (p. 407,) like several other star-fishes, does not have free swimming larvæ, but retains and protects the eggs by holding them by means of the suckers around the mouth, curving the body around them at the same time. In this position the eggs hatch and pass through a metamorphosis different from that of *Asterias*, though somewhat analogous to it. The development of this species was described by Professor M. Sars many years ago. Some of the Ophiurans are viviparous, among them the *Amphipholis elegans* (p. 418) found in this region, but others have free-swimming larvæ, and pass through a metamorphosis similar to that of *Asterias*, though the larvæ are quite different. Some of the Holothurians are also viviparous, while others have free-swimming larvæ, but the young of most of the species of this region are still unknown.

The Acalephs all swim free in one stage or another of their existence. Some of the Hydroids, like *Sertularia* and allied genera, are only free-swimmers while in the early embryonic stages, when they are covered by vibrating cilia; but they soon become fixed and ever after remain attached in one place. Others, like the species of *Obelia*, swim free in the embryonic state, and then develop into attached hydroids, which by budding may produce large branching colonies of similar hydroids, but ultimately they produce another kind of buds, which are developed within capsules or gonothecæ. These soon become elegant, little, circular, and disk-shaped jelly-fishes, which are then discharged and swim free in the water; they soon grow larger, acquire more tentacles, and ovaries or spermaries develop along the radiating tubes, the eggs are formed, discharged, and fertilized, and each egg may develop into a ciliated embryo, which in its turn may become attached and start a new hydroid colony. Thus among these animals we find an alternation of generations, complicated by different modes of budding.

In the case of the large red jelly-fish, *Cyanea arctica*, and the common whitish jelly-fish, *Aurelia flavidula*, (Plate XXXVI, fig. 271,) the history is somewhat different. These jelly-fishes produce immense numbers of minute eggs, which are discharged into the water and develop into minute, oblong, ciliated larvæ; these soon become attached by one end and grow up into broad-disked young, like hydroids with long, slender tentacles; each of these after a time sends out stolon-like tubes from the base, and from these tubes buds are developed, each of which grows up into a "scyphostoma," or hydroid-form, like the first one; all these eventually become much elongated, then circular constrictions begin to form along the body, which grow deeper and deeper until they separate the body into a series of concave segments, which are held together by a pedicle in the middle of each, their borders at the same time becoming divided into eight lobes, or four bilobed ones; in the mean time the long tentacles around the upper end or original disk of the "scyphostoma" gradually grow shorter and are finally entirely absorbed; then the first or upper disk breaks off, and finally all the rest, one after another, until a mere stump is left at the base; after becoming detached each of the disks swims about in the water, and gradually develops its mouth, stomach, tentacles, and other organs, and, turning right side up and rapidly growing larger, eventually becomes a large and complicated jelly-fish, like its grandparents or great-grandparents that produced the egg from which the original "scyphostoma" was developed. The stump of the hydroid produces another set of tentacles, even before the separation of all the segments, and grows up again into the elongated or "strobila" form, and again undergoes the same process of transverse division, thus producing successive crops of jelly-fishes. In these cases there are alternations of generations, accompanied both by budding and fissiparity. The young of this species in the "ephyra" stage were found April 17, and at several other times during April, in abundance, by Mr. Vinal N. Edwards. These were less than a quarter of an inch in diameter, and must have become free only a short time before. On April 30 he took young specimens from half an inch to about an inch in diameter. The young of various sizes, up to nearly three inches in diameter, were common at New Haven May 5. All these young specimens were taken in the day-time.

In some jelly-fishes buds may even be produced upon the proboscis of the adult jelly-fish, which develop directly into free jelly-fishes, like the parent. This is the case with the *Dysmorphosa fulgurans*, found in these waters, and with *Lizzia grata*, found farther north.

On the other hand there are many jelly-fishes that do not have a hydroid state, nor bud, nor pass through any marked metamorphosis. This is the case with our *Pleurobrachia rhododactyla*, *Idyia roseola*, and other Ctenophoræ. In these the young, even before hatching, become perfect little jelly-fishes, and swim round and round within the egg by means of the miniature paddles or flappers along their sides. The young are, nevertheless, very different from the adults in form and structure.

It will be apparent, from the preceding remarks, that a complete list of free-swimming animals would necessarily include all the Acalephs of the region, but, as this would uselessly swell the list, only those that have been actually taken at the surface will be here included. Quite a number of the species were not observed by us, but have been recorded by Mr. A. Agassiz, but in some cases he has given neither the time nor date of capture.

A fine large specimen of the beautiful jelly-fish, *Tima formosa*, has been sent to me by Mr. V. N. Edwards, who captured it at Wood's Hole, April 30. He states that the same species was very abundant in February, 1872. It has not been previously recorded as found south of Cape Cod. The specimen received differs from the description given by Mr. A. Agassiz, in having thirty-six tentacles instead of thirty-two.

Among the most common of the larger species in summer were *Mnemiopsis Leidyi*, which occurred in abundance at nearly all hours of the day and evening, and was very phosphorescent at night; *Cyanea arctica*, which ocurred chiefly in the day-time, and was here seldom more than a foot in diameter; *Aurelia flavidula*, (Plate XXXVI, fig. 271,) which was not unfrequently seen in the day-time; *Dactylometra quinquecirra*, (Plate XXXVI, fig. 272,) which was quite common both by night and day in August and September; and *Zygodactyla Grœnlandica*, (Plate XXXVII, fig. 275,) which was common in July, both in the day and evening, but was seldom seen later in the season.

The two species last named, and also the *Cyanea arctica*, were frequently found to be accompanied by several small fishes, of different sizes up to three inches long, which proved to be young "butter-fishes,' *Poronotus triacanthus*. These fishes swim beneath the broad disk of these jelly-fishes, surrounded on all sides by the numerous tentacles, which probably serve as a protection from larger fishes that are their enemies, for the tentacles of the jelly-fishes are capable of severely stinging the mouths of most fishes, evidently causing them great pain. As many as ten or twelve of these fishes were often found under a single jelly-fish, and in one case twenty-three were found under a *Cyanea* about ten inches in diameter. They do not appear to suffer at all from contact with the stinging-organs of the tentacles, and are, perhaps, protected from them by the thick coating of tenacious mucus which constantly covers the skin, and gives them their common English name. Mr. A. Agassiz states* that he constantly observed a "Clupeoid" fish under the *Dactylometra* in this region, which had essentially the same habits, according to his account, as the species observed by us, though, if a Clupeoid, it must have been a very different fish.

He says, however, that the fishes observed by him were occasionally devoured by the jelly-fish: "It is strange that the fish should go there for shelter, for every once in a while one of them pays the penalty by being swallowed, without this disturbing the others in the least; they in their turn find food in the lobes of the actinostome, and even eat the folds themselves, until their turn comes to be used as food. I have seen in this way three fishes eaten during the course of as many days.

* Catalogue of North American Acalephæ, p. 49.

The specimens measured about an inch in length." The fishes found by us were from a quarter of an inch to three inches long, and we never saw them swallowed, and never found them in the stomachs of any among the several dozen jelly-fishes, of the different kinds that we found accompanied by the fishes, although we found young squids and other kinds of marine animals in a half-digested condition. It is possible that the observation of Mr. Agassiz was made on them when kept in confinement, and that the fishes devoured were not in a perfectly healthy and natural condition, so as to resist the stings of the nettling organs. But if his fish belonged to a family different from ours, the difference may be peculiar to the respective fishes. Yet our observations afford only negative evidence, and it may be that this is one of the peculiarities of this remarkable companionship; though, if so, we should suppose that the race of *Poronotus* would soon become extinct, for we never observed the young under any other circumstances. The adult fishes of this species, when five or six inches long, were often taken in the pounds in considerable numbers.

Among the mouth-folds and lobes of the ovaries, beneath the disk of *Cyanea*, we very often found large numbers of living specimens of a delicate little jelly-fish, nearly globular in form, the *Margelis Carolinensis*, which we also frequently took in the towing-nets in the evening.

In the winter season the *Mnemiopsis Leidyi* is often abundant in Long Island Sound, and I have also observed it in New York harbor in February, in large numbers. At Wood's Hole Mr. V. N. Edwards found the *Pleurobrachia rhododactyla*, both young and nearly full-grown, very abundant in February and March; at Watch Hill, April 13, I found both adult specimens and young ones not more than an eighth of an inch in diameter. It probably occurs through the entire year, for we frequently met with it in mid-summer in Vineyard Sound. Mr. S. I. Smith also found it very abundant at Fire Island, on the south side of Long Island, in September.

In July and August we obtained several large and perfect specimens of the curious "Portuguese man-of-war," *Physalia Arethusa*. This species occurs as far west as Watch Hill, Rhode Island, where it was observed by Professor D. C. Eaton. The boatmen at that place state that it is frequent there in summer. The float of this species was generally deep, rich crimson or purple, and the hydroids beneath it were commonly bright blue in the specimens observed by us. The float or air-bag is, however, sometimes blue and sometimes rose-color.

According to Professor Agassiz, (Contributions, vol. IV, p. 335,) the floating bag in windy weather always presents the same side to the wind, and it is upon the windward side that the bunches of very long locomotive hydroids of the lower surface are situated, and these at such times are stretched out to an enormous length, and thus act as anchors to retard the motion by friction in passing through the water. The smaller locomotive hydroids, the feeding hydroids, and the reproductive hydroids, are on the lee side.

This species is capable of stinging the hands very severely if they be brought into contact with the hydroids attached to the lower surface of the floating air-bag.

The *Idyia roseola*, so abundant on the coast of New England north of Cape Cod, was only occasionally met with, and in small numbers, while the *Bolina alata*, which is one of the most abundant species on the northern coast of New England, was not seen at all. The *Aurelia flavidula* is less common than north of Cape Cod, but was found in abundance in Buzzard's Bay, in May, by V. N. Edwards.

Many of the Polyps have free-swimming, ciliated embryos, but others, like many of the sea-anemones, are viviparous, discharging the young ones through the mouth. These young are of different sizes, and furnished with a small but variable number of tentacles, but in most other respects they are similar to their parents. Mr. A. Agassiz has, however, recently ascertained that the young of a species of *Edwardsia* swims free in the water for a considerable period, or until it develops at least sixteen tentacles. In this condition it has been described as a different genus and species, (*Arachnactis brachiolata* A. AG.) Whether the other species of this genus all have free-swimming young is still uncertain; if so, these young must differ considerably among themselves, for *Edwardsia farinacea* V., of this coast, has but twelve tentacles when adult, and *E. elegans* V. has but sixteen, while others have as many as forty-eight tentacles, when full grown. Among the Protozoa there are great numbers of free-swimming forms included among those commonly known as Ciliated Infusoria, but those of our coast have been studied but little. The germs of sponges also swim free in the water, by means of cilia. Species of Polycystina would probably be found, if carefully sought for, but we have not yet met with any of them.

List of species taken at the surface of the water on the southern coast of New England.

In this list no attempt has been made to enumerate the numerous species of free Copepod Crustacea, which are very abundant, but have not been carefully studied.

ARTICULATA.

Crustacea.

Pinnotheres ostreum, males and young, (438.)
Cancer irroratus, in the zoea and megalops stages; June, July, (438.)
Platyonichus ocellatus, young and adult; megalops; June, July, (438.)
Callinectes hastatus, young, (438.)
Many other species of Brachyura in the zoea and megalops stages.
Hippa talpoida, young, 5 or 6^{mm} in length; early in September, (339.)
Eupagurus, several species in the larval stages; July to September.
Gebia affinis, young, 4^{mm} long; early in September.
Homarus Americanus, larvæ and young; July, (395.)
Crangon vulgaris, larvæ and young; June and July.

Virbius zostericola, larvæ and young; July to September.
Palæmonetes vulgaris, larvæ and young; July to September.
Larval forms and young of other species of Macroura.
Squilla empusa, larvæ in different stages; August, (439.)
Mysis Americana, young and adult; April, May, (396.)
Heteromysis formosa, young and adult.
Thysanopoda, sp. Vineyard Sound; April 30, (V. N. Edwards.)
Cumacea, several species.
Lysianassinæ, several species, young and adult.
Urothoë, sp.
Monoculodes, sp.
Calliopius læviusculus, adult and young; summer and winter, (439.)
Pontogeneia inermis, full grown; winter.
Gammarus natator, adult and young; summer and winter, (439.)
Mœra levis.
Ampelisca, sp., young.
Amphithoë maculata, young.
A. longimana, young even 5 or 6^{mm} long.
Hyperia, species; summer, (439.)
Phronima, sp.; September 8, (439.)
Idotea irrorata, (439.)
I. robusta, (439.)
I. phosphorea.
Erichsonia filiformis.
Epelys trilobus.
Tanais filum.
Sapphirina, sp.; September, (439.)
Free Copepods of many genera and numerous species.
Argulus laticauda; August, (439.)
A. latus; July.
A. megalops; September 8.
Caligus rapax; September 8, (439.)
Balanus balanoides, larvæ; April, May, June, (304.)
Lepas fascicularis; June and July, in Vineyard Sound, (382.)
Limulus Polyphemus, young, (340.)

Worms.

Phyllodoce, sp., adult; July 3; evening.
Phyllodoce, sp., young; evening.
Eulalia, sp., young; September 3; evening.
Eulalia, sp., young; evening.
Eumidia, sp., young; September 8; evening.
Eteone, sp., young; evening.
Autolytus cornutus, male, female, and asexual forms; July 29 to August 18; evening. Watch Hill; April 13, asexual form, (440.)
Autolytus, sp., asexual individuals, (398.)

Gattiola, sp., young; September 3; evening.
Syllis (?), sp., young; September 3; evening.
Rhynchobolus Americanus, young; September 3; evening.
Nereis virens, adult males; April; day-time, (440.)
N. limbata, adult males filled with milt, September 3, evening; September 5, at Fire Island, day. Females, September 3, (few;) young, common, August, September, evening, (440.)
N. pelagica, young; August, September; evening.
Nectonereis megalops; July 3, 11; September 3, 8; evening, (440.)
Podarke obscura, adult; June 26 to August; evening, (440.)
Spio setosa, young; evening.
Scolecolepis viridis, young; evening.
Polydora ciliatum, young; September 3; evening.
Nicolea simplex, young; August, September; evening.
Amphitrite ornata, young; evening.
Lepræa rubra, young; evening.
Polycirrus eximius, young; August, September; evening.
Spirorbis, sp., young; evening.
Tomopteris, sp., young; evening.
Sagitta elegans, adult; July 1, September 8; day-time, (440.)
Sagitta, sp., adult and young; January 30 to May 5; day, (440.)
Balanoglossus aurantiacus; larvæ in the "tornaria" state, (351.)
Meckelia ingens; specimens up to ten inches long; evening, (349.)
Pontonema marinum, adult; February; day-time.
Several other small Nematodes with the last.
Slender round worm, up to six inches long; June 29, July 13; evening.
Young of many other worms; undetermined.

MOLLUSCA.

Cephalopods.

Ommastrephes illecebrosa, adult; July, August, (441.)
Loligo Pealii; June to September; young, July, August, (440.)
L. pallida, adult; October, November, (441.)

Pteropods.

Clione papilionacea, adult; April 13, April 30, (444.)
Styliola vitrea, adult; September 8; day-time, (443.)
Spirialis Gouldii, adult; August; evening, (443.)
Diacria trispinosa, (444.)
Cavolina tridentata, (444.)

Lamellibranchs.

Teredo navalis, larvæ; May, June, (386.)
Mytilus edulis, larvæ; April, (308.)
Ostræa Virginiana, larvæ; June, July, (310.)
Larvæ of many other species, undetermined.

Ascidians.

Salpa Cabotti, adults and young; August and September, (445.)
Doliolum, sp.; summer, (A. AGASSIZ,) (446.)
Appendicularia, sp., (like A. furcata;) summer, (A. AGASSIZ,) (446.)
Appendicularia, sp., (like A. longicauda;) summer, (A. AGASSIZ.)
Larvæ of fixed Ascidians, (445.)

RADIATA.

Echinoderms.

Strongylocentrotus Dröbachiensis, larvæ, (447.)
Asterias arenicola, larvæ; evening, (447.)
A. vulgaris, larvæ; evening, (447.)

Acalephs.

Mnemiopsis Leidyi; February, July to September; day-time, (449.)
Lesueuria hyboptera, adult; September; day-time.
Pleurobrachia rhododactyla, adult and young; January to May, July to September; day-time and evening, (448.)
Idyia roseola, adult; September; day-time, (451.)
Cyanea arctica, adult; August, September; day-time. Young in the "ephyra" stages; April; young of all sizes up to four inches across; May, (449.)
Aurelia flavidula; August, September; day-time, young; May, (449.)
Dactylometra quinquecirra, adult and young; July to September; day and evening, (449.)
Trachynema digitale, young; Wood's Hole, July 1; day-time.
Tiaropsis diademata; Wood's Hole; April 17, (V. N. Edwards.)
Oceania languida, medusæ; June to September; day-time.
Eucheilota ventricularis, young medusæ; evening.
E. duodecimalis, medusa; July.
Obelia, several species, medusæ; evening chiefly, (447.)
Rhegmatodes tenuis, medusæ; September; evening.
Zygodactyla Grœnlandica, medusæ; June to September; day and evening, (449.)
Æquorea albida, medusæ; September; evening.
Tima formosa, adult; February, 1872; April 30, 1873, (449.)
Eutima limpida, medusæ; September; evening.
Lafoëa calcarata, medusæ; September; evening.
Nemopsis Bachei, medusæ; June to September; evening.
Bougainvillia superciliaris, medusæ, April, May, June; evening.
Margelis Carolinensis, medusæ; August and September, chiefly in the evening, (450.)
Dysmorphosa fulgurans, medusæ; evening, (448.)
Modeeria, sp., medusæ.
Turritopsis nutricula, medusæ; July to September; evening.

Stomotoca apicata, medusæ.
Willia ornata, young medusæ; last of September.
Dipurnea conica, medusæ; July; evening.
Gemmaria gemmosa, medusæ; evening.
Pennaria tiarella, medusæ; August, September.
Ectopleura ochracea, medusæ; September.
Nanomia cara, August, September; evening.
Physalia Arethusa, July to September; day, (450.)
Velella mutica, August; day.

Polyps.

Edwardsia, sp., larvæ in the "Arachnactis" stage; September; evening, (451.)

PROTOZOA.

Numerous kinds of ciliated infusoria, (451.)

List of species taken at the surface in winter, December to March.

Crustacea.

Crangon vulgaris, young.
Mysis Americana.
Anonyx, (?,) sp.
Calliopius læviusculus, (439.)
Pontogeneia inermis.
Gammarus natator.
Monoculodes, sp.
Several species and genera of Copepods, very abundant.
Larvæ of Balanus, December 21, January 7 and 8.

Annelids, &c.

Nereis virens, adult males.
Sagitta, sp., adult, abundant, (440.)
Pontonema marinum, adult.
Other Nematodes, undetermined.

Acalephs.

Pleurobrachia rhododactyla, young and adult, abundant, (450.)
Mnemiopsis Leidyi, adult, abundant, (450.)
Cyanea arctica, young; March.
Tima formosa, adult, (449.)

II. 10.—ANIMALS PARASITIC ON FISHES, ETC.

Large numbers of fishes were examined, both internally and externally, for parasites, and a large collection of such parasites was made. The internal parasites were collected mainly by Dr. Edward Palmer, and will be of great interest when carefully studied and described. As yet, nothing more than a casual examination of them has been made. These internal parasites were found in nearly all kinds of fishes, chiefly in the stomach and intestines, but also very frequently in the flesh, or among the abdominal viscera, or in the air-bladder, or even in the eyes, &c. The internal parasites were mostly worms, but these belong to four very distinct orders.

1st. The "round-worms," *Nematodes*.

These are related to the round-worms so frequent in the intestines of children, and also to the notorious *Trichina* of man and the hog. One or more species are found in the intestine and stomach of nearly every kind of fish, and frequently, also, in the liver, peritoneum, eyes, and various other organs. One species, two or three inches long, is very frequently found coiled up spirally in the flesh of the cod. Another large species is frequently found in the flesh of the tom-cod, or frost-fish. Although these are not dangerous to man, they are very disagreeable when found in fish intended for food.

A species belonging to this group is very frequently found in the body-cavity of one of our species of *Sagitta* (see page 440).

2d. The flat-worms or "flukes," *Trematodes*.

These are short, more or less broad, depressed worms, which are provided with one, two, or more suckers, for adhering firmly to the membranes. They pass through very remarkable transformations, as do most of the other parasitic worms. Species belonging to this group are common in the stomach, œsophagus, and intestine, and also encysted or in follicles in the mouth, liver, peritoneum, and various other parts of the body.

3d. The thorn-headed worms, *Acanthocephala*.

These have an elongated roundish body, with a proboscis at the anterior end, covered with hooks, or recurved spines. The proboscis and front end of the body can be withdrawn and thrust out at pleasure. Such worms are very common in the stomachs and intestines of fishes, and are, perhaps, the worst parasites that torment them. The young of these worms also occur quite frequently, encysted in the liver, peritoneum, throat, mouth, and other organs.

4th. The "tape-worms," or *Cestodes*.

These are long flat worms, divided into many distinct segments, and are very frequently found in the intestines of most fishes. There are numerous species of them, ranging in size from less than an inch to many feet in length.

Although parasitic worms are found in nearly all kinds of fishes, they are most frequent and in the greatest variety in the large and very voracious kinds, such as sharks, rays, the angler or goose-fish, salmon, blue fish, cod, haddock, &c.

Nor are other marine animals free from these internal parasites. Certain species have been found in crustacea, others in mollusks, &c. Mr. A. Agassiz has briefly described, but not named, a remarkable worm that he found very common in the jelly-fish, *Mnemiopsis Leidyi*, and the young of this or a different species was observed by me in the same Acaleph. It appeared to be a species of *Scolex*. It was pale purple, with light yellowish orange stripes. I have previously mentioned a round worm (*Ascaris?*) which frequently occurs in winter in one of our species of *Sagitta*.

Most of the species that, in the adult state, inhabit fishes, live while young, or in the larval stages, in smaller fishes, or in other animals, upon which the larger fishes feed, and from which they thus derive their parasites.

Besides the parasitic worms there are also many internal parasites that belong to the Protozoa.

The *external* parasites of fishes are also numerous. They are chiefly crustacea and leeches.

Among the Crustacea there are a few species of Amphipods that are parasitic. One of these, *Laphystius sturionis*, lives upon the gills of fishes and upon the surface of the body. It was found on the gills of the "goose-fish," (*Lophius*,) in Vineyard Sound, and on the back of skates at Eastport. It is remarkable in having large claws developed on the third and fourth pairs of legs, those of the first and second being small. Its color is light red.

Certain Isopod crustacea, belonging to the genus *Livoneca* (Plate VI fig. 29) and allied genera, live in the mouths and on the gills of fishes, clinging firmly to the membrane of the roof of the mouth, or other parts, by means of their strong sharp claws. These are generally unsymmetrical in form. The species of the genus *Bopyrus* live on the gills, under the carapax of shrimp and other crustacea, producing large tumors. A species is common on species of *Hippolyte* in the Bay of Fundy; and a species has been found in this region. The genus *Cepon* is allied to the last, and our species occurs under the carapax of the "fiddler-crabs" in this region.

Among the Entomostraca the number of parasitic species is still greater, but most of these live on the external surface and gills of fishes, though some of them occur also in the mouth. The species of *Pandarus* and allied genera adhere firmly to the skin, and are provided with a proboscis. They are very common on sharks, but occur also on other fishes. A *Pandaru*([illegible]te VII, fig. 31) and *Nogagus Latreillii* (Plate VII, fig. 32) were both found on "Atwood's shark," the "man-eater" of this region, associated also with *Nogagus tenax*. The species of "*Nogagus*" are merely the males of other genera, for no one has yet determined both males and females of the various species. The young of one species, *Caligus rapax*, were found swimming free at the surface.

The species of *Argulus* and allied genera are less strictly parasitic, or rather they adhere less closely, and apparently leave the fishes at pleasure and migrate from one to another. Three species belonging to this group were taken at the surface with the towing-nets. The Lerneans are remarkable creatures. The females are generally very curious in form and very much larger than the more active and less abnormal males, and they are very low in structure, the reproductive system being enormously developed at the expense of nearly all the other organs. They live upon the exterior and gills of fishes, with the head deeply buried in the flesh, and subsist by sucking the blood of their victims. The *Lernæonema radiatum* (Plate VII, fig. 30) is very common on the menhaden, and is also found on the alewives.

There are many kinds of parasitic leeches. One of the most remarkable is the *Branchiobdella Ravenelii*, (Plate XVIII, fig. 89.) This genus is peculiar in having broad, foliaceous, lobed or scolloped gills along the sides of the body. The large species figured was found several times on the large "sting-rays," several of them usually occurring together, on a large spot which had become sore and much inflamed by their repeated bites. It is a very active species.

The *Cystobranchus vividus* is a much smaller and quite slender leech, which has small, papilliform, whitish gills that alternately contract and expand along the sides of the body, each surrounded by a semicircular white spot. The colors are brownish or purplish, with three rows of small white spots on the back. This species is frequent on the common minnow, (*Fundulus pisculentus*,) in autumn and winter, and lives both in brackish water and fresh water. With the last, on the minnows, is found another slender leech, destitute of gills; this is the *Ichthyobdella Funduli.* It has, like the last, four ocelli. The color is pale green with darker green and brown specks, often with whitish transverse bands anteriorly, and a white ring behind the head, at the constriction; sometimes there is a narrow pale dorsal line.

A long, slender, sub-cylindrical leech, the *Pontobdella rapax* V., (Plate XVIII, fig. 91,) is quite common on the upper side of the "summer-flounder," (*Chænopsetta ocellaris.*) It is a very active species, dark olive or brown in color, with a row of square or oblong whitish spots along each side; the suckers are pale greenish white. The young are reddish brown, without spots.

A species of *Pontobdella* was found adhering to *Mysis Americana*, near New Haven, May 5, in three instances, but whether this be its normal habit is uncertain.

The *Malacobdella obesa* V. (Plate XVIII, fig. 90) is a large, stout, yellowish white leech, often two inches long, which is quite common in the branchial cavity of the "long clam," (*Mya arenaria.*)

The *Malacobdella mercenaria* V. is another similar species, but smaller and more slender, which lives in the same way in the "round clam" (*Venus mercenaria.*)

The *Myzobdella lugubris* is a small leech, which lives on the "edible crab" (*Callinectes hastatus*,) adhering to the soft membranes between the joints and at the base of the legs.

List of external parasites observed on fishes and other marine animals of Southern New England.

In the following list I have included all the determined species observed in these waters, whether living in the sounds, or in the outer waters, or in the brackish waters of the estuaries, for most of these parasitic species are capable of living in as diverse conditions as do the animals which they infest, and most of the fishes pass from time to time into each of the divisions named, though some, like the cod, are chiefly found in the colder outer waters, and even there only in winter.

The list is undoubtedly very incomplete for it is based chiefly on collections made during two seasons, and mainly in the summer months. In addition to the true parasites I have, for greater convenience, included in the list some that merely live on or with other animals, either for the sake of shelter, or to feed upon their excretions, or to share their food. Some of these would be properly classed as "commensals."

ARTICULATA.

Crustacea.

Pinnotheres ostreum, (p. 367,) in oysters.
P. maculatus, in Mytilus edulis.
Laphystius sturionis, on goose-fish and skate, (457.)
Hyperia, species, on jelly-fishes, (439.)
Nerocila munda, on file-fish.
Conilera concharum.
Livoneca ovalis, on blue-fish, (457.)
Cepon distortus, in branchial cavity of Gelasimus, (457.)
Ergasilus labraces, on striped-bass.
Argulus catostomi, on the sucker, (Catostomus.)
A. laticauda, (457.)
A. latus.
A. megalops.
A. alosæ, on "alewives."
Caligus curtus, on cod-fish.
C. rapax, on sting-ray, (Trygon hastata.)
Lepeophtheirus, sp., on sting-ray.
Lepeophtheirus, sp., on flounder, (Chænopsetta ocellaris.)
Echthrogalus coleoptratus, on mackerel-shark, (Lamna punctata.)
E. denticulatus, on Atwood's shark, (Carcharodon Atwoodi.)
Pandarus Cranchii, (?) on dusky shark, (Platypodon obscurus.)
Pandarus, sp., on Atwood's shark, (Carcharodon Atwoodi.)
Nogagus Latreillii, on Atwood's shark, (457.)
N. tenax, on Atwood's shark, (457.)
Pandarus sinuatus, on the "dog-fish," (Mustelus canis.)
Cecrops Latreillii, on Othagoriscus mola.

Anthosoma crassum, on mackerel-shark.
Lernæa branchialis, on cod-fish.
Penella plumosa, on Diodon pilosus and Rhombus, sp.
Anchorella uncinata, on cod-fish.
Lernæonema radiatum, on menhaden, (458.)
Lernæonema, sp., on a species of Carangus.
Coronula diadema, on whales.

Leeches.

Branchiobdella Ravenelii, on sting-rays; August, September, (458.)
Cystobranchus vividus, on minnows; October to December 18, (458.)
Ichthyobdella Funduli, on minnows; with last, (458.)
Ichthyobdella, sp., dredged off New London, April.
Pontobdella rapax, on flounders, (458.)
Malacobdella obesa, in long clams, (458.)
M. mercenaria, in round clams, (458.)
Myzobdella lugubris, on the edible crab, (458.)
Bdelloura candida, on gills of *Limulus*.

MOLLUSCA.

Gastropods.

Stylifer Stimpsonii, on the green sea-urchin.
Eulima oleacea, on *Thyone Briareus*, (418.)

III.—FAUNA OF THE ESTUARIES, HARBORS, PONDS, AND MARSHES.

The region about Vineyard Sound and Buzzard's Bay, like that of the entire southern coast of New England and the coast farther south, is characterized by large numbers of ponds, lagoons, and estuaries, having a more or less interrupted communication with the sea. These are usually quite shallow, though often of great extent. The bottom is generally muddy, with occasional patches of sand, but at the surface usually consists largely of decaying vegetable and animal *débris* mixed with mud.

The "eel-grass" (*Zostera marina*) grows in the shallower waters in great quantities, sometimes in small scattered patches, at other times covering large areas. Some of these ponds and estuaries receive considerable, though variable, quantities of fresh water from streams flowing into them, while others receive but little, except the surface drainage of the land immediately around them; but in most of them the fresh water is in sufficient quantities to give a "brackish" character to the waters. Owing to the narrow and often shallow channels by which the ponds communicate with the open waters, the tide is usually irregular, and its rise and fall often much less than outside, so that the waters have little tidal motion. The shallowness of the water and the abundant eel-grass also impede the motion caused by the wind, so that these bodies of water are comparatively quiet under ordinary circumstances. The same causes allow the water to become highly heated during the summer. It is evident that the heat and quietness of the waters are unfavorable for the rapid absorbtion of oxygen from the air, while by the rapid decay of the dead materials of the bottom large quantities of carbonic acid and other gases must be evolved, which would in some cases soon render the water fatal to all animal life, were it not for the presence of the eel-grass, *Ulva*, and other plants that flourish in such waters, which, while absorbing the excess of carbonic acid, also help to give the requisite amount of oxygen to the water. During storms the mud of the bottom is quickly disturbed, causing the escape of noxious gases, and rendering the water turbid, while the eel-grass is torn up in large quantities, thus adding to the decaying materials of the bottom and shores. Moreover, in case of rain-storms or spring-freshets, the sudden addition of large volumes of fresh water often causes great changes in the density and character of the water, sufficient to kill species not adapted to such varying and peculiar conditions.

We accordingly find that although animal life is usually very abundant, the number of species that habitually live and prosper in these impure and decidedly brackish waters is comparatively small. But such as do occur are usually found in great quantities, and are remarkable for their hardiness and ability to live under widely varying conditions. Many of them are strictly southern species, which do not extend much farther north; but there are some, like the long clam, muscle, &c., which extend even to the Arctic Ocean and the coasts of Europe.

Many of the estuaries and harbors, and some of the ponds, have a much freer communication with the sea, and then the water is less brackish and generally less impure in other respects, and the number of species of animals becomes much greater. In other cases the water is so little brackish that the fauna is nearly identical with that of the outer bays. A few of these species are almost restricted to the brackish waters, but by far the greater number are able to live in pure sea-water, and are accordingly also found in the bays and sounds. There are various degrees of preference shown by the different species; some are very abundant in the brackish waters and very seldom found outside; some evidently prefer the estuaries but are also abundant in the sounds; some flourish equally well in both situations; many are common in the estuaries but much more abundant in the pure waters of the sounds; and a large number which are occasionally found in the brackish waters, especially where but little freshened, have their proper homes in the pure waters outside.

Most of our food-fishes frequent the ponds and estuaries, either for the sake of food or for the purpose of spawning, and many spend the earlier part of their lives entirely in such waters. It is apparent, therefore, that among the few species of invertebrate animals living in the brackish waters, there are some that are of great importance as food for fishes. It is true that many of the larger fishes frequent the estuaries to prey upon smaller ones, some of which are extremely abundant in these waters. But the small fishes, like minnows, as well as the young of the larger ones, feed chiefly upon the small crustacea, worms, and shells that live in the waters that they inhabit. Therefore the entire value of the estuaries as feeding-grounds for the larger fishes depends directly upon those species of crustacea, &c., that naturally live in brackish water.

In discussing the fauna of the estuaries I have found it most convenient to group the species under the following divisions: 1. Those of sandy shores and bottoms. 2. Those of muddy shores and bottoms. 3. Those inhabiting oyster-beds. 4. Those inhabiting the eel-grass. 5. Those attached to rocks, piles of wharves, floating timber, buoys, &c.

The lists could be greatly extended by including all the species to be found near the mouths of estuaries, or in those harbors and ponds that are scarcely brackish, for in these localities the fauna is nearly identical with that of the bays and sounds, and the lists already given on previous pages will also apply very well to such places.

As a general rule only those species that are abundant, or at least frequent, in waters distinctly brackish, have been included in the lists.

III, 1.—Animals inhabiting the sandy shores and bottoms of brackish waters.

Sandy shores and bottoms are generally less common and less extensive than muddy ones, and occur chiefly toward the mouths of estuaries, or on the more exposed borders of the larger ponds and harbors, where the wave-action is greatest.

When such bottoms are covered with eel-grass, as often happens, the animals are quite numerous, but when destitute of vegetation the species of animals are but few, and mostly of the kinds that burrow. But when there is a mixture of mud with the sand the variety is much greater.

Near high-water mark, colonies of the "sand-fiddler," *Gelasimus pugilator*, (p. 336,) often occur, as on the sandy beaches outside. In the same situations the beach-fleas, *Talorchestia longicornis* and *T. megalophthalma* (p. 336,) also occur, burrowing in the sand; while the *Orchestia agilis* Smith is abundant under the vegetable *débris* at high-water mark.

Several species of salt-water insects also occur, burrowing in the sandy beaches at and below high-water mark. Among these are several beetles, which live in such situations, both in the larval and adult conditions. The *Bledius cordatus* is one of the most abundant of these. This is a small, dark-colored, "rover-beetle," with very short elytra. It makes small, perpendicular holes in the sand near high-water mark, throwing up a little mound of sand around the burrows. A larger species, *Bledius pallipennis*, occurs lower down, at about half-tide mark and makes similar burrows, but they are larger and deeper. This species is yellowish brown in color. The larva of a fly belonging to the Muscidæ, and growing to the length of three-quarters of an inch, occurs beneath the sand at low-water mark, and was also dredged off-shore in three or four fathoms of water.

In the shallow waters and on the flats the common shrimp, *Crangon vulgaris*, (p. 339, Plate III, fig. 10,) is always to be found in abundance where the water is not too much freshened by the rivers. The prawn, *Palæmonetes vulgaris*, (p. 339, Plate II, fig. 9,) is also frequent on the sandy bottoms, though more abundant among the eel-grass, and this species extends far up the estuaries into the mouths of rivers, where the water is but little salt.

The most abundant Annelids are *Nereis virens*, (Plate XI, figs. 47–50,) *N. limbata*, (Plate XI, fig. 51,) *Rhynchobolus dibranchiatus*, (Plate X, figs 43, 44,) *R. Americanus*, (Plate X, figs. 45, 46,) and *Scolecolepis viridis* V., (p. 345,) all of which burrow in the sand at low-water mark in the same way as on the shores of the sounds.

Under vegetable *débris* and stones, at high-water mark, the *Halodrillus littoralis* (p. 324) and *Clitellio irroratus* (p. 324) occur in abundance. The *Lumbriculus tenuis* burrows among the roots of grass at high-water mark.

The most abundant Gastropod shells are *Ilyanassa obsoleta*, (Plate XXI, fig. 13,) *Tritia trivittata*, (Plate XXI, fig. 112,) *Bittium nigrum*, (Plate XXIV, fig. 154,) *Astyris lunata*, (Plate XXI, fig. 110,) which occur on the flats and on the bottom in shallow water, but all are more common among eel-grass. The *Melampus bidentatus* (Plate XXV, figs. 169, 169*a*) is very abundant among the grass and weeds at and just above high-water mark. It contributes largely to the food of the minnows and other small fishes, as well as to that of many aquatic birds. The *Crepidula convexa* (Plate XXIII, fig. 128) is frequent on the dead shells occupied by the small hermit-crab, *Eupagurus longicarpus*, (p. 313,) which is abundant, running over the bottom in shallow water.

The most abundant bivalves are the long clam, *Mya arenaria*, (Plate XXVI, fig. 179,) and *Macoma fusca*, (Plate XXX, fig. 222.) These both occur burrowing in the sand between tides, and both occur far up the estuaries, where the water is very brackish, but they are most abundant where there is a mixture of sand and mud. In the estuaries the long clam is extremely abundant all along the coast from New Jersey to the Arctic Ocean, as well as on all the northern coasts of Europe It also occurs south of Cape Hatteras, as at Beaufort, North Carolina, but in greatly diminished numbers. North of New York it is very extensively used as an article of food. North of Cape Cod it is the common "clam" of the fishermen; and north of Boston it almost entirely displaces, in the markets, the "round-clam," or "quahog," *Venus mercenaria*, which is the common clam at New York and farther south. Along the southern coast of New England both species are abundant, and both are sold in large quantities in the markets. South of New

York the long clam is but little sought as an article of food, except for local use. On the coast of New Jersey it is often called the "maninose clam," from the Indian name (frequently corrupted to "nanny-nose.") It is also sometimes called the "soft-shelled clam," in distinction from the "quahog," which is called "hard-shelled." The "long clams" of certain localities on Long Island Sound, as, for instance, those from Guilford, Connecticut, are of very excellent quality, and are very highly esteemed.

The Guilford clams are assorted into regular sizes, and are bought from the fishermen on the spot by the hundred. Those of large size bring about $3 per hundred; these are retailed in the market at New Haven for 60 cents per dozen. Smaller sizes bring 48 cents and 36 cents per dozen. During unusually low tides in winter clams of extraordinary size are obtained at Guilford, below the zone ordinarily uncovered by the tide; these often weigh a pound or more, and sell for about $1.25 per dozen; occasionally the weight is as much as a pound and a half, and the shells become six or eight inches in length.

The ordinary long clams of small and moderate sizes bring 95 cents, $1.25, and $2 per bushel at wholesale; these retail in our markets at 50 cents to 75 cents per peck, the smallest sizes being cheapest, while the reverse is the case with the round clams.

In New Haven the long clams are chiefly sold in winter, being "out of season" in summer, when the round clams supply the markets. But in New York the long clams are sold during the whole year.

Large quantities of these clams are also collected on the northern coasts of New England and put up for bait, to be used in the cod-fishery at the banks of Newfoundland.

The total amount collected and used annually is probably not less than 1,000,000 bushels.

List of species inhabiting sandy shores and bottoms of estuaries.

ARTICULATA.

Insects.

	Page.		Page.
Larvæ of fly, (Muscidæ)....	463	Bledius cordatus..........	462
Ephydra, sp., larvæ	466	B. pallipennis.............	462
Cicindela, larvæ...........	335	Heterocera undatus	335
Bembidium constrictum....		Phaleria testacea..........	
B. contractum.............		Anurida maritima.........	331
Phytosus littoralis.........	335		

Crustacea.

	Page.		Page.
Gelasimus pugilator.......	462	Orchestia agilis	462
Cancer irroratus...........	312	Talorchestia longicornis....	462
Carcinus granulatus.......	312	T. megalophthalma........	462
Eupagurus longicarpus	463	Epelys trilobus............	370
Palæmonetes vulgaris......	463	Limulus Polyphemus	340
Crangon vulgaris..........	463		

Annelids.

	Page.		Page.
Nereis virens	463	Clymenella torquata	343
N. limbata	463	Cistenides Gouldii	323
Rhynchobolus Americanus	463	Sabellaria vulgaris	321
R. dibranchiatus	463	Lumbriculus tenuis	463
Spio robustus	345	Clitellio irroratus	463
Scolecolepis viridis	463	Halodrillus littoralis	463
S. tenuis	345		

Nemerteans.

	Page.		Page.
Meckelia ingens	349	Meckelia rosea	350

MOLLUSCA.

Gastropods.

	Page.		Page.
Ilyanassa obsoleta	463	Odostomia trifida	307
Tritia trivittata	463	Bittium nigrum	463
Eupleura caudata	371	Crepidula convexa	463
Astyris lunata	463	Melampus bidentatus	463

Lamellibranchs.

	Page.		Page.
Mya arenaria	463	Lævicardium Mortoni	358
Macoma fusca	463	Solenomya velum	360
Angulus tener	358	Mytilus edulis	307
Tottenia gemma	359	Modiola plicatula	307
Venus mercenaria	463	Pecten irradians	361

III. 2.—Animals inhabiting the muddy shores and bottoms of brackish waters.

The bottoms of the sheltered estuaries, ponds, and harbors, are almost invariably muddy, throughout the greater part of their extent, from low-water mark to their greatest depths, or, in other words, wherever the waves do not act with considerable force. The shores between tides are also muddy in the more protected localities, where the waves do not have sufficient power to remove the fine sediments. The upper and narrower parts of nearly all the estuaries in this region are, on this account, muddy, for the rapidity of the tide is seldom sufficient to entirely remove the fine sediments brought down by the streams.

A large part of the muddy bottoms is generally covered in summer by extensive patches of eel-grass. Over other portions large beds of oysters are always planted, thus greatly modifying the natural conditions of such localities and introducing a large number of species not properly belonging to the true muddy bottoms.

The shores of the muddy estuaries and ponds, or lagoons, are usually low, flat, and bordered by more or less extensive salt-marshes, with the surface generally just above high-water mark of ordinary tides, but liable to inundation by unusually high tides. These marshes are always traversed by winding and sluggish tidal streams of brackish water and by smaller ditches, and the surface is often diversified by small pools or ponds of impure brackish water, in which there is generally a deep deposit of soft, slimy mud and decaying organic matter, which often becomes putrid, and exhales fetid gases. All such waters, whether in the ditches or pools, and however filthy they may be, are inhabited by certain kinds of invertebrate animals, and they are also frequented by multitudes of minnows and other small fishes, which undoubtedly find abundant food in such places.

In these brackish pools and ditches we find certain beetles, both in the adult and larval stages. Among these the most conspicuous is *Hydrophilus quadristriatus* HORN., a large, black species, which appears to be common. The larva of the salt-marsh musquito (*Culex*, sp.,) also lives in such situations, and the adults in August, September, and October, so swarm in these marshes as to render it extremely unpleasant to go on or near them. The larvæ of an *Ephydra* also occurs, and many other insects will doubtless be found in these places when carefully sought for.

One Amphipod, the *Gammarus mucronatus*, commonly lives in the most brackish pools and among the grass on the marshes. The prawn, *Palæmonetes vulgaris*, (Plate II, fig. 9,) is also very abundant in these pools and ditches, even where the water is but little salt, and also occurs in immense numbers on the muddy bottoms and among the eel-grass of the estuaries. In the pools there are also myriads of small Entomostraca of many kinds, upon which the prawn and other species feed, while the Entomostraca find an abundance of ciliated Infusoria and other microscopic animals for food.

We find several species of crabs burrowing in muddy banks along the shores of the estuaries, as well as along banks of the streams and ditches in the salt-marshes. The most abundant of these is the marsh fiddler-crab, *Gelasimus pugnax*, which is often so abundant that the banks are completely honey-combed and undermined by them. These holes are of various sizes up to about three-quarters of an inch in diameter, and descend more or less perpendicularly, often to the depth of two feet or more. Occasionally in summer these crabs will leave their holes and scatter over the surface of the marshes, which at such times seem to be perfectly alive with them, but when disturbed they will scamper away in every direction and speedily retreat to their holes, but occasionally, at least, they do not find their own, for sometimes the rightful owner will be seen forcibly ejecting several intruders. It is probable that at such times of general retreat each one gets into the first hole that he can find. Associated with this "fiddler" another related crab, the *Sesarma reticulata*, is occasionally found in considerable numbers. This is a stout-looking, reddish brown crab, with a squarish carapax; its large claws are stout and nearly equal in both sexes, instead of being very unequal, as in the male "fiddlers." It lives in holes like the "fiddlers," but its holes are usually much larger, often an inch or an inch and a half in diameter. It is much less active than the "fiddlers," but can pinch very powerfully with its large claws, which are always promptly used when an opportunity occurs.

The *Carcinus granulatus* (p. 312) of large size may often be found concealed in the cavities under the banks undermined by the two preceding species, along the ditches and streams in the salt-marshes. On the marshes farther up the estuaries, and along the mouths of rivers and brooks, and extending up even to places where the water is quite fresh, another and much larger species of "fiddler-crab" occurs, often in abundance; this is the *Gelasimus minax*. It can be easily distinguished by its much larger size and by having a patch of red at the joints of the legs. Its habits have been carefully studied by Mr. T. M. Prudden of New Haven, but his interesting account of them has not yet been published. He has also investigated its anatomy. According to Mr. Prudden this species, like *G. pugilator*, (see p. 336,) is a vegetarian. He often saw it engaged in scraping up and eating a minute green algoid plant, which covers the surface of the mud. The male uses its small claw exclusively in obtaining its food and conveying it to the mouth. The female uses either of her small ones indifferently. In enlarging its burrows Mr. Prudden observed that these crabs scraped off the mud from the inside of the burrow by means of the claws of the ambulatory legs, and having formed the mud into a pellet, pushed it up out of the hole by means of the elbow-like joint at the base of the great claw, when this is folded down. He also ascertained that this crab often constructs a regular oven-like arch of mud over the mouth of its burrow. This arch-way is horizontal, and large and long enough to contain the crab, who quietly sits in this curious door-way on the lookout for his enemies of all kinds.

This species can live out of water and without food for many days. It can also live in perfectly fresh water. One large male was kept in my laboratory in a glass jar containing nothing but a little siliceous sand, moistened with pure fresh water, for over six months. During this whole period he seemed to be constantly in motion, walking round and round the jar and trying to climb out. He was never observed to rest or appear tired, and after months of confinement and starvation was just as pugnacious as ever.

Although some of the colonies of this species live nearly or quite up to fresh water, others are found farther down on the marshes, where the water is quite brackish, and thus there is a middle ground where this and *G. pugnax* occur together. This was found by Mr. Prudden to be the case, both on the marshes bordering West River and on those of Mill River near New Haven. They are abundant along both these streams. The holes made by this species are much larger than those of *G. pugnax*. Some of them are an inch and a half to two inches in diameter.

The "blue crab" or common edible crab, *Callinectes hastatus*, (p. 367,) frequents the brackish streams and estuaries, where it is often taken in large quantities for the markets. These are usually brought to market early in May, but the "soft-shelled" ones, which are more highly esteemed, are taken later. These soft-shelled individuals are merely those that have recently shed their old shells, while the new shell has not had time to harden. The period of shedding seems to be irregular and long continued, for soft-shelled crabs are taken nearly all summer. The young and half-grown specimens of this crab may often be found in considerable numbers hiding in the holes and hollows beneath the banks during the flood-tide. When disturbed, they swim away quietly into deeper water. These small crabs are devoured by many of the larger fishes. During flood-tide the large crabs swim up the streams like many fishes, and retreat again with the ebb. They feed largely on fishes, and often do much damage by eating fishes caught in set-nets, frequently making large holes in the nets at the same time.

The "mud-crabs," *Panopeus Sayi* (p. 312) and *P. depressus*, (Plate I, fig. 3,) are very common in all the muddy estuaries and harbors. *P. Harrisii* also occurs in similar places; it is far less common, and apparently usually lives higher up toward high-water mark, under stones, &c., but it has been found on the salt-marshes at the mouth of Charles River, according to Dr. A. A. Gould.

The *Orchestia palustris* SMITH, is found on the salt-marshes, where it occurs under drift-wood, vegetable *débris*, &c., extending its range nearly or quite up to fresh water, and at times living in places that are almost dry, above high-water mark.

The *Squilla empusa* (p. 369) burrows in muddy shores and bottoms at or below low-water mark.

The *Gebia affinis* (p. 368, Plate II, fig. 7) also lives in similar places in deep burrows, as described on a previous page.

The "horseshoe-crab," *Limulus Polyphemus* (p. 340,) is also a common inhabitant of muddy bottoms, in estuaries, where it grows to great size.

The most common Annelids are partly the same as those given above for the sandy shores. The *Nereis virens* is generally very abundant; the two species of *Rhynchobolus* are common; and also *Lumbriconereis opalina*, (Plate XIII, figs. 69, 70;) *Cirratulus grandis*, (Plate XV, figs. 80, 81;) *Polycirrus eximius*, (p. 320, Plate XVI, fig. 85;) *Chætobranchus sanguineus*, (p. 320;) and several other less conspicuous species.

Among the Gastropods by far the most abundant species is the *Ilya-*

nassa obsoleta, (p. 354, Plate XXI, fig. 113,) which creeps over the flats and muddy bottoms in countless multitudes, sometimes almost covering the entire surface. When left by the tide, on the flats, especially in cold weather, they will creep into the small pools and depressions of the surface, where they often huddle together in great crowds, sometimes forming many layers, one above another. This is probably the most abundant shell, of any considerable size, on the coast of the United States. It occurs abundantly from the Gulf of Mexico to Massachusetts Bay. It is essentially a scavenger, and owing to its vast numbers its services in that line must be of great value. It occurs far up the estuaries, where the water is decidedly brackish, but flourishes equally well on the outer shores.

The *Littorinella minuta* (Plate XXIV, fig. 140) also occurs in vast numbers on the mud-flats, and in the pools and ditches of the salt-marshes, but it is a small and inconspicuous species. It is, however, not overlooked by the small fishes and various aquatic birds, for they feed largely upon it.

The *Melampus bidentatus* (Plate XXV, figs. 169, 169*a*) is also extremely abundant on the muddy salt-marshes, creeping over the general surface, or in the shallow pools and ditches, and among the grass, creeping up the stalks. In shallow water, where not too brackish, the *Bulla solitaria* (Plate XXV, fig. 161) is sometimes found in considerable numbers, creeping over soft, muddy bottoms. It is a favorite article of food with the flounders.

Among the Lamellibranchs, one of the most common species is the *Modiola plicatula*, (Plate XXXI, fig. 258,) which occurs everywhere on the muddy banks at and above high-water mark, and also over the salt-marshes, along the borders of ditches and streams, and wherever there is sufficient moisture, partially imbedding its shell in the mud or among the roots of grass, and anchoring itself by means of a stout byssus. The long clam, *Mya arenaria*, (p. 463) and the *Macoma fusca*, (Plate XXX, fig. 222) are almost everywhere abundant on the shores between tides.

The "round clam," *Venus mercenaria*, (p. 359, Plate XXVI, fig. 184,) occurs on the muddy bottoms in shallow water, often in great abundance, especially where the mud is somewhat firm, or where there is an admixture of sand, and the water is not very much freshened. This clam is usually taken in such places by means of long-handled tongs, and sometimes with the dredge. It is especially abundant in the estuaries and harbors opening into Long Island Sound. The quantity of this clam taken annually for food is enormous, but it is impossible, at present, to get reliable statistics, either for this or the long clam, for they are mostly taken and sold, a few bushels at a time, by individual fishermen, and the traffic is diffused along the whole coast, from Florida to Boston; but it is probable that more than 1,500,000 bushels are annually consumed.

In the New Haven markets the round clams retail at $2 to $3 per bushel for the small ones, and $1 to $2 per bushel for the large ones.

The common muscle, *Mytilus edulis*, (p. 307, Plate XXXI, fig. 234,) is also extremely abundant on the muddy bottoms, forming immense beds in many places. It is taken in vast quantities for fertilizing the land, but is seldom used as food on our coast, although it is used extensively in some parts of Europe.

The muddy bottoms of the estuaries, ponds, and harbors, especially when composed largely of organic matter in a living state, afford the best localities for "planting" oysters, and they are extensively utilized for this purpose. The oysters thus planted are mostly brought from farther south, but young "natives" are also transplanted on a large scale in some localities.

It is, however, very certain that the oysters did not originally grow on muddy bottoms, for the young cannot maintain themselves during early life unless attached to some solid substance.

Therefore, where large oyster-beds have been planted, the bottom should no longer be classed as "muddy," but rather as a "shelly bottom," for a large number of animals, in addition to those of true muddy bottoms, live among or attached to the oysters.

Along the peaty and clayey banks, especially where undermined by the waves, even nearly up to high-water mark, the *Petricola pholadiformis* (p. 372, Plate XXVI, fig. 199,) and *Pholas truncata*, (Plate XXVII, fig. 200,) are often found in their deep burrows in considerable numbers. The *Tagelus gibba* (Plate XXVI, fig. 181, and Plate XXX, fig. 217,) burrows at and below low-water mark on the muddy and argillaceous shores of the estuaries, as well as on the shores of the bays. On muddy bottoms, toward the outer parts of the estuaries and harbors, the *Mulinia lateralis* (Plate XXVI, fig. 184, B) often occurs in great abundance. And in similar places, even where the bottom consists largely of decaying vegetable matter, the *Tellina tenta* (Plate XXX, fig. 225) and *Solenomya velum* (Plate XXIX, fig. 210) are sometimes found in considerable numbers. The *Callista convexa* (Plate XXX, fig. 219) also occurs in similar places.

The Ascidians, Bryozoa, and Radiata are almost entirely wanting on the muddy shores and bottoms of estuaries, unless in localities where eel-grass or oyster-beds afford them suitable stations; but such localities will be discussed farther on.

List of species inhabiting the muddy shores and bottoms of brackish waters.

ARTICULATA.

Insects.

	Page.		Page.
Cicindela marginata	335	Culex, sp	466
Hydrophilus quadristriatus	466	Ephydra, sp	466

Crustacea.

Annelids.

Nemerteans.

Nematodes.

MOLLUSCA.

Gastropods.

Lamellibranchs.

	Page.		Page.
Pholas truncata	470	Callista convexa	470
P. costata	433	Mulinia lateralis	470
Mya arenaria	469	Solenomya velum	470
Macoma fusca	469	Nucula proxima	432
Tellina tenta	470	Argina pexata	309
Angulustener	358	Modiola plicatula	469
Tagelus gibba	470	M. hamatus	374
Petricola pholadiformis	470	Mytilus edulis	470
Venus mercenaria	469	Ostræa Virginiana	310

III. 3.—ANIMALS INHABITING OYSTER-BEDS IN BRACKISH WATERS.

Although the oyster-beds are generally planted on bottoms that were originally muddy, when covered wholly or partially with living oysters or with dead oyster-shells, such bottoms may properly be regarded as "shelly bottoms" analogous to the natural shelly bottoms of the outer waters. The shells of the oysters afford suitable attachment for various shells, bryozoa, ascidians, hydroids, sponges, &c., which could not otherwise maintain their existence on muddy bottoms, while other kinds of animals, such as crabs, annelids, &c., find shelter beneath the shells or in their interstices. Some species have apparently been introduced from farther south with the oysters; among these are *Modiola hamatus* and *Panopeus Herbstii*, neither of which is positively known to be fully naturalized on our shores.

In planting the oysters they are more or less uniformly scattered over the bottom, from somewhat above low-water mark to the depth of ten or twelve feet. The oysters thus planted are brought mostly from the waters of Virginia and Maryland in spring. During the summer they usually increase greatly in size, and often become very fat and improve in flavor. They are taken up in the fall, for if left exposed to the freezing weather of our winters, at least all those in very shallow water would be killed. They often double in bulk during the summer. Besides the immense quantities of oysters thus brought from farther south to be "planted" in our waters, large quantities of young "natives" are also collected from the localities where they naturally breed, and are planted on muddy bottoms in the brackish waters, where they grow very rapidly, usually attaining a size suitable for the market in two or three years.

These "native oysters," although of the same species as those brought from the south, are more hardy, and will live through the winter if covered by a depth of water sufficient to prevent them from freezing. The young oysters that attach themselves to stones, ledges, &c., between tides, often in great abundance, nearly all perish by freezing during the winter. They mostly become an inch to an inch and a half in diameter during the first summer. The period of spawning lasts for some time, but most of it seems to be done in May, June, and July. The young, after swimming about for a short time, attach themselves to any suitable hard object, such as rocks, shells, timber, brush, &c. On our coast very few attempts have been made to raise the young oysters by artificial means, because the young oysters, of a size suitable to plant, can generally be bought at a price less than the actual cost of raising them. The time will doubtless come, however, when this will no longer be the case, and then the methods so successfully employed on the coast of France may be resorted to with great advantage.

The young oysters must find some solid substance to which they can attach themselves, before losing their locomotive organs, otherwise they will fall to the bottom and perish in the mud. It is evident, therefore, that although the oysters planted on muddy bottoms of the right kind will grow most rapidly, owing to the great abundance of their microscopic food in the mud and turbid water; yet such localities are unfavorable for breeding-grounds, because the young, or "spat," will find no suitable objects to which they can attach themselves, unless, by chance, to the shells of the old oysters. Therefore, if it be desired to have the oysters in such localities produce the young ones necessary to maintain the bed permanently, it will be necessary to place hard objects on the bottom, to which they may adhere. Stones, broken bricks, &c., may be used for this purpose, but nothing is better than old oyster-shells, and they are generally cheaper than anything else.

On the coast of France bundles of twigs or fagots, prepared tiles, and other objects have been used to catch the young, and they are allowed to remain on such objects until they become large enough to be removed and planted elsewhere.

It is obvious that the best breeding-grounds are on hard bottoms, where there are large quantities of dead shells, pebbles, &c., to which the young will be sure to adhere. But such bottoms are not the best localities for the rapid growth and fattening of the oysters. Therefore it is always found profitable to transplant the young oysters, when large enough, from hard bottoms to the muddy bottoms of the estuaries, where their natural food most abounds.

All muddy bottoms are not equally adapted for this purpose. The great differences to be found in the muddy bottoms of various localities have already been mentioned on a previous page. (See p. 430.) Those bottoms that are composed mainly of tenacious clay are unsuitable, both because the oysters become imbedded too deeply in the clay, and because such mud contains but little organic matter. Those that consist of clay or sand mixed with decaying vegetable matter, and have a black, putrid layer just beneath the surface are also unsuitable and should be avoided. Those that consist of very deep, soft, pasty mud, though the mud itself may be of good quality, are apt to allow the oysters to sink too deeply beneath the surface and thus become smothered in the mud.

The most suitable localities are those sheltered places where there is a firm substratum of sand or gravel, overlaid with a few inches of soft, flocculent mud, consisting largely of living microscopic animals and plants, Infusoria, Diatoms, &c. Such localities are to be found in most of our shallow estuaries, harbors, and brackish ponds, and on such grounds the oysters grow and become fat with surprising rapidity.

The character of such bottoms is very liable to be changed by storms, especially in winter, either by the removal of the organic mud to some other part of the bottom or shore, or by the washing in of silt or clay in quantities sufficient to cover the bottom and destroy the living organisms. Thus it happens that a locality may be an excellent oyster-ground one year and comparatively worthless the next, or a poor locality may in the next year become a good one. And on this account the great reputation that the oysters of a particular locality often acquire in a favorable year may not belong to them in subsequent years, for the quality of the oysters changes with the character of the food and bottom where they grow. I have already mentioned several of the more important enemies of the oysters on former pages. (See pp. 306, 326.) The star-fishes, which are among the most destructive of these, do not flourish in brackish waters, and this is, therefore, a great advantage.

The quantity of oysters taken from our waters is far greater than is generally supposed by those not familiar with this important business. The best statistics are necessarily very incomplete, but they are sufficient to show the almost incredible magnitude of this industry, which is, moreover, rapidly increasing as the facilities for transporting the oysters to all parts of the country, even to the Pacific coast, are multiplied.

According to the official report of Hunter Davidson, commissioner, upon the oyster-fisheries, &c., of Maryland, January, 1872,* the quantity of oysters taken in Maryland waters in the year 1869–'70 was 11,233,475 bushels, which, at an average value of 35 cents per bushel, would amount to $4,031,716. To catch and convey these to market 8,070 men were employed on the water; 7,190,400 bushels were taken by 642 vessels (tonnage 14,436) engaged in dredging, and employing 4,060 hands. The balance, 2,043,075 bushels, were taken by 1,647 boats or "canoes," using tongs and rakes, and employing 3,410 hands.

In 1870–'71, 597 vessels, (tonnage 13,425,) engaged in dredging, and employing 3,775 hands, took 6,686,400 bushels; and 1,649 "canoes" took, with tongs, 2,261,403 bushels, employing 3,507 hands; making the total amount for the year, 10,947,803 bushels, valued at $3,831,731. Many of these oysters were sold at $1 to $1.50 per bushel, while others were sold for less than twenty-five cents, but it is probable that the estimated average value (thirty-five cents) is considerably below the actual value.

The quantity taken in the waters of Virginia is probably quite as large as that from Maryland.

Large quantities are also taken along the coast of New Jersey, Long

* Report on the Oyster-Fisheries, Potomac River Shad and Herring Fisheries, and the Water-fowl of Maryland, to his excellency the governor and other commissioners of the State oyster-police force, January, 1872.

Island, and Connecticut. It is, therefore, probable that the total amount taken on the coast north of Cape Hatteras is not less than 30,000,000 bushels annually, having a value of more than $20,000,000. In making this estimate we should allow for the great increase in bulk and value of many of the Maryland and Virginia oysters that are transplanted to northern waters, and allowed to grow before using. The average value of the northern oysters, both native and transplanted, is probably more than seventy-five cents per bushel. It is, therefore, probable that the above estimate is considerably too low.

The great oyster-markets of the country are Baltimore and New York. In Baltimore immense quantities of oysters are put up in kegs and cans to supply the distant parts of our own country and also to ship to nearly all foreign countries. In 1867 it was estimated that more than 10,000 persons were employed in this branch of the business. There were then thirty packing-houses, employing 4,500 openers. In addition to the packing business great quantities of oysters are sold at Baltimore and sent away in the shell. The total quantity sold at Baltimore exceeded 7,000,000 bushels, of which about 5,000,000 bushels came from Maryland waters, and the balance from Virginia. Of these over 1,000,000 bushels were sent to New York, 700,000 to Fair Haven, Connecticut, where an extensive packing business is carried on, 450,000 to Philadelphia, 350,000 to Boston.

The oyster trade of New York, several years ago, was estimated at over $8,000,000, employing 2,500 vessels, and it has greatly increased since that estimate was made.

Among the most common shells that are found attached to oysters are *Crepidula fornicata* (Plate XXIII, figs. 129, 129*a*) and *C. unguiformis*, (Plate XXIII, fig. 127.) They both occur together on the upper as well as the under valves, and in all cases retain their ordinary characters, except that the latter is more regular in form, and usually has the upper surface slightly convex, instead of being much distorted and with a concave upper surface, as the larger specimens that live on the inside of dead univalves usually are. Its color, when living on the oysters, is always white, while the *C. fornicata* is always more or less marked with brown.

The common muscle, *Mytilus edulis*, (p. 307) frequently occurs attached to oysters, and when it accumulates on the oyster-beds in large quantities it is very injurious. The *Modiola hamatus* (p. 374) is a very peculiar-looking muscle, having a broad, often hatchet-shaped, distorted shell, covered with prominent radiating ribs, many of which are forked. Its color is yellowish or brownish. It somewhat resembles *Modiola plicatula*, but is broader and has coarser ribs. This muscle is sometimes found in New Haven Harbor, living on the oyster-beds in considerable numbers, and of full size, attached to the oysters, either singly or in clusters, by the byssal threads. It has been observed only in the summer and fall and it may not have survived the winters, for it is possible that all the individuals may have been brought from the south, in the spring, when quite small, attached to the oysters. It may be, however, that it has really become naturalized on our shores. It is very common in the Gulf of Mexico, and on other parts of the southern coast. The *Anomia glabra* (p. 311, Plate XXII, figs. 241, 242, 242*a*) is also very commonly found adhering to oysters.

The hard sandy tubes of *Sabellaria vulgaris* (p. 321, Plate XVII, figs 88, 88*a*) and the calcareous tubes of *Serpula dianthus* (p. 322) are very frequent upon oyster-shells, and occasionally those of *Potamilla oculifera*, (p 322, Plate XVII, fig. 86,) *Scionopsis palmata*, (p. 321,) and other species are met with. Many other Annelids are to be found burrowing or hiding beneath the oysters. The common green star-fish, *Asterias arenicola*, (p. 326, Plate XXXV, fig. 269,) occasionally occurs on the oyster-beds near the mouths of estuaries, but is seldom sufficiently abundant in the brackish waters to do serious damage to the oyster-beds.

In the brackish waters the " drill," *Urosalpinx cinerea*, (p. 306, Plate XXI, fig. 116,) is the worst enemy of the oyster, and is sometimes so numerous as to do very serious damage.

Several species of Hydroids grow adhering to oysters. The most abundant of these, in brackish water, is usually *Halecium gracile* V., (p. 328,) but two or three species of *Obelia* and some other forms occur.

Of Bryozoa, one of the most common species is the *Escharella variabilis*, (p. 312, Plate XXXIII, fig. 256,) which forms calcareous incrustations. The *Bugula turrita*, (p. 311, Plate XXXIV, figs 258, 259,) and *Vesicularia dichotoma* V. (p. 404) are also common. The *Alcyonidium hirsutum*, (p. 404,) which forms soft fleshy crusts over the surface of the shells, is quite frequently seen.

The common red sponge (p. 330) is often abundant on the oyster-beds where the water is not much freshened.

List of species inhabiting oyster-beds in brackish waters.

ARTICULATA.

Insects.

	Page.
Chironomus oceanicus	379

Crustacea.

	Page.		Page.
Pinnotheres ostreum	367	E. longicarpus	313
Cancer irroratus	312	Crangon vulgaris	339
Panopeus Herbstii	472	Mysis Americana	370
P. Sayi	312	Melita nitida	314
P. depressus	312	Ampelisca, sp	431
Carcinus granulatus	312	Unciola irrorata	340
Libinia canaliculata	368	Corophium cylindricum	370
Eupagurus pollicaris	313	Epelys trilobus	370

Annelids.

Nemerteans and Planarians.

Nematodes.

MOLLUSCA.

Gastropods.

Lamellibranchs.

Ascidians.

	Page.		Page.
Cynthia partita	311	Molgula Manhattensis	311

Bryozoa.

	Page.		Page.
Bugula turrita	476	Vesicularia dichotoma	476
Escharella variabilis	476	Alcyonidium hirsutum	476
Membranipora lineata	406	Pedicellina Americana	405

RADIATA.

Echinoderms.

	Page.
Asterias arenicola	476

Acalephs.

	Page.		Page.
Obelia gelatinosa	391	Halecium gracile	476
O. diaphana	327	Sertularia argentea	408
O. pyriformis	390		

Polyps.

	Page.		Page.
Metridium marginatum	329	Sagartia leucolena	329

PROTOZOA.

Sponges.

	Page.		Page.
Tedania, species	330	Red branching sponge	476
Halichondria, sp	330		

III. 4.—ANIMALS INHABITING EEL-GRASS IN BRACKISH WATERS.

A large portion of the shallow parts of nearly all the harbors, estuaries, and ponds is occupied by a dense growth of eel-grass, *Zostera marina*, in summer. This plant flourishes both on sandy and muddy bottoms. During the fall and winter it is mostly torn up and drifted away by storms, but in the spring a new crop starts up and grows very rapidly, the narrow, ribbon-like leaves often becoming six feet or more in length during the summer.

These tracts of eel-grass are the favorite resorts of a considerable number of animals, which seek these places either for food or concealment and shelter, or for both combined. Other species, including certain hydroids, bryozoa, and ascidians, grow attached to the leaves of the eel-grass.

Many small fishes frequent the patches of eel-grass, and find there abundance of food and unusual safety from their enemies.

Among the most common Crustacea found among the eel-grass are the edible crab, *Callinectes hastatus*, (p. 367;) *Panopeus Sayi*, (p. 312;) *P. depressus*, (Plate I, fig. 3;) *Eupagurus longicarpus*, (p. 313;) the prawn, *Palæmonetes vulgaris*, (p. 369, Plate II, fig. 9;) the common shrimp, *Crangon vulgaris*, (p. 339, Plate III, fig. 10;) the green shrimp, *Virbius zostericola*, (p. 369, Plate III, fig. 11;) *Mysis stenolepis*, (p. 370, Plate III, fig. 12;) *M. Americana*, (p. 370;) *Idotea irrorata*, (p. 316, Plate V, fig. 23;) *Melita nitida*, (p. 314.) The common prawn (Plate II, fig. 9) has its true home among the eel-grass, and here it occurs in countless numbers. Its translucent body, marked with irregular, ill-defined, dark blotches and spots, admirably adapts it for concealment among the discolored and dead leaves of the plant, at or near the bottom.

Where the eel-grass grows on sandy bottoms the common shrimp is scarcely less abundant. The *Virbius* is often abundant, associated with the common prawn, and having similar habits. All these shrimps and prawns are eagerly devoured by the fishes. The *Idotea irrorata* is generally very abundant, and clings firmly to the leaves of the eel-grass lengthwise. Its body is generally curiously and variously colored with green and brown, &c., and these colors are often so arranged as to imitate very perfectly the colors of the eel-grass when partially dead or discolored. Sometimes the right or left half of the body will be bright green, while the opposite half will be dark brown. In other cases there will be a dorsal bright green stripe, while the sides will be dark brown, just like one of the leaves of the eel-grass that is discolored at the edges, but green in the middle. More commonly these colors are irregularly disposed in blotches.

The *Erichsonia attenuata* HARGER, is a remarkably slender species, which also lives clinging to the eel-grass. Its colors are green and brown, and quite variable.

Several species of Amphipods are also abundant among the eel-grass. One of the most common of these is the *Gammarus mucronatus*, (p. 466,) which is easily distinguished by the dorsal teeth on the abdominal segments. *Microdeutopus minax* SMITH, is a very small species, which sometimes occurs in great abundance in the small brackish ponds. It is remarkable for its relatively large and very broad hands, armed beneath with three prominent teeth. The hands are nearly as large as the entire body.

Among the Mollusks several interesting species occur. The *Ilyanassa obsoleta*, (p. 371, Plate XXI, fig. 113;) *Bittium nigrum*, (p. 305, Plate XXIV, fig. 154;) and *Astyris lunata*, (p. 306, Plate XXI, fig. 110,) are generally the most abundant species. The *Nassa vibex* (p. 371, Plate XXI, fig. 114) is met with occasionally, living on and about the roots of eel-grass, but it is an uncommon shell in our waters, though quite abundant on the southern coasts. The *Crepidula convexa* (p. 371, Plate XXIII, fig. 128) may be found, both adhering to the leaves of eel-grass and attached to shells occupied by the smaller hermit-crabs.

The curious little naked mollusk, *Elysiella catulus*, (Plate XXV, fig. 171,) is often quite common on the leaves of eel-grass in our harbors. It also has the power of floating with the bottom of the foot at the surface of the water. Its small size and bright green color, like that of the growing leaves of the *Zostera*, cause it to be easily overlooked.

The related species, *Elysia chlorotica*, (Plate XXV, fig. 172,) appears to have similar habits, but is much less common. Its color is also green. The pretty *Doto coronata* (p. 400, Plate XXV, fig. 170) also occasionally occurs on the leaves of eel-grass.

A green Planarian is frequent on the eel-grass, and also a bright red species.

List of species inhabiting the eel-grass in brackish waters.

ARTICULATA.

Insects.

	Page.
Chironomus oceanicus	379

Crustacea.

	Page.		Page.
Panopeus depressus	479	Melita nitida	479
P. Sayi	479	Microdeutopus minax	479
Callinectes hastatus	479	Amphithoë valida	315
Carcinus granulatus	312	A. longimana	370
Libinia canaliculata	368	A. compta	370
L. dubia	368	Corophium cylindricum	370
Eupagurus longicarpus	479	Caprella geometrica	382
Crangon vulgaris	479	Idotea irrorata	479
Virbius zostericola	479	Erichsonia attenuata	479
Palæmonetes vulgaris	479	Epelys trilobus	370
Mysis stenolepis	479	Balanus eburneus	381
M. Americana	479	Limulus Polyphemus	340
Gammarus mucronatus	479		

Annelids.

	Page.		Page.
Lepidonotus squamatus	320	Nicolea simplex	321
Podarke obscura	319	Scionopsis palmata	321
Autolytus cornutus	397	Polycinus eximius	320
Nereis limbata	318	Spirorbis, sp	323

Nemerteans and Planarians.

	Page.		Page.
Polinia glutinosa	324	Planarian, (red sp.)	480
Cerebratulus, sp	324	Planarian, (dark green sp.)	480

MOLLUSCA.

Gastropods.

	Page.		Page.
Illyanassa obsoleta	479	Littorinella minuta	469
Nassa vibex	479	Crepidula convexa	479
Astyris lunata	479	Doto coronata	480
Anachis avara	306	Elysia chlorotica	480
Bittium nigrum	479	Elysiella catulus	480
Triforis nigrocinctus	305		

Lamellibranchs.

	Page.		Page.
Argina pexata	309	Pecten irradians	361
Mytilus edulis	470	Ostræa Virginiana	472

Ascidians.

	Page.		Page.
Molgula Manhattensis	311	Botryllus Gouldii	375

Bryozoa.

	Page.		Page.
Bugula turrita	311	Escharella variabilis	312
Vesicularia dichotoma	404	Membranipora, lineata	406

RADIATA.

Acalephs.

	Page.		Page.
Obelia diaphana	327	Hydractinia polyclina	328
Obelia, sp	476		

Polyps.

	Page.
Sagartia leucolena	329

III. 5.—Animals living on or among piles of wharves, bridges, floating timber, rocks, etc., in brackish waters.

The piles of wharves in brackish harbors are often inhabited by an abundance of animal life. The same species are mostly to be found also on piles of wharves in the purer waters of the sounds, and many of them have, therefore, already been mentioned in a previous place, (p. 378.) There are some of these species, however, that appear to flourish best in waters that are decidedly brackish.

Among the most conspicuous of these is the beautiful Tubularian

Parypha crocea, (p. 390, Plate, XXXVI, fig. 274,) which grows in large tufts, several inches in height, and often covers large surfaces of the piles and timbers at and just below low-water mark. Associated with this the *Obelia gelatinosa* (p. 391) often occurs in large quantities. This is a large and very beautiful species, having a large dark colored stem, composed of numerous united tubes, but the terminal branches are white and delicate, and the cells have an elegant bell-shaped form, with a toothed margin. It grows to the length of a foot or more. This species occurs on the piles of Long Wharf, in New Haven Harbor, in great abundance, associated with the preceding; at this place the water is not only quite brackish, but is very impure, on account of sewerage, &c.

Other species of *Obelia* also occur in similar places. The *Balanus eburneus* is a very abundant barnacle in brackish waters, growing upon piles, timbers, oyster-stakes, and every other kind of fixed wood-work, and also upon the bottoms of vessels and floating timber. As already remarked (p. 381) it is capable of living even in fresh water. The *Balanus balanoides* also occurs where the water is less brackish. The piles and timbers of the wharves are often badly damaged by the perforations of *Teredo navalis* (p. 384, Plate XXVI, fig. 183) even where the water is very brackish.*

The *Limnoria lignorum* (p. 379) also attacks wood-work in waters that are somewhat brackish.

Lists of species inhabiting piles of wharves, floating timbers, &c., in brackish waters.

ARTICULATA.

Insects.

	Page.		Page.
Chironomus oceanicus.....	331	Anurida maritima.........	331

Crustacea.

	Page.		Page.
Panopeus depressus.......	312	Jæra copiosa..............	315
Microdeutopus minax......	479	Idotea irrorata............	316
Amphithoë compta........	370	Limnoria lignorum........	482
Corophium cylindricum....	370	Balanus balanoides........	482
Caprella, sp...............	316	B. eburneus...............	482

* Since the account of the *Teredo navalis*, on page 384, has been in type, I have learned some additional facts in regard to it from Mr. V. N. Edwards. The statement that the buoys are taken up every six months does not apply to the spar-buoys, which are taken up only once a year, in April and May. Mr. Edwards states that the *Teredos* would destroy an unpainted spar-buoy in one year, but when painted with verdigris they will only work where the paint becomes rubbed off. They grow to full size in one year. They first attack buoys or piles just below the water's edge, but eventually will destroy the entire submerged part of the spar-buoys. He thinks that some of them live through the winter.

Annelids.

	Page.		Page.
Nereis limbata	318	Potamilla oculifera	322
Autolytus cornutus	397	Sabella microphthalma	323
Sabellaria vulgaris	321	Fabricia Leidyi	323
Nicolea simplex	321	Serpula dianthus	322
Polycirrus eximius	320	Spirorbis, sp	323

Turbellarians.

	Page.		Page.
Monocelis agilis	325	Nemertes socialis	324
Polinia glutinosa	324		

Nematodes.

	Page.		Page.
Pontonema marinum	325	P. vacillatum	326

MOLLUSCA.

Gastropods.

	Page.		Page.
Bela plicata	383	L. palliata	305
Ilyanassa obsoleta	468	Odostomia bisuturalis	307
Tritia trivittata	354	Bittium nigrum	305
Urosalpinx cinerea	306	Cerithiopsis Greenii	383
Astyris lunata	306	Triforis nigrocinctus	305
Anachis avara	306	Alexia myosotis	383
Rissoa aculeus	306	Melampus bidentatus	469
Skenea planorbis	383	Æolidia pilata	383
Littorina rudis	305		

Lamellibranchs.

	Page.		Page.
Teredo navalis	482	Modiola plicatula	307
Argina pexata	309	Anomia glabra	311
Mytilus edulis	307	Ostræa Virginiana	310

Ascidians.

	Page.		Page.
Molgula Manhattensis	311	Botryllus Gouldii	389
Cynthia partita	311		

Bryozoa.

	Page.		Page.
Vesicularia dichotoma	389	Bugula turrita	311
Escharella variabilis	312	Pedicellina Americana	405

RADIATA.

Hydroids.

	Page.		Page.
Obelia gelatinosa..........	482	Halecium gracile..........	328
O. pyriformis.............	390	Parypha crocea	482
O. diaphana	327		

Polyps.

	Page.		Page.
Sagartia leucolena.........	329	Metridium marginatum....	329

IV.—Fauna of the ocean shores and outer cold waters.

All along this coast, from Cape Cod to Stonington, Connecticut, there is a belt or current of cold water which impinges directly against the outer islands and the open coast, especially where there are points of land projecting outward toward the deeper waters. This is especially noticeable at Gay Head, on Martha's Vineyard, No Man's Land, Cuttyhunk Island, Montauk Point, Block Island, Point Judith, and Watch Hill. This cold water is undoubtedly derived from the Arctic current, which passes slowly southward in deep water off our coast, but whether an actual current, distinguishable from the tidal currents, exists in the waters of moderate depth along the coast is still uncertain. The tidal currents apparently have the effect of bringing the cold water of the outside regions up into the shallower localities along the shores, and it is probable that the presence of the cold water in moderate depths is due to the joint action of the tides and the slow-moving Arctic current, which impinges more or less against and upon the slope of the submerged eastern border of the continent. But the position, extent, and temperature of this cold water along our shores varies greatly, according to the direction of the tidal currents and the surface currents caused by the wind. We have shown, on a former page, that at times these local winds and tidal currents are able even to bring Gulf Stream water and its characteristic animals directly upon this coast, even as far westward as Watch Hill, Rhode Island, where the *Physalia* is often cast ashore in summer. At such times the cold current must necessarily be wholly displaced, or disguised by intermixture with the warmer waters. When the tide is flowing from Long Island Sound, Vineyard Sound, or other large bodies of warm water, the cold waters will also be displaced and the temperature raised even at the distance of twenty or thirty miles from the shore in summer. In winter there is comparatively little effect from the Gulf Stream, owing to the prevalence of northerly winds, and there is also far less effect from the warm waters of the shallow bays and sounds carried by the tides. Therefore the full effect of the northern current is felt only in winter, and it doubtless adds to the cold proper to the season and land climate.

In winter and early spring we accordingly find numerous species of northern animals and algæ which disappear partially or wholly in many of these localities in summer. In April, May, and June, the cod and haddock resort in large numbers to the banks and reefs off Stonington, Watch Hill, No Man's Land, and other similar places, but are quite unknown there later in the summer.

In consequence of the varying temperatures of the currents which alternately pass over certain of these localities, there is a very peculiar admixture of northern and southern species, side by side. This is particularly the case on the reefs between Watch Hill and Fisher's Island, where the southern *Astrangia Danæ* is associated with the northern *Alcyonium carneum*, *Cribrella sanguinolenta*, and many other northern forms.

The temperature of the bottom-water during the last of August and first of September was found to vary from 57° F. to 63°, in sixteen to twenty-nine fathoms off Martha's Vineyard and Buzzard's Bay, (see chart.) The surface temperatures were at the same time 62° to 64°, and occasionally as high as 67°, when affected by warmer currents.

IV. 1.—SPECIES INHABITING ROCKY SHORES OF THE OPEN COAST.

The principal localities under this head at which we have made collections are No Man's Land, Cuttyhunk Island, Gay Head, and Watch Hill, Rhode Island. Dr. J. E. Leidy has published a partial list of the species found at Point Judith,* and we have more or less information concerning the fauna of several other similar localities. In all these places the assemblage of animals is nearly the same, and in general not very different from what we find on the rocky shores of the sounds and bays, (see p. 303.) A large part of the species of these shores have, therefore, already been mentioned in connection with the fauna of the bays and sounds.

There are, however, many species that are characteristic of the latter, which are found but rarely, or not at all, on the colder and more exposed outer shores; and these are characterized by the abundance of some northern species which are rare or wanting on the inner shores, or which occur there only in winter.

Among the most abundant species of shells are *Purpura lapillus*, (p. 306, Plate XXI, figs. 118, 119;) *Littorina palliata*, (p. 305, Plate XXIV, fig. 138;) *L. rudis*, (p. 305, Plate XXIV, fig. 137;) *Acmæa testudinalis*, (p. 307, Plate XXIV, figs. 158, 159;) and *Lacuna vincta*, (p. 305, Plate XXIV, fig. 139,) all of which occur adhering to the rocks or algæ, even in the most exposed situations. These are all hardy northern species, which extend their range to Greenland or beyond, and although all of them are to be found, more or less frequently, on the inner shores, they are there less abundant and generally of smaller size. The *Littorina palliata* is extremely abundant on the *Fucus*, and individuals were found at Watch Hill, copulating, April 12. The *Lacuna vincta* breeds still

* Journal of the Academy of Natural Sciences of Philadelphia, 2d series, vol. iii, 1855.

earlier in the season, for its eggs were found attached to algæ and eel-grass at the date named. The eggs of this species are small, yellowish white, imbedded in a gelatinous mass, having an annular form, but showing a break or suture on one side. These annular egg-masses are attached by one side to the surfaces of flat algæ or eel-grass in large numbers; they are from .12 to .20 of an inch in diameter.

The *Æolis papillosa* was found at Watch Hill, under stones, April 12, and with it were long, much convoluted, gelatinous cords, filled with minute pale red or salmon-colored eggs, which probably belong to this species, which is a northern one, and has not hitherto been recorded as from south of Cape Cod. It is very abundant in the Bay of Fundy, and similar egg-clusters are found there under rocks during the entire summer.

Among and between the stones the northern purple star-fish, *Asterias vulgaris* (p. 432) is often found at low-water, and also the green sea-urchin, *Strongylocentrotus Dröbachiensis* (p. 406, Plate XXXV, fig. 268) during the spring tides.

The *Balanus balanoides* (p. 305) is quite as abundant on the most exposed rocks as elsewhere. The minute bivalve young of this species were found just attaching themselves to the lower surfaces of rocks in immense numbers at Watch Hill on the 12th of April.

Beneath the stones the rock-crab, *Cancer irroratus*, (p. 312,) is very common, and occasionally the much rarer *Cancer borealis* is found dead on these shores. It was thus found at Gay Head and No Man's Land, but it is doubtful whether it lives above low-water mark. In the lower part of the fucus zone the large *Gammarus ornatus* (p. 314, Plate IV, fig. 15) is always to be found in great abundance under stones, and in the upper half of the fucus zone the smaller species, *Gammarus annulatas* (p. 314) and *Gammarus marinus* often occur in great numbers, associated with *Jæra copiosa* (p. 315) and *Idotea irrorata* (p. 316, Plate V, fig. 23.) The *Gammarus marinus* occurs higher up than either of the other species, and is sometimes abundant even near high-water mark, where the soil beneath the stones is barely moist at low-water. The *Amphithoë maculata* (p. 315, Plate IV, fig. 16) is also a common species under stones; and both green and reddish brown varieties occur.

Another species of *Amphithoë*, of smaller size, was found swimming free in the rocky pools at Watch Hill, April 12. In this the general color was red, or brownish red; the body was transversely banded with pale flesh-color or whitish, alternating with bands of dark red or brown, which are made up of minute crowded specks; the antennæ are annulated with pale red, and are thickly specked, on the bands and at the base, with darker red. The *Hyale littoralis* (p. 315) is a small but very active Amphipod, which is often abundant near high-water mark on the rocky shores, clinging to the *Fucus* and other algæ, or swimming in the tide-pools. It is capable of leaping actively like the beach-fleas, (*Orchestia agilis*,) which it somewhat resembles in form. The color is very variable; it is often bright yellowish green, but frequently dark green, brownish green, or brown.

The *Nereis virens* (p. 317, Pl. XI, figs. 47–49) is very abundant in burrows beneath the rocks. The males of this species, six to ten inches or more in length, and of a dark green color, were found at Watch Hill, April 12, in great numbers, swimming about in the pools of water among the rocks, with an undulatory motion, and discharging their milt in large quantities. Various other Annelids burrow or build tubes beneath the stones. *A. planaria* and *Leptoplana folium* creep over their lower surfaces.

Attached to the stems of *Fucus* at low-water, several Hydroids may usually be found, but the *Sertularia pumila* (p. 327, Pl. XXXVII, fig. 279) is by far the most abundant. The *Obelia geniculata* is also very common, attached to *Laminaria* and other algæ. Various Bryozoa occur attached to stones and to *Fucus* and other algæ. The *Alcyonidium hispidum* (p. 312) is one of the most abundant species, and usually invests the stems and fronds of *Fucus vesiculosus*, but also often covers broad surfaces of the rocks. The *A. hirsutum* is often associated with the preceding species on the rocks; it forms broad, thin, soft crusts, covered with small soft prominences, but is without the spines or bristles seen in the latter. The Zoöids are also much smaller.

The *Farrella familiaris* is a singular and delicate species, which occurs both on the under side of rocks and on algæ. The body is small, fusiform, attached by a long and very slender, flexible pedicel. When it surrounds the stems of small algæ, the whitish pedicels project outward in all directions, and thus produce the appearance of a delicate chenille-cord. This is a northern and European species. It was also dredged on Saint George's bank in 1872.

List of species found on the outer rocky shores.

ARTICULATA.

Crustacea.

	Page.		Page.
Cancer irroratus	486	Gammarus marinus	486
Cancer borealis	486	Amphithoë maculata	486
Panopeus depressus	312	Amphithoë, sp	486
Panopeus Sayi	312	Caprella, sp	316
Homarus Americanus	492	Jæra copiosa	486
Orchestia agilis	315	Idotea irrorata	486
Hyale littoralis	486	I. phosphorea	316
Calliopius læviusculus	315	Erichsonia filiformis	316
Gammarus ornatus	486	Balanus balanoides	486
Gammarus annulatus	486		

Annelids.

	Page.		Page.
Lepidonotus squamatus.....	320	Cirrhinereis fragilis........	397
Harmothoë imbricata........	321	Clymenella torquata.......	343
Phyllodoce cantenula.......	494	Polycirrus eximius	320
Eteone robusta.............	349	Sabellaria vulgaris.........	321
Autolytus cornutus.........	397	Potamilla oculifera........	322
Nereis virens...............	487	Fabricia Leidyi	323
N. pelagica.................	319	Serpula dianthus..........	322
Ophelia simplex............	319	Spirorbis, sp.............	323

Turbellaria.

	Page.		Page.
Planaria, species	487	Nemertes socialis..........	324
Leptoplana folium..........	487	Nemertes, sp..............	498
Procerodes frequens........	325	Monocelis agilis...........	325

Nematodes.

	Page.		Page.
Pontonema marinum........	325	Pontonema vacillatum.....	326

MOLLUSCA.

Gastropods.

	Page.		Page.
Buccinum undatum.........	494	L. neritoidea..............	495
Tritia trivittata............	354	Bittium nigrum...........	305
Urosalpinx cinerea.........	306	Acmæa testudinalis	485
Purpura lapillus............	485	Doris bifida...............	307
Astyris lunata	306	Polycera Lessonii..........	400
Littorina palliata...........	485	Dendronotus arborescens...	495
L. rudis	485	Æolis papillosa............	486
Lacuna vincta..............	485	Tergipes despectus........	495

Lamellibranchs.

	Page.		Page.
Saxicava arctica...........	309	Mytilus edulis	307
Mya arenaria	309	Modiola modiolus..........	309
Kellia planulata	310	Anomia glabra............	311

Ascidians.

	Page.		Page.
Cynthia partita............	311	Amarœcium pellucidum....	401
Molgula Manhattensis......	311		

Bryozoa.

	Page.		Page.
Alcyonidium hirsutum......	487	Bugula flabellata...........	311
A. hispidum	487	Membranipora pilosa......	406
Vesicularia gracilis.........	389	M. lineata	406
V. cuscuta..................	404	Escharella variabilis.......	312
V. fusca	420	Discopora coccinea........	333
Farrella familiaris..........	487	Lepralia, sp...............	420
Tubulipora flabellaris.......	405	Cellepora ramulosa........	312
Crisia eburnea.............	311	Pedicellina Americana.....	405

RADIATA.

Echinoderms.

	Page.		Page.
Strongylocentrotus Dröbachiensis	496	Asterias vulgaris...........	496
		Cribrella sanguinolenta....	407

Acalephs.

	Page.		Page.
Obelia pyriformis	390	Sertularia pumila	487
O. geniculata	487	S. argentea	408
O. flabellata................	390	Pennaria tiarella..........	327
O. diaphana................	327	Clava leptostyla...........	328
Campanularia flexuosa......	327	Hydractinia polyclina.....	228

Polyps.

	Page.		Page.
Metridium marginatum......	329	Sagartia leucolena.........	329

IV. 2.—Species inhabiting the sandy shores of the open coast.

Owing to the force of the waves the sand and gravel of the exposed shores are kept in constant motion in stormy weather, and are often disturbed to a considerable depth, especially in winter. Therefore the conditions are very unfavorable for the existence of animal life. The fauna of such shores is, accordingly, very meager, as compared with that of the more sheltered sandy shores of the bays and sounds.

It often happens that one may examine these sandy beaches for a mile or more at low-water without finding more than half a dozen species of animals that actually live on them, though many may be found thrown up by the waves from below low-water mark.

In coves or other localities that are somewhat sheltered, the number of species is greater, and most of them are identical with those found on the sandy shores of the sounds.

Toward high-water mark the *Talorchestia longicornis* (p. 336) and *T.*

megalophthalma (p. 336) are everywhere common, burrowing in the sand. The *Cancer irroratus* (p. 338) and *Platyonichus ocellatus* (p. 338) are rather common at and just below low-water mark. The *Hippa talpoida* (p. 338, Plate II, fig. 5) is occasionally found, and the young sometimes occur in large numbers, burrowing in the sand at low-water mark. The common shrimp, *Crangon vulgaris*, (p. 339, Plate III, fig. 10,) is usually abundant where there are sheltered sandy flats.

The Annelids are less numerous than on the sandy shores of the sounds, but such as do occur are mostly of the same species. One of the most interesting is the *Nerine agilis*, (p. 346,) which is very remarkable for the rapidity with which it burrows in the sand.

The Mollusks are few in number. One of the most abundant of the Gastropods is the *Lunatia heros*, (p. 353, Plate XXIII, figs. 133–136,) which burrows just beneath the surface of the sand, at and below low-water mark. The *Neverita duplicata* (p. 354, Plate XXIII, fig. 130) is also occasionally found, but is much less abundant than in the bays.

Of Lamellibranchs there are but few species that can maintain themselves in such situations. Among these the "long clam," *Mya arenaria*, (p. 463,) the "razor-shell," *Ensatella Americana*, (p. 356,) and the "surf-clam," *Mactra solidissima*, (p. 358,) are the most common.

Very few, if any, Radiates are to be found on the exposed sandy shores, unless thrown up by the waves from deeper water. In places that are somewhat protected from the violence of the surf, the *Leptosynapta Girardii* (p. 361, Plate XXXV, figs. 265, 266) is often found burrowing in the sand at low-water mark. Sometimes, in similar places, the "sand-dollar," *Echinarachnius parma*, (p. 362, Plate XXXV, fig. 267,) is found in large numbers at extreme low-water mark.

There are no Hydroids and Polyps that properly inhabit such shores.

List of species inhabiting the sandy shores of the open coast.

ARTICULATA.

Crustacea.

	Page.		Page.
Ocypoda arenaria, (young)...	337	Crangon vulgaris..........	490
Cancer irroratus	490	Orchestia agilis	336
Cancer borealis.............	486	Talorchestia longicornis....	489
Platyonichus ocellatus......	490	T. megalophthalma........	489
Hippa talpoida.............	490	Unciola irrorata...........	340
Eupagurus pollicaris	313	Idotea cæca...............	340

Annelids.

	Page.		Page.
Nereis virens	317	Scolecolepis viridis........	345
N. limbata.................	318	Clymenella torquata.......	343
Rhynchobolus Americanus..	342	Amphitrite ornata	320
Nerine agilis...............	490	Polycirrus eximius	320

MOLLUSCA.

Gastropods.

	Page.		Page.
Sycotypus canaliculatus	399	C. unguiformis	354
Tritia trivittata............	354	Lunatia heros.............	490
Crepidula fornicata.........	355	Neverita duplicata	490

Lamellibranchs.

	Page.		Page.
Ensatella Americana	490	Mya arenaria	490
Siliqua costata..............	426	Mactra solidissima........	490

RADIATA.

Echinoderms.

	Page.		Page.
Leptosynapta Girardii......	490	Echinarachnius parma.....	490

IV. 3.—ANIMALS INHABITING ROCKY BOTTOMS OFF THE OPEN COAST.

The fauna of the rocky bottoms in these outer waters is rich and interesting, and decidedly northern in character, though there is usually an admixture with southern species.

The principal localities where dredgings were made on this kind of ground are: First, off Gay Head and Devil's Bridge, at localities marked on the chart, 53, *a*, *b*, *c*, *d*; 55, *a*, *b*, *c*; 56, *a*, *b*, *c*, *d*; 57, *a*, *b*, *c*, *d*; 58, *a*, *b*, *c*; 59, *a*, *b*, *c*; 60, *a*, *b*, *c*; 61, *a*, *b*, *c*; 62, *a*, *b*, *c*; 63, *a*, *b*; 83, *a*, *b*, *c*. Second, between Gay Head and No Man's Land, and to the westward of the latter island, at localities 82, *a*, *b*; 84, *a*, *b*, *c*, *d*; at these localities cod are caught in the spring. Third, on and about the rocky reef extending from Watch Hill, Rhode Island, to Fisher's Island, and forming, in part, the physical boundary of the eastern end of Long Island Sound; this is also a locality where cod and haddock are caught in spring. The dredgings at this place were made by Professor D. C. Eaton, Mr. C. A. Burt, and myself, April 13, 1873. Fourth, a locality off Cuttyhunk Island, where dredgings were made, April, 1872, by Mr. T. M. Prudden, Mr. T. H. Russell, and others.

The four localities named are characterized by a similar fauna, but each one yielded some species not found in the others, though more numerous dredgings might have revealed them. The reef off Watch Hill is of peculiar interest on account of the singular blending of the northern and southern faunæ at that place, as mentioned above. It seems to be nearly at the extreme western range of many northern species, though some of them may occur sparingly in certain favorable localities still farther westward, in Long Island Sound itself. Many northern algæ were also collected there by Professor Eaton, in abundance, and some of them have not been found farther westward, and others but rarely. Among these were *Ptilota elegans* and *Delesseria sinuosa*, both of which were abundant on the reef in four or five fathoms, associated with large quantities of *Phyllophora Brodiæi*, and *P. membranifolia; Euthora cristata* and *Lithothamnion polymorphum* also occurred. The "dulse," *Rhodymenia palmata*, *Laminaria digitata*, *L. saccharina*, and *L. longicrura*, all of which are decidedly northern species, were large and abundant.

A similar assemblage of algæ was also found on the rocks, in shallow water, off Gay Head, though some of the species just named were not found there.

Among the Crustacea of these localities, the most important is the lobster, *Homarus Americanus*, (p. 395,) which finds its proper habitat in such places. It is very abundant off Gay Head, and among the reefs and rocks off Watch Hill and Stonington, Connecticut. It also occurs plentifully in similar localities off New London, Connecticut, and still farther west in Long Island Sound. At all these and many other localities large quantities are caught for the markets. They are nearly all taken in "lobster pots" baited with refuse fish, &c.

The lobster fishing begins in this region in the latter part of March or early in April, according to the season. By the middle of April they are usually taken in large quantities and shipped alive to New York, New Haven, and other cities. The extent of this trade is enormous even in this region, while north of Cape Cod, along the whole northern coast of New England, and on the shores of Nova Scotia, the lobster is taken in still larger quantities. At present we have no reliable data for estimating the number annually caught, but it probably amounts to several millions.

In winter the supply comes from the northern coasts of Massachusetts and Maine, where they may be taken in moderately deep water at all seasons. According to Captain N. E. Atwood* they do not come into shallow water at Provincetown until June and remain there until October, when they disappear again. He also states that those that visit that locality are nearly all females; "they appear to come near the shore for the purpose of depositing their young, after which they pass away and others in turn take their places, as is indicated by the change that is constantly taking place, for when the fishermen are catching great quantities of large, good hard-shell lobsters, and they are unusually abundant, perhaps the next day there will be a new kind, smaller and not of so good quality, the former ones having passed away and others come to take their places." "In Boston the number of lobsters sold annually cannot be much short of a million. The male lobster is preferred and is the most salable, as this city has always been supplied from the northern shore of Massachusetts and coast of Maine, where the

* Proceedings Boston Society of Natural History, vol. x, p. 11, 1866.

males are most plentiful. It is a great advantage to the fishermen that the people prefer males. In New York it is very different in this particular, that city being supplied from Cape Cod after June, and the female lobster thus considered much the best. I have sold many lobsters in New York, and males sell at only about half price; the male is much poorer than the female in meat." Captain Atwood states, in the same place, that northward and eastward of Plymouth, Massachusetts, "three-quarters at least are males at all seasons of the year." Among those that I have examined from New London, Waterford, and Stonington, Connecticut, in our markets, I have not noticed any marked inequality in the number of the sexes. Mr. Smith examined the lobsters in the market at Provincetown on two occasions in August and September, without finding any decided differences in the number of males and females. He also repeatedly examined those in the fish-markets at Eastport, Maine, in summer, with the same result. It is possible therefore, that the fishermen do not correctly distinguish the sexes, when the females are without eggs, and that an erroneous opinion has thus become current among them.

There is a great difference in the breeding season on different parts of the coast. The lobsters from New London and Stonington often lay their eggs as early as the last of April or first of May; while at Halifax, Mr. Smith found females with recently laid eggs in September. At Eastport, Maine, the females carry their eggs in mid-summer. In the male the genital orifices are in the bases of the last pair of legs; in the female they are at the bases of the middle pair. This will always serve to distinguish the sexes, but they also differ in the structure of the abdominal appendages.

The rock-crab, *Cancer irroratus*, (p. 312,) is very common on these bottoms, and *C. borealis* (p. 395) also inhabits them, judging from the large dead specimens found on the adjacent beaches, but we only dredged a few small living specimens. One of these was taken on the reef between Watch Hill and Fisher's Island, in 4 or 5 fathoms, among algæ. It is more convex, and much more hairy than the preceding species, and the teeth along the sides of the carapax are quite different.

A large and handsomely colored shrimp, *Pandalus annulicornis* (Plate II, fig. 6,) often occurs in the deeper waters, outside, but is far more common farther north, as in the Bay of Fundy. The common shrimp, *Crangon vulgaris*, (p. 339, Plate III, fig. 10,) is common, especially where there are spots of sand among the rocks. The little bright-colored shrimp, *Hippolyte pusiola*, (p. 395,) is frequently met with among the red algæ. The *Unciola irrorata*, (p. 340, Plate IV, fig. 19,) and *Amphithoë maculata*, (p. 315, Plate IV, fig. 16,) together with several other Amphipods, are common, especially among the red algæ, and some of them are handsomely marked with red and other bright colors.

Among these are *Podocerus fucicola*, which is a small species and quite variable in color; some of those from the reef at Watch Hill had a transverse dorsal band of red or orange on each segment, and similar ones on the epimera, and were minutely specked with dark brown; the antennæ and legs were annulated with white and light red or orange. Another species of *Podocerus* was still more abundant among the red algæ; in this the males and females differ greatly in size, form, and color. The females are much smaller and stouter than the males; their colors were generally red and white, in strong contrast, though some were purplish and more like the males in color; most of the females have the head and few anterior segments dark red; then a band of white; then three or four bands of dark red, on the middle of the body, which are often confluent into a large dorsal spot of red or brown; these are followed by a broad white band or spot; the abdominal rings are alternately banded with red and white; part of the epimera are red. The antennæ and legs are more or less annulated and spotted with red. The eyes are black. In the male the color is generally reddish or purplish brown, but irregularly specked with darker brown, and with the intervals between the segments pale red.

Species of *Caprella* occur in considerable numbers, clinging, in grotesque attitudes, upon the delicate algæ and hydroids. The *Idotea irrorata*, (p. 316, Plate V, fig. 23,) is also very common, living among the algæ, and *Erichsonia filiformis* (p. 316, Plate VI, fig. 26,) is often associated with it.

The Annelids living upon such bottoms are difficult to obtain, since they mostly burrow beneath the stones or live in tubes attached to the rocks. The few species obtained are, with few exceptions, not different from those found in the sounds, on similar bottoms. The *Autolytus cornutus*, (p. 397, Plate XIII, figs. 65, 66,) and another species of the same genus were found in abundance, living in tubes attached to the fronds of *Laminaria* among hydroids, (*Obelia geniculata.*) On the same fronds were long, crooked tubes, formed of grains of sand and small bits of shells, belonging to *Nicolea simplex*, (p. 397.)

Burrowing in the corals of *Astrangia Danæ* we found, on the reef off Watch Hill, the singular Annelid named *Naraganseta coralii* by Dr. Leidy, who obtained his specimens at Point Judith. The specimens found by us were mostly very dark greenish brown or black, but some had dark, orange-colored branchiæ. The *Lepidonotus angustus*, *Phyllodoce gracilis*, *P. catenula*, and *Eumidia Americana* are new and interesting species. *Nereis fucata* occurs rarely.

Of Gastropods many species already enumerated as inhabitants of the rocky shores occur also on the rocky bottoms in abundance, but there are a number of additional species. One of the largest is the "whelk," *Buccinum undatum*, (Plate XXI, fig. 121.) This is a decidedly northern and arctic shell, found also on all the northern coasts of Europe, though several authors believe that the American and European shells are distinct species.

One of the most interesting of the northern shells that occur here is the *Leptochiton ruber*, (p. 399, Plate XXV, fig. 166.) This adheres to rocks and stones that are incrusted by the red nullipore *Lithothamnion polymorphum*, with which its red color, of various shades, agrees very closely. It is a far more abundant shell in the Bay of Fundy, where it also lives among the same nullipore. Among the other less common northern species, met with on these bottoms, are *Rissoa exarata; Lacuna neritoidea;* and *Astyris rosacea.*

Several very interesting species of naked mollusks (*Nudibranchs*) occur on these bottoms, creeping over algæ and hydroids, and feeding upon the latter. One of the most conspicuous of these is the *Dendronotus arborescens*, which is a northern form, and had not been found south of Cape Cod until this spring, when we dredged it on the reef off Watch Hill, in four or five fathoms. It can be easily distinguished by the two rows of large arborescently-branched gills along the back; by the branched lobes of the tentacle-sheaths and the arborescently divided branch on their outer side, near the base; and by the very narrow and almost linear foot, which is adapted for creeping over hydroids.

The *Onchydoris pallida* was dredged by Messrs. Prudden and Russell, off Cuttyhunk Island, in April, 1872. It has not been previously recorded from south of Cape Cod, but it is common in the Bay of Fundy. It can easily be recognized by its pale yellow color, and the long, blunt-conical papillæ that cover its back.

The *Æolis papillosa* and *Tergipes despectus* were both found at Watch Hill this spring, April 13, and are new additions to the fauna of southern New England. The former was found, with its eggs, among the roots of *Laminaria*; the latter was abundant in four or five fathoms, creeping over *Obelia geniculata*, which was abundant on the fronds of *Laminaria.* Its eggs, inclosed in small masses of gelatinous matter were attached to the *Obelia* in large numbers. The *Doto coronata*, (Plate XXV, fig. 170,) was associated with the *Tergipes* on the *Obelia.* An undetermined species of *Æolis*, with bright red branchiæ, was dredged off Gay Head, on a rocky bottom.

The Lamellibranchs are not of much interest, and scarcely any are peculiar to this kind of bottom. The *Modiola modiolus* (p. 309, Plate XXXI, fig. 237) is one of the most common and characteristic species. The northern scaly or spiny *Anomia aculeata* (Plate XXXII, figs. 239, 240) is common; it adheres to rocks, shells, and the roots and stems of large algæ.

Among the Ascidians there are several northern species, not before found so far south. The *Cynthia carnea* (Plate XXXIII, figs. 247, 248) was found off Gay Head in ten fathoms. The young specimens were numerous on the stones and shells. In contraction they are low and flat, with a thin margin; the color is light red, or flesh-color. With this a few young specimens of *Cynthia echinata* were found. These are peculiar in being covered by stellate spines. The color of the young specimens is pink, the apertures rose-red. The *Molgula papillosa* also occurred sparingly with the last two species. This is also a northern species, common in the Bay of Fundy. Among the compound Ascidians the only species found here that did not occur also in Vineyard Sound was *Amarœcium pallidum*, a small species, which forms small rounded or turbinated whitish masses, of a firm gelatinous appearance, but with fine grains of sand imbedded in the substance. It is a common species in the Bay of Fundy.

The Bryozoa are represented by numerous species, some of which are very abundant. The *Membranipora pilosa* (Plate XXXIV, figs. 262, 263) is one of the most abundant. It incrusts, and often entirely covers, the fronds of various algæ, especially of *Phyllophora Brodiæi*, *P. membranifolia*, *Rhodymenia palmata*, *Delesseria sinuosa*, &c. On the reef off Watch Hill it was particularly abundant on these and other algæ, shells, &c. It is easily distinguished by the single long spine at the proximal end of the cell, and by the shorter ones along the sides. With the preceding, *Crisia eburnea*, (p. 311, Plate XXXIV, figs. 260, 261;) *Tubulipora flabellaris*; *Cellepora ramulosa*, (p. 312;) and a species of *Discopora*, allied to *D. coccinea*, were very abundant, adhering to the more slender red algæ. A species of *Lepralia*, of a reddish color, and forming both incrusting and lichen-like corals, was common. In this the apertures of the cells are large, operculated, broadest proximally, and each one has a short, stout, conical spine at its proximal border, which is scarcely visible except in a profile view.

The *Bugula Murrayana*, which forms clusters of broad, thin, flexible fronds nearly two inches high, was dredged several times. It is very common in the Bay of Fundy. An incrusting species of *Alcyonidium*, perhaps identical with *A. gelatinosum* of Europe, occurred on the red algæ. A species of *Cellularia*, allied to *A. ternata*, was also obtained.

The Echinoderms are represented by the common green sea-urchin, *Strongylocentrotus Dröbachiensis*, (p. 406, Plate XXXV, fig. 268,) which is common off Gay Head, and as far as off New London, though far less abundant than in the Bay of Fundy; by the common red or purple star-fish, *Asterias vulgaris*, (p. 407,) which was abundant off Gay Head and on the reef off Watch Hill; *Cribrella sanguinolenta*, (p. 407,) which is not uncommon as far west as the Watch Hill reef, and off New London; and by the *Ophiopholis aculeata*, (Plate XXXV, fig. 270,) which was only once met with off Gay Head, but of which we dredged several specimens on the reef off Watch Hill. The last-named species is extremely abundant in the Bay of Fundy and northward, from low-water to the depth of more than one hundred fathoms.

The Hydroids are very numerous on the rocky and stony bottoms, attached to algæ, stones, shells, ascidians, &c. One of the most abundant is *Obelia geniculata*, (p. 407,) which grows on the fronds of *Laminaria*, *Rhodymenia*, and other algæ; it often nearly covers one or both sides of the broad fronds of *Laminaria*, for the distance of two or three feet, the creeping stems forming an intricate net-work from which the upright stems arise in great abundance to the height of an inch or more. This species was particularly abundant on the reef off Watch Hill, and those obtained on the 13th of April were loaded with the reproductive capsules, (gonothecæ.)

At the same place we obtained luxuriant specimens of *O. flabellata*, (p. 390,) some of which were eight or ten inches long and profusely branched; these also bore reproductive capsules at the same date.

The curious *Antennularia antennina* was dredged off Gay Head in eight fathoms, where a number of large and fine specimens were obtained. This species had not been previously recorded from America, but it is not uncommon in the Bay of Fundy.

The Alcyonoid Polyps are represented by the northern *Alcyonium carneum*, (Plate XXXVIII, fig. 283,) which we dredged off Gay Head, off Cuttyhunk, and on the reef at Watch Hill. This species grows up into lobed or arborescently branched forms, with the delicate, translucent polyps mostly clustered toward the ends of the branches. The general color is translucent, pale yellow, or salmon, sometimes more or less tinged with orange or red. Among the Actinoids there is a species of *Edwardsia*, (*E. lineata* V.,) which is as yet undescribed. It occurred in considerable numbers crowded into the openings and interstices between ascidians, worm-tubes, &c. It is peculiar in having no distinct naked basal portion, at least in the numerous specimens hitherto seen, for in all cases the rough epidermis extended entirely over the base. The tentacles are long, slender, thirty or more, and each usually has a flake-white line down the center. The disk is usually marked with radiating white lines. This species was dredged off Gay Head and also on the reef off Watch Hill.

The Sponges are numerous on the outer rocky bottoms, and belong to about a dozen species, most of which are still undetermined; but they are nearly all northern forms, common in the Bay of Fundy.

One of the most common is the *Chalina oculata*, which forms thick, upright, more or less flattened stalks, which, as they grow larger, fork and divide into more or less numerous, and often digitate branches, which vary greatly in form and thickness; scattered over the surface are round orifices, about a tenth of an inch in diameter. The color is dull orange-red, when living, but the color disappears when the animal matter is removed, leaving the sponge white. The texture is open and quite delicate. Another very curious species, (*Polymastia?*) when young, forms yellowish white incrustations over stones and shells; later, it rises at several points into long, slender, round, tapering, finger-like prolongations, which do not branch, but are often so grouped as to give a digitate appearance to the whole. This was dredged off Gay Head in 18 to 20 fathoms, and is also common in the Bay of Fundy. One of the most abundant species of this region forms very irregularly shaped, uneven, pale yellow masses, attached to the stems and fronds of *Phyllophora* and other small algæ, and often, as it grows larger, spreading over and entirely covering and destroying the algæ. The large openings (oscula) are irregularly scattered over the surface and quite unequal in size, varying from less than .05 to .10 of an inch or more in diameter. The texture is rather close when dried, showing a finely reticulated texture at the surface. This appears to belong to the genus *Tedania*. Another species, apparently of the same genus, occurs with the last, and has the same habits, but its color is pale buff, or yellowish white, and its texture is much firmer and more compact. Another species, occurring with the last two on the *Phyllophora*, at Watch Hill, forms small, irregular, deep yellow masses, of a soft and somewhat gelatinous consistency.

Foraminifera of several species are abundant, attached to the fronds of the red algæ, to the rough integument of Ascidians, to stones, shells, worm-tubes, &c., but they have not yet been identified.

List of species inhabiting the stony and rocky bottoms on the open coast.

ARTICULATA.

Crustacea.

	Page.		Page.
Cancer irroratus	493	Mœra levis	315
C. borealis	493	Amphithoë maculata	493
Libinia canaliculata	339	Unciola irrorata	493
Eupagurus longicarpus	313	Cerapus rubricornis	565
E. Bernhardus	501	Podocerus fucicola	493
Homarus Americanus	492	Podocerus, species	494
Crangon vulgaris	493	Caprella, species	494
Hippolyte pusiola	493	Idotea irrorata	494
Pandalus annulicornis	493	I. phosphorea	316
Lysianassinæ, (one species)	431	Erichsonia filiformis	494
Pontogeneia inermis	452	Balanus crenatus	396

Annelids.

	Page.		Page.
Lepidonotus squamatus	320	Clymenella torquata	343
L. Augustus	494	Naraganseta coralii	494
Harmothoë imbricata	321	Sabellaria vulgaris	321
Phyllodoce gracilis	494	Polycirrus eximius	320
P. catenula	494	Nicolea simplex	494
Eumidia Americana	494	Potamilla oculifera	322
Autolytus cornutus	494	Sabella microphthalma	323
Autolytus, species	494	Spirorbis spirillum	323
Nereis pelagica	319	S. porrecta?	504
N. fucata	494	Serpula dianthus	322
Lumbriconereis fragilis	501		

Nemerteans and Planarians.

	Page.		Page.
Nemertes, species	505	Leptoplana folium	487

MOLLUSCA.

Gastropods.

Lamellibranchs.

Ascidians.

Bryozoa.

RADIATES.

Echinoderms.

	Page.		Page.
Strongylocentrotus Dröbachiensis	496	A. arenicola	326
Asterias vulgaris	496	Cribrella sanguinolenta	496
		Ophiopholis aculeata	496

Acalephs.

	Page.		Page.
Clytia Johnstoni	408	Sertularia argentea	408
C. intermedia	408	S. cupressina	408
Orthopyxis caliculata	408	Hydrallmania falcata	408
Platypyxis cylindrica	408	Plumularia, species	407
Campanularia volubilis	408	Antennularia antennina	497
C. flexuosa	327	Eudendrium ramosum	408
Obelia geniculata	496	E. dispar	408
O. dichotoma	407	Pennaria tiarella	327
O. flabellata	497	Thamnocnidia tenella	407
O. diaphana	327	Hydractinia polyclina	328

Polyps.

	Page.		Page.
Alcyonium carneum	497	Edwardsia lineata	497
Metridium marginatum	329	Astrangia Danæ	408

PROTOZOA.

Sponges.

	Page.		Page.
Chalina oculata	497	Polymastia (?)	497
Tedania, two species	498	Grantia ciliata	330
Renieria, species	330	Leucosolenia botryoides (?)	391
Cliona sulphurea	421		

IV. 4.—FAUNA OF THE SANDY AND GRAVELLY BOTTOMS OFF THE OPEN COAST.

The bottom off the southern shores of Nantucket and Martha's Vineyard is sandy or gravelly over large areas, from low-water mark down to 25 fathoms or more. Tracts of similar bottom occur off Cuttyhunk Island and farther west. In many of these places, especially in the shallower waters, near shore, the material of the bottom is nearly pure siliceous sand, varying in fineness from coarse gravel to the finest sand, and as these sands are generally loose and moved by the storm-waves, in shallow water, their inhabitants are but few. In deeper water, at depths of 20 to 25 fathoms or more, the material is usually a very fine sand, often firmly compacted, and not infrequently mixed with more or less fine mud. Such localities are favorable for a much greater variety of animals, and especially for many burrowing annelids, crustacea, and bivalve shells. Bottoms of this character pass by insensible gradations into the true muddy bottoms, so that it is very difficult to make any sharp distinction between them, or between the animals that inhabit them. Several localities at which we dredged were quite intermediate in character, so that it is difficult to decide in which division they should be put. Yet there is a very wide difference between the animals of the pure sandy and of the soft muddy bottoms. Most of the localities where the bottom was of this mixed or intermediate character, and of very fine material, have been classed with the muddy bottoms, because the animals inhabiting them agree more closely with those of the true muddy bottoms than with those of the genuine sandy ones. But in each case I shall endeavor to give an idea of the fauna of typical localities of pure sand, of true mud, of muddy sand, and of sandy mud, so that the more general lists given under the sandy and muddy bottoms, respectively, need not cause confusion.

The special localities where dredgings were made on sandy bottoms are as follows: line 80, *a*, 16½ fathoms, siliceous sand; *b*, 18½ fathoms, siliceous sand; 81, *a*, *b*, 16½ fathoms, sand; 85, *a*, *b*, 15½ fathoms, siliceous sand and gravel; 86, *a*, *b*, 25 fathoms, sand and gravel, with some mud and small stones; off Watch Hill, 6 to 8 fathoms, loose siliceous sand, with some stones. Besides these a few other dredgings were made on similar bottoms, but not recorded.

Among the Crustacea that are characteristic of the true sandy bottoms are *Platyonichus ocellatus*, (p. 388, Plate I, fig. 4,) which is, however, more common in the sounds; *Eupagurus Bernhardus*, a decidedly northern hermit crab; *Crangon vulgaris*, (p. 339, Plate III, fig. 10;) *Ptilocheirus pinguis; Idotea Tuftsii.* Where the bottom is of loose siliceous sand, the common *Unciola irrorata* (p. 340, Plate IV, fig. 19) frequently occurs, usually associated with but few others, except a species of *Anonyx*, or some closely allied genus, which seems to live exclusively on such bottoms. This last species is rather stout, pale grayish or yellowish white, usually tinged with purple on the back The posterior portion is more decidedly purple, together with the caudal appendages and some of the last epimera. This was dredged off Watch Hill.

Several interesting species occurred on the bottoms of fine compact mud and sand, in 20–29 fathoms. Among these were *Phoxus Kroyeri*, which is a northern species; *Siphonœcetes cuspidatus* SMITH, an undescribed species; *Byblis serrata* SMITH, another very interesting new species; undetermined species of *Ampelisca*, &c.

Few Annelids are peculiar to true sandy bottoms. Among those of most interest are *Sthenelais picta* V., (p. 348;) *Lumbriconereis fragilis*, a northern and European species; *Anthostoma acutum* V.; and *Scolecolepis cirrata*. The last is a northern species found in the Bay of Fundy and north to the Arctic Ocean, and also on the northern coasts of Europe.

The color is chocolate-brown, with bright red, ligulate, dorsal branchiæ on the anterior third of the body. The two large tentacles exceed in length three times the breadth of the body; they are often coiled up, and are greenish in color. This worm is three or four inches long.

A large purple *Meckelia* (*M. lurida* V.) was dredged in two localities.

Among the Mollusks there are but few species that are characteristic of these bottoms, and probably none that are peculiar to them, unless some of the Ascidians should prove to be so. The *Molgula arenata* (p. 426, Plate XXXIII, fig. 251) is often common even on loose siliceous sand and gravel, with which it forms a coating over its body. The *Molgula producta* was dredged in some numbers on a bottom of fine sand, with some mud. The integument is thin, translucent, closely covered with a layer of fine sand; the tubes are transparent, whitish or flesh-color, sometimes pink at the ends; anal tube with four, and branchial with six, flake-white, longitudinal stripes, and often with a circle of flake-white spots at the base outside, and other spots within. The anal orifice is square, but the branchial is either subcircular or squarish, in expansion, and destitute of distinct lobes or papillæ, in this respect differing from all the other species of the genus. The branchial tube is generally a little the longest, and both of them are somewhat tapered, with a swollen base.

The *Glandula arenicola* is another nearly globular Ascidian, which lives, like the two preceding, free in the sand, and covers itself with a closely-adherent coating of sand. This species grows to be about half an inch in diameter, and can easily be distinguished from the last by its much smaller tubes, both of which have small square orifices, and by its thicker and firmer integument, in which the sand appears to be somewhat imbedded. At the base there are some slender fibers for anchoring it more securely in the sand. This was dredged by Mr. Prudden, off Cuttyhunk Island, in 1872. Messrs. Smith and Harger dredged it in great abundance last year on St. George's Bank, on a bottom of clear siliceous sand, in 28 fathoms. Dr. Dawson has also dredged it in Murray Bay, in the St. Lawrence River. It is, therefore, a decidedly northern species.

Another species of *Glandula* also occurred on the true sandy bottoms. The specimens of this were all small, mostly less than a fifth of an inch in diameter, and the integument was densely covered by rather coarse and very firmly adherent grains of sand, in several layers; the sand completely concealed the tubes from view in all the specimens observed, and it was not sufficiently studied while living to afford an accurate description.

The Bryozoa and Hydroids that are found on the sandy bottoms are mostly attached to dead shells and small stones that are scattered over the surface.

Of Echinoderms several species occur on the hard bottoms of fine, compact sand, or sandy mud, but most of these are more at home on rocky bottoms.

On the bottoms of loose siliceous sand the *Echinarachnius parma* (p. 362, Plate XXXV, fig. 267) is often very abundant. Several hundred are sometimes obtained at a single cast of the dredge. At locality 81, *b*, off the south coast of Martha's Vineyard, in 21 fathoms, on a bottom of clear siliceous sand, Dr. A. S. Packard dredged a fine specimen of a rare and little known Holothurian, the *Stereoderma unisemita*. This has not been found before, so far as known to me, since the two original specimens were described twenty years ago. One of those was from the Banks of Newfoundland, and the other was supposed to have been from off Massachusetts Bay. As both the original specimens appear to have been lost or destroyed, this rediscovery was of considerable interest. This specimen was about three inches long, and half an inch in diameter, fusiform, tapering to each end; the body and suckers were pale flesh-color, and the integument is filled with a great abundance of small calcareous plates.

Most of the Polyps and Sponges that occur on these sandy bottoms are attached to the scattering dead shells and small stones or pebbles, and belong properly on the rocky and stony bottoms. One large and fine sponge seems, however, to be peculiar to the sandy bottoms. This is a firm, siliceous sponge, with a very compact and fine texture. It is quite irregular in shape, but often grows in the form of elongated, compressed masses, attached by one edge; these masses are often six inches or more in length and one or two in thickness, and perhaps two or three high. Some of the largest specimens consist of two or three such crest-like plates or lobes attached together at base. When living the color is bright sulphur-yellow or lemon-yellow, and the surface is nearly smooth. One fine living specimen, of large size, was dredged by Dr. Packard off the southern shore of Martha's Vineyard, at locality 80, *b*, on a bottom of clear siliceous sand. Numerous specimens were also found thrown on Edgartown beach. These were mostly bleached out white and more or less worn. This species has not yet been identified. I have specimens of it from the coast of Virginia.

A very curious organism, of which the nature is still uncertain, but which was supposed, at the time it was taken, to belong to the sandy Foraminifera, was often extremely abundant in the clear siliceous sand. They were nearly circular, somewhat flattened or biscuit-shaped, and entirely covered by adherent grains of sand, except that there were several dark-colored, hook-like processes projecting from the circumference. The size was generally less than a fifth of an inch in diameter, and more frequently not more than .12 to .15 of an inch. When dried they became very friable, and the sand fell asunder at a slight touch, so that they then appeared like mere lumps of sand, but they retain their firmness when preserved in alcohol. They were often so abundant in the fine sand that when a dredge-full was washed through a moderately fine sieve several hundreds or thousands would sometimes remain in the sieve.

List of species inhabiting sandy and gravelly bottoms.

In the following list I have included nearly all the species that ordinarily occurred on those bottoms in which sand predominated, even though some of them are more strictly muddy-bottom species. Others belong more properly on rocky, stony, or shelly bottoms, but are introduced here because they occur attached to the scattered shells and stones that are always liable to be met with on sandy bottoms.

In order to designate those species that are more strictly characteristic of the clear sandy bottoms, I have prefixed to them a dagger, (thus: †.) To show the character of the fauna on the bottoms of mixed or intermediate character, I have selected a single locality, 86, *b*, southwest of Cuttyhunk Island and opposite the mouth of Buzzard's Bay, where the depth was twenty-five fathoms, and the bottom consisted of fine sand mixed with some mud and gravel, with a few small scattered stones, and have prefixed an asterisk (thus: *) to such species as occurred at that particular locality, though most of them occurred also at other localities.

ARTICULATES.

Crustacea.

	Page.		Page.
†Cancer irroratus	312	*Phoxus Kroyeri	501
C. borealis	493	*Ampelisca, sp	507
Panopeus depressus	312	Byblis serrata	501
†Platyonichus ocellatus	501	Mœra levis	315
Hyas coarctatus	548	*†Unciola irrorata	501
†Eupagurus pollicaris	313	*Ptilocheirus pinguis	501
†E. Bernhardus	501	†Anonyx (?), sp	501
†Homarus Americanus	492	*Siphonœcetes cuspidatus	501
*Pandalus annulicornis	493	†Idotea Tuftsii	501
†*Crangon vulgaris	501	Epelys montosus	370
*Diastylis quadrispinosa, and other species of Cumacea	507		

Annelids.

	Page.		Page.
Lepidonotus squamatus	320	†*Scolecolepis cirrata	501
*Harmothoë imbricata	321	*Ampharete gracilis	508
†Sthenelais picta	501	†*Clymenella torquata	343
*Nephthys ingens	431	*Nicomache dispar	512
Phyllodoce catenula	494	*Ammochares, sp	508
Nereis plagica	397	*Trophonia affinis	507
*Ninoë nigripes	508	*Ammotrypane fimbriata	508
†Lumbriconeris fragilis	501	*Cistenides Gouldii	323
*Rhynchobolus dibranchiatus	341	*Potamilla oculifera	322
†Anthostoma acutum	501	*Euchone elegans	433
		*Spirorbis porrecta?	498

Nemerteans and Planarians.

	Page.		Page.
*Meckelia lurida	502	*Leptoplana folium	487
Nemertes, (?) red sp.	498		

Sipunculoids.

	Page.
*Phascolosoma cæmentarium	416

MOLLUSCA.

Gastropods.

	Page.		Page.
*Neptunea pygmæa	508	Crepidula fornicata	355
Buccinum undatum	494	C. unguiformis	355
Astyris lunata	306	†Lunatia heros	426
Anachis avara	306	Rissoa exarata	495
†*Tritia trivittata	354	*Margarita obscura	508
*Crucibulum striatum	417		

Lamellibranchs.

	Page.		Page.
†Mya arenaria, (young)	472	†Astarte castanea	432
†*Ensatella Americana	356	†A. quadrans	509
†Siliqua costata	358	*A. undata	508
Corbula contracta	418	†*Cyclocardia borealis	418
Clidiophora trilineata	432	†*C. Novangliæ	418
*Lyonsia hyalina	358	*Yoldia sapotilla	509
*Periploma papyracea	509	*Nucula proxima	432
Cochlodesma Leanum	418	Scapharca transversa	309
†Angulus tener	358	*Modiolaria corrugata	509
*Cumingia tellinoides	418	Pecten tenuicostatus	509
*Callista convexa	432	Anomia aculeata	495
*Cardium pinnulatum	423		

Ascidians.

	Page.		Page.
*Cynthia partita	311	†Glandula arenicola	502
†Molgula arenata	502	†Glandula, sp.	502
†*M. producta	502	*Amarœcium pallidum	496
*M. Manhattensis	311		

Bryozoa.

	Page.		Page.
*Crisia eburnea	311	Bugula Murrayana	496
*Caberea Ellisii	420	*Cellepora ramulosa	312

RADIATA.

Echinoderms.

	Page.		Page.
†Stereoderma unisemita.....	503	Asterias vulgaris..........	496
†*Echinarachnius parma....	503	*Cribrella sanguinolenta...	407
Strongylocentrotus Dröbachiensis	406	Ophiopholis aculeata......	496

Acalephs.

	Page.		Page.
*Platypyxis cylindrica.......	408	*Plumularia, sp...........	407
*Clytia Johnstoni..........	408	Hydractinia polyclina.....	328
Eudendrium ramosum......	408		

Polyps.

	Page.		Page.
Edwardsia lineata..........	497	Alcyonium carneum.......	497

PROTOZOA.

Sponges.

	Page.		Page.
Chalina oculata............	497	†Massive siliceous sponge ..	503
Polymastia (?)	497		

IV. 5.—FAUNA OF THE MUDDY BOTTOMS OFF THE OPEN COAST.

Within the depths to which our dredgings extended, very few true muddy bottoms occur. The deposits of mud on the open coast usually begin to occur only at the depths of twenty-five to thirty fathoms, and even at these depths there is a considerable admixture with fine siliceous sand. The central and deeper portion of the depression in line with the axis of Vineyard Sound is, however, occupied off to the west of Gay Head and No Man's Land by a deposit of fine, soft, sticky mud, filled with the tubes of Annelids and Amphipods, (*Ampelisca*, &c.) Dredgings were made on this bottom at localities 85, *c*, in 18 fathoms; *d*, 19 fathoms; *e*, 11 fathoms. On September 9, the temperature at 85, *c*, was 58° Fahrenheit at the bottom, and 62° at the surface; at *d*, it was 57° at the bottom and 62° at the surface; at *e*, it was 59° at the bottom and 63° at the surface. This muddy bottom abounded in Annelids, small Crustacea, and bivalve shells.

In several other localities, where the bottom was a mixture of mud and fine sand, the mud seemed to predominate and to determine the character of the life, so that such localities have been classed with the muddy bottoms, though the fauna differed considerably from that of the soft muddy bottoms referred to above. In the following list, however, I have specially designated the species found in the typical localities of each kind.

The principal localities where we dredged on the bottoms of fine sandy mud are as follows: 80, *c*, south of Martha's Vineyard, in 21 fathoms; 84, *b*, southwest of Gay Head, in 16 fathoms; 87, *a*, *b*, about fifteen miles east of Block Island, in 29 fathoms. At the last locality the temperature, on September 14, was 62° F. at the surface, and 59° at the bottom.

Among the Crustacea none was more abundant on the soft, muddy bottoms than a small species of *Ampelisca*, which inhabits soft, flabby tubes, covered with fine mud. When taken out of the water these tubes are always collapsed and flat, and they were so abundant in the mud that it was almost impossible to wash it through the sieves, because they soon became completely clogged up with the tubes. When a quantity of the mud was left in a bucket of water these Crustacea would come out of the tubes and rise to the surface in large numbers. This species is generally quite pale, or nearly white. Its body is much compressed.

Another variety, or perhaps a distinct species, found with the last, is pale flesh-color, with a row of bright red spots along the middle of the back; the antennæ were specked with red; eyes bright red; epimera reticulated with red lines; and the legs and caudal appendages are more or less marked with red.

The *Unciola irrorata*, (p. 340,) *Ptilocheirus pinguis*, and other Amphipods, were associated with the preceding species.

The *Diastylis quadrispinosa* (Plate III, fig. 13) was very abundant on the soft muddy bottoms, together with other species of Cumacea, not yet identified. It is pale flesh-color, with a reddish purple patch at the posterior part of the carapax, and two small spots of pink.

The Annelids were very numerous, both on the soft muddy bottoms and in the sandy mud. One of the most conspicuous species is the *Aphrodita aculeata*, which was common in the soft mud. This is a large, stout Annelid, the largest specimen obtained measuring about 3 inches in length, and about half as much in breadth. It is remarkable for the exceedingly numerous and long setæ of many kinds, which cover its sides and back, except along a narrow dorsal space; some of these setæ are stout, and nearly an inch long, with sharp points, and barbed near the end, and they curve over the back much like the quills of a porcupine, and are liable to inflict painful wounds, if the creatures are carelessly handled. These setæ usually reflect bright, iridescent colors.

Several other northern European species, found also in the Bay of Fundy and at Saint George's Banks, were also met with. Among these were *Lumbriconereis fragilis*, *Scolecolepis cirrata*, *Melinna cristata*, *Terebellides Stroëmi*, and several more common species.

The *Nephthys ingens* (p. 431, Plate XII, figs. 59–60) is a very abundant species on these bottoms and grows to a large size.

The curious *Sternaspis fossor* (Plate XIV, fig. 74) is quite common; and the *Trophonia affinis* (Plate XIV, fig. 75) was dredged several times.

Many other species were also common, or even abundant, in the various localities, and quite a number proved to be undescribed, and therefore their descriptions will be found in the systematic catalogue accompanying this report. Among these were *Lycidice Americana*, *Ninoë nigripes*, *Anthostoma*, sp., *Acutum*, *Ammotrypane fimbriata*, *Travisia carnea*, Eone gracilis, *Brada setosa*, *Nicomache dispar*, *Rhodine attenuata*, a species of *Ammochares*, *Ampharete gracilis*, *Euchone elegans*, and a species of *Nematonereis*.

Several species of *Nemerteans* also occur on these bottoms. The largest and most interesting is a large species of *Meckelia*, (*M. lurida*, V.) This grows to the length of 8 or 10 inches, and .25 broad; its color is deep chocolate-brown, with paler margins. It generally breaks up into numerous fragments when caught. Another species, belonging, perhaps, to the genus *Cerebratulus*, but not sufficiently studied while living, was 2 or 3 inches long in extension, and .05 to .08 of an inch broad. Its color was dark olive-green, darkest anteriorly, the head with a white margin. The lateral fossæ of the head were long and deep; the eyes inconspicuous, perhaps wanting; proboscis emitted from a terminal pore; the ventral orifice, or mouth, placed well forward. Both this and the preceding were found at the 29-fathom locality, in sandy mud, but the former also occurred in soft mud, in 19 fathoms.

One of the most abundant Gastropods is *Neptunea pygmæa*, (Plate XXI, fig. 115,) which is a rather northern shell, very common in the Bay of Fundy. The specimens from this region are, however, quite as large as any that I have seen from farther north. The small disk-shaped egg-capsules of this shell were found in great abundance early in September attached to various bivalve shells, as well as to the shells of the *Neptunea* itself.

Buccinum undatum, (Plate XXI, Fig. 121;) *Bela harpularia*, (Plate XXI, fig. 108;) *Lunatia immaculata*, (Plate XXIII, fig. 131;) *Margarita obscura*, (Plate XXIV, fig. 156;) *Astyris rosacea;* and *Cylichna alba*, (Plate XXV, fig. 163,) are all northern shells, which were met with in small numbers on the muddy bottoms.

The Lamellibranchs were quite abundant. One of the most conspicuous is the northern *Cyprina Islandica*, (Plate XXVIII, fig. 201,) which was quite common at several localities, especially in soft mud.

Many of the shells from the deeper dredgings in this region are northern and even arctic species, several of which have been supposed not to occur south of Cape Cod. Among these northern forms are *Macoma proxima*, of which we dredged a few small specimens; *Cyclocardia borealis* and *C. Novangliæ* (p. 418,) both of which were common; *Astarte undata*, (Plate XXIX, fig. 203,) which was dredged in considerable abundance at several localities. A large proportion of the shells of this species, obtained here, were quite different in appearance from the varieties that occur in such abundance in the Bay of Fundy. The latter,

Fig. 3.

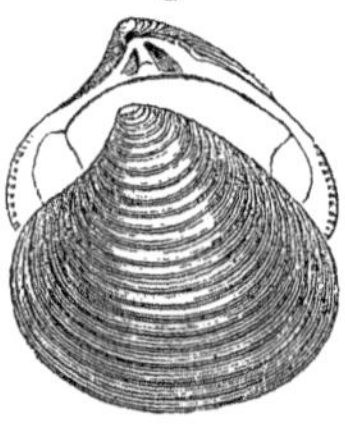

although quite variable in form and sculpture, are generally compressed; those from this region are mostly rather swollen, and often decidedly obese. These correspond with the type-specimen of *A. lutea* PERKINS, from New Haven, (fig. 3,) which I have been able, through the kindness of Dr. Perkins, to compare directly with our specimens. This form is, perhaps, sufficiently well marked to be designated a sa variety, (*lutea*,) but many specimens intermediate between this and the ordinary forms occurred. This variety resembles the European *A. sulcata* more closely than do any of the other varieties of our species, but in the character of the hinge, lunule, beaks, and sculpture, it differs decidedly from any European specimens that I have seen. The *Astarte quadrans* (Plate XXIX, fig. 205) was rarely met with. Good-sized specimens of the large scollop, *Pecten tenuicostatus*, were dredged off Gay Head on hard bottoms, and also on the muddy bottom, in 29 fathoms, and in several other localities. The northern *Anomia aculeata* (Plate XXXII, figs. 239, 240) occurred adhering to dead shells. The *Modiolaria corrugata* (Plate XXXI, fig. 235) was dredged several times in the deepest localities, but *M. lævigata*, recorded by Mr. Sanderson Smith, was not met with by us; nor *Leda tenuisulcata*, which has been found off Newport, Rhode Island. The *Nucula delphinodonta* (Plate XXX, fig. 229) was common on soft muddy bottoms. The *Lucina filosa* (Plate XXIX, fig. 212) appeared to be not uncommon on similar bottoms, but most of the specimens obtained were less than an inch in diameter. Small specimens of *Periploma papyracea* (Plate XXVII, fig. 197) were frequently dredged. The specimens of *Thracia truncata* (Plate XXVII, fig. 195) were few and small. The *Cryptodon obesus* V., (Plate XXIX, fig. 214,) was first discovered in this region, but all the specimens were of large size and dead, though mostly quite fresh. I have since seen smaller specimens from Labrador, &c. *C. Gouldii* (Plate xxix, fig. 213,) is more common. *Yoldia sapotilla* (Plate XXX, fig. 231) was generally abundant, especially in the soft mud, but *Y. obesa* was only met with once, and in small numbers, in 29 fathoms; *Y. thraci-formis* we did not meet with, but Dr. Simpson records it from off Long Island.

Of Ascidians very few species occur. The most abundant is *Eugyra pilularis*, (Plate XXXIII, fig. 249,) which, in contraction, looks like a round ball of mud, for it completely covers itself with a thick coating of fine sand or mud, which is held in place partly by delicate fibrous processes from the integument, those from the base being longer, and serving to anchor the little creature in the sand by attaching a considerable quantity of sand to themselves. When the sand is removed, the integument is found to be thin and quite translucent, the tubes, when extended, are long and transparent, close together, and inclosed by a naked band which surrounds the base of both. It is also very

Figure 3. Original figure of *Astarte lutea*, natural size. From the Proceedings of the Boston Society of Natural History.

common in the Bay of Fundy, &c. The *Molgula producta* (p. 502) also occurred on the sandy mud at the 29-fathom locality.

The Echinoderms appear to be very scarce on these bottoms. The only one of special interest was the *Molpadia oölitica*, a small, round, rather slender species, about an inch and a half long, of a uniform flesh-color. Of this only one specimen was dredged, at the 29-fathom locality, fifteen miles east of No Man's Land, by Dr. Packard. It had not been observed alive before, the only specimens previously known having been taken from the stomachs of fishes.

The most interesting Hydroid that lives on the muddy bottoms is *Corymorpha pendula*, (Plate XXXVI, fig. 273.) This is a very beautiful species, which grows singly, with the bulb-like base of the stem inserted into the mud.

Two interesting species of Polyps were found on the muddy bottoms. One of these, the *Edwardsia farinacea*, occurred only on the soft muddy bottom off Gay Head, in 19 fathoms. It is a cylindrical species, about an inch long, and .10 or .12 of an inch in diameter, remarkable for having only 12 tentacles, which are equal, unusually short, thick, and blunt. The coating of mud in the middle region is thin and easily removed.

The single specimen obtained here had only 10 tentacles, but in other respects it agrees essentially with those found on similar bottoms at several localities in the Bay of Fundy, all of which had 12 tentacles. The body is whitish or flesh-color, the naked portion below the tentacles; in the specimen from off Gay Head, was striped with 10 longitudinal lines or bands of brown, corresponding with the tentacles; these bands were varied with flake-white specks and mottlings, the spots of white becoming more distinct near the tentacles; these bands were alternately lighter and darker. Tentacles translucent at tip, tranversely barred on the inside, with about five brown bands and spots, the lower ones often V-shaped or W-shaped, and some of them extend around to the outside of the tentacles; alternating with these brown bands were bars and spots of yellow and of white. The disk was pale yellow, varied with small brown spots, mostly forming radiating rows from the mouth to the bases of the tentacles, and there were two spots of brown between the bases of adjacent tentacles; mouth with ten lobes, which were also brown, with a fine light line extending from between them to the intervals between the tentacles. The specimens from the Bay of Fundy vary considerably in color, but the above is one of the more frequent styles of coloration.

The *Epizoanthus Americanus* (Plate XXXVIII, figs. 286, 287) is a very singular species, which either lives attached to stones, as in the deeper parts of the Bay of Fundy and off Saint George's Bank, in 430 fathoms, or else it attaches itself to univalve shells, inhabited by hermit-crabs. All those obtained in this region had the latter habit, and were from the 29-fathom place, fifteen miles east of Block Island, on sandy mud. After one original young polyp has found lodgment and attached itself to the shell, its base begins to expand over the surface of the shell, and from this basal membrane buds arise, which soon grow larger and become like the parent polyp, while the basal membrane continues to extend itself and new buds to develop, until the whole shell becomes incrusted by the membrane, inside and out, while a number of beautiful polyps arise from the upper side of the shell, and turn their mouths in different directions. The number of the polyps in these colonies varies, according to the size of the shell, from three to ten or more. Finally, by some chemical process, the polyps, or rather their basal membranes, dissolve the shell entirely, and apparently absorb it into themselves. And yet the membranes retain the spiral form of the shell very perfectly, and the hermit crab eventually actually lives inside the membranes of the polyps, which continue to grow and even to enlarge the chamber for the use of the crab, so that it need not change its habitation for a larger one as it grows older. When fully expanded these polyps are about an inch high, and are capable of changing their form considerably, but they are generally more or less cylindrical, or else hour-glass shaped. There are 38 or more tentacles, in full grown ones, and they are subequal, long, slender, acute, arranged in two close circles, and usually held in a recurved position, (as in fig. 287,) with those of the outer circle more recurved than those of the inner ones; corresponding with the bases of the alternate tentacles there is an outer circle of triangular points or lobes, covered externally, like the rest of the exterior of the body, with adherent and imbedded grains of fine sand. The mouth is bilabiate, often somewhat raised on a conical protrusion of the disk, the lips many-lobed, or plicate. The integument of the body when fully expanded is translucent, pale flesh-color, or salmon-color; disk and tentacles salmon-color, or pale orange, sometimes white, the lips and inside of the mouth brighter orange.

List of species inhabiting bottoms composed of soft mud and sandy mud off the outer coast.

In the following list those species that were found on the soft, sticky mud, in 11 to 19 fathoms, off Gay Head, are designated by the sign ‡, prefixed to their names. Those that occurred at 87, *a*, *b*, in 29 fathoms, fine sandy mud, fifteen miles east of Block Island, are designated by an asterisk prefixed.

ARTICULATA.

Crustacea.

	Page.		Page.
‡ Libinia canaliculata	339	* ‡ Ampelisca, sp	507
Eupagurus longicarpus	313	* Byblis serrata	501
* Pandalus annulicornis	493	* ‡ Ptilocheirus pinguis	507
Hippolyte pusiola	395	* ‡ Unciola irrorata	507
Crangon vulgaris	339	* Siphonœcetes cuspidatus	501
* ‡ Diastylis quadrispinosa	507	‡ Epelys montosus	370
Phoxus Kroyeri	501	E. trilobus	370
* Mœra levis	315	Anthura brachiata	573

Annelids.

	Page.		Page.
* ‡ Aphrodita aculeata	507	‡ Travisia carnea	508
* Harmothoë imbricata	321	Brada setosa	508
Lepidonotus squamatus	320	* ‡ Trophonia affinis	507
* ‡ Nephthys ingens	507	‡ Sternaspis fossor	507
N. bucera	416	* Cirrhinereis fragilis	397
‡ Eumidia, sp	397	* ‡ Clymenella torquata	343
Phyllodoce, sp	397	* Ammochares, sp	508
* Nereis pelagica	397	* Nicomache dispar	508
‡ Lycidice Americana	508	Rhodine attenuata	508
* ‡ Lumbriconereis fragilis	507	Cistenides Gouldii	323
* Nematonereis, sp	508	* Ampharete gracilis	508
* Ninoë nigripes	508	Melinna cristata	507
‡ Eone gracilis	508	* Terebellides Stroëmi	507
‡ Anthostoma acutum	508	‡ Polycirrus eximius	320
Anthostoma, sp	508	Potamilla oculifera	322
* Scolecolepis cirrata	507	* ‡ Euchone elegans	508
‡ Ammotrypane fimbriata	508	* Spirorbis, sp	397

Nemerteans and Planarians.

	Page.		Page.
* ‡ Meckelia lurida	508	* Polinia glutinosa	324
Cerebratulus, (?) green sp	508	* Leptoplana folium	487

Sipunculoids.

	Page.
* ‡ Phascolosoma cæmentarium	416

MOLLUSCA.

Gastropods.

	Page.		Page.
Bela harpularia	508	Crepidula unguiformis	355
‡ Buccinum undatum	508	C. fornicata	355
* ‡ Neptunea pygmæa	508	* Lunatia heros, var. triseriata	354
* Tritia trivittata	354	* L. immaculata	508
Astyris lunata	306	* Margarita obscura	508
* Astyris rosacea	508	* Cylichna alba	508
* Crucibulum striatum	399		

Lamellibranchs.

	Page.		Page.
Ensatella Americana	356	* ‡ Clidiophora trilineata	432
* Siliqua costata	358	* ‡ Lyonsia hyalina	358
‡ Corbula contracta	418	* ‡ Periploma papyracea	509

Ascidians.

Bryozoa.

RADIATA.

Echinoderms.

Acalephs.

Polyps.

B.—LISTS OF SPECIES FOUND IN THE STOMACHS OF FISHES—FOOD OF FISHES.

In the following lists I have brought together the principal results of the various recorded examinations of stomachs of fishes in this region, up to the present time, whether done in connection with the United States Fish Commission or independently. The special dates and localities are given in each case.

The observations from June to September, 1871, were made in connection with the work of the commission. Those from May to July, 1872, are based on collections made at Wood's Hole by Mr. Vinal N. Edwards, for Professor Baird. Those at Great Egg Harbor, New Jersey, April, 1871, were made by Mr. S. I. Smith and the writer while on an independent visit to that place.* The observations made at Eastport, Maine, in 1872, are not included in this report.

The names of the fishes used in this list are those adopted by Professor Baird, and agree, for the most part, with those used by Professor Theodore Gill in his Catalogue of the Fishes of the Eastern Coast of North America.

STRIPED BASS; ROCK-FISH, OR "ROCK;" (*Roccus lineatus.*)

At Great Egg Harbor, New Jersey, April, 1871, several specimens, freshly caught in seines, with menhaden, &c., contained *Crangon vulgaris* (shrimp) in large quantities.

A specimen caught at Wood's Hole, July 22, 1872, contained a large mass of "sea-cabbage," *Ulva latissima*, and the remains of a small fish.

Specimens taken at Wood's Hole, August, 1871, contained crabs, *Cancer irroratus;* and lobsters, *Homarus Americanus.*

WHITE PERCH; (*Morone Americana.*)

Numerous specimens caught with the preceding at Great Egg Harbor, New Jersey, contained *Crangon vulgaris.*

BLACK BASS; SEA-BASS; (*Centropristis fuscus.*)

Specimens caught in Vineyard Sound, June 10, contained the common crab, *Cancer irroratus;* the mud-crab, *Panopeus Sayi;* three species of fishes.

Another caught May 25 contained a squid, *Loligo pallida.*

SCUP; PORGEE; (*Stenotomus argyrops.*)

Forty young specimens, one year old, taken at Wood's Hole in August, contained large numbers of Amphipod Crustacea, among which were *Unciola irrorata*, *Ampelisca*, sp., &c.; several small mud-crabs, *Panopeus depressus; Idotea irrorata; Nereis virens*, and numerous other Annelids of several species, too much digested for identification.

---

* The results of the observations made at Great Egg Harbor were published by the writer in the American Naturalist, vol. v, p. 397, 1871.

Other specimens, opened at various times, show that this fish is very general feeder, eating all kinds of small Crustacea, Annelids, bivalve and univalve mollusks, &c.

TAUTOG; BLACK FISH; (*Tautoga onitis.*)

Specimens caught at Wood's Hole, May 23, contained the common rock-crab, *Cancer irroratus;* hermit-crabs, *Eupagurus longicarpus;* shells, *Tritia trivittata*, all crushed.

Others caught May 26 contained *Eupagurus pollicaris; E. longicarpus;* the barnacle, *Balanus crenatus;* the squid, *Loligo Pealii; Tritia trivittata.* Others taken May 29 had *Cancer irroratus;* mud-crabs, *Panopeus depressus;* lady-crabs, *Platyonichus ocellatus;* shells, *Tritia trivittata, Crepidula fornicata, Argina pexata*, and the scollop, *Pecten irradians;* barnacles, *Balanus crenatus*, all well broken up.

Another taken May 31 contained *Platyonichus ocellatus; Tritia trivittata.*

Others taken June 3 contained the mud-crab, *Panopeus depressus;* triangular crab, *Pelia mutica; Crepidula unguiformis; Triforis nigrocinctus;* the common muscle, *Mytilus edulis;* and the "horse-muscle," *Modiola modiolus.*

Another, on June 10, contained the common rock-crab, *Cancer irroratus;* mud-crab, *Panopeus Sayi; Nucula proxima;* several ascidians, *Cynthia partita* and *Leptoclinum albidum.*

Two caught July 8 and 15 contained small lobsters, *Homarus Americanus; Crepidula fornicata; Bittium nigrum;* a bryozoan, *Crisia eburnea;* sand-dollars, *Echinarachnius parma.*

A specimen caught in August contained long-clams, *Mya arenaria;* muscles, *Mytilus edulis; Petricola pholadiformis.*

WEAK-FISH; SQUETEAGUE; (*Cynoscion regalis.*)

Several caught in seines at Great Egg Harbor, New Jersey, April, 1871, with menhaden, &c., contained large quantities of shrimp, *Crangon vulgaris*, unmixed with other food.

Specimens taken at Wood's Hole, in July, often contained sand-crabs, *Platyonichus ocellatus;* and very frequently squids, *Loligo Pealii.*

KING-FISH; (*Menticirrus nebulosus.*)

Four specimens taken in seines at Great Egg Harbor, April, 1871, contained only shrimp, *Crangon vulgaris.*

Others taken at Wood's Hole, May 29, were filled with *Crangon vulgaris.*

Specimens taken in July contained rock-crabs, *Cancer irroratus;* squids, *Loligo Pealii.*

RUDDER-FISH; (*Palinurichthys perciformis.*)

A specimen caught at Wood's Hole, in August, contained a small *Squilla empusa;* and young squids, *Loligo Pealii.*

MACKEREL; (*Scomber vernalis.*)

Specimens taken July 18, twenty miles south of No Mans Land, contained shrimps, *Thysanopoda*, sp.; larval crabs in the zoëa and megalops stages of development; young of hermit-crabs; young of lady-crabs, *Platyonichus ocellatus;* young of two undetermined Macroura; numerous small Copepod Crustacea; numerous shells of a Pteropod, *Spirialis Gouldii.*

SMALL TUNNY; (*Orcynus thunnina.*)

One specimen caught at Wood's Hole, in August, contained eleven squids, *Loligo Pealii.*

BONITO; (*Sarda pelamys.*)

Specimens taken at Wood's Hole, in August, contained an abundance of shrimp, *Crangon vulgaris.*

BLUE-FISH; HORSE-MACKEREL; (*Pomatomus saltatrix.*)

Specimens caught at Wood's Hole, in August, frequently contained squids, *Loligo Pealii;* also various fishes.

Off Fire Island, Long Island, August, 1870, Mr. S. I. Smith saw blue-fishes feeding eagerly on the free-swimming males (heteronereis) of *Nereis limbata*, (p. 318,) which was then very abundant.

SEA-ROBIN; (*Prionotus Carolinus.*)

A specimen caught at Wood's Hole, May 27, contained shrimp, *Crangon vulgaris;* and a small flounder.

Another caught May 29 contained Amphipod Crustacea, *Anonyx* (?), sp.; and *Crangon vulgaris.*

Specimens dredged in Vineyard Sound, in August, contained mud-crabs, *Panopeus Sayi;* rock-crabs, *Cancer irroratus;* and several small fishes.

TOAD-FISH; (*Batrachus tau.*)

Several specimens examined at Great Egg Harbor, New Jersey, April, 1871, contained young edible crabs, *Callinectes hastatus* of various sizes up to those with the carapax two inches broad; shrimp, *Crangon vulgaris;* prawn, *Palæmonetes vulgaris; Ilyanassa obsoleta;* various fishes, especially the pipe-fish, *Syngnathus Peckianus;* and the anchovy, *Engraulis vittatus.*

A specimen caught at Wood's Hole, in July, contained the common rock-crab, *Cancer irroratus.*

GOOSE-FISH; ANGLER; (*Lophius Americanus.*)

A specimen caught in Vineyard Sound, in June, contained crabs, *Cancer irroratus;* and squids, *Loligo Pealii.*

COD; (*Gadus morrhua, var.*)

The cod-fishes devour a great variety of Crustacea, Annelids, Mollusks, star-fishes, &c. They swallow large bivalve shells, and after digesting the contents spit out the shells, which are often almost uninjured. They are also very fond of shrimps, and of crabs, which they frequently swallow whole, even when of large size. The brittle star-fishes (*Ophiurans*) are also much relished by them. I have taken large masses of the *Ophiopholis aculeata* from their stomachs on the coasts of Maine and Labrador; and in some cases the stomach would be distended with this one kind, unmixed with any other food.

In this region I have not been able to make any new observations on the food of the cod. This deficiency is partially supplied, however, by the observations made by me on the coast of Maine, &c., coupled with the very numerous observations made at Stonington, Connecticut, many years ago, by Mr. J. H. Trumbull, who examined large numbers of the stomachs of cod and haddock, caught within a few miles of that place, for the sake of the rare shells that they contained. This collection of shells, thus made, was put into the hands of the Rev. J. H. Linsley, who incorporated the results into his "Catalogue of the Shells of Connecticut," which was published after his death, and in a somewhat unfinished state, in the American Journal of Science, Series I, vol. xlviii, p. 271, 1845. In that list a large number of species are particularly mentioned as from the stomachs of cod and haddock, at Stonington, all of which were collected by Mr. Trumbull, as he has informed me, from fishes caught on the fishing-grounds near by, on the reefs off Watch Hill, &c. Many other northern shells, recorded by Mr. Linsley as from Stonington, but without particulars, were doubtless also taken from the fish-stomachs by Mr. Trumbull. There was no record made of the Crustacea, &c., found by him at the same time.

The following list includes the species mentioned by Mr. Linsley as from the cod. For greater convenience the original names given by him are added in parentheses, when differing from those used in this report:

List of mollusks, &c., obtained by Mr. J. H. Trumbull, from cod-fish caught near Stonington, Connecticut.

GASTROPODS.

Sipho Islandicus (?), young, (Fusus corneus.)
Ptychatractus ligatus, (Fasciolaria ligata.)
Turbonilla interrupta, (Turritella interrupta.)
Turritella erosa.
Rissoa exarata, (?), (Cingula arenaria.)
Lunatia immaculata, (Natica immaculata.)
Amphisphyra pellucida, (Bulla debilis.)
Chiton marmoreus, (?), (Chiton fulminatus.)

LAMELLIBRANCHS.

Martesia cuneiformis, (Pholas cuneiformis.)
Periploma papyracea, (Anatina papyracea.)
Thracia truncata.

Tagelus divisus, (Solecurtus fragilis.)
Semele equalis, (?), (Amphidesma æqualis.)
Ceronia arctata, (Mesodesma arctata.)
Montacuta elevata, (Montacuta bidentata.)
Callista convexa, young, (Cytherea morrhuana.)
Cardium pinnulatum.
Cyprina Islandica.
Gouldia mactracea, (Astarte mactracea.)
Yoldia sapotilla, (Nucula sapotilla.)
Y. limatula, (N. limatula.)
Nucula proxima.
N. tenuis.
Modiolaria nigra, (Modiola nexa.)
Crenella glandula, (M. glandula.)
Pecten tenuicostatus, young, (Pecten fuscus.)

ECHINODERMS.

Echinarachnius parma.

HADDOCK; (*Melanogrammus æglifinus.*)

The haddock is not much unlike the cod in the character of its food. It is, perhaps, still more omnivorous, or, at least, it generally contains a greater variety of species of shells, &c.; many of the shells that it habitually feeds upon are burrowing species, and it probably roots them out of the mud and sand.

A complete list of the animals devoured by the haddock would doubtless include nearly all the species belonging to this fauna. We have had few opportunities for making observations on the food of the haddock south of Cape Cod, but have examined many from farther north.

A specimen taken at Wood's Hole, November 6, 1872, contained a large quantity of *Gammarus natator*, and a few specimens of *Crangon vulgaris*. Another from Nantucket contained the same species.

The following species of shells were mentioned by Mr. Linsley, in his catalogue, as from the haddock:

List of mollusks obtained from stomachs of haddock, at Stonington, Connecticut, by Mr. J. H. Trumbull.

Neptunea pygmæa, (Fusus Trumbulli.)
Astyris zonalis, (Buccinum zonale.)
Bulbus flavus, (?), (Natica flava.)
Margarita obscura,
Actæon puncto-striata, (Tornatella puncto-striata.)
Cylichna alba, (Bulla triticea.)
Serripes Grœnlandicus, (?), (Cardium Grœnlandicum.)

The above list doubtless contains only a small portion of the species collected by Mr. Trumbull, but they are all that are specially recorded.

As an illustration of the character and diversity of the haddock's food, I add a list of the species taken from the stomach of a single specimen, from the Boston market, and doubtless caught in Massachusetts Bay, September, 1871.

GASTROPODS.

Natica clausa.
Margarita Grœnlandica.

LAMELLIBRANCHS.

Leda tenuisulcata.
Nucula proxima.
N. tenuis.
Crenella glandula.

ECHINODERMS.

Psolus phantapus.
Lophothuria Fabricii.

In addition to these there were fragments of shrimp, probably *Pandalus annulicornis*, and numerous Annelids, too much digested for identification.

TOM-COD; FROST-FISH; (*Microgadus tom-codus.*)

Several specimens from New Haven Harbor, January 30, contained numerous Amphipods, among which were *Mœra levis; Gammarus, sp.; Ampelisca, sp.;* an undetermined Macrouran; numerous Entomostraca; the larva of *Chironomus oceanicus.*

A lot taken in a small pond at Wood's Hole, in March, by Mr. Vinal N. Edwards, contained the common shrimp, *Crangon vulgaris;* large numbers of the green shrimp, *Virbius zostericola;* the prawn, *Palæmonetes vulgaris;* large quantities of Amphipods, especially of *Gammarus annulatus, G. natator, Calliopius læviuscula*, and *Microdeutopus minax;* and smaller numbers of *Gammarus ornatus* and *G. mucronatus.*

Another lot of twelve, taken in April at the same place, contained most of the above, and in addition several other Amphipods, viz: *Mœra levis, Pontogeneia inermis, Ptilocheirus pinguis*, and *Caprella;* also *Nereis virens*, and various small fishes.

OCELLATED FLOUNDER; SUMMER FLOUNDER; (*Chænopsetta ocellaris.*)

Several specimens taken in the seines, at Great Egg Harbor, New Jersey, in April, contained large quantities of shrimp, *Crangon vulgaris* and *Mysis Americana;* one contained a full-grown *Gebia affinis.*

One caught at Wood's Hole, June 6, contained twenty-six specimens of *Yoldia limatula;* and numerous shells of *Nucula proxima, Angulus tener*, and *Tritia trivittata;* and Amphipod Crustacea belonging to the genus *Ampelisca.*

Specimens caught at Wood's Hole, in July, contained rock-crabs, *Cancer irroratus; Pinnixa cylindrica; Crangon vulgaris;* squids, *Loligo Pealii; Angulus tener; Nucula proxima;* and many "sand-dollars," *Echinarachnius parma.*

WINTER FLOUNDER; (*Pseudopleuronectes Americanus.*)

A specimen caught at Wood's Hole, in August, contained large numbers of *Bulla solitaria.*

SPOTTED FLOUNDER; (*Lophopsetta maculata.*)

Numerous specimens caught in seines at Great Egg Harbor, April, 1871, contained large quantities of shrimp, especially *Mysis Americana* and *Crangon vulgaris;* the prawn, *Palæmonetes vulgaris;* numerous Amphipods, *Gammarus mucronatus;* one contained a *Gebia affinis.*

MINNOW; (*Fundulus pisculentus.*)

Specimens caught in July, at Wood's Hole, contained large numbers of *Melampus bidentatus*, unmixed with other food.

SEA-HERRING; (*Clupea elongata.*)

Specimens taken in Vineyard Sound, May 20, contained several shrimp, *Crangon vulgaris*, about 1.5 inches long; *Mysis Americana*, and large numbers of an Amphipod, *Gammarus natator;* also small fishes.

SHAD; (*Alosa tyrannus.*)

Several specimens taken in the seines, at Great Egg Harbor, April, 1871, contained finely-divided fragments of numerous Crustacea, among which were shrimp, *Mysis Americana.*

Several from the mouth of the Connecticut River, May, 1872, contained fragments of small Crustacea, (*Mysis*, &c.)

HICKORY SHAD; (*Pomolobus mediocris.*)

Several specimens taken in the seines at Great Egg Harbor, April, 1872, contained large quantities of fragmentary Crustacea; one contained recognizable fragments of shrimp, *Crangon vulgaris.*

MENHADEN; (*Brevoortia menhaden.*)

A large number of specimens freshly caught in seines at Great Egg Harbor, April, 1871, were examined, and all were found to have their stomachs filled with *large quantities of dark mud.* They undoubtedly swallow this mud for the sake of the microscopic animal and vegetable organisms that it contains. Their complicated and capacious digestive apparatus seems well adapted for this crude and bulky food.

FILE-FISH; (*Ceratacanthus aurantiacus.*)

A specimen taken at Wood's Hole, in August, contained a quantity of the finely-divided stems and branches of a Hydroid, *Pennaria tiarella.*

DUSKY SHARK; (*Eulamia obscura.*)

Several specimens caught at Wood's Hole, in July and August, contained lobsters, *Homarus Americanus;* rock-crabs, *Cancer irroratus.*

BLUE SHARK; (*Eulamia Milberti.*)

A large specimen caught at Wood's Hole, in August, contained a quantity of small bivalve-shells, *Yoldia sapotilla.*

TIGER-SHARK; (*Galerocerdo tigrina.*)

Specimens caught at Wood's Hole, in August, contained large univalve shells, *Buccinum undatum* and *Lunatia heros.*

DOG-FISH; (*Mustelus canis.*)

Several specimens caught at Wood's Hole, in August, contained lobsters, *Homarus Americanus;* spider-crabs, *Libinia canaliculata;* rock-crabs, *Cancer irroratus.*

SAND-SHARK; (*Eugomphodus littoralis.*)

Many specimens taken at Wood's Hole, in July and August, contained lobsters, *Homarus Americanus,* in abundance; *Cancer irroratus;* and squids, *Loligo Pealii.*

COMMON SKATE; "SUMMER SKATE;" (*Raia diaphana.*)

A specimen taken at Wood's Hole, May 14, contained rock-crabs, *Cancer irroratus;* a young skate; a long slender fish, (*Ammodytes ?.*) Another, caught in July, contained *Cancer irroratus.*

PEAKED-NOSE SKATE; (*Raia lævis ?.*)

Specimens caught in Vineyard Sound, May 14, contained numerous shrimps, *Crangon vulgaris;* several *Conilera concharum;* several Annelids, among them *Nephthys ingens; Meckelia ingens;* two specimens of *Phascolosoma Gouldii;* razor-shells, *Ensatella Americana,* (the "foot" only, of many specimens;) a small fish, *Ctenolabrus burgall.* Specimens taken at Menemsha, in July, contained large numbers of crabs, *Cancer irroratus;* and of lobsters, *Homarus Americanus.*

STING-RAY; (*Trygon centroura.*)

Specimens caught at Wood's Hole, in July and August, contained large numbers of crabs, *Cancer irroratus;* squids, *Loligo Pealii;* clams, *Mya arenaria; Lunatia heros.*

LONG-TAILED STING-RAY; (*Myliobatis Freminvillei.*)

Specimens taken in Vineyard Sound, in July, contained an abundance of lobsters, *Homarus Americanus;* crabs, *Cancer irroratus;* also clams, *Mya arenaria;* and *Lunatia heros.*

"RABBIT-FISH."

A specimen taken at Wood's Hole, in July, contained a lobster, *Homarus Americanus.*

"FOG-FISH."

A specimen caught at Wood's Hole, July 1, contained hermit-crabs, *Eupagurus pollicaris.*

C.—THE METAMORPHOSES OF THE LOBSTER, AND OTHER CRUSTACEA.—BY S. I. SMITH.

Most of the larger crustaceans of our coast, whatever may be their habits when adult, are, in the early stages of their existence after hatching from the eggs, essentially free-swimming animals, living a large part of the time near the surface of the water. In this stage they are constantly exposed to the attacks of other predaceous animals, and, as they occur in vast numbers, afford food for many valuable fishes. They are most abundant at the surface in calm, clear weather, and they especially resort, like the young of many other marine animals, to spots and streaks of smooth water where the tidal currents meet.

Very little has yet been written upon the forms or habits of the young crustaceans of our own coast; but, in connection with the investigations carried on in Vineyard Sound and Buzzard's Bay, a great amount of material for such work was collected. This material has not yet been fully studied, and only a sketch of some of the more important results is presented in this report. During the few weeks in June and July, in which I was myself at Wood's Hole, the time was so fully occupied in collecting, that very little time was left for studying the animals while alive; hence most of the observations which follow, except occasionally those on color, have been subsequently made from specimens preserved in alcohol. While at Wood's Hole, I was much assisted in obtaining these young animals by every one then associated there in the work of the commission; and I would especially acknowledge such assistance from Dr. W. G. Farlow, Mr. V. N. Edwards, and Capt. John B. Smith. After I left, the collecting was kept up as before, and many valuable notes were made by Professors Verrill and J. E. Todd.

Special attention was given to the early stages of the lobster, as perhaps the most important crustacean found on our coast, and I have gone more fully into the account of its early history than that of any other species. As this will serve as an example to illustrate the development of most of the other Macrourans, it is presented first.

Numerous specimens of the free-swimming young of the lobster, in different stages of growth, were obtained in Vineyard Sound during July, but it was too late for any observations upon the young within the egg. This deficiency was partially supplied by a few observations at New Haven in 1872. Eggs taken May 2, from lobsters captured at New London, Connecticut, had embryos well advanced, as represented in fig. 4. In this stage the eggs are slightly elongated spheroids, about 2.1^{mm} in the longer diameter, and 1.9^{mm} in the shorter. One side is rendered very opaque dark green by the unabsorbed yolk mass, while the other shows the eyes as two large black spots, and the red pigment spots on the edge of the carapax, bases of the legs, &c., as irregular lines of pink markings.

In a side view of the embryo, the lower edge of the carapax (*b*, figure) is clearly defined and extends in a gentle curve from the middle of the eye to the posterior border of the embryo. This margin of the carapax is marked with dendritic spots of red pigment. The whole dorsal portion, fully one-half the embryo, is still occupied by the unabsorbed portion of the yolk, (*a*, *a*,) of which the lower margin, represented in the figure by a dotted line, extends from close above the eye in a curve nearly parallel with the lower margin of the carapax, but with a sharp indentation a little way behind the eye. The eyes (*c*) are large, nearly round, not entirely separated from the surrounding tissues, and with a central portion of black pigment. The antennulæ (*d*) are simple, sack-like appendages, arising from just beneath the eyes, with the terminal portion turned backward and marked with several large dendritic spots of red pigment. The antennæ (*e*) are but little larger than the antennulæ and are sack-like and without articulations, but the scale and flagellum are separated and bent backward, the scale being represented by the large and somewhat expanded lobe, and the flagellum by a shorter and slender lobe which arises from near the base of the scale. The mandibles, both pairs of maxillæ, and the first and second pairs of maxillipeds are not sufficiently developed to be seen without removing the antennæ and the edge of the carapax, and are only represented by several small lobes, of which the anterior, apparently representing the mandibles, are distinctly defined, while those that follow are much smaller, indistinct, and confused. The first and second maxillipeds are each represented by a small lobe divided at the extremity. The external maxillipeds (*f*) are well developed and almost exactly like the posterior cephalothoracic legs. Both the branches are simple and sack-like, the main branch, or endognathus,† much larger and slightly longer than the outer branch, or exognathus, which is quite slender. The five pairs of

Fig. 4.*

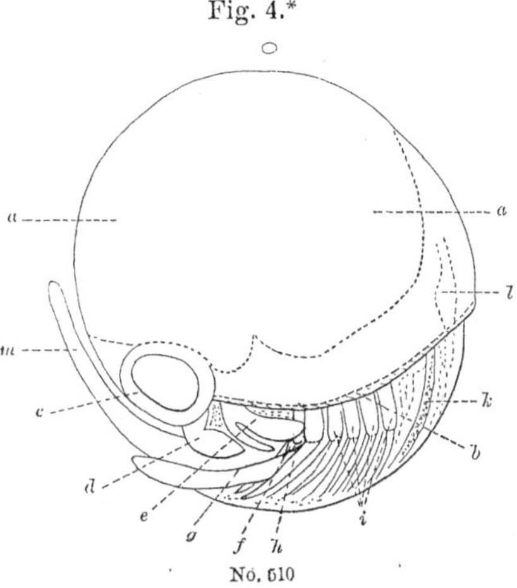

*Embryo, some time before hatching, removed from the external envelope and shown in a side view enlarged twenty diameters; *a*, *a*, dark-green yolk mass still unabsorbed; *b*, lateral margin of the carapax marked with many dendritic spots of red pigment; *c*, eye; *d*, antennula; *e*, antenna; *f*, external maxilliped; *g*, great cheliped which forms the big claw of the adult; *h*, outer swimming branch or exopodus of the same; *i*, the four ambulatory legs with their exopodal branches; *k*, intestine; *l*, heart; *m*, bilobed tail seen edgewise. [Drawn by S. I. Smith.]

† To prevent confusion, the terms here used are those proposed by Milne Edwards to designate the different branches of the cephalothoracic appendages: *endopodus*, for the main branch of a leg; *exopodus*, for the accessory branch, (*a* in fig. *D*, Plate IX;) *epipodus*, for the flabelliform appendage, (*b*;) and *endognathus*, *exognathus*, and *epignathus*, for the corresponding branches of the mouth organs.

cephalothoracic legs (*g*, *h*, *i*) are all similar and of about the same size, except the main branch of the first pair, (*g*,) which is much larger than that of the others, but is still sack-like and entirely without articulations. The outer or exopodal branches of all the legs are slender, wholly unarticulated, sack-like processes, while the inner or main (endopodal) branches of the four posterior pairs are similar, but much stouter and slightly longer processes arising from the same bases. The bases of all the legs are marked with dendritic spots of red pigment like those upon the lower margin of the carapax.

The abdomen (*m*) is curved round beneath the cephalothorax, the extremity extending between and considerably in front of the eyes. The segments are scarcely distinguishable. The extremity, as seen from beneath the embryo, is slightly expanded into a somewhat oval form, and very deeply divided by a narrow sinus, rounded at the extremity. The lobes into which the tail is thus divided are narrow, and somewhat approach each other toward the extremities, where they are each armed along the inner edge with six small obtuse teeth.

The heart (*l*) is readily seen, while the embryo is alive, by its regular pulsations. It appears as a slight enlargement in the dorsal vessel, just under the posterior portion of the carapax. The intestine (*k*) is distinctly visible in the anterior portion of the abdomen as a well defined, transparent tube, in which float little granular masses. This material within the intestine is constantly oscillating back and forth as long as the embryo is alive.

The subsequent development of the embryo within the egg was not observed. The following observations on the young larvæ, after they have left the eggs, have all been made upon specimens obtained in Vineyard Sound, or the adjacent waters, during July. These specimens were mostly taken at the surface in the day-time, either with the towing or hand net. They represent three quite different stages in the true larval condition, besides a later stage approaching closely the adult. The exact age of the larvæ of the first stage was not ascertained, but was probably only a few days, and they had, most likely, molted not more than once. Between the third stage, here described, and the last, there is probably an intermediate form wanting.

First stage.—In this stage, (Plate IX, Figs. A, B, C, D,) the young are free-swimming Schizopods about a third of an inch (7.8 to 8.0^{mm}) in length, without abdominal appendages, and with six pairs of pediform cephalothoracic appendages, each with the exopodus developed into a powerful swimming organ. The general appearance is represented in the figures. The eyes are bright blue; the anterior portion and the lower margin of the carapax and the bases of the legs are speckled with orange; the lower margin, the whole of the penultimate, and the basal portion of the ultimate segment of the abdomen, are brilliant reddish orange.

The antennulæ (Fig. *C*.) are short and sack-like, with a single articulation at the base, and three setæ at the tip. The antennæ have large well developed scales, furnished along the inner margin with long plumose hairs, but the flagellum is shorter than the scale, not divided into segments, and has three plumose setæ at tip. The mandibles are unlike on the two sides; the inferior edges are armed with acute teeth, except at the posterior angle, where there is a small molar area; the palpi are very small, with the three segments just indicated. The exognathus in both pairs of maxillæ is composed of only one article, and is furnished with several setæ at tip. In the first maxillipeds the exognathus is an unarticulated process, furnished with short plumose hairs on the outer side. The second maxillipeds have the principal branch cylindrical, not flattened and appressed to the inner mouth organs as in the adult; the exognathus is short, and as yet scarcely flabelliform; and the epignathus is a simple process, with not even the rudiment of a branchia. The external maxillipeds are pediform, the endognathus as long as and much resembling the endopodi of the posterior legs, while the exognathus is like the exopodi of all the legs, being half as long as the endognathus, and the terminal portion furnished along the edges with long plumose hairs. The epignathus and the branchiæ are very rudimentary, represented by minute sack-like processes. The anterior cephalothoracic legs, (Fig. *D*,) which in the adult develop into the big claws, are exactly alike, and no longer than the external maxillipeds. The pediform branch is, however, somewhat stouter than in the other legs, and subcheliform. The legs of the second and third pairs are similar to the first, but not as stout. The legs of the fourth and fifth pairs are still more slender, and styliform at the extremity, as in the adult.

The exopodal branches of all the legs and of the external maxillipeds are quite similar, and differ very little in size. In life, while the animal is poised at rest in the water, they are carried horizontally, as represented in Figure *B*, or are curved up over the carapax, sometimes so as almost to cover it. The blood circulates rapidly in these appendages, and they undoubtedly serve, to a certain extent, as respiratory organs, as well as for locomotion. By careful examination, small processes were found representing the normal number of branchiæ to each leg.* These rudimentary branchiæ, however, differ somewhat in different specimens, being very small, and scarcely distinguishable, in what appear to be younger individuals, from the rudimentary epipodi, while in others, apparently older, they are further developed, being larger, more cellular in structure than the epipodi, and even showing an approach to crenulation in the margins, as shown in Figure *D*.

The abdomen is slender, the second to the fifth segments each armed with a large dorsal spine, curved backward, and with the lateral angles

* The number of branchiæ, or branchial pyramids, in the American lobster is twenty on each side; a single small one upon the second maxilliped, three well developed ones upon the external maxilliped, three upon the first cephalothoracic leg, four each upon the second, third, and fourth, and one upon the fifth.

produced into long spines, and the sixth segment with two dorsal spines. The proportional size and the outline of the last segment are shown in Figure *B;* its posterior margin is armed with a long and stout central spine, and each side with fourteen or fifteen plumose spines or setæ, which are articulated to the margin.

In this stage the young were first taken July 1, when they were seen swimming rapidly about at the surface of the water among great numbers of zoëæ, megalops, and copeopods. Their motions and habits recall at once the species of *Mysis* and *Thysanopoda*, but their motions are not quite as rapid and are more irregular. Their bright colors render them conspicuous objects, and they must be readily seen and captured by fishes. They were frequently taken at the surface in different parts of Vineyard Sound from July 1 to 7, and several were taken off Newport, Rhode Island, as late as July 15, and they would very likely be found also in June, judging from the stage of development to which the embryos had advanced early in May in Long Island Sound. Besides the specimens taken in the open water of the Sound, a great number were obtained July 6, from the well of a lobster-smack, where they were swimming in great abundance near the surface of the water, having undoubtedly been recently hatched from the eggs carried by the female lobsters confined in the well. Some of these specimens lived in vessels of fresh sea-water for two days, but all efforts to keep them alive long enough to observe their molting failed. They appeared, while thus in confinement, to feed principally upon very minute animals of different kinds, but were several times seen to devour small zoëæ, and occasionally when much crowded, so that some of them became exhausted, they fed upon each other, the stronger ones eating the weaker.

Second stage.—In the next stage the young lobsters have increased somewhat in size, and the abdominal legs of the second to the fifth segments have appeared. The rostrum is much broader, and there are several teeth along the edges. The basal segments of the antennulæ have become defined, and the secondary flagellum has appeared, but is not subdivided into segments. The antennæ and mouth organs have undergone but slight changes. The first cephalothoracic legs are proportionally larger and stouter than in the first stage, and have become truly cheliform. The succeeding legs have changed little. The epidodi of all the legs and of the external maxillipeds have increased in size, and the branchial processes are distinctly lobed along the edges, and have begun to assume the form of true branchiæ. The segments of the abdomen have the same number of spines, but they are relatively somewhat smaller, and the last segment is relatively smaller and broader at base. The appendages of the second to the fifth segments differ considerably in size in different specimens, but are nearly as long as the segments themselves; their terminal lamellæ, however, are represented only by simple sack-like appendages, without sign of segmentation, or clothing of hairs or setæ. The penultimate segment is still without appendages.

Specimens in this stage were taken only twice, July 1 and 15. They have the same habits and general appearance as in the first stage, but are readily distinguished by the possession of rudimentary abdominal legs. In color they are almost exactly the same, only the orange-colored markings are perhaps a little less intense.

Third stage.—In the third stage (Plate IX, figs. *E*, *F*, *G*,) the larvæ are about half an inch (12 to 13^{mm}) in length, and the integument is of a much firmer consistency than in the earlier stages. The antennulæ are still rudimentary, and considerably shorter than the rostrum, although the secondary flagellum has increased in length, and begins to show division into numerous segments. The antennæ retain the most marked feature of the early stages—the large size of the scale—but the flagellum is much longer than the scale, and begins to show division into segments. The mandibles, maxillæ, and first and second maxillipeds have changed very little, although in the second maxillipeds the extremity of the exognathus begins to assume a flagelliform character, and the branchia is represented by a small process upon the side of the epignathus. The external maxillipeds have begun to lose their pediform character. The anterior legs have increased enormously in size, and those of the second and third pairs have become truly chelate, while the swimming exopodal branches of all the legs, as well as of the external maxillipeds, are relatively much smaller and more unimportant. The epipodi (fig. *G*) are furnished with hairs along the edges, and begin to assume the characters of these appendages in the adult. The branchiæ (fig. *G*) have developed rapidly, and have a single series of well-marked lobes along each side. The abdomen still has the spines characteristic of the earlier stages, though all of them are much reduced in size. The appendages of the second to the fifth segments have become conspicuous, their lamellæ have more than doubled in length, and the margins of the terminal half are furnished with very short ciliated setæ. The appendages of the penultimate segment (fig. *F*) are well developed, although quite different from those in the adult. The outer lamella wants wholly the transverse articulation near its extremity, and both are margined, except the outer edge of the outer lamella, with long plumose hairs. The last segment is relatively smaller and more quadrangular in outline, and the spines of the posterior margin are much smaller.

The only specimens procured in this stage were taken July 8 and 15. In color they were less brilliant than in the earlier stages, the orange markings being duller and whole animal slightly tinged with greenish brown.

In the next stage observed, the animal, about three-fifths of an inch (14 to 17^{mm}) long, has lost all its schizopodal characters, and has assumed the more important features of the adult lobster. It still retains, however, the free-swimming habit of the true larval forms, and was frequently taken at the surface, both in the towing and hand net. Although resembling the adult in many features, it differs so much that, were it an adult form, it would undoubtedly be regarded as a distinct genus. The rostrum is bifid at tip, and armed with three or four teeth on each side toward the base, and in some specimens with a minute additional spine, on one or both sides, close to the tip. The flagella of the antennulæ extend scarcely beyond the tip of the rostrum. The antennal scale is very much reduced in size, but is still conspicuous and furnished with long plumose hairs along the inner margin, while the flagellum is as long as the carapax. The palpi of the mandibles have assumed the adult character, but the mandibles themselves have not acquired the massive molar character which they have in the older animal. The other mouth-organs have nearly the adult form. The anterior legs, although quite large, are still slender and just alike on the two sides, while all the cephalothoracic legs retain a distinct process in place of the swimming exopodi of the larva. The lateral angles of the second to the fifth abdominal segments are prolonged downward into long spiniform teeth, the appendages of these segments are proportionately much longer than in the adult, and the margins of their terminal lamellæ are furnished with very long plumose hairs. The lamellæ of the appendages of the penultimate segment are oval, and margined with long plumose hairs. The terminal segment is nearly quadrangular, as wide at the extremity as at the base, the posterior margin arcuate, but not extending beyond the prominent lateral angles, and furnished with hairs like those on the margins of the lamellæ of the appendages of the penultimate segment.

In color they resemble closely the adult, but the green color of the back is lighter, and the yellowish markings upon the claws and body are proportionately larger.

In this stage, the young lobsters swim very rapidly by means of the abdominal legs, and dart backward, when disturbed, with the caudal appendages, frequently jumping out of the water in this way like shrimp, which their movements in the water much resemble. They appear to be truly surface animals, as in the earlier stages, and were often seen swimming about among other surface animals. They were frequently taken from the 8th to the 28th of July, and very likely occur much later.

From the dates at which the different forms were taken, it is probable that they pass through all the stages here described in the course of a single season. How late the young, after reaching the lobster-like form, retain their free-swimming habit was not ascertained.

The young of the different kinds of shrimp, *Crangon vulgaris*, *Palæmonetes vulgaris*, and *Virbius zostericola*, when hatched from the egg, are free-swimming animals, similar in their habits to the young of the lobster. In structure, however, they are quite unlike the larvæ of the lobster, and approach more the zoëa stages of the crabs, which are described farther on. When they first leave the egg, they are without the five pairs of cephalothoracic legs, the abdomen is without appendages, and much as it is in the first stage of the young lobster, while the maxillipeds are developed into long locomotive appendages, somewhat like the external maxillipeds of the first stage of the young lobster. While yet in the free-swimming condition the cephalothoracic legs are developed, the maxillipeds assume the adult form, and the abdominal limbs appear. The young of these shrimp are very much smaller than the young of the lobster, but they remain for a considerable time in this immature state, and were very frequently taken at the surface in the towing-net.

The young of *Crangon vulgaris* are hatched in the neighborhood of Vineyard Sound, in May and June, and arrive at the adult form before they are more than 4 or 5^{mm} long. Specimens of this size were taken at Wood's Hole, at the surface, on the evening of July 3. Later in the season much larger specimens were frequently taken at the surface both in the evening and day-time.

The young of *Palæmonetes vulgaris* did not appear till near the middle of July. Soon after hatching, the young are 3^{mm} long. The cephalothorax is short and broad with a slender spiniform rostrum in front, an enormous compound eye each side at the anterior margin, and a small simple eye in the middle of the carapax. The antennulæ are quite rudimentary, being short and thick appendages projecting a little way in front of the head; the peduncle bears at its extremity a very short obtuse segment representing the primary flagellum, and inside, at the base of this, a much longer plumose seta. The antennæ are slightly longer, than the antennulæ; the short peduncle bears a stout appendage, corresponding to the antennal scale, the terminal portion of which is articulated and furnished with long plumose setæ, and on the inside at the base of the scale, a slender process corresponding to the flagellum, and terminated by a long plumose seta. The first and second pairs of maxillæ are well formed and approach those of the adult. The three pairs of maxillipeds are all developed into powerful locomotive appendages; the inner branches, or endognathi, being slender pediform appendages terminated by long spines, while the outer branches, or epignathi, are long swimming appendages like the swimming branches of the legs of the young lobsters in the first stage. Both branches of the first maxillipeds are considerably shorter than those of the following pairs, but otherwise like them, and the inner branch of the second pair is somewhat shorter than that of the third, but its outer branch is about as long as that of the third pair. The five pairs of cephalothoracic legs are wanting or only represented by a cluster of minute sack-like processes just behind the outer maxillipeds. The abdomen is long and slender, wholly without appendages beneath, and the last segment is expanded into a short and very broad caudal lamina, the posterior margin of which is truncate with the lateral angles rounded; these angles each bear three, and the posterior margin itself eight more stout plumose setæ, the setæ of the posterior margin being longer than those upon the angles, and separated by broader spaces in which the margin is armed with numerous very small setæ. They arrive at the adult form before they are more than 5^{mm}

long, and they were often taken at the surface until 8 to 12^{mm} in length, the larger ones being taken in the first part of September.

The young of *Virbius zostericola* appear at about the same time as those of *Palæmonetes*, or a very little later, and pass through quite similar changes. The young attain the adult form when not more than 3^{mm} in length, and were frequently taken at the surface, both in the daytime and the evening, until they were 10^{mm} long, those 8 to 10^{mm} long being common in late August and early September.

The larval forms of several other Macrourans were taken at different times, but none of these were abundant, and I have not been able to connect them with the adult forms of any of the common species of the New England coast.

The young of *Gebia affinis*, only 4^{mm} long, but with nearly the form of the adult, was taken at the surface on the evening of September 3. The young of *Callianassa Stimpsoni*, about 4^{mm} long and with nearly all the adult characters, was also taken at the surface early in September.

The hermit-crabs (species of *Eupagurus*) when first hatched have much resemblance to the young of shrimp at the same period, and have similar habits. The young of one of the species, after it has passed through the earlier stages, and when it is about 3^{mm} long, and has all the cephalothoracic appendages similar to those of the adult, has still a symmetrical abdomen, like that of a shrimp, with long swimming-legs upon the second, third, fourth, and fifth segments, and broad laminated appendages upon the penultimate segment. Young, in this and the earlier stages, were common at the surface in Vineyard Sound during the last of August and the first of September.

Hippa talpoida probably passes through a metamorphosis similar to that of the hermit-crabs. The young attain nearly the adult form before they are more than 5 or 6^{mm} long, and specimens of this size were taken at the surface in Vineyard Sound on the evening of September 3. I have also found, early in September, the young a little larger upon the outer shores of Fire Island Beach, where they were left in large numbers by a high tide, and soon buried themselves in the sand.

All, or at least nearly all, the species of Brachyura living on the coast of New England pass through very complete and remarkable metamorphoses. The most distinct stages through which they pass were long ago described as two groups of crustaceans, far removed from the adult forms of which they were the young. The names zoëa and megalops, originally applied to these groups, are conveniently retained for the two best marked stages in the development of the crabs.

The young of the common crab, (*Cancer irroratus*,) in the earlier or zoëa stage, when first hatched from the egg, are somewhat like the form figured on Plate VIII, (fig. 37, the latest stage of the zoëa of *Cancer irroratus*, just before it changes to the megalops,) but the spines upon the carapax are all much longer in proportion, and there are no signs of the abdominal legs or of any of the future legs of the megalops and crab. In this stage they are very small, much smaller than in the stage figured. After they have increased very much in size, and have molted probably several times, they appear as in the figure just referred to. The terminal segment of the abdomen, seen only in a side-view in the figure, is very broad and divided nearly to the base by a broad sinus, each side the margins project in long, spiniform, diverging processes, at the base of which the margin of the sinus is armed with six to eight spines on each side. When alive they are translucent, with deposits of dark pigment forming spots at the articulations of the abdomen and a few upon the cephalothorax and its appendages. In this stage they were taken at the surface in Vineyard Sound, in immense numbers, from June 23 to late in August. They were most abundant in the early part of July, and appeared in the greatest numbers on calm, sunny days.

Several zoëæ of this stage were observed to change directly to the megalops form, (Plate VIII, fig. 38.) Shortly before the change took place they were not quite as active as previously, but still continued to swim about until they appeared to be seized by violent convulsions, and after a moment began to wriggle rapidly out of the old zoëa skin, and at once appeared in the full megalops form. The new integument seems to stiffen at once, for in a very few moments after freeing itself from the old skin the new megalops was swimming about as actively as the oldest individuals.

In this megalops stage the animal begins to resemble the adult. The five pairs of cephalothoracic legs are much like those of the adult, and the mouth-organs have assumed nearly their final form. The eyes, however, are still enormous in size, the carapax is elongated and has a slender rostrum and a long spine projecting from the cardiac region far over the posterior border, and the abdomen is carried extended, and is furnished with powerful swimming-legs as in the Macroura. In color and habits they are quite similar to the later stage of the zoëæ from which they came; their motions appear, however, to be more regular and not so rapid, although they swim with great facility. In this megalops the dactyli of the posterior cephalothoracic legs are styliform, and are each furnished at the tip with three peculiar setæ of different lengths and with strongly curved extremities, the longest one simple and about as long as the dactylus itself, while the one next in length is armed along the inner side of the curved extremity with what appear to be minute teeth, and the shortest one is again simple.

According to the observations made at Wood's Hole, the young of *Cancer irroratus* remain in the megalops stage only a very short time, and at the first molt change to a form very near that of the adult. Notwithstanding this, they occurred in vast numbers, and were taken in the towing-nets in greater quantities even than in the zoëa stage. Their time of occurrence seemed nearly simultaneous with that of the zoëæ, and the two forms were almost always associated. The exact time any particular individual remained in this stage was observed only a few times. One full-grown zoëa (like the specimen figured) obtained June 23, and placed in a vessel by itself, changed to a megalops between 9 and 11½ a. m. of June 24, and did not molt again till the forenoon of June 27, when it became a young crab of the form described farther on. Of two other zoëæ obtained at the same time, and placed together in a dish, one changed to a megalops between 9 and 11½ a. m. of June 24, the other during the following night; these both changed to crabs during the night of June 26 and 27.

The following memorandum on a large number of the same lot of both stages of the young, kept together in a vessel of fresh sea-water, also indicates the rapidity of these changes. In the columns "zoëa" and "megalops" the total number of individuals in each of these stages is given; under "crabs" the number which had appeared since the last observation, and under "dead" the number which had died since the last observation:

Time of observation.	Zoëa.	Megalops.	Crabs.	Dead.
June 23, 7 p. m.	15	22	0	0
June 24, 5 a. m.	5	23	2	7
June 24, 9 a. m.	4	22	2	0
June 24, 11½ a. m.	2	22	1	1
June 24, 7 p. m.	1	22	1	0
June 25, 6 a. m.	0	20	0	3
June 25, 2 p. m.	....	19	1	0
June 26, 6 a. m.	....	16	1	2
June 27, 6 a. m.	....	14	2	0
June 27, 2½ p. m.	....	12	0	2
June 27, 7 p. m.	....	11	0	1
June 28, 7 a. m.	....	9	2	0
June 28, 4 p. m.	....	4	3	2
June 29, 7 a. m.	....	2	2	....

In the two or three instances in which the change from the megalops to the young crab was actually observed, the megalops sank to the bottom of the dish and remained quiet for some time before the molting took place. The muscular movements seemed to be much less violent than in the molting at the close of the zoëa stage, and the little crab worked himself out of the megalops skin quite slowly. For a short time after their appearance the young crabs were soft and inactive, but the integument very soon stiffened, and in the course of two or three hours they acquired all the pugnacity of the adult. They swam about with ease and were constantly attacking each other and their companions in the earlier stages. Many of the deaths recorded in the above memorandum were due to them, and on this account they were removed from the vessel at each observation. In this early stage the young crabs are quite different from the adult. The carapax is about 3^{mm} long and slightly less in breadth. The front is much more prominent than in the adult, but still has the same number of lobes and the same general form. The antero-lateral margin is much more longitudinal than in the adult, and is armed with the five normal teeth, which are long and acute, and four very much smaller secondary teeth alternating with the normal ones. The antennæ and ambulatory legs are proportionally longer than in the adult. The young crabs in this stage were once or twice taken in the towing-net, but they were not common at the surface, although a large number were found, with a few in the megalops stage, among hydroids upon a floating barrel in Vineyard Sound, July 7.

The young of *Platyonichus ocellatus* in the zoëa and megalops stages were frequently taken in the towing-net from the last of June till August, but they were much less abundant than the young of *Cancer irroratus*. On June 29, however, they occurred in great numbers. Twenty-two out of forty of those in the zoëa state changed to the megalops during the first twenty-four hours, and in the same time ten out of fifty in the megalops stage changed to the adult form, so that they probably do not remain in the megalops state longer than the young of *Cancer irroratus*. They apparently do not molt during the megalops stage.

The megalops of the *Platyonichus* is about the size of that of *Cancer irroratus*, and resembles it much in general appearance, but the carapax is much broader in proportion, the rostrum is a little longer, and there is a marked prominence at the anterior margin of the orbit, representing the lateral tooth of the front of the adult, and a similar prominence, representing the stout postorbital tooth, at the posterior angle of the orbit. The spine upon the cardiac region is rather more slender than in the megalops of the *Cancer*. The chelipeds are more elongated, and much like those of the adult *Platyonichus*, except that they want the stout spines of the latter. The dactyli of the posterior legs already approach in form those of the adult, being expanded into narrow oval plates a fourth as broad as long. The tips of each of these dactyli are furnished with four peculiar setæ of different lengths and with strongly curved extremities, the longest and two shortest of which are simple, while next to the longest one is furnished along the inner side of the curved extremity with little, closely set, sack-like appendages.

Another megalops, belonging apparently to some swimming-crab, was several times taken in the towing-net, in Vineyard Sound, from August 11 to September 3, and was also taken by Mr. Harger and myself, east of George's Bank, latitude 41° 25′ north, longitude 63° 55′ east, September 14. It would fall in the genus *Cyllene* of Dana, and is closely allied to his *Cyllene furciger* (Crust. U. S. Expl. Expd., p. 494, Plate XXXI, fig. 8) from the Sooloo Sea. In one specimen the carapax, including the rostrum, is 2.0^{mm} long, excluding rostrum, 1.6^{mm}, breadth, 1.1^{mm}. The front is quite narrow between the bases of the ocular peduncles, and has a long and slender rostrum. There are no prominences either side of the orbit and no dorsal spine upon the carapax. The fourth segment of the sternum is armed each side, just within the bases of the legs, with a long and broad spine projecting backward and slightly outward, as in *Cyllene furciger*. The chelipeds and ambulatory legs are long and slender, and the dactyli of the posterior pair of legs are expanded and lamellar, as in the megalops of *Platyonichus*. The abdomen is about as long as the carapax excluding the rostrum, and the fifth segment is armed with a stout spine each side of the postero-lateral angles.

A very large megalops, quite different in structure from those already mentioned, is occasionally found thrown upon outer beaches on the southern coast of New England and Long Island, but is apparently much more common upon the coast of the Southern States. This is undoubtedly the young of *Ocypoda arenaria*, and was long ago described by Say (Journal Acad. Nat. Sci., Philadelphia, vol. i, p. 157, 1817) as *Monolepis inermis*, and it is partially figured by Dana, (Crust. U. S. Expl. Exp., Plate XXXI, fig. 6.) The carapax is very convex above, broader behind, and has no dorsal spine. The front is deflexed sharply downward and a little backward, and the extremity is tricuspidate, the median tooth being long and narrowly triangular, while the lateral teeth are small and obtuse. The sides are high and impressed so as to receive the three anterior pairs of ambulatory legs. The third pair of ambulatory legs are closely appressed along the upper edge of the carapax and extend forward over the eyes, their dactyli being curved down over the eyes and along each side of the front. The posterior legs are small and weak, and each is folded up and lies in a groove on the latero-posterior surface of the carapax. The external maxillipeds have almost exactly the same structure as in the adult *Ocypoda*, and, as in the adult *Ocypoda*, there is a tuft of peculiar hairs between the bases of the second and third ambulatory legs. I have specimens of this megalops from Block Island, and have myself collected it, late in August, at Fire Island Beach, Long Island. In the largest specimen from the last locality the carapax is 6.4^{mm} long and 5.6^{mm} broad.

A large number of young specimens of the *Ocypoda*, collected at Fire Island Beach, indicate plainly that they had only recently changed from this megalops. The smallest of these specimens, in which the carapax is 5.6 to 6.0^{mm} long and 6.1 to 6.5^{mm} broad, differ from the adult so much that they might very easily be mistaken for a different species. The carapax is very slightly broader than long, and very convex above. The front is broad, not narrowed between the bases of the ocular peduncles, and triangular at the extremity. The margin of the orbit is not transverse but inclines obliquely backward. The ambulatory legs are nearly naked, and those of the posterior pair are proportionately much smaller than in the adult.

The adult *Ocypoda* is terrestrial in its habits, living in deep holes above high-water mark on sandy beaches, but the young in the zoëa state are undoubtedly deposited in the water, where they lead a free-swimming existence like true pelagic animals, until they become full-grown in the megalops state. Say mentions that his specimens were found cast upon the beach by the refluent tide and "appeared desirous to protect themselves by burrowing in the sand, in order to wait the return of the tide," but they were more likely awaiting the final change to the terrestrial state. The tufts of peculiar hairs between the bases of the second and third ambulatory legs, and, in the adult, connected with the respiration, are present in the full-grown megalops, and are undoubtedly provided to fit the animal for its terrestrial existence as soon as it is thrown upon the shore. The young in the magalops stage occur on the shore of Long Island, in August, and perhaps earlier. At Fire Island Beach in 1870 no specimens of *Ocypoda* were discovered till the last of August, and those first found were the smallest ones obtained; by the middle of September, however, they were common on the outer beach, and many of them were twice as large as those first obtained. Although careful search was made along the beach for several miles, not a specimen of the adult or half-grown crab could be found; every individual there had evidently landed and developed during the season. Probably all those living the year before had perished during the winter, and it is possible that this species never survives long enough to attain its full growth, so far north.

A small megalops, taken in the towing-nets in considerable numbers at Wood's Hole on the evening of September 3, resembles in several characters the megalops of *Ocypoda*, and is probably the young of one of the species of *Gelasimus*. The carapax is 1.0^{mm} long and 0.7 broad. The front is narrowly triangular, deflexed perpendicularly, somewhat excavated between the eyes, and terminates in a long, slender, and acute tip. The sides are high and impressed for the reception of the three anterior ambulatory legs as in the megalops of *Ocypoda*, although in the alcoholic specimens examined the legs are not closed against the sides. The posterior ambulatory legs are small, and lodged in grooves on the surface of the carapax, much as in the megalops of *Ocypoda*. The external maxillipeds are very much like those of the megalops of *Ocypoda*.

A peculiar megalops, belonging apparently to some Grapsoid group of crabs, was several times taken in the towing-net in Vineyard Sound from August 5 to September 3, on the latter date in the evening. In these the carapax is 1.2 to 1.3^{mm} in length and 0.9 to 1.0^{mm} in breadth. The front is broad, concave above between the eyes; the middle portion projects obliquely downward and terminates in a short, obtuse rostrum; while the lateral angles project forward into a prominent tooth above each eye, so that, when seen from above, the frontal margin appears transverse and tridentate, the teeth being separated by considerable spaces. There are no dorsal spines or tubercles upon the carapax. The sides are high, and are apparently impressed for the reception of the anterior ambulatory legs. The posterior ambulatory legs are subequal with the others and have styliform dactyli. The ischial and meral segments of the external maxillipeds are short and broad.

Another megalops, of which several specimens were taken in the towing-net, in Vineyard Sound, August 5, has a remarkable, elongated and tuberculated carapax. The carapax, including the rostrum, is 1.3^{mm} long and 0.84^{mm} broad, is armed above with several large tubercles, and the posterior margin is arcuate and armed with a median tubercular prominence. The front is somewhat excavated above and expanded each side in front of the eyes, the anterior margin being transverse, as seen from above, with a short and spiniform rostrum curved obliquely downward. The chelipeds have slender hands and the ambulatory legs are long and slender, the posterior pair being subequal with the others, and all having the dactyli styliform. The abdominal legs are very long.

Several other forms of zoëa and megalops were taken in Vineyard Sound and vicinity, but, as they were not traced to the adult forms and were none of them very abundant, they are not here described.

Squilla empusa passes through a remarkable metamorphosis, but none of the earliest stages were observed. Specimens in one of the later larval stages (Plate VIII, fig. 36) were taken at the surface in Vineyard Sound, August 11. These are nearly 6^{mm} long. The carapax is proportionally much larger than in the adult, covering completely the whole cephalothorax, has a long slender rostrum projecting far in front of the eyes, and the lateral angles projecting backward in two slender processes as long as the rostrum. There is also on each side, just behind the eye, a small tooth on the margin of the carapax, and another similar one on the posterior margin just beneath each of the posterior processes. The eyes are very large and almost spherical. The antennulæ are short, projecting scarcely beyond the eyes, and biramous, one of the flagella being short and unsegmented, the other longer and composed of three segments. The antennæ are still without flagella, and the scale is quite small. The first pair of legs (the appendages corresponding to the first pair of maxillipeds in the Macroura, &c.) are well developed, long, and slender, like those of the adult. The great claws are proportionally larger than in the adult, and have very much the same structure. Of the six succeeding pairs of cephalothoracic legs, only the three anterior, subcheliform ones are as yet developed, and these are quite small, those of the third pair being smaller than the others, and projecting but slightly beyond the carapax; the three posterior, styliform legs are entirely wanting, or represented only by slight sack-like protuberances. The abdomen is not quite as long as the cephalothorax, including the rostrum and posterior processes, and the five anterior segments are subequal in length, smoothly rounded above, and furnished with well developed swimming-legs, much like those of many macrouranas. The sixth segment is much shorter than the others, and has rudimentary appendages scarcely longer than the segment itself. In these appendages the spiniform process from the base is long and simple, not biramous, as in the adult, and the lamellæ are small, much shorter than this process, and the outer one has no articulated terminal portion. The terminal segment is as long as the four preceding segments, about as broad as long, the lateral margins slightly convex in outline, and each armed with two sharp teeth, while the posterior margin is concave in outline, with the lateral angles projecting into sharp teeth, between which the edge is armed with about twenty small and equal slender spines.

D.—CATALOGUE OF THE MARINE INVETEBRATE ANIMALS OF THE SOUTHERN COAST OF NEW ENGLAND, AND ADJACENT WATERS.—BY A. E. VERRILL, S. I. SMITH, AND OSCAR HARGER.

In the following catalogue nearly all the marine invertebrates which are known to inhabit the coast between Cape Cod and New York are included, except those belonging to certain groups which have not yet been studied by any one, sufficiently for their identification. Such are chiefly minute or microscopic species, belonging to the Entomostraca, Foraminifera, Ciliated Infusoria, &c., together with the intestinal worms of fishes and other animals. Our sponges, also, have hitherto received very little attention, and it has not yet been possible to identify but a small number of the species. It is not to be supposed, however, that the list is complete in any group, for every season in the past has served to greatly increase the number of species in almost every class and order, and this will doubtless be the case for many years to come. But as no attempt has hitherto been made to enumerate the marine animals of this region, excepting the shells and radiates, it is hoped that this catalogue will prove useful, both to show what is already known concerning this fauna, and to serve as a basis for future work in the same direction.

In some instances species that have not actually been found on the part of the coast mentioned, but which occur on the shores of Long Island and New Jersey, under such circumstances as to render it pretty certain that they will also be found farther north, have been included in the catalogue, but the special localities have always been given in such cases.

In order not to make the list too long, only those synonyms are given which are really necessary to make apparent the origin of the names, and to refer the student to some of the best descriptions and figures in the works that are generally most accessible, and in which more complete synonymy may be found.

For the same reason, in describing the new species, the descriptions have been made as brief as seemed consistent with the purpose in view, viz: to enable students and others who may not be experienced naturalists to identify the species that they may meet with. To this end, the portions of the descriptions relating to strictly microscopic parts have frequently been omitted, when more obvious characters, sufficient to distinguish the species, could be found.

References to the plates at the end of this volume have been inserted, and also to the pages in the first part of the report where brief descriptions, remarks on the habits, or other information may be found.

The catalogue of the Crustacea was prepared by Mr. S. I. Smith and Mr. Oscar Harger. The rest of the catalogue is by Professor A. E. Verrill, with the exception of the descriptions of the insects, which have been furnished by Dr. A. S. Packard and Dr. G. H. Horn; the Pycnogonids, which have been determined by Mr. S. I. Smith; and a few of the Bryozoa, which were identified by Professor A. Hyatt, who also furnished most of the figures of the species belonging to that class.

Hitherto there has been no attempt to enumerate the marine invertebrates of the entire southern coast of New England. Several partial lists have been published, however, and these have been of considerable use in the preparation of the following catalogue.

In the Report on the Invertebrata of Massachusetts, by Dr. A. A. Gould, 1841, numerous localities for shells on the southern coast of Massachusetts are mentioned.

A catalogue of the shells of Connecticut, by James H. Linsley, was published in the American Journal of Science, vol. 48, 1845. In "Shells of New England," 1851, Dr. William Stimpson gave much accurate information concerning the distribution of our Mollusca. In 1869 Dr. G. H. Perkins published a very useful catalogue, in the Proceedings of the Boston Society of Natural History, vol. xiii, p. 109, entitled "Molluscan Fauna of New Haven."

The "Report on the Mollusca of Long Island, New York, and of its Dependencies," by Sanderson Smith and Temple Prime, in the Annals of the Lyceum of Natural History, vol. ix, p. 377, 1870, also contains much useful information.

A paper by Dr. Joseph Leidy, entitled "Contributions toward a Knowledge of the Marine Invertebrate Fauna of the Coasts of Rhode Island and New Jersey," in the Journal of the Philadelphia Academy, vol. iii, 1855, although very incomplete, contains the only published lists of the Annelids and Crustacea of this region. In his "Catalogue of North American Acalephæ," 1865, Mr. A. Agassiz has enumerated all the species discovered on this coast up to that time. Other papers will also be referred to in the synonymy.

ARTICULATA.

INSECTA.

The insects included in the following catalogue have mostly been determined by A. S. Packard, jr., M. D., and by George H. Horn, M. D., who have also kindly furnished descriptions of the new species. Our thanks are also due to Dr. H. A. Hagen, who has identified some of the species. The Pycnogonids have been determined by Mr. S. I. Smith.

DIPTERA.

CHIRONOMUS HALOPHILUS Packard, sp. nov. (p 415.)

Full-grown larvæ were dredged in 10 fathoms in Vineyard Sound, several miles from land, among compound Ascidians, (A. E. V.;) and several young larvæ were dredged in 8 to 10 fathoms in Wood's Hole Passage, September 10, (A. S. P.)

"This is a true *Chironomus*, the body being long and slender, with the usual respiratory filaments at the end of the body. Head red as usual, chitinous; antennæ slender, ending in two unequal spines; eyes black, forming conspicuous dots; mandibles acute, three-toothed.

From lower side of antepenultimate segment arise two pairs of long fleshy filaments, twice as long as the diameter of body, not containing tracheæ, so far as I can see; and from the end of penultimate segment a dorsal minute tubercle, forming a cylindrical papilla, giving rise to eight respiratory hairs about as long as the segment is thick; anal legs long and slender, with a crown of about twelve spines. Two prothoracic feet, as usual. In one larva the semi-pupa was forming; length, 11^{mm}, (.45 inch.)

This species belongs in the same section of the genus with *Chironomus plumosus*, figured by Reaumer, (vol. iv, Pl. 14, figs. 11 and 12; and vol. v.)"—A. S. P.

CHIRONOMUS OCEANICUS Packard. (p. 331.)

Proceedings of the Essex Institute, vol. vi, p. 42, figs. 1–4, 1869.

Specimens apparently belonging to this species have been obtained near New Haven, at low-water mark, among confervæ. It occurs at Salem, Massachusetts; Casco Bay; and the Bay of Fundy, from low-water mark to 20 fathoms.

CULEX, species undetermined. (p. 466.)

A species of mosquito is excessively abundant on the salt-marshes in autumn, and the larvæ inhabit the brackish waters of the ditches and pools.

MUSCIDÆ.—Larvæ of an undetermined fly. (p. 415.)

This larva was found living beneath the surface of the sand, at low-water mark, on the shore of Great Egg Harbor, at Beesley's Point, New Jersey, April 28, 1871. (A. E. V.) The same larva, or an allied species, was found May 5, under stones below high-water mark. "Specimens were brought to me from New Jersey, and kept living in sea-water for some time. The following description is from the living specimens: Body white, long, slender, cylindrical, tapering gradually from the penul-penultimate segment toward the head; thirteen segments, counting the head as one. Segments smooth, thickened at the hinder edge, the sutures being distinct; tegument very thin and transparent, allowing the viscera to be easily distinguished. The terminal segment of the body is conical; seen from beneath it is nearly a fourth longer than broad, the end subacute and deeply cleft by a furrow which diminishes in size and depth to beyond the middle of the segment, where it fades out. This conical extension is flattened vertically above; from the middle of the same ring project the supra-anal, conical, fleshy tubercles, one-fourth the length of the entire ring, which give rise to two main tracheæ running to the head, and which separate and close together at the will of the animal. When extended the prothoracic ring is considerably longer than the others. Head one-third as large as prothorax, and a little more than half as wide. Length, 9^{mm}.

I cannot detect any spiracles on either of the thoracic rings. The tracheæ are not nearly so regular as in the larvæ of the *Anthomyia ceparum*, with living specimens of which I placed it side by side; head much the same, showing it may be of this family. Minute antennæ present; no traces of them in *Anthomyia*, and their presence throws a doubt whether it be a muscid."—A. S. P.

ERISTALIS, species undetermined.

One large-sized larva was found in Vineyard Sound among algæ in April, by Mr. Vinal N. Edwards.

EPHYDRA, species undetermined. (p. 466.)

Packard, Proceedings Essex Institute, vol. vi, p. 50.

Shores of Narragansett Bay, puparium found under sea-weeds by Dr. T. d'Orexmieul. According to Dr. Packard, "scarcely distinguishable from *E. halophila* Packard, which lives in salt brine at the salt-works in Gallatin County, Illinois."

COLEOPTERA.*

A number of species of tiger-beetles (*Cicindela*) are common on the sandy shores and beaches just above high-water mark, and some of them are seldom found away from the sea-shore, while others are also found far inland. The larvæ of some of these, and perhaps of all, live below high water, but this has not yet been observed in the case of several

* The Coleoptera were mostly determined by Dr. George H. Horn.

in the following list, which includes those most characteristic of the sea-shores.

CICINDELA GENEROSA Dejean. (p. 336.)

Spécies Général des Coléoptères, vol. v, p. 231, (teste Lec.;) Gould. Boston Journal Nat. Hist., vol. i, p. 42. Pl. 3, fig. 2.

Adult common on sandy beaches at high-water mark; larvæ burrowing in sand below high-water mark, in company with the species of *Talorchestia.*

CICINDELA DORSALIS Say. (p. 364.)

Journal Academy Nat. Sciences of Philadelphia, vol. i, p. 20; Gould, op. cit., p. 47.

Martha's Vineyard, on the sandy beaches.

CICINDELA MARGINATA Fabricius. (p. 470.)

Systema Eleutheratorum, vol. i, p. 241; Gould, op. cit., p. 48.

Barren spots in salt marshes that are occasionally covered by the tides.

CICINDELA REPANDA Dejean. (p. 364.)

Spécies Gén. des Coléoptères, vol. i, p. 74.

With the last, and on sandy beaches at Martha's Vineyard, &c.

CICINDELA HIRTICOLLIS Say. (p. 364.)

Trans. Amer. Phil. Society, new series, vol. i, p. 411, Pl. 13, fig. 2.

With last, also at a distance from the coast.

CICINDELA DUODECIMGUTTATA Dejean.

Spéc. Gén. des Coléop., vol. i, p. 73; Gould, op. cit., p. 51.

Sandy beaches near the salt water; appears both in spring and autumn.

GEOPINUS INCRASSATUS (Dej.) (p. 364.)

Spécies Gén. des Coléopères, vol. iv, p. 21.

Several specimens were found on the outer beach of Great Egg Harbor, New Jersey, burrowing in sand between tides. This species is not confined to the coast, but occurs even west of the Mississippi in sandy places, (Horn.)

BEMBIDIUM CONSTRICTUM Leconte. (p. 464.)

Annals Lyceum Nat. Hist., N. Y., vol. iv, p. 362.

Between tides at Great Egg Harbor, New Jersey.

B. CONTRACTUM Say. (p. 464.)

Trans. Amer. Phil. Soc., vol. ii, p. 85.

Between tides at Great Egg Harbor. This and the preceding occur also along the margins of streams emptying into the ocean. (Horn.)

HYDROPHILUS (TROPISTERNUS) QUADRISTRIATUS Horn. (p. 466.)

Trans. Amer. Entomol. Soc., 1871, p. 331.

In brackish pools, near Beesley's Point, New Jersey, associated with *Palæmonetes vulgaris* and other brackish-water species.

"Elongate oval, more attenuate in front, black, with slight olivaceous tinge; surface densely, finely, and equally punctured. Head with a sigmoid row of coarse punctures on each side, meeting at the vertex. Antennæ and palpi testaceous. Thorax with a small fovea on each side, near the anterior margin, behind and within the eyes, and an angulate row of punctures on each side near the middle, and a few coarse punctures very irregularly disposed. Elytra with four striæ of moderate punctures, the first two sutural and extending nearly from base to apex, inclosing at base a short scutellar row; the outer two rows subhumeral, obliterated at base, extending nearly to apex, and becoming confused, extending toward the inner rows. Body beneath black, opaque, and pubescent, abdomen with a row of brownish patches at the sides of each segment. Legs pale testaceous, femora at base and tarsi black. Length, .38 inch; (9.5^{mm}.)

Resembles *lateralis* in form, but more narrowed in front than behind. The elytra are evenly punctured, and the body along the median line moderately convex. It differs from all our species by the four distinct striæ of punctures on each elytron. The outer two correspond in position with the eighth and ninth, and traces of a third, fourth, and fifth are visible at base."—Horn.

PHILHYDRUS REFLEXIPENNIS Zimmermann.

Trans. Amer. Entomol. Soc., 1869, p. 250.

Great Egg Harbor, between tides.

This and the next occur also inland. (Horn.)

P. PERPLEXUS, Leconte.

Proc. Philad. Acad. Nat. Sci., 1855, p. 371.

Great Egg Harbor, between tides.

PHYTOSUS LITTORALIS Horn. (p. 464.)

Trans. Amer. Entomol. Soc., 1871, p. 331.

"Head brownish testaceous, moderately shining, sparsely clothed with yellowish hairs, front feebly concave; parts of mouth and antennæ testaceous, the latter darker at tip. Thorax paler than the head, as broad as long, disk depressed, sides strongly rounded in front, behind the middle sinuate; base truncate, feebly emarginate at middle, and but slightly broader than half the width of thorax at middle; surface sparsely punctured and pubescent. Elytra pale testaceous, sparsely punctured and pubescent, short, sides strongly divergent behind; body apterous. Abdomen elongate oval, broader behind the middle, piceous, shining, and very sparsely pubescent. Legs pale testaceous. Last segment of abdomen ♂ slightly prolonged at middle and sinuate on each side. Length, .08 inch, (2^{mm}.)

The male resembles in its several characters *P. Balticus* Kraatz, of Europe, but the median prolongation of the last abdominal segment is broader. The penultimate segment is subcarinate along the median line behind. The mandibles in the present species are much more exsert than in the species from California.

This is an interesting addition to our insect fauna. Its occurrence has been looked for on the ground of the occurrence of a species on the Pacific Coast, for, as a rule, (rapidly losing its exceptions,) any genus represented in Europe and on the Pacific Coast will have a representation in the Atlantic faunal region."—Horn.

This species was found burrowing in sand, between tides, at Beesley's Point, New Jersey.

BLEDIUS CORDATUS (Say.) (p. 462.)

Trans. Amer. Phil. Soc., vol. iv, p. 461.

This small species occurred in considerable abundance near Beesley's Point. It forms its small burrows in the loose sand at and just below high-water mark, in company with *Talorchestia longicornis*, *Scyphacella arenicola* SMITH, &c. It throws up a small heap of sand around the opening of its burrows, which are much smaller than those of the following species.

"This species is somewhat variable in the form of the elytral dark spot. The elytra are pale testaceous or nearly white in color, and normally with a cordate space of brownish color, and with the apex in front. This spot may become a narrow median fusiform space, or be divided so that the suture is pale; the spot frequently becomes larger by the apex of the cordate spot, extending to the scutellum and along the basal margin."—Horn.

BLEDIUS PALLIPENNIS (Say.) (p. 462.)

Journal Acad. Nat. Sci., Philad., vol. iii, p. 155.

Shores of Great Egg Harbor, near Beesley's Point, common, burrowing perpendicularly in moist sand considerably below high-water mark. The holes are round, with a small heap of sand around the orifice. This species is also found far inland. (Horn.)

HETEROCERUS UNDATUS Melsheimer. (p. 464.)

Proc. Acad. Nat. Sci., Philad., vol. ii, p. 98.

Beesley's Point, burrowing in sand, between tides. This species occurs also on the margins of inland streams. (Horn.)

PHALERIA TESTACEA Say.

Long's Expedition, vol. ii, p. 280.

Somer's Point, on the shore of Great Egg Harbor, between tides.

NEUROPTERA.

MOLANNA, species undetermined. (p. 379.)

This larva was found in a firm, straight, flattened, tapering tube, made of grains of sand, and attached to the piles of a wharf, below high-water mark, at Menemsha Bight, on Martha's Vineyard, October, 1871, by Dr. Edward Palmer.

ANURIDA MARITIMA (Guerin.) (p. 331.)

This Podurid is very abundant on the under surfaces of large stones from high-water mark to about half tide, New Haven, Wood's Hole, Nantucket; also on the coasts of Europe and Greenland. (Fabricius.)

ARACHNIDA.

CHERNES OBLONGUS Say. (p. 331.)

Hagen, Record of American Entomology for 1868, p. 51.

Under stones near low-water mark, at Wood's Hole, (S. I. S.,) several specimens were found together. This species is recorded from Florida and Georgia. I am not aware that it has been observed below high-water mark before. These specimens were identified by Dr. Hagen.

TROMBIDIUM, species. (p. 331.)

Several species of mites belonging to this or allied genera are found beneath stones near high-water mark, or even running over the *fuci* and rocks near low-water mark, but it is uncertain whether they become submerged by the rising tide or rise on its surface.

BDELLA MARINA Packard, sp. nov. (p. 331.)

Savin Rock, near New Haven, under stones between tides.

"Elongated pyriform, of the usual form of the genus, the body being thickest at the insertion of the third pair of legs. Body with a few scattered hairs, especially toward the end. Palpi twice as long as labium, hairy toward the tip, four-jointed, basal joint not so long as second, third, and fourth conjointly; second a third shorter than third. Mandibles very acutely conical, projecting one-fourth their length beyond the beak, with about four hairs on the outer side; tips very slender acute, corneous. Legs rather hairy; fourth pair but little longer than the others. Claws consisting of two portions, the basal much compressed, subovate, with about six hairs on the under edge, and carrying a stout curved claw. Beak half as long as the body is wide. Length 2.5^{mm}.

"It differs from Say's *Bdella oblonga* ('from Georgia, under bark of trees,' &c.) in its pyriform shape, the shorter first joint of the palpi, and much shorter beak."—A. S. P.

PYCNOGONIDEA.

PHOXICHILIDIUM MAXILLARE Stimpson. Plate VII, fig. 35. (p. 415.)

Marine Invertebrata of Grand Manan, p. 37, 1853.

Common in Vineyard Sound and the Bay of Fundy.

PALLENE, species. (p. 421.)

A small species, perhaps young, found upon piles of the wharf at Wood's Hole, and dredged in Vineyard Sound, in 14 fathoms, off Tarpaulin Cove on Ascidians, and off Holmes's Hole on Hydroids; also off Watch Hill, Rhode Island, and New Haven.

CRUSTACEA.

The following catalogue of the Crustacea has been prepared by Mr. S. I. Smith, excepting the portion relating to the Isopoda, which has been written by Mr. O. Harger.* The list is by no means complete, even for the higher groups which are treated, and no attempt has been made to enumerate the Ostracoids and free-swimming Copepods. Among the Amphipods, the difficult group of Lysianassinæ has not been studied, as the species require careful comparison with those of our northern coast and of Europe. The same is true of the species of *Ampelisca*, and partially of some other genera. In several cases species are omitted which are as yet only represented in our collections by imperfect, young, or too few specimens. The catalogue is intended, however, to include every species which has been mentioned, on good authority, in any published work as inhabiting the southern coast of New England.

BRACHYURA.

GELASIMUS MINAX Leconte. (p. 467.)

Proceedings Acad. Nat. Sci., Philadelphia, vol. vii, 1855, p. 403; Smith, Trans. Conn. Acad., vol. ii, p. 128, Pl. 2, fig. 4, Pl. 4, fig. 1, 1870.

Southern coast of New England to Florida. This species, the largest of our "fiddler-crabs," lives upon salt marshes, usually farther from the sea than the others, and frequently where the water is most of the time nearly fresh.

GELASIMUS PUGNAX Smith. (p. 466.)

Trans. Conn. Acad., vol. ii, p. 131, Pl. 2, fig. 1, Pl. 4, fig. 2. *G. vocans*, var. A, De Kay, Nat. Hist. of New York, p. 14, Pl. 6, fig. 10, 1844, (not *Cancer vocans* Linné.) *G. pugilator* Leconte, loc. cit., p. 403, (not of Bosc.)

From Cape Cod to Florida, the Gulf of Mexico, and the West Indies. It makes its burrows only upon salt marshes, but is often seen in great companies wandering out upon muddy or sandy flats, or even upon the beaches of the bays and sounds.

GELASIMUS PUGILATOR Latreille. (p. 336.)

Nouveau Dictionnaire d'Hist. nat., 2è édit., tome xii, p. 520, 1817; Smith, Trans. Conn. Acad., vol. ii, p. 136, Pl. 4, fig. 7, 1870. *Ocypode pugilator* Bosc, Hist. nat. des Crust., tome i, p. 167, 1820. *Gelasimus vocans* DeKay, op. cit., p. 14, Pl. 6, fig. 9.

Cape Cod to Florida, upon muddy and sandy flats and beaches.

OCYPODA ARENARIA Say. (pp. 337, 534.)

Journal Acad. Nat. Sci., Philadelphia, vol. i, p. 69, 1817; Edwards, Hist. nat. des Crust., tome ii, p. 44, Pl. 19, figs. 13, 14.

This species, which is common upon the sandy beaches from New Jersey southward, and which I have found upon Fire Island Beach, Long

* The description of *Scyphacella arenicola* and the reference of *Idotea triloba* to *Epelys* are taken from Mr. Smith's unpublished manuscript, and his name, therefore, appears as authority in these cases.

Island, will very likely be found rarely upon the beaches at Nantucket, and on the southern part of Cape Cod. It lives in deep burrows, above the reach of tides, upon sandy beaches. It is readily distinguished from the "fiddlers" by the nearly equal claws or hands, which are alike in both sexes, and by its color, which is almost exactly like the sand upon which it lives. It is carnivorous and very active, running with great rapidity when pursued.

The synonymy of this species is in much confusion, and I have not attempted to rectify it here, although there are apparently several names which antedate that of Say. The Brazilian species, usually called *rhombea* appears to be identical with ours, and if it is really the *rhombea* of Fabricius, his name should undoubtedly be retained.

SESARMA RETICULATA Say. (p. 467.)

Journal Acad. Nat. Sci., Philadelphia, vol. i, pp. 73, 76, Pl. 4, fig. 6, 1817; p. 442, 1818; Smith, Trans. Conn. Acad., vol. ii, p. 156.

From Long Island Sound to Florida, usually upon salt marshes and associated with *Gelasimus pugnax.*

PINNIXA CYLINDRICA Say. Plate I, fig. 1. (p. 367.)

Journal Acad. Nat. Sci., Philadelphia, vol. i, p. 452, 1818.

Vineyard Sound and Long Island Sound to South Carolina.

PINNOTHERES OSTREUM Say. Plate I, fig. 2, male. (p. 367.)

Loc. cit., p. 67, Pl. 4, fig. 5, 1817; DeKay, op. cit., p. 12, Pl. 7, fig. 16.

Massachusetts to South Carolina.

PINNOTHERES MACULATUS Say. (p. 434.)

Loc. cit. p. 450, 1818.

It lives in *Mytilus edulis* on the New England coast, and is found from Cape Cod to South Carolina.

CANCER IRRORATUS Say. (pp. 312, 530.)

Loc. cit., p. 59, Pl. 4, fig. 2, 1817; Stimpson, Annals Lyceum Nat. Hist., New York, vol. vii, p. 50, 1859. *Platycarcinus irroratus* Edwards, Hist. nat. des Crust., tome i, p. 414, 1834; DeKay, op. cit., Pl. 2, fig. 2. *Cancer Sayi* Gould, Report on the Invertebrata of Massachusetts, 1st edit., p. 323, 1841. *Platycarcinus Sayi* DeKay, op. cit., p. 7. *Cancer borealis* Packard, Memoirs Boston Nat. Hist. Soc., vol. i, p. 303, 1867.

Labrador to South Carolina.

CANCER BOREALIS Stimpson. (pp. 486, 493.)

Loc. cit., p. 50, 1859. *Cancer irroratus* Gould, op. cit., p. 322.

Nova Scotia to Vineyard Sound and No Man's Land. It very likely occurs both north and south of these limits, as it seems to be rare or local, and is often, perhaps, confounded with the far more common *C. irroratus*, although it is a perfectly distinct species.

PANOPEUS HERBSTII Edwards. (p. 472.)

Op. cit., vol. i, 403, 1834; Smith, Proceedings Boston Soc. Nat. Hist., vol. xii, p. 276, 1859.

Long Island Sound to Brazil, but not common north of New Jersey. It is readily distinguished from the following species, by the tubercle on the subhepatic region, just below the first lobe of the antero-lateral border of the carapax; by the postorbital tooth being separated from the second tooth of the antero-lateral margin by a rounded sinus; and by the dactylus of the larger cheliped having a stout tooth near the base within.

PANOPEUS DEPRESSUS Smith. Plate I, fig. 3. (p. 312.)

Loc. cit., p. 283, 1859.

From Cape Cod to Florida, and often carried with oysters much farther north. It is, perhaps, native in Massachusetts Bay.

PANOPIUS SAYI Smith. (p. 312.)

Loc. cit., p. 284, 1859.

Associated with the last, and having the same range. It is easily distinguished from the last species by its narrower, more convex, and swollen carapax, and by the more projecting and arcuate front. The terminal segment of the abdomen of the male is also quite different in the two species; in *P. Sayi* it is broader than the preceding segment, about two-thirds as long as broad, the edges slightly concave, and the tip abruptly triangular, while in *P. depressus* it is narrower than the preceding segment, about three-fourths as long as broad, the edges convex, and the tip broadly rounded.

PANOPEUS HARRISII Stimpson. (p. 313.)

Loc. cit., p. 55, 1859. *Pilumnus Harrisii* Gould, op. cit., p. 326, 1841.

Massachusetts Bay to Florida.

CARCINUS GRANULATUS (Say, sp.) (p. 312.)

Cancer granulatus Say, loc. cit., p. 61, 1817. *Carcinus mænas* Gould, op. cit., p. 321; DeKay, op. cit., p. 8, Pl. 5, figs. 5, 6. (?) *Carcinus mænas* Leach, Edwards, &c.

Cape Cod to New Jersey, and perhaps much farther south. Our species may, very likely, be the same as the *Carcinus mænas* of Europe, but its not extending north on our own coast throws some doubt upon this until there has been a careful comparison of specimens from the two sides of the Atlantic.

PLATYONICHUS OCELLATUS Latreille. Plate I, fig. 4. (pp. 338, 533.)

Encyclopédie méthodique, tome xvi, p. 152; DeKay, op. cit., p. 9, Pl. 1, fig. 1, Pl. 5, fig. 7. *Cancer ocellatus* Herbst, Krabben und Krebse, Band iii, erstes Heft, p. 61, Pl. 49, fig. 4, 1799. *Portunus pictus* Say, loc. cit., p. 62, Pl. 4, fig. 4, 1817.

Cape Cod to Florida.

CALLINECTES HASTATUS Ordway. (pp. 367, 468.)

Boston Journal Nat. Hist., vol. vii, p. 568, 1863. *Lupa hastata* Say, loc. cit., p 65, 1817. *Lupa diacantha* DeKay, op. cit., p. 10, Pl. 3, fig. 3.

Cape Cod to Florida, and occasionally in Massachusetts Bay.

LIBINIA CANALICULATA Say. (p. 368.)

Loc. cit., p. 77, Pl. 4, fig. 1, 1817; DeKay, op. cit., p. 2, Pl. 4, fig. 4; Streets Proceedings Acad. Nat. Sci., Philadelphia, 1870, p. 105, 1871.

Found as far north as Casco Bay, on the coast of Maine, and common from Massachusetts Bay southward, at least as far as Florida.

LIBINIA DUBIA Edwards. (p. 368.)

Op. cit., tome i, p. 300, Pl. 14 *bis*, fig. 2, 1834; Streets, loc. cit., p. 104.

Cape Cod to Florida.

PELIA MUTICA Stimpson. (p. 415)

Annals Lyceum Nat. Hist., New York, vol. vii, p. 177, 1860. *Pisa mutica* Gibbes, Proceedings Amer. Association Adv. Sci., 3d meeting, p. 171, 1850.

Vineyard Sound to Florida.

HYAS COARCTATUS Leach. (p. 504.)

Trans. Linn. Soc., London, vol. xi, p. 329, 1815. Régne animal de Cuvier, 3me édit., Pl. 32, fig. 3. *Lissa fissirostra* Say, loc. cit., p. 79, 1817.

Leidy mentions this species as having been found on the coast of New Jersey, and Say mentions it from the coast of Long Island, but it seems to be rare south of Cape Cod. It lives in deep water from Cape Cod northward, and on the European coast, and is frequently found in the stomachs of the cod-fish.

HETEROCRYPTA GRANULATA Stimpson. (p. 315.)

Annals Lyceum Nat. Hist., New York, vol. x, p. 102, 1871. *Cryptopodia granulata* Gibbes, loc. cit., p. 173; and Proceedings Elliott Soc., Charleston, vol. i, p. 35, wood cut.

This species, dredged several times in Vineyard Sound, was before known only from North Carolina to Florida and the West Indies.

ANOMOURA.

HIPPA TALPOIDA Say. Plate II, fig. 5. (pp. 338, 530.)

Loc. cit., p. 160, 1817.

Cape Cod to Florida.

EUPAGURUS POLLICARIS Stimpson. (p. 313.)

Annals Lyceum Nat. Hist., New York, vol. vii, p. 92, 1859. *Pagurus pollicaris* Say, loc. cit., p. 162, 1817; Gould, op. cit., p. 329; DeKay, op. cit., p. 19, Pl. 8, fig. 21.

Massachusetts to Florida.

EUPAGURUS BERNHARDUS Stimpson. (p. 501.)

Loc. cit., p. 89, 1859. *Pagurus Bernhardus* (Linné sp.,) Fabricius, Entomologia systematica, vol. ii, p. 469, 1793; Gould, op. cit., p. 329; DeKay, op. cit., p. 20.

Vineyard Sound, &c., in deep water, more abundant north of Cape Cod, and extending to Northern Europe on one side, and to Puget Sound on the other.

EUPAGURUS PUBESCENS Stimpson.

Loc. cit., p. 89, 1859; and Proceedings Acad. Nat. Sci., Philadelphia, 1858, p. 237, 1859. *Pagurus pubescens* Kroyer, Naturh. Tidsskrift, Bind ii, p. 251, 1838.

This species has been taken in deep water off the coast of New Jersey, and will, doubtless, be found off Long Island and Vineyard Sounds. It extends northward to Greenland and Northern Europe.

EUPAGURUS LONGICARPUS Stimpson. (p. 339.)

Proceedings Acad. Nat. Sci., Philadelphia, 1858, p. 237, 1859. *Pagurus longicarpus* Say, loc. cit., p. 163, 1817; Gould, op. cit., p. 330; DeKay, op. cit., p. 20, Pl. 8, fig. 22.

Massachusetts Bay to South Carolina.

MACROURA.

GEBIA AFFINIS Say. Plate II, fig. 7. (pp. 367, 530.)

Loc. cit., p. 195, 1817.

Long Island Sound to South Carolina.

CALLIANASSA STIMPSONI Smith, sp. nov. Plate II, fig. 8. (p. 369.)

Carapax smooth and shining. Greater cheliped (fig. 8) about three times as long as the carapax; carpus and hand convex on both sides; carpus sometimes considerably longer, sometimes not at all longer than broad; both fingers of the same length, and about as long as the basal portion of the dactylus; the prehensile edge of the dactylus without a strong tooth or tubercle at base. Smaller cheliped about half as long as the greater; carpus and hand about equal in length; fingers equal, slender, as long as the basal portion of the propodus. Abdomen smooth and shining above, gradually increasing in breadth to the fifth segment; second segment longest, much longer than broad; third and fifth equal in length; fourth shorter, and sixth a little longer than third or fifth; telson much broader than long, shorter than the fourth segment.

Length of a large specimen, 61^{mm}; length of carapax, 15; length of larger cheliped, 44.

In the character of the chelipeds this species seems to be closely allied to *C. longimana* Stimpson, from Puget Sound.

Our species ranges from the coast of the Southern States north to Long Island Sound.

HOMARUS AMERICANUS Edwards. (pp. 395, 492, 522.)

Hist. nat. des. Crust., tome ii, p. 334, 1837. *Astacus marinus* Say, loc. cit., p. 165, 1817, (not of Fabricius.)

New Jersey to Labrador.

CRANGON VULGARIS Fabricius. Plate III, fig. 10. (pp. 339, 529.)

Supplementum Entomologiæ system., p. 410, 1798. *Crangon septemspinosus* Say, loc. cit., p. 246, 1818.

North Carolina to Labrador and Europe. In depth it extends from low water to 60 or 70 fathoms, and probably much deeper.

HIPPOLYTE PUSIOLA Kroyer. (p. 395.)

Monografisk Fremstlling Hippol., p. 319, Pl. 3, figs. 69–73, 1842.

Vineyard Sound and northward to Greenland and Europe.

VIRBIUS ZOSTERICOLA Smith, sp. nov. Plate III, fig. 11. (p. 369.)

Female: Short and stout. Rostrum about as long as the carapax, and reaching nearly, or quite, to the tip of the antennal scale; the upper edge nearly straight and unarmed, except by two, or rarely three, teeth at the base; under edge with three (sometimes two or four) teeth on the anterior half. Carapax smooth and armed with a stout (supra-orbital) spine on each side at the base of the rostrum and above and a little behind the base of the ocular peduncle, a small (antennal) spine on the anterior margin beneath the ocular peduncle, and a stout (hepatic) spine behind the base of the antennæ. Inner flagellum of the antennula extending very slightly beyond the tip of the antennal scale; outer flagellum considerably shorter. Abdomen geniculated at the third segment; the posterior margin of the third segment prominent above, but not acute.

The males differ from the females in being smaller, much more slender, and in having the rostrum narrower vertically.

The color in life is very variable. Most frequently the entire animal is bright green, sometimes pale, or even translucent, tinged with green. Others were translucent, specked with reddish brown, and with a broad median band of dark brown extending the whole length of the body.

Length of female, 20–26^{mm}; male 15–20.

It is at once distinguished from *V. pleuracanthus* Stimpson, to which, in many characters, it is closely allied, by its very much longer rostrum.

Among eel-grass about Vineyard Sound, and probably common at other points on the coast.

Virbius pleuracanthus Stimpson, (Annals Lyceum Nat. Hist., New York, vol. x, p. 127, 1871,) abundant upon the coast of New Jersey, will very likely be found farther north. In habit it is similar to the species just described.

PANDALUS ANNULICORNIS Leach. Plate II, fig. 6. (p. 493.)

Malacostraca Podophthalmata Britanniæ, Pl. 40, 1815.

Deep water in Vineyard Sound, off Newport, &c.

North of Cape Cod it is common, and extends to Greenland and Europe. In depth it extends down to 430 fathoms at least.

PALÆMONETES VULGARIS Stimpson. Plate II, fig. 9. (pp. 479, 529.)

Annals Lyceum Nat. Hist., New York, vol. x, p. 129, 1871. *Palæmon vulgaris* Say, Journal Acad. Nat. Sci., Philadelphia, vol. i, p. 224, 1818.

Massachusetts to South Carolina.

PENÆUS BRASILIENSIS Latreille.

Edwards, Hist. nat. des Crust., tome ii, p. 414; Gibbes, loc. cit., p. 198; Stimpson, Annals Lyceum Nat. Hist., New York, vol. x, p. 132.

According to Stimpson, this species has been found in the Croton River at Sing Sing, New York, by Professor Baird. It will therefore be very likely to occur in the rivers of Southern New England. It is common on the coast of the Southern States, and extends to Brazil.

SQUILLOIDEA.

SQUILLA EMPUSA Say. (pp. 369, 536.)

Loc. cit., p. 250, 1818; Dekay, op. cit., p. 32, Pl. 13, fig. 54; Gibbes, Proceedings Amer. Assoc., 3d meeting, p. 199.

Florida to Cape Cod.

The young of this species is figured on Plate VIII, fig. 36.

MYSIDEA.

MYSIS STENOLEPIS Smith, sp. nov. Plate III, fig. 12. (p. 370.)

Male: Anterior margin of the carapax produced into a very short, broad, and obtusely rounded rostrum, and each side at the inferior angle into a prominent, acutely triangular tooth, between which and the base of the ocular peduncle there is a broad and deeply rounded sinus. Peduncle of the antennula about a third as long as the carapax along the dorsal line; the sexual appendage slender, tapering, nearly as long as the peduncle; inner flagellum half as long as the outer. Antennal scale rather longer than the carapax along the dorsal line, narrow, about ten times as long as broad, tapering to a slender and acute point, both edges ciliated and nearly straight; flagellum about as long as the rest of the animal. Abdomen somewhat geniculated between the first and second segments; sixth segment about twice as long as the fifth. Appendages of the fourth segment reaching nearly to the distal extremity of the sixth segment; inner ramus slender, slightly longer than the base; outer ramus naked, composed of six segments; the first, third, and fourth subequal in length, and together equaling about three-fourths of the entire length; the second, fifth, and sixth subequal; penultimate segment armed with a stout spine on the outside at the distal extremity, and the last segment terminated by a similar spine. Inner lamella of the appendages of the sixth segment extending slightly beyond the telson, narrow and tapering to an obtuse tip; outer lamella narrow, linear, about seven times as long as broad, nearly a third longer than the inner, both edges ciliated and nearly straight, and the tip narrow and somewhat truncated. Telson considerably longer than the sixth segment, tapering slightly, the sides nearly straight, and each armed with about twenty-four spines; the extremity cleft by a deep sinus rounded at bottom, and its margins convex posteriorly and armed with very numerous slender spines.

Length of a male from tip of rostrum to extremity of telson, 23.2^{mm}; length of carapax along the dorsal line, 6.5; length of antennal scale, 6.7; length of telson, 3.8. Length of female, 30^{mm}.

The females differ but little from the males except in the usual sexual characters. The figure, (Plate III, fig. 12,) made from a small female specimen, does not properly represent the anterior margin of the carapax.

In life the young females are semi-translucent, a spot on each ocular peduncle, the peduncles and inner flagella of the antennulæ, the antennal scale, the telson and caudal lamellæ more or less blackish from deposits of black pigment, while each segment of the abdomen is marked with a rudely stellate spot of black.

Large males of this species were found in the autumn among eel-grass, at New Haven, Connecticut, and the young abundantly in the same situation in May. Young females were collected in abundance during June and July, among the eel-grass in the shallow bays and coves about Vineyard Sound, while adult females, with the marsupial pouches filled with young, were collected, at Wood's Hole, in abundance, April 1, by Mr. V. N. Edwards.

MYSIS AMERICANA. Smith, sp. nov. (p. 396.)

Anterior margin distinctly rostrated, but only slightly projecting; evenly rounded, the inferior angle projecting into a sharp tooth. Antennulæ, in the male, with the densely ciliated sexual appendage similar to that in *M. vulgaris* of Europe; the outer flagellum nearly as long as the body, the inner slightly shorter. Antennal scale about three-fourths as long as the carapax, about nine times as long as broad, tapering regularly from the base to a very long and acute tip; both margins ciliated. Appendages of the fourth segment of the abdomen in the male similar to those in *M. vulgaris*. The outer ramus is slender and naked, and its pair of terminal stylets are equal in length, slender, curved toward the tip, and the distal half armed with numerous short setæ; the ultimate segment of the ramus itself is little more than half as long as the stylets, the penultimate segment four or five times as long as the terminal. Inner lamella of the appendages of the sixth segment about as long as the telson, narrow, slightly broadened at the base, and tapering to a slender but obtuse point; outer lamella once and a half as long as the inner, and eight times as long as broad, slightly tapering, the extremity subtruncate. Telson triangular, broadened at base, the lateral margins slightly convex posteriorly, and armed with stout spines alternating with intervals of several smaller ones; the tip very narrow, truncate, armed with a stout spine each side, and two small ones filling the space between their bases. Length 10 to 12^{mm}.

This species was found, in April, at Beesley's Point, New Jersey, in pools, upon salt-marshes, and at the same locality the stomachs of the spotted flounder were found filled with them. Professor D. C. Eaton found it in great abundance among sea-weeds, &c., just below low-water mark, at New Haven, Connecticut, May 5, 1873. It was also taken in the dredge, in 4 to 6 fathoms, at New Haven, Connecticut, and in 25 fathoms off Vineyard Sound, and has been found in the stomachs of the shad, mackerel, &c.

HETEROMYSIS FORMOSA Smith, gen. et sp. nov. (p. 396.)

Body rather short and stout. Carapax broad behind and tapering anteriorly; the anterior margin produced into an obtusely triangular rostrum. Ocular peduncles short and thickened nearly to the base. Peduncle of the antennula stout, extending to the tip of the antennal scale; the terminal segment in the male wanting the usual elongated sexual process, but having in its place a very dense tuft of long hairs; inner flagellum nearly as long as the carapax; outer flagellum stout at base and more than twice as long as the inner. Antennal scale about three and a half times as long as broad, not quite reaching to the extremity of the peduncle of the antennula, ovate, obtuse at the tip, external margin without a spine and ciliated like the inner; peduncle elongated, penultimate segment considerably longer than the ultimate; flagellum nearly as long as the entire body. Mandibles, maxillæ, first and second maxillipeds, as in *Mysis*. The first pair of legs (second pair of gnathopoda) differ remarkably from those in all the described genera of Mysidæ. The whole leg is stouter than in the succeeding pairs, and the terminal portion, corresponding to the multiarticulate portion of the inner branch (endopodus) in *Mysis*, &c., consists of only three segments including the terminal claw; the first of these segments is stout, slightly shorter than the preceding (meral) segment, and armed with stout spines along the distal portion of the inner margin; the second segment is very short, not longer than broad, and closely articulated to the preceding segment so as to admit of very little motion; the ultimate article is a long, slightly curved claw, freely articulated to the preceding segment. In the five posterior pairs of legs the terminal portion of the inner branch is multiarticulate as in *Mysis*, in the first composed of five segments, besides a stout terminal claw like that in the preceding pair, and in the four remaining pairs of six segments and a slender terminal claw. The exopodal branches of all the legs are well developed.

Abdomen a little more than twice as long as the carapax, the sixth segment a little longer than the fifth. The appendages of the first five segments alike in both sexes; short, rudimentary, and like the same appendages in the female *Mysis*. Inner lamella of the sixth segment projecting very slightly beyond the extremity of the telson, broad, ovate; outer lamella only a little longer than the inner, about two-sevenths as long as broad, inner margin quite convex, outer very slightly, tip rounded. Telson short, broad at base, and narrowed rapidly toward the extremity, the width at base about two-thirds the length, at the extremity only a third as wide as at base; the lateral margins each armed with twelve to fourteen spines, which increase in size distally, and a very long terminal spine; the posterior margins cleft by a sinus deeper than broad, and armed with numerous small spines.

In life the males are semitranslucent and nearly colorless, while in the females the antennulæ, the flagella of the antennæ, the ocular peduncles, the thorax with the marsupial pouch, and the articulations of the caudal appendages are beautiful rose color.

Length of a male, 6.0^{mm}; carapax along the dorsal line, 1.8; antennal scale, 0.70; telson, 0.90. Length of a female, 8.5^{mm}; carapax, 2.5; antennal scale, 0.88; telson, 1.16.

The absence of the sexual appendages from the antennulæ of the male, the peculiar structure of the anterior legs, and the similarity of the abdominal appendages in the two sexes, at once separate the genus *Heteromysis* from all known allied genera.

THYSANOPODA, species. (452.)

A great number of small specimens were taken from the stomach of mackerel caught twenty miles off No Man's Land, July 18, 1871.

Several were also caught swimming at the surface in Vineyard Sound, April 30, 1873, by V. N. Edwards.

A single specimen of a species apparently the same as this was taken at New Haven, Connecticut, May 5, 1873, by Professor D. C. Eaton.

CUMACEA.

DIASTYLIS QUADRISPINOSA, G. O. Sars. Plate III, fig. 13. (p. 507.)

Öfversigt af Kongl. Vet.-Akad. Förh., 1871, Stockholm, p. 72.

Dredged in 23 fathoms of Martha's Vineyard and in 29 fathoms of Buzzard's Bay. It is also found in the Bay of Fundy. Sars's specimens were dredged by the Josephine expedition in 18 fathoms off Skinnecock Bay, Long Island, and in 30 to 35 fathoms, latitude 39° 54′ north, longitude 73° 15′ west, off the coast of New Jersey.

Our specimens agree well with Sars's description, except that the second segment of the inner ramus of the lateral caudal appendages has but three, or rarely four, spines upon the inner margin, while in Sars's specimens there were five.

DIASTYLIS SCULPTA Sars.

Loc. cit., p. 71.

With the last species, in 18 fathoms, off Skinnecock Bay, according to Sars.

DIASTYLIS ABBREVIATA Sars.

Loc. cit., p. 74.

Rare in 30 to 35 fathoms, off the coast of New Jersey, with the first species, (Sars.)

EUDORELLA PUSILLA Sars.

Loc. cit., p. 79.

Not infrequent in 18 fathoms, off Skinnecock Bay, (Sars.)

EUDORELLA HISPIDA Sars.

Loc. cit., p. 80.

Rare in 30 to 35 fathoms, with the other species mentioned, off the coast of New Jersey, (Sars.)

AMPHIPODA.

ORCHESTIA AGILIS Smith, sp. nov. Plate IV, fig. 14. (p. 314.)

Male: Antennula not quite reaching the distal extremity of the penultimate segment of the antenna; second and third segments of the peduncle about equal in length, and each slightly longer than the first; flagellum about as long as the two last segments of the peduncle. Antenna less than half as long as the body; segments of the peduncle stout and swollen, the ultimate longer than the penultimate; flagellum stout, compressed vertically, much shorter than the peduncle, composed of twelve to fifteen segments. Propodus in the second pair of legs short and thickened laterally, the palmary margin with a small prominence on the outer edge of the posterior angle, behind which the tip of the dactylus closes, and along the inner edge, inside the dactylus, with a thin ridge, which is broken by a small notch near the posterior angle, so that the margin when viewed laterally shows a broad lobe next the base of the dactylus and two small, rounded lobes next the posterior angle, the tip of the dactylus resting between the small lobes; dactylus slender, curved so as to fit closely the palmary margin, and furnished with very minute setæ along the prehensile margin. Posterior thoracic legs slightly longer than the preceding; carpus in full-grown specimens short, much swollen, and thickened so as to be nearly cylindrical.

Female: Carpus and hand in the second pair of legs unarmed; propodus short, slightly spatulate in outline, with a pair of minute setæ at the base of the dactylus, which is very short, not reaching the extremity of the propodus.

Length: male, 10–15^{mm}; female, 10–14.

Bay of Fundy to New Jersey.

ORCHESTIA PALUSTRIS Smith, sp. nov. (p. 468.)

Male: Antennulæ reaching slightly beyond the distal extremity of the penultimate segment of the peduncle of the antennæ. Antennæ less than half as long as the body; peduncle slender; flagellum slender, longer than the peduncle, composed of eighteen to twenty-six segments. Propodus in the second pair of legs nearly oval in outline, the palmary margin spinous, regularly curved to the posterior angle, which projects on the outer edge in a slight, rounded prominence, within which the tip of the dactylus closes; dactylus slender, curved so as to nearly fit the palmary margin, and furnished with minute setæ along the prehensile margin. Posterior thoracic legs slightly longer than the preceding; carpus and propodus both long and slender.

The female differs from the male as in the last species.

Length, male, 15–22^{mm}; female, 12–18^{mm}.

Cape Cod to New Jersey, and very likely farther north and south.

TALORCHESTIA LONGICORNIS Smith. (p. 336.)

Talitrus longicornis Say, loc. cit., p, 384, 1818. *Orchestia longicornis* Edwards, His. nat. des. Crust., tome iii, p. 18, 1840; De Kay, op. cit., p. 36, Pl. 7, fig. 19.

Cape Cod to New Jersey, and probably farther south.

TALORCHESTIA MEGALOPHTHALMA Smith. (p. 336.)

Orchestia megalophthalma Bate, Catalogue Amphip. Crust., British Museum, p. 22, 1862.

Cape Cod to New Jersey, and probably farther south.

Talitrus quadrifidus, De Kay, (op. cit., p. 36, Pl. 14, fig. 27,) may be based on the female of one of the preceding species, but it so is badly described and figured as to be indeterminable.

HYALE LITTORALIS Smith. (p. 315.)

Allorchestes littoralis Stimpson, Marine Invertebrata of Grand Manan, p. 49., Pl. 3, fig. 36, 1853; Bate, Catalogue Amphip. Crust., British Museum, p. 48, Pl. 8, fig. 2, 1862.

This species was found at New Haven, Connecticut., by Professor Verrill, May 5, 1873, and is one of the inhabitants of rocky shores, piles of wharves, &c. I have found it at Provincetown, Massachusetts, and it is abundant in the Bay of Fundy. It is undoubtedly abundant on the whole New England coast, but its station upon the shore is so high up on the beach that it is likely to be overlooked.

LYSIANASSA, species. (p. 431.)

A species of this genus, as restricted by Boeck, was several times dredged in Vineyard Sound and Buzzard's Bay.

Several other species of *Lysianassinæ* were taken in Vineyard Sound and the neighboring region, but they have not yet been sufficiently studied to be enumerated. The species of this group are much less common and the individuals smaller on the coast of Southern New Eng-and than they are upon the coast of Maine and farther north.

LEPIDACTYLIS DYTISCUS Say. (p. 339.)

Loc. cit., p. 380, 1818.

Georgia to Cape Cod.

PHOXUS KROYERI Stimpson. (p. 501.)

Marine Invertebrata of Grand Manan, p. 58, 1853.

Rare in Vineyard Sound and usually in deep water. Common in the Bay of Fundy.

UROTHOË, species. (p. 452.)

A species with long, slender antennæ and very large black eyes, and apparently belonging to this genus, was taken in great numbers at the surface at Wood's Hole, on the evening of July 3, and on one or two other occasions. In life it was whitish, slightly tinged with orange-yellow.

MONOCULODES, species. (p. 452.)

A single specimen taken at the surface in Vineyard Sound, December 21, by Mr. V. N. Edwards.

LAPHYSTIUS STURIONIS Kroyer. (p. 457.)

Nat. Tidsskrift, vol. iv, p. 157, 1842. *Darwinia compressa* Bate, Report Brit. Assoc., 1855, p. 58; Catalogue Amphip. Crust., Brit. Mus., p, 108, Pl. 17, fig. 7; Bate and Westwood, Brit. Sessile-eyed Crust. vol. i, p. 184, wood cut.

A parasitic amphipod, apparently quite identical with this species of Europe, was found in the mouth of a goose-fish (*Lophius Americanus*) taken in Vineyard Sound. A species, apparently the same, was also taken from the back of a skate (*Raia lævis*) in the Bay of Fundy the past summer. It is readily distinguished by its broad depressed form, and by having the third to fifth pairs of legs very stout and their distal segments forming powerful talon-like claws, while the first and second pairs are small and slender.

CALLIOPIUS LÆVIUSCULUS Boeck. (p. 315.)

Crust. Amphipoda borealia et arctica, p. 117, 1870. *Amphithoë læviuscula* Kroyer Grönlands Amfipoder, p. 53, Pl. 3. fig. 13, 1838. *Calliope læviuscula* Bate, Catalogue Amphip. Crust. Brit. Mus., p. 148, Pl. 28, fig. 2, 1862; Bate and Westwood, op. cit., vol. i, p. 156, wood cut.

Vineyard Sound and northward to Greenland, Northern Europe, and Spitzbergen.

PONTOGENEIA INERMIS Boeck. (p. 452.)

Op. cit., p. 114, 1870. *Amphithoë inermis* and *crenulata*, Kroyer, Grönlands Amfipoder, pp. 47, 50, Pl. 3, figs. 11, 12, 1838. *Iphimedia vulgaris* Stimpson, Marine Invertebrata of Grand Manan, p. 53, 1853. *Atylus inermis, crenulatus*, and *vulgaris* Bate, Catalogue Amphip. Crust. Brit. Mus., pp. 138, 139, 142, Pl. 27, figs. 5, 6, 1862. *Atylus vulgaris* Packard, Memoirs Boston Soc. Nat. Hist., vol. i, p. 298, 1867. (Not *Atylus* (*Paramphitoë*) *inermis* Packard, loc. cit., p. 298, Pl. 8, fig. 3.)

Taken at the surface in Vineyard Sound, in March, by Mr. V. N. Edwards. It is abundant, in company with *Calliopius læviusculus*, about the Bay of Fundy in pools left by the tide, and ranges north to Labrador and Greenland.

GAMMARUS ORNATUS Edwards. Plate IV, fig. 15. (p. 314.)

Annales des Sci. nat., tome xx, 1830, p. 367, Pl. 10, figs. 1–10; Hist. nat. des Crust., tome iii, p. 47; Bate, op. cit., p. 212, Pl. 37, fig. 8. *Gammarus locusta* Gould, op. cit., p. 334. *Gammarus pulex* Stimpson, Marine Invert. Grand Manan, p. 55.

New Jersey to Greenland.

GAMMARUS ANNULATUS Smith, sp. nov. (p. 314.)

Anterior margin of the head produced each side beneath the antennulæ into a truncated lobe, which extends farther forward than in *G. ornatus;* eyes scarcely reniform, less elongated than in *G. ornatus*, and their lower margins not reaching, by considerable, the anterior border of the truncated lobe. Antennæ longer than the antennulæ; the ultimate segment of the peduncle longer than the penultimate; the flagellum much more slender, the segments more elongated and with fewer hairs, than in *G. ornatus*. Hands of the first pair of legs more elongated than in *G. ornatus*, and the palmary margins very oblique. Propodus in the second pair very narrow and elongated, subcylindrical, slightly flattened on the inner side, the palmary margin longitudinal, and scarcely distinct from the posterior margin. Fourth segment of the abdomen with a median fascicle of two large and two small spines, but no lateral fascicles. Fifth and sixth segments with both median and lateral fascicles of spines.

Color in life grayish white, the posterior margins of the segments bordered with brown, giving the body an annulated appearance.

Length, 12–18^{mm}.

New Haven, Connecticut, and Eastport, Maine, and doubtless abundant at other points on the coast.

This species closely resembles the fresh-water *G. fasciatus*, but is distinguished from it by the proportions of the segments of the peduncles of the antennæ, and by wanting the lateral fascicles of spines upon the fourth segment of the abdomen.

GAMMARUS NATATOR Smith, sp. nov. (p. 439.)

Male: Eyes large, enlongated, but only slightly reniform. Antennula short and stout, about three-sevenths as long as the body; flagellum but little longer than the peduncle; secondary flagellum nearly half as long as the primary. Antenna considerably longer than the antennula; penultimate segment of the peduncle reaching to the extremity of the peduncle of the antennula; ultimate segment of the peduncle longer than the penultimate; flagellum about two-thirds as long as the peduncle. Both antennulæ and antennæ are furnished with very long hairs, of which many on the antennulæ are plumose. First, second, and third epimera margined on the inferior edges with long cilia. First pair of legs more slender than the second; propodus oval, twice as long as broad, palmary margin continuous with the inferior, with a very narrow lamellar edge, a stout obtuse spine in the middle, and two smaller ones at the inferior angle; dactylus strongly curved. In the second pair the propodus is more than half as broad as long, and somewhat rectangular in outline, except that the palmary margin is slightly oblique; the palmary margin has a narrow lamellar edge, with a slight emargination in the middle, from which a stout obtuse spine arises, and at the inferior angle there are two or three smaller spines, as in the first pair. The inferior edges of the carpi and propodi of both pairs of legs are thickly clothed with long hairs. Natatory legs reaching to the tips of the telson. Second and third segments of the abdomen with the sides produced backward, and the postero-inferior angle acute. Fourth segment with only a median fascicle of spines; fifth and sixth segments with median and lateral fascicles. Rami of the posterior caudal stylets lanceolate, five or six times as long as broad, the outer extending beyond the inner by the length of its terminal article, which is very slender, almost spiniform, the edges of both rami clothed with long plumose hairs. Each division of the telson nearly three times as long as broad.

In the female the hands of the first and second pairs of legs are smaller and slenderer, and the propodi somewhat oval and nearly alike in both pairs; otherwise the females do not differ from the males, except that the rami of the posterior caudal stylets are, perhaps, a very little shorter and broader in proportion.

Length, 10–12^{mm}.

Vineyard Sound, in vast numbers at the surface of the water, usually among floating sea-weeds and eel-grass. Also from stomach of mackerel, May 20.

GAMMARUS MARINUS Leach. (p. 486.)

Trans. Linnean Soc., London, vol. xi, p. 359, 1815; Bate, Catalogue Amphip. Crust., Brit. Mus., p. 215, Pl. 38, fig. 4; Bate and Westwood, Brit. Sessile-eyed Crust., vol. i, p. 370, wood-cut.

A species which I cannot distinguish, by the published figures and descriptions, from this common species of Europe, was not uncommon, associated with *Amphithoë maculata*, under stones at the Wepecket Islands, Gull Island, Cuttyhunk Island, and at other places on Vineyard Sound and Buzzard's Bay. It has also been found at Watch Hill, Rhode Island, and at New Haven, Connecticut, by Professor Verrill. It is at once distinguished from all the other species of our coast by its slender form, slender antennæ, by having the sides of the second and third segments of the abdomen narrow and not produced or acute at the postero-inferior angle, and by having the outer rami of the posterior caudal stylets four or five times as long as the inner.

GAMMARUS MUCRONATUS Say. (p. 479.)

Loc. cit., p, 376, 1818; De Kay, op. cit., p. 37. *Gammaracanthus mucronatus* Bate, op. cit., p. 203.

Readily distinguished from the other species of the coast by having the posterior margin of each of the anterior segments of the abdomen produced into a slender, spiniform, dorsal tooth. In life, it is translucent, tinged with green, or yellowish green, minutely specked with brown or black; these black or brown markings and the green color being frequently so arranged as to give the antennæ and legs a banded appearance. Our species cannot be referred to Bate's genus *Gammaracanthus*, for the dorsal margin is not distinctly carinated, and the third, fourth, and fifth segments of the abdomen are furnished with fascicles of spines.

Usually in brackish water, North Carolina to Cape Cod, and, according to Say, from Florida also.

MŒRA LEVIS Smith, sp. nov. (p. 315.)

Eyes nearly round; black in alcoholic specimens. Antennula two-thirds as long as the body; first and second segments of the peduncle equal in length, third about two-thirds as long as the second; flagellum about as long as the peduncle. Antenna about as long as the peduncle of the antennula; ultimate and penultimate segments equal in length, antepenultimate very short; flagellum much shorterthan the peduncle. Legs of the first pair small; carpus as broad as the propodus, but little longer than broad, the posterior margin straight and furnished with fascicles of stout hairs; palmary margin nearly transverse, slightly arcuate, and armed with short setæ; dactylus slender and fitting closely the palmary margin. Legs of the second pair larger; carpus short, as broad as the base of the propodus, the posterior angle thickly clothed with stout hairs; propodus in the male stout, broadest distally, the palmary margin expanded toward the inferior angle and excavated on the inner side to receive the long and strongly curved dactylus; in the female, elongated, slightly narrowed distally, the posterior margin continuous and nearly parallel with the palmary, and furnished with fascicles of stout hairs. Fifth pair of legs but little longer than the third or fourth; sixth and seventh much longer than the fifth, subequal, stout, their meral and carpal segments considerably expanded, especially in the male. Ultimate caudal stylets projecting a little beyond the preceding pairs; rami short, broad, and with spinous tips; the outer ramus slightly longer and broader than the inner, and its outer margin armed with a very few fascicles of spinules. Telson reaching to the bases of the rami of the posterior caudal stylets, nearly as broad as long, and cleft two-thirds of the way to the base.

Length, 5–7^{mm}.

New Jersey, Long Island Sound, Vineyard Sound.

MELITA NITIDA Smith, sp. nov. (p. 314.)

Eyes small, round, black. Antennula about two-thirds as long as the body; first segment of the peduncle slightly shorter than the second, which is nearly twice as long as the last; flagellum longer than the peduncle. Antenna shorter than the antennula, but the peduncle considerably longer than the peduncle of the antennula, the penultimate segment being scarcely shorter than the penultimate segment of the antennula, while the ultimate segment is subequal with it. First pair of legs with the carpus longer and broader than the propodus; propodus oblong, slightly curved; dactylus very small but stout, curved, and attached in a notch in the middle of the extremity of the propodus, not closing upon the extremity of the propodus but projecting inward. Second pair of legs stout; carpus short, triangular; propodus somewhat oval, the palmary margin oblique, arcuate, continuous with the posterior margin, and armed with a series of minute spines and with numerous stiff hairs, the clothing of hairs continuing round upon the posterior margin to the carpus; dactylus curved, tip resting within the palmary margin. Third pair of legs slightly longer than the fourth. Three posterior pairs slender, the fifth somewhat shorter than the sixth and seventh, which are subequal, and have the anterior margins of the bases armed with small spines and the posterior margins minutely serrate. None of the dorsal margins of the segments of the abdomen serrate or emarginate, but the margin of the fifth segment armed with several slender spines on each side near the median line of the dorsum. Penultimate caudal stylets not quite reaching the tip of the preceding pair. The ultimate pair very long and armed with fascicles of spines along the margins. Divisions of the telson slender, spinous at the tips.

In life dark greenish slate-color, changing in alcohol to dark slate.

Length, 7–9^{mm}.

New Jersey to Cape Cod.

AMPELISCA. Plate IV, fig. 17. (pp. 431, 507.)

The species of this genus found upon our coast have not yet been carefully studied. At least two species were taken in Vineyard Sound and Buzzard's Bay. The genus is readily recognized, but the species are difficult to distinguish.

BYBLIS SERRATA Smith, sp. nov. (p. 501.)

Female: Dorsum rounded above, with no trace of a longitudinal carina upon the abdomen; third segment of the abdomen broadly rounded at the postero-lateral angle. Antennula about as long as the peduncle of the antenna; fourth segment of the peduncle of the antenna longer than the fifth. Inferior margins of the epimera of the first and second pairs of legs serrate, with slender and acute teeth alternating with the marginal cilia; carpus in the first pair scarcely if any longer than the propodus; carpus in the second pair very much longer than the propodus. In the third and fourth pairs of legs the dactylus as long as the propodus. Basal segment in the seventh pair of legs expanding distally, the posterior margin nearly straight, the anterior and inferior margins evenly arcuated, and reaching as far as the distal end of the carpus; carpus about as long as the ischium and merus together, a little less than twice as long as broad, and armed with long spines upon the anterior and distal margins, but the posterior margin wholly unarmed; propodus almost as long as the carpus, and nearly four times as long as broad, anterior margin unarmed, the posterior armed upon the outside with two transverse rows of three or four spines, decreasing in size as they recede from the margin, the distal end with a spine each side the slender dactylus. Rami of the first pair of caudal stylets equal, as long as the base; outer rami of the second pair shorter than the inner; rami of the posterior pair equal, longer than the bases, reaching to the tips of the rami of the first pair. Telson as long as the breadth at base, cleft rather more than half its length, the lateral margins arcuate, and rapidly converging toward the evenly rounded extremity.

Alcoholic specimens are pale yellowish, the epimera, bases of the posterior legs, and the sides of the abdomen specked and mottled with numerous points of dark pigment crowded irregularly together.

Length, 10–12^{mm}.

Deep water off Vineyard Sound and Buzzard's Bay.

PTILOCHEIRUS PINGUIS Stimpson. (p. 431.)

Marine Invertebrata of Grand Manan, p. 56, 1853. *Protomedia pingus* Bate, Catalogue Amphip. Crust. Brit. Mus., p. 170, Pl. 31, fig. 2, 1862.

Common on the whole coast of New England upon muddy bottoms

and north to Labrador. In depth it extends down to 150 fathoms, and probably much farther.

MICRODEUTOPUS MINAX Smith, sp. nov. (p. 479.)

Antennula about two-thirds as long as the body; first segment of the peduncle stout, about as long as the head; second segment a little longer and much more slender; third segment nearly half as long as the first; flagellum slender, about a third longer than the peduncle; secondary flagellum very small, consisting usually of but one segment. Antenna about two-thirds as long as the antennula; ultimate and penultimate segments of the peduncle equal in length, and each fully twice as long as the antepenultimate; flagellum scarcely as long as the last segment of the peduncle. Hands of the first pair of legs in the male greatly developed; carpus very large, scarcely longer than the breadth in the middle; superior margin strongly arcuate, the inferior angle produced into a stout process opposed to the propodus, and the inferior margin arcuate and armed distally with two teeth, a large and prominent one at the base of the terminal process, the other small, obtuse, or even obsolete; propodus not more than half as long as the carpus, much longer than broad, the inferior margin with two broad obtuse teeth; dactylus stout, a little shorter than the propodus. Legs of the second pair with the basal segment broad and squamiform; carpus elongated; propodus as long as the carpus and as broad as its distal portion, rectangular, about two and a half times as long as broad; dactylus short and hooked at the tip. In the female the hands of the first pair of legs are only moderately developed; carpus broad; propodus scarcely as broad as the carpus, rectangular, the palmary margin somewhat oblique, and the inferior margin armed with a spine at the obtusely rounded inferior angle. In the second pair the basal segment is not expanded but narrow; the carpus and propodus much as in the male, except that they are clothed with numerous long, plumose hairs. The bases of the first and second pairs of caudal stylets are armed with a long, slender, spiniform process, arising from the distal end just below the bases of the rami. The outer rami of the posterior stylets are a little longer than the inner. All the stylets extend to the same point.

Length, about 4^{mm}.

Long Island Sound and Vineyard Sound.

Another species of *Microdeutopus* was collected in Vineyard Sound, but it was not abundant.

AUTONOE, species. (p. 415.)

A species belonging apparently in this genus, as defined by Boeck, was common in Vineyard Sound, living in tubes in masses of a compound Ascidian (*Amouroucium pellucidum* Verrill) in 3 to 8 fathoms. It is 6 or 7^{mm} in length, and in life the antennulæ and antennæ are obscurely banded and specked with pink; the body above, except upon the fifth segment and the posterior part of the abdomen, is almost black, the color extending down upon the epimera, while the legs and caudal appendages are semi-translucent. The eyes are large and black.

AMPHITHOË MACULATA Stimpson. Plate IV, fig. 16. (p. 315.)

Marine Invertebrata of Grand Manan, p. 53, 1853.

Vineyard Sound to the Bay of Fundy and Labrador.

AMPHITHOË VALIDA Smith, sp. nov. (p. 315.)

Male: Eyes round, black in alcoholic specimens. Antennulæ and antennæ subequal in length. Peduncle of the antennula extending scarcely beyond the distal extremity of penultimate segment of the peduncle of the antenna; the second segment but little longer than the first; ultimate segment short and slender. Ultimate and penultimate segments of the peduncle of the antenna subequal in length. First pair of legs short, compressed; carpus as broad as the propodus; propodus broad, oval in outline, the posterior and palmary margins forming a continuous, nearly semicircular curve; dactylus fitting closely the palmary margin. Second pair of legs very large; carpus small; propodus oblong, broadest at the distal extremity, very large and thickened, the outer surface convex, the inner flattened, palmary margin transverse, with a broad, low, median tooth, and a rounded prominence at the inferior angle, within which the tip of the very stout and strongly curved dactylus closes.

The female differs in having the hands of the first pair of legs slightly more elongated, and those of the second pair smaller than in the male, and the palmary margin slightly oblique.

Color in life, bright green.

Length, 10–13^{mm}.

New Jersey and Long Island Sound.

AMPHITHOË LONGIMANA Smith, sp. nov. (p. 370.)

Male: Eyes round, and, in specimens preserved in alcohol, black. Antennula slender and as long as the body; second segment of the peduncle a little longer than the first; third segment about half as long as the second; flagellum about twice as long as the peduncle. Antenna considerably stouter and slightly shorter than the antennula, the peduncle about twice as long as the flagellum; third segment of the peduncle a little more than half as long as the first segment of the peduncle of the antennula; fourth segment nearly three times as long as the third; fifth considerably longer than the fourth; flagellum a little longer, or sometimes only as long, as the fifth segment of the peduncle. Hands of the first and second pairs of legs stout and much elongated. Carpus in the first pair nearly as long as the first segment of the peduncle of the antennula, narrow; propodus much more than twice as long as broad, as wide and long as the carpus, of the same width throughout, slightly curved, and the very short palmary margin transverse; dactylus stout, very little curved, more than half as long as the propodus, and projecting far beyond its inferior edge; the posterior margins of both propodus and carpus densely clothed with long, stiff hairs. Carpus in the second pair of legs short, with an angular prominence upon the posterior side; propodus as long as in the first pair, and much broader, the palmary margin oblique, projecting at the inferior angle, just inside of which there is a deep sinus in the margin. Posterior edges of the bases of the sixth and seventh pairs of legs unarmed.

In the female the antennæ are shorter and not quite as stout, and the hands of the first and second pairs of legs are very much shorter, smaller, and much less hairy; in the first pair the carpus and propodus are very much shorter and proportionally broader, and the palmary margin of the propodus more oblique; in the second pair the propodus is short and somewhat oval, with a slight prominence at the inferior angle of the palmary margin.

Length, 6–9^{mm}.

New Jersey; Great South Bay, Long Island; Vineyard Sound. Common among eel-grass in sheltered situations. The young, even 5 or 6^{mm} long, were taken at the surface in Vineyard Sound several times.

AMPHITHOË COMPTA Smith, sp. nov. (p. 370.)

Eyes small, round, red in life, but fading in alcohol to whitish. Antennula slender, as long as the body; first segment of the peduncle as long as the head; second slightly longer than the first; last a third as long as the second; flagellum very slender, nearly three times as long as the peduncle. There is a rudimentary secondary flagellum, not longer than the first two segments of the primary flagellum and very slender. Antenna a little shorter than the antennula; the peduncle very little shorter than that of the antennula; last two segments about equal in length, the penultimate reaching as far as the same segments of the antennula; flagellum about as long as the peduncle. First and second pairs of legs, in the male, about equal in size, as long as the head and thorax together, and clothed on both margins with long, plumose hairs. Carpus in the first pair longer than, and as broad as, the propodus, the distal extremity truncate and right-angled at the inferior margin; the propodus much longer than broad, the palmary margin oblique, very nearly straight, and armed at the inferior angle upon the inner side with a stout spine. Carpus in the second pair narrower than in the first, the distal extremity obliquely rounded at the inferior angle; propodus as long as the carpus and no broader, the palmary margin less oblique than in the first pair, without any spine, and the inferior angle slightly projecting; dactylus, strongly curved and closing by the margin of the propodus. In the female the legs of the first and second pairs are nearly alike in form, very much smaller and weaker than in the male, and only sparsely clothed with mostly simple hairs, except upon the inferior margin of the carpus in the second pair. In both pairs the carpus is about as long and broad as the propodus; the propodus is short, narrowed toward the carpus, the palmary margin oblique, convex in outline, with the inferior angle rounded and armed with a stout spine on the inside. Second and third segments of the abdomen produced into a slight angular prominence at the postero-inferior angle. The posterior edges of the bases of the sixth and seventh pairs of legs not serrated but armed with two to four small spines. First and second pairs of caudal stylets extending scarcely beyond the posterior pair. In the first pair there is a long, slender spine projecting from the distal extremity of the base beneath the rami.

Length of largest specimen examined, 13^{mm}

North Carolina to Cape Cod. Common among eel-grass. Taken at surface in Vineyard Sound.

PODOCERUS FUCICOLA Smith. (p. 493.)

Cerapus fucicola Stimpson, Marine Invertebrata of Grand Manan, p. 48, Pl. 3, fig. 34, 1853.

This species was dredged by Professor Verrill, in 4 to 5 fathoms, off Watch Hill, Rhode Island, in April, 1873. It is common in the Bay of Fundy.

PODOCERUS, species. (p. 494.)

Another species of the same genus was taken in abundance with the last. It is a large and dark-colored species.

CERAPUS RUBRICORNIS Stimpson. Plate IV, fig. 18.

Marine Invertebrata of Grand Manan, p. 46, Pl. 3, fig. 33, 1853; Bate, Catalogue Amphip. Crust. Brit. Mus., p. 256, Pl. 45, fig. 4.

Not common south of Cape Cod, but very abundant in the Bay of Fundy and north to the coast of Labrador. In depth it extends down to 100 fathoms at least.

CERAPUS MINAX Smith, sp. nov.

Antennulæ and antennæ about equal in length, rather more than half as long as the body. Second pair of legs greatly developed in the male, the hand nearly half as long as the body; carpus elongated, narrow, nearly three times as long as the breadth in the middle, the posterior angle projecting into a broad process about as long as the dactylus, and armed on the inside with a tooth nearly as stout as the distal part of the process itself, but projecting only about half as far; propodus about half as long as the carpus, twice as long as broad; dactylus considerably shorter than the propodus, the tip in most of the larger specimens furnished with a pencil of long hairs. In the female the hand in the second pair of legs is small; the carpus produced into a long process on the inferior edge of the propodus to the palmary margin; propodus short, broad, somewhat oval, the palmary margin arcuate and armed with several short spines on the portion next the carpal process.

Length, about 4^{mm}.

Long Island Sound, Vineyard Sound.

? CERAPUS TUBULARIS Say. (p. 396.)

Loc. cit., p. 49, Pl. 4, fig. 7–11, 1817.

Several specimens of a small amphipod, dredged, June 27, in Vineyard

Sound, among masses of a large compound Ascidian, (*Amouroucium pellucidum*,) in eight to ten fathoms, off Nobska Point, are probably this species, but unfortunately females only were obtained, while Say describes and figures the male alone. In our specimens, the antennulæ and antennæ are spotted with very dark purplish-brown, the anterior part of the body almost black, the middle and posterior portions spotted with black, or very dark purplish brown. They are between 4 and 5^{mm} long and inhabit unattached tubes as described by Say. The tubes are regularly cylindrical, quite thin and delicate, black, about 5^{mm} long, and 0.4^{mm} in diameter, and are carried about by the animal very much as the larvæ of some of the Phryganeidæ carry about their tubes in fresh water. In the structure of the caudal appendages, our specimens are quite different from the species usually referred to *Cerapus*, but I have not thought best to make any changes in nomenclature until the discovery of the male shall make it certain whether our specimens belong to the species described by Say.

COROPHIUM CYLINDRICUM Smith. (p. 370.)

Podocerus cylindricus, Say loc. cit., p. 387, 1818, (*not* of Bate, Catalogue Amphip. Crust. Brit. Mus., p. 256.)

New Jersey to Vineyard Sound. Very abundant among weeds and hydroids about piles of wharves, and almost everywhere in shallow water.

Length, about 4^{mm}.

SIPHONŒCETES CUSPIDATUS Smith, sp. nov. (p. 501.)

Male: Head produced into a long, slender, acute rostrum, and each side between the antennula and antenna into a long lobe rounded at the end where the eye is situated, and contracted toward the base. Antennula reaching about to the middle of the fourth segment of the peduncle of the antenna; segments of the peduncle equal in length; flagellum scarcely longer than a segment of the peduncle, and composed usually of five segments. Antenna a little longer than the body; third segment of the peduncle a little longer than any segment of the peduncle of the attennula; fourth segment nearly twice as long as the third; last segment nearly one-half longer than the third; flagellum a little shorter than the last segment of the peduncle. Legs much like Kroyer's figures of *S. typicus*, those of the first pair with the carpus twice as long as broad; propodus slightly narrower and a little longer than the carpus, the posterior edge furnished with long hairs and several stout spines. Legs of the second pair much stouter. Posterior caudal stylets with the terminal process fully as long as the ramus itself, the ramus as broad as long, the extremity obtusely rounded and furnished with very long hairs. Telson broader than long, transversely elliptical.

In the female the antennæ and second pair of legs are more slender than in the male.

In alcoholic specimens the antennulæ are marked with narrow bands of black or dark brown upon each segment of the flagellum and at both ends of the second and third segments of the peduncle, and the antennæ are obscurely banded and tinged with a lighter color.

Length, about 6^{mm}.

It inhabits tubes constructed of grains of sand.

In deep water off Vineyard Sound and Buzzard's Bay.

UNCIOLA IRRORATA Say. Plate IV, fig. 19. (p. 340.)

Loc. cit., p. 389, 1818 ; Stimpson, Marine Invertebrata of Grand Manan, p. 45.

This species grows to a much larger size than described by Say, being frequently 15^{mm} in length.

New Jersey to the Bay of Fundy, and probably much farther north, and from low water to more than 400 fathoms in depth.

HYPERIA, species. (p. 439.)

A large species of *Hyperia* was several times found upon the large red jelly-fish (*Cyanea*) in Vineyard Sound. The same species is common in the Bay of Fundy, but has not been identified with certainty.

Another species of *Hyperia* was taken at the surface, in company with *Salpa*, in Vineyard Sound, early in September.

PHRONIMA, species. (p. 439.)

A species of this peculiar genus was taken at the surface, in company with *Salpa*, off Gay Head, early in September. It is closely allied to the *P. Atlantica* of Guérin. According to Professor Verrill's notes it is, in life, translucent, scarcely tinged with yellowish white, and nearly invisible in the water ; the eyes red.

Another form allied to the last was taken with it, and is possibly the male of the same species, but differs from it, and from the characters usually assigned to the genus, in possessing well-developed antennulæ. In life, according to Professor Verrill, it was translucent whitish, the body spotted with dark brown, and the eyes blackish.

THYROPUS, species.

A single specimen of a species of this genus was taken with the *Phronima* and *Salpa*, off Gay Head, early in September.

CAPRELLA GEOMETRICA Say. Plate V, fig. 20. (p. 480.)

Loc. cit., p. 390, 1818; Bate, Catalogue Amphip. Crust. British Mus., p. 357, Pl. 56, fig. 8.

North Carolina to Vineyard Sound, especially among eel-grass ; very abundant in Great Egg Harbor, New Jersey, April, 1871.

CAPRELLA, species. (p. 316.)

A larger species of *Caprella*, which is common in the Bay of Fundy, was frequently dredged in Vineyard Sound.

ISOPODA.

SCYPHACELLA Smith, gen. nov.

Near *Scyphax*, Dana.* Antenna composed of eight distinct segments,

* U. S. Exploring Expedition, Crust., p. 734, Pl. 48, fig. 5.

with a geniculation at the articulation of the fourth with the fifth segment; terminal portion, corresponding to the flagellum, composed of three closely articulated segments, besides a minute apical one; mandibles slender, without palpi; exposed portion of the maxillipeds formed of only two segments; the basal one with a narrow, elongated portion, which is abruptly narrowed at the articulation of the terminal segment, and sends a slender process beneath it to the middle of its inner margin; the terminal segment much narrower than the basal, and tapering toward the extremity; legs subequal, the posterior not shorter than the others; terminal segment of the abdomen produced between the posterior caudal appendages, which are short and essentially as in the allied genera.

This genus differs from *Scyphax* most notably in the form of the maxillipeds, which in *Scyphax* have the terminal segment broad and serrately lobed, while in our genus it is elongated, tapering, and has entire margins. In *Scyphax*, also, the posterior pair of thoracic legs are much smaller than the others, and weak; the last segment of the abdomen is truncated at the apex, and the articulations between the segments of the terminal portion of the antennæ are much more complete than in our species. The general form and appearance of the genera are the same, and the known species agree remarkably in habits, the *Scyphax*, according to Dana, occurring on the beach of Parua Harbor, New Zealand, and found in the sand by turning it over for the depth of a few inches.

SCYPHACELLA ARENICOLA Smith, sp. nov. (p. 337.)

Body elliptical; abdomen not abruptly narrower than the thorax; the whole dorsal surface, except the extremity of the abdomen, covered with small, depressed tubercles, which give rise to minute spinules; eyes prominent, round; antenna a little longer than the breadth of the body; first and second segments short, equal; third, fourth, and fifth successively longer, the fifth being rather longer than the terminal portion, which is more slender than the fifth segment, tapers regularly to the tip, and is composed of three successively much shorter segments, and a very short, somewhat spiniform, but obtuse, terminal one; all the segments, except the minute terminal one, scatteringly beset with spinules; legs beset with small spines; the ischial, meral, carpal, and propodal segments subequal; terminal process of the last segment of the abdomen narrow, triangular, with the apex slightly rounded, and the dorsal surface a little concave; posterior caudal appendages much shorter than the abdomen; rami slightly unequal, the outer stout, spinulose, the inner a little shorter and much more slender.

Color, in life, nearly white, with chalky white spots and scattered, blackish dots arranged irregularly. Eyes black.

Length, 3–4^{mm}.

Found at Somers's and Beesley's Points, on Great Egg Harbor, New Jersey, in April, 1871, burrowing in the sand of the beaches, just above ordinary high-water mark, in company with several species of *Staphylinidæ*, and will very likely be found on Long Island and the southern coast of New England.

PHILOSCIA VITTATA Say.

Jour. Acad. Nat. Sci., Philadelphia, vol. i, p. 429, 1818.

Under rubbish below high-water mark, Connecticut and New Jersey.

SPHÆROMA QUADRIDENTATA Say. Plate V, fig. 21. (p. 315.)

Jour. Acad. Nat. Sci. Philadelphia, vol. i, p. 400, 1818.

Massachusetts to Florida.

IDOTEA CÆCA Say. Plate V, fig. 22. (p. 340.)

Loc. cit., p. 424, 1818. Gould, Invertebrata of Massachusetts, p. 337, 1841.

Massachusetts to Florida.

IDOTEA TUFTSII Stimpson. (p. 340.)

Marine Invertebrata of Grand Manan, p. 39, 1853.

Bay of Fundy and off New London, Connecticut.

IDOTEA IRRORATA Edwards. Plate V, fig. 23. (p. 316.)

Hist. nat. des Crust., vol. iii, p. 132, 1840. *Stenosoma irrorata* Say, loc. cit., p. 423, 1818; Gould, Invertebrata of Massachusetts, p. 338, 1841.

Bay of Fundy to Great Egg Harbor, New Jersey.

IDOTEA ROBUSTA Kroyer. Plate V, fig. 24. (p. 439.)

Naturhist. Tidssk., 2d R., Bind ii, p. 108, 1846; Stimpson, Proceedings Acad. Nat. Sci., Philadelphia, 1862, p. 133.

South shore of Long Island to the Arctic Ocean. A pelagic species.

IDOTEA PHOSPHOREA Harger, sp. nov. (p. 316.)

Resembling *I. irrorata* in size and shape, but easily distinguished from that species by the pointed abdomen.

Antennæ less than half the length of the body, antennulæ attaining the end of the third segment of the antennæ. Front slightly excavated with the lateral angles salient. Head about twice as broad as long, turgid, and usually with a pair of tubercles on the vertex. Eyes placed a little before the middle of the lateral margin, hemispherical, black. First segment of thorax produced laterally around the back part of the head nearly to the eyes, showing no epimeral sutures. Second segment much longer on the median line, but shorter at the sides than the first; the epimera occupy the anterior two-thirds of the lateral margin. Third segment slightly longer than the second; the epimera occupying still more of the lateral margin. Fourth segment of about the same length as third; the epimera occupying nearly or quite all the lateral margin. The remaining three thoracic segments gradually decrease in size; the epimera occupy the whole lateral margin and increase in size posteriorly. The first two abdominal segments are distinct and acute at the sides. The third is similar to these at the sides, but is only separated from the last by an incision reaching about half way to the median line, Last segment entire, ovate behind, and cuspidate. The style on the second pair of branchial plates in the male is slender, surpasses the laminæ, and reaches the middle of the terminal cilia; it is obliquely truncated at the end.

Many of the specimens, especially the smaller ones, are furnished with a row of prominent tubercles along the back, and sometimes with lateral rows.

Length, 10–25 mm; breadth, 3–7.5mm.

Long Island Sound to Bay of Fundy.

ERICHSONIA FILIFORMIS Harger. Plate VI, fig. 26. (p. 316.)

Stenosoma filiformis Say, loc. cit., p. 424, 1818.

Small, slender, and nearly linear in outline. Antennulæ not quite attaining the fourth segment of the antennæ, which are six-jointed, and more than half as long as the body, with the first segment short, second and third increasing in length, last three segments about equal; head elevated between the eyes, where it is surmounted by a bifid tubercle; first and second thoracic segments with a lateral salient angle behind the evident angulated epimera; third and fourth segments with their lateral borders emarginate, and the epimera concealed or rarely visible from above at the emargination; last three thoracic segments angulated in front of the epimera, which are also angular. This arrangement, especially in the smaller specimens, gives the appearance of fourteen serrations on each side of the thorax. There is a row of tubercles along the median line. Abdominal segments consolidated into a single piece, which is furnished with a divergent tooth on each side near the base, and is expanded and obtusely triangular at the apex. The style on the second pair of branchial plates in the male is strong and curved, surpasses the cilia, and is acute and sharply serrate near the end.

Length, 5–9mm

Vineyard Sound to Great Egg Harbor, New Jersey.

ERICHSONIA ATTENUATA Harger, sp. nov. Plate VI, fig. 27. (p. 370.)

Body smooth, narrowly linear in outline. Antennulæ slightly surpassing the second segment of the antennæ, which are more than half the length of the body, and have the last segment longest. Head excavated in front; eyes small, black, prominent; first thoracic segment short; second, third, and fourth segments about equal in length, twice as long as the first; third segment broadest, last three segments gradually decreasing in length. Epimera visible from above only in the last two or three segments, but the sutures are evident, except in the first segment, and their position moves gradually from the anterior portion of the segment in the second to the posterior in the seventh segment. Abdominal segments consolidated into a single piece, which is slightly dilated laterally near the base, and obtusely triangular at the tip. The style on the second pair of branchial plates in the male is straight, slightly surpasses the cilia, and is acute at the end.

The color in life is usually uniform dark green, sometimes with an obscure dorsal stripe of a lighter color.

Length, 15^{mm}.

Abundant among eel-grass at Great Egg Harbor, New Jersey, and also found at New Haven, Connecticut.

EPELYS TRILOBUS Smith. Plate VI, fig. 28. (p. 370.)

Idotea triloba Say, loc. cit., p. 425, 1818.

Great Egg Harbor, New Jersey to Vineyard Sound.

EPELYS MONTOSUS Harger. (p. 370.)

Idotea montosa Stimpson, Marine Invert., Grand Manan, p. 40, 1853.

Bay of Fundy to Long Island Sound.

JÆRA COPIOSA Stimpson. (p. 315.)

Loc. cit., p. 40, Pl. 3, fig. 29, 1853. *J. nivalis* Packard, Memoirs Boston Soc. Nat. Hist., vol. i, 296, (*non* Kroyer.)

Long Island Sound to Labrador.

LIMNORIA LIGNORUM White. Plate VI, fig. 25. (p. 379.)

Pop. Hist. Brit. Crust., p. 227, Pl. 12, fig. 5. *Cymothoa lignorum* Rathke, Skrivt. af Naturh. Selsk., vol. 101, t. 3, f. 14, 1799, (teste Bate and Westwood.) *Limnoria terebrans* Leach, Trans. Linn. Soc., London, vol. xi, p. 371, 1815. Gould, Invertebrata of Massachusetts, p. 388, 1841.

Great Egg Harbor, New Jersey, to the Bay of Fundy and Europe.

NEROCILA MUNDA Harger, sp. nov. (p. 459.)

Elongated, oval, smooth, and polished. Antennæ and antennulæ nearly equal in length, about as long as the head. Head flattened, about one-third broader than long, slightly narrowing anteriorly, produced and broadly rounded in front, subequally trilobed behind, the middle lobe largest. Eyes black, consisting of an irregularly rounded patch of rather indistinct ocelli visible both above and below. First thoracic segment longer than the others, excavated in front for the three lobes of the head; epimeral sutures of this segment indistinct, but the posterior lateral angles of the segment are somewhat produced and broadly rounded. The next three segments have this angle produced so as to become a small tooth in the fourth thoracic segment; in the last three segments it is much produced, becoming a long acute tooth in the seventh. The epimera of the second segment are rounded behind; the remaining epimera are slightly angular behind, becoming more acute posteriorly; those of the second, third, and fourth segments extend backward about as far as the segment to which they belong, but in the last three segments the produced angles of the segments surpass the epimera, so that the angle of the sixth segment nearly attains the end of the seventh epimeron.

The abdomen is composed of six segments, the first five short and about equal in length; the sixth equal in length to the other five, truncate in front and rounded behind. The spines beneath the abdomen, or "abdominal epimera," are acute, the second a little more slender than the first, and extending not quite to the posterior angle of the fourth abdominal segment. The internal plate of the caudal stylets is oval and obliquely truncate, shorter than the external, which is narrow, ovate, acute behind, extending about half its length beyond the tip of the abdomen and longer than the preceding segment of the stylet. Claws of the anterior feet strongly hooked, those of the posterior feet feebly so.

Color, in alcohol, brown, with two narrow dorsal bands of lighter color.

Length, 15^{mm}; breadth, 7^{mm}.

This species is allied to *N. bivittata*, but differs from that species as figured by Milne Edwards, (Atlas du Règne animal de Cuvier, Crust., Plate 66, fig. 5,) in the shortness of three posterior epimera, the regularly rounded terminal segment of the abdomen, and the shape of the caudal stylets.

A single specimen was obtained on the dorsal fin of *Ceratacanthus aurantiacus*.

CONILERA CONCHARUM Harger. (p. 459.)

Æga concharum Stimpson, Marine Invert. Grand Manan, p. 42, 1853.

Vineyard Sound; Charleston, South Carolina.

LIVONECA OVALIS Harger. Plate VI, fig. 29. (p. 457.)

Cymothoa ovalis Say loc. cit., p. 394, 1818.

These animals are usually distorted, and not, as represented in the figure, symmetrical on the two sides.

The specimen figured was taken from a blue-fish near the gill.

ANTHURA BRUNNEA Harger, sp. nov. (p. 426.)

Nearly uniform in size throughout, but slightly narrower anteriorly. Antennulæ and antennæ nearly equal in length, scarcely longer than the head. Front projecting between and each side of the bases of the antennulæ into prominent angles. Eyes small and situated in the sides of the lateral prominences. Thoracic segments smooth and shining above; the third with a slight semicircular depression on the middle of the anterior margin. This depression is still more strongly marked on the three following segments. First segment slightly longer and narrower than the others; second to fifth about equal; sixth and seventh considerably shorter; the seventh about three-fourths the length of the sixth; all the segments carinated below. Dorsal surface of the basal portion of the abdomen similar to the posterior segment of the thorax, showing no indication of segments. Terminal portion flat, smooth, and narrowly ovate at tip. Appendages of the penultimate segment lamelliform, similar in form to the terminal plate but not quite equaling it. First pair of feet short and thickened. All the feet slightly hairy.

In life whitish mottled with dull, purplish brown above. Eyes black, retaining their color in alcohol. Length, 14–15^{mm}.

Great Egg Harbor, New Jersey, and Vineyard Sound.

ANTHURA BRACHIATA Stimpson. (p. 511.)

Marine Invertebrata of Grand Manan, p. 43, 1853.

This species is greatly constricted at the articulations of the second thoracic segment, and by that character is easily distinguished from *A. brunnea*.

Bay of Fundy to Vineyard Sound.

TANAIS FILUM Stimpson. (p. 381.)

Marine Invertebrata of Grand Manan, p. 43, 1853.

Bay of Fundy to Vineyard Sound.

CEPON DISTORTUS Leidy. (p. 557.)

Jour. Acad. Nat. Sci. Phila., vol. iii, p. 149, Pl. 11, figs. 26–32, 1855.

Branchial cavity of *Gelasimus pugilator*, Atlantic City, New Jersey.

ENTOMOSTRACA.

The Ostracoda and the minute Copeopoda of our coast have not yet been sufficiently studied by any one for us to attempt to enumerate even the more common species.

COPEOPODA.

SAPPHIRINA, species. Plate VII, fig. 33. (p. 439.)

A beautiful species of this remarkable genus was taken off Gay Head, Martha's Vineyard, September 2 and 8.

PHYLLOPODA.

ARTEMIA GRACILIS Verrill.

Amer. Jour. Sci., 2d series, vol. xlviii, p. 248, 1869; Proceedings Amer. Assoc. Adv. Sci., vol. xviii, p. 235, figs. 1 and 2, 1870.

In tubs of concentrated sea-water at New Haven, Connecticut; Charlestown, Massachusetts; and in salt-vats at Falmouth, Massachusetts.

SIPHONOSTOMA.

ERGASILUS LABRACES Kroyer. (p. 459.)

Nat. Tidsskrift, 1863–'64, p. 303, Pl. 11, fig. 2, (teste Zoological Record for 1865.)

According to Kroyer, found upon the striped bass (*Roccus lineatus*) from Baltimore, and liable, therefore, to occur on the coast of New England.

ARGULUS CATOSTOMI Dana and Herrick. (p. 459.)

Amer. Jour. Sci., 1st series, vol. xxx, p. 383, 1836, and vol. xxxi, p. 297, plate, 1837.

Parasitic on the "sucker" (*Catostomus*) in Mill River, near New Haven, Connecticut.

ARGULUS LATICAUDA Smith, sp. nov. (p. 452.)

Carapax orbicular, longer than broad; antero-lateral margin with a deep sinus from which a deep sulcus extends to the center of the carapax; sinus of the posterior margin about twice as deep as broad, extending a little less than a third of the length of the carapax. Eyes large. Body scarcely projecting beyond the posterior margin of the carapax. Tail orbicular, slightly longer than broad, its posterior sinus narrow, extending scarcely a fourth the length. Antennulæ and antennæ much as in *A. Catostomi*, to which the species bears considerable resemblance. The squamiform appendage upon the base of the prehensile legs expands into a broad posterior margin, which is divided into three broad, closely approximated lobes, of which the extremities are broad, truncated, and slightly and irregularly excavated; the terminal portion of the leg is much as in *A. Catostomi*, the ultimate segment longer than the penultimate and armed at the tip with two claws. Natatory legs short, the anterior ones not projecting beyond the carapax.

In alcoholic specimens most of the carapax is opaque and black with a thick deposit of pigment.

Length of entire animal, in the largest specimen, 5^{mm}; length of carapax, 3.7; breadth of carapax, 3.2; length of tail, 1.3; breadth of tail, 1.1.

Found among algæ in Vineyard Sound.

A small specimen taken at surface early in September had the opaque portions of the carapax dark brown in life, and in alcohol it retains about the same color.

ARGULUS LATUS Smith, sp. nov. (p. 452.)

Carapax large, orbicular, broader than long; the antero-lateral border with a broad shallow sinus; the sinus of the posterior margin not deeper than broad, its depth scarcely more than a fifth of the length of the carapax. Body projecting considerably beyond the posterior margin of the carapax. Tail a third as long as the carapax, about two-thirds as broad as long, the lateral margins slightly curved and nearly parallel, the sinus very broad and extending more than a third of the whole length. Disks of the sucking legs about a fourth as wide as the carapax. Squamiform appendage upon the base of the prehensile legs with a pappilose area upon the expanded distal portion, the posterior margin without teeth or lobes, but the outer margin of the expanded portion armed with numerous very small teeth; ultimate segment longer than the penultimate, and apparently without any hooks at the tip. Natatory legs all long, even the anterior projecting beyond the sides of the carapax.

Color of alcoholic specimens yellowish white.

Length, 3.0^{mm}; length of carapax, 2.2; breadth of carapax, 2.5; length of tail, 0.7; breadth of tail, 0.45.

Taken at the surface, in Vineyard Sound, July 1.

ARGULUS MEGALOPS Smith, sp. nov. (p. 452.)

Carapax subelliptical, longer than broad; the antero-lateral margin with a deep sinus; the posterior lobes of the carapax, each side of the shallow and narrow sinus, broady rounded. Eyes very large, their diameter a tenth as great as the breadth of the carapax. Body projecting much beyond the posterior margin of the carapax. Tail somewhat ovate, about two-thirds as broad as long, the sinus only a small notch, extending not more than a tenth of the length. Natatory legs very long, all projecting beyond the carapax. Squamiform appendages upon the bases of the prehensile legs, with a pappilose area upon the expanded portion, and the posterior margin armed with three rather slender teeth, separated by broad spaces; the terminal segment of the leg armed with two small hooks.

Color of alcoholic specimens, yellowish white.

Length, 2.2^{mm}; length of carapax, 1.3; breadth of carapax, 1.0; length of tail, 0.7; breadth of tail, 0.47.

Vineyard Sound, taken at the surface, July 8.

ARGULUS ALOSÆ Gould. (p. 459.)

Invertebrata of Massachusetts, p. 340, 1841.

Parasitic upon the alewife in Massachusetts Bay, according to Gould.

CALIGUS CURTUS Müller. (p. 459.)

Entomostraca, p. 130, Pl. 21, figs. 1, 2, 1785; Kroyer, Nat. Tidsskrift, vol. i, p. 619, Pl. 6, fig. 2, 1837. *Caligus Mülleri* Leach, Encycl. Brit., Suppl., vol. i, p. 405, Pl. 20, figs. 1–8, 1816, (teste Baird et al.;) Baird, British Entomostraca, p. 271, Pl. 32, figs. 4, 5. *Caligus Americanus* Pickering and Dana, Amer. Jour. Sci., vol. xxxiv, p. 225, Pl. 3–5, 1838; Dana, U. S. Expl. Expd., Crust., Pl. 93.

Abundant upon the cod-fish of our coast and of Europe. It is probably the *Caligus piscinus* of Gould and other American writers.

CALIGUS RAPAX Edwards. (p. 457.)

Hist. nat. des Crust., tome iii, p. 453, Pl. 38, fig. 9–12, 1840; Baird, op. cit., p. 270, pl. 32, figs. 2, 3; Steenstrup and Lütken, Bidrag til Kundskab om det aabne Havs Snyltekrebse og Lernæer, p. 359, Pl. 2, fig. 4, 1861.

Vineyard Sound, on the sting ray, (*Trygon centroura*,) and small specimens, both male and female, taken at the surface at Wood's Hole, September 3, in the evening. These specimens from the surface, according to Professor Verrill's notes, were light flesh color, thickly speckled with minute brown spots, the eyes bright red.

LEPEOPHTHEIRUS, species. (p. 459.)

A species with a long tail, and somewhat like the *L. gracilis*, (Van Benaden sp.,) was found upon the sting ray (*Trygon centroura*) taken in Vineyard Sound.

LEPEOPHTHEIRUS, species. (p. 459.)

A species with a very short tail, and approaching Heller's genus *Anuretes*. South shore of Long Island, upon a flounder, (*Chænopsetta ocellaris*.)

The *Lepeophtheirus salmonis* Kroyer, is found upon the salmon of the northern coast of New England.

ECHTHROGALEUS COLEOPTRATUS Steenstrup and Lütken. (p. 459.)

Op. cit., 380. *Dinematura coleoptrata* Guérin, Icnographie du Règne animal, Crust. Pl. 35, fig. 6. *Dinemoura alta* Baird, British Entomostraca, p. 285, Pl. 33, figs. 6, 7.

Vineyard Sound, September 19, from the back fin of the mackerel-shark, (*Lamna punctata*.) It has been found upon the English coast and off the Azores.

ECHTHROGALEUS DENTICULATUS Smith, sp. nov. (p. 459.)

Carapax broader than long, with a very slight median emargination in the outline of the front. Posterior portion of the body scarcely longer and not quite as wide as the carapax. Dorsal plates, or elytra, covering much more than half the genital segment, their inner and posterior margins armed with a regular series of small teeth. The posterior lobes of the genital segment somewhat triangular and each terminated by a stout spine. Dorsal plate of the tail elongated, obtusely rounded at the extremity, and exposed from above by the very broad sinus in the genital segment. The tail itself broad, somewhat rectangular, but narrowed distally and not projecting behind the dorsal plate; the terminal lamellæ nearly as long as the tail, narrow, linear, nearly three times as long as broad, and armed at the tip with several setæ.

Length, 9^{mm}; breadth of carapax, 5.1; length of elytra along the inner margin, 2.5.

Vineyard Sound, on Atwood's shark, (*Carcharias Atwoodi*.)

? PANDARUS CRANCHII Leach. (p. 459.)

Dict. des Sci. nat., tome xiv, p. 535, 1819, (teste Edwards et al.;) Edwards, Règne animal de Cuvier, 3me éd., Crust., Pl. 78, fig. 2; Steenstrup and Lütken, op. cit., Pl. 11, fig. 22.

A number of specimens of a *Pandarus*, taken from a dusky shark (*Eulamia obscura*) on the south side of Long Island in 1870, differ only very slightly from the figures and descriptions of *P. Cranchii* quoted above.

PANDARUS, species. Plate VII, fig. 31. (p. 457.)

Vineyard Sound, on Atwood's shark, (*Carcharias Atwoodi*.) It is, perhaps, only a variety of the last species, but differs considerably from it, wanting almost wholly the series of spines upon the posterior margin of the carapax, having the caudal appendages shorter and obtuse, besides some slight differences in the natatory legs.

NOGAGUS LATREILLII Leach. Plate VII, fig. 32. (p. 457.)

Dict. des. Sci. nat., tome xiv, p. 536, 1819, (teste Edwards et al.;) Règne animal de Cuvier, Crust., Pl. 79, fig. 3; Hist. nat. des Crust., tome iii, p. 459; Steenstrup and Lütken, op. cit., p. 384, Pl. 9, fig. 18.

Vineyard Sound, in company with the last species, on Atwood's shark.

All the species of *Nogagus* are males of the allied genera, *Pandarus*,

Echthrogaleus, &c., and are only provisionally retained in a separate group, until it can be determined to which of these genera the different species really belong. This species is probably a *Pandarus*, and very likely the male of the last species.

Our specimens differ slightly from the figures given by Steenstrup and Lütken, the dentiform prominences on the sides of the genital segment in our specimens being much smaller than represented in their figures, the segments of the tail somewhat shorter and broader, and the terminal lamellæ also shorter and broader, while in other respects they agree well. Steenstrup and Lütken's specimens were taken from sharks caught in latitude 31° north, longitude 76° west, (in the Gulf Stream, off the South Carolina coast,) and in latitude 40° south, longitude 31° west, while Leach's came from latitude 1° south, longitude 4° east.

NOGAGUS TENAX Steenstrup and Lütken. (p. 457.)

Op. cit., pp. 384, 388, Pl. 10, fig. 20, 1861.

Vineyard Sound, with the last species, upon Atwood's shark. It has nearly as extended a range as the last species.

It is very different from the last species, having the branches of the posterior pair of natatory legs each composed of a single segment, and the tail also composed of a single segment, which is broader than long, and has the short, truncate caudal lamellæ attached to its obliquely truncated posterior angles. Length, 4.5^{mm}.

This species probably belongs to a different genus from the last, and is perhaps the male of *Echthrogaleus denticulatus*, with which it was associated. Both species of *Nogagus*, the *Pandarus* and *Echthrogaleus denticulatus*, were, however, all found on the same specimen of the shark, so that the association of males and females in one or two instances is not very good proof of their identity.

PANDARUS SINUATUS Say. (p. 459.)

Loc. cit., p. 436, 1818.

This species is apparently, as far as can be judged from Say's description, allied to *P. bicolor* Leach, a European species, which is probably not congeneric with the species which we have previously mentioned.

CECROPS LATREILLII Leach. (p. 459.)

Encyl. Brit., Suppl., vol. i, p. 405, Pl. 20, 1816, (teste Edwards et al.;) Edwards, Hist. nat. des Crust., tome iii, p. 475; Baird, op. cit., p. 293, Pl. 34, figs. 1, 2.

According to Gould, (op. cit., p. 341,) this species has been found upon the sun-fish (*Orthagoriscus mola*) taken on the coast of Massachusetts.

ANTHOSOMA CRASSUM Steenstrup and Lütken. (p. 460.)

Op. cit., p. 367, Pl. 12, fig. 24, 1861. *Caligus crassus* Abildgaard, (teste Steenstrup and Lütken,) Naturh. Selsk. Skr., Bind iii, p. 49, pl. 5, [1794 ?] (teste Kroyer.) *Anthosoma Smithii* Leach, Encycl. Brit., Suppl., vol. i, p. 406, Pl. 20, 1816, (teste Edwards et al.;) Kroyer, Nat. Tidsskrift, vol. i, p. 295, Pl. 2, fig. 2, 1836; Edwards, Hist. nat. des Crust., tome iii, 493, Pl. 39, fig. 5; Règne animal de Cuvier, Crust., Pl. 79, fig. 3; Baird, op. cit., p. 299, Pl. 33, fig. 9.

According to Gould, (op. cit., p. 341,) *Anthosoma Smithii* has been found upon the mackerel-shark (*Lamna punctata*) taken on the coast of Massachusetts.

LERNÆA BRANCHIALIS Linné. (p. 460.)

Systema Naturæ; Edwards, Hist. nat. des Crust., tome iii, p. 528; Steenstrup and Lütken, op. cit., p. 403, Pl. 13, fig. 28.

Found attached to the gills of the cod in the Bay of Fundy, and, undoubtedly, extends as far south as that fish. It is common in Northern Europe.

PENELLA PLUMOSA DeKay. (p. 460.)

Op. cit., p. 60, 1844.

Found, according to DeKay, upon *Diodon pilosus*, and a species of *Rhombus*.

ANCHORELLA UNCINATA Nordmann. (p. 460.)

Mikrographische Beitrage, Heft ii, p. 102, Pl. 8, figs. 8–12, Pl. 10, figs. 1-5, 1832; Baird, op. cit., p. 337, Pl. 35, fig. 9. *Lernæa uncinata* Müller, Zoologia Danica, vol. i, Pl. 33, fig. 2, 1788, (teste Nordmann el al.;) Van Benaden, Poissons des côtes de Belgique, Mémoires Acad. Royale Belgique, tome xxxiii, Pl. 2, fig. 7, 1871.

Found upon cod-fish taken at New London, Connecticut. It is a common European species.

LERNEONEMA RADIATA Stp. and Ltk. Plate VII, fig. 30. (p. 458.)

Op. cit., p. 400, 1861. *Lerneocera radiata* Leseur, Journal Acad. Nat. Sci., Philadelphia, vol. iii, p. 288, Pl. 11, fig. 1, 1824.

At Great Egg Harbor, New Jersey, and in Vineyard Sound and Buzzard's Bay, very common upon the menhaden, (*Brevoortia Menhaden.*)

LERNEONEMA ?, species. (p. 460.)

A species belonging to this, or a closely-allied genus, was found upon a species of *Carangus* taken in Vineyard Sound.

According to Gould, (op. cit., p. 341,) *Penella filosa* Cuvier, (Guérin, op. cit., Zoophytes, Pl. 9. fig. 3; Edwards, Hist. nat. des Crust., tome iii, p. 525,) has been found upon *Orthagoriscus mola*, and might, therefore, occasionally occur south of Cape Cod. The same author also mentions (p. 341) *Chondracanthus cornutus* Cuvier, (Nordmann, op. cit., p. 111, Pl. 9, figs. 5–10; Edwards, Hist. nat. des Crust., tome iii, p. 500, Pl. 40, figs. 18–22,) and *Branchiella Thynni* Cuvier, (Edwards, op. cit., tome iii, p. 512; Steenstrup and Lütken, op. cit., p. 420, Pl. 15, fig. 36,) as occurring upon the coast of Massachusetts.

CIRRIPEDIA.

BALANUS AMPHITRITE Darwin. (p. 381.)

Monograph of the Cirripedia, pp. 240, 614, Pl. 5, fig. 2, 1854.

Found upon the bottoms of ships, but probably does not live long after arriving upon our coast. It is found in all the tropical and warmer temperate seas.

Balanus tintinnabulum Linné, (Darwin, op. cit., pp. 194, 611, Pl. 1, 2, fig. 1,) occurs with the last species, but has not been noticed living. It has about the same range as the *B. amphitrite*.

BALANUS EBURNEUS Gould. (p. 381.)

Op. cit., p. 15, Pl. 1, fig. 6, 1841, Darwin, op. cit., pp. 248, 614, Pl. 5, fig. 4.

From Massachusetts Bay to Florida and the West Indies. It sometimes occurs in brackish or even fresh water. Professor J. Wyman found it living about 50 miles up the St. John's River, Florida, where the water was fresh enough to drink, and the specimens lived well when transferred to a vessel of perfectly fresh water.

BALANUS IMPROVISUS Darwin.

Op. cit., pp. 250, 614, Pl. 6, fig. 1.

Darwin gives this species as occurring in England, Nova Scotia, United States, West Indies, and South America, so that it undoubtedly occurs upon the coast of New England.

BALANUS CRENATUS Bruguière. (p. 381.)

Encyclop. Method., 1798, (teste Darwin;) Darwin, op. cit., pp. 261, 615, Pl. 6, fig. 6. *Balanus rugosus* Gould, op. cit., p. 16, Pl. 1, fig. 10.

Dredged abundantly in Vineyard Sound. It ranges from the arctic regions of the Atlantic to the Cape of Good Hope and the West Indies.

BALANUS BALANOIDES Stimpson. (p. 305.)

Marine Invertebrata of Grand Manan, p. 39, 1853; Darwin, op. cit., pp. 267, 615 Pl. 7, fig. 2. *Lepas balanoides* Linné, Systema Naturæ, 1767, (teste Darwin.) *Balanus ovularis* and *elongatus* Gould, op. cit., pp. 17, 18, Pl. 1, figs. 7, 8.

Extremely abundant between tides. It inhabits the whole North Atlantic.

CORONULA DIADEMA De Blainville. (p. 460.)

Dict. des Sci. nat., 1824, (teste, Darwin;) Gould, op. cit., p. 12; Darwin, op. cit., pp. 417, 623, Pl. 15, fig. 3, Pl. 16, figs. 1, 2, 7. *Lepas diadema* Linné, Systema Naturæ, 1767, (teste Darwin.)

Attached to whales taken on the coast, both north and south of Cape Cod. It is found throughout the whole North Atlantic.

LEPAS FASCICULARIS Ellis and Solander. Plate VII, fig. 34. (p. 382.)

Zoophytes, 1786, (teste Darwin;) Darwin, op. cit., p. 92, Pl. 1, fig. 6.

Found in vast numbers in Vineyard Sound, in June and July, and frequently taken in the Bay of Fundy in August.

LEPAS PECTINATA Spengler. (p. 382.)

Darwin, op. cit., p. 85, Pl. 1, fig. 3. *Anatifa dentata* Gould, op. cit., p. 21, Pl. 1, fig. 11.

Attached to ships' bottoms, but probably does not live long after arriving on our coast. It lives throughout the warmer parts of the Atlantic.

LEPAS ANATIFERA Linné. (p. 382.)

Systema Naturæ, 1767, (teste Darwin;) Darwin, op. cit., p. 73, Pl. 1, fig. 1.

Occurs in the same way as the last species. It is common to the Atlantic, Pacific, and Indian Oceans, and the Mediterranean.

LEPAS ANSERIFERA Linné. (p. 382.)

Systema Naturæ, 1767, (teste Darwin;) Darwin, op. cit., p. 81, Pl. 1, fig. 4. *Anatifa striata* Gould, op. cit., p. 20.

This species probably occurs in the same way as the last. It has the same range.

CONCHODERMA AURITA Olfers. (p. 392.)

Darwin, op. cit., p. 141, Pl. 3, fig. 4. *Lepas aurita* Linné, Systema Naturæ, 1767, (teste Darwin.) *Otion Cuvieri* Gould, op. cit., p. 23.

On ships' bottoms, &c. It ranges through all the seas.

CONCHODERMA VIRGATA Olfers. (p. 392.)

Darwin, op. cit., p. 146, Pl. 3, fig. 2. *Lepas virgata* Spengler, 1790, (teste Darwin.) *Cineras vittata* Gould, op. cit., p. 22.

Occurs in the same way, and has the same range as the last species.

XIPHOSURA.

LIMULUS POLYPHEMUS Latreille. (p. 340.)

Hist. des Crust., (teste Edwards,) Hist. nat. des Crust., tome iii, p. 549; Say, loc. cit., p. 433; Gould, op. cit., p. 339; Packard, Memoirs Boston Soc. Nat. Hist., vol. ii, p. 155, Pl. 3–5, 1872, (on the development;) A. Milne Edwards, Annales des Sci. nat., 5e sér., tome xvii, nos. 1 et 2, Dec., 1872, Pl. 5–16, (on the anatomy.) *Monoculus Polyphemus* Linné, Systema Naturæ; *Polyphemus occidentalis* Lamark, Hist. des Anim. sans vert.; De Kay, op. cit., p. 55, Pl. 11, fig. 50. *Limulus australis* Say, loc. cit., p. 436. *Xiphosura Polyphemus* White, List of Crust. in British Mus., p. 121, 1847.

Casco Bay, on the coast of Maine, to Florida.

ANNELIDA.

POLYCHÆTA.

APHRODITA ACULEATA Linn. (p. 507.)

Systema Naturæ, ed. xii, vol. i, p. 1084, 1767; Malmgren, Öfvers. af Kong. Vet.-Akad. Förhandlingar, 1865, p. 52; Johnston, Catalogue of British Non-Parasitical Worms, p. 101, Pl. 9, 1865; Quatrefages, Histoire naturelle des Annelés, vol. i, p. 191, 1865.

Off Gay Head in 15 to 19 fathoms, mud; Bay of Fundy, 10 to 106 fathoms, mud; St. George's Bank, 50 fathoms; northward to Labrador. Northern coasts of Europe to Great Britain and Mediterranean.

LEPIDONOTUS SQUAMATUS Leach. Plate X, figs. 40, 41. (p. 320.)

Aphrodita squamata Linn., Syst. Nat., ed. x, p. 665; ed. xii, p. 1084. *Polynöe squamata* Savigny, Syst. Annel., 20 (t. Quatr.); Quatr., op. cit., p. 218. *Aphrodita punctata* Müll., Zoöl. Dan. Prod., p. 218 (t. Malmgren). *Lepidonotus squamatus* Malmgren, op. cit., p. 56; Johnston, op. cit., p. 109, Pl. 7, fig. 1. *Lepidonote armadillo* Leidy, Marine Invert. of Rhode Island and New Jersey, p. 16, Pl. 11, fig. 54. *Polynöe dasypus* Quatr., op. cit., vol. i, p. 226.

Great Egg Harbor, New Jersey; New Haven; Watch Hill, Rhode Island; Vineyard Sound, &c. Very common north of Cape Cod to Labrador and Iceland; northern coasts of Europe; Great Britain; France.

In the Bay of Fundy it occurs abundantly from above low-water mark to the depth of 80 fathoms.

LEPIDONOTUS SUBLEVIS Verrill, sp. nov. Plate X, fig. 42. (p. 320.)

Body oblong, somewhat narrowed toward each end, entirely covered by twelve pairs of large scales, or "elytra," which, with the exception of the first and last pairs, are broad oval, evenly rounded posteriorly, the outer lateral edge with a fine fringe; the posterior margin smooth. Their surface is iridescent and nearly smooth throughout, and destitute of tubercles, but has minute rounded granules, and appears punctate under a lens. The scales of the last pair are elongated, with the inner edge curved inward, but without a distinct emargination, such as is seen in the preceding species. Setæ numerous, slender but stiff, amber-yellow. Scales usually reddish or greenish brown, finely specked with dark brown. Length up to 30^{mm}; breadth, 8^{mm}.

This species is easily distinguished from the last by its nearly smooth scales, the form of the last pair, and the lighter-colored and more slender setæ.

Savin Rock, near New Haven; Vineyard Sound.

LEPIDONOTUS ANGUSTUS Verrill, sp. nov. (p. 494.)

Body elongated, narrow, of nearly uniform width throughout, convex above. Twelve pairs of elytra, which are only slightly imbricated and hardly cover the back completely, there being often a narrow naked dorsal space, but when the elytra are closely appressed the back is nearly covered. The elytra are rather small, regularly oval, except those of the terminal pairs; outer edge irregularly fringed; surface covered with small, slightly prominent, roundish granules. Posterior elytra with a deep emargination on the inner margin. Head larger and relatively broader than in *L. squamatus*, convex, with well-rounded sides, eyes larger and farther apart. Antennæ rather short. Setæ shorter than in either of the preceding species, of nearly uniform length, rather rigid, light amber-colored, forming short dense fascicles. Color variable; in one specimen the scales were yellowish gray and brownish, varied with dark specks, and with a central subcircular or somewhat crescent-shaped white spot, surrounded by a circle of dark brown specks, which form an irregular dark spot on the inner border of the pale central spot.

Reefs off Watch Hill, Rhode Island, in 4 or 5 fathoms, among rocks and algæ.

HARMOTHÖE IMBRICATA Malmgren. (p. 321.)

Nordiska Hafs-Annulater, op. cit., p. 67, 1865, Pl. 9, fig. 8, A–E. *Aphrodita imbricata* Linn., Syst. Nat., ed. xii, p. 1084, 1767. *Aphrodita cirrata* Müller, Prodr. Zoöl. Dan., No. 2644 (t. Malmgren); Fabricius, Fauna Grœnlandica, p. 308, Pl. 1, fig. 70. *Lepidonote cirrata* Œrsted, Grön. Ann. Dorsib., 1843, p. 14, Pl. 1, figs. 1, 5, 6, 11, 14, 15; Stimpson, Invertebrata of Grand Manan, p. 36, 1853. *Polynöe cirrata* Sars, Arch. für. Naturg., vol. xi, 1845, p. 11, Pl. 1, figs. 12–21 (embryology).

New Haven; Watch Hill, Rhode Island; Vineyard Sound; Massachusetts Bay; Bay of Fundy and northward to Greenland; Iceland; and Spitzbergen. Northern coasts of Europe; Scotland. In the Bay of Fundy it is common from above low-water mark to 60 fathoms; in Vineyard Sound, from low-water mark to 15 fathoms; 25 fathoms off Buzzard's Bay.

STHENELAIS PICTA Verrill, sp. nov. (p. 348.)

(?) *Sigalion Mathildæ* Leidy, Marine Invert. Fauna of the Coasts of Rhode Island and New Jersey, p. 16, Pl. 11, f. 53, from Journal Philadelphia Acad., series ii, vol. iii, 1855 (*non* Aud. and Edw.) (?) *Sthenelais Leidyi* Quatr., op. cit., vol. i, p. 278 (no description).

Body depressed, much elongated, nearly uniform in breadth throughout; back convex; ventral surface flat. The whole dorsal surface is closely covered by the imbricated scales, of which there are more than 150 pairs. These, with the exception of the anterior and posterior pairs, are broadly lunate, with a deep emargination in the center of the anterior edge; the posterior and lateral margins are broadly rounded; the outer lateral edge is laciniately fringed; the posterior edge is smooth; the whole surface of the anterior scales is covered with minute, slightly elevated granules; farther back, the exposed portion of the surface of the scales is smooth, and the microscopic granules are restricted to the anterior and inner portions. The scales of the anterior pair are oval, and have their entire outer and anterior margins minutely but irregularly denticulate.

The head is small, rounded, contracted behind the posterior eyes and in front of the anterior ones; the eyes are near together, in a quadrangle; those in the anterior pair are a little farther apart, and lateral. The head is prolonged anteriorly into a narrow elliptical or oval portion, which forms the base of the median antennæ; close to and below each of the anterior eyes a prominent, membranous, ciliated process arises. The feet of the first pair, which are directed forward, are elongated, and bear a pair of slender, elongated, dorsal cirri, which are nearly as long as the antennæ; a much shorter, slender cirrus from the lower lobe, with a small, thin, membraneous process below; and a large fascicle of long, slender setæ, as long as the median antennæ. The palpi are slender, longer than the antennæ; lateral feet prominent, projecting beyond the scales; setæ light yellow.

Color variable, generally light gray, with a dark brown median dorsal band, each scale often bordered on the posterior and inner edges with brown, which is connected with a blackish angular spot near the anterior margin, the rest of the scale being transparent and whitish; head dark brown, with a red central spot and a round whitish spot on each side. Length up to 150^{mm}; breadth usually about 4^{mm}.

Vineyard Sound, low-water mark to 14 fathoms; off Martha's Vineyard, 21 fathoms, sand; off New Haven, 4 to 5 fathoms, shelly. Great Egg Harbor (Leidy).

This species differs considerably in the form of the head, antennæ, &c., from the figure given by Leidy. His description is insufficient to determine whether he observed the same species.

NEPHTHYS INGENS Stimpson. Plate XII, figs. 59, 60. (p. 431.)

Marine Invertebrata of Grand Manan, p. 33, in Smithsonian Contributions, 1853.

Long Island Sound, off New Haven, 3 to 8 fathoms, mud, common; off Block Island, in 29 fathoms; Bay of Fundy, 10 to 60 fathoms.

This species is readily distinguished by the form of the head and position of the small antennæ; by the large median dorsal papilla on the proboscis, and the smaller ventral one; by the very prominent and widely separated rami of the posterior feet; and the dark color of the setæ. It grows to the length of 130^{mm} or more.

NEPHTHYS PICTA Ehlers. Plate XII, fig. 57. (p. 348.)

Die Borstenwürmer, vol. i, p. 632, Pl. 23, figs. 9, 35, 1868.

Vineyard Sound, low-water mark to 8 fathoms, muddy and shelly. Nahant; Charleston (Ehlers).

NEPHTHYS BUCERA Ehlers. Plate XII, fig. 58. (p. 416.)

Die Borstenwürmer, vol. i, p. 617, Pl. 23, fig. 8.

Vineyard Sound, 8 to 10 fathoms, shelly; Watch Hill, Rhode Island, 4 to 5 fathoms, among rocks and sand. Massachusetts Bay (Ehlers).

This species is remarkable both for the form of the head and the length of the setæ, which often exceed the diameter of the body.

NEPHTHYS CILIATA Rathke.

Beiträge zur Fauna Norwegens, p. 170, 1843; Malmgren, op. cit., p. 104, Pl. 12, figs. 17, A–C, 1865; Quatrefages, op. cit., p. 429 (*Nephtys*); Ehlers, Borstenwürmer, vol. i, p. 629, Pl. 23, fig. 36, 1868. *Nereis ciliata* Müller, Zoölog. Danica, vol. iii, p. 17, Pl. 89, figs. 1–4 (t. Ehlers). *Nephthys borealis* Œrsted, Annulat. Danicor. consp., p. 32, 1843 (t. Malmgren).

Ehlers gives Edgartown as a locality for this species. It is a northern form, found at Iceland, Greenland, Spitzbergen, and along the northern coasts of Europe and Great Britain. Stimpson records it from the

Bay of Fundy, in 40 fathoms, mud. It was dredged near St. George's Bank in 85, 110, and 150 fathoms, mud, by Dr. A. S. Packard, on the "Bache," 1872.

EUMIDIA AMERICANA Verrill, sp. nov. (p. 494.)

Body long and slender. Head triangular, subcordate, broad and slightly emarginate posteriorly, the sides rapidly converging, the front end narrow and rounded, with four slender antennæ, which are as long as the head; odd median antenna long and slender, tapering, as long as or longer than the head. Eyes moderately large, round, convex, near the posterior margin of the head. Tentacular cirri long and slender; crowded. Proboscis elongated, subclavate, enlarging to the end, which is surrounded by about fourteen triangular papillæ; the basal two-thirds covered with small, slender, prominent papillæ, which are not crowded, but arranged in longitudinal rows; this part of the proboscis is, in the preserved specimens, longitudinally ridged and transversely wrinkled; the terminal third is nearly smooth, but usually minutely granulous. The lateral lamellæ, or branchiæ, are ovate-lanceolate, leaf-like, with curved tips; posteriorly they are larger and more acute. Length up to 50^{mm}; breadth, 1.5^{mm}.

Vineyard Sound, 8 to 12 fathoms, among compound ascidians.

EUMIDIA VIVIDA Verrill, sp. nov.

Head relatively a little longer than in the preceding species, with the sides more convex, and the front rounded; antennæ long and slender. Eyes brownish, very large, about twice as large as in the preceding species. Proboscis long, slender, clavate, nearly smooth, but with a few minute, distant papillæ; the terminal orifice surrounded by about eighteen very small papilliform denticulations. Branchiæ of the anterior segments long and narrow lanceolate; of the middle segments ovate. Length up to 45^{mm}; breadth, 1.5^{mm}.

Vineyard Sound, 8 to 12 fathoms, among ascidians.

EUMIDIA PAPILLOSA Verrill, sp. nov.

Head short, rounded, convex, emarginate posteriorly, the sides convex; antennæ not very slender; median odd one stout, tapering, acute, as long as the head. Eyes large; brown. Tentacular cirri rather stout, those of the two posterior pairs more than twice as long as the others. Proboscis long, clavate, densely covered with short, rounded papillæ, and with a circle of minute papillæ at the orifice.

Length up to 40^{mm}; breadth, 2^{mm}.

Vineyard Sound, 6 to 10 fathoms, among compound ascidians.

EULALIA PISTACIA Verrill, sp. nov.

Body moderately slender, depressed. Head convex, shorter than broad; in preserved specimens, sides well rounded, posterior margin slightly emarginate; median odd antenna small, slender, considerably shorter than the head. Eyes large, brown. Tentacular cirri moderately long; the four posterior ones considerably longer than the others. Branchiæ narrow lanceolate anteriorly; ovate and leaf-like on the middle segments; longer and lanceolate posteriorly. Proboscis long, more or less clavate, smooth, but often showing longitudinal striations, and sometimes with a few very minute scattered papillæ toward the end; the orifice surrounded by a circle of numerous minute papillæ. Color bright yellowish green (epidote-green or pistachio-green), often with obscure darker markings posteriorly, and at the base of the appendages. Length up to 40^{mm}; breadth, 1.5^{mm}.

Vineyard Sound, 6 to 12 fathoms, among compound ascidians; off New Haven, 4 to 5 fathoms, among hydroids.

EULALIA GRANULOSA Verrill, sp. nov.

Body not very slender, considerably stouter than in the preceding species, and less tapering anteriorly. Head short cordate, decidedly emarginate behind, broader than long; sides prominently rounded; front small, rounded. Antenæ short; odd one slender, originating between the eyes, more than half the length of the head. Eyes large, round, convex, dark brown. Proboscis long, clavate, thickly covered throughout with round, scarcely prominent, crowded, rather large granules, each of which has a dark central spot; orifice surrounded by a circle of small papillæ. Tentacular cirri slender, acute, the two posterior pairs long, reaching the eighth segment. Lateral appendages large and prominent for the genus. Branchiæ of upper ramus rather large, ovate, leaf-like anteriorly; larger and obliquely ovate, with acuminate tips, farther back; branchiæ of lower ramus similar in form and nearly as large. Color bright grass-green. Length 55^{mm}, or more; breadth, 2^{mm}; length of proboscis, 6^{mm}.

Off New Haven, 4 to 5 fathoms, among hydroids.

EULALIA ANNULATA Verrill, sp. nov.

Body moderately slender, convex, tapering to both ends. Head longer than broad, somewhat oblong, truncate behind, the sides but little convex, narrowing but little to the obtusely rounded front. Proboscis covered with small prominent papillæ. Eyes two, large, dark brown or blackish, rather near together. Odd median antenna slender, more than half as long as the head, placed far in advance of the eyes; frontal antennæ rather large, about the same in length, but much stouter than the median one, with slender tips. Tentacular cirri very unequal, the two upper pairs much longer than the others, not very slender, reaching to the seventh or eighth segment in preserved specimens; the two lower pairs not more than one-third as long. Dorsal branchiæ narrow and acute throughout; the anterior ones are narrow lanceolate, with subacute tips; those farther back become still more elongated, narrow lanceolate, or almost linear lanceolate, with acuminate tips, and in length equal to half the diameter of the body; posteriorly they become somewhat wider, with acute, curved tips. Caudal cirri small, narrow lanceolate, about as long as the posterior lateral lamellæ, or branchiæ. Color of preserved specimens pale greenish or bluish gray, with narrow annulations of golden brown, and iridescent. Length 50^{mm}, or more; breadth about 1.25^{mm}.

Vineyard Sound, 4 to 12 fathoms, among ascidians.

EULALIA GRACILIS Verrill, sp. nov.

Body very long and slender, with the segments deeply incised; posterior segments elongated. Head small, elongated, truncate behind; posterior angles not prominent, oblong, tapering but little toward the front, which is obtusely rounded; sides not swollen. Eyes of moderate size, brown, situated close to the posterior margin of the head. The four frontal antennæ are more than half as large as the head, rather stout, tapering, and the head is slightly constricted behind them; odd median one, small, slender, inconspicuous, about one-third the length of the head, placed considerably in advance of the eyes. Tentacular cirri rather stout, the two upper ones longest, rather more than twice as long as the head; the posterior pair, when extended backward, reaches the fifth setigerous segment in preserved specimens; the two lower ones are considerably stouter and smaller, nearly equal, and are somewhat longer than the head in alcoholic specimens. Branchiæ of the anterior segments short, oval, obtuse at the tip; posteriorly larger, elongated oval, leaf-like. Color light greenish brown or olive, with a row of dark brown spots along each side of the dorsal surface of the body.

Length up to 65^{mm}; breadth about 1^{mm}.

Vineyard Sound, 6 to 14 fathoms, among ascidians and hydroids.

This species is very active in its motions. In general appearance it resembles certain species of *Phyllodoce*, for which it might easily be mistaken, owing to the small size and translucency of the odd median antenna, which is not easily observed, especially with living specimens. The position of the tentacular cirri is, however, sufficient to distinguish the genus from *Phyllodoce* and *Eumidia*. The form of the head is quite peculiar, but somewhat resembles that of *Phyllodoce gracilis*, and also the preceding species.

One specimen of the *Eulalia gracilis* was found in which fissiparity was apparently about to take place. In this, one of the segments was larger than the rest, and had developed a distinct pair of eyes. The specimen unfortunately died before the separation took place.

PHYLLODOCE GRACILIS Verrill, sp. nov. Pl. XI, fig. 56. (p. 494.)

(?) *Phyllodoce maculata* A. Agassiz, Annals Lyceum New York, vol. viii, p. 333, fig. 53, 1866 (*non* Müller, *nec* Œrsted).

Body very long and slender. Head longer than broad, decidedly cordate behind, with the posterior angles well rounded; the sides swelling out opposite the eyes, then narrowing to near the antennæ, where there is a slight constriction, and expanding slightly at the end, which is obtusely rounded. Eyes very large, brown, wide apart, and sub-lateral, connected by a curved band of brown specks; antennæ rather large and long, about one-third as long as the head. Tentacular cirri large, the two posterior much the longest, reaching to about the eighth setigerous segment. Branchiæ of anterior segments broad oval or sub-circular, rounded at the end; posterior ones larger, broad oval, narrowed to the end. Proboscis with a large, swollen, basal portion, on which are twelve longitudinal rows of large, prominent, obtuse papillæ, about seven in each row; and a terminal smooth portion, which is somewhat longer, and about as broad at the end as the basal portion, but considerably narrower at its commencement; the orifice is surrounded by a circle of large, rounded papillæ. Color greenish, with a median dorsal row of dark brown spots, and another less conspicuous row along each side of the back, at the base of the lateral appendages.

Length up to 75^{mm}; breadth, 1 to 1.25^{mm}.

Watch Hill, Rhode Island, in 4 or 5 fathoms, rocky bottom.

The figure (56) copied from one of those given by Mr. Agassiz does not agree perfectly with the specimens described, but probably represents the same species. The head, as figured, is more oblong and the eyes nearer together than in my specimens; the tentacular cirri are less crowded. The anterior ones, in the preserved specimens at least, appear to arise from beneath the base of the head. Some of these differences may be due to the different states of extension and contraction; for the species in this family are all quite changeable in form during life, and usually contract very much in alcohol.

PHYLLODOCE CATENULA Verrill, sp. nov. (p. 494.)

Head somewhat longer than broad, slightly cordate posteriorly, with the posterior angles well rounded, and the sides full and convex; front broadly rounded, and with a slight emargination in the middle. Eyes large, dark brown, placed on the dorsal surface of the head; antennæ rather long, slender. Tentacular cirri long and slender, the two posterior much longer than the others. Branchiæ of anterior segments broad ovate, with rounded tips; farther back larger and longer, ovate, leaf-like, with acuminate tips. Proboscis with twelve rows of papillæ on the basal portion, which are prominent, somewhat elongated, obtuse, seven or eight in the lateral rows, those in each row close together. Color of body and branchiæ pale green, with a median dorsal row of dark brown spots, one to each segment; and two lateral rows, in which there is a spot at the base of each "foot;" head pale, or greenish white.

Length up to 75^{mm}; breadth about 1.5^{mm}.

Watch Hill, Rhode Island, in 4 to 6 fathoms, among rocks and algæ, and in tide-pools; Wood's Hole, at surface, evening, July 3. Very common in the Bay of Fundy, from low-water to 50 fathoms.

This species is closely allied to *P. pulchella* Malmgren, from Northern Europe, but differs somewhat in the form of the head, which is shorter and rounder in the latter; the branchiæ also differ in form. It is a very active species, and secretes a large quantity of mucus.

ETEONE ROBUSTA Verrill, sp. nov. (p. 488.)

Body large, stout, depressed, broadest in the middle, tapering gradually to each end. Head small, about as long as wide, convex, with a median depression; the sides rounded; front obtusely rounded. The four frontal antennæ are very small, short, obtuse, less than half the diameter of the head. Eyes very small, black. Tentacles very small and short, tapering, their length about one-half the diameter of the head, the two pairs about equal. Branchiæ small, sessile, anteriorly very small, oval, obtuse; in the middle region rounded, sub-oval. Color dark green, with the anterior portion somewhat paler, and with light green transverse bands between the segments; lateral appendages pale green.

Length, 125^{mm}; breadth in middle, 5^{mm}; length of head, 0.6^{mm}.

Watch Hill, Rhode Island, under stones, between tides, April 12, 1873.

ETEONE LIMICOLA Verrill, sp. nov. (p. 349.)

Body very long and slender, tapering gradually to both ends; depressed, and with deeply incised, elongated segments posteriorly; less depressed and with shorter and less distinct segments anteriorly. Head small, about as broad as long, the posterior angles well rounded, the sides with a slight constriction in advance of the eyes, narrowing rapidly; front narrow, convex; antennæ slender, about half the length of the head. Eyes minute, inconspicuous. Tentacular cirri about equal to the length of the head. Lateral appendages small on the anterior segments, becoming much more prominent farther back; anterior branchiæ very small, ovate, sessile; those farther back much larger, and narrow ovate. Color, when living, light green throughout.

Length about 80^{mm}; breadth, including appendages, 1.5^{mm}.

Great Egg Harbor, New Jersey, in mud at low-water.

ETEONE SETOSA Verrill, sp. nov.

Body long and slender, resembling the preceding in form, but somewhat less slender. Head shorter and broader, the posterior angles prominently rounded; two slight notches or emarginations on the posterior margin, the middle portion extending farther back than the lateral; sides rapidly tapering; front narrow. Antennæ less than half the length of the head. Eyes small, but quite distinct. Tentacular cirri scarcely as long as the head. Lateral appendages a little prominent on the anterior segments, but much less so than farther back; setæ numerous. The branchiæ are small, sessile, and inconspicuous anteriorly; larger and ovate farther back.

Length up to 75^{mm}; breadth about 2^{mm}.

Vineyard Sound, 6 to 12 fathoms, among ascidians.

ETEONE, species undetermined.

A small and slender species was dredged off Gay Head, in 19 fathoms, soft mud.

Another very peculiar species of *Eteone* was obtained at Great Egg Harbor, New Jersey. In this the head is depressed and elongated, tapering, with short antennæ. The anterior part of the body is round and with the lateral appendages very small, closely appressed, and not at all prominent, giving to this part of the body a smooth appearance; on this part of the body the branchiæ are very small, lunate, sessile, closely appressed; farther back they become much larger, and rounded or ovate, while the setigerous lobe becomes prominent, and the setæ much longer and more numerous.

PODARKE OBSCURA Verrill, sp. nov. Pl. XII, fig. 61. (p. 319.)

Body convex above, flat below, with the segments deeply incised at the sides, moderately slender in full extension, but capable of great contraction, tapering gradually to the caudal extremity, and less toward the head. Head small, broader than long, emarginate in front, sides forming rounded angles; posterior margin nearly straight. Antennæ five, subequal, the outer pair articulated upon a short, thick basal segment; the odd median one is somewhat shorter, articulated upon a small basal segment, which arises in front of the anterior pair of eyes. Tentacular cirri long, slender, six on each side, two arising from each of the first three annulations, on each side; those on the middle are longest, those on the first shortest. Eyes four, small, red; those on each side close together, but those of the anterior pair are farthest apart. Proboscis with a large, swollen basal portion, and a smaller cylindrical terminal portion, the surface nearly smooth. Lateral appendages, or "feet," elongated, biramous. The upper branch is short, conical, bearing at its extremity a long, slender dorsal cirrus, nearly as long as the breadth of the body, or even exceeding it, and having a short basal joint; the setæ of the upper ramus are very few and small. The lower branch is much larger and longer, thick at base, tapering somewhat to the obtuse end, from which a small, terminal, obtuse, papilliform process arises; the short, acute, ventral cirrus arises from about the terminal third, and is less than half as long as the dorsal cirrus; the setæ are numerous and long, forming a broad, fan-shaped fascicle, in which the middle setæ are considerably longer than the upper and lower ones, and in length about equal to the setigerous lobe; these setæ are all compound, the middle ones having a very long, slender, acute terminal joint, and the shorter ones beneath having a much shorter terminal joint. Last segment small, rounded, bearing two long, slender anal cirri, much longer than the dorsal cirri. Color variable, most commonly very dark brown or blackish; sometimes dark brown with transverse bands of light flesh-color between the segments, and two intermediate transverse whitish lines on each segment.

Length up to 40mm when extended; breadth, including setæ, 3mm.

Wood's Hole, among eel-grass and at the surface, very abundant, especially at night, in July and August; also under stones, between tides.

AUTOLYTUS CORNUTUS A. Agassiz. Pl. XIII, figs. 65, 66. (p. 397.)

Journal Boston Society of Natural History, vol. vii, p. 392, Plates 9–11, 1863.

Great Egg Harbor, New Jersey; New Haven; Watch Hill; Vineyard Sound; Massachusetts Bay; Eastport, Maine. Low-water mark to 15 fathoms.

AUTOLYTUS, species undetermined. (p. 398.)

Off New Haven, 4 to 6 fathoms, shelly, among hydroids.

AUTOLYTUS, species undetermined.

Females, filled with eggs, of a large species of this genus were taken at the surface of Vineyard Sound, April 30, by Mr. V. N. Edwards. These were about 40mm in length, as preserved in alcohol, and rather stout, tapering to each end. The head is small, short, rounded in front. The eyes are small, and the two pairs are near together. The odd median antenna is more than twice as long as the breadth of the head; the lateral ones are about half as long; the first six setigerous segments have short setæ; the following ones have a fascicle of long, slender ones, equal to the breadth of the body.

SYLLIS, species undetermined. (p. 453.)

A single specimen from Vineyard Sound. The body is about 12mm long; the antennæ are not very long; the palpi short; the dorsal cirri are rather long, and, like the antennæ, regularly beaded; the ventral cirri are small, tapering; the setæ are numerous, rather short.

GATTIOLA, species undetermined. (p. 453.)

Young specimens were taken several times in Vineyard Sound, at the surface. Adult specimens of a fine species of this genus were dredged in the Bay of Fundy in 1872, in 80 fathoms.

NEREIS VIRENS Sars. Pl. XI, figs. 47–50. (p. 317.)

Beskrivelser og Iakttagelser, etc., p. 58, Pl. 10, fig. 27, a, b, c, 1835 (t. Malmgren). *Nereis grandis* Stimpson, Invertebrata of Grand Manan, p. 34, fig. 24, 1853. *Nereis Yankiana* Quatrefages, Hist. des Annelés, i, p. 553, Pl. 17, figs. 7, 8 1865; *Alitta virens* Malmgren, op. cit., p. 183; Annulata polychæta, p. 56, Pl. 3, figs. 19, A–E, 1867.

New Haven, at low water; Watch Hill; Vineyard Sound; Massachusetts Bay; Eastport, Maine; northward to Labrador. Northern coasts of Europe to Great Britain.

NEREIS LIMBATA Ehlers. Pl. XI, fig. 51. (p. 318.)

Die Borstenwürmer, vol. i, p. 567, 1868.

Charleston, South Carolina, to Massachusetts Bay; half-tide mark to 4 to 6 fathoms in Long Island Sound.

NEREIS PELAGICA Linn. Pl. XI, figs. 52–55. (p. 319.)

Systema naturæ, ed. x, p. 654; ed. xii, p. 1086; Malmgren, Annulata polychæta p. 47, Pl. 5, figs. 35, A–D, 1867; Ehlers, op. cit., p. 511, Pl. 20, figs. 11–20, 1868. *Heteronereis grandifolia* Malmgren, Nordiska Hafs-Annulater, p. 108, Pl. 11, figs. 15, 16, B, B[1], C; Ann. polychæta, p. 60, Pl. 5, figs. 31, A–D; *Heteronereis arctica* Œrsted, Grœnland's Annul. dorsibr., p. 27, Pl. 4, figs. 50*, 51, 60, Pl. 5, figs. 65, 68 70*, male (t. Ehlers); *Heteronereis assimilis* Œrsted, op. cit., p. 28, Pl. 4, figs. 54, 61, Pl. 5, fig. 72, female (t. Ehlers).

Off New Haven; Watch Hill; Vineyard Sound; northward to Labrador. Greenland; Iceland; Spitzbergen; northern coasts of Europe to Great Britain. In the Bay of Fundy from low-water mark to 106 fathoms, common.

NEREIS FUCATA Aud. and Edwards. (p. 494.)

Histoire nat. litt. de la France, vol. ii, p. 188 (teste Malmgren); *Lycoris fucata* Savigny, Syst. des Annélides, p. 31, 1820 (t. Ehlers); Descr. de l'Égypte, éd. 2, xxi, p. 357 (t. Malmgren); *Nereilepas fucata* Malmgren, Annulata polychæta, p. 53, Pl. 3, figs. 18–18 E; Johnston, Catalogue, p. 158, fig. 30, 1865. *Heteronereis glaucopis* Malmgren, Nordiska Hafs-Annulater, Öfvers. af Kongl. Vet. Akad. Förh., 1865, p. 181, Pl. 11, figs. 16, 16 A; Annulata polychæta, p. 60, Pl. 4, figs. 26, 27, 1867. *Nereis fucata* Ehlers, Borstenwürmer, vol. i, p. 546, Pl. 21, figs. 41–44.

A specimen was dredged at Watch Hill, Rhode Island, in 4 to 6 fathoms, among rocks and algæ, which agrees well with Malmgren's description and figure of *Heteronereis glaucopis*. Ehlers regards the latter as the heteronereis-form of *N. fucata*.

NEREIS, species undetermined.

Head sub-conical; antennæ small, slender; palpi small, shorter, and thicker; two upper pairs of tentacular cirri moderately elongated, subequal, lower ones very small. Posterior eyes elongated and on the upper side of the head; anterior pair small, lateral. Feet terminated by four small papillæ; dorsal and ventral cirri small, slender.

The only specimen observed is preserved in alcohol; it is a female filled with eggs. Vineyard Sound, 6 to 8 fathoms.

NECTONEREIS Verrill, genus nov.

Head prominent, depressed, oval, rounded in front, bearing two pairs of large eyes on the upper and lateral surfaces, and a pair of small antennæ beneath; palpi small or rudimentary. Tentacular cirri four on each side, as in *Nereis*. Proboscis small, similar to that of *Nereis*, but more simple; furnished with a pair of terminal hooks; with two anterior clusters of denticles on the upper side, and with five small clusters below, in a ring extending nearly half-way around it. Anterior part of body fusiform, consisting of about fourteen segments, on which the feet are divided into small, rounded lobes, with small ventral cirri; and with long dorsal cirri, those on the first seven segments swollen and gibbous toward the end, with a small acute terminal portion. Posterior part of the body composed of numerous short segments, on which the feet are furnished with lamelliform appendages.

This remarkable annelid bears some resemblance, in the structure of the body and "feet," to *Heteronereis*, and there is probably another form to which it bears the same relation that *Heteronereis* bears to *Nereis*; but the structure of the head is very unlike that of any known genus, and, indeed, would not allow it to be placed in the family of *Nereidæ* without modifying the family-characters. There are are no large palpi, corresponding to those of *Nereis*, and nothing to represent them, unless two small lobes close to the mouth be considered rudimentary palpi.

NECTONEREIS MEGALOPS Verrill, sp. nov. Plate XII, figs. 62, 63. (p. 440.)

Body slender, consisting of two parts; the anterior portion, containing fourteen setigerous segments, is broadest in the middle, tapering both ways, and separated from the posterior portion by a distinct constriction; the posterior portion is much longer and more slender, tapering gradually to the end, and consists of very numerous short segments, which are furnished with complex lateral appendages, with thin lamellæ and compound bladed setæ. Head broad oval, somewhat convex, and very smooth above; the lateral margins a little convex; the front obtusely rounded. Eyes very large, convex; the anterior ones largest, lateral and partially dorsal, oval; in contact with the posterior ones, which are somewhat smaller and more dorsal. Two small decurved antennæ, with swollen bases, are on the ventral side of the head; two small, rounded processes in front of the mouth. Tentacular cirri slender, the upper pair much the longest; the rather short lower pair arising near the mouth; the two intermediate pairs arise behind and close to the anterior eyes; all are slightly annulated. The "feet" on the first seven segments have a large dorsal cirrus, increasing in length from the first to the seventh, narrow at base, swollen and gibbous toward the end, with a slender, oblique, terminal portion; on the seven following segments the dorsal cirri are smaller, slender, tapering; the ventral cirri are small, with swollen bases on the first five segments, slender and tapering on the rest; the intermediate lobes of the feet are small and rounded, but more elongated on the first five segments. Setæ of different forms, many of them with a slender, often curved, acute terminal piece.

The lateral appendages of the posterior region have, on the upper ramus, a long, slender dorsal cirrus, strongly crenulate-lobed on the lower side; a small, rounded lamelliform process above its base; and a long, lanceolate process arising just below it, and in length equaling the cirrus; an ovate setigerous lobe, bearing a broad fan-shaped fascicle of compound setæ, extending about to the end of the dorsal cirrus; and a lower ovate-lanceolate lamelliform process, with the base expanded and extending backward, the tip reaching to about the outer third of the cirrus; a single strong black spine supports the setigerous lobe. The lower ramus has a rounded setigerous lobe, and a large broadly-rounded lamelliform process, nearly as long as the longest one of the upper ramus and much broader; the setigerous lobe bears a broad fan-shaped fascicle of compound setæ, similar to those of the upper ramus, but a little shorter, and a single black basal spine; the ventral cirrus is slender, and there is a broad, rounded ventral lamella at its base. The setæ are rather stout, with a broad, thin, blade-like, terminal piece, which is generally lanceolate, with a rounded point, and often somewhat curved, but more commonly straight. A few setæ have a slender acute terminal piece. Anal segment with numerous small slender papilliform processes on each side, forming a circle.

Length up to 35^{mm}; breadth about 2.5^{mm}.

Vineyard Sound, swimming actively at the surface, both in the evening and in the brightest sunshine, in the middle of the day; July 3 to August 11.

DIOPATRA CUPREA Claparède. Plate XIII, figs. 67, 68. (p. 346.)

Annélides chétopodes du golfe de Naples, in Mémoires de la Société de Physiques et d'Hist. Nat. de Genève, vol. xix, p. 432, 1868. *Nereis cuprea* Bosc, Hist. nat. des Vers, vol. i, p. 143 (t. Claparède).

Charleston, South Carolina, to Long Island Sound and Vineyard Sound.

MARPHYSA LEIDYI Quatrefages. Plate XII, fig. 64. (p. 319.)

Histoire nat. des Annelés, vol. i, p. 337, 1865 (*M. Leidii*). *Eunice sanguinea* Leidy, Mar. Inv. Fauna of Rhode Island and New Jersey, p. 15, 1855 (*non* Montagu).

Great Egg Harbor, New Jersey, to Long Island Sound and Vineyard Sound. Low-water mark to 10 fathoms.

LYCIDICE AMERICANA Verrill, sp. nov. (p. 508.)

Body depressed, slender, narrowed toward each end; segments well-marked. Head much depressed, oblong, narrowed somewhat toward the front, which is truncate and somewhat emarginate in the middle; lower side bilobed, the lobes well rounded. The two eyes are lateral, just outside the bases of the lateral antennæ. The three antennæ are subequal, nearly as long as the diameter of the head; the odd median one is apparently a little longer than the lateral, and placed slightly farther back. The dorsal cirri are long and slender, exceeding the diameter of the body in living specimens; they have a small lobe near the base. Anal cirri four; the two lower exceeding the diameter of the body; the two upper ones less than half as long. Color light red, with a bright red dorsal vessel and dark brown intestines, showing through in the middle; eyes dark red.

Length, while living, about 40^{mm}; greatest diameter, 1.5^{mm}.

Off Gay Head, in 19 fathoms, soft mud.

NEMATONEREIS, species undetermined. (p. 508.)

A species, apparently belonging to this genus, was dredged in 29 fathoms, east of Block Island. The specimens have been lost or mislaid. In life the head was small, rounded, with one median dorsal antenna, about as long as the diameter of the head. Eyes two, small but conspicuous, dark brown. Dorsal cirri slender.

LUMBRICONEREIS FRAGILIS Œrsted. (p. 507.)

Conspec. Ann. Dan., p. 15, figs. 1, 2, 1843 (t. Malmgren). *Lumbricus fragilis* Müller, Prod. Zool. Dan., p. 216; Zool. Dan., vol. i, p. 22, Pl. 22, figs. 1–3, 1788, (t. Malmgren). *Lumbrinereis fragilis* Malmgren, Annulata polychæta, p. 63, Pl. 14, figs. 83–83, D.

Mouth of Vineyard Sound and deeper waters outside; northward to Nova Scotia and Gulf of Saint Lawrence. Northern coasts of Europe. From low-water mark, in the Bay of Fundy, to 430 fathoms, off Saint George's Bank.

LUMBRICONEREIS OPALINA Verrill, sp. nov. Plate XIII, figs. 69, 70. (p. 342.)

Lumbriconereis splendida Leidy., op. cit., p. 15 (*non* Blainville).

Body cylindrical, much elongated, largest in the middle, tapering gradually toward the head, which is comparatively small; segments well marked. Head conoidal, obtuse, changing much in form during life; in extension considerably longer than broad, and more acute than in the figure. Eyes four, in a transverse row, the two middle ones larger and a little in advance of the others. The lateral appendages, or "feet," consist of a short, obtusely-rounded basal papilla, which bears the setæ; from the posterior and ventral end of this a prominent elongated lobe arises, which is somewhot curved and obtuse. These appendages are longer in the middle of the body than anteriorly. Setæ five to nine in each fascicle, and of several forms; one or two in each fascicle usually have a long, slender, flexible capillary point. Color reddish or brownish, with brilliant iridescence.

Length up to 400^{mm}; diameter in middle, 3^{mm}.

New Haven to Vineyard Sound; low-water mark to 14 fathoms.

LUMBRICONEREIS TENUIS Verrill, sp. nov. (p. 342.)

Body very long, slender, filiform, of nearly uniform diameter throughout, capable of great extension; segments very numerous, well marked. Head a little narrower than buccal segment, depressed, obtusely pointed or rounded in front, without eyes. In the first to ninth pairs the lateral appendages have about six slender lanceolate setæ; those of the ninth pair have two slender spatulate setæ, with about six or seven lanceolate ones; at the sixteenth pair they begin to have recurved spatulate setæ, with two or three hook-like denticles at the end, while two or three lanceolate ones remain; posterior to the twenty-third or twenty-fourth pair only one of the long, slender, acute setæ remains, accompanied by two or three of the spatulate hooks; the latter are about half as long as the former, slender toward the base, but gradually becoming broader toward the end, which is twice as broad, obtusely rounded, and curved back from about the middle; the hooks are nearly terminal on one side, the thin margin projecting beyond them. The basal lobe of the "feet" is very small; the posterior lobe is small but prominent. Color light red to dark red, somewhat iridescent.

Length up to 350^{mm}; diameter, 0.05^{mm} to 1^{mm}.

Great Egg Harbor, New Jersey, to New Haven and Vineyard Sound.

NINOË NIGRIPES Verrill, sp. nov. (p. 508.)

Body elongated, slender, broadest a short distance behind the head, at the middle of the branchiferous segments. Head depressed, elongated, conical, blunt at end, about twice as long as broad. The branchiæ are represented on the first two setigerous segments by a short, flattened lobe, arising from the outer and posterior face of the setigerous lobe. On the two following segments the lobe is divided into two or three parts; on the fifth there are usually three, more elongated, round, and more slender branchiæ, which increase in number and length on the succeeding segments until there are five, six, or more long, slender branchial filaments, which arise from the posterior face of the setigerous lobe, and diverge, forming a somewhat fan-shaped or digitate group; about the twenty-fourth segment the number rapidly diminishes, and after the twenty-seventh or twenty-eighth there remains but one small branchial process. The setigerous lobe is prominent, obtuse, turned forward. The setæ are numerous on the branchial segments, and rather long, of various shapes, but mostly bent, with an acute lanceolate point; posteriorly they are shorter and fewer, and mostly slender, margined setæ, with hooks at the spatulate end. Body flesh-color; the setæ dark, often blackish; branchiæ bright red.

Length of broken specimens, 20^{mm}; breadth anteriorly, 2^{mm}.

Vineyard Sound and Buzzard's Bay, and waters outside; in 8 to 29 fathoms, mud.

STAUROCEPHALUS PALLIDUS Verrill, sp. nov. (p. 348.)

Body rather slender, convex above, flattened below, largest in the middle, tapering slightly toward each end, composed of about seventy segments. Head small, depressed, rounded in front; antennæ four, slender, longer than the breadth of body, the two upper ones longer and more slender than the lower ones, strongly annulated or beaded; lower ones stouter, smooth, tapering. Eyes four, dark red; the posterior pair very small, placed between the bases of the upper antennæ; the anterior pair farther apart, placed between the bases of the upper and lower antennæ. Anal cirri four, the upper pair slender and about twice as long as the lower ones. Dorsal cirri elongated, slender, more than twice as long as the setigerous lobe, absent on the first setigerous segment, very small on the second, but well developed on the third. Setæ rather long and slender. Color pale yellow, with red blood-vessels showing through anteriorly.

Length, 50^{mm}; breadth, 2^{mm}. This species moves like a *Nereis*.

Near New Haven light-house, in sand, at low-water mark.

RHYNCHOBOLUS AMERICANUS Verrill. Plate X, figs. 45, 46. (p. 342.)

Glycera Americana Leidy, op. cit., p. 15, Pl. 11, figs. 49, 50, 1855; Ehlers, Borstenwürmer, vol. i, p. 668, Pl. 23, figs. 43–46, 1868.

Charleston, South Carolina, to Long Island Sound and Vineyard Sound. Low-water mark to 10 fathoms.

I follow Claparède in adopting *Rhynchobolus* for those species of the old genus *Glycera* which have the proboscis armed at the end with four hooks or fangs.

RHYNCHOBOLUS DIBRANCHIATUS Verrill. Plate X, figs. 43, 44. (p. 341.)

Glycera dibranchiata Ehlers, op. cit., pp. 670–702, Pl. 24, figs. 10–28, 1868.

Great Egg Harbor, New Jersey, to Long Island Sound; Vineyard Sound; and Massachusetts Bay. Low-water mark to 8 fathoms.

Ehlers has given a very full anatomical description of this species.

EONE GRACILIS Verrill, sp. nov. (p. 508.)

Body very slender, terete; surface iridescent. Head elongated, acutely conical, composed of eight distinct, rounded annulations, the basal one with a pair of minute reddish eyes; antennæ four, slender. Feet prominent, elongated, more than equal to half the diameter of the body; they are uniramous on about thirty-two segments of the anterior part of the body, and bilobed, with a small obtuse dorsal cirrus; the upper lobe is prominent, more elongated than the lower one, both cylindrical, obtusely pointed; setæ compound, in two small fascicles, long, the free part exceeding the entire length of the foot. On the posterior half of the body there is a small, slightly elevated, mammilliform upper ramus, above the base of the lower ramus, and entirely separate from it, containing two or more small, acute, dark setæ, which project but slightly; the lower ramus is deeply bilobed, the lobes elongated, round, the upper one longest, the lower one acute; on the posterior side of the base of the upper lobe there is a minute, rounded setigerous lobe, and at the junction of the two lobes, on the posterior face, there is another small setigerous lobe; the setæ are long and slender, acute, many of them curved, arranged in small fascicles.

Length, 20^{mm}; diameter less than 1^{mm}.

Off Gay Head, 19 fathoms, in soft mud.

ARICIA ORNATA Verrill, sp. nov. (p. 344.)

Body rather stout, composed of numerous very short segments, much depressed and flattened anteriorly, strongly convex beneath in the middle region, flattened above throughout; breadth nearly the same through a large part of the length, narrowed slightly and gradually toward the posterior end, and abruptly narrowed anteriorly close to the head, which is very small, short, conical, and acute at the tip. On the anterior thirty-two setigerous segments the feet consist of a small upper ramus, having a small, tapering dorsal cirrus and a minute setigerous lobe, bearing a small fascicle of slender and short setæ, and a lower ramus, separated by a narrow space, and consisting of a small upper papilla, and a long transverse row of minute, rounded papillæ, which surmount a narrow, somewhat elevated, crest-like ridge; the first twelve or thirteen segments having shorter rows, so as to leave a broad, naked ventral space, but those farther back having rows of papillæ that nearly meet beneath, and thus entirely covering the sides and ventral surface for a short distance; these crest-like ridges bear close rows of minute, hooked setæ. The branchiæ commence on the upper surface of the fifth setigerous segment, in the form of elongated papillæ, which become more elongated and narrow ligulate farther back. Posterior to the thirty-second segment the papilliform crests of the lower ramus disappear, and the lower ramus consists of an elongated papilliform, and finally cirriform, upper process, with a minute setigerous lobe at its base, bearing fine inconspicuous setæ; and an elongated membranous basal portion, decurrent down on the lateral surface of the segment; the upper ramus is connected at the base by a membranous web with the lower one, and consists of an elongated dorsal cirrus, similar in size and shape to the branchia, and a very small setigerous lobe, bearing a small fascicle of fine setæ. The branchiæ are connected by a slight web-like basal ridge with the dorsal cirri. Thus there are three parallel rows of cirriform or slender ligulate processes along each side of the back, leaving a broad, central, naked space all along the back.

Length up to 60^{mm} or more; breadth, 4^{mm}.

Savin Rock, burrowing in sand at low-water mark, May, 1872.

ANTHOSTOMA ROBUSTUM Verrill, sp. nov. Plate XIV, fig. 76. (p. 343.)

Body large, long, stout, thickest and rounded, or but slightly depressed, anteriorly; tapering rapidly to the head; posterior portion very long, narrowing gradually to the posterior end, flatter or concave above, well rounded below, higher than wide, with three rows of long, erect, ligulate, or narrow lanceolate processes along each side of the back, the four inner rows largest; and a pair of foliaceous processes on the sides of each segment. Head short, conical, acute. Proboscis large, broad, divided into about eighteen long, narrow, digitate, and sulcated lobes, with convoluted margins, broadest at the end, and free for a large part of their length, but united at the base by a membranous web; or it might be described as divided into a lower, two lateral, and two upper main lobes, each of which is again divided into three or four digitations. During life these are all continually changing in form and length, and generally only a few of the processes are protruded at one time. Branchiæ commence on the twenty-sixth setigerous segment as minute papillæ; on the twenty-eighth they become prominent and acute-conical; farther back they become long, lanceolate, thin, foliaceous, as long as the diameter of the body.

On the twenty-three anterior setigerous segments the "feet" are represented by two short, dense, fan-shaped fascicles of setæ on each side. On the twenty-fourth segment a small papilliform lobe, or ventral cirrus, appears below the lower ramus, which rapidly becomes larger on the succeeding segments, becoming quite conspicuous on the twenty-ninth segment; at about the twenty-eighth it becomes broader, and divided into three small lobes, the lowest broadest and thinnest, and a bilobed setigerous lobe is developed. At the thirtieth the ventral lobe becomes broader, somewhat foliaceous, with a rounded outline; farther back this becomes still larger and more foliaceous, with a broadly-rounded flexuous outer border, and the upper branch of the setigerous lobe becomes an elongated ligulate process, directed upward, and similar in form to the branchiæ, though smaller and more slender, but the lower branch remains small and rounded; a small fascicle of long, slender setæ arises from between them. On the twenty-seventh segment an upper cirrus appears on both the upper and lower rami, in the form of a small papilla, which becomes somewhat elongated and tapering at the twenty-ninth; that of the lower ramus continues small throughout, and much shorter than the setigerous or ventral lobes, but that of the upper ramus becomes rapidly larger, longer, and more ligulate, corresponding nearly with the branchiæ in size, form, and rate of increase. On the middle and posterior regions the upper ramus consists of this long, thin, lanceolate cirrus and a fascicle of long, slender setæ, arising from the anterior face of its base, and in length considerably exceeding the cirrus; the setæ are pale yellow. Those of the upper ramus are short anteriorly, and become decidedly longer at the twenty-eighth segment, and on the thirty-second and subsequent segments they form a long, divergent, fan-shaped fascicle; color, when living, ocher-yellow, orange-yellow, to yellowish brown, generally brighter yellow posteriorly. Usually there are two rows of brown spots along the back, and posteriorly there is a dorsal red or reddish brown line; branchiæ blood-red.

Length of large specimens up to 375^{mm} or more; breadth, 10^{mm}; ordinary specimens are about 300^{mm} long and 7^{mm} broad. Owing to the facility with which it breaks up when disturbed, it is difficult to obtain entire specimens of large size.

Great Egg Harbor, New Jersey; New Haven; Wood's Hole; in sand, at low-water.

ANTHOSTOMA FRAGILE Verrill, sp. nov. (p. 344.)

Body long and slender, composed of very numerous segments, very fragile, and prone to divide spontaneously when disturbed; thickest and sub-cylindrical anteriorly, tapering rapidly to the head; posterior part very long and slender, tapering gradually, flattened dorsally. Head distinctly annulated, elongated conical, very acute, with the tip slender and translucent; proboscis short and broad, not extending far beyond the tip of the head, with six or more broad, convoluted, changeable lobes, which are united at the base by a broad membranous expansion. The dorsal branchiæ first appear on the sixteenth setigerous segment as small papillæ; they become well developed and long ligulate at about the twentieth, increasing somewhat in length on the segments farther back. On the first thirteen segments behind the buccal the "feet" are represented by a very small, slightly-elevated lobe, above and below, each bearing a dense fascicle, that of the lower ramus widest, but the length of the setæ about equal in both. On the fourteenth segment a small tubercle appears on both rami; on the sixteenth these become elongated and somewhat cirriform, and the setæ become considerably longer on the fifteenth segment. At about the seventeenth segment the lower ramus becomes distinctly tri-lobed, and at the twentieth four-lobed, with the setigerous lobe bifid, and the two lower lateral lobes conical, acute, and swollen at the base; while the upper ramus is long and ligulate, like the branchiæ, and the setæ are long and slender, the lower fascicle smallest. Farther back the lobes of the lower ramus become still more developed, but keep their acute conical form, and the upper ramus and setæ continue to elongate until, on the posterior part of the body, they exceed in length the diameter of the body. Anal segment oblong, sub-cylindrical, smooth, with two long filiform cirri on the upper side; color, when living, brownish orange, dull yellow, ocher, light reddish, or flesh-color, with a red median dorsal line, and sometimes with the dorsal surface tinged with red posteriorly; a narrow, light ventral line, bordered with reddish. Sometimes the upper surface is maculate with fine polygonal, whitish spots, due, perhaps, to ova contained within the body; there are sometimes two obscure brownish spots on the upper side of the head.

Length up to 125^{mm}; diameter, 3^{mm}.

Great Egg Harbor, New Jersey; New Haven; Watch Hill; Wood's Hole; in sand, between tides, and gregarious.

ANTHOSTOMA ACUTUM Verrill, sp. nov. (p. 501.)

Body long and quite slender, tapering most toward the head, and very gradually posteriorly. Head very acutely pointed, with two rather indistinct reddish spots above, resembling imperfect ocelli. The branchiæ commence at the eleventh setigerous segment as small dorsal papillæ, and become prominent on the thirteenth; on the succeeding segments they become long and ligulate. Anteriorly the feet are represented by an upper ramus, consisting of a very small tuft of setæ, with a very small papilliform lobe above it, and a lower ramus, consisting of a small prominent papilla, with a fascicle of slender setæ, much larger than the upper one. On the fourteenth and succeeding segments the dorsal cirrus of the upper ramus becomes longer, more slender, and ligulate. On the fifteenth segment a small, short, rounded ventral cirrus appears on the lower ramus, and farther back it becomes larger and more prominent, and the setigerous lobe becomes bilobed. Anal segment rounded, obtuse; cirri long and slender. Color light red.

Length up to 40^{mm}; diameter, 2.5^{mm}.

Off Gay Head, 19 fathoms, soft mud; also from the deeper parts of Vineyard Sound.

ANTHOSTOMA, species undetermined. (p. 508.)

Another species, not well studied, was dredged in the deeper waters off Gay Head and Buzzard's Bay. It differs from all the preceding in having eighteen anterior segments without branchiæ.

NERINE AGILIS Verrill, sp. nov. (p. 346.)

Body long and rather slender, anteriorly flattened, posteriorly more rounded. Head long conical, with a slender acute tip; mouth a transverse fissure beneath; eyes four, placed in front of the bases of the two large antennæ, small, black, the anterior ones a little farther apart; antennæ long, slender, with thickened bases, placed on the dorsal surface of the head, with their bases contiguous.

The branchiæ are slender, ligulate, and exist on all the segments except the first. On the first segment the "feet" are represented on each side by two small rounded lobes, bearing very small setæ, and placed just below the bases of the antennæ; on the succeeding twenty segments the lower ramus consists of a larger, somewhat semicircular lobe, bearing a broad cluster of slender, acute setæ, and separate from the upper ramus, which consists of a thin foliaceous process joined to the branchial cirrus, but with a free terminal portion, and bearing a broad, comb-like cluster of long acute setæ, nearly as long as the branchiæ, and much longer than those of the ventral ramus. On the twenty-first setigerous segment a small papilliform ventral cirrus appears on the lower ramus, and farther back it becomes more prominent and separate from the setigerous lobe. In the middle and posterior region the free portion of the cirriform lobe of the upper ramus is longer.

Color reddish or brownish green anteriorly, light green on the sides; branchiæ bright red. Length up to 60^{mm}; breadth, 2^{mm}; length of antennæ, 12^{mm}.

Great Egg Harbor, New Jersey, on the outer beach, burrowing in sand, at low-water mark.

SCOLECOLEPIS VIRIDIS Verrill, sp. nov. (p. 345.)

Body long, slender, depressed; both the upper and lower surfaces flattened, of nearly uniform breadth throughout most of the length, abruptly narrowed at each end, and somewhat tapering and more rounded posteriorly. Head with the central plate longer than broad, forming an acute angle behind, anteriorly suddenly expanding into a wide transverse frontal lobe, broadly rounded in front, with a slight emargination in the middle, the lateral angles prominent and slightly auriculate or recurved. Eyes four, distant, the two pairs nearly parallel. Proboscis small, smooth, rounded. Antennæ slender, twice as long as the breadth of the body. The branchiæ are slender and ligulate anteriorly, and meet over the middle of the back; but farther back they gradually decrease in length, and disappear at about the anterior third. The upper ramus of the feet consists of a broad, thin, foliaceous upper ramus, rounded outwardly, connected, for most of its length, with the branchia, the upper end a little prominent; and a broad cluster of setæ, consisting of a small upper fascicle of slender aciculæ, scarcely as long as the branchia, and a comb-like group of shorter and somewhat stouter bent and acute setæ. The lower ramus consists of a small, thin, rounded process, bearing a transverse row of acute bent setæ, and a ventral tuft of longer and more slender ones. Posteriorly the slender setæ in the dorsal and ventral tufts are considerably longer; and several stouter, recurved, two-hooked, uncinate setæ appear in the transverse rows of acute setæ, both in the upper and lower rami. Anal segment short, truncate or suburceolate, somewhat bilobed; the margin of the orifice crenulated with small rounded lobes, and with four small conical papillæ on the upper side. Color olive-green or bright green, darker posteriorly; branchiæ bright red; antennæ light green, with a row of black specks.

Length up to 100^{mm}; breadth, 3^{mm}.

Great Egg Harbor; New Haven; Watch Hill; Wood's Hole; burrowing in sand, at low-water.

SCOLECOLEPIS TENUIS Verrill, sp. nov. (p. 345.)

Body very long and slender, depressed, especially anteriorly, gradually tapering posteriorly. Head short and broad, slightly three-lobed in front, the central lobe broadly rounded, the lateral ones also rounded, somewhat smaller. Antennæ long and slender. The branchiæ are small, ligulate, and exist only on the anterior segments. The setæ of the dorsal fascicle are long and slender; but those of the first three segments are longer than the others, forming large fan-shaped fascicles directed upward and forward; those of the first segment longest, about twice as long as the breadth of the head. Farther back the setæ of the upper ramus become shorter, the upper ones slender, capillary, the lower ones stouter, somewhat bent, mostly acute, some uncinate. Those of the lower ramus are shorter, setiform, forming large fascicles anteriorly. Farther back the upper ones are partly stouter, somewhat bent, and acute, and partly uncinate, while a small ventral fascicle of slender ones still remains. Posteriorly the setigerous lobes of the feet become very small. Color light green; branchiæ red, tinged with green; antennæ whitish, with a red central line.

Length, 80^{mm}; breadth, 1.25^{mm}.

Great Egg Harbor, New Jersey; burrowing in sand, at low-water.

SCOLECOLEPIS CIRRATA Malmgren. (p. 501.)

Annulata polychæta, p. 91, Pl. 9, figs. 54 A–54 D. *Nerine cirrata* Sars, Nyt. Mag., vol. vi, p. 207 (teste Malmgren).

This is a larger and stouter species than either of the preceding. The front of the head is broadly rounded, with prominent, rounded, lateral angles; the foliaceous lateral appendages are larger and much wider.

Off Block Island, in 29 fathoms, and in the deepest parts of Vineyard Sound, near the mouth; off Saint George's Bank, in 110 and 150 fathoms. Northern coasts of Europe; Spitzbergen; Greenland. In 20–250 fathoms. (Malmgren).

SPIO SETOSA Verrill, sp. nov. Plate XIV, fig. 77. (p. 344.)

Nerine coniocephala? A. Agassiz, Annals Lyceum of Nat. Hist. of New York, vol. viii, p. 333, Pl. x, figs. 39–45, 1866, (*non* Johnston.)

Body long, moderately slender, flattened dorsally, convex below, obtuse anteriorly, slightly tapered toward the posterior end. Head with a prominent median lobe, which is sub-truncate and a little turned up at the front end, with the corners a little prominent and rounded; lateral lobes shorter than the median; on the posterior part of the vertex there is a small median, conical prominence. Eyes four, on the vertex, the posterior pair nearest together; antennæ long. Branchiæ moderately long, slender, ligulate, largest on the anterior segments. On the first three or four segments the upper ramus of the feet has a slender dorsal cirrus, which disappears farther back. The setæ of the upper ramus are long, acute, and form a broad fascicle, in which the upper ones are much longer and more slender, divergent; the lower stouter and more or less bent; they are longest on the first four or five segments, the upper ones considerably exceeding the branchiæ. The lower ramus is small and but slightly elevated; on the anterior segments it bears a small fascicle of short, acute, bent setæ, much shorter than those of the upper ramus, and closely crowded together in two or more rows, with a small ventral tuft of longer and more slender setæ; farther back the acute bent setæ begin to be replaced by uncinate setæ, which, at about the tenth segment, form a complete transverse row, parallel with a row of slightly longer, pointed setæ, while the small ventral tuft of longer acute setæ still remains, and all the setæ in the broad fascicle of the upper ramus are acute and much longer. In the middle region of the body, the uncini of the lower ramus form a close row, containing fifteen to twenty; they are strongly recurved near the end and margined.

Length up to 80^{mm}; diameter about 2.5^{mm}.

New Haven; Wood's Hole; and Naushon Island; in sand, at low-water.

This species appears to be the same as the one studied by Mr. Agassiz, though it differs slightly from his figures, one of which I have copied.

SPIO ROBUSTA Verrill, sp. nov. (p. 345.)

Body stout, broadest anteriorly, tapering posteriorly, but little depressed except anteriorly, very convex beneath, flattened above. Head broad, somewhat angular; the median lobe truncated and slightly emarginate in front; lateral lobes a little shorter, wide, obtuse in front, slightly angulated laterally; a small median, conical elevation on the posterior part of the head. Antennæ long, rather stout. Branchiæ long, narrow, tapering. Upper ramus of the feet with a small, obtuse setigerous lobe, bearing a small fascicle of short setæ, considerably shorter than the branchiæ, even on the anterior segments, and a foliaceous process arising behind the setigerous lobe, broadly rounded on its thin outer edge; the upper end free and obtusely pointed; farther back the setæ are shorter and the foliaceous process smaller and less prominent. The lower ramus on the anterior segments has a small, prominent, semicircular foliaceous process and a small, dense fascicle of short setæ, crowded in several transverse rows; on the eighth and subsequent segments the foliaceous processes become larger and wider, and the setæ more numerous, crowded, and partly uncinate; still farther back the setæ are nearly all uncinate, except a very small ventral tuft of slender ones, and form long, double, transverse rows, projecting but little beyond the surface. Color greenish.

Length, 50^{mm}, or more; breadth, 3^{mm} to 3.5^{mm}.

Wood's Hole and Naushon Island; in sand, at low-water mark.

POLYDORA CILIATUM Claparède (?). Plate XIV, fig. 78. (p. 345.)

A. Agassiz, On the Young Stages of a Few Annelids, in Annals Lyceum Nat. Hist. of New York, vol. viii, pp. 323–330, figs. 26–38, 1866 (embryology).

Naushon Island and Massachusetts Bay; in muddy sand, at about half-tide (A. Agassiz).

The adults of this species were not found by us. The young were frequently taken in the towing-nets.

A young *Polydora*, belonging perhaps to a different species, was dredged off New Haven, in 4 to 6 fathoms, shelly bottom. It was about 12^{mm} long. The color was pale yellow, with small black spots along the sides between the fascicles of setæ; a red dorsal vessel; antennæ white.

OPHELIA SIMPLEX Leidy. (p. 319.)

Marine Invert. Fauna of Rhode Island and New Jersey, p. 16, 1855.

Body short, smooth, iridescent, well rounded above, flat below; usually found coiled up, so that the extremities meet, or nearly so, and resembling in general form the larvæ of certain beetles and flies. Head very acute conical; the buccal segment suddenly enlarges; mouth beneath, with thick evertile lips, the lower one generally protruded as a large rounded lobe. Posterior end terminated by about ten unequal, round, blunt, fleshy, simple papillæ, of which the two ventral ones are considerably longest. The setæ commence opposite the mouth and extend to the posterior end; they form two fan-shaped fascicles on each side of each segment, closely approximate at their origin, but strongly divergent, the upper ones directed upward, the lower ones downward; the setæ are very long and slender on the middle segments, those of the upper fascicles longest, and exceeding half the diameter of the body; anteriorly they are considerably shorter; they are somewhat expanded toward the base, but have long and very slender tips. Dorsal cirri rather long and stout, transparent and wrinkled, blunt at tip, thickened at base; in length nearly equaling a third of the diameter of the body. Color yellowish white, tinged with brownish on the sides.

Length, 8^{mm} to 10^{mm}; diameter, 1.5^{mm}.

Savin Rock, at half-tide. Point Judith, Rhode Island, below low-water mark (Leidy).

The specimen above described was found under stones at Savin Rock, near New Haven, May 5. Its body was completely filled, from one end to the other, with comparatively large yellowish white eggs, which show through the transparent integument of the dorsal side very distinctly.

TRAVISIA CARNEA Verill, sp. nov. (p. 508.)

Body with twenty-four setigerous segments, oblong or fusiform, very changeable, round, usually tapering abruptly to each end. Head small, conical, acute; posterior end terminated by a small, bluntly rounded, or slightly clavate papilla; setæ small and slender. Branchiæ short, slender, commencing on the third setigerous segment and ceasing at the twentieth; longest about one-fourth as long as the diameter of the body. Segments of middle region tri-annulated. Color light red or deep flesh-color; branchiæ bright red.

Length, in extension, about 25^{mm}; 3^{mm} to 4^{mm} in diameter. It can contract to 12^{mm} or less in length.

Off Gay Head, Martha's Vineyard, in 19 fathoms, soft mud.

AMMOTRYPANE FIMBRIATA Verrill, sp. nov. Plate XV, fig. 79. (p. 508.)

Body elongated, slender, smooth, thickest in advance of the middle, tapering gradually to both ends, convex, and well rounded above; lower surface with a median sulcus and rounded margins, separated from the upper surface by a deep groove. Head very acute. Eyes two, small, black. Proboscis small, sub-globular, smooth. Branchiæ long and slender. Caudal appendage spoon-shaped, deeply concave, transversely striated; the outer margin fringed with a row of small, slender papillæ; a pair of slender cirriform processes, about half its length, arises at its ventral base, and a longer single median one is generally concealed in its cavity. Setæ of the anterior segments long and slender, more than half the diameter of the body, shorter farther back. Color, when living, purplish flesh-color, shining and iridescent on the dorsal surface; a row of elongated dark spots on each side between the fascicles of setæ; the setæ dark gray.

Length, 75mm; diameter, 3mm.

Off Buzzard's Bay, in 25 fathoms, mud; Bay of Fundy, 10 to 90 fathoms, mud; near Saint George's Bank, 110 and 150 fathoms, mud.

SCALIBREGMA BREVICAUDA Verrill, sp. nov. (p. 416.)

Body rather short, with a narrow, tapering anterior portion; a swollen middle region; and a narrow, tapering caudal portion; lower surface with a very narrow, smooth median area, divided transversely into a series of small rounded prominences by slight depressions. Head small, transverse, truncate or slightly concave in front, the angles produced and prominent. On the anterior region four segments bear short, tufted branchiæ, close to the base of the upper fascicles of setæ, which are rather long and slender; each of these segments also has a dorsal transverse row of rather large and conspicuous blackish granules on its posterior margin, and also a black spot on the sides below the branchiæ. The surface of all the anterior segments is regularly and rather finely granulous, the granules in transverse rows. The middle region, composed of about ten segments, is thicker, and sometimes much swollen, and the feet are represented only by small fascicles of slender setæ. The caudal region is less than one-half the entire length in preserved specimens, and is rather slender and tapering, composed of about sixteen segments; the rami of the feet consist of a prominent, obtuse papilla, both above and below, with a blackish spot at the end, and bearing a fascicle of slender setæ, in length rather exceeding half the diameter of this part of the body. Color, when living, dark brownish red, tinged with yellow at both ends.

Length, 32mm; diameter, 2.5mm.

Off New Haven, 4 to 6 fathoms, shelly bottom.

TROPHONIA AFFINIS Verrill. Pl. XIV, fig. 75. (p. 507.)

Siphonostomum affine Leidy, op. cit., p. 16 (148), 1855.

Body rather slender and elongated for the genus; skin irregularly rugose, granulous, anteriorly covered with small papillæ. The eight branchiæ are cylindrical, thick, blunt, unequal; two tentacles stouter than the branchiæ, sulcate beneath. On the four anterior segments the upper and lower fascicles of setæ are much elongated and directed forward. On the fifth and following segments those in the upper fascicles are capillary, divergent, six to ten in each fascicle; in the lower fascicles there are about three stout, slightly curved, acute, deep yellow setæ. On the third and fourth segments the setæ of the upper fascicles are longer and larger than those in the lower ones; posteriorly the lower setæ become longer, stouter, and more curved at the tip, the lowest one becoming hook-like.

Length, 60mm; diameter, 3.5mm

Off Block Island, 29 fathoms; off Buzzard's Bay, 25 fathoms, mud. Great Egg Harbor (Leidy).

BRADA SETOSA Verrill, sp. nov. (p. 508.)

Body short, oblong, sub-cylindrical, flattened below, tapering a little toward both ends, which are obtuse; composed of seventeen setigerous segments. Skin covered with small, prominent, acute papillæ. Upper fascicles of setæ long, slender, light colored; lower fascicles larger, composed of stouter, long, dark colored setæ, surrounded at base by small cirriform appendages. Ventral cirrus small.

Length of preserved specimen, 10^{mm}; diameter, 2.5^{mm}.

Off Gay Head, 8 to 10 fathoms, among muscles, &c.

STERNASPIS FOSSOR Stimpson, Plate XIV, fig. 74. (p. 507.)

Marine Invertebrata of Grand Manan, p. 29, fig. 19, 1853.

Off Gay Head, 19 fathoms, soft mud; common in the Bay of Fundy in 10 to 90 fathoms, mud; near Saint George's Bank, 110 fathoms, sandy mud; Casco Bay, 20 fathoms.

CIRRATULUS GRANDIS Verrill, sp. nov. Plate XV, figs. 80, 81. (p. 319).

Body large and stout, anteriorly subcylindrical, somewhat flattened and tapering slightly posteriorly, and rather abruptly tapered anteriorly. Head small, acute, with obscure brownish spots above, but apparently without distinct ocelli. Posterior end obtuse, the orifice surrounded by a thickened, slightly crenulated border. Posterior to the mouth there are about seven rather indistinct annuli (perhaps four biannulated segments) destitute of appendages; the two next segments bear two fascicles of small setæ on each side, and two crowded dorsal clusters of long slender branchial cirri; these clusters nearly meet on the dorsal line, leaving only a narrow naked space, and contain a large number of cirri, usually of various lengths, closely crowded together. Farther back the "feet" consist of small and slightly prominent upper and lower rami, connected by a slightly raised, transverse ridge; each ramus bears a small fascicle of short, slender, acute setæ, in a transverse row; and a few stouter curved spinules, which project but little from the surface; posteriorly the spinules are more numerous and the slender setæ fewer and a little longer, but they are scarcely equal to one-tenth of the diameter of the body. Along nearly the whole length of the body long slender branchial cirri arise from above most of the upper rami, but many of these are generally broken off in preserved specimens. In alcohol the lower surface of the body is generally flat or concave; the "feet" occupy an elevated lateral ridge, often separated from both the ventral and dorsal surface by a deep groove; and the dorsal surface is moderately convex. The annulations are short, very numerous, and distinct. Color, when living, dull yellow, yellowish green, yellowish orange, greenish orange to orange-brown, darkest anteriorly, and often iridescent beneath; sides often with dark brown specks; anterior branchial cirri usually bright orange, with a red central line; lateral ones darker yellow or orange, generally with a central line of bright red, due to the blood-vessels showing through.

Length up to 150^{mm}; diameter, 5^{mm} to 7^{mm}; length of branchial cirri, 60^{mm} to 100^{mm}.

New Haven to Vineyard Sound; low-water to 6 fathoms, in sand and gravel; common.

CIRRATULUS TENUIS Verrill, sp. nov. (p. 416.)

Body slender, elongated, strongly annulated. Head conical, depressed, acute. The first four rings behind the mouth are longer than the rest, and destitute of appendages. The branchiæ and setæ commence at the fifth segment; the branchiæ form a cluster on each side, and are long and filiform; farther back and on the middle region there is usually a pair of branchial cirri on each segment, but posteriorly they become distant and irregular. Setæ long and slender in each ramus, the upper ones exceeding in length the diameter of the body on the anterior and middle regions, but becoming much shorter posteriorly. In alcohol the integument is iridescent. No eyes were detected.

Length, 40^{mm}; diameter, 1.25^{mm}.

Vineyard Sound, 6 to 12 fathoms, among compound ascidians; 23 fathoms off Martha's Vineyard.

CIRRHINEREIS FRAGILIS Quatrefages. (p. 397.)

Histoire naturelle des Annelés, vol. i, p. 464. *Cirrhatulus fragilis* Leidy, op. cit., p. 147 (15), Plate 11, figs. 39–43, 1855.

Point Judith, Rhode Island, under stones at low water (Leidy). Specimens, apparently of this species, were dredged in Vineyard Sound.

NARAGANSETA CORALII Leidy. (p. 494.)

Marine Invertebrate Fauna of Rhode Island and New Jersey, p. 12 (144), Pl. 11, figs. 46–48, 1855; Quatrefages, op. cit., vol. i, p. 468.

New Haven; Watch Hill; Point Judith; in *Astrangia Danæ.*

Our largest specimen had ten pairs of cirri; the first three pairs originate from one segment, the lowest being stouter and lighter colored than the rest.

DODECACEREA, species undetermined. (p. 422.)

A species, belonging apparently to this genus, was dredged off New Haven Harbor, in shallow water, but the specimens are too young for accurate determination.

CLYMENELLA Verrill, gen. nov.

Body elongated, composed of about twenty-two segments exclusive of the cephalic and anal segments. All the segments, except the buccal and three anteanal, setigerous; they bear fascicles of slender setæ above and series of hooks below. The anterior margin of the fourth setigerous segment is prolonged into a thin membranous collar. Proboscis swollen, longitudinally ribbed. Head with a prominent convex median plate, and with a raised border on each side and behind, the lateral and posterior lobes separated by notches. Anal segment funnel-shaped, the edge surrounded by papillæ.

CLYMENELLA TORQUATA Verrill. Plate XIV, figs. 71–73. (p. 343).

Clymene torquatus Leidy, op. cit., p. 14 (146), 1855.

Great Egg Harbor, New Jersey; New Haven; Vineyard Sound; Bay of Fundy; Saint George's Bank, &c. Low-water to 60 fathoms.

NICOMACHE DISPAR Verrill, sp. nov. (p. 512.)

Body elongated, with eighteen setigerous segments. Head elongated, sub-conical, with a small central plate, and a depressed point in front, and with low, narrow, lateral and posterior marginal lobes, separated by slight notches; on the anterior part of each lateral border there is a cluster of small, reddish brown, ocelli-like specks. Buccal lobe coalescent with the cephalic above. Proboscis swollen and plicate. The first two setigerous segments have small fascicles of slender, short setæ above, and a single uncinate seta or hook below on each side. The third segment has much longer setæ in the upper fascicles and two hooks in the lower ones. The fourth has still longer, slender setæ in the upper fascicles, and about eight hooks in each of the lower ones. In the following segments the hooks become much more numerous. There is one short, biannulated, anteanal segment, destitute of setæ. Anal segment suburceolate, as long as broad, cylindrical toward its border, which is furnished on the ventral side with one long, slender cirrus, often as long as the diameter of the anal segment, and two short lateral ones; the rest of the border has a few, mostly very small, distant, unequal, obtuse papillæ or denticulations. The anal orifice is situated at the summit of a small cone, which rises from the bottom of the funnel. The last setigerous segment is longer than the anteanal, and a little longer than any of the ten that precede it, which are all short and subequal, broader than long, those toward the posterior end deeply incised at the intervals between them. The three anterior setigerous segments are shorter than broad; the fourth is twice as long; the fifth is three times as long; the sixth is five times as long. The color, when living, was light red, translucent, with conspicuous bright red blood-vessels, and with a bright red band at about the anterior third. The largest specimen obtained was 50^{mm} long and 2.5^{mm} in diameter after preservation in alcohol. In this specimen the anal segment is long, funnel-shaped, flaring but little toward the margin, and with four or five slight transverse annulations. The buccal segment has two transverse reddish lines on each side.

Off Buzzard's Bay in 25 fathoms; fifteen miles east of Block Island in 29 fathoms, sandy mud. It forms rough tubes of sand, which are not very firm.

MALDANE ELONGATA Verrill, sp. nov. (p. 343.)

Body large and much elongated, cylindrical, obliquely truncated at both ends; with nineteen setigerous segments, those of the middle region elongated; head depressed, with its dorsal surface very oblique; median lobe low, convex, obtusely rounded in front; lateral marginal lobes, or folds, low, rounded, thickened, separated by a shallow emargination from the posterior transverse fold, which is also thickened, little elevated, and divided into two parts by a slight sulcus; from the notch between the lateral and posterior lobes of the head, a lateral oblique sulcus curves downward and backward, and joins the first of the two transverse sulci, which are strongly marked on the ventral side of the buccal segment. Anterior setigerous segments strongly biannulated; the first two are short, the length about equal to the diameter; the next two are considerably longer; and those farther back become very much elongated; the last setigerous segment is short. The segments are considerably swollen where the setæ arise, especially in the middle region. The upper setæ are long and slender, mostly about half the diameter of the body, and form rather large fascicles on most of the segments. The last segment is obliquely truncated, its posterior border surrounding the base of the large anal process, which is obliquely placed, foliaceous, obovate, with the posterior edge broadly rounded, the upper surface concave, and the margin entire. Color dark umber-brown, or reddish brown, iridescent; the swollen parts of the rings are lighter yellowish brown, or grayish brown, the dark red blood-vessels often showing through; near the bases of the setæ there are usually small dark colored specks; head and buccal lobe thickly specked with dark brown or blackish.

Length of largest specimens, 300^{mm}; diameter, 4^{mm} to 5^{mm}; more frequently about half this size.

Savin Rock, near New Haven; in sandy mud at low-water mark, forming thick tubes composed of fine mud.

RHODINE ATTENUATA Verrill, sp. nov. (p. 508.)

Body slender, elongated, with the segments strongly marked, and the first setigerous segment very long. Head elongated, depressed, obtusely rounded in front; median lobe, or ridge, broad and but little elevated, except near the front of the head, where it becomes suddenly narrowed, more convex, with well marked foveæ on each side; lateral lobes rudimentary, scarcely apparent; on the posterior part of the head there is a prominent transverse elevation. Buccal lobe confluent with the cephalic. First setigerous segment swollen anteriorly and about as broad as the head at its anterior end where the setæ arise, but narrowed and gradually attenuated backward, its total length being about eight times its diameter; second and third setigerous segments about equal, nearly twice as long as broad, swollen in the middle, the front margin of each prolonged into a sheath-like collar; the three next segments are short and rounded, about as long as broad, much narrowed at each end, and swollen in the middle; next two about twice as long as broad; succeeding segments more elongated. Anal segment wanting in the specimens examined.

Length about 50^{mm}; diameter about 1^{mm}.

Off Gay Head, 6 to 8 fathoms; fifteen miles east of Block Island, in 29 fathoms, sandy mud.

The *Clymene urceolata* Leidy, from Great Egg Harbor, will probably be found on the New England coast, but we have not met with it. It is peculiar in having an urceolate anal segment, with a smooth margin.

AMMOCHARES, species undetermined. (p. 508.)

A species which constructs slender, flexible tubes, covered with grains of sand, regularly and curiously attached by one end in an imbricated manner, was dredged fifteen miles east of Block Island, in 29 fathoms sandy mud, and in 23 fathoms off Martha's Vineyard. The worm is very slender, flesh-color, with a red dorsal vessel, and two small, red, ocelli-like spots.

NOTOMASTUS LURIDUS Verrill, sp. nov. (p. 342.)

Body long and rather large, composed of numerous segments, nearly cylindrical when living, and tapering but little, except close to the ends. In preserved specimens the anterior region, including about ten segments, is often a little swollen and slightly larger than the rest of the body; at other times it is even more slender than the posterior region. Head small, acute. Proboscis short and broad, swollen; in full expansion nearly twice the diameter of the body, nearly smooth, dark blood-red. The segments of the anterior region are longer than broad, in extension nearly twice as long, biannulated, and each of the annuli is again annulated with several transverse, more or less irregular sulci or furrows; ten of these segments bear fascicles of slender setæ both above and below, the fascicles on the first two setigerous segments being very small, and containing few setæ. The segments following the tenth setigerous one have a small transverse row of slender uncinate setæ above, and a longer lateral transverse row of the same kind of setæ on each side; the "feet," or setigerous lobes, are but little prominent, the upper ones being dorsal and much smaller than the lateral ones. The surface of the body is transversely wrinkled, and covered with minute, irregular reticulations, giving it a slightly granulous appearance. Color, when living, dark purplish brown, with a bluish iridescence anteriorly, and a darker median dorsal line posteriorly; minute, white, raised spots, or slight papillæ, are scattered over the surface.

Length, 150^{mm} or more; diameter, 2^{mm}.

Savin Rock, near New Haven; in muddy sand, at low-water mark.

NOTOMASTUS FILIFORMIS Verrill, sp. nov. (p. 342.)

Body very long and slender, filiform, composed of very numerous short segments. Head very changeable in form, usually long, conical, and very acutely pointed. Proboscis smooth, obovate, or trumpet-shaped, when extended, and bright red. In the anterior region there are eleven setigerous segments, which bear small fascicles of slender setæ in both rami, those in the first five longer and acutely pointed; these segments are short, biannulate; the lower fascicles of setæ are largest and fan-shaped. In the middle region the segments are about as long as broad. Color, pale red to bright red, often mottled with whitish, and more or less yellowish posteriorly.

Length, 100^{mm}; diameter, 1^{mm}.

Great Egg Harbor, low-water to one fathom, in sandy mud; New Haven; Watch Hill; Vineyard Sound.

SABELLARIA VULGARIS Verrill, sp. nov. Plate XVII, figs. 88, 88*a*. (p. 321.)

Body rather stout, thickest anteriorly, tapering backward to the base of the long, slender caudal appendage. Two slender, red, oral tentacles arise near the mouth, between the bases of the operculigerous lobes, and, when extended, reach beyond the bases of the opercula. A single median lanceolate process also arises between the operculigerous lobes. A deep emargination exists on the ventral side, back of the mouth; on each side of this the front margin of the segment is prolonged into a tridentate lobe, the teeth or lobes being unequal, the inner ones largest, the middle ones more slender and acute, the outer one smallest and shortest; beyond these, toward the sides, there is another small acute process; two conical processes also project forward from the lateral margins, and also a fascicle of setæ. The ciliated prehensile cirri, or tentacles, are long and slender when extended, and reach considerably beyond the opercula. The setæ composing the opercula are golden yellow; the outer circle white at base. A row of small conical papillæ surrounds the bases of the opercula. Branchiæ long, lanceolate, acute, longer than the diameter of the body. Color of body yellowish flesh-color, or pale reddish, often with two rows of brown spots along the ventral surface; operculigerous lobes whitish or grayish, specked with blackish; branchiæ reddish or yellowish, with a red central line, often with a greenish tinge, or red centered with green; tentacles pale flesh-color, sometimes purplish; opercula blackish or grayish on the anterior surface, golden yellow on the sides, white at base; caudal process pale red or flesh-color.

Length about 25^{mm}, exclusive of caudal process; 2^{mm} to 2.5^{mm} in diameter.

Great Egg Harbor, New Jersey, to New Haven and Vineyard Sound; low-water to ten fathoms; very common. Eggs are laid in May and June.

CISTENIDES GOULDII Verrill, sp. nov. Plate XVII, figs. 87, 87*a*. (p. 323).

Pectinaria Belgica Gould, Invertebrata of Massachusetts, 1st ed., p. 7, Plate 1, fig. 1 (tube), 1841 (not of European writers). *Pectinaria auricoma* Leidy, op. cit., p. 14 (146), 1855 (not of European writers).

Body rather stout, little curved. Head with the dorsal surface obliquely truncated, its posterior marginal fold with a smooth border. Antennæ long, tapering, acute; frontal membrane or veil semicircular, its edge divided into rather long, slender, acute papillæ, about twenty-eight in number. Cephalic setæ in two broad groups, each containing about fifteen light golden setæ, which are somewhat curved upward, with long, slender, very acute tips, those in the middle of each group much the longest. Tentacles stout, obtuse, flattened, and folded up so as to form a groove beneath. Color light red or flesh-color, handsomely mottled with dark red and blue.

Length up to 40^{mm}; diameter, 7^{mm}

Great Egg Harbor to New Haven and Cape Cod; low-water to 10 fathoms.

This species can easily be distinguished from *C. granulatus*, which is common in the Bay of Fundy, by the cephalic setæ or spines, which are fewer, much stouter, obtuse, and darker colored in the latter.

AMPHARETE GRACILIS Malmgren. Plate XVI, fig. 83. (p. 508).

Nordiska Hafs-Annulater, Ofvers. af kongl. vet. Akad. Förh., 1865, p. 365, Plate 26, figs. 75–75D.

Body flesh-colored, greenish posteriorly, with a conspicuous red median vessel; branchiæ light sea-green.

Length, 25^{mm} to 35^{mm}; diameter, 2.5^{mm} to 3^{mm}; length of branchiæ, 6^{mm} to 9^{mm}.

Off Gay Head, 10 fathoms; off Martha's Vineyard, 23 fathoms; east of Block Island in 29 fathoms; Bay of Fundy, 10 to 90 fathoms; northern coasts of Europe, Bahusia, at Koster Island, in 130 fathoms. Our specimens differ slightly from the description and figures of Dr. Malmgren, especially in usually having but twelve uncigerous segments in the posterior region, instead of thirteen, found by him in the European specimens. This may be due to difference of age or sex. There are, however, thirteen in one of our specimens.

AMPHARETE SETOSA Verrill, sp. nov. (p. 416.)

Body rather thick anteriorly, tapering rapidly backward. Cephalic lobe acute, with a much shorter, small, lateral lobe on each side. Branchiæ eight, transversely wrinkled, rather short; in preserved specimens about equal to the breadth of the body. Palmulæ, or cephalic fascicles of setæ, short and broad, rounded, fan-shaped, the setæ being nearly equal, the ventral ones a little longer than the lateral. Fourteen segments bear small fascicles of long setæ, supported by prominent lobes at the base. The posterior region consists of about ten uncigerous segments. Anal segments small, with two long slender cirri. Color of body translucent, light yellowish green; the anterior part of the body tinged with bright blood-red, due to the circulating fluid, showing through the integument; branchiæ greenish, with a central series of white spots; setæ of the palmulæ, deep yellow.

Length about 20^{mm}; diameter, 2.5^{mm} to 3^{mm}.

Off New Haven, low-water mark to 6 fathoms, shelly. It makes rough tubes about an inch long, covered with coarse sand and mud.

AMAGE PUSILLA Verrill, sp. nov.

Body rather slender. Head obtusely rounded in front; the middle lobe small, and but little larger than the lateral. Eight slender branchiæ, about twice as long as the diameter of the body, arranged in a crowded group; two farther back than the rest; and with no apparent naked median space. Twelve of the setigerous segments bear long fascicles of slender setæ. No "palmulæ," or cephalic setæ. Tentacles numerous and slender. Two small, slender anal cirri.

Length, 12^{mm}; diameter, 1.5^{mm}.

Off New Haven, 5 to 6 fathoms; shelly bottom.

MELINNA CRISTATA Malmgren. (p. 432.)

Nordiska Hafs-Annulater, loc. cit., p. 371, Plate 20, figs. 50–50D. *Sabellides cristata* Sars, Fauna littoralis Norvegiæ, vol. ii, pp. 19, 24, Pl. 2, figs. 1–7, 1856.

Mouth of Vineyard Sound, on muddy bottoms, in the deepest water; Bay of Fundy, on muddy bottoms, in 10 to 90 fathoms; near Saint George's Bank, in 110 and 150 fathoms, mud. Off the Scandinavian coast in 40 to 200 fathoms; Greenland; Spitzbergen.

The tube is soft, flexible, slender, and covered with fine mud.

TEREBELLIDES STROËMI Sars. (p. 507.)

Beskriv. og Iakttag., p. 48, Plate 13, figs. 31, *a–d* (teste Malmgren); Malmgren, Nordiska Hafs-Annulater, loc. cit., p. 396, Plate 48–48D, 1865.

East of Block Island, in 29 fathoms, sandy mud; Bay of Fundy, 10 to 90 fathoms, muddy; near Saint George's Bank, 85 to 150 fathoms. Greenland, 10 to 250 fathoms; Iceland; Spitzbergen; northern coasts of Europe; Adriatic Sea.

AMPHITRITE ORNATA Verrill. Pl. XVI, fig. 82. (p. 320).

Terebella ornata Leidy, Marine Invertebrate Fauna of Rhode Island and New Jersey, loc. cit., p. 14 (146), Plate 11, figs. 44, 45 (setæ), 1855.

Great Egg Harbor, New Jersey, to New Haven and Vineyard Sound; common in sand and gravel at low-water mark.

NICOLEA SIMPLEX Verrill, sp. nov. (p. 321.)

Body elongated, swollen anteriorly, especially above, attenuated posteriorly. Head with a rather large, well rounded, or nearly circular frontal membrane, which has a smooth margin; mouth with a small posterior fold. Tentacles very numerous, crowded, long, and slender. Branchiæ four, rather small; those of the anterior pair somewhat the larger; those of both pairs are repeatedly dichotomously divided from close to the base. The divisions are short and not very numerous, and diverge at a wide angle. Fifteen segments bear small fascicles of slender setæ, commencing at the next behind the last branchiferous segment. The third and fourth setigerous segments of the male bear small, slender lateral cirri. Ventral shields about thirteen; the first six transversely oblong, and nearly equal in width; the last seven narrowing rapidly to the last, which is acutely triangular. Color, when living, light red, or flesh-color.

Length, 35^{mm}; diameter, 3^{mm} to 4^{mm}

New Haven to Vineyard Sound, from low-water to 6 fathoms; off Watch Hill, 4 to 6 fathoms, in tubes composed of bits of shells and grains of sand, attached to *Laminariæ.*

SCIONOPSIS Verrill, gen. nov.

Body composed of numerous segments, of which 17, following the third, bear fascicles of slender setæ, and the following ones have only small uncigerous lobes; second and third segments bear branchiæ, and have their anterior margins prolonged into membranous, collar-like expansions; that of the second forming broad, lateral lobes behind the tentacles; that of the third forming behind the branchiæ a dorsal collar or sheath, beneath which they can be retracted. Branchiæ typically four. Those of the first pair usually larger, but generally one or more are absent, and frequently the anterior ones are smallest, or those of the same pair may be unequal, owing probably to the facility with which they may break off and be reproduced; they are palmately branched and supported on elongated pedicels. Tentacles numerous and crowded.

This genus is allied more closely to *Pista* than to any other yet described, but differs in the structure of the branchiæ and character of the collar formed by the third segment.

SCIONOPSIS PALMATA Verrill, sp. nov. (p. 321.)

Body elongated; rather slender; thickened but not distinctly swollen anteriorly, tapering gradually to the posterior end. The setigerous feet commence at the fourth segment, or next behind the branchial collar, and are all quite prominent, the first three or four being a little smaller than the rest; the setæ are rather long. The uncigerous feet commence on the second setigerous segment. Behind the last setigerous segment the uncigerous feet are smaller, somewhat prominent, and extend to the anal segment. Ventral shields about 20; the most anterior ones are transversely oblong; the succeeding ones squarish, gradually tapering to the last, which are very narrow. Anal segment tapering; its orifice with a crenulated margin. Branchiæ large, with numerous palmate divisions arising from the summit of the stout and rather long pedicels.* There are usually five or more main divisions in good-sized specimens, these spread outward from one point, are recurved at the ends, and flexuous and bipinnately branched, the lower pinnæ being longest each time, and the ultimate divisions very numerous, fine, slender, and acute. The branchiæ of the posterior pair, in normal specimens, are considerably smaller, with the divisions less numerous, and the ramuli longer and more delicate. The pedicels of the anterior branchiæ are about as long as the diameter of the body, and are very contractile, as well as the branches, so that the gills can be contracted into a small compass and withdrawn under the dorsal collar, beneath which the pedicels arise. This branchial collar is formed by the prolongation of the margin of the third segment; on each side of the median line above, it is divided into two narrow, lanceolate processes directed forward; exterior to these there are two other wider and usually less prominent angles or lobes; laterally, the collar is prominent, with a broadly rounded, thin margin, which forms another angle on each side beneath; on the ventral side its edge recedes and is but little raised. The tentacular collar, formed by the second segment, expands into a broad, rounded, prominent lobe on each side; and on the ventral surface becomes narrower, though still prominent, and recedes in a broad, rounded sinus behind the posterior lobe of the mouth. The cephalic segment is bordered by a rather broad frontal membrane, emarginate above, and broadly rounded laterally. Tentacles very numerous, long, and slender. Color, light red, brownish red to dark reddish brown; the annulations often darker; the upper surface is usually more or less specked with flake-white; along each side, below, there is usually a row of squarish spots, brighter red than the rest of the body, each pair connected by a narrow, transverse line of red between the ventral shields, which are dull yellowish red; the segments along the sides are often bordered with red; branchiæ usually green, specked on the outer sides of the branches with flake-white, and with internal blood-red vessels, showing distinctly in all the divisions; the pedicel is usually bright red; tentacles, flesh-color.

Length up to 70^{mm}; diameter, 3^{mm}.

Great Egg Harbor to New Haven and Vineyard Sound; low-water mark to one fathom.

LEPRÆA RUBRA Verrill, sp. nov. (p. 382.)

Body elongated, somewhat swollen anteriorly, rapidly tapering to the very long, slender, posterior portion. All the segments posterior to the branchiæ bear small fascicles of slender setæ, as well as uncini; posterior to the twenty-fifth setigerous segment the uncigerous feet become

*In mentioning this species, on page 321, it was stated that it has but three gills, and, in fact, this is the most frequent number. Among the numerous examples examined, I have only recently found a specimen with both pairs of gills in their normal condition.

much narrower and more prominent; anteriorly they are very broad. Ventral plates rather broad anteriorly, those posterior to the seventh or eighth suddenly narrowed. Branchiæ in three pairs, small, finely arborescently divided, the divisions numerous; posterior pair considerably smaller than the others. Cephalic lobe with a somewhat prolonged frontal border, broadly rounded in front, with an entire margin. Color bright red; tentacles flesh-color.

Length, 50^{mm} or more; diameter, 2.5^{mm} to 3^{mm}.

Vineyard Sound; Wood's Hole on piles of wharves just below low-water mark.

POLYCIRRUS EXIMIUS Verrill. Plate XVI, fig. 85. (p. 320).

Torquea eximia Leidy, op. cit, p. 14 (146), Plate 11, figs. 51, 52 (setæ), 1855.

In this species there are twenty-five setigerous segments, bearing small fascicles of long, slender setæ; about seventy posterior segments bear uncini only; anteriorly the uncini commence on the eighth setigerous segment. There are nine ventral shields, divided by a median ventral sulcus. The frontal lobe of the head is large, elongated oval or elliptical. The posterior lobe of the mouth is large, rounded. Body and tentacles bright blood-red; the body is often more or less yellowish posteriorly.

Great Egg Harbor to New Haven and Vineyard Sound; low-water to 10 fathoms.

A species of this genus was also dredged in 19 fathoms off Gay Head, but its identity with the above is uncertain. Another species, remarkable for its brilliant blue phosphorescence, is common in the Bay of Fundy. The *P. eximius* does not appear to be phosphorescent.

CHÆTOBRANCHUS Verrill, genus nov.

Allied to *Polycirrus* and, like the latter, destitute of blood-vessels. Body much elongated, composed of very numerous segments, nearly all of which bear fascicles of setæ. Segments of the middle region bear simple, or more or less branched, branchial cirri, each of their divisions tipped with slender setæ; these cirri are wanting on the anterior and posterior segments, the first and last ones being smaller and more simple than the rest. The cephalic segment expands into a broad, tentacular or frontal lobe, which is rounded or emarginate anteriorly, and often more or less scolloped laterally. Tentacles crowded, very numerous, long and slender in extension, capable of being distended by the blood, as in *Polycirrus*, &c.

CHÆTOBRANCHUS SANGUINEUS Verrill, sp. nov. (p. 320.)

Body greatly elongated, much attenuated posteriorly, more or less swollen anteriorly, but narrowed toward the head, the thickest portion being usually between the tenth and fifteenth segments. The branchial cirri commence at about the ninth segment, those of the first pair being short, simple cirri; those on the next segment are once forked; those on the next have three or four branches; farther back they divide dichotomously above the base into numerous branches, all of which are supported upon a short basal pedicel, which may be a little elongated in expansion, the total length of the branchiæ being then greater than the diameter of the body; the branches are clustered, slender, delicate, and elongated, and each one is terminated by a small fascicle of slender, sharp, serrate setæ two to four or more in a group, so that the entire appendage may be regarded as a very remarkable enlargement and modification of the setigerous lobes of the "feet."

On the segments anterior to the ninth the setigerous lobes of the feet are short, conical, swollen at base, and bear a small fascicle of setæ; the ventral surface of the anterior segment is somewhat raised, and divided by a series of sulci or wrinkles into several lobes or crenulations, which are somewhat prominent and papilliform at the posterior margin of each segment, and have a granulous surface. There is a distinct median ventral sulcus. Between the adjacent branchial cirri anteriorly there are, on each side, four or more thickened, somewhat raised, squarish organs, with a granulous and apparently glandular structure; farther back these are reduced to two, then to one, and finally disappear on the segments of the posterior region, which is very long, slender, attenuated, composed of very numerous short segments, with only rudimentary appendages; after the branchial cirri become reduced to simple processes they still continue, on about forty segments, gradually decreasing in length and size; beyond this small setæ still exist on the segments, till near the end of the body. Anal segment small and simple, the orifice with slightly crenulated margins. Frontal membrane large and broad, versatile in form, often with a deep emargination in front, each lateral lobe divided into two or three subordinate lobes, or unequal scollops, the edges undulated; at other times the front edge and sides are broadly rounded and entire. The mouth is furnished with a large elongated ovate lobe, which is rounded, free, and prominent posteriorly. Tentacles very long, much crowded, and very numerous; in extension usually as long as the body. Color of body, anteriorly, deep blood-red; posteriorly, more or less mottled or centered with yellow, owing to the internal organs showing through the integument; tentacles and branchial cirri bright blood-red.

Length up to 350^{mm}; diameter 5^{mm} to 7^{mm} or more anteriorly; length of tentacles, in extension, 400^{mm} or more.

Great Egg Harbor to New Haven and Vineyard Sound; common at low-water mark, in mud.

POTAMILLA OCULIFERA Verrill. Plate XVII, fig. 86. (p. 322).

Sabella oculifera Leidy, op. cit., p. 13 (145), Plate 11, figs. 55–61, 1855.

Great Egg Harbor to New Haven; Vineyard Sound, low-water mark to 25 fathoms, off Buzzard's Bay. In the Bay of Fundy from low-water mark to 60 fathoms.

Closely related to *P. reniformis* of Northern Europe, and possibly identical with it.

SABELLA MICROPHTHALMA Verrill, sp. nov. (p. 323.)

Body rather short and stout, narrowed slightly anteriorly, tapering rapidly close to the posterior end, composed of about sixty segment, depressed, moderately convex above, flat below, especially when preserved in alcohol; anterior region composed of eight setigerous segments, having moderately long fascicles of setæ; posterior region composed of about fifty short segments, bearing very small fascicles of setæ; anal segment small, simple, with two very small ocelli-like spots; ventral shields of the anterior segments short, transversely narrow, oblong; median sulcus very distinct in the posterior region, dividing the ventral shields into two nearly rectangular parts, which are broader than long. Branchiæ numerous and long, often half as long as the body, connected by a slight web close to the base; the stalks smooth, with numerous minute ocelli, in two irregular rows; pinnæ numerous, long and slender; tips of the branchiæ without pinnæ. Collar broadly interrupted above, flaring and reflexed at the sides, with rounded upper angles, erect and sinuous at the latero-ventral margins, reflexed below, forming two short, rounded lobes, separated by a narrow but deep central sinus, within which there is a short bilobed organ. Tentacles thin, lanceolate, acute, in preserved specimens not so long as the diameter of the body. The anterior segment is divided by a deep dorsal sulcus, which is not conspicuous on the succeeding segments. Color of body greenish yellow, dull olive-green, or greenish brown; branchiæ pale yellowish, greenish, or flesh-color, often with numerous transverse bands of lighter and darker green, which extend to the pinnæ, and sometimes blotched with brown; collar translucent, specked with flake-white; ocelli dark reddish brown. Specimens, apparently belonging to this species, were taken from wood bored by *Teredo*, near New Haven. These had the body olive-green, specked with flake-white anteriorly, on the ventral side, especially on the first two segments; branchiæ mottled with greenish brown and white and specked with flake-white; ocelli brown, numerous.

Length, 30^{mm}; diameter, 2.5^{mm} to 3^{mm}. Preserved specimens are about 20^{mm} long, 2.5^{mm} broad.

New Haven to Vineyard Sound; low-water mark to 5 fathoms.

EUCHONE ELEGANS Verrill, sp. nov. Plate XVI, fig. 84. (p. 432).

Body rounded, slender, gradually tapered backward; the anterior region, which forms about one-half of the entire length, consists of eight setigerous segments; these are biannulated and divided by a dorsal, longitudinal sulcus, and by a lateral sulcus on each side below the uncigerous lobes. The middle region consists of thirteen shorter biannulated segments, which bear small fascicles of setæ on the lower rami; these are divided by a ventral sulcus, and also by the lateral ones. The caudal region consists of about ten very short segments; all of which, except the last, bear small fascicles of setæ. These segments are margined by a rather broad membrane, wider and rounded anteriorly, narrowing to the end. Collar broad, with a nearly even margin, often somewhat sinuous at the sides, divided above and below, the lobes rounded at the angles. The collar is a little broader below than above. Branchiæ long, slender, recurved in expansion, connected by a broad and very thin membrane, continued as thin borders of the branchiæ to their tips, which are destitute of pinnæ for some distance. Body pale flesh-color, with a darker median line, reddish anteriorly, darker greenish or brownish, posteriorly; branchiæ pale yellowish or greenish, each with a flake-white spot near the base outside. Other specimens were greenish gray, with green branchiæ. Some were flesh-color, with a bright-red dorsal vessel; the branchiæ flesh-color, without the white spots at the base.

Length, in extension, about 20^{mm}; diameter of body, 1.5^{mm}.

Deep water off the mouth of Vineyard Sound; off Martha's Vineyard, in 21 and 23 fathoms; off Block Island, in 29 fathoms, sandy mud, abundant. Cosco Bay, 7 to 20 fathoms.

This species makes slender tubes, covered with fine sand.

FABRICIA LEIDYI Verrill, sp. nov. (p. 323.)

Body very small and slender, tapering a little to both ends, in extension considerably exsert from the slender tube; eleven segments bear fascicles of setæ; the segments are about as long as broad, slightly constricted at the articulations, with the anterior margin a little prominent; anal segment small, tapered to a blunt point, bearing two small, dark ocelli. Branchiæ six, subequal, forming three symmetrical pairs, each one with five to seven slender pinnæ on each side; the basal pinnæ are about as long as the main stem, the others successively shorter, so that all reach to about the same level. Tentacles short, thick, bluntly rounded at the end, strongly ciliated. At the base of the branchiæ, on each side, is a red, pulsating vesicle, the pulsations alternating in the two; just back of these, on the first segment, are two brown ocelli; a little farther back, and near together, on the dorsal side, are two auditory vesicles, each with a round central corpuscle. The fourth and eleven succeeding segments bear small fascicles of acute, bent setæ, about as long as half the diameter of the body; on the middle segment there are about four or five setæ in a fascicle; on the ninth, three; on the tenth, two; on the eleventh, one or two, in the specimens examined. Intestine rather wide, but narrowed at the eighth setigerous segment, and after that slender, bordered by a red blood-vessel on each side. In the fourth setigerous segment there are three globular granulated organs. color, yellowish white, tinged with red by the circulating fluid.

Length about 3^{mm}; diameter about 0.25^{mm}; expanse of branchiæ, 0.8^{mm}. The specimens measured may be immature.

New Haven to Vineyard Sound, common at and below low-water mark; Cisco Bay.

SERPULA DIANTHUS Verrill, sp. nov. (p. 322.)

Body elongated, gradually attenuated to the posterior end; the posterior region considerably flattened; dorsal surface covered with minute papillæ and having a finely pubescent appearance under a lens. Collar broad and long, in living specimens sometimes one-third as long as the body; the posterior portion free dorsally, and in expansion about as long as the attached portion, extending backward and gradually narrowing to the end; the margins thin and undulated; the anterior border is divided into a broad revolute dorsal lobe, with an undulated margin, and two narrower lateral lobes, which are broadly revolute laterally, with the margin rounded and nearly even. Seven segments bear rather large fascicles of long, acute setæ. The first fascicle is remote from the next, and directed downward and forward, with the setæ longer than in the others; the six following fascicles are broad, and are directed downward and backward. The uncinate setæ form long transverse rows anteriorly, but toward the posterior end they form short rows. Operculum funnel-shaped, longitudinally striated externally, with a long, slender pedicel; the upper surface is concave, with about thirty small, acute denticles around the margin; an inner circle of about twelve long, slender papillæ, incurved at tips and united at base, arises from the upper surface of the operculum. On the left side is a small rudimentary operculum, club-shaped at the end, with a short pedicel. Branchiæ are long rather slender, united close to the base, about eighteen on each side, in mature specimens, those toward the ventral border considerably longer, than the upper ones; tips naked for a short distance, slender, and acute; pinnæ very numerous, slender. Colors quite variable, especially those of the branchiæ; the branchiæ are frequently purplish brown, transversely banded with flake-white, alternating with yellowish green, the pinnæ usually having the same color as the portion from which they arise; on the exterior of the branchiæ the purple bands are often divided by a narrow longitudinal line of whitish; operculum brownish green on the outer surface, purplish on the sides, with white longitudinal lines toward the margin, greenish white at base; pedicel purplish, banded with white; collar pale translucent greenish, veined with darker green; body deep greenish yellow, the dorsal surface light yellow. Many other styles of coloration occur, some of which are described on page 322.

Length up to 75^{mm}; diameter about 3^{mm}.

Great Egg Harbor to New Haven and Cape Cod; low-water mark to 8 fathoms.

The tubes are long, variously crooked, and often contorted, sometimes solitary, frequently aggregated into masses four or five inches in diameter. They are nearly cylindrical, with irregular lines of growth, and sometimes with faint carinations.

SERPULA DIANTHUS, var. CITRINA Verrill. (p. 322.)

I have applied this name to a very marked color-variety, in which the branchiæ are lemon-yellow or orange-yellow, without bands, but usually with a reddish central line; the operculum is usually yellow; collar and base of branchiæ bright yellow; body light yellow.

Found with the preceding, and often in the same cluster of tubes.

VERMILIA (?), species undetermined. (p. 416.)

The species thus indicated forms slender, more or less crooked, angular tubes, with two distinct carinations on the upper surface; they are about half an inch long, attached firmly by one side along their whole length. The branchiæ form a wreath, with about six on each side; pinnæ long and slender; two or more of the branchiæ bear pink, sack-like appendages. The branchiæ are reddish brown, annulated with narrow bands of white.

Diameter of tubes, about 1.25^{mm}; of expanded branchiæ, 4^{mm}. The specimens have been lost, and no observations were recorded concerning the operculum, so that the genus is still uncertain.

Long Island Sound, off New Haven, in 4 to 6 fathoms, on shells.

SPIRORBIS BOREALIS Daudin (?).

Rec. des mém. de mollusques, 1800. *Serpula spirorbis* Linné, Systema Naturæ, ed. xii, p. 1265. (?) *Spirorbis spirillum* Gould, Invertebrata of Mass., ed. i, p. 8, 1841; A. Agassiz, Annals Lyceum Nat. History of New York, vol. viii, p. 318, Plate 7, figs. 20–25 (embryology), 1866 (not of Linné and other European writers).

New Haven to Cape Cod, the Bay of Fundy, and northward; abundant on *Fucus*, *Chondrus crispus*, and other algæ, at low-water mark.

Whether this, our most common species, be identical with the European species known by this name is still uncertain.

The animals of the various species of *Spirorbis* are still very imperfectly known, and many species have been described from the tubes alone. Accurate descriptions or figures of the animals are necessary before the species can be determined satisfactorily.

This species has nine branchiæ, five on one side and four on the other, with the operculum. The branchiæ are large and broad with long pinnæ, the basal ones shorter, the distal ones increasing in length to near the end, so that each branchial plume is somewhat obovate in outline; the tips are naked only for a short distance. The branchial wreath, in full expansion, is about as broad as the entire shell. The operculum is oblique and one-sided, and supported on a long clavate pedicel, which is transversely wrinkled, and expands gradually into the operculum at the end, the enlargement being chiefly on one side; the outer surface is roughly granulous and usually covered with adhering dirt. The collar is broad, and has three fascicles of setæ on each side. The branchiæ are pale greenish white, centered with brighter green, due to the circulating fluid.

This is the species mentioned in the early part of this report (p. 332) under the name of *S. spirillum*. The true *spirillum* of Linné as a translucent tube, and is found in deeper water, on hydroids, &c.

SPIRORBIS LUCIDUS Fleming.

Edinburgh Encyclop., vol. vii, p. 68; Johnston, Catalogue of British Non-Parasitical Worms, p. 349; Malmgren, Annulata polychæta, p. 123. *Serpula lucida* Montagu, Test. Brit., p. 506 (t. Johnston). *Serpula porrecta* Fabricius, Fauna Grœnlandica, p. 378 (*non* Müller). *Spirorbis sinistrorsa* Montagu, op. cit., p. 504; Gould, Invertebrata of Massachusetts, ed. i, p. 9, Plate 1, fig. 4, 1841.

Deeper parts of Vineyard Sound, near the mouth, in 10 to 12 fathoms, on hydroids and bryozoa; off Gay Head, 10 fathoms; off Buzzard's Bay, in 25 fathoms, on *Caberea Ellisii;* off Block Island, in 29 fathoms, on *Caberea;* Casco Bay, 6 to 20 fathoms, on algæ, &c.; Bay of Fundy, 10 to 80 fathoms, on hydroids; Saint George's Bank, 30 to 60 fathoms. Greenland; northern coasts of Europe.

This species forms small, translucent, glossy, reversed spiral tubes, coiled in an elevated spire, the last whorls usually turned up, or even erect and free.

There are six branchiæ, which are large and broad, with long, slender pinnæ, which do not decrease in length till near the end; the naked tips are short and acute. The operculum is sub-circular, somewhat obliquely attached to the slender pedicel, which is about half as long as the extended branchiæ, and enlarges rather suddenly close to the operculum; the outer surface of the operculum appears nearly flat, and is covered with adherent dirt. The collar is broad, with undulated and revolute edges. The three fascicles of setæ are long and slender. Ocelli two, conspicuous. The animal, in expansion, is usually much exsert from the tube. Anterior part of the body bright red; branchiæ pale greenish; their bases and posterior part of the body bright epidote-green.

It is the species catalogued as *S. porrecta (?)* on pages 498 and 504.

OLIGOCHÆTA.

CLITELLIO IRRORATA Verrill, sp. nov. (p. 324.)

Body very slender, the largest about 60^{mm} long, 0.75^{mm} in diameter, distinctly annulated. Head conical, a little elongated, subacute; setæ commencing on the first segment; those on the anterior segments in fascicles of two or three, very short, small, in length not one-third the diameter of the body, more or less curved like an italic *f*, obtusely pointed at the end; some of them are but slightly bent at the tip, others are strongly hooked; farther back there are three or four setæ in the fascicles, and they are somewhat longer, and two or more in many of the fascicles are forked, the others simple, spinous, more or less curved; in the upper fascicles posteriorly, and sometimes throughout the whole length, there are two or three much longer, very slender, hair-like, flexible bristles, but these are often absent from most of the segments, perhaps accidentally. The intestine is voluminous, slightly constricted at the articulations; two bright red blood-vessels, distinctly visible through the integuments, run along the intestine, one above and one below, following its flexures, without contractile lacunæ.

New Haven to Wood's Hole and Casco Bay, under stones in the upper part of the fucus-zone, and nearly up to high-water mark.

The above description was made from living specimens taken at Savin Rock, near New Haven.

Some of the specimens obtained at Wood's Hole appear to differ somewhat from this description, but the differences may be chiefly due to their being taken in the breeding season. In these the anterior fascicles consist of two short setæ, which are slightly curved in the form of an italic *f*, and are subacute, not bifid at tips. At the ninth to twelfth setigerous segments a thickening occurs, forming a clitellus; on the ninth segment the setæ are replaced by a small mammiform, bilobed organ; on the tenth there is a pair of prominent obtuse papillæ, swollen at base. On the posterior segments only two setæ were observed in each of the four fascicles, but they were longer, more slender, and more curved at the tip than the anterior ones. In each of the segments slender cæcal tubes, forming about two loops on each side, were noticed. Length, about 35^{mm}.

LUMBRICULUS TENUIS Leidy.

Marine Invertebrate Fauna of Rhode Island and New Jersey, p. 16 (148), Plate 11, fig. 64, 1855.

Point Judith, Rhode Island, abundant about the roots of grasses on the shore of a sound (Leidy). We did not obtain this species.

HALODRILLUS Verrill, genus nov.

Body long and slender. Blood white or colorless. Setæ small, acute, in four fan-shaped fascicles on each segment. The alimentary canal consists of a pyriform pharynx, followed by a portion from which several (five to seven) rounded or pyriform cæcal lobes, of different sizes, arise on each side and project forward and outward; these are followed by a large two-lobed portion, beyond which the intestine is constricted then thickened and convoluted, and covered with polygonal, greenish, glandular cells, which become fewer farther back, where the intestine becomes a long, narrow, convoluted tube. In the anterior part of the body, around the stomach and cæcal lobes, there are numerous convolutions of slender tubes. The blood-vessels running along the intestine contain a colorless fluid.

HALODRILLUS LITTORALIS Verrill, sp. nov. (p. 324.)

Body round, slender, moderately long, tapering to both ends, but thickest toward the anterior end, tapering more gradually posteriorly. Head small, conical, moderately acute, or obtuse, according to the state of contraction; mouth a transverse, slightly sinuous slit beneath. The setæ commence with four fascicles on the first segment behind the buccal; the setæ are slightly curved, forming rounded, fan-shaped fascicles of four to six setæ, the middle setæ being longer than the upper and lower ones; posteriorly the setæ are less numerous. Caudal segment tapered, obtuse, or slightly emarginate at the end, with a simple orifice. The blood contains minute, oblong corpuscles. Color milk-white. Length, 25^{mm} to 40^{mm}; diameter, 0.5^{mm} to 1^{mm}.

New Haven; Wood's Hole; Casco Bay, Maine; very common under dead sea-weeds and stones near high-water mark.

ENCHYTRÆUS TRIVENTRALOPECTINATUS Minor.

American Journal of Science, vol. xxxv, p. 36, 1863.

In this species, according to Minor, there are three pairs of ventral fascicles of setæ before the dorsal ones commence; the pharynx extends to the fourth pair of ventral fascicles, from which a narrow œsophagus extends to a little back of the sixth pair; here a gradual enlargement of the alimentary canal occurs, ending abruptly just back of the eighth in a narrow, twisted tube, and this gradually enlarges at the ninth ventral fascicle into a moderate sized alimentary canal. No eyes. Length, about 10^{mm}.

New Haven, near high-water mark (Minor).

BDELLODEA.

Comparatively few leeches have hitherto been met with in this region. Many additional species, parasitic on fishes, undoubtedly remain to be discovered.

BRANCHIOBDELLA RAVENELII Diesing. Plate XVIII, fig. 89. (p. 458.)

Sitzungsberichte der kais. Akad. der Wissenschaften, Wien, xxxiii, p. 482, 1859. *Phyllobranchus Ravenelii* Girard, Proceedings of the American Association for the Advancement of Science for 1850, vol. iv, p. 124, 1851. (?) *Branchellion Orbiniensis* Quatrefages, Annals des sci. natur., sér. 3, vol. xviii, pp. 279–325, Plate 6, figs. 1–13, Pl. 7–8, 1852 (anatomy).

In describing this species Mr. Girard mistook the anterior for the posterior end, and described the large posterior sucker, or acetabulum, as the head. The color is dark brown, purplish, or dark violaceous, specked with white.

Vineyard Sound, on a stingray (*Myliobatis Freminvillei*), in several instances; a number usually occurred together. Charleston, South Carolina, on a "skate," species unknown (Girard). Atlantic Ocean, on a torpedo (Quatrefages).

CYSTOBRANCHUS VIVIDUS Verrill. (p. 458.)

American Journal of Science and Arts, ser. 3, vol. iii, p. 126, fig. 1, 1872.

New Haven, on the minnow (*Fundulus pisculentus*), both in fresh and brackish water; November and December.

ICHTHYOBDELLA FUNDULI Verrill. (p. 458.)

American Journal of Science and Arts, loc. cit., p. 126.

New Haven, on *Fundulus pisculentus*, with the last.

PONTOBDELLA RAPAX Verrill, sp. nov. Plate XVIII, fig. 91. (p. 458.)

Body, in extension, long and slender, rounded, thickest behind the middle, attenuated anteriorly. Acetabulum nearly circular, not much wider than the body. Head small, obliquely truncated, rounded. Color dark olive, with a row of square or oblong white spots along each side; head and acetabulum whitish, tinged with green. The young are reddish brown.

Length, 30^{mm} to 40^{mm}; diameter, 1.5^{mm} to 2^{mm}.

Vineyard Sound, on the ocellated flounder, (*Chænopsetta ocellaris*).

PONTOBDELLA, species undetermined. (p. 458.)

Body slender, cylindrical, strongly annulated; the largest seen was about 12^{mm} long and 0.75^{mm} in diameter when extended. Head obliquely campanulate, attached by a narrow pedicel-like neck. Acetabulum oblique, round, only a little wider than the body. Color pale greenish or greenish white, with scattered microscopic specks of blackish. No distinct ocelli, but there are several dark stellate pigment-spots on the head, similar to those on the body. Perhaps all the specimens are immature.

Savin Rock, New Haven, on *Mysis Americanus*, below low-water mark.

MYZOBDELLA LUGUBRIS Leidy. (p. 458.)

Proceedings of the Academy of Natural Sciences of Philadelphia, vol. v, p. 243, 1851; Diesing, op. cit., p. 489.

Parasitic on the edible crab (*Callinectes hastatus*), attached about the bases of the legs. We have not obtained this species on the coast of New England, but it may be expected to occur here.

MALACOBDELLA OBESA Verrill, sp. nov. Plate XVIII, fig. 90. (p. 458.)

Body stout, broad, thick, convex above, flat below, broadest near the posterior end, narrowing somewhat anteriorly; the front broadly rounded, with a median vertical slit, in which the mouth is situated. Acetabulum large, rounded, about as broad as the body. Intestine convoluted posteriorly, visible throug the integument. Between the intestine and lateral margins, especially posteriorly, the skin is covered with small stellate spots, looking like openings, within and around which are large numbers of small round bodies, like ova. Color yellowish white. Length, 30^{mm} to 40^{mm}; breadth, 12^{mm} to 15^{mm}.

Salem, Massachusetts; Long Island Sound; parasitic in the branchial cavity of the long clam (*Mya arenaria*).

MALACOBDELLA MERCENARIA Verrill, sp. nov. (p. 458.)

Malacobdella grossa Leidy, Proceedings Academy Natural Sciences of Philadelphia, vol. v, p. 209 (*non* Blainville).

Body, in extension, elongated, oblong, with nearly parallel sides, or tapering slightly anteriorly; anterior end broad, obtusely rounded, emarginate in the center, but not deeply fissured. In contraction the body is broader posteriorly. Dorsal surface a little convex; lower side side flat. Acetabulum round, rather small, about half the diameter of the body in the contracted state, but nearly as broad when the body is fully extended. The intestine shows through the integument distinctly; it is slender, and makes about seven turns or folds. Color pale yellow, with minute white specks beneath and on the upper surface anteriorly, giving it a hoary appearance; middle of the dorsal surface irregularly marked with flake-white; laterally reticulated with fine white lines.

Length in extension, 25^{mm}; breadth, 4^{mm}; in partial contraction, 18^{mm} long; 5^{mm} to 6^{mm} wide.

New Haven, parasitic in the branchial cavity of the round clam (*Venus mercenaria*), October, 1871. Philadelphia, in the same clam (Leidy).

GYMNOCOPA.

TOMOPTERIS, species undetermined. (p. 453.)

Young specimens of a species of this genus were taken in the evening in Vineyard Sound. They are too immature for accurate identification.

A large and fine species of *Tomopteris* was taken by Mr. S. I. Smith, in Eastport harbor, in July, 1872. This was about 40^{mm} in length. An excellent drawing of it was made by Mr. Emerton from the living specimens. It is, perhaps, the adult state of the Vineyard Sound species.

CHÆTOGNATHA.

SAGITTA ELEGANS Verrill, sp. nov. (p. 440.)

Body slender, thickest in the middle, tapering slightly toward both ends. Head somewhat broader than the neck, and about equal to the body where thickest, slightly oblong, a little longer than broad, obtuse, rounded in front or sub-truncate, sometimes with a slightly prominent small central lobe or papilla; the anterior part of the head rises into a crest-like median lobe considerably higher than the posterior part; ocelli two, minute, widely separated, on the posterior half of the head; the anterior lateral borders of the head are slightly crenulated. The fascicles of setæ or spinules on the sides of the head each contain about eight setæ, which are considerably curved, with acute tips, and reach as far as the anterior border of the head. Caudal fin ovate; its posterior edge broadly rounded. The posterior lateral fins commence just in advance of the ovaries, and extend back considerably beyond them, so as to leave a naked space somewhat less than their length between their posterior ends and the caudal fin; on this naked part, just in advance of the caudal fin, are two small, low, lateral papillæ connected with the male organs; two other smaller papillæ are situated at about the posterior third of the lateral fins. The median lateral fins are about equal in length to the posterior ones, and separated from them by a naked space less than their own length; the distance from the anterior end of the middle fins to the anterior border of the head is equal to twice the length of the fins; the length of the latter is about one-sixth of the entire length of the body. The color is translucent whitish, nearly diaphanous.

Length, about 16^{mm}; diameter, about 0.9^{mm}.

Wood's Hole and Vineyard Sound, at surface, July 1; off Gay Head, among *Salpæ*, September 8, in the day-time.

SAGITTA, species undetermined. (p. 440.)

A much larger and stouter species than the preceding was taken in abundance by Mr. Vinal N. Edwards, in Vineyard Sound, at various dates, from January to May.

Its length is generally 25^{mm} to 30^{mm} I have not seen it living.

GEPHYREA or SIPUNCULOIDS.

PHASCOLOSOMA CÆMENTARIUM. Verrill Plate XVIII, fig. 92. (p. 416.)

Sipunculus cæmentarius Quatrefages, op. cit., vol. ii, p. 628, 1865. *Phascolosoma Bernhardus* Pourtales, Proceedings American Association for Advancement of Science for 1851, p. 41, 1852. *Sipunculus Bernhardus* Stimpson, Invertebrata of Grand Manan, p. 28 (*non* Forbes.)

Deeper parts of Vineyard Sound, 10 to 15 fathoms; off Block Island, 29 fathoms; Bay of Fundy, 2 to 90 fathoms, abundant; near Saint George's Bank, 45 to 430 fathoms.

PHASCOLOSOMA, species undetermined. (p. 353.)

A species similar to the last in size and form, with a thick integument, thickly covered throughout with small rounded papillæ or granules, but without the dark chitinous hooks seen on the posterior part of the latter.

Vineyard Sound.

PHASCOLOSOMA GOULDII Diesing. Plate XVIII, fig. 93. (p. 353.)

Revision der Rhyngodeen, op. cit., p. 764, 1859. *Sipunculus Gouldii* Pourtales, Proceedings of American Association for the Advancement of Science for 1851, vol. v, p. 40, 1852; Keferstein, Zeitschrift für wissenschaftliche Zoologie, vol. xv, p. 434, Plate 33, fig. 32, 1865, and vol. xvii, p. 54, 1867.

New Haven to Massachusetts Bay, at Chelsea Beach; common in sand and gravel at low-water mark.

SCOLECIDA.

TURBELLARIA.

RHABDOCŒLA or NEMERTEANS.

BALANOGLOSSUS AURANTIACUS Verrill. (p. 351.)

Stimpsonia aurantiaca Girard, Proceedings Academy of Natural Sciences of Philadelphia, vol. vi, p. 367, 1854. *Balanoglossus Kowalevskii* A. Agassiz, Memoirs American Academy of Arts and Sciences, vol. ix, p. 421, Plates 1–3, 1873.

Fort Macon, North Carolina, to Naushon Island. Charleston, South

Carolina (Girard). Newport, Rhode Island, to Beverly, Massachusetts (A. Agassiz). In sand between tides.

A reexamination of living specimens of the southern form will be necessary before their identity with the northern one can be positively established. I am unable to separate them with preserved specimens. See page 351; also American Journal of Science, ser. 3, vol. v, p. 235.)

NEMERTES SOCIALIS Leidy. (p. 324.)

Marine Invert. Fauna of Rhode Island and New Jersey, p. 11 (143), 1855.

Great Egg Harbor to New Haven and Vineyard Sound. Very common under stones, between tides.

NEMERTES VIRIDIS Diesing.

Sitzungsberichte der kais. Akad. der Wissenschaften, vol. xlv, p. 305, 1862. *Planaria viridis* Müller, Zoöl. Dan. Prodromus, 2684, 1776 (t. Fab.); Fabricius, Fauna Grœnlandica, p. 324, 1780. *Notospermus viridis* Diesing, Syst. Helminth, vol. i, p. 260, 1850. *Nemertes olivacea* Johnston, Mag. of Zoology and Botany, vol. i, p. 536, Pl. 18, fig. 1. *Borlasia olivacea* Johnston, Catalogue British Non-parasitical Worms, p. 21, Pl. 2[b], fig. 1, 1865. *Nemertes obscura* Desor, Boston Journal of Natural History, vol. vi, pp. 1 to 12, Plates 1 and 2, 1848. *Polia obscura* Girard in Stimpson's Marine Invertebrata of Grand Manan, p. 28, 1853.

Body very changeable in form; in full extension long and slender, sub-terete, tapering toward both ends, the length being sometimes 150^{mm} to 200^{mm}, while the diameter is 2^{mm} to 3^{mm}; in contraction the body becomes much shorter and stouter, more or less flattened, and obtuse at the ends, large specimens often being only 30^{mm} or 40^{mm} long and 4^{mm} to 5^{mm} broad. The head is flattened, more or less bluntly rounded, and is furnished with a row of small dark ocelli on each side, which vary in number and size according to the age, the large specimens often having six or eight on each side, while the small ones have but three or four, and the very young ones have only a single pair. The lateral fossæ of the head are long and deep, in the form of slits, and extend well forward to near the terminal pore. The latter in some states of contraction appears like a slight vertical slit or notch, but at other times appears circular; the proboscis is long, slender toward the base, clavate toward the end, the terminal portion transversely wrinkled. The ventral opening or mouth is situated opposite to or a little behind the posterior ends of the lateral fossæ; it is ordinarily small and elliptical, with a distinct lighter colored border, but is capable of great dilation when the creature is engaged in swallowing some annelid nearly as large as itself.

In alcoholic specimens the body is usually thickened and rounded anteriorly, more slender and somewhat flattened farther back, often acute at the posterior end; head obtusely rounded or sub-truncate, with a small terminal pore and two lateral fossæ, which are short and extend forward very near to the terminal pore; ventral opening or mouth small and round, situated slightly behind the posterior ends of the lateral fossæ; ocelli not apparent. The color, when living, is very variable, most commonly dark olive-green or blackish green above, and somewhat lighter below, the head margined with lighter; frequently the color is dark liver-brown or reddish brown, and the back is usually crossed by faint pale lines, placed at unequal distances.

Buzzard's Bay and Vineyard Sound, under stones, between tides, and in 4 to 6 fathoms, rocky bottoms, very common; Casco Bay and Bay of Fundy; and northward to Labrador and Greenland. Also on the northern coasts of Europe to Great Britain. Abundant under stones between tides, and in shallow water.

The specimens referred to on page 324 as probably belonging to *Cerebratulus*, were most likely identical with this species.

NEMERTES (?) species undetermined (*a*). (p. 498.)

Body elongated, moderately stout; head not distinct from the body. Color uniform bright brownish red.

Length, 25^{mm}.

Off Watch Hill, Rhode Island, among rocks, in 4 to 6 fathoms. A species, apparently the same, also occurred in 25 fathoms off Buzzard's Bay.

This was red with two dark red spots anteriorly. No ocelli were detected.

NEMERTES, (?), species undetermined (*b*).

Body slender, sub-terete; head not distinct from body. Ocelli inconspicuous, apparently about three in a row on each side of front of head. Color of head and body, above, brownish red, with a whitish ring around the neck, which recedes in the middle, above.

Length, 8^{mm}.

Off Watch Hill, with the preceding.

This is, perhaps, a species of *Cosmocephala*.

NEMERTES, species undetermined (*c*).

Body slender; head not separated by a constriction. Ocelli very numerous, arranged in a long cluster on each side of the head. Color uniform olive-green above and below.

Length, 35^{mm}; breadth, 1.3^{mm} to 2^{mm}.

New Haven Harbor, on the piles of a wharf, in brackish water.

TETRASTEMMA ARENICOLA Verrill, sp. nov. Plate XIX, fig. 98. (p. 351.)

Body sub-terete, long, slender, slightly depressed, of nearly uniform width; the head is very versatile, usually sub-conical or lanceolate, flattened, occasionally becoming partially distinct from the body by a slight constriction at the neck. Ocelli four, those in the anterior pair nearer together. The lateral fossæ are long and deep slits on the sides of the head; mouth or ventral pore small, often sub-triangular, situated just back of the posterior ends of the lateral fossæ. Body deep flesh-color or pale purplish. Length, about 100^{mm}, in extension.

Savin Rock, near New Haven, in sand at low-water mark.

This species is, perhaps, not a true *Tetrastemma*. It is here only provisionally referred to that genus.

MECKELIA INGENS Leidy. Plate XIX, figs. 96, 96*a*. (p. 349.)

Marine Invertebrate Fauna of Rhode Island and New Jersey, p. 11 (143), 1855. (?) *Meckelia Pocohontas* Girard, Proceedings of Academy of Natural Sciences of Philadelphia, vol. vi, p. 366, 1854.

Fort Macon, North Carolina; Great Egg Harbor to New Haven and Vineyard Sound. Low-water mark to 8 fathoms. Charleston, South Carolina (Girard).

MECKELIA LACTEA Leidy. (p. 350.)

Proceedings of Academy of Natural Sciences of Philadelphia, vol. v, p. 243, 1851.

Great Egg Harbor to New Haven and Vineyard Sound. Low-water mark to 10 fathoms. Perhaps the young of the preceding species.

MECKELIA ROSEA Leidy. (p. 350.)

Proceedings Academy Natural Sciences of Philadelphia, vol. v, p. 244, 1851.

Great Egg Harbor to New Haven and Vineyard Sound. Common in sand at low-water mark.

MECKELIA LURIDA Verrill, sp. nov. (p. 508.)

Body long, large, stout, much depressed throughout, and thin posteriorly, somewhat thickened anteriorly. Head changeable in form, often acute; lateral fossæ long. Ventral opening large, elongated. Proboscis long, slender, emitted from a terminal pore. In some specimens there was a slender, acute, caudal papilla. Color deep chocolate-brown, with lighter margins. Length, 150^{mm} to 250^{mm}; breadth up to 10^{mm} or more.

Off Gay Head, 19 fathoms, soft mud; off Buzzard's Bay, 25 fathoms; off Block Island, 29 fathoms, sandy mud; Casco Bay, 10 to 68 fathoms.

CEREBRATULUS (?), species undetermined (*a*). (p. 508.)

This is a dark olive-green species, with paler margins, the anterior part darkest.

Off Block Island, in 29 fathoms; off Gay Head, in 19 fathoms, soft mud.

COSMOCEPHALA OCHRACEA Verrill, sp. nov. Plate XIX, figs. 95, 95*a*. (p. 325.)

Body elongated, moderately slender, somewhat flattened but thick, and with the margins rounded, obtuse at both ends or subacute posteriorly; broadest and often swollen anteriorly; gradually and slightly tapering posteriorly; the integument is translucent and the internal median organs show quite distinctly; lateral organs voluminous, extending the whole length of the body along each side, and showing through as dull yellowish white mottlings. Head continuous with the body, obtuse; a slight groove, usually appearing as a whitish line on each side, runs obliquely across the ventral and lateral surface of the head, diverging from the mouth and curving somewhat forward at the sides; terminal pore small and inconspicuous; mouth, or ventral pore, small. Ocelli numerous, arranged as in the figure, but varying somewhat in number. (See p. 325.) Color dull yellowish, or yellowish white, often tinged with deeper yellow or orange anteriorly, with the median line lighter; a reddish internal organ shows through as an elongated red spot between the posterior ocelli.

Length, 50^{mm} to 70^{mm}; breadth, 2.5^{mm} to 3^{mm}.

New Haven to Vineyard Sound; under stones, between tides.

POLINA GLUTINOSA Verrill, sp. nov. Plate XIX, fig. 97. (p. 324.)

Body rather slender and elongated in extension, usually broadest in the middle and tapering to both ends, but quite versatile in form; head not distinct, usually obtuse; posterior end narrower, usually obtuse or slightly emarginate; integument soft, secreting a large quantity of mucus; the lateral organs extend to the head. Ocelli numerous, variable in number, usually eight or ten on each side, arranged in three pairs of short, oblique, divergent rows, two to four in each; terminal pore of the head moderately large; no lateral fossæ could be detected. There appears to be a terminal opening at the posterior end. Color dull yellow or pale orange yellow, sometimes brighter orange, especially anteriorly; posteriorly usually lighter, with a faintly marked dusky or greenish median line.

Length, 25^{mm} to 30^{mm} in extension; breadth, 1.3^{mm} to 2^{mm}.

Great Egg Harbor to New Haven and Vineyard Sound; low-water mark to 6 fathoms.

MONOCELIS AGILIS Leidy. (p. 325.)

Marine Invert. Fauna of Rhode Island and New Jersey, p. 11 (143), 1855. *Monops* (?) *agilis* Diesing, Sitzungsberichte der kais, Akad. der Wissenschaften, vol. xlv, p. 232, 1862 (*non Monops agilis* Schultze, sp.)

New Haven; Point Judith, Rhode Island, at low-water, creeping on *Mytilus edulis* (Leidy).

ACELIS CRENULATA Diesing.

Op. cit. p. 206. *Acmostomum crenulatum* Schmarda, Neue wirbell. Th., vol. i, p. 1, 3, Pl. 1, fig. 2 (t. Diesing).

Hoboken, New Jersey, in brackish water (Schmarda).

GENUS UNDETERMINED.

Body very long and slender, almost filiform, slightly flattened, with rounded sides; the flat sides are longitudinally striated, the narrower rounded sides are marked with numerous short, distinct, separate, transverse lines or depressions, corresponding to opaque internal organs. In one of the smaller specimens one end is acute conical, terminated by a slender incurved point; the other end is obtusely rounded, depressed and translucent at the end, apparently with a transverse orifice beneath. The largest specimen, and one of the smaller, has one end corresponding in form to that last described; the other is rounded, a little enlarged, subtruncate, apparently with a terminal orifice. A yellowish internal organ, with transverse divisions, runs along each side internally. In life the color was grayish white, with four very slender double longitudinal lines of dark slate-color.

Length of largest specimens, in alcohol, 80^{mm}; diameter, 0.7^{mm}; smallest ones, 40^{mm}; diameter, 0.5^{mm}.

Wood's Hole, swimming very actively at the surface in the evening, June 29 and July 13, 1871.

This species was taken by Mr. S. I. Smith, who recorded the color. I did not observe it myself in the living state. The above description was made from preserved specimens. Its characters cannot all be made out satisfactorily with alcoholic specimens, and its generic and family affinities are uncertain. In general appearance, when living and moving, it resembles *Gordius* and *Rhamphogordius*.

DENDROCŒLA or PLANARIANS.

STYLOCHOPSIS LITTORALIS Verrill, sp. nov. Plate XIX, fig. 99. (p. 325.)

Body flat with thin margins, very changeable in form, broad oval, elliptical or oblong, rounded or sub-truncate at the ends, often with the margins undulated. The tentacles are small, round, obtuse, translucent, each containing an elongated group of about ten or twelve minute black ocelli on the anterior surface. The tentacles are situated at about the anterior fourth of the body, and are separated by about one-fourth of its breadth. Dorsal ocelli about eight, forming four groups of two each, in advance of the tentacles; marginal ocelli numerous, small, black, most conspicuous beneath, and most numerous on the anterior portion, arranged in two or more irregular rows near the margin, extending back to the middle of the sides or beyond. Color pale greenish or brownish yellow, veined or reticulated with lighter, and with a light median stripe posteriorly; beneath flesh-color, with a median elongated light spot, narrowest in the middle, due to internal organs.

Length, 8^{mm}; breadth, about 6^{mm}.

New Haven to Vineyard Sound; under stones, between tides.

PLANOCERA NEBULOSA Girard. Plate XIX, fig. 100. (p. 325.)

Proceedings of the Academy of Natural Sciences of Philadelphia for 1853, vol. vi, p. 367, 1854.

Savin Rock near New Haven, under stones at low-water. Charleston, S. C. (Girard).

LEPTOPLANA FOLIUM Verrill, sp. nov. (p. 487.)

Body very flat, with the margin thin and undulated; outline versatile, usually cordate or leaf-like, broadest and emarginate posteriorly, the posterior borders well rounded, and the side a little convex, narrowing to an obtuse point at the anterior end; sometimes oblong or elliptical, and but little narrowed anteriorly; the posterior emargination is usually very distinct, often deep, and sometimes in contraction has a small projecting angular point in the middle, but at times the emargination nearly disappears. Ocelli in four groups, near the anterior end; the two posterior clusters are smaller than the anterior and wider apart; the anterior clusters are very near the others, and close together, almost blending on the median line, and are composed of numerous very minute crowded ocelli, less distinct than those of the other clusters. Color pale yellowish flesh-color, veined with dentritic lines of darker flesh-color, or with whitish; an indistinct pale reddish spot behind the anterior ocelli; an interrupted longitudinal whitish stripe in the middle, due to the internal organs, and a small median whitish stripe posteriorly.

Length, 20^{mm} to 25^{mm}; breadth, 10^{mm} to 15^{mm}.

Off Watch Hill, 4 to 6 fathoms, among rocks and algæ; off Block Island, in 29 fathoms; off Buzzard's Bay, in 25 fathoms.

PLANARIA GRISEA Verrill, sp. nov. (p. 487.)

Body elongated and usually oblong in extension, often long oval or somewhat elliptical, obtusely pointed or rounded posteriorly; head subtruncate in front, often a little prominent in the middle; the angles are somewhat prominent, but not elongated. Ocelli two, black, each surrounded by a reniform, white spot. Color yellowish green or grayish, with a central whitish stripe in the middle of the back, surrounded by darker; head margined with whitish.

Length, in extension, 12^{mm}; breadth, 3^{mm}.

Watch Hill, Rhode Island, under stones, between tides.

PROCERODES WHEATLANDII Girard. (p. 325.)

Proceedings Boston Soc. Natural History, vol. iii, p. 251, 1851; Stimpson, op. cit., p. 6, 1857. *Planaria frequens* Leidy, Marine Invert. Fauna of Rhode Island and New Jersey, p. 11, 1855. *Procerodes frequens* Stimpson, op. cit., p. 6; this Report, p. 325.

New Haven to Casco Bay. Point Judith (Leidy). Manchester, Massachusetts (Girard). Abundant under stones, between tides.

FOVIA WARRENII Girard. (p. 480.)

Proceedings of the Boston Society of Natural History, vol. iv, p. 211, 1852; Stimpson, Prodromus, p. 6, 1857. *Vortex Warrenii* Girard, op. cit., vol. iii, pp. 264 and 363, 1851; Diesing, op. cit., vol. xiv, p. 229, 1862.

A small, narrow, oblong, red Planarian, apparently belonging to this species, was collected at Wood's Hole, among eel-grass, and also in Casco Bay. Chelsea, Massachusetts (Girard).

BDELLOURA CANDIDA Girard. (p. 460.)

Proceedings Boston Society Natural History, vol. iv, p. 211, 1852. *Vortex candida* Girard, op. cit., vol. iii, p. 264, (for 1850), 1851. *Bdelloura parasitica* Leidy, Proceedings Academy Natural Sciences of Philadelphia for 1851, vol. v, p. 242, 1852; Stimpson, Prodromus, p. 6, 1857.

Great Egg Harbor; New Haven; Massachusetts Bay. Parasitic on the gills of the "horseshoe-crab" (*Limulus Polyphemus*).

BDELLOURA RUSTICA Leidy.

Proceedings Acad. Natural Sciences of Philadelphia, vol. v, p. 242, 1852; Stimpson, Prodromus, p. 6, 1857.

Great Egg Harbor, on *Ulva latissima* (Leidy).

NEMATODES.

PONTONEMA MARINUM Leidy. Plate XVIII, fig. 94. (p. 325.)

Marine Invertebrate Fauna of Rhode Island and New Jersey, p. 12 (144), 1855.

Great Egg Harbor to New Haven and Vineyard Sound; very abundant from above low-water mark to 10 fathoms.

PONTONEMA VACILLATUM Leidy. (p. 326.)

Marine Invertebrate Fauna of Rhode Island and New Jersey, p. 12 (144), 1855.

Great Egg Harbor to Vineyard Sound, with the preceding.

Various other small, free Nematodes are frequently met with, but they have not been carefully examined.

Numerous species are also parasitic in the stomach, intestine, muscles and other organs of fishes, crustacea, worms, &c. (See page 456.)

MOLLUSCA.

CEPHALOPODA.

DIBRANCHIATA.

OMMASTREPHES ILLECEBROSA. (p. 441.)

Loligo illecebrosa Lesueur, Journal Acad. Natural Sciences, Philadelphia, vol. ii, p. 95, Plate 10, 1821; Gould, Invertebrata of Massachusetts, ed. i, p. 318, 1841; Dekay, Natural History of New York, Mollusca, p. 4, 1843. *Ommastrephes sagittatus* Binney,* in Gould's Invertebrata of Mass., ed. ii, p. 510, 1870, but *not* Plate 25, fig. 339 (*non* Lamarck, sp.)

A large specimen, taken at Eastport, Maine, was ten inches long, exclusive of the arms. When preserved in alcohol the caudal-fin was rather more than one-third of the length of the head and body together; its width was equal to about three-fourths of its length. The colors of this specimen were described on page 442. A small specimen from Newport, R. I., agrees in color and most other respects with the larger specimens, but differs somewhat in the proportions, especially of the caudal fin, probably owing to its immaturity. This specimen, in alcohol,

* Binney's, Plate xxvi, Figs. 341–344, erroneously referred to *Loligopsis pavo*, apparently represents this species.

is 84^{mm} long, exclusive of the arms; the body is 72^{mm} long, 15^{mm} broad; the caudal fin is 25^{mm} long and 36^{mm} broad.

A fresh specimen, caught in Casco Bay, had the following proportions: Length of head and body, not including the arms, 221^{mm}; length of caudal fin, 86^{mm}; breadth of fin, 90^{mm}; diameter of body, 35^{mm}; length of upper arms, 80^{mm}; of second pair, 100^{mm}; of third pair, 100^{mm}; of extensile arms, 182^{mm}; of the ventral pair, 90^{mm}.

Greenport, Long Island, (Sanderson Smith); Newport, Rhode Island; Provincetown, Massachusetts; Casco Bay; Mount Desert, Maine; Bay of Fundy.

Ommastrephes Bartramii (Lesueur, sp.) is found in the Gulf Stream off our coasts, and may sometimes occur accidentally on our shores. It is a more slender and elongated species than the preceding, with a relatively shorter caudal fin. It is also darker colored. The figure given by Binney in the last edition of Gould's Invertebrata of Massachusetts (Plate 25, fig. 340) does not represent this species.

LOLIGO PEALII Lesueur. Plate XX, figs. 102–105. (p. 440.)

Journal Acad. Natural Sciences, Philadelphia, vol. ii, p. 92, Pl. 8, 1821; Dekay, Natural History of New York, Mollusca, p. 4, Pl. 38, fig. 354 (copied from Lesueur); Binney, in Gould's Invertebrata of Mass., ed. ii, p. 514 (Pl. 25, fig. 340,) probably represents this species, certainly not *O. Bartramii.*)

South Carolina to Massachusetts Bay. Very common in Long Island Sound and Vineyard Sound.

The young, from an inch to two inches in length, were taken from the middle of July to the last of August in great numbers, at the surface, in Vineyard Sound, by Mr. Vinal N. Edwards.

LOLIGO PUNCTATA Dekay.

Natural History of New York, Mollusca, p. 3, Pl. I, fig. 1, 1843; Binney, in Gould's Invertebrata of Mass., ed. ii, p. 513.

This is probably identical with the preceding species. The slight differences noticed are probably sexual, but as I have not been able to fully satisfy myself in regard to this, I have not thought it proper to unite them at this time.

Long Island Sound.

LOLIGO PALLIDA Verrill, sp. nov. Plate XX, figs. 101, 101*a*. (p. 441.)

Body stout, tapering rapidly backward. Anterior border of mantle with a prominent, obtusely rounded, median dorsal lobe, from which the margin recedes on each side; on the lower side the margin is concave in the middle, with a projecting angle on each side. Caudal fin large, about as broad as long, more than half as long as the body. Siphon large and stout; upper pair of arms considerably smaller and shorter than the others, slender at tips, margined along the inner dorsal ridge with a thin membrane. Second pair of arms stouter and longer, triquetral, slightly margined on the outer angle. Third pair much stouter and considerably longer, with a membranous fold along the middle of the outer surface, which expands into a thin membrane toward the end. Tentacular arms long and slender, in extension longer than the body, the portion that bears suckers forming about one-third the whole length; in the female the larger suckers on the middle of this portion are not so large as the largest on the other arms, and are arranged in about four rows; those near the tips of the arms are very small and crowded. In the male the principal suckers of the tentacular arms are very much larger than in the female, and considerably exceed those of the other arms; they form two alternating rows along the middle of the arm, and external to them there is a row of smaller suckers on each side, alternating with them; the suckers toward the tips are very numerous, small, and crowded; outside of the suckers, on each side, there is a marginal membrane with a scolloped edge; another membranous fold runs along the outer surface and expands into a broad membrane near the end; the arms of the ventral pair are intermediate in length between those of the second and third pairs. Ground-color of body, head, arms, and fins pale, translucent, yellowish white; entire ventral surface pale, with small, distant, brownish circular spots, which are nearly obsolete on the siphon and arms; the upper surface is covered with pale brown, unequal, circular spots which are not crowded, having spaces of whitish between them; the spots are more sparse on the head and arms, but somewhat clustered above the eyes. The general appearance of the animal when fresh is unusually pale and gelatinous. The "pen" is broad, quill-shaped, translucent, and amber-colored. A medium-sized male specimen preserved in alcohol measures 145^{mm} from the base of the dorsal arms to the posterior end of the body; length of body, 120^{mm}; length of caudal fin, 70^{mm}; breadth of fin, 75^{mm}; length of first pair of arms, 42^{mm}; of second pair, 50^{mm}; of third, 60^{mm}; of tentacular arms, 150^{mm}; of ventral pair, 53^{mm}.

Long Island Sound.

The *Spirula Peronii* Lamarck, (*Spirula fragilis* in Binney's Gould, p. 516, fig. 755), is occasionally cast up, on the outer beaches of Nantucket, but it probably does not occur alive in our waters.

GASTROPODA.

PECTINIBRANCHIATA.

BELA HARPULARIA Adams. Plate XXI, fig. 108. (p. 508.)

H. and A. Adams, Genera of Recent Mollusca, vol. i, p. 92, 1858; Gould's Invertebrata of Mass., ed. ii, p. 352, fig. 191. *Fusus harpularius* Couthouy, Boston Journal Natural History, vol. ii, p. 106, Pl. 1, fig. 10, 1838; Gould's Invertebrata of Mass., ed. i, p. 291, fig. 191, 1841. *Mangelia harpularia* Stimpson, Shells of New England, page 48, 1851.

Massachusetts Bay to Labrador and Greenland. Off Gay Head, 10 to 19 fathoms; in the Bay of Fundy frequent in from 1 to 80 fathoms. Fossil in the Post-Pliocene "Leda-clays" of Labrador (Packard); and Canada (Dawson)

BELA PLEUROTOMARIA Adams.

H. and A. Adams, Genera of Recent Mollusca, vol. i, p. 92, 1858; Gould, Invert. of Mass., ed. ii, p. 355, fig. 625. *Fusus pleurotomarius* Couthouy, Boston Journal of Natural History, vol. ii, p. 107, Plate 1, fig. 9, 1838. *Fusus rufus* Gould, Invert. of Mass., ed. i, p. 190, fig. 192 (*non* Montagu). *Buccinum pyramidale* Ström, N. A. Dan. iii, p. 296, fig. 22 (t. Loven). *Defrancia Vahlii* (Beck) Möller, 1842 (t. Loven). *Mangelia pryamidalis* Stimpson, Shells of New England, p. 49.

Off the coast of Long Island, in 46 fathoms (Stimpson). Massachusetts Bay to Labrador; in Casco Bay and the Bay of Fundy not uncommon in 18 to 60 fathoms. Greenland (Möller). Finmark (Lovén). Fossil in the Post-Pliocene deposits of Canada, Labrador, Great Britain, and Scandinavia.

The identification of this species with the *Buccinum pyramidale* Ström, is somewhat uncertain; if correct, the latter name has priority.

BELA PLICATA Adams. Plate XXI, fig. 107. (p. 383.)

H. and A. Adams, Genera of Recent Mollusca, vol. i, p. 92, 1858. *Pleurotoma plicata* C. B. Adams, Boston Journal of Natural History, vol. iii, p. 318, Plate 3, fig. 6; Gould, Invert. of Mass., ed. i, p. 282, fig. 187; ed. ii, p. 350, fig. 612. *Pleurotoma plicosa* C. B. Adams, Contributions to Conchology, vol. i, p. 54, 1850; Jay, Catalogue, ed. iv, p. 327. *Pleurotoma brunnea* Perkins, Proc. Boston Soc. Nat. History, vol. xiii, p. 121, 1869.

Near New Haven, rare. Huntington and Greenport, Long Island (Sanderson Smith). New York (Dekay). Dartmouth, Massachusetts, and New Bedford Harbor, in mud, (C. B. Adams). Beaufort, N. C. (Dr. E. Coues). Indian Pass, Florida (E. Jewett).

MANGELIA CERINA. (p. 432.)

Verrill, American Journal of Science, vol. iii, p. 210, 1872. *Pleurotoma cerinum* Kurtz and Stimpson, Proceedings of the Boston Society of Natural History, vol. iv, p. 115, 1851; Stimpson, Shells of New England, p. 49, Pl. 2, fig. 2, 1851.

Shell elongated, fusiform, rather acute at apex, composed of about seven whorls; apical whorls smooth, the others angulated in the middle and decidedly flattened just below the suture; suture distinct, but shallow, undulated; the body whorl has about eleven prominent, longitudinal, sub-acute plications or ribs, separated by wide, concave interspaces. The ribs are most prominent at the angulation above the middle of the lower whorl, and do not extend on the flattened sub-sutural band. The whole surface is covered by fine, raised, revolving lines, often alternately larger and smaller, separated by wider striæ, and crossed by fine, distinct lines of growth, rendering them slightly nodulous. The revolving lines are most distinct on the sub-sutural band, and are often nearly obsolete over the summits of the ribs. Outer lip acute, with a decided angle at about the posterior fourth, where it recedes to form a decided, rounded notch, at and just above the angle; middle portion nearly straight, gradually curving and receding toward the anterior end; canal short, straight, and somewhat contracted. Color whitish, or slightly yellow; inner surface light wax-yellow. Length, 6.5^{mm}; breadth, 3^{mm}; length of aperture, 3^{mm}.

Vineyard Sound, 3 to 10 fathoms; near New Haven. New Bedford, Mass., and Charleston, S. C. (Stimpson). Staten Island; Greenport and Huntington, Long Island, low water to 3 fathoms, (S. Smith). Beaufort, N. C. (Coues). Fossil in the Post-Pliocene of South Carolina.

PLEUROTOMA BICARINATUM Couthouy. Plate XXI, fig. 106. (p. 418.)

Boston Journal of Natural History, vol. ii, p. 104, Plate 1, fig. 11, 1838; Gould, Invert. of Mass., ed. i, p. 281, fig. 186; ed. ii, p. 349, fig. 618. *Mangelia bicarinata* Stimpson, Shells of New England, p. 49. *Defrancia bicarinata* H. and A. Adams, Genera of Mollusca, vol. i, p. 95.

Stonington, Conn. (Linsley). Vineyard Sound, 6 to 12 fathoms, rare; Massachusetts Bay; Bay of Fundy. This is a rare and imperfectly known species. I have never had opportunities to examine the living animal.

The generic relations of this and the two preceding shells are still doubtful.

BUCCINUM UNDATUM Linné. Plate XXI, fig. 121. (p. 494.)

Systema Naturæ, ed. xii, p. 1204. Gould, Invertebrata of Massachusetts, ed. i, p. 305; ed. ii, p. 366, fig. 634. *Buccinum undulatum* Möller, in Kroyer's Tidsskrift, vol. iv, p. 84, 1842 (t. Stimpson). Stimpson, Review of the Northern Buccinums, in Canadian Naturalist, October, 1865. *Buccinum Labradorense* Reeve, Conch. Icon., vol. iii, Buc. i, 5, 1846 (t. Stimpson).

Mouth of Vineyard Sound and off Gay Head, 6 to 19 fathoms. Off New Jersey, north latitude 40°, west longitude 73°, in 32 fathoms, sandy bottom, (Captain Gedney).

Near Stonington, Conn. (Linsley); Montauk Point, Long Island, and Little Gull Island (S. Smith). Not common south of Cape Cod, except on the outer islands and in deep water; common in Massachusetts Bay; and very abundant on the coast of Maine, and northward to Greenland. On the European coast it occurs from Iceland and the North Cape to France, and from low water to 650 fathoms. In the Bay of Fundy it is abundant from above low-water mark to 100 fathoms.

As a fossil it is common in the Post-Pliocene deposits of Maine, Canada, Labrador, and Great Britain. Mr. Desor obtained it from the Post-Pliocene formation of Nantucket Island.

The ordinary American specimens from shallow water differ considerably in form from the typical European specimens, but the species is quite variable on both coasts, and I have examined large specimens from Saint George's Bank and La Have Bank, dredged by Mr. S. I. Smith, which differ very little from the common European form, and it is easy to form series connecting these with our common shore specimens. I am, therefore, unable to agree with Dr. Stimpson, who considered our shell distinct from the European, and adopted the name *undulatum* for it.

NEPTUNEA CURTA Verrill.

Fusus corneus Say, Amer. Conch., iii, Plate 29, 1831 (*non* Linné, Pennant, etc.). *Fusus Islandicus* Gould, Invert. of Mass., ed. i, p. 284; ed. ii, p. 371, fig. 638 (*non* Chemnitz, Gmelin, etc.). *Fusus curtus* Jeffreys, British Conchology, vol. iv, p. 336, 1867.

Massachusetts Bay to Labrador. Casco Bay, 6 to 50 fathoms; common in the Bay of Fundy from low-water mark to 80 fathoms. Linsley reports it, as *F. corneus*, from fish-stomachs at Stonington, Connecticut. In the Yale Museum are dead shells of this species, which have been occupied by *Eupaguri*, found on Fire Island Beach, on the south side of Long Island, by Mr. S. I. Smith. It probably inhabits the deep water off Block Island.

The dentition of this species is decidedly buccinoid. The central plates are transversely oblong, deeply concave above, with the lateral angles produced; below armed with three small, nearly equal, short teeth, the central one largest, beyond which, on each side, it is concave, the outer angles being a little prominent. The lateral plates are large, with an outer, very strong, curved tooth, and two much smaller, slightly curved ones near the inner end, the innermost being slightly the largest.

The dentition agrees very closely with that of *N. antiqua*, the type both of the genus *Neptunea*, Bolton, 1798, and *Chrysodomus*, Swainson, 1840, but it is very different from that of *Sipho Berniciensis* (*S. Islandicus* Trosch.), which Troschel refers to the Faciolaridæ. The latter is evidently the type of a genus (*Sipho*) very distinct from *Neptunea;* but among the European species, *gracilis*, *propinqua*, *buccinata*, and the true *Islandica* (as described by Jeffreys) are closely related to *curta*, and belong to the genus *Neptunea*, in the family Buccinidæ.

NEPTUNEA (*Neptunella*) PYGMÆA. Plate XXI, fig. 115. (p. 508.)

> *Fusus Islandicus, var. pygmæus*, Gould, Invert. of Mass., ed. i, p. 284, fig. 199, 1841. *Tritonium pygmæum* Stimpson, Shells of New England, p. 46, 1851. *Fusus Trumbullii* Linsley, Amer. Journal Science, ser. i, vol. xlviii, p. 28, fig. 1, 2, 1845 (*non* Gould, 1848). *Fusus pygmæus* Gould, Invert. of Mass., ed. ii, p. 372, fig. 639. *Neptunea* (*Sipho*) *pygmæa* H. and A. Adams, Genera Recent Mollusca, vol. i, p. 81, 1858. *Chrysodomus pygmæus* Dall, Proc. Boston Soc. Nat. Hist., vol. xiii, p. 242, 1870.

Deep water off New London and Stonington, Connecticut, northward to the Gulf of Saint Lawrence. East of Block Island, 29 fathoms, sandy mud; off Buzzard's Bay, 25 fathoms; off Gay Head, 19 fathoms, mud, abundant and large; off Edgarton, 18 to 20 fathoms; Casco Bay, 10 to 40 fathoms, common; Eastport, Maine, and Bay of Fundy, low water to 100 fathoms (A. E. V.). Near Saint George's Bank, 40 to 150 fathoms; east of Saint George's Bank, 430 fathoms; and off Halifax (S. I. Smith).

The odontophore in this species is long and slender; the dentition is buccinoid. The middle plate is small, transversely oblong, concave above, below convex, with one very small central tooth; lateral plates relatively large and strong, with a large, curved outer tooth, and a smaller bifid inner tooth, widely separated from the outer one.

The peculiarities in the dentition of this species, in connection with the singular wooly or velvety epidermis, indicate that this species should form the type of a sub-genus, or perhaps even a distinct genus. For the group I would propose the name *Neptunella*.

FULGUR CARICA Conrad. Pl. XXII, fig. 127. (p. 355.)

Proceedings of the Academy of Nat. Sciences, Philadelphia, vol. vi, p. 319, 1853; Gill, on the Genus Fulgur and its Allies, in American Journal of Conchology, vol. iii, p. 145, 1867. *Murex carica* Gmelin, Syst. Nat., p. 3545, 1788. *Fulgur eliceans* (*pars*) Montfort, Conch. Syst., vol. ii, p. 503, 1810, fig. (t. Gill). *Pyrula carica* Lamarck, Anim. sans Vert., ed. i, vol. vii, p. 138, 1822; Gould, Invert. of Mass., ed. i, p. 296. *Busycon carica* Gould, op. cit., ed. ii, p. 383, fig. 646; Stimpson, in American Journal of Conchology, vol. i, p. 61, 1865.

Eastern coast of the United States; northward to Cape Cod; southward to northern Florida, and west Florida. Abundant in Vineyard Sound, in 1 to 10 fathoms; also in Long Island Sound, near New Haven. Nantucket (Adams); St. Augustine, Florida (H. S. Williams); west Florida (E. Jewett.) It occurs in the Miocene formation of Maryland and Virginia, and in the Post-Pliocene deposits of Virginia, North Carolina, South Carolina, and Florida.

SYCOTYPUS CANALICULATUS Gill. (p. 355.)

American Journal of Conchology, vol. iii, p. 149, 1867. *Murex canaliculatus* Linné, Syst. Nat., ed. xii, p. 1222. *Pyrula canaliculata* Lamarck, Anim. sans Vert., vol. vii, p. 137, 1822; Gould, Invert. of Mass., ed. i, p. 294, fig. 206. *Busycon canaliculatum* H. and A. Adams, Genera of Recent Mollusca, vol. i, p. 151, 1858; Gould, Invert. of Mass., ed. ii, p. 380, fig. 645. *Fulgur canaliculata* Say, Journal Acad. Nat. Sciences, Philadelphia, vol. ii, 1822; Conrad, Proc. Phil. Acad., vol. vi, p. 219, 1853.

Eastern coast of the United States; northward to Cape Cod and Nantucket; southward to Georgia and Northern Florida, Western Florida, and northern shores of Gulf of Mexico. Abundant in Vineyard Sound, Long Island Sound, &c., in 1 to 8 fathoms. St. Augustine, Florida (H. S. Williams). Found fossil in the Post-Pliocene of Virginia, North and South Carolina, and Northern Florida; in the Pliocene of South Carolina; and Miocene of Maryland.

NASSA VIBEX Say. Plate XXI, fig. 114. (p. 371).

Journal Academy Nat. Sciences, Philadelphia, vol. ii, p. 231, 1822; Gould, Invertebrata of Mass., ed. ii, p. 365, fig. 633. *Nassa fretensis* Perkins, Proceedings Boston Soc. Nat. History, vol. xiii, p. 117, figure, 1869 (variety).

Eastern coast of the United States; northward to Vineyard Sound; southward to Florida, and the Gulf of Mexico; not abundant north of Cape Hatteras. In Vineyard Sound and Long Island Sound, found sparingly in shallow water among eel-grass. New Bedford (Adams). Lloyd's Harbor, Huntington, and Northport, Long Island (S. Smith); Egmont Key, Florida (Jewett). It has been found in the Pliocene and Post-Pliocene of South Carolina.

Some of Say's original specimens were from South Carolina, others from Great Egg Harbor, New Jersey. At the latter locality I have also collected among eel-grass, in shallow water, the variety described by Dr. Perkins as *N. fretensis*, which is the most common form in all the more northern localities. Specimens intermediate between these and the ordinary southern forms are, however, of frequent occurrence, and the typical form also occurred in Vineyard Sound, with the variety.

TRITIA TRIVITTATA Adams. Plate XXI, fig. 112. (p. 354.)

H. and A. Adams, Genera of Recent Mollusca, vol. i, p. 122, 1858. *Nassa trivittata* Say, Journal Acad. Natural Sciences, Philadelphia, vol. ii, p. 231; Gould, Invert. of Mass., ed. ii, p. 364, fig. 632. *Buccinum trivittatum* Adams, Boston Journal of Nat. Hist., vol. ii, p. 265; Gould, op. cit., ed. i, p. 309, fig. 211.

Gulf of Saint Lawrence to Northern Florida. Eastport, Maine, and Bay of Fundy, 3 to 30 fathoms, not abundant; Casco Bay, 1 to 40 fathoms, abundant; Vineyard Sound and Buzzard's Bay, 0 to 14 fathoms, abundant; off Block Island, 29 fathoms; Long Island Sound, common. Gaspé, Canada (Dawson). Fossil in the Post-Pliocene of Point Shirley, Mass., Nantucket (Desor), Gull Island (Smith), Virginia, South Carolina, and North Carolina; in the Pliocene of South Carolina; and in the Miocene of Maryland, Virginia, and South Carolina.

ILYANASSA OBSOLETA Stimpson. Plate XXI, fig. 113. (p. 468.)

American Journal of Conchology, vol. i, p. 61, Plate 9, figs. 11, 12, 1865. *Nassa obsoleta* Say, Journal Acad. Nat. Sciences, Philadelphia, vol. ii, p. 232, 1822; Binney's Say, p. 77, 1858; Gould, Invertebrata of Mass., ed. ii, p. 362, fig. 631; *Buccinum obsoletum* Gould, Invert. of Mass., ed. i, p. 308, fig. 210; *Tritia obsoleta* H. and A. Adams, Genera, p. 122, 1858.

Eastern and southern coasts of the United States; northward to Casco Bay, Maine, and the mouth of the Kennebeck River, and local in the southern part of the Gulf of Saint Lawrence; southward to Florida and the northern shores of the Gulf of Mexico. Extremely abundant on the whole coast south of Cape Cod; more local farther north, and mostly restricted to sheltered bays and harbors. It has not been found on the eastern part of the coast of Maine nor in the Bay of Fundy. An isolated colony of this species is found on the western and southern shores of the Gulf of Saint Lawrence and Prince Edward's Island (Bell, Dawson).

As a fossil it has been found in the Post-Pliocene deposits at Point Shirley, in Chelsea, Massachusetts (Stimpson); at Nantucket Island (Desor); Virginia; and South Carolina. It is also reported from the Pliocene of South Carolina.

UROSALPINX CINEREA Stimpson. Plate XXI, fig. 116. (p. 306.)

American Journal of Conchology, vol. i, p. 58, Plate 8, figs. 6 and 7, 1865. *Fusus cinereus* Say, Journal Academy Nat. Science, Philadelphia, vol. ii, p. 236, 1822; American Conchology, Plate 29, 1831. *Buccinum plicosum* Menke, Syn., ed. ii, p. 69, 1830, (t. Gould); Gould, Invertebrata of Mass., ed. i, p. 303, fig. 213. *Buccinum cinereum* Gould, op. cit., ed. ii, p. 370, fig. 637.

Eastern coast of the United States; northward to Massachusetts Bay, and local farther north, to the Gulf of Saint Lawrence; southward to Georgia and Northern Florida, and on the west coast of Florida, at Tampa Bay. Abundant in Vineyard Sound, Buzzard's Bay, Long Island Sound, and along the coast of the Middle States, especially on oyster-beds. In Vineyard Sound it occurs from above low-water mark to 8 fathoms. It occurs in some of the shallow and sheltered branches of Casco Bay, especially at the upper end of Quahog Bay, but has not been found on the islands, nor farther eastward along the coast of Maine, nor in the Bay of Fundy. A colony exists, however, in the southern part of the Gulf of Saint Lawrence, associated with the preceding and other southern species. It is found fossil in the Post-Pliocene of Point Shirley, Massachusetts, Nantucket, Gardiner's Island, Virginia, North Carolina, and South Carolina; in the Pliocene of South Carolina; and in the Miocene of Maryland.

EUPLEURA CAUDATA H. and A. Adams. Plate XXI, fig. 117. (p. 371.)

Genera of Recent Mollusca, vol. i, p. 107, 1858; Stimpson, Amer. Journal of Conchology, vol. i, p. 58, Plate 8, fig. 5 (dentition), 1865. *Ranella caudata* Say, Journal Acad. Nat. Sciences, Philadelphia, vol. ii, p. 236, 1822; Gould, Invert. of Mass., ed. i, p. 297, fig. 176; ed. ii, p. 386, fig. 648.

Eastern coast of the United States; northward to Nantucket and Cape Cod; southward to northern Florida, and western Florida, at Tampa Bay. At Vineyard Sound it occurred living in considerable numbers in the shallow ditches on the marshes, as well as in the sound itself, in 1 to 8 fathoms; off New Haven, in 1 to 5 fathoms, not abundant; Great Egg Harbor, frequent among eel-grass in shallow water. Egmont Key, Florida (Jewett).

In the fossil state this species has been found in the Post-Pliocene of Virginia, North and South Carolina, and Florida; in the Pliocene of South Carolina; and in the Miocene of Maryland and South Carolina.

PURPURA LAPILLUS Lamarck. Plate XXI, figs. 118 to 120. (p. 306.)

Anim. sans Vert., ed. i, vol. vi, 1822; ed. ii, vol. x, p. 79; Gould, Invert. of Mass., ed. i, p. 301; ed. ii, p. 360, fig. 630. *Buccinum lapillus* Linné, Syst. Naturæ, ed. xii, p. 1202, 1767.

Watch Hill, Rhode Island; Montauk Point, Long Island; Cuttyhunk Island; shores of Vineyard Sound, at Nobsca Point; northward to the Arctic Ocean. On the European coast southward to Portugal. North-eastern coast of Asia. Sitka (Middendorff). This species is local south of Cape Cod, and has not been found to the eastward of Stonington, Connecticut, in Long Island Sound. It is extremely abundant along the northern coasts of New England and Nova Scotia, often nearly covering the surface of the rocks toward low-water mark, where they are encrusted by *Balanus balanoides*, upon which it chiefly feeds, inserting its proboscis between the opercular valves of the barnacle.

This shell has been found in the Post-Pliocene deposits at Waterville, Maine, and at Gardiner's Island, but is not a common fossil in this country. In England it is found in the Red-Crag and all later formations; it also occurs in the Post-Pliocene deposits of Scandinavia. The fossils show the same variations that are seen in the recent shells.

PTYCHATRACTUS LIGATUS Stimpson.

American Journal of Conchology, vol. i, p. 59, plate 8, fig. 8 (dentition), 1865. *Fasciolaria ligata* Mighels and Adams, Boston Journal of Nat. History, vol. iv, p. 51, Plate 4, fig. 17, 1842; Gould, Invert. of Mass., ed. ii, p. 385, fig. 647.

Casco Bay, Maine, to Labrador. Stonington, Connecticut (Linsley).

Casco Bay, 20 to 40 fathoms; Bay of Fundy, 15 to 60 fathoms. Halifax (Willis); Gaspé (Whiteaves); Murray Bay (Dawson); Mingan (Foote). This shell occurs sparingly at all these localities. It has not been recorded from south of Cape Cod by any one except Linsley, and it must be regarded as a very doubtful member of the fauna of Southern New England until rediscovered.

Dr. Dawson records one broken specimen from the Post-Pliocene of Montreal.

ANACHIS AVARA Perkins. (p. 306.)

Proceedings, Boston Soc. Nat. History, vol. xiii, p. 113, 1869 (in part). *Columbella avara* Say, Journal Acad. Nat. Sciences, Philadelphia, vol. ii, p. 230, 1822; (in part) Gould, Invert. of Mass., ed. i, p. 313; ed. ii, p. 356 (in part).

Cape Cod to Northern Florida; Western Florida and the northern shores of the Gulf of Mexico. Vineyard Sound, from 0 to 10 fathoms; Long Island Sound; Great Egg Harbor, New Jersey; Nantucket (Adams); Fort Macon (Coues); South Carolina (Gibbes); Georgia (Couper); Western Florida (Jewett). North of Cape Cod, it is local and rare; Massachusetts Bay (Stimpson).

Fossil in the Post-Pliocene of North and South Carolina, and in the Pliocene of South Carolina.

Among the shells usually referred to this species there are great variations in form and sculpture, and the color is quite inconstant. The numerous specimens that I have examined from various localities can, however, be arranged in two groups, between which I have found no specimens that can be regarded as truly intermediate, although most of their distinctive characters are variable in each series. For the present, therefore, I have with some hesitation followed Mr. Ravenel in regarding these two principal forms as distinct species. As these species (or varieties) have not been distinguished by most writers, it is probable that some of the northern localities given above should properly go under the next species, which is far more abundant in Vineyard Sound and Long Island Sound than the typical *avara*, while the latter predominates in the collections from Fort Macon, North Carolina, and southward. The figures given by Dr. Gould represent the ordinary northern form of the following species. In the first part of this report both forms are included under *avara*.

From Fort Macon I have specimens that agree perfectly with Say's original description of *avara*. These are less elongated than the next species, and rather fusiform, the thickest part being but little below the middle, with the spire acute. The mature shells have ten flattened whorls; the first three or nuclear whorls are smooth; some of the succeeding ones usually have numerous vertical costæ; the last whorl has 10 to 13 more or less prominent, smooth obtusely rounded, somewhat curved costæ, separated by wider concave intervals, and gradually disappearing below the middle; below the costæ are numerous, well impressed revolving grooves, of which 8 or 10 are wider and deeper than the rest; similar but finer grooves cross the spaces between the costæ, but are mostly obsolete on the costæ; the middle whorls usually have a similar number of costæ, which are less prominent, and often more or less obsolete, while the spaces between are crossed by numerous fine revolving striæ. The canal is short, broad, and nearly straight; the outer lip well rounded, not incurved anteriorly, but with a decided emargination posteriorly. Length of mature shells, 13^{mm}; diameter, 6^{mm}, often smaller.

Specimens of the same size and form from Vineyard Sound and New Haven agree closely with the above description in most respects, but have 14 or 15 costæ on the last whorl, and about 20 on the preceding ones, where the costæ are so crowded that the spaces between are often narrower than the costæ.

ANACHIS SIMILIS Verrill. Plate XXI, fig. 109.

Columbella similis Ravenel, Proc. Acad. Nat. Sci., Philad., 1861, p. 41. *Columbella translirata* Ravenel, op. cit., p. 42. *Columbella avara* (in part) Gould, Invert., ed. i, p. 313, fig. 197; ed. ii, p. 356, fig. 726.

Massachusetts Bay to Georgia. Abundant in Vineyard Sound and Long Island Sound; Great Egg Harbor. Fort Macon (Dr. Yarrow.) This species is usually much more elongated than the preceding, with a more elevated spire, the broadest place being a little above the lower third of the length. Whorls, 10; flattened; the nuclear whorls smooth The canal is longer, and usually distinctly excurved; the outer lip is more or less incurved anteriorly, so as to slightly narrow the canal; the body-whorl has 18 to 20 or more rather regular, obtuse costæ, separated by spaces of about the same width, generally slightly nodular close to the suture; at some distance below the middle of the whorl they gradually disappear, but sometimes there are also smaller intermediate costæ below the middle of the whorl (var. *translirata*); the lower part of the whorl is covered with numerous well-impressed, revolving grooves, which cross the lower ends of the costæ, rendering them nodulous; on the upper part of the whorls the revolving grooves are larger and more distinct than in the preceding species, and usually continue over the costæ; the one next below the suture is usually larger than the rest, and thus produces the subsutural nodules; the grooves are generally least distinct in the middle of the lower whorl, which is sometimes slightly angulated. On the middle whorls there are numerous (usually more than 25) regular costæ, like those of the last one, and crossed by about 5 distinct revolving grooves, more conspicuous in the spaces between; the upper one largest, usually producing a distinct series of nodules on each whorl. Color exceedingly variable, generally dark reddish brown, chestnut, or light yellowish brown, more or less mottled and specked with whitish; there is often a subsutural band of white, or the nodules are white, and also a band of white around the middle of the last whorl, but these are frequently absent. Length of a rather large specimen, 17mm; breadth, 7mm; length of an average specimen, 13mm; breadth, 5mm; length of a slender specimen, 15mm; breadth, 5mm.

ASTYRIS LUNATA Dall. Plate XXI, fig. 110. (p. 306.)

Proceedings Boston Soc. Natural History, vol. xiii, p. 242, 1870. *Nassa lunata* Say, Journal Acad. Nat. Sciences, Philadelphia, vol. v, p. 213, 1826. *Buccinum lunatum* Adams, Boston Journ. Nat. Hist., vol. ii, p. 226; Gould, Invert. of Mass., ed i., p. 312, fig. 196. *Columbella lunata* Gould, op. cit., ed. ii, p. 359, fig. 629. *Fusus Trumbulli* Gould, Amer. Journ. Science, vol. vi, p. 235, fig. 7, 1848, (*non* Linsley). *Buccinum Wheatleyi* Dekay, Nat. Hist. of New York, Mollusca, p. 132, Plate 7, fig. 162, 1843. *Columbella Gouldiana* Ag. MSS.; Stimpson, Shells of New England, p. 48, 1851; Smith, Annals Lyceum Nat. Hist. of New York, vol. viii, p. 398, fig. 5, 1865. *Astyris* "*limata* Say" and *A.* "*Turnbullii* Linsl.," H. and A. Adams, Genera, vol. i, p. 187 (typographical errors).

Massachusetts Bay to Northern Florida and the northern shores of the Gulf of Mexico; local and not abundant north of Cape Cod, at Provincetown, Nahant, and Swampscott, Massachusetts. Very abundant in Vineyard Sound, from low-water to 10 fathoms; and in Long Island Sound; Great South Bay, Long Island; and Great Egg Harbor, New Jersey; Fort Macon, North Carolina, and southward. Estella Pass, Florida (Jewett); Georgia (Couper).

Fossil in the Post-Pliocene deposits of South Carolina; and at Gardiner's Island, New York (S. Smith); and in the Pliocene of South Carolina.

The color-variety, separated by several writers as *C. Gouldiana*, is identical with the *Wheatleyi* of Dekay.

ASTYRIS ZONALIS Verrill. Plate XXI, fig. 111. (p. 399.)

Buccinum zonalis Linsley, American Journal of Science, ser. i, vol. xlviii, p. 285, 1845 (no description); Gould, Amer. Journ. Science, series ii, vol. vi, p. 236, fig. 8, 1848. *Columbella dissimilis* Stimpson, Proceedings Boston Soc. Nat. History, vol. iv, p. 114, 1851; Shells of New England, p. 47, 1851; Gould, Invert. of Mass., ed. ii, p. 358, fig. 628.

Long Island Sound, near New Haven; Vineyard Sound; Casco Bay; Eastport, Maine, 10 to 60 fathoms. Grand Menan, New Brunswick, in 8 fathoms, sand, (Stimpson). Stonington (Linsley).

ASTYRIS ROSACEA H. and A. Adams. (p. 508.)

Genera of Recent Mollusca, vol. i, p. 187, 1858. *Buccinum rosaceum* Gould, American Journal of Science, xxxviii, p. 197, 1840; Invert. of Mass., ed. i, p. 311, fig. 195, 1841. *Columbella rosacea* Stimpson, Shells of New England, p. 47, 1851; Gould, Invert. of Mass., ed. ii, p. 257, fig. 627. (?)*Fusus Holböllii* Möller, Naturhistorisk Tidsskrift, vol. iv, p. 88, 1842.

East of Block Island, 29 fathoms, fine sandy mud; Stonington, Connecticut (Linsley); Massachusetts Bay to Gulf of Saint Lawrence; Isles of Shoals, 20 fathoms, and West Isles, 10 fathoms (Stimpson); Casco Bay, 10 to 20 fathoms; Bay of Fundy, 8 to 60 fathoms; Sable Island, Nova Scotia (Willis); Grand Menan, in deep water, (Stimpson).

The identity of *A. Holböllii*, from Greenland, with this species, is very doubtful, for it was described as smooth, with a firm corneus, fusco-luteus epidermis.

LUNATIA HEROS Adams. Plate XXIII, figs. 133 to 136. (p. 353.)

H. and A. Adams, Genera of Recent Mollusca, vol. i, p. 207, 1858; Gould, Invert. of Mass., ed. ii, p. 338, figs. 608, 609. *Natica heros* Say, Jour. Acad. Nat. Sci., Philadelphia, vol. ii, p. 248, 1822; Gould, Invert., ed. i, p. 231. *Natica triseriata* Say, op. cit., vol. v. p. 209 (color-variety); Gould, Invert., ed. i, p. 233. *Lunatia triseriata* Gould, op. cit., ed. ii, p. 340, fig. 610.

Georgia to Gulf of Saint Lawrence and southern coast of Labrador. Coast of New Jersey, near Great Egg Harbor, abundant and large, (A. E. V.) ;southern side of Long Island, at Fire Island beach, abundant, (S. I. Smith); Long Island Sound, at New Haven, not common; Vineyard Sound, abundant from low-water to 10 fathoms; Casco Bay, common; Bay of Fundy, common from low-water to 40 fathoms; Saint George's Bank, common, (S. I. Smith); Gaspé (Dawson); Georgia (Couper). The variety *triseriata* has the same distribution, and is the more common form in the deeper waters, but is also found on the sand-flats at low-water. It is common in Casco Bay and Bay of Fundy, in 1 to 40 fathoms; off Martha's Vineyard, 10 to 20 fathoms; and off New London, Connecticut, 10 fathoms.

This species has been found fossil in the Miocene of Maryland, Virginia, and South Carolina; in the Pliocene of South Carolina; and in the Post-Pliocene of Canada and South Carolina.

LUNATIA IMMACULATA Adams. Plate XXIII, fig. 131. (p. 508.)

H. and A. Adams, Genera of Recent Mollusca, vol. i, p. 207. *Natica immaculata* Totten, American Journal of Science, ser. i, vol. xxviii, p. 351, fig. 6, 1835; Gould, Invertebrata, ed. i, p. 234, fig. 168, 1841. *Mamma* (?) *immaculata* Gould, ed. ii, p. 344, fig. 614.

Stonington, Connecticut, and eastern end of Long Island, to Gulf of Saint Lawrence. Off Martha's Vineyard, 20 fathoms; east of Block Island, 29 fathoms. Stonington (Linsley); Off Napeague Point, Long Island (S. Smith); Newport, R. I. (Totten). Massachusetts Bay, Casco Bay, and Bay of Fundy, 5 to 80 fathoms, common; often found living at low-water mark in the Bay of Fundy.

NEVERITA DUPLICATA Stimpson. Plate XXIII, fig. 130. (p. 354.)

Smithsonian Check List, p. 5, 1860; Gould, Invert. of Mass., ed. ii, p. 345, fig. 615. *Natica duplicata* Say, Jour. Acad. Nat. Sciences, Philadelphia, vol. ii, p. 247, 1822; Gould, Invert., ed. i, p. 236, fig. 164, 1841. *Lunatia duplicata* H. and A. Adams, Genera Recent Mollusca, vol. i, p. 207, 1858.

Massachusetts Bay to Northern Florida; northwestern Florida to Yucatan. Local and not common north of Cape Cod. Abundant at Nantucket; Vineyard Sound; Long Island Sound; southern coast of Long Island; New Jersey; and southward. Saint Augustine, Florida (Williams). Tampa Bay, Florida, and Egmont Key, abundant, (Jewett). Texas (Schott). Near Vera Cruz, Mexico (coll. T. Salt).

Fossil in the Miocene of Maryland, Virginia, North and South Carolina; Pliocene of South Carolina; and Post-Pliocene of Virginia, North Carolina, South Carolina, Saint John's River, and Tampa Bay, Florida.

NATICA PUSILLA Say. Plate XXIII, fig. 132. (p. 417.)

Journal Acad. Nat. Sciences, Philadelphia, vol. ii, p. 257, 1822; Stimpson, Shells of New England, p. 43, 1851; Gould, Invert. of Mass., ed. ii, p. 344, fig. 613, (*not* of ed. i); Sanderson Smith, in Annals Lyc. Nat. History, New York, vol. ix, p. 396, fig. 4, 1870.

Vineyard Sound to Northern Florida. In Vineyard Sound and Buzzard's Bay this species is common in 2 to 10 fathoms. Huntington and Gardiner's Bay, Long Island, 4 to 5 fathoms, (S. Smith). South Carolina (Kurtz). Fort Macon, North Carolina (Coues). Georgia (Couper).

Acrybia flava H. and A. Adams, = *Natica flava* Gould, Invert., ed. i, p. 239, fig. 162; *Bulbus flavus* Gould, op. cit., ed. ii, p. 347, fig. 616. This species was catalogued by Linsley (1845) as from the stomachs of haddock taken off Stonington, Connecticut. It has not been subsequently recorded from south of Cape Cod by any one. It is not improbable that there was some mistake, either in respect to the locality or the identity of the specimens referred to by Linsley. It is an arctic species, found in the Bay of Fundy and at Saint George's Bank; northward to Greenland (Möller, as *N. nana*).

Natica clausa Brod. and Sowerby, was erroneously given by Mr. Perkins (Proc. Boston Soc. Nat. Hist., vol. xiii, p. 162) as from "Stonington, Connecticut, Linsley." It does not occur in Mr. Linsley's list, nor has it been found living, to my knowledge, south of Cape Cod. It occurs in Massachusetts Bay and northward to the Arctic Ocean. It is not uncommon in the Bay of Fundy from 6 to 109 fathoms; and in Casco Bay from 9 to 60 fathoms. One small dead specimen was dredged by us in 19 fathoms, off Gay Head.

CERITHIOPSIS GREENII Verrill. Plate XXIV, fig. 153. (p. 383.)

Cerithium Greenii C. B. Adams, Boston Journal of Natural History, vol. ii, p. 287, Plate 4, fig. 12, 1838; Gould, Invert., ed. i, p. 579, fig. 184. *Bittium Greenii* H. and A. Adams, Genera, vol. i, p. 287, 1858; Gould, Invert., ed. ii, p. 322, fig. 591.

Massachusetts Bay to South Carolina. Vineyard Sound and Buzzard's Bay, 3 to 10 fathoms; Long Island Sound, near New Haven. Dartmouth Harbor (Adams); Boston Harbor (Stimpson); Long Island (S. Smith); Fort Macon, North Carolina (Coues). Also reported from Bermuda.

Jeffreys (in Annals and Mag. Nat. Hist., Oct., 1872, p. 244) regards this as identical with the European *C. tubercularis*, and gives it a northern distribution. Both opinions appear to be incorrect.

CERITHIOPSIS EMERSONII Adams. Plate XXIV, fig. 151. (p. 417.)

H. and A. Adams, Genera, p. 240, 1858; Gould, Invert., ed. ii, p. 387, fig. 649 *Cerithium Emersonii* C. B. Adams, op. cit., p. 284, Plate 4, fig. 10, 1838; Gould, Invert., ed. i, p. 275, fig. 180.

Cape Cod to South Carolina. Vineyard Sound and Buzzard's Bay, 3 to 10 fathoms, shelly. Nantucket (Adams); Huntington and Greenport, Long Island (S. Smith). Fossil in the Miocene of North Carolina, (Conrad). Jeffreys (in British Conchology, vol. iv, p. 257) regards this species as identical with *Cerithium metula* Lovén, 1846, on the authority of Danielssen. This appears to be an erroneous identification.

CERITHIOPSIS TEREBRALIS Adams. Plate XXIV, fig. 150. (p. 417.)

H. and A. Adams, Genera, vol. i, p. 241, 1858; Gould, Invert., ed. ii, p. 389, fig. 650. *Cerithium terebrale* C. B. Adams, Boston Journal Nat. Hist., vol. iii, p, 320, Plate 3, fig. 7, 1840; Gould, Invert., ed. i, p. 276, fig. 181. *Cerithium terebellum* C. B. Adams, Catalogue Genera and Species of Recent Shells in Collection of C. B. A., p. 13, 1847.

Cape Cod to South Carolina. Vineyard Sound and Buzzard's Bay, 2 to 12 fathoms, not uncommon. New Bedford, Massachusetts (Adams). Greenport and Huntington, Long Island (S. Smith). Fort Macon, North Carolina (Coues).

TRIFORIS NIGROCINCTUS Stimpson. Plate XXIV, fig. 152. (p. 305.)

Smithsonian Check-List, p. 5, 1860; Gould, Invert., ed. ii, p. 323, fig. 592. *Cerithium nigrocinctum* C. B. Adams, Boston Jour. Nat. Hist., vol. ii, p. 286, Plate 4, fig. 11, 1838; Gould, Invert., ed. i, p. 277, fig. 182.

Cape Cod to South Carolina. Vineyard Sound and Buzzard's Bay, low-water to 10 fathoms, not uncommon; near New Haven; and Great Egg Harbor, New Jersey. Dartmouth, Massachusetts (Adams). Huntington and Greenport, Long Island (S. Smith). Fort Macon (Coues).

BITTIUM NIGRUM Stimpson. Plate XXIV, fig. 154. (p. 305.)

Smithsonian Check-List, p. 5, 1860; Gould, Invert., ed. ii, p. 321, fig. 590. *Pasithea nigra* Totten, American Jour. of Science, vol. xxvi, p. 369, Plate 1, fig. 7, 1834. *Cerithium reticulatum* Totten, op. cit., vol. xxviii, p. 352, fig. 8, 1835 (*non* Da Costa). *Cerithium Sayi* Menke (t. Gould); Gould, Invert., ed. i, p. 278, fig. 183.

Massachusetts Bay to South Carolina; local north of Cape Cod, in Boston Harbor (Totten), and in the Gulf of Saint Lawrence, at Pictou and Prince Edward's Island (Dawson). It is not found on the coast of Maine nor in the Bay of Fundy. Vineyard Sound and Buzzard's Bay, abundant, low-water to 8 fathoms, among algæ and eel-grass; Long Island Sound; and Great Egg Harbor, New Jersey, abundant. Fort Macon (Coues).

The *Bittium alternatum* (*Turritella alternata* Say, 1822) is a very closely related species, and probably identical with this.

Turritella erosa Couthouy, recorded, with a mark of doubt, by Linley, as from the stomach of a cod, off Stonington, Conn., was perhaps incorrectly identified. It may have been a worn *Cerithiopsis terebralis*. The true *T. erosa* is a decidedly northern species, common in Casco Bay and the Bay of Fundy, and extending northward to the Arctic Ocean, and southward on the northern coasts of Europe, and on the North Pacific coast of America. It has not been recorded from south of Cape Cod by any one except Linsley.

VERMETUS RADICULA Stimpson. Plate XXIV, fig. 157. (p. 417.)

Shells of New England, p. 37, 1851; Gould, Invert., ed ii, p. 316, fig. 584. *Vermetus lumbricalis* Gould, ed. i, p. 246, and various other American authors, (*non* Lamarck).

Cape Cod to Florida. Vineyard Sound and Buzzard's Bay, 3 to 10 fathoms, not uncommon; Long Island Sound. Fort Macon, North Carolina, common, (Coues).

Fossil in the Post-Pliocene of North Carolina.

CÆCUM PULCHELLUM Stimpson. Plate XXIV, fig. 158. (p. 417.)

Proceedings Boston Society of Natural History, vol. iv, p. 112, 1851; Shells of New England, p. 36, Plate 2, fig. 3, 1851; Gould, Invert., ed. ii, p. 315, fig. 583.

Vineyard Sound, 1 to 4 fathoms, and dead on shore at Nobsca Beach. New Bedford (Stimpson). Greenport, Long Island, 10 fathoms, sand, (S. Smith).

Dead shells of this species readily lose the outer layer, in which the annulations are formed; they then become white and smooth, without any trace of annulations, and might be mistaken for a different species.

CÆCUM COOPERI Smith.

Sanderson Smith, Annals Lyceum Nat. Hist., New York, vol. vii, p. 154, 1860; op. cit., vol. ix, p. 393, fig. 3, 1870, (*non* Carpenter, 1864). *Cæcum costatum* Verrill, American Journal of Science, vol. iii, p. 283, 1872; this Report, p. 417.

Vineyard Sound, 8 to 10 fathoms. Gardiner's Bay, Long Island, 4 to 5 fathoms, sand, (Smith).

The first description of this species was formerly overlooked by me; as it antedates the description of the Californian species to which Dr. Carpenter gave the same name, the present species must be called *Cooperi*.

In the adolescent stage of growth this species enlarges rather rapidly, and has 12 or 13, distinct, elevated, rounded costæ, narrower than the intervals between; the circular grooves are numerous, unequal, interrupted over the costæ, and broader toward the aperture. The aperture is rounded within; its margin is stellated externally by the costæ.

CREPIDULA FORNICATA Lamarck. Plate XXIII, fig. 129. (p. 417.)

Animaux sans Vert., vol. vii, p. 641; Say, Journal Acad. Nat. Sciences, Philadelphia, vol. ii, p. 225, 1822; Gould, Invert., ed. i, p. 158, fig. 17; ed. ii, p. 271, fig. 532(?). *Patella fornicata* Linné, Syst. Nat., ed. xii, p. 1257.

Casco Bay, Maine, to Florida, and the northern shores of the Gulf of Mexico. Local north of Massachusetts Bay; in the southern part of the Gulf of Saint Lawrence, at Prince Edward's Island, &c. Halifax (Willis). Saint George's Bank (S. I. Smith). It is common in the shallow and sheltered parts of Casco Bay, but has not been found east of the Kennebeck River, on the coast of Maine, nor in the Bay of Fundy. Very abundant in Vineyard Sound and Buzzard's Bay, from low-water to 12 fathoms; in Long Island Sound, near New Haven, low-water to 6 fathoms; Great Egg Harbor, New Jersey; and everywhere southward. Egmont Key and Tampa Bay, Florida (E. Jewett).

Fossil in the Miocene of Maryland, North and South Carolina; Pliocene of South Carolina; and Post-Pliocene of North and South Carolina, Gardiner's Island, New York, and Nantucket Island.

The *fornicata* of Linné was described as a Mediterranean species, and may not be identical with the American shell.

CREPIDULA PLANA Say. Plate XXIII, fig. 127.

Journal Acad. Nat. Sciences, Philadelphia, vol. ii, p. 226, 1822; Gould, Invert., ed. i, p. 159, fig. 16; ed. ii, p. 272, fig. 533. *Crepidula unguiformis* Stimpson, Shells of New England, p. 30, 1851; this Report, pp. 355, 417 (*non* Lamarck, 1822).

Massachusetts Bay to Florida and the northern shores of the Gulf of Mexico. Local and less abundant farther north, in Casco Bay, Maine; Nova Scotia (Willis); Gulf of Saint Lawrence (Bell, Dawson); and Saint George's Bank (S. I. Smith). Not found on the eastern part of the coast of Maine, nor in the Bay of Fundy. Very common in Vineyard Sound, Buzzard's Bay, and Long Island Sound, from low-water mark to 12 fathoms, on the *outside* of oysters, *Limuli*, and various dead shells, as well as on the *inside* of various dead univalve shells; in all these situations frequently associated with the preceding species, but no intermediate forms have been observed.

Fossil in the Miocene of North and South Carolina; Pliocene of South Carolina; and in the Post-Pliocene of Gardiner's Island, New York, North Carolina, South Carolina, and Florida.

The Mediterranean shell, *C. unguiformis* Lamarck, is a distinct species.

CREPIDULA CONVEXA Say. Plate XXIII, fig. 128. (p. 355.)

Journal Acad. Nat. Sciences, Philadelphia, vol. ii, p. 227, 1822; Gould, Invert., ed. i, p. 160, fig. 15; ed. ii, p. 273, fig. 534. *Crepidula glauca* Say, op. cit., p. 226; Gould, Invert., ed. ii, p. 274, fig. 535; ed. i, p. 151, fig. 14. *Crepidula acuta* H. C. Lea, American Jour. Science, ser. i, vol. xlii, p. 108, Plate 1, fig. 4, 1842.

Massachusetts Bay to Florida. Less abundant and local farther north; at Quahog Bay, Maine; Nova Scotia (Willis); and Gulf of Saint Lawrence. Very common in Vineyard Sound, Buzzard's Bay, Long Island Sound, shores of Long Island, and Great Egg Harbor, New Jersey. Fort Macon, North Carolina (Coues). Georgia (Couper).

Fossil in the Post-Pliocene of Virginia and South Carolina.

The distribution of this species is probably identical with that of *Eupagurus longicarpus* and *Ilyanassa obsoleta*, with which it is nearly always associated. At Quahog Bay, Maine, this species occurs on the back of the dead shells of *I. obsoleta*, which are occupied by the hermit-crab, just as in the waters of Southern New England; and these, with numerous other southern forms associated with them, constitute a genuine southern colony, occupying a warm, sheltered bay, surrounded on all sides by the northern fauna.

The depressed variety (*glauca*) is found chiefly on broad and nearly flat surfaces of large bivalve shells, stones, &c. The very convex varieties adhere mainly to the surfaces of small convex univalves.

CRUCIBULUM STRIATUM Adams. Plate XXIII, figs. 125, 126. (p. 417.)

H. and A. Adams, Genera of Recent Mollusca, vol. i, p. 366; Gould, Invert., ed. ii, p. 275, fig. 536. *Calyptræa (Dispotæa) striata* Say, Journ. Acad. Nat. Sciences Philadelphia, vol. v, p. 216, 1836. *Crucibulum (Dispotæa) striata* H. and A. Adams, Genera, vol. i, p. 366, 1858.

Bay of Fundy to New Jersey. Eastport Harbor and Bay of Fundy, low-water mark to 30 fathoms, common; Frenchman's Bay and Mount Desert, Maine, 3 to 10 fathoms, common; Casco Bay, Maine, 6 to 40 fathoms; Vineyard Sound and Buzzard's Bay, 3 to 12 fathoms, not uncommon. Gardiner's Bay and Montauk Point, Long Island (S. Smith). Off New London, Conn. (coll. T. M. Prudden). Saint George's Bank (S. I. Smith). Northern New Jersey (Say).

LITTORINA IRRORATA Gray. (p. 372.)

Zoology of Captain Beechey's Voyage, p. 138, Plate 38, fig. 1, 1839. Gould, Invert., ed. ii, p. 311, fig. 579. *Turbo irroratus* Say, Journal Acad. Nat. Sciences, Philadelphia, vol. ii, p. 239, July, 1822; Binney's Say, p. 81. *Phasianella sulcata* Lamarck, Animaux sans Vert., ed. i, vol. vii, p. 54, Aug., 1822; ed. ii, vol. ix, p. 244. *Littorina sulcata* Deshayes, in Lamarck, op. cit., vol. ix, p. 203, 1843.

Vineyard Sound to Florida and the northern shores of the Gulf of Mexico. Vineyard Sound, sparingly; Long Island Sound, near New Haven, rare. Stratford, Connecticut, on high sedge (Linsley). Huntington, Long Island (S. Smith). Comparatively rare and local north of Maryland; very abundant farther south.

Many of the shells of this species found on our shores have undoubtedly been brought from Virginia and Maryland with the southern oysters planted in our waters, but it is probably indigenous in certain localities.

LITTORINA RUDIS. Plate XXIV, fig. 137. (p. 305.)

Gould, Invert., ed. i, p. 257, fig. 165, 1841; ed. ii, p. 304, fig. 575. *Turbo rudis* Maton, Nat. Hist. and Antiq. West. Count., vol. i, p. 277, 1797, (t. Jeffreys); Donovan, British Shells, vol. i, Plate 33, fig. 3, 1800, (t. Gould.) *Turbo obligatus* Say, Jour. Acad. Nat. Sci., Philad., vol. ii, p. 241, 1822. *Turbo vestitus* Say, op. cit., p. 241, 1822 (variety *tenebrosa*). *Littorina Grönlandica* Möller, in Kroyer's Tidsskrift, vol. iv, p. 82, 1842. *Turbo tenebrosus* Montagu, Test. Brit., p. 303, Plate 20, fig. 4, 1803 (variety). *Littorina tenebrosa* Gould, ed. i, p. 259, fig. 166; ed. ii, p. 306, fig. 576.

Among the additional names that appear to have been applied to the various states of this variable species are: *L. saxatilis* Johnson; *Turbo sulcatus* Leach; *Turbo jugosus* Montagu; *L. patula* (*var.*) Jeffreys; *L. neglecta* Bean; *T. ventricosus* Brown; *L. marmorata* Pfeiffer; *Nerita littorea* Fabricius (*non* Linné); *L. Grönlandica* Möller, Lovén, Mörch; *L. rudissima* Bean; *L. zonaria* Bean; *L. neglecta* Bean, etc.

Great Egg Harbor, New Jersey, northward to the Arctic Ocean; Greenland; Iceland; Spitzbergen. Northern coasts of Europe to Great Britain and Spain. Local south of Long Island Sound; abundant on all the rocky shores of Southern New England, from New York to Cape Cod, and at the eastern end of Long Island; local at Great Egg Harbor, among *Fucus*, on the stones of an old pier. Extremely abundant on all the northern shores of New England and northward. Fossil in the Post-Pliocene of Canada, Great Britain, and Scandinavia.

LITTORINA PALLIATA. Plate XXIV, fig. 138. (p. 305.)

Gould, Invert. of Mass., ed. i, p. 260, fig. 167, 1841; ed. ii, p. 309, fig. 578. *Turbo palliatus* Say, op. cit., p. 240, 1822. *Littorina neritoidea* Dekay, Mollusca New York, p. 105, Plate 6, figs. 109–111 (*non Turbo neritoidea* Linné). *Littorina littoralis* Stimpson, Shells of New England, p. 33, (*non* Forbes and Hanley; *non Nerita littoralis* Linné). *Turbo littoralis* Fabricius, Fauna Grœnlandica, p. 402, 1780 (*non* Linné). *Littorina arctica* Möller, Kroyer's Tidsskrift, vol. iv, p. 82, 1842. (?) *Littorina limata* Lovén, Ofversigt af Kongl. Vet.-Akad. Förhandlingar, vol. iii, p. 154, 1846. *Littorina Peconica* S. Smith, Annals Lyceum Nat. Hist., New York, vol. vii, p. 155, 1860.

Great Egg Harbor, New Jersey, to the Arctic Ocean; Greenland, Spitzbergen, Finmark, and Norway. Very abundant from New York to Cape Cod and northward, wherever *Fuci* grow on rocks between tides; local and less abundant south of Long Island Sound.

Fossil in the Post-Pliocene of Great Britain and Scandinavia.

Should this species prove to be identical with *L. obtusata* (Linné, sp.) of Europe, as there is reason to anticipate, its range will be nearly coincident with that of *L. rudis*, with which it is always found associated on our coast. Several writers have already united the two forms, but no satisfactory comparisons of large series of specimens, from many localities on both coasts, have been made.

LACUNA VINCTA Turton. Plate XXIV, fig. 139. (p. 305.)

Gould, Invert., ed. i, p. 262, figs. 169, 178*, 1841; ed. ii, p. 302, fig. 573. *Turbo vincta* Montagu, Test. Brit., p. 307, Plate 20, fig. 3, (t. Gould). *Trochus divaricatus* Fabricius, Fauna Grönlandica, p. 392, 1780 (*non* Linné). *Lacuna divaricata* Lovén, op. cit., p. 155, 1846; Jeffreys, British Conchology, vol. iii, p. 346.

According to Jeffreys, the following are among the synonyms or varieties of this species: *Turbo canalis* Montagu; *T. quadrifasciata* Mont.; *Phasianella fasciata*, *P. bifasciata*, *P. cornea*, and *P. striata* Brown; *Lacuna solidula* Lovén; *L. labiosa* Lovén; *L. frigida* Lovén.

New York to the Arctic Ocean; Greenland, Iceland, Lapland, Scandinavia, Great Britain, France; on the Pacific coast of America southward to Puget Sound. Long Island Sound, common, but rather local; Watch Hill, Rhode Island, among algæ, in 4 to 5 fathoms; Vineyard

Sound; Buzzard's Bay. Very abundant north of Massachusetts Bay, in Casco Bay, Bay of Fundy, Labrador, etc. Staten Island and Long Island (S. Smith).

Fossil in the Post-Pliocene of northern Great Britain and Scandinavia.

Lacuna neritoidea Gould.

American Journ. of Science, vol. xxxviii, p. 197, 1840; Invert., ed. i, p. 263, fig. 170; ed. ii, p. 303, fig. 574.

This species is a very doubtful inhabitant of this region, having been recorded by no one except Linsley, 1845, who reports it from Long Island Sound (Oyster River and Long Beach, Stratford, Connecticut). I have never been able to find it in the same region, nor has any one else had better success. Linsley's specimens may have been incorrectly named. It occurs in Massachusetts Bay; at Cape Elizabeth, Casco Bay; Grand Menan Island, etc.; northward to Greenland; and on the northern shore of Europe.

LITTORINELLA MINUTA Stimpson. Plate XXIV, fig. 140. (p. 469.)

Researches upon the Hydrobiinæ and Allied Forms, p. 42, May, 1865, in the Smithsonian Miscellaneous Collections. *Turbo minutus* Totten, American Journ. Science, ser. i, vol. xxvi, p. 369, fig. 6, 1834. *Cingula minuta* Gould, Invert., ed. i, p. 265, fig. 171. *Rissoa minuta* Gould, op. cit., ed. ii, p. 298, fig. 566. *Ecrobia minuta* (provisional name) Stimpson, op. cit., p. 42, 1865. ? *Cingula modesta* Lea, Boston Journal of Natural History, vol. v, p. 288, Plate 24, fig. 5.

The tentacles in this species are rather short, scarcely exceeding the breadth of the head, slightly tapering, blunt; the eyes are on low prominences on the outer side of the bases of the tentacles; rostrum large, stout, transversely wrinkled, longer than the tentacles, tapering somewhat, but divided at the end by a deep emargination into two rounded lobes, which are often somewhat expanded. Foot short and broad, subtruncate anteriorly, with the angles broad and but little produced, posterior end broadly rounded.

New Jersey to Nova Scotia and Gulf of Saint Lawrence. Abundant along the brackish and muddy shores of Long Island Sound, Buzzard's Bay, Vineyard Sound, Massachusetts Bay, Casco Bay, and Bay of Fundy.

It is not confined to brackish waters, but often occurs also on the ocean shores, under stones between tides.

LITTORINELLA LÆVIS Verrill.

Cingula lævis Dekay, Natural History of New York, Mollusca, p. 111, Plate 6, fig. 118 (poor), 1843. *Odostomia limnoidea* (Dekay, MSS.), Linsley, Amer. Journ. Science, ser. i, vol. xlviii, p. 284, 1845 (no description). (?)*Rissoa Stimpsoni* S. Smith, Annals Lyceum Nat. Hist., New York, vol. ix, p. 393, fig. 2, 1870.

Long Island Sound, near New Haven. Stratford, Connecticut (Linsley); near New York (Dekay); Greenport, Long Island (S. Smith).

RISSOA ACULEUS Stimpson. Plate XXIV, fig. 141. (p. 306.)

Proc. Boston Soc. Nat. Hist., vol. iv, p. 15, 1851; Shells of New England, p. 34; Gould, Invert., ed. ii, p. 299, fig. 568. *Cingula aculeus* Gould, Invert., ed. i, p. 266, fig. 172, 1841. *Trochus striatellus* Fabricius, Fauna Grönl., p. 393, (*non* Linné). (?)*Rissoa saxatilis* Möller, Index Mollusca Grönl., in Kroyer's Tidsskrift, vol. iv, p. 82, 1843. (?)*Rissoa arctica* Lovén, Ofversigt af Kongl., Vet.-Akad. Förhandlingar, vol. iii, p. 156, 1846.

Long Island Sound to Greenland. New Haven, Connecticut, and vicinity, common. Watch Hill, Rhode Island; Vineyard Sound; Stratford, Connecticut (Linsley); Gull Island (Smith). Common on the shores of Massachusetts Bay, Casco Bay, and Bay of Fundy.

Lovén's *R. arctica* was from Finmark, and, to judge from the descriptions, may not be identical with our species. Mr. Jeffreys regards it as a variety of *R. striata* of Europe. He also unites the American shell with *R. striata*, thus: "The variety *arctica* (under the specific name *aculeus* given to it by Professor Stimpson) inhabits the northern sea-board of the United States." (See British Conchology, vol. iv, p. 38). It is natural to infer that a writer who does not appear to have seen the accurate description and figure of this species published in the well-known work of Dr. Gould, ten years previous to Dr. Stimpson's earliest publications, cannot have devoted much time or attention to the American shells, and therefore his opinions should not have too much weight in such cases.

In reality, our shell differs widely from *R. striata*. It agrees more nearly with the English *R. proxima* (Alder, Forbes and Hanley), but apparently differs from it in the soft parts. The foot in our shell is broadly and slightly rounded anteriorly, with the angles only slightly produced, and tapers backward to a bluntly-rounded posterior end. The tentacles are long, slender, slightly tapering, with blunt tips. The eyes are situated near their bases on the dorso-lateral aspect, and are scarcely elevated above the general surface. The snout is rather long, often a little expanded at the end, and divided by a deep emargination into two lobes, which often, in a dorsal view, show a slight emargination on their outer surface. No opercular cirrus was observed. This species belongs to the genus *Onoba* of H. and A. Adams. The *R. saxatilis* was described by Möller as having the whorls *smooth*, but he refers to *T. striatellus* of Fabricius, which had spiral striations, as in our species.

RISSOA EXARATA Stimpson. (p. 495.)

Proceedings Boston Soc. Nat. Hist., vol. iv, p. 15, 1851; Shells of New England, p. 34, Plate 1, fig. 3, 1851; Gould, Invert., ed. ii, p. 301, fig. 571. *Cingula arenaria* Mighels and Adams, Boston Jour. Nat. Hist., vol. iv, p. 49, Plate 4, fig. 24, 1842 (*non* Montagu, sp.). *Rissoa Mighelsii* Stimpson, Proc. Bost. Soc. Nat. Hist., vol. iv, p. 15, 1851; Shells of New England, p. 34; Gould, Invert., ed. ii, p. 301, (but not figure 570, which is probably *R. sulcosa*).

Stonington, Connecticut, to Gulf of Saint Lawrence. Watch Hill, Rhode Island, 4 to 5 fathoms, among rocks and algæ (white variety); Casco Bay,

6 to 25 fathoms; Bay of Fundy, 4 to 20 fathoms. Fossil in the Post-Pliocene of Canada. This species is usually brownish or chestnut-color, but is also frequently white.

Rissoa eburnea Stimpson, has been recorded (as *Rissoella* (?) *eburnea*) by Dr. G. H. Perkins, from Long Island Sound, near New Haven, but I have seen no undoubted shells of this species from any locality south of Massachusetts Bay. The shell referred to by Dr. Perkins was beach-worn, and may have been some other species. The figure given in the second edition of Gould's Invertebrata (fig. 564, p. 297), does not represent this species. See the figure in Stimpson's Shells of New England, Plate 1, figs. 1, 1*a*. This shell appears to be a *Jeffreysia*.

From Huntington, Long Island, I have seen a shell closely resembling *Rissoa latior* Stimpson, (M. and Adams, sp.), if not identical with it.

SKENEA PLANORBIS. Plate XXIV, fig. 142. (p. 383.)

Forbes and Hanley, British Mollusca, vol iii, p. 156, Plate 74, figs. 1–3, and Plate G, G, figs. 1 and 1*a* (animal); Stimpson, Shells of New England, p. 35; Gould, Invert., ed. ii, p. 296, fig. 563. *Turbo planorbis* Fabricius, Fauna Grönl., p. 394, 1780. *Skenea serpuloides* Gould, Invert., ed. i, 247, fig. 189.

Long Island Sound to Greenland, Iceland, Spitzbergen, Scandinavia; and northern and eastern coasts of Europe generally, to England and France. Near New Haven, Connecticut, common; Watch Hill, Rhode Island; Cuttyhunk Island. Very common on all rocky shores in Massachusetts Bay, Casco Bay, and Bay of Fundy. Fossil in the Post-Pliocene of Scotland and Scandinavia.

STYLIFER STIMPSONII Verrill. (p. 460.)

American Journal of Science, vol. iii, pp. 210 and 283, 1872.

Shell white, short, swollen, broad oval; spire short, rapidly enlarging. Whorls four or five, the last one forming a large part of the shell; convex, rounded, with the suture impressed, surface smooth, or with very faint striæ of growth; a slightly impressed revolving line just below the suture. Aperture large and broad. Length about .15 of an inch; breadth, .12.

Parasitic on the dorsal surface of *Strongylocentrotus Dröbachiensis*, from off New Jersey, in 35 fathoms (Captain Gedney); and Saint George's Bank, north latitude 41° 25′, west longitude 65° 50′, 3″, in 60 fathoms, (S. I. Smith).

EULIMA OLEACEA Kurtz and Stimpson. Plate XXIV, fig. 149. (p. 418.)

Proceedings Boston Soc. Nat. Hist., vol. iv, p. 115, 1851; Stimpson, Shells of New England, p. 39, Plate 1, fig 6, 1851; Gould, Invert., ed. ii, p. 332, fig. 603.

Vineyard Sound to Beaufort, North Carolina. In Vineyard Sound it is not uncommon on *Thyone Briareus*, in 4 to 10 fathoms. Buzzard's Bay (Stimpson).

ODOSTOMIA PRODUCTA Gould. Plate XXIV, fig. 143. (p. 418.)

Invert., ed. i, p. 270, fig. 175, 1841; ed. ii, p. 325, fig. 593. *Jaminia producta* Adams, Boston Journal Nat. Hist., vol. iii, p. 322, Plate 3, fig. 8, 1840.

Vineyard Sound to New Jersey.

ODOSTOMIA FUSCA Gould. Plate XXIV, fig. 144. (p. 307.)

Invert., ed. i, p. 270, fig. 176; ed. ii, p. 325, fig. 594. *Pyramis fusca* Adams, op. cit., vol ii, p. 282, Plate 4, fig. 9, 1839.

Cape Cod to New Jersey.

This species is referred both to *Turbonilla* and *Odostomia* by H. and A. Adams, in the same work (Genera Moll., pp. 231, 232).

ODOSTOMIA DEALBATA Stimpson.

Smithsonian Check-List, p. 5, 1860; Gould, Invert., ed. ii, p. 327, fig. 595. *Chemnitzia dealbata* Stimpson, Proc., Boston Soc. Nat. Hist., vol. iv, p. 114, 1851; Shells of New England, p. 41.

Long Island Sound to Boston Harbor. New Haven, Connecticut (Perkins). Boston (Stimpson).

ODOSTOMIA BISUTURALIS Gould. (p. 307.)

Invert., ed. ii, p. 327, (not fig. 597). *Turritella bisuturalis* Say, Journ. Acad. Nat. Sci., Philadelphia, vol. ii, p. 244, 1822. *Chemnitzia bisuturalis* Stimpson, Shells of New England, p. 42. *Jaminia exigua* Couthouy, Boston Journ. Nat. Hist., vol. ii, Plate 1, fig. 7, 1838. *Odostomia exigua* Gould, Invert., ed. i, p. 272, fig. 177.

New Jersey to Massachusetts Bay. Boston (Say); Chelsea (Couthouy); Staten Island; Greenport, and Huntington, Long Island (S. Smith). Not uncommon in Long Island Sound, Vineyard Sound, and Buzzard's Bay.

The figure (597) in the second edition of Gould's Invertebrata does not represent this species, but apparently a variety of *O. trifida*.

ODOSTOMIA TRIFIDA Gould. Plate XXIV, figs. 145, 146. (p. 307.)

Invert., ed. i, p. 274, fig. 179, 1841; ed. ii, p. 328, fig. 598. *Actæon trifidus* Totten, Amer. Journ. Science, ser. i, vol. xxvi, p. 368, Plate 1, figs. 4, *a*, *b*, 1834.

New Jersey to Massachusetts Bay. Staten Island (S. Smith); Lynn, Massachusetts (Haskell). Common in Long Island Sound, Vineyard Sound, and Buzzard's Bay.

ODOSTOMIA IMPRESSA Stimpson. Plate XXIV, fig. 147. (p. 418.)

American Journ. Science, vol. xxiv, p. 444, 1860; Gould, Invert., ed. ii, p. 330, fig. 600. *Odostomia insculpta* Dekay, Nat. Hist. N. Y., Mollusca, p. 115, Plate 31, fig. 297, 1843. *Turritella impressa* Say, Journ. Acad. Nat. Sci., Philadelphia, vol. ii, p. 244, 1822; Binney's Say, p. 84. *Chemnitzia impressa* Stimpson, Shells of New England, p. 42, 1851.

Long Island Sound to South Carolina. Near New Haven, Connecticut, rare. East River (Dekay); Maryland (Say); Beaufort, North Carolina (Stimpson, Coues).

ODOSTOMIA SEMINUDA Gould. Plate XXIV, fig. 148. (p. 418.)

Invert., ed. i, p. 273, fig. 178, 1841; ed. ii, p. 329, fig. 599. *Jaminia seminuda* C. B. Adams, Boston Journal Nat. Hist. vol. ii, p. 280, Plate 4, fig. 13, 1839. *Chemnitzia seminuda* Stimpson, Shells of New England, p. 42, 1851. *Turbonilla seminuda* H. and A. Adams, Genera Moll., vol. i, p. 231.

Massachusetts Bay to South Carolina. Common in Vineyard Sound and Buzzard's Bay, in 2 to 10 fathoms; Long Island Sound, less common. Massachusetts Bay (Stimpson). Greenport and Huntington, Long Island (S. Smith). Fort Macon, North Carolina (Coues).

TURBONILLA INTERRUPTA Adams. (p. 418.)

H. and A. Adams, Genera, vol. i, p. 231, 1858; Gould, Invert., ed. ii, p. 231, fig. 601 (bad figure). *Turritella interrupta* Totten, Amer. Jour. Science, ser. i, vol. xxviii, p. 352, fig. 7, 1835; Gould, Invert., ed. i, p. 268, fig. 173 (incorrect).

Cape Cod to South Carolina. Quite common in Vineyard Sound and Buzzard's Bay, in 3 to 10 fathoms; Long Island Sound, off Thimble Islands and New Haven, 3 to 5 fathoms, rather rare. Huntington and Greenport (S. Smith). Dartmouth, Massachusetts (Adams). Newport, Rhode Island (Totten). Fort Macon, North Carolina (Coues).

I have received from Prof. E. S. Morse specimens of this shell obtained from mud in the harbor of Portland, Maine, but they are dead and bleached. I am not aware that it has been found living so far north on our coast. Fossil in the Post-Pliocene of South Carolina.

Lovén records this species as from the coast of Norway, but possibly his shell is a different species, or else a variety of *T. rufa* of Southern Europe, which is certainly very closely related to our species, and is considered the same by Jeffreys. If so, the name given by Totten has precedence of *rufa* (Philippi, 1836). Farther and more extensive comparisons must be made before the identity of the two forms can be established.

The figure given in the first edition of Gould's Invertebrata, and copied in the second edition, does not correctly represent this shell, and was, perhaps, drawn from some other species, for it does not agree with Gould's description, which is accurate. The spire, as represented, is too acute and too rapidly tapered; the last or body whorl is too large; the aperture has not the right form; and the peculiar sculpture is not brought out at all. Totten's figure, though somewhat coarse, is characteristic.

TURBONILLA ELEGANS Verrill. Plate XXIV, fig. 155. (p. 418.)

American Journal of Science, ser. iii, vol. iii, pp. 210, 282, Plate 6, fig. 4, 1872.

Shell light yellowish, elongated, moderately slender, acute. Whorls ten or more, well rounded, not distinctly flattened; suture rather deeply impressed; surface somewhat lustrous, with numerous rounded vertical costæ, narrower than the concave interspaces, fading out below the middle of the last whorl; and with numerous fine revolving grooves, which are interrupted on the costæ, but distinct in the intervals; on the upper whorls there are about five; and on the lower half of the last whorl usually five or six distinct and continuous ones. Aperture broad oval, anteriorly rounded and slightly effuse; outer lip thin, sharp; columella nearly straight at base within, slightly revolute outwardly, regularly curved anteriorly where it joins the outer lip, and not forming an angle with it. The epidermis is thin, light yellow, sometimes with a darker, yellowish, revolving band on the middle of the last whorls, and also with the revolving striæ darker.

Vineyard Sound, 6 to 10 fathoms; Long Island Sound, near New Haven, 5 fathoms.

TURBONILLA AREOLATA Verrill, sp. nov.

Shell small, slender, with eight or more whorls, slightly obelisk-shaped, owing to the more rapid narrowing of the upper whorls; apical or nuclear whorl very small, reversed; the other whorls are moderately convex, somewhat flattened in the middle, and crossed by numerous rather crowded, narrow, transverse costæ, of which there are twenty-five or more on the lower whorls; interstices interrupted by numerous rather conspicuous, revolving, impressed lines, of which there are about six on the upper whorls; these divide the interstices into series of pretty regular, small, squarish pits, but do not cross the costæ; the body-whorl is subangulated below the middle, where the costæ disappear, below which the base is marked only by fine revolving lines; suture impressed. Aperture oval, acute posteriorly, rounded and slightly spreading anteriorly; outer lip sharp, thin, slightly angulated below the middle, rounded and slightly effuse anteriorly; columella smooth, somewhat curved, scarcely forming an angle at its junction with the outer lip. Length, 4^{mm}; breadth, 1.5^{mm}.

Long Island Sound, near New Haven.

The crowded costæ and numerous spiral lines produce a closely cancellated appearance, which is sufficient to distinguish this from the two preceding species. From the following it differs much in sculpture, form, shape of aperture, and columella, and especially in the minute size of the apical whorl.

TURBONILLA COSTULATA Verrill, sp. nov.

Shell small, long conical, translucent, glossy white, banded faintly with pale brown, subacute, with a relatively large, smooth, reversed apical whorl; the other whorls are six or more, flattened, and but slightly convex, enlarging regularly, crossed by numerous straight, smooth, rounded, transverse costæ, of which there are upward of twenty on the lower whorls; interstices rather narrower than the costæ, deep, and interrupted by numerous very minute revolving lines, which are scarcely visible under an ordinary pocket-lens, and do not cross the costæ; suture impressed. The body-whorl is subangulated below the middle, the costæ vanishing at the angulation; the base is covered with numerous microscopic revolving lines; on the body-whorl there are two revolving bands of pale brown, one above and one below the angulation. Aperture long ovate, acute posteriorly, a little angulated on the outer side, rounded and slightly prolonged anteriorly. Outer lip thin and sharp, round and slightly effuse anteriorly; columella smooth, nearly straight, but scarcely forming an angle where it joins the outer lip. Length, 4^{mm}; breadth, 1.5^{mm}.

Somewhat resembles *T. interrupta*, but the costæ are more crowded, the spiral lines are very much finer and more numerous, and the nuclear-whorl is much larger.

Long Island Sound, near New Haven, Conn.

TURBONILLA STRICTA Verrill, sp. nov.

Shell white, subulate, very acute, with a very minute reversed apical whorl; whorls ten, besides the nucleus, gradually and regularly enlarging, flattened or only very slightly convex, crossed by straight, obtuse, transverse costæ, of which there are about sixteen or eighteen on the lower whorls; the two upper whorls are nearly smooth; suture impressed. Aperture irregularly oblong-ovate, acute posteriorly, rounded anteriorly; outer lip flattened, thickened internally, in mature shells, and minutely crenulate within; columella smooth, nearly straight, thickened, forming an angle where it joins the outer lip. Length, 4.5^{mm}; breadth, 1^{mm}.

Long Island Sound, off New Haven, Connecticut.

This is probably the shell recorded from this region as *T. nivea* (Stimpson, sp.) by Dr. G. H. Perkins. It differs from the *nivea* in the form of the aperture and lip, and in being smaller and much more acute, though having the same number of whorls.

TURBONILLA EQUALIS Verrill.

Turritella æqualis Say, Journal Acad. Nat. Sciences, vol. v, p. 208, 1826; Binney's Say, p. 119.

"Shell subulate, white; volutions ten, each with about twenty-two, transverse, elevated, obtuse, equal lines, with interstitial grooves of the same diameter; suture distinct, impressed; aperture rounded at base, and destitute of any distinct emargination. Length one-fifth of an inch." (Say.)

My specimens agree well with the above description. The shell is very slender and acute, with a small distinctly reversed apical whorl; the remaining nine whorls are somewhat flattened, and all are crossed by obtuse, transverse costæ, which are a little oblique, especially at the upper ends, close to the sutures; on the body-whorl there are about twenty, but fewer on the upper ones; at the base of the body-whorl they vanish, leaving it smooth; the interstices between the costæ are deep and apparently smooth. The aperture is round ovate, well rounded or sub-circular anteriorly; the inner lip having a raised and thin margin. Length, 4.5mm; breadth, 1.25mm. Vineyard Sound, 6 to 8 fathoms.

Menestho albula Möller (Fabricius, sp.), was recorded by Linsley (as *Pyramis striatula* Couth.) from the stomachs of ducks at Bridgeport, Connecticut. It has not been found south of Cape Cod by any one else, and as it is a rare deep-water shell on our northern coast, it is not likely to have been obtained by ducks. It is found in Massachusetts Bay, Casco Bay, Bay of Fundy, and northward to Greenland. Linsley's shell may have been *Odostomia impressa*.

SCALARIA LINEATA Say. Plate XXI, fig. 123. (p. 418.)

Journal Acad. Nat. Sciences, Philadelphia, vol. ii, p. 242, 1822; Binney's Say, pp. 83, 180, Plate 27, lower left figure; Gould, Invert., ed. i, p. 250; ed. ii, p. 312, fig. 580.

Vineyard Sound, Buzzard's Bay, and Long Island Sound; southward to South Carolina and Georgia. Fossil in the Post-Pliocene of North and South Carolina.

SCALARIA MULTISTRIATA Say. Plate XXI, fig. 122. (p. 418.)

Journ. Acad. Nat. Sciences, Philadelphia, vol. v, p. 208, 1826; Amer. Conchology, iii, Plate 27; Binney's Say, pp. 119, 180, Plate 27, lower right figure; Gould, Invert., ed. ii, p. 313, fig. 581.

Vineyard Sound, Buzzard's Bay and Long Island Sound; southward to Florida. Fossil in the Post-Pliocene of South Carolina.

SCALARIA ANGULATA Say.

American Conchology, iii, Plate 27, upper figures, 1831, as a variety of *S. clathrus*; Sowerby, Thes. Conch., part iv, p. 86, Plate 32, fig. 5, 1844. *Scalaria Humphreysii* Kiener, Iconographie des Coquilles Viv., p. 15, Plate 5, fig. 16, 1838–9.

Connecticut to Florida. Stonington (Linsley); Greenport, Long Island (S. Smith). Outer beach at Great Egg Harbor, New Jersey (A. E. V.); Fort Macon and Beaufort, North Carolina, common, (Stimpson, Coues); South Carolina (Kiener). Rare and perhaps accidental north of New Jersey.

SCALARIA GRŒNLANDICA Perry.

Conch., 1811, (t. Mörch); Sowerby, Thesaurus Conch., part iv, p. 101, Plate 34. figs. 105, 106, 1844; Gould, Invert., ed. i, p. 249, fig. 170*; ed. ii, p. 314, fig, 582. *Turbo clathrus Grœnlandicus* Chemnitz, Conch., xi, t. 1878, 1879 (t. Gould). *Scalaria subulata* Couthouy, Boston Jour. Nat. Hist., vol. ii, p. 93, Plate 3, fig. 4, 1838.

Cape Cod to the Arctic Ocean, and northern coasts of Europe, southward to Bergen. South Shoals, off Nantucket (Agassiz, t. Stimpson). Common in Casco Bay and Bay of Fundy, from 10 to 109 fathoms. Fossil in the Post-Plicoene of Nantucket, rare, (Desor); and in the Red-Crag, Norwich-Crag, and later deposits in Great Britain.

Janthina fragilis Lamarck; Gould, Invert., ed. i, p. 240; ed. ii, p. 277. This has been found cast ashore at Nantucket, but probably does not occur living so far north. It inhabits the Gulf Stream farther south.

RHIPIDOGLOSSA.

MARGARITA OBSCURA Gould. Plate XXIV, fig. 156. (p. 508.)

Invert., ed. i, p. 253, fig. 171*, 1841; ed. ii, p. 283, fig. 545. *Turbo obscurus* Couthouy, Boston Journ. Nat. Hist., vol. ii, p. 100, Plate 3, fig. 2, 1838.

Stonington, Connecticut, to Labrador. Rare and confined to the outer waters south of Cape Cod; off Martha's Vineyard, 20 to 25 fathoms. Stonington, from haddock's stomach, (Linsley). Common in Massachusetts Bay, Casco Bay, and in the Bay of Fundy, from extreme low-water mark to 100 fathoms. East of Saint George's Bank, in 430 fathoms, (S. I. Smith).

Margarita ornata Dekay, N. Y. Mollusca, p. 107, Plate 6, fig. 104, 1843, was described as occurring in the vicinity of New York, but I have not met with it in Long Island Sound.

DOCOGLOSSA.

ACMÆA TESTUDINALIS Forbes and Hanley. Plate XXIV, figs. 159, 159*a*. (p. 307.)

British Mollusca, vol. ii, p. 434, Plate 62, figs. 8, 9, and Plate A A, fig. 2; Carpenter, Report of British Association for 1856, pp. 219, 366, 1857; Dall (subgenus, *Collisella* Dall), American Journal of Conchology, vol. vi, p. 249, 1871. *Lottia testudinalis* Gould, Invert., ed. i, p. 153, fig. 12. *Tectura testudinalis* Gould, Invert., ed. ii, p. 267, fig. 529. *Patella testudinalis* Müller, Prodromus Zool. Danica, p. 227, 1776.

Variety *alveus*. (fig. 159 *a*). *Patella alveus* Conrad, Journal Acad. Nat. Sciences, Philadelphia, vol. vi, Plate 11, fig. 20, 1831. *Lottia alveus* Gould, Invert., ed. i, p. 154, fig. 13. *Tectura alveus* Gould, Invert., ed. ii, p. 269, fig. 530.

Long Island Sound to the Arctic Ocean; circumpolar. It extends southward on the European coasts to Southern Sweden, England, and Ireland; in the North Pacific, southward to Sitka and the Island of Jesso, Japan. It is comparatively rare and local south of Cape Cod; at New Haven, very rare; Watch Hill, Rhode Island; Martha's Vineyard, Cuttyhunk, and adjacent islands. Huntington and Greenport, Long Island (S. Smith). Fossil in the Post-Pliocene of Labrador (Packard); Greenland, Scandinavia, and Great Britain.

POLYPLACOPHORA.

CHÆTOPLEURA APICULATA Carpenter. Plate XXV, fig. 167.

Chiton apiculatus Say, Amer. Conch., part vii, appendix, (?) 1834; Binney's Say, p. 231; Gould, Invert., ed. i, p. 146, fig. 20; ed. ii, p. 258, fig. 522. *Leptochiton apiculatus*, this Report, p. 399.

Cape Cod to Eastern and Western Florida. Common in Vineyard Sound and Buzzard's Bay, in 3 to 12 fathoms, shelly. Off New London, Connecticut (coll. T. M. Prudden).

Dr. P. P. Carpenter informs me that this species belongs to the genus *Chætopleura* of Gray (*non* Adams).

TRACHYDERMON RUBER Carpenter. Plate XXV, fig. 166.

Chiton ruber Lowe, Zoöl. Journ., vol. ii, p. 101, Plate 5, fig. 2 (t. Gould); Gould, Invert., ed. i, p. 149, fig. 24; ed. ii, p. 260, fig. 523. *Leptochiton ruber* H. and A. Adams, Genera, vol i, p. 473; this Report, p. 399.

Off New London, Connecticut, to the Arctic Ocean and northern coasts of Europe. Rare and local in the colder outer waters south of Cape Cod. Off New London, 8 fathoms; off Watch Hill, 5 fathoms. Stonington (Linsley). Very common in Casco Bay and Bay of Fundy, from low-water mark to 40 fathoms.

Dr. Carpenter assures me that this species should be referred to *Trachydermon.*

Linsley records "*Chiton fulminatus* Couth." (= *C. marmoreus* Gould, Invert., ed. ii, p. 261, fig. 524) as from cod-fish taken off Stonington, Connecticut, but as it has not been confirmed from south of Cape Cod, this must be regarded as a doubtful identification. This species is found from Massachusetts Bay northward to the Arctic Ocean and northern coasts of Europe. It is common in the Bay of Fundy, from low-water mark to 40 fathoms, on "nullipore" (*Lithothamnion*).

"*Chiton albus*" (= *Trachydermon albus*, t. Carpenter) has been mentioned as from this region, but probably erroneously. White specimens of *C. apiculata* are often mistaken for it, when superficially examined. The genuine *albus* is a northern species, with about the same distribution as the preceding. It is abundant in the Bay of Fundy, from low-water to 80 fathoms.

PULMONATA.

MELAMPUS BIDENTATUS Say. Plate XXV, figs. 169, 169*a*. (p. 463.)

Journal Acad. Nat. Sciences, Philadelphia, vol. ii, p. 245, 1822; Gould, Invert., ed. ii, p. 467, fig. 721. *Auricula bidentata* Gould, Invert., ed. i, p. 117, fig. 131. *Melampus corneus* Stimpson, Shells of New England, p. 51, 1851.

Massachusetts Bay to Florida, and along the northern shores of the Gulf of Mexico to Texas. Very common on the shores of Vineyard Sound, Buzzard's Bay, Long Island, and Long Island Sound. Fossil in the Post-Pliocene of South Carolina.

ALEXIA MYOSOTIS Pfeiffer. Plate XXV, fig. 168. (p. 383.)

Pfeiffer, Mon. Auric. Viv., p. 148, (t. Binney); Gould, Invert., ed. ii, p. 463, figs. 718, 719. *Auricula myosotis* Draparnaud, Tabl. Moll. Fr., p. 53. *Auricula denticulata* Gould, Invert., ed. i, p. 199, fig. 129 (*non* Montfort).

New Jersey to Nova Scotia; also on the Atlantic and Mediterranean coasts of Europe. It is common at Eastport, Maine; Portland, Maine; and at the mouth of West River, near New Haven, Connecticut; also near New York City.

TECTIBRANCHIATA.

BULLA SOLITARIA Say. Plate XXV, fig. 161. (p. 371.)

Journal Acad. Nat. Sciences, Philadelphia, vol. ii, p. 245, 1822; Binney's Say, p. 84; Gould, Invert., ed. i, p. 162, fig. 92; ed. ii, p. 222, fig. 513. *Bulla insculpta* Totten, American Journ. Science, vol. xxviii, p. 350, fig. 4, 1835.

Massachusetts Bay to South Carolina. Common in the muddy lagoons and salt-ponds along the shores of Vineyard Sound, Buzzard's Bay, and Long Island Sound. Abundant in a small pond near Holmes' Hole; in New Haven Harbor, in ditches near Fort Hale.

CYLICHNA ORYZA Stimpson. Plate XXV, fig. 161. (p. 432.)

Smithsonian Check List, p. 4, 1860; Gould, Invert., ed. ii, p. 221, fig. 512. *Bulla oryza* Totten, Amer. Jour. Science, vol. xxviii, p. 350, fig. 5, 1835; Gould, Invert., ed. i, p. 168, fig. 93.

Cape Cod to South Carolina. Not uncommon in Vineyard Sound, Buzzard's Bay, and Long Island Sound. This species was recorded as from Casco Bay by Dr. Mighels, but as this habitat has not been confirmed subsequently, it was probably based on an erroneous identification. Fossil in the Post-Pliocene of Canada (Dawson).

CYLICHNA ALBA Lovén. Plate XXV, fig. 163. (p. 508.)

Ofversigt af Kongl. Vet.-Akad. Förhandlingar, vol. iii, p. 142, 1843; Gould, Invert., ed. ii, p. 220, fig. 511. *Volvaria alba* Brown, Ill. Conch. G. B., iii, p. 3, figs. 43, 44. *Bulla triticea* Couthouy, Boston Jour. Nat. Hist., vol. ii, p. 88, Plate 2, fig. 8, 1838; Gould, Invert., ed. i, p. 165, fig. 98.

Near Block Island, northward to the Arctic Ocean; northern coasts of Europe to Bergen; and on the northwest coast of America, south to Sitka. Fossil in the Post-Pliocene of Canada and Great Britain.

Most of the specimens of this shell dredged in the Bay of Fundy are opaque, yellowish brown or chestnut color, but those from Casco Bay are nearly all clear white and translucent, although of equal size.

UTRICULUS CANALICULATUS. Plate XXV, fig. 160. (p. 432.)

Stimpson, Smithsonian Check-List, p. 4, 1860; Gould, Invert., ed. ii, p. 219, fig. 510. *Volvaria canaliculata* Say, Jour. Acad. Nat. Sciences, Philadelphia, vol. v, p. 211, 1826; Binney's Say, p. 121. *Bulla canaliculata* Gould, Invert., ed. i, p. 166, fig. 97. *Tornatina canaliculata* H. and A. Adams, Genera, vol. ii, p. 13.

Massachusetts Bay to South Carolina. Common in Buzzard's Bay and Vineyard Sound, in 2 to 8 fathoms; less common in Long Island Sound. Fort Macon, North Carolina, abundant, (Dr. Yarrow). Fossil in the Post-Pliocene of North and South Carolina; and the Pliocene of South Carolina.

AMPHISPHYRA DEBILIS Verrill. Plate XXV, fig. 162. (p. 432.)

Bulla debilis Gould, Amer. Journ. Science, ser. i, vol. xxxviii, p. 196, 1840; Invert., ed. i, p. 164, fig. 95, 1841. *Diaphana debilis* Gould, Invert., ed. ii, p. 216, fig. 507. *Bulla pellucida* Brown, 1844. *Amphisphyra pellucida* Lovén, op. cit., p. 143, 1846. *Bulla hyalina* Turton, Mag. Nat. Hist., vol. vii, p. 353, 1834, (t. Jeffreys), (*non* Gmelin).

Cape Cod to the Arctic Ocean; and on the northern coasts of Europe, southward to Great Britain, Madeira, etc. Stonington, Connecticut, from stomach of cod (Linsley). Not uncommon in Casco Bay and Bay of Fundy, and northward, in 6 to 50 fathoms. Very rare south of Cape Cod. Fossil in the Post-Pliocene of Canada, Great Britain, Norway, and Sweden.

ACTÆON PUNCTO-STRIATA Stimpson. Plate XXV, fig. 165.

Shells of New England, p. 51, 1851; H. and A. Adams, Genera, vol. ii, p. 5. *Tornatella puncto-striata* C. B. Adams, Boston Jour. Nat. Hist., vol. iii, p. 323, Plate 3, fig. 9, 1840; Gould, Invert., ed. i, p. 245, fig. 188; ed. ii, p. 224, fig. 515.

Cape Cod to South Carolina. Vineyard Sound, and Buzzard's Bay, not uncommon; Long Island Sound, rare; Huntington and Greenport, Long Island (S. Smith).

DORIDELLA Verrill.

Body smooth, oval, convex. Dorsal tentacles retractile, without sheaths. Head prominent, the lateral angles prolonged anteriorly as short oral palpi or tentacles. Foot broad, cordate. Branchiæ tufted, situated near the posterior end, on the right side, in the groove between the mantle and foot.

DORIDELLA OBSCURA Verrill. Plate XXV, figs. 173 *a*, *b*. (p. 400.)

American Journal of Science, vol. 1, p. 408, figs. 2, 3, November, 1870.

Body broad oval, 7.5^{mm} long and 5^{mm} broad; back convex, smooth. Foot broad, cordate in front. Oral disk broad, emarginate or with concave outline in front; the angles somewhat produced, forming short, obtusely pointed, tentacle-like organs, which in extension project beyond the front edge of the mantle. Dorsal tentacles small, stout, retractile. The branchiæ consist of a tuft of slender filaments, usually concealed by the edge of the foot. Color of body dark brown, lighter toward the edge, as if covered with nearly confluent blackish or brown spots, the whitish ground-color showing between them; foot, oral disk, and dorsal tentacles white; the central part of the body, beneath, with a three-lobed yellow spot due to the internal organs. Young specimens are flesh-color or yellowish brown above, specked with darker brown.

Vineyard Sound and Long Island Sound to Great Egg Harbor, New Jersey. Savin Rock, at low-water, under stones; off South End, 4 to 5 fathoms, shelly.

NUDIBRANCHIATA.

DORIS BIFIDA Verrill. Plate XXV, fig. 176. (page 307.)

American Journal of Science, vol. 1, p. 406, 1870.

Outline broad oval, widest anteriorly, about 25^{mm} long by 12^{mm} broad, in extension; back very convex, mantle covered with numerous, scattered, small but prominent, pointed papillæ. Tentacles rather long, thickest in the middle, the outer half strongly plicated with about twenty folds, but with a smooth tip, the base surrounded by small papillæ. Gills retractile into a single cavity, united together by a partial web, deeply frilled, much subdivided, bipinnate, the subdivisions fine and slender. Foot very broad, in extension projecting back beyond the mantle about a quarter of an inch, slightly tapering, rounded and slightly notched at the end. Oral disk or veil crescent-shaped, the front a little prominent, the sides extended backward, and forming a curve continuous with that of the foot.

Color purplish brown, sprinkled with white specks; tentacles deep brown, specked with white, tips yellowish; gills purplish at base, the edges and tips usually yellow; foot similar in color to mantle, but lighter.

Long Island Sound, at Savin Rock, near New Haven, to Eastport, Maine, under stones, at low-water mark.

ONCHIDORIS PALLIDA Verrill. (p. 495.)

American Journal of Science, vol. 1, p. 403, 1870; vol. iii, p. 212, 1872. *Doris pallida* Ag. MSS.; Stimpson, Invert. of Grand Manan, p. 26, 1853; Gould, Invert., ed. ii, p. 229, Plate 20, figs. 284, 287, 288, 291.

Off Cuttyhunk Island; Massachusetts Bay; Casco Bay; Bay of Fundy. In Eastport Harbor, not uncommon, from low-water mark to 30 fathoms.

POLYCERA LESSONII D'Orbigny. (p. 400.)

Magazine de Zoöl., vol. vii, p. 5, Plate 105 (t. Gould); Alder and Hancock, Brit. Nud. Moll., Fam. 1, Plate 24; Gould, Invert., ed. ii, p. 226, Plate 17, figs. 242--248. *Doris illuminata* Gould, Invert., ed. i, p. 4, 1841.

Long Island Sound to Labrador; European coasts, from Sweden to France and Great Britain. Savin Rock, near New Haven, Connecticut, at low-water, and off South End in 4 to 5 fathoms; Watch Hill, Rhode Island, 3 to 6 fathoms. Common in Casco Bay and Bay of Fundy, from low-water mark to 20 fathoms.

DENDRONOTUS ARBORESCENS Ald. and Hancock. (p. 495.)

British Nud. Moll., Fam. 3, Plate 3, 1850; Gould, Invert., ed. ii, p. 234, Plate 22, figs. 311–313. *Doris arborescens* Müller, Zoöl. Dan. Prod., p. 229, 1776; Fabricius, Fauna Grönl., p. 346, 1780. *Tritonia arborescens* Cuvier; Gould, Invert., ed. i, p. 5. *Tritonia Reynoldsii* Couthouy, Boston Journ. Nat. Hist., vol. ii, p. 74, Plate 2, figs. 1–4, 1838.

Watch Hill, Rhode Island, in 4 to 5 fathoms, common on *Laminaria* among *Obeliæ;* northward to Greenland; on the European coasts south to Great Britain and France; Sitka (Middendorff). Very common in the Bay of Fundy and Casco Bay, from above low-water mark to 60 fathoms. Rare and local south of Massachusetts Bay.

DOTO CORONATA Lovén. Plate XXV, fig. 170. (p. 400.)

Arch. Scand. Nat., p. 151 (t. Stimpson); Öfvers. af Kongl. Vet.-Akad. Förhandlingar, vol. iii, p. 139, 1846; Alder and Hancock, Brit. Nud. Moll., Fam. 3, Plate 6; Gould, Invert., ed. ii, p. 236, Plate 16, figs. 233–237. *Doris coronata* Gmelin, Syst. Nat., p. 3105, 1790.

New Jersey to Labrador; on the northern European coasts, southward to Great Britain, Holland, and France. Great Egg Harbor, New Jersey, 1 fathom, (A. E. V. and S. I. Smith); Long Island Sound, near New Haven; off Gay Head, Martha's Vineyard; off Watch Hill, Rhode Island, 4 to 5 fathoms, on *Obelia.* Common in Massachusetts Bay, Casco Bay, and Bay of Fundy, from low-water mark to 15 fathoms.

Æolis papillosa Lovén. (p. 495.)

Öfvers. af Kongl. Vet.-Akad. Förh., vol. iii, p. 139, 1846; Gould, Invert., ed. ii, p. 238, fig. 518, and Plate 18, figs. 257–263. *Limax papillosus* Linné, Syst. Nat., ed. xii, vol. i, p. 1082, 1767. *Æolis farinacea* Gould, MSS.; Stimpson, Invert. Grand Manan, p. 25, 1853.

Rhode Island to the Arctic Ocean; northern coasts of Europe to Great Britain. Rare south of Cape Cod; Watch Hill, among roots of *Laminariæ*; very common in Casco Bay and Bay of Fundy, from above low-water mark to 20 fathoms.

Æolis, or Montagua. Species undetermined. (p. 495.)

A species about an inch long, with bright red, fusiform branchiæ, arranged in seven or eight transverse clusters on each side. Foot with prominent and acute auricles anteriorly.

Off Gay Head, 4 to 5 fathoms, rocks.

Montagua pilata Verrill. (p. 383.)

Æolis pilata Gould, Invert., ed. ii, p. 243, Plate 19, figs. 270, 277, 279, 281, 1870. *Æolidia pilata*, this Report, p. 383. (See errata.)

Long Island Sound to Massachusetts Bay. Abundant in New Haven Harbor, on piles of Long Wharf.

Montagua vermifera Verrill.

Æolis vermiferus S. Smith, Annals Lyc. Nat. Hist., N. Y., vol. ix, p. 391, 1870.

Greenport, Long Island (Smith). Long Island Sound, off Thimble Islands, 4 to 5 fathoms, among rocks.

The specimens from Thimble Islands differ somewhat from the original description. They were about half an inch long; moderately stout; the foot lanceolate, rapidly tapered posteriorly to a point, but not produced far beyond the branchiæ, nor slender-pointed; anteriorly the angles are somewhat produced, triangular, and pointed, their length equal to about half the breadth of the foot. Head rounded; tentacles rather stout, obtuse; the oral longer than the dorsal ones; the latter are transversely wrinkled. The branchial papillæ are fusiform, moderately stout, obtuse, arranged in about twelve transverse rows on each side, forming six clusters, the two rows forming each cluster separated by a narrow elliptical naked space, narrower than the spaces between the clusters; in each anterior row there are six or seven papillæ, the upper ones larger, the lowest short and blunt. Foot translucent, white, with a flake-white streak on the upper side posteriorly; body pale yellowish, minutely specked with greenish and flake-white; back of the dorsal tentacles there is, on each side, an orange patch, and there are others along the back; papillæ dark brown internally, irregularly specked with flake-white externally, forming toward the end an ill-defined white ring; the extreme tips are white; tentacles similar in color to the body.

MONTAGUA GOULDII Verrill, sp. nov.

Body elongated, rather slender; foot with the anterior angles only slightly prominent, and obtusely rounded; posteriorly it tapers gradually to an elongated slender point. Tentacles long, slender, not serrate, the dorsal ones a little longer than the oral; eyes small, black; branchial papillæ fusiform, moderately stout, grouped in eight or more tranverse rows on each side, the rows being grouped two by two, so as to form transverse clusters, with two rows each, the rows of the clusters being separated by spaces narrower than those between the clusters. Color of body light yellow or tinged with pale orange; tentacles pale orange, with a flake-white stripe on the posterior surface; branchial papillæ dark brown or reddish brown internally, with a ring of opaque white close to the tips.

Length about 20mm.

Off Thimble Island, in 4 to 5 fathoms, with the preceding species.

This is nearly allied to *M. Mananensis* Stimpson, but the angles of the foot are less produced and not acute, and the proportions of the tentacles are different. Dr. Gould seems to have confounded this species with *M. diversa* (*Æolis diversa* Couth.), and one of his figures (Plate 19, fig. 280) apparently represents this species; but certainly does not represent *M. diversa*, which was originally described and figured as having the oral tentacles longer than the dorsals (See Gould's figs. 267, 268, copied from Couthouy.)

CORYPHELLA GYMNOTA Verrill.

> *Eolis* (*Tergipes*) *gymnota* Couthouy, Boston Jour. Nat. Hist., vol. ii, p. 69, Plate 1, fig. 3, 1838; Gould, Invert., ed. i, p. 7; ed. ii, p. 249, Plate 16, figs. 238–241. *Montagua gymnota* H. and A. Adams, Genera, vol. ii, p. 74. *Cavolina gymnota*, this Report, p. 383. (See errata.)

Wood's Hole to Boston, Massachusetts.

TERGIPES DESPECTUS Adams. (p. 495.)

> H. and A. Adams, Genera, vol. ii, p. 76, 1858. *Eolidia despecta* Johnston, Lond. Mag. Nat. Hist., vol. viii, p. 378, fig. 35e. *Eolis despecta* Alder and Hancock, Brit. Nud. Moll., Fam. 3, Plate 37. *Æolis* (*Tergipes*) *despecta* Gould, Invert., ed. ii, p. 248, Plate 16, figs. 222–225.

Stonington, Connecticut, to Bay of Fundy and northward; northern coasts of Europe to Great Britain. Off Watch Hill, 4 to 5 fathoms, on *Laminaria*, among hydroids, abundant; Casco Bay; Eastport Harbor.

HERMÆA CRUCIATA A. Agassiz, MSS. Plate 25., fig. 175.

> Gould, Invert., ed. ii, p. 253, Plate 17, fig. 256.

Naushon Island (A. Agassiz).

ELYSIA CHLOROTICA Gould. Plate XXV, fig. 172. (p. 480.)

> Invert., ed. ii, p. 255, Plate 17, figs. 251–255, 1870.

Great Egg Harbor, New Jersey, in pools on salt-marsh at low-water (A. E. V. and S. I. Smith). Cambridge, Massachusetts (Agassiz).

ELYSIELLA CATULUS Verrill. Plate XXV, fig. 171. (p. 480.)

American Journ. Science, vol. iii, p. 284, Plate 7, figs. 5, 5[a], 1872. *Placobranchus catulus* Agassiz, MSS.; Gould, Invert., ed. ii, p. 256, Plate 17, figs. 249, 250, 1870.

Great Egg Harbor, New Jersey, to Massachusetts Bay. New Haven Harbor and Wood's Hole, among eel-grass, common.

PTEROPODA.

GYMNOSOMATA.

CLIONE PAPILLONACEA Pallas. (p. 444.)

Spicil. Zoöl., x, p. 37, Plate 1, figs. 18, 19, (?) 1774. *Clio limacina* Phipps, Voyage to North Pole, p. 195, 1774 (t. Gould). *Clio retusa* Müller, Prod. Zoöl. Dan., 2742, 1776 (*non* Linné); Fabricius, Fauna Grönlandica, p. 334, 1780 (description excellent). *Clio borealis* Brugiere, Encyc. Meth., Vers., i, p. 502, 1792 (t. Gould). *Clione borealis* Gray, Brit. Mus. Pteropoda, p. 36, 1850; Stimpson, Shells of New England, p. 27, 1851; H. and A. Adams, Genera, vol. i, p. 62, Plate 7, fig. 7. *Clione limacina* Stimpson, Smithsonian Check-Lists, p. 4, 1860; Binney in Gould, Invert., ed. ii, p. 507, fig. 754 (poor). *Clio Miquelonensis* Rang, Ann. Sci. Nat., ser. i, vol. v, p. 285, Plate 7, fig. 2, 1825.

New York to the Arctic Ocean; on the northern coasts of Europe south to Great Britain. Off Stonington, Connecticut (A. E. V. and D. C. Eaton); Vineyard Sound (V. N. Edwards); Portland, Maine (C. B. Fuller).

The synonymy of this species has been greatly and unnecessarily confused. The *Clio retusa* of Linné was a southern Pteropod, having a triquetral shell. In a foot-note on page 1094 of the twelfth edition of the Systema Naturæ, he states that he had not seen the genus *Clio*, but adopts it from Brown. He gives three species mentioned by Brown, all having shells.

THECOSOMATA.

STYLIOLA VITREA Verrill. Plate XXV, fig. 178. (p. 443.)

American Journ. Science, vol. iii, p. 284, Plate 6, fig. 7, 1872.

Shell smooth, polished, diaphanous, almost glassy, long conical, rather slender, slightly curved toward the acute apex; animal white; locomotive organs obovate, with the end broadly rounded, and bearing slender tapering tentacle-like processes near the middle of the anterior edge; intermediate lobe short, rounded in front.

Length of shell, 11.5^{mm}; diameter, 2^{mm}.

Taken among *Salpæ*, off Gay Head, Martha's Vineyard, in the afternoon, September 9, 1871.

Several other species of this and other related genera were taken by Messrs. S. I. Smith and Oscar Harger, off Saint George's Bank, in 1872, on the United States steamer Bache. These may occasionally occur also in the vicinity of Nantucket and Martha's Vineyard.

CAVOLINA TRIDENTATA. Plate XXV, fig. 177. (p. 444.)

H. and A. Adams, Genera, vol. i, p. 51, Plate 6, figs. 1, 1[a]; Verrill, op. cit., p. 284. *Anomia tridentata* Forskal, Fauna Arab., p. 124, 1775; Icon., Plate 40, fig. b, (t. Lamarck). *Hyalæa cornea* Lamarck, Syst. des Anim., p. 140, 1801. *Hyalæa tridentata* Lamarck, Anim. sans Vert., ed. ii, vol. vii, p. 415.

Mediterranean Sea and the warmer parts of the Atlantic. The shells were dredged off Martha's Vineyard, at two localities, in 19 and 22 fathoms.

DIACRIA TRISPINOSA Gray. (p. 444.)

British Museum Pteropoda; H. and A. Adams, Genera, i, p. 52, Plate 6, fig. 2[a]; Gould, Invert., ed. ii, p. 504. *Hyalæa trispinosa* Lesueur, in Blainville, Dict. des Sci. Nat., vol. xxii, p. 82, 1824; Forbes and Hanley, Brit. Moll., vol. ii, p. 380, Plate 5, fig. 3; Stimpson, Shells of New England, p. 27.

Gulf Stream and warmer parts of the Atlantic generally. Occasionally cast ashore at Nantucket (Stimpson).

SPIRIALIS GOULDII Stimpson. (p. 443.)

Proc. Boston Soc. Nat. Hist., vol. iv, p. 8, 1851; Shells of New England, p. 27, Plate 1, fig. 4. *Heterofusus balea* and *H. retroversus* Binney, in Gould, Invert., ed. ii, p. 505, Plate 27, figs. 345–349, (not of European writers). *Spirialis Flemingii* A. Agassiz, Proc. Boston Soc. Nat. Hist., vol. x, p. 14, 1865, (not of Forbes). *Heterofusus Alexandri* Verrill, Amer. Jour. Science, vol. iii, p. 281, 1872 (young).

Near Naushon Island and Nahant, Massachusetts (A. Agassiz). Twenty miles off No Man's Land, in stomach of herring, (S. I. Smith). Off Saint George's Bank, in Gulf Stream, (S. I. Smith and O. Harger). The identity of this species with the *Limacina balea* Möller, of Greenland, is very questionable. The description of the latter is brief, and no mention is made of the spiral sculpture, which is an important character of *S. Gouldii*.

LAMELLIBRANCHIATA.

DIMYARIA.

TEREDO NAVALIS Linné. Plate XXVI, fig. 183. Plate XXVII, fig. 186. (pp. 384, 482.)

Systema Naturæ, ed. xii, p. 1267, 1767; Tryon, Proc. Acad. Nat. Sciences, vol. xiv, p. 468, 1862; Gould, Invert., ed. ii, p. 28, fig. 355; Jeffreys, Brit. Conch., vol. iii, p. 171.

Coast of United States, from Florida to Vineyard Sound; coasts of Europe, from Sweden (Christiania) and Great Britain to Sicily; Algeria and the Black Sea (Jeffreys); Senegal. Great Egg Harbor, New Jersey; New Haven Harbor, in piles of wharves; Wood's Hole, in piles of wharf; Vineyard Sound and Buzzard's Bay, in cedar buoys.

This is the most abundant species on our Atlantic coast, south of Massachusetts Bay, where it also probably occurs.

TEREDO MEGOTARA Hanley. Plate XXVII, fig. 188. (p. 387.)

Forbes and Hanley, Brit. Conch., vol. i, p. 77, Plate 1, figs. 1, 2; Plate 18, figs. 1, 2; vol. iv, p. 247; Tryon, op. cit., p. 466, 1862; Jeffreys op. cit., p. 176; Gould, Invert., ed. ii, p. 30, fig. 357.

Massachusetts Bay to South Carolina. Common in floating drift-wood, in the North Atlantic; north to Greenland, Iceland, and Spitzbergen; coasts of Scandinavia and Great Britain. Fossil in the Post-Pliocene of Scandinavia.

TEREDO THOMSONII Tryon. Plate XXVII, fig. 187. (p. 387.)

Proc. Acad. Nat. Sci., Philadelphia, vol. xv, p. 28, Plate 2, figs. 3, 4, 5, 1863; Gould, Invert., ed. ii, p. 31, fig. 358.

New Bedford, Massachusetts, in cedar buoys (Tryon). Provincetown, Massachusetts, in whale-ship (Atwood).

TEREDO DILATATA Stimpson.

Proc. Boston Soc. Nat. Hist., vol. iv, p. 113, 1851; Shells of New England, p. 26; Tryon, op. cit., p. 464, 1862; Gould, Invert., ed. ii, p. 32, fig. 359.

Massachusetts to South Carolina (Tryon). Cape Ann, in buoys, (Stimpson). Provincetown, Massachusetts (Gould). Greenport, Long Island (S. Smith). I have not met with this species south of Cape Cod.

XYLOTRYA FIMBRIATA Jeffreys. Plate XXVII, fig. 189. (p. 387.)

Annals and Mag. Nat. Hist., ser. iii, vol. vi, p. 126, 1860; Tryon, op. cit., p. 478, 1862; Gould, Invert., ed. ii, p. 34, fig. 361. *Teredo palmulata* Forbes and Hanley, Brit. Moll., vol. i. p. 86, Plate 2, figs. 9–11, (*non* Lamarck). *Xylotrya palmulata* Stimpson, Check-List, p. 3, 1860; Perkins, Proc. Boston Soc. Nat. Hist., vol. xii, p. 141, 1869.

Long Island Sound to Florida; Pacific coast, at the Straits of Fuca; Europe. In an old submerged wreck near New Haven. From the hull of the "Peterhoff," used in the blockade of the southern coast during the late war. Frequent in vessels from foreign ports.

PHOLAS TRUNCATA Say. Plate XXVII. fig. 200. (p. 372.)

Journal Acad. Nat. Sciences, Philadelphia, ser. i, vol. ii, p. 321, 1822; Binney's Say, p. 107; Hanley, Recent Shells, p. 6, Plate 9, fig. 26; Tryon, op. cit., p. 202; Gould, Invert., ed. ii, p. 38, fig. 364.

Vineyard Sound to Florida. Payta, Peru (Tryon). Common on the shores of Long Island Sound, near New Haven. The large specimens from Sable Island (Gould), mentioned by Tryon, were not this species, but *Z. crispata*.

PHOLAS COSTATA Linné. (p. 433.)

Systema Naturæ, ed. xii, p. 1111, 1762; Tryon, Proc. Acad. Nat. Sciences, Philadelphia, xiv, p. 201, 1862; Gould, Invert., ed. ii, p. 37, fig. 363.

Caribbean Sea to Buzzard's Bay. Southern Europe (Linné). New Bedford Harbor, living, (Gould); Wood's Hole, Massachusetts, dead shells dredged, (A. E. V.); Long Island Sound. Atlantic City, New Jersey (Tyron). Specimens from the east and west coasts of Florida; and from near Vera Cruz, Mexico (coll., Mr. Salt), are also in the museum of Yale College.

ZIRPHÆA CRISPATA Mörch, 1853. (p. 433.)

H. and A. Adams, Genera, vol. ii, p. 327, Plate 89, figs. 5, 5*a*, 1858; Tryon, op. cit., p. 211, 1862. *Pholas crispata* Linné, Syst. Nat., ed. xii, p. 1111, 1767; Gould, Invert., ed. i, p. 27. *Zirfæa crispata* Gray, Figures of Moll. Anim., Plate 338, fig. 5, and 339, fig. 5, 1857; Ann. and Mag. Nat. Hist., ser. ii, vol. viii, p. 385, 1851; Gould, Invert., ed. ii, p. 39, fig. 365.

Stonington, Connecticut, to Gulf of Saint Lawrence; Iceland; northern coasts of Europe, south to France, and the southern coasts of Great Britain; west coast of North America, south to California. Charleston, South Carolina (Stimpson, t. Gould). New Jersey (t. Gould). Wood's Hole, dead shells dredged, (A. E. V.). Common in Casco Bay, in 10 to 20 fathoms, perforating hard clay and sunken but sound wood; also in the Bay of Fundy, in 8 to 70 fathoms, in hard clay. Mr. C. B. Fuller has obtained fine large specimens in submerged tree-stumps at extreme low-water mark on Jewell's Island, Casco Bay. Fossil in the Post-Pliocene of Maine, Scandinavia; and in the Coralline and Red Crags of Great Britain. Its occurrence at Charleston, South Carolina, needs confirmation.

Martesia cuneiformis Gray, 1851; Tryon, op. cit., p. 219. *Pholas cuneiformis* Say, Jour. Acad. Nat. Sci., Philad., vol. ii, p. 322, 1822.

This species was found by Mr. Perkins in oyster-shells, near New Haven, but it was probably brought from farther south (Maryland or Virginia) in the oysters. It inhabits the coasts of Florida and the West Indies.

Diplothyra Smithii Tryon, op. cit., p. 450, 1862.

This species was described from specimens found in oyster-shells at Staten Island, where they were supposed to have lived. If really indigenous there, it may be expected to occur in Long Island Sound.

SAXICAVA ARCTICA Deshays. Plate XXVII, fig. 192. (p. 309.)

Elem. Conch., Plate xii, figs. 8, 9 (t. Gould); Forbes and Hanley, Brit. Moll., vol. i, p. 141, Plate 6, figs. 4–6; Gould, Invert., ed. ii, p. 89, fig. 397. *Mya arctica* Linné, Syst. Nat., ed. xii, p. 1113, 1767. *Mytilus rugosus* Linné, Syst. Nat., ed. xii, p. 1156. *Saxicava rugosa* Lamarck, Anim. sans Vert., ed. ii, vol. vi, p. 152; Gould, Invert., ed. ii, p. 87; Jeffreys, Brit. Conch., vol. iii, p. 81. *Mytilus pholadis* Linné, Mant. Plant., p. 548. *Saxicava pholadis* Lamarck, op. cit., vol. vi, p. 152. (?) *Saxicava distorta* Say, Jour. Acad. Nat. Sci., Philad., vol. ii, p. 318, 1822; Gould, ed. i, p. 62.

Georgia and South Carolina to the Arctic Ocean; northern coasts of Europe to the Mediterranean; Pacific Coast of America, south to Santa Barbara, California. Various other parts of the world are given as localities by different authors. On our coast this shell is very common from Massachusetts Bay to Labrador, occurring from low-water mark to 50 fathoms or more. In Casco Bay it is extremely abundant in rocky, cavernous pools, among the ledges at low-water mark, and mostly attached by a byssus, associated with *Modiola modiolus*. I also found specimens in 10 to 15 fathoms, perforating recent and sound shells of *Cyprina Islandica*. In the Gulf of Saint Lawrence, near Anticosti Island, where limestone abounds, I have found it burrowing in the limestone in large numbers. South of Cape Cod it is far less abundant, though not uncommon in Long Island Sound. Var. *distorta* (Say) is common from Fort Macon to Georgia, and is possibly a distinct species. Fossil in the Post-Pliocene of Maine, New Brunswick, Canada, Anticosti, Labrador, Scandinavia, and Great Britain; in the Coralline and Red Crags of England, etc. Var. *distorta* is found in the Miocene of Maryland.

MYA ARENARIA Linné. Plate XXVI, fig. 179. (pp. 357, 463.)

Systema Naturæ, ed. xii, p. 1112, 1767; Gould, Invert., ed. i, pp. 40, 359; ed. ii, p. 55, fig. 375. *Mya mercenaria* and *M. acuta* Say, Journal Acad. Nat. Sci., Philadelphia, vol. ii, p. 313, 1822.

South Carolina to the Arctic Ocean; northern coasts of Europe, south to England and France; northeastern coast of Asia, south to China and Japan (Hakodadi). Sitka (Middendorff). South Carolina (Gibbs). Fort Macon, North Carolina (Dr. Yarrow). Comparatively scarce south of Cape Hatteras. Very abundant from New Jersey northward, both in brackish estuaries and on the open coasts. Particularly large and fine in Long Island Sound (see p. 463). Casco Bay and Bay of Fundy, from half-tide mark to 40 fathoms, those dredged being all young. Fossil in the Post-Pliocene of Scandinavia, Greenland, Labrador, Canada, New England, Virginia, South Carolina, etc.; in the Red-Crag and all later formations in Great Britain; and in the Miocene of Virginia.

CORBULA CONTRACTA Say. Plate XXVII, fig. 191. (p. 418.)

Journal Acad. Nat. Sciences, Philadelphia, vol. ii, p. 312, 1822; Gould, Invert., ed. i, p. 43, fig. 37; ed. ii, p. 60, fig. 377.

Cape Cod to Florida. Common, living, in Vineyard Sound and Buzzard's Bay, in 5 to 19 fathoms; Long Island Sound, near New Haven, not uncommon in shallow water. Georgia (Couper). Fossil in the Post-Pliocene of Virginia, North and South Carolina; and in the Pliocene of South Carolina. A closely related species occurs in the Miocene of Maryland.

LYONSIA HYALINA Conrad. Plate XXVII, fig. 194. (p. 358.)

American Marine Conchology, p. 51, Plate 11, fig. 2, 1831; Gould, Invert., ed. ii, p. 64, fig. 380. *Mya hyalina* Conrad, Jour. Acad. Nat. Sci., Philadelphia, vol. vi, p. 261, Plate 11, fig. 12, 1831. *Osteodesma hyalina* Couthouy, Boston Jour. Nat. Hist., vol. ii, p. 166, 1839; Gould, Invert., ed. i, p. 46, fig. 31.

Florida to Gulf of Saint Lawrence. Common in Long Island Sound, Buzzard's Bay, Vineyard Sound, Massachusetts Bay, Casco Bay, and Bay of Fundy; low-water mark to 30 fathoms; Beaufort, North Carolina (Coues).

CLIDIOPHORA TRILINEATA Carpenter. Plate XXVII, fig. 193. (p. 418.)

Proc. Zoöl. Soc., London, 1864, p. 597; Mollusks of W. N. America, p. 226. *Pandora trilineata* Say, Journ. Acad. Nat. Sciences, Philadelphia, vol. ii, p. 261, 1822; Gould, Invert., ed. i, p. 44; ed. ii, p. 62, fig. 379.

Florida to Gulf of Saint Lawrence. Common in Long Island Sound; off Block Island, 29 fathoms; Buzzard's Bay; Vineyard Sound; Casco Bay; and Bay of Fundy; low water mark to 30 fathoms; Great Egg Harbor, New Jersey, 1 fathom. Beaufort, North Carolina (Coues, Yarrow). Fossil in the Post-Pliocene of Virginia and South Carolina; and in the Pliocene of South Carolina. A closely-related form, *C. crassidens* (Conrad, sp.), occurs in the Miocene of Virginia.

PERIPLOMA PAPYRACEA Verrill. Plate XXVII, fig. 197. (p. 509.)

Amer. Journal Science, vol. iii, pp. 213, 285, Plate 7, figs. 1, 1[a], 1[b] (animal and hinge), 1872. *Anatina papyratia* Say, op. cit., p. 314, 1822. *Anatina papyracea* Gould, Invert., ed. i, p. 47, fig. 28; ed. ii, p. 66, fig. 382. *Anatina fragilis* Totten (name provisional), Amer. Jour. Science, vol. xxviii, p. 347, fig. 1, 1835.

New Jersey to Labrador. Anticosti Island (A. E. V.); not uncommon in Massachusetts Bay, Casco Bay, and Bay of Fundy, 10 to 100 fathoms. Less frequent south of Cape Cod; off Block Island, in 29 fathoms, (A. S. Packard); Newport, Rhode Island (Totten); Greenport, Long Island (S. Smith). Chateau Bay, Labrador (Packard).

This species, when young, is liable to be confounded with *Thracia myopsis* Beck = *T. Couthouyi* Stimpson (see Plate XXVII, fig. 196), but they are easily distinguished by the structure of the hinge. The latter occurs in Massachusetts Bay, Bay of Fundy, etc., northward to Greenland, but has not been recorded from south of Cape Cod.

COCHLODESMA LEANUM Couthouy. Plate XXVII, fig. 198. (p. 418.)

Boston Jour. Nat. Hist., vol. ii, p. 170, 1839; Stimpson, Shells of New England, p. 22; Gould, Invert., ed. i, p. 49, figs. 29, 30; ed. ii, p. 68, fig. 383. *Anatina Leana* Conrad, Jour. Acad. Nat. Sciences, vol. vi, p. 263, Plate 11, fig. 11, 1831.

North Carolina to the Gulf of Saint Lawrence. Vineyard Sound and Long Island Sound, not uncommon in 3 to 10 fathoms; Casco Bay and Eastport, Maine, rarely obtained alive; banks off Nova Scotia (Willis); Saint George's Bank (S. I. Smith and O. Harger). A related species, *C. antiquatum* (*Periploma antiquata* Conrad), occurs in the Miocene of Virginia.

THRACIA CONRADI Couthouy. (p. 426.)

Boston Jour. Nat. Hist., vol. ii, p. 153, Plate 4, fig. 2, 1839; Gould, Invert., ed. i, p. 50; ed. ii, p. 69, fig. 384. *Thracia declivis* Conrad, Amer. Mar. Conch., p. 44, Plate 9, fig. 2, 1831 (not of Pennant).

Long Island to Gulf of Saint Lawrence. Vineyard Sound, 6 to 8 fathoms; Casco Bay, 6 to 15 fathoms; Frenchman's Bay, near Mount Desert, Maine, 3 to 8 fathoms. Eastport, Maine, in 6 fathoms, and Grand Menan (Stimpson); Nahant, Massachusetts (Haskell); Rhode Island

and Buzzard's Bay (Gould); Labrador (Packard). Fossil in the Post-Pliocene (Leda-clay) at Saco, Maine (Fuller).

This species burrows so deeply in the mud or sand that it is seldom taken alive with the dredge.

THRACIA TRUNCATA Mighels and Adams. Plate XXVII, fig. 195. (p. 509.)

Boston Jour. Nat. Hist., vol. iv, p. 38, Plate 4, fig. 1, 1842; Gould, Invert., ed. ii, p. 72, fig. 386.

Long Island to Greenland. Off Block Island, 29 fathoms; Casco Bay, 10 to 20 fathoms; Bay of Fundy. Off Long Island, 37 fathoms, (Gould). Greenland, in 60 fathoms, (Mörch).

ENSATELLA AMERICANA Verrill. Plate XXVI, fig. 182; Plate XXXII, fig. 245. (p. 356.)

American Jour. Science, vol. iii, pp. 212, 284, 1872. *Solen Americanus* Gould, Invert., ed. ii, p. 42, 1870 (provisional name). *Solen ensis* Gould, op. cit., ed. i, p. 28; and ed. ii, p. 40 (*non* Linné); Dekay, Nat. Hist. New York, Moll., p. 242, Plate 33, fig. 313. *Ensis Americana* H. and A. Adams, Genera, vol ii, p. 342.

Florida to Labrador. Common at Great Egg Harbor, New Jersey; Long Island Sound; Buzzard's Bay; Vineyard Sound; Massachusetts Bay; Casco Bay; Bay of Fundy; Gulf of Saint Lawrence; low-water mark to 20 fathoms, sandy. Fort Macon, North Carolina, abundant, (Coues). Georgia (Couper). Labrador, rare (Packard). Saint George's Bank (S. I. Smith).

Fossil in the Post-Pliocene of Portland, Maine; Point Shirley, Massachusetts; Nantucket; Virginia; and South Carolina; in the Pliocene of South Carolina; and Miocene of Maryland; North and South Carolina.

In this species the siphonal tubes, in mature shells, protrude about 35^{mm}, and are united together for about half their length, beyond which they are round and divergent, subequal. Both orifices are surrounded by a similar circle of numerous papillæ, of three sizes; the larger ones are enlarged in the middle, acute at tips, with a large black spot on each side of the base; alternate with these are somewhat smaller ones of the same form and with similar basal spots; alternating with the primary and secondary ones are small tapering papillæ, less than half the length of the longest; numerous slender tapering papillæ are also scattered irregularly over the sides of the free portions of both tubes, in some cases in irregular rows of four to six, while on the ventral side of the branchial tube two rows of alternating papillæ extend along the whole length of the siphon. The mantle is closed ventrally for most of its length; there is a posterior opening for the protrusion of the foot, and a small opening just in advance of it, and another opening near the middle of the ventral border; the latter is fringed with small conical papillæ. Foot long; the end bulbous, obliquely truncated and beveled laterally.

Solen viridis Say. This species has been recorded from the southern coast of New England by several writers (Stonington, Connecticut, Linsley; Rhode Island, Conrad), but I have myself met with no authentic New England specimens. It may, however, occur rarely and perhaps accidentally. It is not uncommon on the outer beach at Great Egg Harbor, New Jersey, and farther south, to Florida.

SILIQUA COSTATA Adams. Plate XXXII, fig. 244. (p. 358.)

H. and A. Adams, Genera, vol. ii, p. 345, 1858. *Solen costatus* Say, Jour. Acad. Nat. Sci., Philad., vol. ii, p. 315, 1822; Hanley, Recent Shells, p. 15, Plate 9, fig. 28 (*non Leguminaria costata* Schum., 1817 = *Siliqua radiata* Linné, sp.). *Solen Sayii* Gray, Griffith's Cuvier, xii, Plate 31, fig. 3 (t. Gould). *Machæra costata* Gould, Invert., ed. i, p. 34, and fig. on p. 24, 1841; ed. ii, p. 47, fig. 370.

Cape Hatteras to Gulf of Saint Lawrence. Rare or local north of Casco Bay. Not observed in the Bay of Fundy. Common in Massachusetts Bay; Vineyard Sound; Great Egg Harbor, New Jersey. Comparatively rare in Long Island Sound, near New Haven; Fire Island Beach, Long Island (S. I. Smith). Coney Island, etc. (S. Smith). Rimouski, Gulf of Saint Lawrence, common, (Bell). Banks off Nova Scotia (Willis). The earliest name for this genus appears to be *Siliqua* Muhlfeldt, 1811. It was named *Leguminaria* by Schumacher in 1817, and *Machæra* by Gould, in 1841. The latter name is, moreover, preoccupied by *Machæra* Cuvier, 1832.

TAGELUS GIBBUS Gray. Plate XXVI, fig. 181; Plate XXX, fig. 217. (p. 373.)

Proc. Zoöl. Soc., London, xv, 1847; Dall, Proc. Boston Soc. Nat. Hist., vol. xiii, p. 251, 1870. *Solen gibbus* Spengler, Skrivt. Nat. Selks., vol. iii, p. 104, 1794 (t. Gould). *Solen Guineensis* Chemnitz, Conch., xi, p. 202, Plate 198, fig. 1937, 1799. *Solen Caribæus* Lamarck, Anim. sans Vert., ed. ii, vol. vi, p. 58. *Solecurtus Caribæus* Gould, Invert., ed. i, p. 30. *Solecurtus gibbus* Forbes and Hanley, Brit. Moll., vol. i, p. 267; Gould, Invert., ed. ii, p. 43, fig. 367. *Siliquaria notata* Schumacher, Essai d'un Nouv. Syst. des Habit. des Vers test., p. 129, Plate 7, figs. 2, 3, 1817 (not the genus *Siliquaria* Brug.; Lamarck, 1801). *Siliquaria gibba* H. and A. Adams, Genera, p. 347, Plate 93, figs. 5, 5*a*, 1858.

Caribbean Sea, West Indies, and Gulf of Mexico to Cape Cod. Similar if not identical species are found on the Pacific coast of Central America, and on the west coast of Africa. Vineyard Sound and Buzzard's Bay, not uncommon; Great Egg Harbor, New Jersey, abundant. Fort Macon, North Carolina, very common (Coues). Alabama (Mighels). Fossil in the Post-Pliocene of Virginia, South Carolina, and Florida; in the Pliocene of South Carolina; and in the Miocene of North and South Carolina.

The name, *Siliquaria* Schumacher, 1817, adopted for this genus by several recent writers cannot be retained, because preoccupied by Brugiere, 1791, and by Lamarck (see Syst. des Anim., 1801, p. 98) for a genus of *Vermetidæ*.

This genus is widely different from the restricted genus *Solecurtus*

Blainv., 1824,=*Macha* Oken, 1835, and undoubtedly belongs to the *Tellinidæ*, near *Psammobia*, as shown by the structure of the soft parts. (See page 373 and Plate xxvi, fig. 181).

TAGELUS DIVISUS. Plate XXX, fig. 218. (p. 435.)

Dall, op. cit., p. 251, 1870. *Solen divisus* Spengler, op. cit., p. 96, 1794 (t. Gould). *Solen bidens* Chemnitz, op. cit., p. 203, Plate 198, fig. 1939, 1799. *Solen fragilis* Pulteney, Dorset Catal., p. 28, Plate 4, fig. 5, 1799 (t. Gould). *Solen centralis* Say, Journ. Acad. Nat. Sci., Philad., vol. ii, p. 316, 1822. *Solecurtus bidens* Forbes and Hanley, op. cit., vol. i, p. 266; Stimpson, Shells of New England, p. 22. *Solecurtus divisus* Gould, Invert., ed. ii, p. 44, fig. 368. *Macha divisa* Gray, Catal. Brit. Moll., p. 160. *Leguminaria Floridana* Conrad, Proc. Acad. Nat. Sci., Philad., vol. iv, p. 121, 1848. *Mesopleura bidentata* Conrad, Catal. Solenidæ, Amer. Jour. Conch., vol. iii, Appendix, p. 23, 1867.

Gulf of Mexico and West Indies to Cape Cod. Vineyard Sound and Buzzard's Bay, not common. Rhode Island, rather common, (Gould). Fort Macon, North Carolina, common, (Coues). Tampa Bay, Florida, (Conrad, Jewett).

MACOMA FRAGILIS Adams. Plate XXX, fig. 222.

H. and A. Adams, Genera, vol. ii, p. 400, 1858.

Var. fusca = *Macoma fusca* Adams. (p. 359.)

Genera, vol. ii, p. 400; Gould, Invert., ed. ii, p. 93, fig. 400. *Psammobia fusca* Say, Jour. Acad. Nat. Sci., Philad., vol. v, p. 220, 1826. *Sanguinolaria fusca* Conrad, Amer. Mar. Conch., p. 34, Plate 7, fig. 1, 1831; Gould, Invert., ed. i, p. 66, fig. 42.

Var. fragilis.

Venus fragilis O. Fabricius, Fauna Grönlandica, p. 413, 1780. *Tellina Grönlandica* Beck, Lyell, in Trans. Geol. Soc., London, vol. v, p. 137, Plate 16, fig. 8, 1841. *Macoma Grönlandica* Packard, Mem. Boston Soc., vol. i, pp. 235, 243, etc., 1866; Dawson, Notes on Post-Pliocene Geology of Canada, p. 72, from Canadian Naturalist, vol. vi, 1872. *Tellina Fabricii* Hanley; Sowerby, Thesaurus, p. 112, (t. Mörch).

Georgia to Greenland. Var. *fusca* is abundant on the entire coast of New England, Long Island, and New Jersey. Georgia (Say, Couper). Var. *fragilis* is abundant from Long Island Sound and Massachusetts Bay to Labrador. The two forms grade into one another insensibly.

A closely related but apparently distinct species, *M. Balthica* (Linné, sp.), is abundant in the Baltic and elsewhere on the northern coasts of Europe, and has been regarded as identical by several writers. Another similar form, *inconspicua* (Sowerby), occurs on the northwest coast of America, but is regarded as distinct by Dr. P. P. Carpenter and others.

As a fossil, *var. fragilis* is abundant in the Post-Pliocene deposits of New England, New Brunswick, Canada, Labrador, and Greenland; *var. fusca* occurs in the Post-Pliocene of New England, Virginia, North Carolina, and South Carolina.

MACOMA SABULOSA Mörch.

Tellina (Macoma) sabulosa Mörch, in Naturh. Bidrag til Beskr. af Grönland, p. 90, 1857. *Tellina sabulosa* Spengler, Skrivt. Nat., vol. iv, part 2, 1798. *Tellina proxima* Gray, Zoöl. Beechey's Voyage, p. 154, Plate 44, fig. 4, 1839. *Tellina sordida* Couthouy, Boston Jour. Nat. Hist., vol. ii, p. 59, Plate 3, fig. 11, 1839. *Sanguinolaria sordida* Gould, Invert., ed. i, p. 67, 1841. *Tellina lata* Lovén, Öfvers. af Kongl. Vet.-Akad., Förhand., vol. xi, p. 195, 1846 (not *Tellina lata* Gmelin, 1790, which is a *Thracia*, t. Mörch). *Tellina calcarea* Lyell, Phil. Trans., 1836 (not Chemnitz, 1782 = a *Mactra*, t. Mörch). *Macoma proxima* Gould, ed. ii, p. 95, fig. 401; this Report, p. 503. *Macoma calcarea* Adams; Dawson, op. cit., p. 73.

Connecticut to the Arctic Ocean; northern coasts of Europe; North Pacific; south on the coast of Asia to Hakodadi, Japan; and, perhaps (as *M. expansa*, a doubtful variety), on the west coast of America south to Puget Sound. Off Block Island, in 29 fathoms, rare; Casco Bay, 3 to 60 fathoms, not uncommon; Quahog Bay, Maine, 3 to 5 fathoms, soft mud, large and abundant; Bay of Fundy, 4 to 80 fathoms. Stonington and Stratford, Connecticut (Linsley); Saint George's Bank (S. I. Smith). Fossil in the Post-Pliocene of Maine, New Brunswick, Canada, Labrador, Scandinavia, and Great Britain.

The *Tellina tenera* Leach, 1818 (*non* Say), has been regarded as a synonym of this species by most writers; Mörch considers it identical with *M. fragilis*.

ANGULUS TENER. Plate XXVI, fig. 180; Plate XXX, fig. 223. (p. 358.)

Tellina (Angulus) tenera H. and A. Adams, Genera, vol. ii, p. 398, 1858. *Angulus tener* Verrill, Amer. Jour. Science, vol. iii, p. 290, Plate 6, figs. 1, 1*a*, 1872. *Tellina tenera* Say, Jour. Acad. Nat. Sci., Philad., vol. ii, p. 303, 1822; Hanley, Recent Shells, p. 65, Plate 9, fig. 38; Gould, Invert., ed. i, p. 68, fig. 44; ed. ii, p. 97, fig. 403.

Florida to Gulf of Saint Lawrence. Common on the coast of New Jersey, Long Island, Long Island Sound, Buzzard's Bay, Vineyard Sound, Massachusetts Bay; less common in Casco Bay and Bay of Fundy. Gaspé, Canada (Dawson). Fort Macon, North Carolina (Coues). A closely-allied form (*A declivis* = *Tellina declivis* Conrad, Journ. Acad. N. Sc., Phil., vol. vii, p. 131) occurs in the Miocene of Virginia.

ANGULUS TENELLUS Verrill. Plate XXX, fig. 224.

Angulus modestus Verrill, Amer. Jour. Science, vol. iii, pp. 210, 285, Plate 6, figs. 2, 2*a*, 1872; this Report, p. 418, (*non* Carpenter, 1864).

Shell smooth, shining, more or less iridescent, with very fine concentric striæ. Form similar to that of *A. tener*, but more oblong, and with the anterior dorsal margin nearly straight, or even slightly concave; the beaks are at about the posterior third, and scarcely prominent; the posterior end slopes rapidly, and is subtruncate at the end; the ventral margin is but slightly convex in the middle, and sub-parallel with the dorsal margin. The shell is often a little thickened, and firmer than in *A. tener*, but is sometimes as thin. Color, pink, light straw-color, or white; often banded concentrically with these colors. The hinge-margin is stouter and the teeth stronger than in *A. tener*, and different in relative size and proportions; the ligament-plate is also longer.

Long Island Sound and Vineyard Sound; 4 to 10 fathoms, mud and sand.

TELLINA TENTA Say. Plate XXX, fig. 223. (p. 432.)

American Conchology, Part vii, Plate 65, fig. 3, 1837; Binney's Say, p. 228; Hanley, Recent Shells, p. 65, Plate 14, fig. 10; Gould, Invert., ed. i, p. 68, fig. 43; ed. ii, p. 96, fig. 402. *Tellina (Peronæa) tenta* H. and A. Adams, Genera, vol. ii, p. 499, 1858.

Cape Cod to South Carolina. Vineyard Sound and Buzzard's Bay, 2 to 10 fathoms, mud, common; Long Island Sound; Great Egg Harbor. Greenport, Long Island (S. Smith); Fort Macon, North Carolina (Coues); South Carolina (Say).

Fossil in the Post-Pliocene of South Carolina.

Tellina versicolor Cozzens.

Jay, Catalogue Shells, ed. ii, p. 12, 1836; Dekay, Nat. Hist. New York, Moll., p. 208, Plate 26, fig. 272.

Glass House Point, near New York (Cozzens); Stratford, Connecticut (Linsley).

I have met with no shells corresponding precisely with the description of this species.

GASTRANELLA Verrill.

American Journal of Science, vol. iii, p. 286, 1872.

"Shell oblong, more or less irregular, and sometimes with the ventral margin inflexed; pallial sinus large; ligament external, elongated. Right valve with two small cardinal teeth; the posterior one thin, directed obliquely backward. Left valve with two cardinal teeth; the posterior one stout, bilobed; the anterior one smaller. No distinct lateral teeth. Animal with long, slender, separate siphonal tubes, with a simple circle of papillæ at the ends; mantle well open anteriorly; foot ligulate. The curious little shell for which this genus is constituted apparently resembles *Gastrana* more than any other described genus."

GASTRANELLA TUMIDA Verrill. Plate XXVII, fig. 190. (p. 418.)

American Jour. Sci., vol. iii, pp. 210, 286, Plate 6, figs. 3, 3*a*, 1872.

Shell small, variable in form, swollen above, more or less elongated oval, or oblong, with rounded ends, compressed posteriorly. The beaks are rounded, somewhat prominent, incurved but not approximate, and directed somewhat forward; the anterior dorsal margin is deeply concave in front of the beaks, but without a distinct lunule, at the anterior end regularly rounded or a little prolonged, compressed; ventral margin slightly convex, or nearly straight and sub-parallel with the dorsal margin, or incurved, in the different specimens; posterior end broadly rounded in some, decidedly prolonged in others; dorsal posterior margin usually nearly straight for at least half its length, sometimes a little convex and gradually sloping throughout. Surface with fine, somewhat irregular, concentric striæ, slightly iridescent. Color white, with the umbos purple. Length, 4^{mm}; height, 2.5^{mm}.

Long Island Sound, near New Haven, 4 to 6 fathoms, shelly and gravelly bottom, among hydroids and sponges (A. E. V.).

Abra æqualis Say.

American Conch., Part iii, Plate 28; outer figures, 1831; Binney's Say, p. 182, same plate; Stimpson, Check-List, p. 3, 1860. *Amphidesma æqualis* Say, Journ. Acad. Nat. Sci., Philadelphia, vol. ii, p. 307, 1822; American Conch., Part iii, Plate 28; Binney's Say, pp. 100, 182. *Semele equalis* Verrill, Amer. Jour. Science, vol. iii, p. 210, 1872.

Florida and Gulf of Mexico to Cape Hatteras; rare and local farther north. Stonington, Connecticut, from cod-stomachs (Linsley). Fort Macon, North Carolina, abundant (Coues, Yarrow). Texas (Rœmer). Charleston, South Carolina (Say).

The occurrence of this southern species at Stonington needs confirmation. I have seen no specimens from north of Cape Hatteras.

Fossil in the Miocene of North and South Carolina.

CUMINGIA TELLINOIDES Conrad. Plate XXX, fig. 221. (p. 418.)

Journ. Acad. Nat. Sci., Philad., vol. vii, p. 234, 1837; Gould, Invert., ed. i, p. 56, fig. 36; ed. ii, p. 79, fig. 390. *Mactra tellinoides* Conrad, Journ. Acad. Nat. Sci., Philad., vol. vi, p. 258, Plate 9, figs. 2, 3, 1831.

Cape Cod to Florida. Common in Vineyard Sound and Buzzard's Bay, 3 to 12 fathoms; Long Island Sound, less common. Fort Macon, North Carolina (Coues, Yarrow). Florida (Conrad). Fossil in the Post-Pliocene of Nantucket Island, South Carolina, and North Carolina; in the Pliocene of South Carolina; and in the Miocene of Virginia and South Carolina.

CERONIA ARCTATA Adams. (p. 426.)

H. and A. Adams, Genera, vol. ii, p. 414, 1858; Gould, Invert., ed. ii, p. 80, fig. 391. *Mactra arctata* Conrad, Journ. Acad. Nat. Sci., Philad., vol. vi, p. 257, Plate 11, fig. 1, 1831. *Mesodesma arctata* Gould, Invert., ed. i, p. 57, fig. 39.

Long Island to River Saint Lawrence. Stonington, Connecticut (Linsley). East Hampton and Montauk, Long Island (S. Smith). Nantucket (Gould). Common in Massachusetts Bay; Casco Bay, and Eastport, Maine, rare. Nova Scotia (Willis).

Donax fossor Say.

Journal Acad. Nat. Sciences, Philadelphia, vol. ii, p. 306, 1822; Binney's Say, pp. 99, 226, Plate 61, fig. 2.

This species may possibly occur occasionally on the Southern New England coast, but I am not aware of any authentic instances. I have found it quite common living on the outer beach at Great Egg Harbor, New Jersey, and it has been found as far north as the southern side of Long Island.

MACTRA SOLIDISSIMA Chemnitz. Plate XXVIII, fig. 202. (p. 358.)

Conch., x, p. 350, Plate 170, fig. 1656, 1788; Gould, Invert., ed. i, p. 51; ed. ii, p. 73, fig. 387. *Mactra gigantea* Lam., Anim. sans Vert., ed. ii, vol. vi, p. 97. *Mactra similis* Say, Journ. Acad. Nat. Sci., Philadelphia, vol. ii, p. 309, 1822; Binney's Say, p. 101. *Spisula solidissima* Gray, Charlesworth's Mag. Nat. Hist., vol. i, p. 373, 1837; H. and A. Adams, vol. xi, p. 378. *Hemimactra solidissima* Conrad, Amer. Journ. Conch., vol. iii, appendix, p. 32; Perkins, Proc. Bost. Soc. Nat. Hist., vol. xiii, p. 346, 1869. *Spisula Sayi* Gray, op. cit., p. 373.

Florida and Gulf of Mexico to Labrador. Very abundant on the outer beach at Great Egg Harbor, New Jersey; Long Island; Long Island Sound; Vineyard Sound; Cape Cod; Massachusetts Bay; Casco Bay; Bay of Fundy, low water-mark to 10 fathoms, sandy. Fort Macon, North Carolina (Coues); Labrador (Packard); St. George's Bank (S. I. Smith); West Florida (Jewett); Texas (Rœmer).

Fossil in the Post-Pliocene at Point Shirley, Chelsea, Massachusetts (Stimpson); and apparently in the Miocene of North and South Carolina (Conrad, as "*M. similis?*").

MULINIA LATERALIS Gray. Plate XXVI, fig. 185, B. (p. 373.)

Charlesworth's Mag. of Nat. Hist., vol. i, p. 376, 1837; Meek, Smithsonian Check-Lists, Miocene, p. 11, 1864. *Mactra lateralis* Say, Journ. Acad. Nat. Sci., Philad., vol. ii, p. 309, 1822; Gould, Invert., ed. i, p. 54, figs. 34, 35; ed. ii, p. 77, fig. 389. *Standella lateralis* H. and A. Adams, Genera, vol. ii, p. 382, 1858; Conrad, Proc. Philad. Acad., vol. xiv, p. 573, 1862.

Massachusetts Bay to Florida, and on the northern shores of the Gulf of Mexico to Galveston, Texas. Very abundant in Long Island Sound; common in Buzzard's Bay and Vineyard Sound, 1 to 15 fathoms, mud. Boston and near Lynn, Massachusetts (Gould). Fort Macon, North Carolina (Coues). Georgia (Couper). Texas (Rœmer).

Fossil in the Post-Pliocene of Virginia, North Carolina, South Carolina, and Florida (Saint John's River); in the Pliocene of South Carolina; and in the Miocene of Virginia, North and South Carolina.

PETRICOLA PHOLADIFORMIS Lamarck. Plate XXVII, fig. 199. (p. 372.)

Anim. sans Vert., ed. i, vol. v., p. 505, 1818; ed. ii, vol. vi, p. 159; Say, Amer. Conch., Part vi, Plate 60, fig. 1, 1834; Binney's Say, p. 222 (same plate); Hanley, Recent Shells, p. 52, Plate 13, fig. 49; Gould, Invert., ed. i, p. 63; ed. ii, p. 90, figs. 398, 399. *Petricola fornicata* Say, Journ. Acad. Nat. Sci., Philadelphia, vol. ii, p. 319, 1822. *Petricola dactylus* Say, Amer. Conch., Part vi, Plate 60, fig. 2 (*non* Sowerby, Hanley, etc.); Gould, Invert., ed. i, p. 65; ed. ii, p. 92, fig. 41.

Florida and Gulf of Mexico to Massachusetts Bay; local and more rare farther north, at Quahog Bay, Maine; and in the southern part of the Gulf of Saint Lawrence, as at Prince Edward's Island (Dawson); Nova Scotia (Willis). Very common in Long Island Sound, near New Haven; Buzzard's Bay; Vineyard Sound (Lackey's Bay, etc.); and Massachusetts Bay (Chelsea, Nahant, etc.). Fort Macon (Coues);

Florida (Conrad); Texas (Rœmer); Cuba (D'Orbigny). Fossil in the Post-Pliocene of Virginia, South Carolina, and Florida; and in the Pliocene of South Carolina. A similar form, if not identical (*P. Carolinensis* Conrad), occurs in the Miocene of South Carolina.

A species scarcely to be distinguished from this was sent to me in large numbers from La Paz, Gulf of California, by Captain Pedersen.

VENUS MERCENARIA Linné. Plate XXVI, fig. 184 (animal). (p. 359.)

Systema Naturæ, ed. xii, p. 1131, 1767; Gould, Invert., ed. i, p. 85, fig. 67; ed. ii, p. 133, fig. 445. *Mercenaria violacea* Schumacher, Essai d'un Nouveau Syst., p. 135, Plate 10, fig. 3, 1817; Adams, Genera, vol. ii, p. 419. *Mercenaria mercenaria* Chenu, Man. Conch., vol. ii, p. 82, figs. 356–358, 1862. *Crassivenus mercenaria* Perkins, Proc. Boston Soc. Nat. Hist., vol. xiii, p. 147, 1869. *Venus notata* Say, Journ. Acad. Nat. Sci., Philadelphia, vol. ii, p. 271, 1822 (variety); Gould, Invert., ed. i, p. 87, fig. 67; ed. ii, p. 135, fig. 446. *Venus præparca* Say, op. cit., p. 271, 1822; Binney's. Say, p. 95.

Florida to Massachusetts Bay; more rare and local farther north, at Quahog Bay, Maine; Nova Scotia (Willis); and in the southern part of the Gulf of Saint Lawrence, to the Bay of Chaleur. It is not found on the coast of Maine, east of Kennebeck River, nor in the Bay of Fundy. Very common in Vineyard Sound, Buzzard's Bay, Long Island Sound, and southward. Fort Macon (Coues); South Carolina (Gibbes); Georgia (Couper); Texas (Rœmer). Fossil in the Post-Pliocene of Point Shirley, Nantucket Island, Gardiner's Island, Virginia, and South Carolina; in the Pliocene of South Carolina; and in the Miocene of Maryland, Virginia, North and South Carolina.

CALLISTA CONVEXA Adams. Plate XXX, fig. 219. (p. 432.)

H. and A. Adams, Genera, vol. ii, p. 425, 1858. *Cytherea convexa* Say, Journ. Acad. Nat. Sci., Phil., vol. iv, p. 149, Plate 12, fig. 3, 1824 (fossil); Gould, Invert., ed. i, p. 84, fig. 49; ed. ii, p. 131, fig. 444 (recent). *Dione convexa* Deshayes, Catal. Conch. Biv., British Museum, p. 71, 1853. *Cytherea morrhuana* Linsley, Amer. Jour. Sci., vol. xlviii, p. 276, 1845 (no description); Gould, op. cit., ser. ii, vol. vi, p. 233, 1848 (young). *Cytherea Sayana* Conrad, Amer. Jour. Sci., ser. i, vol. xxiii, p. 345, 1833 (recent); Fossils of the Medial Tertiary of the U. S., p. 13, Plate 7, fig. 3, 1838 (fossil). *Cytherea Sayii* Perkins, Proc., Boston Soc. Nat. Hist., vol. xiii, p. 147, 1869. *Callista (Caryatis) convexa* Römer; Verrill, Amer. Jour. Sci., vol. xlix, p. 277, March, 1870.

New Jersey to Gulf of Saint Lawrence. Fort Macon, North Carolina, dead valves on the beach, plenty, but perhaps fossil, (Coues, Yarrow). Great Egg Harbor, New Jersey; Long Island Sound; Vineyard Sound, and Buzzard's Bay, 2 to 10 fathoms, mud, common; Casco Bay, 3 to 8 fathoms, mud, adult, living; Eastport, Maine, rare. Nova Scotia (Willis); Prince Edward's Island (Dawson).

Fossil in the Post-Pliocene of Virginia and North Carolina; in the Pliocene of South Carolina; and in the Miocene of Maryland, North and South Carolina.

The name *Sayana* given to this species in 1833 (loc. cit.) by Mr. Conrad, was accompanied by a short description of recent specimens from Rhode Island and New Jersey. He gave *C. convexa* Say as a synonym, however, remarking that it "appears not to differ from the *C. convexa* of Say, but I have changed the name because M. Brogniart had previously applied it to a very dissimilar species." More recently, however, he has indicated his belief that the two are distinct (Catal. Miocene Shells, in Proc. Phil. Acad., vol. xiv, p. 575, 1862), although he recognizes the "*Sayana*" as a Miocene shell, but he has not pointed out the differences, if any exist, so far as known to me. Should the recent shell prove to be distinct from the fossil one described by Say, it should therefore bear the name *Callista Sayana*.

In this species the animal is white, or pale salmon-color. The border of the mantle sometimes protrudes considerably beyond the edge of the shell, and is delicately undulated or frilled; the siphon tubes, in full expansion, are smooth and rather longer than the shell, and are united quite to the ends; the orifices are simple, without apparent papillæ, and the branchial is considerably larger than the other; a well-marked groove extends along the whole length of the siphon, indicating the partition between the tubes.

TOTTENIA GEMMA Perkins. Plate XXX, fig. 220. (p. 359.)

Proc. Boston Soc. Nat. Hist., vol. xiii, 1869 (in errata); by error, *Tottentiana* (p. 148). *Venus gemma* Totten, Amer. Jour. Science, vol. xxvi, p. 367, figs. 2*a*, *d*, 1834. *Gemma gemma* Deshayes, Catal. Conch. Biv., British Museum, p. 113, 1853; H. and A. Adams, Genera, vol. ii, p. 419, Plate 107, fig. 3. *Gemma Totteni* Stimpson, Check-List, p. 3, 1860.

South Carolina to Labrador. Very abundant in Long Island Sound, Buzzard's Bay, Vineyard Sound, Nantucket, and Massachusetts Bay; common in Casco Bay, and at Grand Menan Island. Nova Scotia (Willis). Prince Edward's Island (Dawson). Indian Harbor, Labrador (Packard). Fort Macon, North Carolina (Coues).

An allied species (*T. sphærica* H. C. Lea, sp.) occurs in the Miocene of Virginia.

TOTTENIA MANHATTENSIS Verrill.

Venus Manhattensis Prime, in Jay's Catalogue of Shells, ed. iv, supplement, p. 466, 1852. *Venus* (*Gemma*) *Manhattensis* Prime, Annals Lyc. Nat. Hist. N. Y., vol. vii, p. 482 (figure), 1862. *Gemma Manhattensis* Gould, Invert., ed. ii, p. 138, fig. 449.

North Carolina to Vineyard Sound. Hell Gate (Prime). Greenport and Huntington, Long Island (S. Smith). Near New Haven, rare. Fort Macon, North Carolina (Yarrow).

I have seen but few specimens of this shell, and am not fully satisfied that it is distinct from the preceding. Its color is not constant, some specimens being pale straw-color, others purplish. Mr. Prime originally described it as white.

CYPRINA ISLANDICA Lamarck. Plate XXVIII, fig. 201. (p. 508.)

Animaux sans Vert., ed. ii, vol. vi, p. 290; Gould, Invert., ed. i, p. 82; ed. ii, p. 443. *Venus Islandica* Linné, Syst. Nat., ed. xii, p. 1131.

Eastern end of Long Island to the Arctic Ocean; on the northern European coasts southward to England. Off Block Island, 29 fathoms, sandy mud; off Gay Head, Martha's Vineyard, 19 fathoms, soft mud; common in Casco Bay, 10 to 80 fathoms; Bay of Fundy, 6 to 90 fathoms; Saint George's Bank, 45 fathoms; and Gulf of Saint Lawrence. Montauk, Long Island (S. Smith). Fossil in the Post-Pliocene of Scandinavia, Scotland, England, Sicily, and other parts of Europe. In North America it appears not to have been found fossil hitherto, and it must, therefore, be rare in our northern Post-Pliocene or glacial deposits, if not altogether absent.

CARDIUM PINNULATUM Conrad. Plate XXIX, fig. 209. (p. 505.)

Journal Acad. Nat. Sciences, Philadelphia, ser. i, vol. vi, p. 260, Plate 11, fig. 8, 1831; Gould, Invert., ed. i, p. 90, fig. 57; ed. ii, p. 141, fig. 452.

Long Island Sound to Southern Labrador. Near New Haven, Connecticut, rare; Buzzard's Bay and Vineyard Sound, 4 to 12 fathoms, common; very common in Massachusetts Bay, Casco Bay, Bay of Fundy, and Gulf of Saint Lawrence, 2 to 80 fathoms. Labrador, south of Straits of Belle Isle (Packard). Huntington, Gardiner's and Peconic Bays, Long Island (S. Smith.) Off New London, Connecticut, (coll. T. M. Prudden). Fossil in the Post-Pliocene of New Brunswick.

LÆVICARDIUM MORTONI. Plate XXIX, fig. 208. (p. 358.)

Perkins, Proc. Boston Soc. Nat. Hist., vol. xiii, p. 150, 1869. *Cardium Mortoni* Conrad, op. cit., vol. vi, p. 259, Plate 10, figs. 5, 6, 7; Gould, Invert., ed. i, p. 91; *Liocardium Mortoni* Stimpson, Check-List, p. 2, 1860; Gould, Invert., ed. ii, p. 143, fig. 453.

Florida and northern shores of the Gulf of Mexico to Cape Cod; rare and local farther north. Common in Long Island Sound, Buzzard's Bay, Vineyard Sound, and about Nantucket. Dartmouth Lakes, Halifax, Nova Scotia (Willis, t. Gould). West Florida (Jewett). Fort Macon (Coues). Fossil in the Post-Pliocene of South Carolina.

Serripes Grönlandicus Beck (*Aphrodite Grönlandica* Stimpson; Gould, Invert., ed. ii, p. 144, fig. 454). This species was recorded as from Stonington, Connecticut, by Linsley, but has not since been found south of Cape Cod, and must, therefore, be regarded as a doubtful inhabitant of our waters. It occurs from Massachusetts Bay to the Arctic Ocean, but is rare south of the Gulf of Saint Lawrence and Labrador. Casco Bay and Mount Desert, Maine, 8 to 30 fathoms, rare, (A. E. V.).

CYCLOCARDIA BOREALIS Conrad. Plate XXIX, fig. 216. (p. 418.)

Amer. Journ. Conchology, vol. iii, p. 191, 1867. *Cardita borealis* Conrad, Amer. Mar. Conch., p. 39, Plate 8, fig. 1, 1831; Gould, Invert., ed. i, p. 94, fig. 59; ed. ii, p. 146, fig. 455. *Actinobolus borealis* H. and A. Adams, Genera, vol. ii, p. 487, 1858.

(?) *Venericardia cribraria* Say, Amer. Conch., Part v, cover, 1832; Binney's Say, p. 205. (?) *Venericardia granulata* Say, Jour. A. Nat. Sci., Philadelphia, vol. iv, p. 142, Plate 12, fig. 1. *Cardita granulata* Conrad, Fossils of Medial Tert. of U. S., p. 13, Plate 7, fig. 1.

New Jersey to Labrador. Common in the deeper parts of Vineyard Sound, near its mouth, and off Gay Head and Buzzard's Bay, 10 to 25 fathoms; off Block Island, 29 fathoms; very common in Casco Bay, Bay of Fundy, and Gulf of Saint Lawrence, 3 to 80 fathoms. Sandy Hook, and Montauk, Long Island (S. Smith). Off New London, Connecticut (T. M. Prudden). Saint George's Bank, 25 to 65 fathoms, (S. I. Smith). Straits of Belle Isle, 50 fathoms; Chateau Bay, 50 fathoms; Long Island, Labrador, 15 fathoms, (Packard). A species, regarded as identical by Dr. Carpenter, occurs on the North Pacific coast of America as far south as Catalina Island, and on the northeast coast of Asia.

Fossil in the Post-Pliocene of Gardiner's Island; Nantucket and Point Shirley, Massachusetts; and Labrador. The Miocene form, *C. granulata* (Say, sp.) is very closely allied to this, if not identical. It is found in Virginia and Maryland.

CYCLOCARDIA NOVANGLIÆ Morse. Plate XXIX, fig. 215. (p. 418.)

Actinobolus (Cyclocardia) Nova-angliæ Morse, First Annual Report of Trustees of Peabody Acad. of Science, Salem, p. 76, cut, 1869. *Cyclocardia Novangliæ* Verrill, Amer. Journ. Science, vol. iii, p. 211, 1872.

Connecticut to Gulf of Saint Lawrence. Mouth of Vineyard Sound and off Gay Head, 10 to 25 fathoms; Casco Bay, and Bay of Fundy, 3 to 40 fathoms, not uncommon. Off New London, Connecticut (T. M. Prudden).

ASTARTE UNDATA Gould. Plate XXIX, fig. 203. (p. 508.)

Invert., ed. i, p. 80, fig. 46, 1841 (provisional name); Philippi, Abbildungen und Beschr. neuer oder wenig gek. Conch., vol. ii, p. 1, Plate 1, fig. 1, 1850; Verrill, Amer. Jour. Science, vol. iii, p. 213, 1872. *Crasina latisulca* Hanley, Recent Shells, p. 87, Plate 14, fig. 35, 1843. *Astarte sulcata* Gould, Invert., ed. i, p. 78, fig. 46, 1841 (not of European writers); ed. ii, p. 119, fig. 432 (poor figure, from an old, deformed shell).

Var. *lutea* = *Astarte lutea* Perkins, Proc. Boston Soc. Nat. Hist., vol. xiii, p. 150, figure, 1869.

Long Island Sound to the southern part of the Gulf of Saint Lawrence. Off Gay Head and Buzzard's Bay, and in the deeper parts of Vineyard Sound, 8 to 25 fathoms, common; off Block Island, 29 fathoms; very common in Casco Bay and Bay of Fundy, 5 to 100 fathoms; Saint George's Bank, 20 to 85 fathoms. Off New London, Connecticut, (T. M. Prudden). Southern part of Gulf of Saint Lawrence (Whiteaves). Var. *lutea* occurs rarely near New Haven (Perkins); and more frequently off Gay Head and in Vineyard Sound, 8 to 19 fathoms, with the ordinary varieties. It resembles the European *sulcata* more than the common or typical varieties do, but passes insensibly into the ordinary forms. The shells referred to *undata*, by Dawson and Whiteaves, from

Gaspé, Canada, are not this species, but a short variety of *A. elliptica.* The latter is a much more northern shell, and I have dredged but one specimen on the New England coast (off Casco Bay, 65 fathoms).

Fossil at Point Shirley, Massachusetts, in the Post-Pliocene, (Stimpson, as *A. sulcata*); and at Gardiner's Island (S. Smith).

ASTARTE CASTANEA Say. Plate XXIX, fig. 204. (p. 432.)

American Conchology, Part i, 1830, Plate 1; Binney's Say, p. 150, Plate 1; Gould, Invert., ed. i, p. 76, fig. 45; ed. ii, p. 117, fig. 431. *Venus castanea* Say, Journ. Acad. Nat. Sci., Philad., vol. ii, p. 273, 1822; Binney's Say, p. 96. *Crassina castanea* Lamarck, Anim. sans Vert., ed. ii, vol. vi, p. 258; Hanley, Recent Shells, p. 88, Plate 9, fig. 27.

Great Egg Harbor, New Jersey, to Nova Scotia. Common on the shores of Long Island, Nantucket, Martha's Vineyard, and Cape Cod; Long Island Sound, not very common; Vineyard Sound and Buzzard's Bay, 5 to 20 fathoms, frequent; Casco Bay and Bay of Fundy, 5 to 20 fathoms, not common. Massachusetts Bay, abundant, (t. Gould). Saint George's Bank, 25 to 40 fathoms, (S. I. Smith). Halifax and Sable Island, Nova Scotia (Willis). Off Cape Sable, Nova Scotia (A. E. V.). Off New London, Connecticut (T. M. Prudden). Fossil in the Post-Pliocene at Nantucket and Point Shirley, Massachusetts.

ASTARTE QUADRANS Gould. Plate XXIX, fig. 205. (p. 509.)

Invert., ed. i, p. 81, fig. 48, 1841; ed. ii, p. 123, fig. 434; Verrill, Amer. Journ. Sci., vol. iii, p. 287, 1872. *Astarte Portlandica* Mighels, Boston Journ. Nat. Hist., vol. iv, pp. 320, 345, Plate 16, fig. 2, 1843 (variety); Gould, Invert., ed. ii, p. 127, fig. 441.

Stonington, Connecticut, to Gulf of Saint Lawrence. Mouth of Vineyard Sound, and off Martha's Vineyard, 19 to 25 fathoms, rare; Massachusetts Bay; Casco Bay; Bay of Fundy, in 6 to 40 fathoms, not uncommon. Saint George's Bank (S. I. Smith). Gulf of Saint Lawrence (Whiteaves).

Var. *Portlandica* occurs, with intermediate forms, in Casco Bay and Bay of Fundy, 10 to 25 fathoms, not common.

GOULDIA MACTRACEA Gould. Plate XXIX, figs. 206, 207. (p. 418.)

Invert., ed. ii, p. 128, fig. 442, 1870. *Astarte mactracea* Linsley, Amer. Jour. Sci., vol. xlviii, p. 275 (figure), 1845; Gould, op. cit., ser. ii, vol. vi, p. 233, figs. 1. 2, 1848. (?)*Astarte lunulata* Conrad, Jour. Acad. Nat. Sciences, Philad., vol. vii, p. 151, 1837; Fossils of the Medial Tertiary of the U. S., p. 45, Plate 21, fig. 8, 1840; *Gouldia lunulata* Conrad, Catal. of Miocene Shells, in Proc. Acad. Nat. Sci., Philad., vol. xiv, p. 578, 1862.

Florida and northern shores of the Gulf of Mexico to Cape Cod. Common, living, and of large size, in Vineyard Sound and Buzzard's Bay, especially at Wood's Hole, 3 to 10 fathoms. Stonington, in stomach of cod (Linsley). Huntington and Greenport, Long Island (S. Smith). Off New London, Connecticut (coll. T. M. Prudden). Fort Macon (Coues). South Carolina (Kurtz). West Florida (E. Jewett). Tampa Bay (Conrad).

Fossil (*G. lunulata*) in the Post-Pliocene of North and South Carolina; in the Pliocene of South Carolina; and in the Miocene of Maryland and Virginia. The fossil shell is probably identical with the recent one, but I have not had suitable specimens of the former for comparison; if identical, the species should be called *G. lunulata*.

LUCINA FILOSA Stimpson. Plate XXIX, fig. 212. (p. 509.)

Shells of New England, p. 17, 1851; Gould, Invert., ed. ii, p. 98, fig. 404. *Lucina radula* Gould, Invert., ed. i, p. 69 (*non* Montagu, sp.). ? *Lucina contracta*, Say, Jour. Acad. Nat. Sciences, Philad., vol. iv, p. 145, Plate 10, fig. 8; Conrad, Fossils of the Medial Tertiary of U. S., p. 40, Plate 20, fig. 5, 1840.

Stonington, Connecticut, to Maine. Off Block Island, 29 fathoms, sandy mud; off Gay Head, 19 fathoms, soft mud; Casco Bay and Portland Harbor. Stonington (Linsley). Boston Harbor (Stimpson). Phillip's Beach (Holder). Rhode Island (Conrad, as *L. contracta*).

Fossil in the Post-Pliocene of Gardiner's Island (S. Smith). *L. contracta* occurs in the Miocene of Virginia; it was formerly regarded by Conrad as identical with the recent shell from Rhode Island, but is probably a distinct, though closely-allied species. Mr. Jeffreys identified this species with *L. borealis* (Linné) of Europe; the latter is also found on the Pacific coast at Vancouver Island and Catalina Island (Cooper and P. P. Carpenter).

CYCLAS DENTATA. Plate XXIX, fig. 211. (p. 418.)

Lucina dentata Wood, General Conchology, p. 195, Plate 46, fig. 7, 1815; Gould, Invert., ed. ii, p. 99, fig. 45. *Lucina divaricata* Gould, Invert., ed. i, p. 70, (*non* Linné, sp). *Lucina strigilla* Stimpson, Shells of New England, p. 17, 1851.

Brazil and West Indies to Cape Cod. Not uncommon, dead, but rarely obtained living, in Vineyard Sound, 6 to 14 fathoms. Coney Island (S. Smith). Nantucket (Gould). St. George's Bank (S. I. Smith). Fort Macon, North Carolina, abundant, (Coues, Yarrow). Georgia (Couper).

Fossil in the Post-Pliocene of North Carolina, South Carolina, and Florida; and in the Pliocene of South Carolina. The same, or a closely-related species, (*L. Conradi* D'Orb., Prod., iii, p. 117, 2194, t. Conrad, in Proc. Acad. Nat. Sci., Phil., 1862, p. 577=*L. divaricata* Conrad, Fossils of Med. Tert., p. 38, Plate 20, fig. 3) occurs in the Miocene of Virginia.

CRYPTODON GOULDII Adams. Plate XXIX, fig. 213. (p. 509.)

H. and A. Adams, Genera, vol. ii, p. 470, 1858; Gould, Invert., ed. ii, p. 100, fig. 406. *Lucina Gouldii* Philippi, Zeitsch. f. Malak., 1845, p. 74 (t. Gould). *Thyasira Gouldii* Stimpson, Shells of New Eng., p. 17, 1851. *Lucina flexuosa* Gould, Invert., ed. i, p. 71, fig. 52 (*non* Montagu, sp.).

Stonington, Connecticut, to Gulf of Saint Lawrence. Off Block Island, 29 fathoms; Buzzard's Bay, 6 fathoms, mud; common in Massachusetts Bay, Casco Bay, and Bay of Fundy, 5 to 60 fathoms, muddy and sandy. Nova Scotia (Willis). Gaspé, Canada (Whiteaves). Murray Bay (Dawson). Gulf of Saint Lawrence, 20 to 300 fathoms (Whiteaves). Greenland (Mörch). Labrador, 15 to 50 fathoms, (Packard). Fossil in the Post-Pliocene at Montreal, rare, (Dawson); Brunswick, Maine (Packard).

Possibly some of the Gulf of Saint Lawrence specimens may belong to the following species.

CRYPTODON OBESUS Verrill. Plate XXIX, fig. 214. (p. 509.)

American Journ. Science, vol. iii, pp. 211, 287, Plate 7, fig. 2, 1872.

Shell white, irregularly and rather coarsely concentrically striated, much swollen in the middle; the transverse diameter nearly equal to the length; the height considerably exceeding the length. The beaks are prolonged and turned strongly to the anterior side. The lunular area is rather large and sunken, somewhat flat, in some cases separated by a slight ridge into an inner and an outer portion. Anterior border with a prominent rounded angle; ventral margin prolonged and rounded in the middle; posterior side with two strongly-developed flexures, separated by deep grooves. Interior of shell with radiating grooves, most conspicuous toward the ventral edge.

Length of the largest specimen, 15^{mm}; height, 18^{mm}; thickness, 13^{mm}. The smaller specimens have about the same proportions.

Six single valves, some of them quite fresh, were obtained off No-man's Land at different localities. They were all right valves, and the smallest was 12.5^{mm} of an inch in height. The specimen from Labrador agrees nearly in form and structure, and is only 5.75^{mm} in height and 5^{mm} in length.

This species appears to be more nearly related to *C. flexuosus* of Europe than to *C. Gouldii*. The European species is nearly intermediate between the two American shells in form; but judging from the specimens that I have had opportunities to examine, the three forms ought to be kept distinct. *C. Gouldii* is a thinner and more delicate shell, more rounded, relatively much longer, and is seldom more than 6^{mm} to 7^{mm} in breadth.

Block Island to Labrador. East of Block Island, in 29 fathoms, fine sandy mud; off Gay Head, 19 fathoms, mud; Casco Bay, 60 fathoms, mud. Labrador (Packard). East of Saint George's Bank, 430 fathoms (S. I. Smith).

Turtonia minuta Stimpson.

Shells of New England, p. 16, 1851 (*non* Alder, Forbes and Hanley, etc.); Gould, Invert., ed. ii, p. 85, fig. 395. *Venus minuta* Fabricius, Fauna Grönlandica, p. 412, 1780. *Turtonia nitida* Verrill, Amer. Journ. of Sci. vol. iii, p. 286, Plate 7, figs. 4, 4*a*, 1872.

Massachusetts Bay to Greenland. Common under stones and in rocky pools at low-water, in Massachusetts Bay and Casco Bay. Although this species has not yet been found south of Cape Cod, so far as I am aware, it will probably be found hereafter on the more exposed rocky shores, as at Point Judith, Watch Hill, or on some of the outer islands.

The American specimens of this shell differ so widely in form, and especially in the structure of the hinge, from all the European specimens with which I have compared them, as well as from the descriptions and figures, that I cannot regard them as identical. Dr. Gould has well defined the form and external characters of our shell. I have seen no European specimens so elongated in form as the American examples seen by me invariably are, but depend less on the external form than on the structure of the hinge for distinguishing them. (See the greatly enlarged figure in the Amer. Journal of Science).

Having had opportunities to study northern specimens of this shell, since I gave it the name *nitida*, I have become fully satisfied that the original shell described by Fabricius is identical with the American species, rather than with the European. His description corresponds well with our best specimens. The European species, if, as I believe, distinct from ours, should, therefore, retain the name *T. purpurea* (Montagu, sp.); and *minuta* should be restored to the American form.

KELLIA PLANULATA Stimpson. Plate XXX, fig. 226. (p. 310.)

Shells of New England, p. 17, 1851; Gould, Invert., ed. ii, p. 83, fig, 393. *Kellia rubra* Gould, Invert., ed. i, p. 60, (*non* Montagu, sp.).

Long Island Sound to Greenland. Near New Haven, Connecticut, rare; Vineyard Sound and Buzzard's Bay, 1 to 8 fathoms, not common; Casco Bay; Eastport, Maine, 8 to 15 fathoms; Bay of Fundy. Montauk and Greenport, Long Island, low-water to 6 fathoms, mud; and Gull Island, low-water, under stones, (S. Smith). Boston Harbor, 5 fathoms, shelly, (Stimpson). Sable Island, Nova Scotia (Willis). Greenland (Mörch).

MONTACUTA ELEVATA Stimpson. (p. 418.)

Shells of New England, p. 16, 1851; Gould, Invert., ed. ii. p. 86, fig. 396. *Montacuta bidentata* Gould, Invert., ed. i, p. 59, 1841 (*non* Montagu, sp., 1803).

Long Island Sound to Massachusetts Bay. Savin Rock, near New Haven, rare; Naushon Island, Vineyard Sound, rare. Greenport, Long Island (S. Smith). New Bedford (Gould). Chelsea Beach (Stimpson).

LEPTON FABAGELLA Conrad.

Marine Conchology, p. 53, Plate 11, fig. 3, 1831; Dekay, Nat. History of New York, Mollusca, p. 243, Plate 32, fig. 307, A, B.

Rhode Island (Conrad).

I have not seen specimens of this shell. It seems to be rare and little known.

A closely-related species (*L. mactroides* Conrad, Fossils Medial Tert., p. 19, Plate X, fig. 5, 1839) is found in the Miocene of Maryland.

SOLENOMYA VELUM Say. Plate XXIX, fig. 210. (p. 360.)

Journal Acad. Nat. Sciences, Philad., vol. ii, p. 317, 1822 (*Solemya*); Gould, Invert., ed. i, p. 35; ed. ii, p. 48, fig. 371.

North Carolina to Nova Scotia. Great Egg Harbor, New Jersey; Long Island Sound, near New Haven, low-water to 6 fathoms, not uncommon;

very common in Buzzard's Bay and Vineyard Sound, 1 to 5 fathoms, especially in soft mud, in coves; Chelsea Beach, etc., Massachusetts Bay, common; Casco Bay, rare. Nova Scotia (Willis). Huntington and Greenport, Long Island, rare, (S. Smith).

SOLENOMYA BOREALIS Totten.

Amer. Jour. Science, vol. xxvi, p. 366, fig. 1, *h*, *i*, 1834 (*Solemya borealis*); Gould, Invert., ed. i, p. 36; ed. ii, p. 50, fig. 372.

Connecticut to Nova Scotia. Newport, Rhode Island (Totten). Chelsea and Nahant, Massachusetts (Gould). Casco Bay and Portland Harbor rare; Vineyard Sound, at Cuttyhunk Island, rare. Stonington, Connecticut (Linsley).

This species may prove to be only the mature state of the preceding, but I have never seen specimens intermediate in character.

YOLDIA LIMATULA Stimpson. Plate XXX, fig. 232. (p. 432).

Shells of New England, p. 9, 1851; H. and A. Adams, Genera, vol. ii, p. 548, Plate 126, figs. 5, 5*b*, 1858; Gould, Invert., ed. ii, p. 154, fig. 462. *Nucula limatula* Say, Amer. Conch., ii, Plate 12, middle figures, 1831; Gould, Invert., p. 98, fig. 62. *Leda limatula* Stimpson, Shells of New England, p. 10, 1851.

North Carolina to Gulf of Saint Lawrence. Common in Long Island Sound; Buzzard's Bay; Vineyard Sound; Casco Bay, in 2 to 12 fathoms, soft mud; less common in the Bay of Fundy, 4 to 30 fathoms. Beaufort, North Carolina (Stimpson, Coues). Huntington and Greenport, Long Island (S. Smith). Nova Scotia (Willis). The specimens from Long Island Sound are as large and fine as the northern ones.

Fossil in the Post-Pliocene of Canada, Virginia, North and South Carolina; and in the Pliocene of South Carolina. An allied species (*Y lævis* Say, sp., Conrad) occurs in the Miocene of Maryland and South Carolina.

Yoldia myalis Stimpson; Gould, Invert., ed. ii, p. 160, fig. 467; *Nucula myalis* Couthouy, 1838. This is often confounded with *Y. limatula*, though quite distinct. It is a more arctic species, ranging from Massachusetts Bay to the Arctic Ocean and Spitzbergen, but it has not been found south of Cape Cod, so far as known to me. The shells reported as such, that I have seen, are *Y. limatula*. Gould reports the latter as from Nordland (McAndrew), but we suspect that *Y. myalis* or *Y. sapotilla* may have been, in this case, mistaken for *Y. limatula*.

YOLDIA SAPOTILLA Stimpson, 1851. Plate XXX, fig. 231. (p. 509.)

H. and A. Adams, Genera, vol. ii, p. 548; Gould, Invert., ed. ii, p. 159, fig. 466. *Nucula sapotilla* Gould, Invert., ed. i, p. 100, fig. 61, 1841; Hanley, Recent Shells, p. 170, Plate 20, fig. 3. *Leda* (*Yoldia*) *sapotilla* Stimpson, Shells of New England, p. 10, 1851. *Yoldia arctica* Mörch, op. cit., p. 93, 1857 (t. Dawson, from specimen; *non Y. arctica* Sars).

Long Island to the Arctic Ocean, comparatively rare and local, chiefly in deep water, south of Cape Cod. Off Gay Head, 19 fathoms, soft mud; off Buzzard's Bay, 25 fathoms, sand; east of Block Island, 29 fathoms, fine sandy mud; common in Casco Bay and Bay of Fundy, 4 to 100 fathoms, mud. Greenport, Long Island (S. Smith). Massachusetts Bay (Gould). Nova Scotia (Willis). Labrador (Packard). Greenland (Mörch).

This species seems to be unknown among our Post-Pliocene shells. Having examined several hundred specimens from many different localities and depths, I am satisfied that it is perfectly distinct from *Y. limatula*, with which certain writers are inclined to unite it.

Yoldia Gouldii.

Nucula Gouldii DeKay, Nat. Hist. New York, Mollusca, p. 180, Plate 13, fig. 221, 1843.

This was originally described by Dekay as from Long Island Sound. I have seen no specimens corresponding with the description in all respects. It is, perhaps, a short variety of *Y. sapotilla.*

YOLDIA OBESA Stimpson, 1851. (p. 509.)

H. and A. Adams, Genera, vol. ii, p. 548, 1858; Gould, Invert., ed. ii, p, 155, fig. 463. *Leda obesa* Stimpson, Proc. Boston Soc. Nat. Hist., vol. iv, p. 13, 1851; Shells of New England, p. 10, Plate 2, fig. 1, 1851. *Nucula navicularis* Mighels, Boston Journal Nat. History, p. 323, 1843 (*non* Couthouy, Gould).

Block Island to Gulf of Saint Lawrence. East of Block Island, 29 fathoms, rare; Casco Bay and off Cape Elizabeth, 30 to 95 fathoms; Bay of Fundy, 40 to 100 fathoms, rare; near Saint George's Bank, 110 and 150 fathoms (Packard). Massachusetts Bay (Stimpson).

YOLDIA THRACIFORMIS Stimpson, 1851. (p. 509.)

Smithsonian Check-List, p. 2, 1860; H. and A. Adams, Genera, vol. ii, p. 548, 1858 (*thraciæformis*); Gould, Invert., ed. ii, p. 157, fig. 465; Mörch, op. cit., p. 21, 1857. *Nucula thraciæformis* Storer, Boston Jour. Nat. History, vol. ii, p. 122, figure, 1838; Gould, Invert., ed. i, p. 97, fig. 66. *Leda thraciæformis* Stimpson, Shells of New England, p. 9, 1851. *Nucula navicularis* Couthouy, Boston Journ. Nat. History, vol. ii, p. 178, Plate 4, fig. 4, 1839, (young); Gould, Invert., ed. i, p. 103. *Yoldia angularis* Möller, op. cit., p. 92, 1842 (t. Mörch).

Long Island to Greenland. Off Fire Island, south of Long Island, in 10 fathoms; and off Race Point, Cape Cod, in 30 fathoms, (Stimpson). Not uncommon, and of large size, in Casco Bay, 15 to 95 fathoms; and Bay of Fundy, 10 to 100 fathoms; near Saint George's Bank, 85 fathoms (Packard).

LEDA TENUISULCATA Stimpson. (p. 509.)

Shells of New England, p. 10, 1851; Gould, Invert., ed. ii, p. 161, fig. 468. *Nucula tenuisulcata* Couthouy, Boston Journ. Nat. Hist., vol. ii, p. 64, Plate 3, fig. 8, 1838. *Nucula minuta* Gould, Invert., ed. i, p. 101, 1841 (*non* Fabricius, sp).

Rhode Island to Gulf of Saint Lawrence. Common in Massachusetts Bay, Casco Bay, and Bay of Fundy, 6 to 80 fathoms. Nova Scotia (Willis). Newport, Rhode Island (t. S. Smith). Southern part of the Gulf of Saint Lawrence (Whiteaves). Particularly abundant in Eastport Harbor, 10 to 30 fathoms; Saint George's Bank and vicinity, 40 to 150 fathoms (Smith, Packard). Fossil in the Post-Pliocene at Saco and Portland, Maine (Packard); ? Canada (Dawson, as *L. pernula*, var).

NUCULA PROXIMA Say. Plate XXX, fig. 230. (p. 418.)

Journ. Acad. Nat. Sciences, Philad., vol. ii, p. 270, 1822; Gould, Invert., ed. i, p. 103, fig. 63; ed. ii, p. 150, fig. 458.

South Carolina to Gulf of Saint Lawrence. Common in Long Island Sound, Buzzard's Bay, and Vineyard Sound, 2 to 19 fathoms; off Buzzard's Bay and Block Island, 25 to 29 fathoms; common in Massachusetts Bay, Casco Bay, and Bay of Fundy, 4 to 80 fathoms; very abundant in Trenton Bay, Mount Desert, Maine, 10 fathoms, soft mud. Nova Scotia (Willis). Saint George's Bank (S. I. Smith). Fort Macon, North Carolina (Coues). Long Island, abundant, (S. Smith). Fossil in the Post-Pliocene of North and South Carolina; in the Pliocene of South Carolina; and in the Miocene of Maryland and South Carolina.

NUCULA DELPHINODONTA Mighels. Plate XXX, fig. 229. (p. 509.)

Boston Journal Nat. Hist., vol. iv, p. 40, Plate 4, fig. 5, 1842; Gould, Invert., ed. ii, p. 153, fig. 461. *Nucula corticata* Möller, Naturhistorisk Tidsskrift, vol. iv, p. 90, 1842. ? *Nucula radiata* Dekay, Nat. Hist. New York, Moll., p. 179, Plate 12, fig. 216, 1843.

Rhode Island to Greenland. East of Block Island, 29 fathoms; off Gay Head, 19 fathoms, soft mud; Massachusetts Bay, common; Casco Bay, 6 to 95 fathoms, common; Frenchman's Bay, Mount Desert, common; Bay of Fundy and Eastport Harbor, 10 to 100 fathoms, mud, common; Nova Scotia (Willis); Gulf of St. Lawrence (Whiteaves). Greenland (Möller, Mörch). Northern Europe (t. Jeffreys).

Nucula tenuis Turton (Montagu, sp.)

Gould, Invert., ed. i., p. 105, fig. 64; ed. ii, p. 149, fig. 457.

This species was recorded as from cod-stomachs, at Stonington, Connecticut, but was not met with by us. Its occurrence south of Cape Cod needs confirmation. It is an arctic species; common in Casco Bay and the Bay of Fundy, in 10 to 100 fathoms, mud; and northward to the Arctic Ocean. Also on the northern coasts of Europe, south to Great Britain. It is also found in the Post-Pliocene of New England and Canada.

SCAPHARCA TRANSVERSA. Plate XXX, fig. 228. (p. 309.)

H. and A. Adams, Genera, vol. ii, p. 538, 1858. *Arca transversa* Say, Jour. Acad. Nat. Sci., Philad., vol. ii, p. 269, 1822; Gould, Invert., ed. i, p. 96; ed. ii, p. 148, fig. 456*a*.

Florida to Cape Cod. Long Island Sound, near New Haven, low-water to 8 fathoms; Buzzard's Bay and Vineyard Sound, 2 to 10 fathoms; Great Egg Harbor, New Jersey, 1 fathom. Nantucket (Gould). Long Island, abundant; Greenport, 3 to 10 fathoms (S. Smith). Fort Macon, North Carolina (Coues). South Carolina (Kurtz). Georgia (Couper).

Fossil in the Post-Pliocene of Nantucket, Gardiner's Island, Virginia, North and South Carolina; and in the Miocene of Virginia and North Carolina. According to Gould, found fossil at Provincetown, Massachusetts, in an artesian boring, 120 to 200 feet beneath the surface, (Post-Pliocene ?)

ARGINA PEXATA Gray. Plate XXX, fig. 227. (p. 309.)

Proc. Zoöl. Soc., London, 1847; H. and A. Adams, Genera, vol. ii, p. 540, Plate 125, figs. 7, 7*a*, 1858. *Arca pexata* Say, Jour. Acad. Nat. Sciences, Philad., vol. ii, p. 268, 1822; Gould, Invert., ed. i, p. 95, fig. 60; ed. ii, p. 147, fig. 456.

Florida and northern shores of Gulf of Mexico to Cape Cod; rare and local farther north, in Massachusetts Bay. Very common in Long Island Sound, low-water to 10 fathoms; Buzzard's Bay; Vineyard Sound; Great Egg Harbor, New Jersey. On beach at Provincetown, Massachusetts (S. I. Smith). Staten Island and Long Island, abundant (S. Smith). Fort Macon, North Carolina (Yarrow). Georgia (Couper). West Florida (Jewett). Texas (Rœmer).

Fossil in the Post-Pliocene of Gardiner's Island (?) (S. Smith); in the Miocene of South Carolina.

ARCA PONDEROSA Say.

Journ. Acad. Nat. Sciences, Philadelphia, vol. ii, p. 267, 1822; Binney's Say, p. 92.

This species occurs on the beach at Edgartown, Martha's Vineyard, associated with the other common sand-dwelling shells of that region. The valves are apparently tolerably fresh, though worn, and no fossil shells have been found in that vicinity. It occurs in the same way on the southern side of Long Island, near Fire Island (S. I. Smith and S. Smith). But I am not aware that it has been found living north of Cape Hatteras; nevertheless, it may occur locally in shallow water off shore. The specimens found may possibly have been washed out from submerged Post-Pliocene deposits.

It is found living at Fort Macon, North Carolina, and southward to the Gulf of Mexico.

HETEROMYARIA.

MYTILUS EDULIS Linné. Plate XXXI, fig. 234. (pp. 307, 432.)

Systema Naturæ, ed. xii, p. 1157, 1767; Gould, Invert., ed. i, p. 121, fig. 82; ed. ii, p. 183, figs. 483, 484. *Mytilus borealis* Lamarck, Anim. sans Vert., ed. ii, vol. vii, p. 46; Dekay, Nat. Hist. N. Y., Moll., p. 182, Plate 13, fig. 222, Plate 24, fig. 256. *Mytilus pellucidus* Pennant, Brit. Zoöl., vol. iv, p. 237, Plate 66, fig. 3, (t. Gould) = variety *pellucidus* Gould, Invert., ed. ii, p. 184, fig. 484. *Mytilus notatus* Dekay, op. cit., p. 182, Plate 13, fig. 223, 1843.

Circumpolar: Arctic Ocean south to North Carolina, on the American coast; south to Great Britain, France, and the Mediterranean and Black Seas, on the European coast; south to Monterey and San Francisco, on the North Pacific coast; south to China and Japan, on the Asiatic coast. Very abundant in Great Egg Harbor, New Jersey, Long

Island Sound, Buzzard's Bay, Vineyard Sound, Massachusetts Bay, Casco Bay, Bay of Fundy (littoral to 50 fathoms), and northward. Fort Macon, North Carolina (Coues).

Fossil in the Post-Pliocene of Greenland, Labrador, Canada, Lake Champlain, Maine, New Brunswick, Point Shirley, Massachusetts, and Saint John's River, Florida; in the Post-Pliocene of Scandinavia, Russia, and Great Britain; in the Red Crag and all later formations in England.

MODIOLA MODIOLUS Turton. Plate XXXI, fig. 237. (p. 309.)

British Bivalves, p. 199, Plate 15, fig. 3, 1822; Gould, Invert., ed. i, p. 123; ed. ii, p. 186, fig. 485; Dekay, op. cit., p. 185, Plate 24, fig. 257. *Mytilus modiolus* Linné, Syst. Nat., ed. xii, p. 1158. (?)*Modiola papuana* Lamarck, Anim. sans Vert., ed. ii, vol. vii, p. 17; Say, Amer. Conch., Plate 45.

Circumpolar: Greenland southward to New Jersey; on the European coast from Spitzbergen southward to Great Britain and France; in the North Pacific southward to Monterey, California, on the American coast; and southward to Northern Japan on the Asiatic coast. Long Island Sound, not very common; Vineyard Sound and Buzzard's Bay, not abundant; common in Massachusetts Bay; abundant in Casco Bay and Bay of Fundy, low-water to 80 fathoms. Staten Island and Long Island (S. Smith). Fossil in the Post-Pliocene of Point Shirley, Massachusetts, Montreal, Canada, Scotland, Ireland, Sicily, etc.; in the Coraline Crag, Red Crag, and later formations in England.

MODIOLA PLICATULA Lamarck. Plate XXXI, fig. 238. (p. 307.)

Anim. sans Vert., ed. i, 1819; ed. ii, vol. vii, p. 22; Gould, ed. i, p. 125, fig. 81; ed. ii, p. 188, fig. 486; Dekay, op. cit., p. 184, Plate 14, fig. 258; Hanley, Recent Shells, p. 240. *Mytilus plicatus* Deshayes, Encyclop. Meth., Plate 220, fig. 5; Stimpson, Shells of New England, p. 12. *Modiola semicosta* Conrad, Jour. Acad. Nat. Sci., Philad., vol. vii, p. 244, Plate 20, fig. 7, (t. Gould). *Mytilus demissus* Dillyn, Catal. Recent Shells, vol. i, p. 314 (t. Gould). *Brachydontes plicatulus* H. and A. Adams, Genera, vol. ii, p. 517; Perkins, op. cit., p. 156.

Georgia, to Casco Bay, Maine; more rare and local farther north; in the southern part of the Gulf of Saint Lawrence, and on the coast of Nova Scotia; nor observed on the coast of Maine east of the Kennebeck River, nor in the Bay of Fundy. Very abundant at Egg Harbor, New Jersey, Long Island Sound, Buzzard's Bay, and Vineyard Sound; less abundant in Massachusetts Bay, near Salem, Massachusetts, etc.; local in sheltered muddy coves about Casco Bay and Quahog Bay, Maine. Mouth of the Kennebeck River (C. B. Fuller). Prince Edward's Island (Dawson). Nova Scotia (Willis). Fort Macon, North Carolina (Coues). Georgia (Couper).

MODIOLA HAMATUS Verrill. (pp. 374, 475.)

American Journ. Science, vol. iii, p. 211, Plate 7, fig. 3, 1872. *Mytilus hamatus* Say, Journ. Acad. Nat. Sci., Philadelphia, vol. ii, p. 265, 1822; American Conchology, Plate 50; Binney's Say, pp. 91, 204, Plate 50. *Aulacomya hamatus* Adams, Genera, vol. ii, p. 513. *Brachydontes hamatus* Perkins, op. cit., p. 156, 1869.

Long Island Sound to Florida, and the shores of the Gulf of Mexico to Vera Cruz. New Haven, common on oysters, living, but perhaps introduced from Virginia. New York Harbor, on oysters, (S. Smith). Fort Macon, North Carolina (Yarrow). Georgia (Couper). Tampa Bay, Florida (Conrad, Jewett). Texas (Rœmer). Near Vera Cruz (coll. T. Salt, in Yale museum).

MODIOLARIA NIGRA Lovén. Plate XXXI, fig. 236. (p. 433.)

Öfvers. af Kongl. Vet.-Akad., Förhandl., vol. iii, p. 187, 1846; Mörch, Naturhist. Bidrag, Grönland, p. 93, 1857; H. and A. Adams, Genera, vol. ii, p. 515, 1858; Gould, Invert., ed. ii, p. 190, figs. 487, 488. *Modiola nigra* Gray, Appendix to Parry's Voyage, p. 244, 1824; Hanley, Recent Shells, p. 242. *Mytilus discrepans* Stimpson, Shells of New England, p. 12, 1851 (not of European authors). *Modiola nexa* Gould, Invert., ed. i, p. 128, fig. 86 (young).

Circumpolar: Greenland, southward to Long Island; Spitzbergen, southward to Great Britain and Holland; Behring's Straits, southward to Okhotsk. Not uncommon and of good size in Vineyard Sound, 10 to 15 fathoms, off Gay Head, etc.; common in Casco Bay and Bay of Fundy, of large size, low-water to 60 fathoms; Stonington, Connecticut, in stomach of cod, (Linsley).

Fossil in the Post-Pliocene of Maine, Canada, Labrador, and Northern Europe.

MODIOLARIA DISCORS Beck.

Lovén, Öfvers. af Kongl. Vet.-Akad. Förhandl., vol. iii, p. 187, 1846; Gould, Invert., ed. ii, p. 83, figs. 489, 490. *Mytilus discors* Linné, Syst. Nat., ed. xii, p. 1159; Stimpson, Shells of New England, p. 12, (*non* Gould, ed. i). *Mytilus discrepans* Montagu, Test. Brit., p. 169. *Modiola discrepans* Lamarck, Anim. sans Vert., ed. ii, vol. vii, p. 23; Gould, Invert., ed. i, p. 129, fig. 83. *Modiola lævigata* Gray, Appendix to Parry's Second Voyage, p. 245. *Mytilus levigatus* Stimpson, Shells of New England, p. 12. *Modiolaria lævigata* Lovén, op. cit., p. 187, 1846; Stimpson, Check-List, p. 2, 1860; this Report, p. 509.

Circumpolar: Greenland, southward to Long Island; Finmark, southward to Great Britain; Behring's Straits, southward to Puget Sound. Very common in Casco Bay and Bay of Fundy, low-water to 100 fathoms; not uncommon in Massachusetts Bay; rare and local south of Cape Cod. Saint George's Bank and vicinity, common, (S. I. Smith, Packard). Gardiner's Bay, Long Island, rare, (S. Smith). North of Hebrides, in 530 fathoms, (t. Jeffreys).

Fossil in the Post-Pliocene of Canada, Greenland, and Northern Europe. I am unable to separate *M. lævigata*, as a species, from the ordinary New England form, usually referred to *M. discors*, the differences being due chiefly to age. The common European form of *discors* shows more differences, but is probably only a dwarf variety of the same species.

MODIOLARIA CORRUGATA Mörch. Plate XXXI, fig. 235. (p. 509.)

Op. cit., p. 94, 1857; Stimpson, Check-List, Smithsonian Inst., p. 2, 1860; Gould, Invert., ed. ii, p. 193, fig. 491. *Mytilus corrugatus* Stimpson, Shells of New England, p. 12, 1851. *Mytilus discors* Gould, Invert., ed. i, p. 130, fig. 84 (*non* Linné, sp.).

Long Island to Greenland and Northern Europe. Off Martha's Vineyard and Buzzard's Bay, 20 to 25 fathoms, rare; Casco Bay, 15 to 95 fathoms, not common; Bay of Fundy, 10 to 100 fathoms, frequent. Saint George's Bank (S. I. Smith, A. S. Packard). Gardiner's Bay, 5 fathoms, one specimen, (S. Smith). Off New London, Connecticut (T. M. Prudden). Gulf of Saint Lawrence (Whiteaves). Murray Bay (Dawson). Nova Scotia (Willis). Labrador (Packard). Arctic Ocean, near Behring's Straits, 30 fathoms, (Stimpson, N. P. Expl. Exp., t. Gould).

Fossil in the Post-Pliocene of Canada (Dawson).

CRENELLA GLANDULA Adams. Plate XXXI, fig. 233. (p. 418.)

H. and A. Adams, Genera, vol. ii, p. 515, 1858; Gould, Invert., ed. ii, p. 194, fig. 492. *Modiola glandula* Totten, American Journal Science, ser. i, vol. xxvi, p. 367, figs. 3, e, f, g, 1834; Gould, Invert., ed. i, p. 131, fig. 87 (*pars*). *Mytilus decussatus* Stimpson, Shells of New England, p. 11, 1851, (*non* Montagu, sp.); Dekay, op. cit., p. 186, Plate 22, fig. 248.

Connecticut to Gulf of Saint Lawrence. Buzzard's Bay and Vineyard Sound, 5 to 15 fathoms, not uncommon; off Gay Head, 19 fathoms, soft mud; off Block Island, 29 fathoms, sandy mud; common in Massachusetts Bay, Casco Bay, and Bay of Fundy, 3 to 60 fathoms. Halifax (Willis). Gulf of Saint Lawrence, at Gaspé (Whiteaves). Gardiner's Bay, Long Island (S. Smith). Stonington (Linsley). Off New London, Connecticut (T. M. Prudden). Sandy Hook, New Jersey (Ferguson). Fossil in the Post-Pliocene at Montreal, Canada (Dawson). A related species, *C. æquilaterata* Conrad (H. C. Lea, sp.) occurs in the Miocene of Virginia.

This species was undoubtedly confounded with *C. decussata* (Montagu, sp.) by both Gould and Stimpson. The genuine *decussata* is quite common in Casco Bay, Bay of Fundy, and Gulf of Saint Lawrence, and is usually associated in those waters with *C. glandula*. It is a northern, and common European species, and is also recorded from the North Pacific coast of America by Dr. P. P. Carpenter. It also occurs in Greenland (Mörch).

MONOMYARIA.

PECTEN IRRADIANS Lamarck. Plate XXXII, fig. 238. (p. 374.)

Anim. sans Vert., ed. i, 1819; ed. ii, vol. vii, p. 143; Gould, Invert., ed. ii, p. 199, fig. 496. *Pecten concentricus* Say, Journ. Acad. Nat. Sci., Philad., vol. ii, p. 259, 1822; Gould, Invert., ed. i, p. 134, fig. 88; Dekay, op. cit., p. 172, Plate 9, fig. 205.

Florida and the northern shores of the Gulf of Mexico to Cape Cod; rare and local farther north in Massachusetts Bay; and Nova Scotia (Willis). Very common in Vineyard Sound, Buzzard's Bay, shores of Long Island and Connecticut, New Jersey, and southward. Tampa Bay, Florida (Conrad, E. Jewett). Texas (Rœmer).

Fossil in the Post-Pliocene of North Carolina and Tampa Bay, Florida; in the Pliocene of South Carolina; and in the Miocene of

Maryland. Dug up from beneath the mud in the harbor of Portland, Maine, in a semi-fossil state by the mud-dredging machines (Fuller).

PECTEN ISLANDICUS Chemnitz.

Conch., vii, p. 304, Plate 65, figs. 615, 616, 1784, (t. Gould); Lamarck, op. cit., ed. ii, vol. vii, p. 145; Gould, Invert., ed. i, p. 133, fig. 87; ed. ii, p. 198, fig. 495. *Ostrea Islandica* Müller, Zoöl. Dan. Prod., No. 2990, 1776; Fabricius, Fauna, Grönl., p. 415, 1780. *Pecten Pealii* Conrad, Amer. Mar. Conch., p. 12, Plate 2, fig. 2, 1831.

Arctic Ocean south to Cape Cod, local and rare farther south; on the northern European coasts, south to Bergen, Norway, and Great Britain. Not uncommon and of good size in Casco Bay, 20 to 70 fathoms; common in the Bay of Fundy, low-water to 100 fathoms. Saint George's Bank, 40 to 65 fathoms, (S. I. Smith). More common farther north. Stonington, Connecticut, in an eel-pot, (Linsley). I am not aware that any one except Linsley has recorded it from the southern coast of New England.

Fossil in the Post-Pliocene of Maine (abundant), New Brunswick, Canada, Labrador, Greenland, Scandinavia, Denmark, Scotland, etc. Naples (Jeffreys). Mr. Sanderson Smith reports fragments from Gardiner's Island.

PECTEN TENUICOSTATUS Mighels. (p. 509.)

Mighels and Adams, Proceedings Boston Soc. Nat. Hist., vol. i, p. 49, 1841; Boston Journal of Natural History, vol. iv, p. 41, Plate 4, fig. 7, 1842 (young); Gould, Invert., ed. ii, p. 196, fig. 494. *Pecten Magellanicus* Lamarck, Anim. sans Vert., ed. ii, vol. vii, p. 134 (? *non* Gmelin, sp.); Hanley, Recent Shells, p. 274; Gould, Invert., ed. i, p. 132. *Pecten fuscus* Linsley, Amer. Jour. Sci., ser. i, vol. xlviii, p. 278, 1845; Gould, ser. ii, vol. vi, p. 235, fig. 6, 1848 (young). *Pecten brunneus* Stimpson, Shells of New England, in errata, 1851.

New Jersey to Labrador. Rare and local south of Cape Cod. Not uncommon in Massachusetts Bay and Casco Bay, 4 to 80 fathoms; abundant in Frenchman's Bay, Mount Desert, Maine, in 3 to 10 fathoms; common in Passamaquoddy Bay and Bay of Fundy, 1 to 109 fathoms. Saint George's Bank, 45 fathoms, (S. I. Smith). Nova Scotia (Willis). Labrador, 2 to 15 fathoms, (Packard). Off Block Island (Gould). Stonington, Connecticut, in cod stomachs, (Linsley, as *P. fuscus*). Coney Island and Sandy Hook, New York (S. Smith).

Fossil in the Post-Pliocene near Saint John, New Brunswick, and Gardiner's Island, New York. A closely related species occurs in the Miocene of Virginia.

ANOMIA GLABRA Verrill. Plate XXXII, figs. 241, 242, 242[a]. (p. 311.)

American Jour. Science, vol. iii, p. 213, 1872. *Anomia ephippium* (*pars*) Linné, Syst. Nat., ed. xii, p. 1150; Gould, Invert., ed. i, p. 138; ed. ii, p. 204, fig. 497. *Anomia electrica* Gould, Invert., ed. i, p. 140; ed. ii, p. 205, fig. 499, adult, (*non* Linné.) *Anomia squamula* Gould, Invert., ed. i, p. 140; ed. ii, p. 206, young, (*non* Linné.)

Florida to Cape Cod; rare and local farther north, in Massachusetts Bay, Casco Bay, and on the southern coast of Nova Scotia, off Cape

Sable, 8 fathoms. Not observed on the eastern part of the coast of Maine, nor in the Bay of Fundy. Very common in Long Island Sound, Buzzard's Bay, Vineyard Sound; along both shores of Long Island; New Jersey, and southward; low-water to 12 fathoms. Southern part of Saint George's Bank, 20 fathoms, (S. I. Smith).

Fossil in the Post-Pliocene of North and South Carolina; and in the Pliocene of South Carolina.

Linné gave "Pennsylvania" as one of the localities for his *A. ephippium*, and, therefore, probably confounded our shell with the European species, as most subsequent writers have done. Gould has well described our species in its different states, under the names quoted above, figures 499 of the second edition (our figures 241, 242), represent the ordinary adult form, which is everywhere abundant on the southern shores of New England. The specimens from Eastport, Maine, referred to *A. ephippium* by Gould, were undoubtedly the smooth or squamose variety of the following species.

ANOMIA ACULEATA Gmelin. Plate XXXII, figs. 239, 240, 240[a]. (p. 495.)

Syst. Nat., p. 3346, 1790; Gould, Invert., ed. i, p. 139, fig. 90; ed. ii, p. 204, fig. 498.

Long Island to Labrador, and northern coasts of Europe. Off Stonington, Connecticut, 4 to 5 fathoms rocky; off Gay Head, 10 fathoms, scarce; very common in Casco Bay, Bay of Fundy, and northward, low-water to 80 fathoms. Greenport and Montauk, Long Island (S. Smith).

Varieties of this species occur frequently in the Bay of Fundy and Casco Bay, in which the aculeate scales are more or less abortive, or even entirely absent, leaving the surface either nearly smooth or irregularly squamose, but such varieties are easily distinguished from the young of the preceding species.

This may possibly be a variety of the true *ephippium* of Europe, as supposed by many writers, but I believe it to be perfectly distinct from *A. glabra*.

OSTREA VIRGINIANA Lister. (pp. 310, 472.)

Favanne, Conch., Plate 41, fig C 2, 1780 (t. Gould); Gould, Invert., ed. i, p. 136; ed. ii, p. 202; Verrill, Amer. Jour. Science, vol. iii, p. 213, 1872. *Ostrea Virginica* Gmelin, Syst. Nat., p. 3336, 1790; Lamarck, Anim. sans Vert., ed. ii, vol. vii, p. 225. *Ostrea borealis* Lamarck, op. cit., p. 220; Gould, Invert., ed. i, p. 137; ed. ii, p. 203; Dekay, op. cit., p. 169, Plate 10, figs. 203, 204. *Ostrea Canadensis* Bruguière, Encycl. Meth., Plate 180, figs. 1–3; Lamarck, op. cit., p. 226; Hanley, Recent Shells, p. 299.

Florida and the northen shores of the Gulf of Mexico to Massachusetts Bay; local farther north, off Damariscotta, Maine, and in the southern part of the Gulf of Saint Lawrence, at Prince Edward Island, in Northumberland Straits, and Bay of Chaleur. Not found along the eastern shores of Maine, nor in the Bay of Fundy. Abundant in the ancient Indian shell-heaps on the coast of Massachusetts, on the islands in Casco Bay, and at Damariscotta. The shells, in a semi-fossil state, have been dug up from deep beneath the mud in the harbor of Portland, Maine, in large quantities, but native oysters appear to be entirely extinct in Casco Bay. Very abundant in Long Island Sound; in the upper part of Buzzard's Bay; rare and local in Vineyard Sound; very abundant on the shores of Maryland and Virginia. Mouth of Saint John's River, and in Tampa Bay, Florida (Conrad). Texas (Rœmer).

Fossil in the Post-Pliocene at Point Shirley, Massachusetts, Nantucket Island (abundant), Gardiner's Island; in the Pliocene of South Carolina; and in the Miocene of Virginia and South Carolina.

The occurrence of large quantities of oyster-shells beneath the harbor mud at Portland, associated with *Venus mercenaria*, *Pecten irradians*, *Turbonilla interrupta*, and other southern species, now extinct in that locality, and the occurrence of the first two species in the ancient Indian shell-heaps, on some of the islands in Casco Bay, though not now found living among the islands, indicates that the temperature of those waters was higher at a former period than at present. These facts also point to the most satisfactory explanation of the existence of numerous southern shells, associated with the oyster and *Venus mercenaria* in the southern part of the Gulf of Saint Lawrence, though not now found in the intermediate waters, along the coast of Maine, nor in the Bay of Fundy.

All the various forms of this species, upon which the several nominal species, united above, have been based by Lamarck and others, often occur together in the same beds in Long Island Sound, and may easily be connected together by all sorts of intermediate forms. Even the same specimen will often have the form of *borealis* in one stage of its growth, and then will suddenly change to the *Virginiana* style, and, perhaps, later still, will return to the form of *borealis*. Or these different forms may be assumed in reverse order. Great variations in the number and size of the costæ and undulations of the lower valve occur, both in different specimens from the same locality, and even in the same specimen, at different stages of growth. All these variations occur in precisely the same way in the shells taken from the ancient Indian shell-heaps along our entire coast, from Florida to Maine.

TUNICATA.

SACCOBRANCHIA.

CIONA TENELLA Verrill. (p. 419.)

American Journal Science, ser. iii, vol. i, p. 99, figs. 12, 13, 1871. *Ascidia tenella* Stimpson, Proc. Bost. Soc. Nat. Hist., iv, p. 228, 1853; Inv. of Grand Manan, p. 20, 1853; Binney, in Gould, Invert., ed. ii, p. 24, 1870. ?*Ascidia ocellata* Ag., Proc. Amer. Assoc. for Adv. Sci., ii, p. 159, 1850 (description insufficient); Binney, in Gould, Invert., ed. ii, p. 24, Plate 24, fig. 332, 1870.

Cape Cod to Gulf of Saint Lawrence; rare and local south of Cape

Cod. Common in Casco Bay and Bay of Fundy, low-water to 100 fathoms. New Bedford, Massachusetts (L. Agassiz).

MOLGULA MANHATTENSIS Verrill. Plate XXXIII, fig. 250. (pp. 311, 445.)

Amer. Jour. Science, vol. i, p. 54, Jan., 1871; Tellkampf, Annals Lyc. Nat. Hist., New York, vol. x, p. 83, 1872. *Ascidia Manhattensis* Dekay, Report on the Natural History of New York, Mollusca, p. 259, 1843; Binney, in Gould's Invertebrata of Massachusetts, ed. ii, p. 25, 1870 (copied from Dekay). *Ascidia amphora* Ag., MSS.; Binney, op. cit., p. 25, Plate 24, fig. 333.

North Carolina to Casco Bay, Maine. Very common in Great Egg Harbor, New Jersey, Long Island Sound, Buzzard's Bay, Vineyard Sound, and Massachusetts Bay. Less common in Casco Bay. Great South Bay, Long Island, abundant, (S. I. Smith).

MOLGULA PELLUCIDA Verrill. (p. 426.)

Amer. Jour. Science, vol. iii, p. 289, Plate 8, fig. 2, 1872.

Body subglobular with a smooth, thin, pellucid test. Tubes terminal, contiguous, much swollen at base, long, divergent, tapering, reticulated within by longitudinal and circular white lines (muscular fibers). Branchial aperture with six papillæ. Intestine conspicuously visible through the test; stomach covered by deep orange-colored hepatic glands. Ovaries large, whitish. Color of test, pale hyaline bluish; tubes toward the ends, dull neutral tint.

Diameter of the largest specimens about 25^{mm}.

North Carolina to Massachusetts Bay. Massachusetts Bay (L. Agassiz). Long Island (Coll. Peabody Academy of Science). Bird Shoal near Beaufort, North Carolina (Dr. H. C. Yarrow).

Mr. Binney has published (Plate 22, figs. 315, 316) characteristic colored figures of this species under the name of *M. producta* (Stimpson), which is a very different, sand-covered species.

MOLGULA PRODUCTA Stimpson. (p. 502.)

Proc. Boston Society Natural History, vol. iv, p. 229, 1852; Verrill, op. cit., p. 289, Plate 8, fig. 6, 1872; Binney, in Gould, p. 21 (not the figures, which are *M. pellucida*).

Off Buzzard's Bay, 25 fathoms, sandy. Massachusetts Bay, low-water to 6 fathoms, (Stimpson).

MOLGULA ARENATA Stimpson. Plate XXXIII, fig. 251. (p. 419.)

Proc. Boston Soc. Nat. Hist., vol. iv, p. 230, 1852; Binney, in Gould, Invert., ed. ii, p. 21; Verrill, Amer. Jour. Sci., vol. iii, Plate 8, fig. 5, 1872.

Long Island Sound, near New Haven, 3 fathoms, sand; Vineyard Sound and Buzzard's Bay, 5 to 15 fathoms, sand and gravel. Nantucket (Stimpson).

MOLGULA PAPILLOSA Verrill. (p. 495.)

Amer. Jour. Science, vol. i, p. 57, fig. 4, b, 1871; op. cit., vol. iii, p. 211, Plate 8, fig. 4, 1872.

Body free, nearly globular, or transversely suboval, usually slightly compressed laterally. Integument rather thin, translucent, the surface, both of the tubes and body, entirely covered by particles of sand, broken shells, foraminifera, etc., which adhere firmly. When cleaned the whole surface is thickly covered with prominent granule-like papillæ and numerous slender fibrous processes; the granules are most conspicuous on the tubes, where they usually have a rusty color. The tubes are long, subequal, and their bases are separated by a space usually greater than their diameters; they are quite divergent, both of them curving outward, the anal tube most abruptly. The branchial tube is cylindrical, somewhat longer than the anal, equal to or exceeding the diameter of the body, the orifice surrounded by six rather long and slender, conical, divergent papillæ. The anal tube often bends suddenly outward, tapers slightly, and has a small square aperture, surrounded by a circle of dull reddish brown. In contraction the tubes are not retracted, but are usually shortened to about one-half their length. In life the body, when cleaned, is pale grayish, with an almost transparent integument, through which the convolutions of the dark intestine are conspicuous.

The largest specimens are about 10^{mm} in diameter.

Off Martha's Vineyard, 10 fathoms, stony; Casco Bay and Bay of Fundy, 10 to 20 fathoms.

EUGYRA PILULARIS Verrill. Plate XXXIII, fig. 249. (p. 509.)

Amer. Jour. Science, vol. iii, p. 211, Plate 8, fig. 3, 1872. *Molgula pilularis* Verrill, op. cit., vol. i, p. 56, fig. 4, c, 1871.

Body unattached, globular, covered with a thin layer of mud, and, when the tubes are retracted, looking like a small soft ball. Integument of the body, when cleaned, very thin, soft, nearly transparent, thickly covered with minute granules, and minutely fibrous, usually concealed by the adhering particles of mud and fine sand, but this can be easily removed. The tubes are naked, smooth, nearly transparent, subconical, slender, as long as the diameter of the body, originating close together, and but slightly divergent, both of them nearly straight; they can be wholly retracted, and their bases are surrounded and connected by a narrow, naked, oval or oblong band, which is usually conspicuous when the tubes are withdrawn; in partial contraction, the tubes are conical, subpellucid, reticulated with white lines. The branchial tube is a little shorter than the anal, the aperture surrounded by six acute, conical papillæ, and twelve small, dark, brownish spots. Anal tube a little smaller, slightly longer, a little tapering, with a small square aperture, surrounded by four small lobes and four small, reddish brown eye-spots.

In life the body, when cleaned, is transparent grayish, the dark intestine showing through very distinctly; tubes greenish at base.

Diameter usually about 5^{mm}, seldom more than 6^{mm} or 8^{mm}.

Off Gay Head, Martha's Vineyard, 19 fathoms, soft mud; Casco Bay,

10 to 20 fathoms; Bay of Fundy, off Grand Menan, Eastport Harbor, and South Bay, 6 to 20 fathoms, soft mud. Gulf of Saint Lawrence (Whiteaves).

GLANDULA ARENICOLA Verrill. (p. 502.)

Amer. Jour. Science, ser. iii, vol. iii, pp. 211, 288, 1872.

Body subglobular, rather higher than broad, the whole surface covered with grains of sand, forming a continuous layer. When the sand is removed the surface of the test is reticulately wrinkled and pitted, not furnished with fibers, except at base, where there are a few long, slender, thread-like white ones. Tubes terminal, near together, in the alcoholic specimens short, forming low verrucæ, swollen at base, the ends a little prominent and naked. Apertures square, with four small lobes. The test is tough and opaque. Height, about 12^{mm}; breadth, 10^{mm}; often larger.

Murray Bay, Gulf of Saint Lawrence (Dr. J. W. Dawson). Saint George's Bank, 28 fathoms, sand, abundant, (S. I. Smith). Off Cuttyhunk Island and Buzzard's Bay (T. H. Prudden).

GLANDULA. Species undetermined. (p. 502.)

Vineyard Sound and off Martha's Vineyard, 10 to 20 fathoms, sand.

CYNTHIA PARTITA Stimpson. Plate XXXIII, fig. 246. (p. 311.)

Proc. Bost. Soc. Nat. History, vol. iv, p. 231, 1852; Binney, op. cit., p. 18; Verrill, Amer. Jour. Science, vol. iii, p. 213, 1872. (?) *Cynthia rugosa* Agassiz, Proc. Amer. Assoc., vol. ii, p. 159, 1850 (description inadequate); Binney, op. cit., p. 20 (copied from the preceding). *Cynthia stellifera* Verrill (var.), Amer. Jour. Science, vol. i, p. 93, figs. 5, 6, a, b, 1871.

North Carolina to Massachusetts Bay. Common in Long Island Sound, Vineyard Sound, and Buzzard's Bay, low-water to 15 fathoms. Boston Harbor, 4 fathoms (Stimpson). Off New London, Connecticut (T. M. Prudden).

CYNTHIA CARNEA Verrill. Plate XXXIII, figs. 247, 248. (p. 495.)

American Jour. Science, ser. iii, vol. i, p. 94, figs. 7, 8, 9, 1871. *Ascidia carnea* Agassiz, Proc. American Assoc. for Adv. Sci., ii, p. 159, 1850 (description insufficient); Binney, in Gould's Invertebrata of Mass., ed. ii, p. 25, Plate 24, figs. 334, 335, 1870 (young). (?) *Cynthia gutta* Stimpson, Proc. Boston Soc. Nat. Hist., vol. iv, p. 231, 1852 (young); Binney, op. cit., p. 19, 1870. *Cynthia placenta* (*pars*) Packard, Mem. Boston Soc. Nat. Hist., vol. i, p. 277, 1867; Binney, op. cit., p. 19, Plate 23, figs. 322, 1870; Verrill, Amer. Jour. Sci., vol. xlix, p. 424, 1870.

Martha's Vineyard to Labrador. Off Gay Head, 10 fathoms, stony; common in Eastport Harbor and Bay of Fundy, low-water to 109 fathoms; Casco Bay, less common, 10 to 40 fathoms. Massachusetts Bay (Stimpson). Labrador (Packard).

This species is closely allied to *C. rustica* (Linné, sp.) from Iceland, and may eventually prove to be identical.

CYNTHIA ECHINATA Stimpson. (p. 495.)

Invert. of Grand Menan, p. 20, 1854; Binney, op. cit., p. 18, Plate 23, fig. 326; Verrill, Amer. Jour. Science, vol. i, p. 96, 1871; vol. iii, p. 213, 1872. *Cynthia hirsuta* (young) Agassiz, op. cit., 1850; Binney, in Gould, Invert., ed. ii, p. 20, Plate 24, fig. 336. *Ascidia echinata* Linné, Syst. Nat., ed. xii, p. 1087, 1767. *Ascidia echinata* Fabr., Fauna Grœnl., p. 331, 1780; Rathke, Zoölogica Danica, vol. iv, p. 10, Plate 130, fig. i, 1806; Möller, Index Mollusc. Grœnl., in Kroyer's Nat. Tidsskrift, vol. iv, p. 95.

Martha's Vineyard to Greenland, Iceland, and northern coasts of Europe. Off Martha's Vineyard, 10 fathoms, stony, rare; common in Casco Bay and Bay of Fundy, low-water to 109 fathoms, attached to stones, shells, and other ascidians. Saint George's Bank (S. I. Smith). Banks of Newfoundland (T. M. Coffin). Labrador (Packard).

BOLTENIA. Species undetermined.

Boltenia reniformis Dekay, Nat. Hist. New York, Mollusca, p. 260, Plate 34, fig. 324 (*non* Macleay).

New York Harbor (t. Dekay.)

The description and figure of the single poor specimen seen by Dekay are insufficient for its determination. I have not met with the genus south of Cape Cod, and the locality given may possibly be incorrect.

PEROPHORA VIRIDIS Verrill. (p. 388.)

American Jour. Science, ser. iii, vol. ii, p. 359, 1871.

Colonies composed of numerous nearly sessile individuals, which are small, about 2.5^{mm} to 3^{mm} high, connected by slender stolons, and thickly covering the surfaces over which they creep. Test compressed, seen from the side, scarcely higher than broad, oval, elliptical, or sub-circular, often one-sided or distorted, with a short pedicle, or subsessile at base. Branchial orifice large, terminal; anal lateral or subterminal, both a little prominent, with about 16 angular lobes, alternately larger and smaller. Test transparent; mantle beautifully reticulated with bright yellowish green; intestine yellow.

Vineyard Sound, 2 to 12 fathoms, on algæ and ascidians, common; Little Harbor, Wood's Hole, on piles of wharves, at and below low-water mark, very abundant.

BOTRYLLUS GOULDII Verrill. Plate XXXIII, figs. 252, 253. (p. 375.)

Amer. Jour. Science, ser. iii, vol. i, figs. 14, 19, 1871. *Botryllus stellatus* Gould, Rep. on Inv. of Mass., 1st ed., p. 320, 1841 (*non* Pallas). *Botryllus Schlosseri* Binney, in Gould, Inv. Mass., ed. ii, p. 3, Plate 23, fig. 319, 1870 (*non* Pallas); Dall, Proc. Bost. Soc. Nat. Hist., xiii, p. 255, 1870.

This species commonly forms thick, fleshy, translucent incrustations on sea-weeds and zoöphytes, the form which it assumes depending upon the shape of the object. The masses are often several inches in length and half an inch or more in width. The animals are short oval, as seen at the surface, and form circular or elliptical groups, of from five to sixteen or more, surrounding circular or elliptical cloacal orifices. The "marginal tubes" or buds are numerous in all parts of the common tissue, the enlarged ends appearing as oval or pyriform spots, lighter than the ground-color. The branchial openings are small and circular, surrounded by a light halo. The animals differ considerably in form, according to the state of contraction.

The color is extremely variable; several of the color-varieties have been named and described on pages 375, 376.

Brooklyn, New York, to Boston, Massachusetts. Very abundant at Wood's Hole, Waquoit Pond, and other similar localities along the shores of Vineyard Sound and Buzzard's Bay; abundant at the mouth of Charles River, near Boston. Watch Hill, Rhode Island, and Brooklyn, New York (D. C. Eaton).

AMARŒCIUM PELLUCIDUM Verrill. (p. 401.)

Amouroucium pellucidum Verrill, Amer. Jour. Science, ser. iii, vol. i, p. 290, 1871; vol. iii, p. 211. *Alcyomdium ? pellucidum* Leidy, Jour. Acad. Nat. Science, Philad., ser. ii, vol. iii, 1855, p. 142, Plate 10, fig. 25, (mutilated zooid).

Colonies large, complex, consisting of a large number of small, elongated, clavate colonies, arising from a common base, and more or less separate laterally and at summit, thus forming large aggregated hemispherical or irregular masses, often six inches in diameter, the surface generally covered thickly with adhering sand, but frequently naked over the summits of the colonies, or even over large surfaces of the masses, when, as often happens, the central colonies coalesce; when naked, the tissue is smooth, translucent, gelatinous-looking, and soft. The small side-colonies are long, with a slender stolon-like base, curving outward and ascending, enlarging gradually to the summit, which is more or less convex, usually with a single central cloacal orifice, surrounded by an irregular circle of individual zoöids, varying in number according to the size or age of the colony to which they belong. The zoöids, when mature, are long and slender, varying greatly in length in each colony, according to the state of development of the post-abdomen; the largest are often 20^{mm} to 25^{mm} in length. The stomach is bright orange-red, and quite conspicuous; the slender post-abdomen exceeds in length the rest of the body, but is not more than half the diameter of the thorax, and is slightly constricted at base. In young individuals, not half grown, the post-abdomen forms nearly half the whole length, and is very slender. The branchial aperture has six, short, round papillæ; the anal is situated a short distance from the end of the body, and has short inconspicuous lower lobes, with an elongated, pointed lobe above. The branchial sac is oblong, with numerous longitudinal and transverse vessels and a broad ventral duct. The stomach is about as broad as long, subglobular, with the ends truncated and the surface covered with numerous, interrupted, longitudinal, glandular ridges. The post-abdomen is nearly filled by the large, elongated ovary, which extends nearly to the posterior end on the dorsal or atrial side, and contains numerous closely-packed ovules of comparatively large size, and the conspicuous male organs, extending through the whole length on the ventral or branchial side, in the form of a slightly-convoluted duct. The posterior end terminates in a small, obtuse papilla. The atrium, or cloacal cavity, often contain eggs in which the embryos are well developed, and, in some cases, the free, tadpole-shaped larvæ. The tunic is specked with numerous, minute, purplish brown pigment-cells.

One of the zoöids measured 7.5^{mm} in length; thorax, 2^{mm}; abdomen, 1.5^{mm}; post-abdomen, 4^{mm}; diameter of thorax, .8^{mm} to .9^{mm}; of abdomen, about the same; of post-abdomen, .375^{mm} to .5^{mm}.

North Carolina to Vineyard Sound. Very abundant in Vineyard Sound, in 6 to 12 fathoms.

AMARŒCIUM STELLATUM Verrill. (p. 402.)

Amouroucium stellatum Verrill, Amer. Journal of Science, ser. iii, vol. i, p. 291, 1871.

Masses large, variable in form, often in the form of thick vertical plates, or erect crest-like lobes, frequently irregular; surface nearly smooth, naked; tissue firm and cartilage-like externally, somewhat translucent, generally pale yellow or flesh-color by transmitted light. The fronds are often six inches or more in breadth and height, and from half an inch to an inch thick. The zoöids are grouped in more or less regular, and generally simple, circular, stellâte clusters, scattered over the whole surface, and usually containing from six to twenty individuals, arranged around a central, sub-circular cloacal orifice; in contraction the position of each individual is indicated by an oval spot, more transparent than the common tissue, with a small flake-white spot around the branchial orifice. The individual zoöids are elongated and slender; the post-abdomen more slender, usually considerably exceeding in length the rest of the body, and but slightly constricted proximally; the thorax and abdomen are shorter and stouter than in the preceding species; branchial sac with about twelve transverse vessels; stomach oblong-oval, with numerous longitudinal glandular folds, which are bright orange-red in life; intestine large, light orange or yellow. Branchial tube elongated, bright orange; the orifice with six prominent rounded lobes. Anal orifice subterminal, with a prominent ligulate process above, and several small lobes below.

North Carolina to Cape Cod. Very abundant in Vineyard Sound, in 5 to 15 fathoms, on gravelly and shelly bottoms. Fort Macon, North Carolina (Dr. Yarrow).

AMARŒCIUM CONSTELLATUM Verrill. (pp. 388, 403.)

American Journal of Science, ser. iii, vol. ii, p. 359, 1871 (*Amouroucium*).

Masses thick, turbinate, often incrusting, surface usually convex, smooth; substance firm, gelatinous, translucent, but softer than in *A. stellatum.* Groups stellate, circular, oval or elliptical, often narrow and elongated, or irregular and complex; zoöids much elongated, slender; the branchial tube short, with six rounded lobes. Branchial sac elongated. Color of the masses usually light orange-red, varying to yellowish and pale flesh-color; the branchial orifices with six radiating white lines. Anal orifices often surrounded by a pale or whitish border; zoöids generally orange-yellow; the orifices and tubes with upper part of the mantle bright orange, or lemon-yellow; branchial sac usually flesh-color or pale yellow, sometimes bright orange; stomach with bright orange-red longitudinal glandular ribs; intestine light orange; mantle with minute opaque white specks. In some specimens the cloacal chamber or "atrium" contained three or four bright purple tadpole-shaped larvæ.

Vineyard Sound, 4 to 12 fathoms, frequent; Wood's Hole, on piles of wharf; off Stonington, Connecticut, 4–5 fathoms.

AMARŒCIUM PALLIDUM Verrill. (p. 496.)

American Journal of Science, ser. iii, vol. i, p. 289, 1871 (*Amouroucium*).

Masses sessile, hemispherical or sub-globular, usually attached by a large base. Surface generally evenly rounded, sometimes irregular in large specimens, smoothish, but thinly covered with minute, firmly adherent particles of fine sand, which are imbedded in the surface of the common tissue and scattered throughout its substance. The cloacal openings are few in number and irregularly placed, except in small specimens, which usually have but one large central opening. The animals are much smaller and more numerous than in the preceding species, often forming somewhat circular groups of six or eight individuals around the cloacal openings; outside of the circular groups they are usually irregularly scattered, but sometimes form linear series of eight or ten, and in young specimens with but one central opening they often form a larger outer circle, which is near the margin, more or less irregular, and composed of numerous individuals. The post-abdomen, in all the numerous examples examined, was small, thick, obtuse, and decidedly shorter than the abdomen and thorax taken together; it often terminates in two slender papillæ. Color of the masses pale yellowish or grayish; stomach dull orange-yellow; ovaries yellowish white.

The larger specimens of this species are 15^{mm} to 25^{mm} in diameter; the largest zoöids are 3^{mm} to 4^{mm} long, by $.75^{mm}$ to 1.25^{mm} in diameter; but many are much smaller.

Martha's Vineyard to Gulf of Saint Lawrence. Off Buzzard's Bay, 25 fathoms, gravel; south of Gay Head, 10 fathoms, stony; Casco Bay, 8 to 40 fathoms; Eastport Harbor and Bay of Fundy, low-water to 80 fathoms.

LEPTOCLINUM ALBIDUM Verrill. (p. 403.)

American Journal of Science, ser. iii, vol. i, p. 446, 1872.

Colonies incrusting stones, dead shells, ascidians, etc., forming broad, thin, irregular, coriaceous crusts, with an uneven surface, filled with minute, white, spherical, calcareous grains or corpuscles, which, under the miscroscope, have the surface covered with projecting points. Surface of the crusts covered with small, irregular, scattered prominences, in which the branchial orifices are situated. Cloacal orifices few and distantly scattered. Systems irregular, the zoöids scattered, but often arranged in rather indistinct concentric groups around the cloacal openings, and connected with them by cloacal ducts, which are variously branched, often showing through the integument as dark dendritic lines, converging toward the cloacal orifices from different directions.

Color white, the zoöids light yellowish.

The colonies often become 200^{mm} to 300$_{mm}$ across; thickness seldom more than 2.5^{mm}, commonly about 1.25 ^{mm}; zoöids .5^{mm} to .75^{mm} long; diameter .25^{mm} to .30^{mm}.

Long Island Sound to Labrador. Thimble Islands, near New Haven, 4 to 6 fathoms, rocky; off Stonington, 4 fathoms, rocky; common in Vineyard Sound, 8 to 15 fathoms; abundant in Casco Bay, 6 to 40 fathoms; abundant in the Bay of Fundy, low-water to 80 fathoms. Banks of Newfoundland (T. M. Coffin). Mingan Islands, 10 fathoms (A. E. V.). Saint George's Bank (S. I. Smith).

LEPTOCLINUM LUTEOLUM Verrill. (p. 403.)

American Jour. Science, loc. cit., p. 446, 1872.

This species forms thin, coriaceous crusts, like the preceding, filled in the same way with similar spherical corpuscles. The branchial orifices open at the summits of low verrucæ. The cloacal orifices are small, with four to six lobes, and distantly scattered. Color deep salmon, or somewhat rosy.

The crusts are of all sizes up to 300^{mm} or more in diameter, and are usually somewhat thicker than in the preceding species, with larger and darker colored zoöids.

Connecticut to Bay of Fundy; off Stonington, Connecticut, 4 fathoms, rocky; Vineyard Sound, 6 to 14 fathoms, common; Casco Bay, 10 to 40 fathoms, common; Bay of Fundy, low-water to 80 fathoms, common.

TÆNIOBRANCHIA.

SALPA CABOTI Desor. Plate XXXIII, figs. 254, 255. (p. 445.)

Proc. Boston Soc. Nat. History, vol. iii, p. 75, 1848 (not described); A. Agassiz, op. cit., vol. xi, p. 17, figs. 1 to 5, 1866; Binney, in Gould, Invert., ed. ii, p. 6, figs. 350 to 354, 1870 (description and figures copied from A. Agassiz).

In the typical variety, as described by Mr. Agassiz, the color is pale pink or rosy; the nucleus deep chestnut. Long Island Sound to Saint George's Bank. Common in Buzzard's Bay and Vineyard Sound. Off Saint George's Bank (S. I. Smith).

Var. *cyanea*. (p. 446.)

Nucleus and the borders of the mantle are bright Prussian-blue; surface of the latter delicately reticulated with fine blue lines.

Vineyard Sound, especially off Gay Head, in September.

DOLIOLUM (species undetermined). (p. 446.)

Vineyard Sound (A. Agassiz).

LARVALIA.

APPENDICULARIA (species undetermined, [a]). (p. 446.)

Allied to *A. longicauda* (t. A. Agassiz), op. cit., p. 23, 1866; Binney, op. cit., p. 13 (copied from A. Agassiz).

Long Island Sound to Massachusetts Bay (A. Agassiz).

APPENDICULARIA (species undetermined, [b]). (p. 446.)

Allied to *A. furcata* (t. A. Agassiz), op. cit., p. 23, 1866; Binney, op. cit., p. 13 (copied).

Long Island Sound to Massachusetts Bay (A. Agassiz).

BRYOZOA OR POLYZOA.

PHYLACTOLÆMATA.

PEDICELLINA AMERICANA Leidy. (p. 405.)

Journal Acad. Nat. Sciences, Philadelphia, ser. ii, vol. iii, p. 143, Plate X, fig. 25, 1855.

New Haven, Connecticut, to Vineyard Sound. Point Judith, Rhode Island (Leidy).

GYMNOLÆMATA.

CYCLOSTOMATA.

CRISIA EBURNEA Lamouroux. Plate XXXIV, figs. 260, 261. (p. 311,)

Polyp. flex., p. 138, 1816; Exp. methodique, p. 6; Johnston, British Zoophytes, ed. i, p. 262, Plate 30, figs. 3, 4; ed. ii, p. 283, fig. 62, and Plate 50, figs. 3, 4; Smitt, Kritisk fört. öfver Skandinaviens Hafs-Bryozoer, in Öfvers. af Kongl. Vet.-Akad. Förhandl., 1865, p. 117, Plate 16, figs. 7 to 19. *Sertularia eburnea* Linné, Syst. Nat., ed. x, p. 810; ed. xii, p. 1316.

Long Island Sound to the Arctic Ocean; Spitzbergen to the Mediterranean (t. Smitt); California (t. Johnston). Common near New Haven, and at Thimble Islands, 1 to 6 fathoms, rocky, and in tide-pools; off Watch Hill, Rhode Island, 4 to 5 fathoms, on algæ; common in Vineyard Sound, 4 to 15 fathoms; very common in Casco Bay and Bay of Fundy, low-water to 80 fathoms.

DIASTOPORA PATINA Smitt. (p. 405.)

Smitt, op. cit., p. 397, Plate 8, figs. 13 to 15. *Tubulipora patina* Lamarck, Animaux sans Vert., ed. i, vol. ii, p. 163; ed. ii, vol. ii, p. 244; Johnston, Brit. Zoöph., ed ii, p. 266, Plate 47, figs. 1 to 3.

Long Island Sound to the Arctic Ocean; northern coast of Europe, from Finmark to Great Britain. Near New Haven, at Thimble Islands, 1 to 5 fathoms; Watch Hill, Rhode Island, 4 to 5 fathoms; Vineyard Sound, off Holmes' Hole, 3 to 4 fathoms; very common in Casco Bay, Bay of Fundy, and northward.

TUBULIPORA FLABELLARIS Smitt. (p. 405.)

Op. cit., p. 401, Plate 9, figs. 6 to 8. *Tubipora flabellaris* Fabricius, Fauna Grœnl., p. 430, 1780 (*non* Johnston, sp.). *Tubulipora phalangea* Johnston, Brit. Zoöph., ed. ii, p. 273, Plate 46, figs. 1, 2.

Long Island Sound to Greenland; northern coasts of Europe to Great Britain. Common at Thimble Islands, 1 to 5 fathoms, on algæ, hydroids, etc.; Watch Hill, Rhode Island; Vineyard Sound; Casco Bay; Bay of Fundy, and northward.

CTENOSTOMATA.

ALCYONIDIUM RAMOSUM Verrill. Plate XXXIV, fig. 257. (p. 404.)

American Journal of Science, vol. iii, p. 289, Plate 8, fig. 10, 1872.

Much branched, when full-grown; the branches round, irregularly dichotomus, usually crooked. Surface glabrous, smooth, or nearly so, the cells rather small and crowded, their margins not elevated; zoöids with sixteen slender tentacles. Color ashy brown, or dull rusty brown.

Diameter of branches, mostly 5^{mm} to 6.5^{mm}. Height, $.250^{mm}$ to $.375^{mm}$.

Great Egg Harbor, New Jersey, to Vineyard Sound; common in Long Island Sound, near New Haven, in 1 to 5 fathoms; Thimble Islands; Watch Hill, Rhode Island, etc.

ALCYONIDIUM HIRSUTUM Johnston. (p. 404.)

British Zoöph., ed. i, p. 303, Plate 42, figs. 1, 2; ed. ii, p. 360, Plate 69, figs. 1, 2; Smitt, op. cit., p. 496, Plate 12, figs. 3 to 8. *Alcyonium hirsutum* Fleming, Brit. Anim., p. 517.

Long Island Sound to the Arctic Ocean; Spitzbergen; northern coasts of Europe to Great Britain. Savin Rock, near New Haven, low-water; Thimble Islands, in tide-pools, on *Fucus*, *Phyllophora*, etc.; Vineyard Sound; and Casco Bay.

ALCYONIDIUM HISPIDUM Smitt. (p. 404.)

Op. cit., p. 499, Plate 12, figs. 22 to 27, 1866. *Flustra hispida* Fabricius, Fauna Grœnl., p. 438, 1780; Johnston, Brit. Zoöph., ed. ii., p. 363, Plate 66, fig. 5. *Flustrella hispida* Gray, Brit. Mus. Catal., part i, p. 108.

Long Island Sound to Greenland; Finmark to Great Britain. Very common at Savin Rock, near New Haven, at low water, encrusting stones, *Fucus*, etc.; Thimble Islands; Watch Hill, Rhode Island; Vineyard Sound; Casco Bay; Bay of Fundy, etc.

ALCYONIDIUM PARASITICUM Johnston. (p. 404.)

British Zoöph., ed. i, p. 304, Plate 41, figs. 4, 5; ed. ii, p. 362, Plate 68, figs. 4, 5; Smitt, op. cit., p. 499, Plate 12, figs. 14–19. *Alcyonium parasiticum* Fleming, Brit. Anim., p. 518.

Rhode Island to Arctic Ocean; northern coasts of Europe to Great Britain. Vineyard Sound, on *Phyllophora*.

(?) ALCYONIDIUM GELATINOSUM Johnston. (p. 496.)

Brit. Zoöph., ed. i, p. 300, Plate 41, figs. 1–3; ed. ii, p. 358, Plate 68, figs. 1–3; Smitt, op. cit., p. 497, Plate 12, figs. 9–13. *Alcyonium gelatinosum* Linné, Fauna Suec., ed. ii, p. 538; Syst. Nat., ed. xii, p. 1295.

Gulf of Saint Lawrence; Spitzbergen to Great Britain. A few small specimens, apparently belonging to this species, were dredged in the deeper parts of Vineyard Sound.

VESICULARIA CUSCUTA Thompson. (p. 404.)

Zoöl. Res., mem. v, p. 97, Plate 2, figs. 1–4; Smitt, op. cit., p. 501, Plate 13, figs. 28, 34, 35. *Sertularia cuscuta* Linné, ed. xii, p. 1311. *Valkeria cuscuta* Fleming, Brit. Anim., p. 550; Johnston, Brit. Zoöph., ed. i, p. 252; ed. ii, p. 374.

New Jersey, northward; northern coasts of Europe to Great Britain. In Vineyard Sound it was found on hydroids attached to floating eel-grass, and was also dredged in 6 to 8 fathoms, on algæ, *Sertularia argentea*, and other hydroids; Great Egg Harbor, New Jersey, low water, on *Sertularia pumila;* Casco Bay, on piles of wharf.

VESICULARIA GRACILIS Verrill. (p. 389.)

Bowerbankia gracilis Leidy, Journal Acad. Nat. Sciences, Philad., ser. ii, vol. iii, p. 142, Plate 11, fig. 38, 1855.

Great Egg Harbor, New Jersey, to Vineyard Sound. Point Judith, Rhode Island (Leidy). Vineyard Sound, 6 to 8 fathoms, on hydroids.

VESICULARIA DICHOTOMA Verrill, new sp. (p. 404.)

Stems clustered, cæspitose, usually one or two inches high, slender, flexible, white, and repeatedly forking. The branches stand in different planes, so as often to produce miniature tree-like or shrub-like forms, many of which generally arise close together, forming crowded tufts upon rocks, oyster-shells, or algæ. When the stem or a branch divides, there is a joint formed at the base of each of the forks, by the interposition of a very short segment of a dark brownish, opaque substance, which contrasts strongly with the white translucent substance of the rest of the stem. Zoöids arranged closely in two subspiral rows of six to twelve each, just below each fork of the stem and branches, and not occupying half the length of the internodes, which are naked and smooth below the crowded clusters of the zoöids; these are smooth, greenish brown, broad oval or obovate in contraction, subcylindrical or elliptical in expansion, entirely sessile, and but little narrowed at the base, and so crowded as to appear imbricated. The tentacles are eight, long and slender, in expansion usually more than half the length of the cell.

Great Egg Harbor, New Jersey, on oysters; Savin Rock, at low-water; off New Haven Light, 4 to 6 fathoms, shelly and rocky; Thimble Islands, in rocky tide-pools; Norwalk, Connecticut, on oysters. This is probably the species recorded by Dr. Leidy from Great Egg Harbor under the name of *Valkeria pustulosa*, which is an allied European species.

VESICULARIA ARMATA Verrill, new sp. (p. 405.)

Cells stout, oval, broad at base, with a short and narrow pedicel, attached either singly or in pairs along slender, filiform, creeping stems, which often anastomose, the branches being mostly opposite. Distal end of cells prolonged into four conical processes, each of which, when perfect, supports a long slender spinule, nearly half as long as the cell. Tentacles not seen. Cells yellowish horn-color, with an oval, dark brown internal organ, visible in most of the cells.

Vineyard Sound, on floating sea-weeds attached to *Sertulariæ*, *Halecium gracile*, etc.; also in 6 to 10 fathoms, rocky, on *Sertularia argentea*.

VESICULARIA FUSCA Smitt. (p. 420.)

Op. cit., p. 502, Plate 13, figs. 37–39, 1866. *Avenella fusca* (?) Dalyell, Rare and Rem. Anim. of Scotland, vol. ii, p. 65; vol. i, Plate 12, fig. 11, (t. Smitt).

Long Island Sound northward; northern coasts of Europe to Great Britain. Off South End, near New Haven, 3 to 5 fathoms, on *Alcyonidium ramosum*.

FARRELLA FAMILIARIS. (p. 487.)

Vesicularia (*Farrella*) *familiaris* Smitt, op. cit., p. 502, Plate 13, fig. 36, 1866. *Plumatella familiaris* Gros, Bulletin Soc. Imp. Mascou, vol. xxii, p. 567, Plate 6, G. figs. 1–10 (t. Smitt). *Farrella pedicellata* Alder, Catal., p. 68, Plate 6, figs. 1–3; Quart. Jour. Miscrosc. Soc., vol. v, p. 24, Plate 14, figs. 1–3.

Long Island Sound to Vineyard Sound and northward; coasts of Scandinavia and Great Britain. Thimble Islands, near New Haven, in tide-pools, on algæ; Casco Bay. Saint George's Bank (S. I. Smith).

CHILOSTOMATA.

Cellularina.

ÆTEA ANGUINA Lamouroux. (p. 405.)

Soc. Phil., 1812, p. 184 (t. Smitt); Polyp. flex., p. 153, Plate 3, fig. 6; Expos. Methodique, p. 9, Plate 65, fig. 15; Smitt, op. cit., p. 280, Plate 16, figs. 2–4, 1867. *Sertularia anguina* Linné, Syst. Nat., ed. xii, p. 1317. *Anguinaria spatulata* Johnston, Brit. Zoöph., ed. ii, p. 290, Plate 50, figs. 7, 8.

Long Island Sound, northward; coasts of Scandinavia and Great Britain. In Vineyard Sound it was common at low-water mark and in 6 to 14 fathoms, on *Phyllophora* and hydroids. Off New Haven, 4 to 6 fathoms, on *Halecium gracile.*

EUCRATEA CHELATA Lamouroux. (p. 405.)

Polyp. Corall. flex., p. 149, Plate 3, fig. 5, 1816; Expos. Meth., p. 8, Plate, 65, fig. 10; Smitt, op. cit., 1865, Plate 5, fig. 3; 1867, p. 281, Plate 16, figs. 7–9; Johnston, Brit. Zoöph., ed. ii, p. 288, fig. 64. *Sertularia chelata* Linné, Systema Nat., ed. x, p. 816. *Cellularia chelata* Pallas, Elench. Zoöph., p. 25, 1766.

Martha's Vineyard northward; northern coasts of Europe to Great Britain. Off Gay Head, 10 fathoms, on hydroids and ascidians. Our specimens differ somewhat from the figures of the European form; the cells are simple, more slender, and more elongated; aperture of primary cells somewhat bilabiate; of lateral cells simple and scarcely raised; no processes were observed on the front of any of the cells; the primary cells taper below into a slender, often crooked pedicel, which is about one-third as long as the cell.

(?) CELLULARIA TERNATA Johnston. (p. 496.)

British Zoöph., ed. ii, p. 335, Plate 59, 1848; Smitt, op. cit., 1867, p. 282, Plate 16, figs. 10 to 26. *Cellaria ternata* Ellis and Solander, Zoöph., p. 30. *Menipea ternata* Busk, op. cit., p. 21, Plate 20, figs. 3 to 5. (?) *Cellularia densa* Desor, Proc. Boston Soc. Nat. Hist., vol. iii, p. 66, 1848 (description inadequate).

Cape Cod to the Arctic Ocean; northern coasts of Europe to Great Britain. Off Gay Head, 10 to 20 fathoms; common in Casco Bay, Bay of Fundy, and at Saint George's Bank, 6 to 100 fathoms. South Shoals, 22 fathoms, (Desor).

CABEREA ELLISII Smitt. (p. 420.)

Op. cit., 1867, p. 287, Plate 17, figs. 55, 56. *Flustra Ellisii* Fleming, Mem. Wern. Soc., vol. ii, p. 251, Plate 17, figs. 1 to 3 (t. Smitt). *Flustra setacea* Fleming, Brit. Anim., p. 536; Johnston, Brit. Zoöph., ed. ii, p. 346. *Cellularia Hookeri* Johnston, Brit. Zoöph., ed. ii, p. 338, Plate 60, figs. 1, 2. *Caberea Hookeri* Busk, op. cit., p. 39, Plate 37, fig. 2.

Martha's Vineyard, northward to the Arctic Ocean; northern coasts of Europe, from Finmark to Great Britain. Mouth of Vineyard Sound, off Gay Head, 8 to 12 fathoms; off Buzzard's Bay, 25 fathoms; very common in Casco Bay, Bay of Fundy, and Saint George's Bank, 6 to 100 fathoms. Labrador (Packard).

BUGULA MURRAYANA Busk. (p. 496.)

Catal. Mar. Polyzoa, Brit. Mus., part i, p. 46, Plate 59; Smitt, op. cit., 1867, p. 292, Plate 18, figs. 19 to 27. *Flustra Murrayana* Bean Mss., Johnston, Brit. Zoöph., ed. i, p. 347, Plate 63, figs. 5, 6. *Flustra truncata* Desor, Proc. Boston Soc. Nat. Hist., vol. iii, p. 66 (*non* Linné).

Martha's Vineyard to Spitzbergen; northern coasts of Europe to Great Britain. Off Gay Head, 10 to 20 fathoms; very common in Casco Bay, Bay of Fundy, and Gulf of Saint Lawrence, 1 to 100 fathoms. Saint George's Bank, 20 to 65 fathoms, (S. I Smith). Labrador (Packard).

BUGULA FLABELLATA Busk. (p. 389.)

Catal. Marine Polyzoa, Brit. Mus., part i, p. 43, Plates 51, 52. *Bugula avicularia*, forma *flabellata*, Smitt, op. cit., 1867, p. 290, Plate 18, fig. 11. *Flustra avicularia* Johnston, Brit. Zoöph., ed. i, p. 286, Plate 36, figs. 3, 4; ed. ii, p. 346, Plate 63, figs. 3, 4.

Vineyard Sound, 6 to 8 fathoms; Wood's Hole, abundant on the piles of wharves. Coasts of Great Britain and Belgium.

BUGULA TURRITA Verrill. Plate XXXIV, figs. 258, 259. (p. 311.)

Cellularia turrita Desor, Proc. Boston Soc. Nat. Hist., vol. iii, p. 66, 1848. *Cellularia fastigiata* Leidy, op. cit., p. 142 (*non* Linné, sp.).

North Carolina to Casco Bay. Very abundant in Great Egg Harbor, New Jersey; Long Island Sound; Buzzard's Bay; and Vineyard Sound, low-water to 15 fathoms; Portland, Maine, on piles of wharf.

Flustrina.

MEMBRANIPORA PILOSA Farre. Plate XXXIV, figs. 262, 263. (p. 496.)

Phil. Trans., 1837, p. 412, Plate 27, figs. 1 to 5; Johnston, Brit. Zoöph., ed. i, p. 280, Plate 34, figs. 10, 12, 1838; ed. ii, p. 327, Plate 56, fig. 6, 1847; Smitt, op. cit., 1867, p. 368, Plate 20, fig. 49. *Flustra pilosa* Linné, Fauna Suec., ed. ii, p. 539 (t. Smitt). *Eschara pilosa* Pallas, Elench, Zoöph., p. 50, 1766. *Hippothoa rugosa* Stimpson, Invert. Grand Manan p. 18 (variety *catenularia*). *Tubipora catenularia* Jameson, Wern. Mem., vol. i, p. 561 (t. Smitt).

Long Island Sound to the Arctic Ocean; Finmark to the Mediterranean. Very abundant near New Haven, at Savin Rock, Thimble Islands, etc., in 1 to 6 fathoms, and in tide-pools, on *Chondrus crispus*, *Phyllophora* and other algæ, stones, etc.; Watch Hill, Rhode Island, 4 to 5 fathoms, on algæ, abundant; Vineyard Sound; Massachusetts Bay; Casco Bay; Bay of Fundy, and northward. The variety *catenularia* is common in Casco Bay and Bay of Fundy, from above low-water mark to 50 fathoms. It occurs on the coasts of Northern Europe at various depths down to 300 fathoms. Fossil in the Post-Pliocene of Canada and Labrador (Dawson).

MEMBRANIPORA LINEATA Busk. (p. 406.)

Catal. Mar. Polyzoa, part ii, p. 58, Plate 61, fig. 1; Smitt, op. cit., 1867, p. 363, Plate 20, figs. 23 to 31. *Flustra lineata* Linné, Systema Nat., ed. xii, p. 1301; Johnston, Brit. Zoöph., ed. ii, p. 349, Plate 66, fig. 4. *Escharina lineata* Leidy, Journ. Acad. Nat. Sciences, Philad., ser. ii, vol. iii, p. 141, Plate 10, fig. 22, 1855.

Great Egg Harbor, New Jersey, to the Arctic Ocean; Spitzbergen to Great Britain, low-water mark to 50 fathoms. Common near New Haven, from low-water mark to 6 fathoms, on stones, oysters, algæ, etc.; Watch Hill; Rhode Island; Vineyard Sound; Casco Bay; Bay of Fundy, and northward.

Fossil in the Post-Pliocene of Canada.

MEMBRANIPORA TENUIS Desor. (p. 420.)

Proc. Boston Soc. Nat. Hist., vol. iii, p. 66, 1848.

Long Island Sound to Cape Cod. Common near New Haven and in Vineyard Sound, low-water to 10 fathoms. Muskeget Channel, in 5 fathoms, (Desor).

Escharina.

ESCHARIPORA PUNCTATA Smitt. (p. 424.)

Op. cit., for 1867, Appendix, p. 4, (separate copies, p. 4), Plate 24, figs. 4–7, 1868. *Lepralia punctata* Hassal, Mag. Nat. Hist., vol. vii, p. 368, Plate 9, fig. 7; vol. ix, p. 407; Johnston, Brit. Zoöph., ed. ii, pp. 312 and 478, Plate 55, fig. 1.

Vineyard Sound, northward; northern coasts of Europe to Southern Norway and Great Britain. Vineyard Sound, 6 to 12 fathoms, on shells, etc., common. Saint George's Bank (S. I. Smith). (?) Fossil in the Post-Pliocene of Canada (Dawson).

ESCHARELLA VARIABILIS Verrill. Plate XXXIII, fig. 256. (p. 419.)

Escharina variabilis Leidy, Jour. Acad. Nat. Sci., Philadelphia, ser. ii, vol. iii, p. 142, Plate 11, fig. 37. *Lepralia variolosa* Desor, op. cit., p. 66, 1848 (*not* of Johnston).

South Carolina to Cape Cod and Massachusetts Bay. Very abundant in Great Egg Harbor; Long Island Sound; Buzzard's Bay; Vineyard Sound; Nantucket Harbor; low-water to 25 fathoms. Saint George's Bank, 20 fathoms, (S. I. Smith). Fort Macon, North Carolina (coll. Dr. Yarrow).

MOLLIA HYALINA Smitt. Plate XXXIV, fig. 264. (p. 420.)

Op. cit., for 1867, Ap., p. 16, (separate copies, p. 16), Plate 25, figs. 84–87, 1868. *Cellepora hyalina* Linné, Syst. Nat., ed. xii, p. 1286. *Lepralia hyalina* Johnston, Brit. Zoöph., ed. ii, p. 301, Plate 54, fig. 1. *Cellepora nitida* Fabricius, Fauna Grœnl., p. 435, 1780.

Long Island Sound to Greenland; Spitzbergen to Great Britain. Common near New Haven and at Thimble Island, in tide-pools and from 1 to 6 fathoms, on algæ; Watch Hill, Rhode Island, 4 to 5 fathoms; Buzzard's Bay and Vineyard Sound, abundant; Casco Bay; Bay of Fundy, and northward. Fossil in the Post-Pliocene of Canada (Dawson).

(?) LEPRALIA PALLASIANA Busk. (p. 496.)

Catal. Mar. Polyzoa, Brit. Mus., part ii, p. 81, Plate 83, figs. 1, 2; Smitt, op. cit., for 1867, Ap., p. 19, (separate copies, p. 19), Plate 26, fig. 93, 1868. *Eschara Pallasiana* Moll, die Seerinde, p. 64, Plate 3, fig. 13 (t. Smitt). *Lepralia pediostoma* Hassal, Ann. and Mag. Nat. Hist., vol. vii, p. 368, Plate 9, fig. 4; vol. ix, p. 407; Johnston, Brit. Zoöph., ed. ii, p. 315, Plate 55, fig. 7. *Escharina pediostoma* Leidy, op. cit., p. 141, Plate 10, fig. 23, 1855.

Rhode Island, northward; northern coasts of Europe to Southern Norway and Great Britain. Watch Hill, Rhode Island, 4 to 5 fathoms, on algæ; Vineyard Sound, 6 to 14 fathoms, on *Phyllophora* and other algæ, shells, etc.

Our specimens do not agree perfectly with the European form. Close to the proximal border of the aperture there is a large, but not very prominent, broad-based spine, or subconical process, which is not conspicuous in a view from above, but is prominent in a side-view. In some specimens a few of the cells have several slender spines around the margin of the aperture.

This may prove to be a species distinct from *S. Pallasiana*, but at present I regard it as a variety.

(?) DISCOPORA COCCINEA Smitt. (p. 496.)

Op. cit., for 1867, Ap., p. 26, (separate copies, p. 26), Plate 27, figs. 162–176. (?) *Cellepora coccinea* Abildgard, Zoöl. Dan., vol. iv, p. 30, Plate 146, figs. 1, 2 (t. Smitt). *Lepralia Peachii* Johnston, Brit. Zoöph., ed. ii, p. 315, Plate 55, figs. 5, 6.

Long Island Sound, northward; northern coasts of Europe to Great Britain. Watch Hill, Rhode Island, 4 to 5 fathoms, on red algæ; Vineyard Sound and Quick's Hole, on algæ, etc., in 4 to 12 fathoms.

Fossil in the Post-Pliocene of Canada (Dawson as *L. Peachii*).

The specimens from our coast, referred to the above species, differ considerably from the typical European forms, and may eventually prove to be a distinct species when a careful direct comparison with a large series of European specimens can be made.

The aperture is usually surrounded by a circle of stout, conical or elongated spinules, variable in number, the one nearest the angle of the aperture, on each side, often stouter; but the spines are often absent. A small semicircular avicularium is often seen near one side of the cell, and distant from the aperture. The tooth or spine at the proximal edge of the cell is elongated and more or less bifid at the end.

Celleporina.

CELLEPORA SCABRA Smitt. (p. 419.)

Op. cit., for 1867, Ap., p. 30, (separate copies, p. 30), Plate 28, figs. 183 to 197, 1868. *Eschara scabra* Fabricius, Nye Zoöl. Bidr., Vid. Selsk. Phys. Skr., Hauniæ, vol. i, p. 29 (t. Smitt). *Millepora reticulata* Fabricius, Fauna Grœnl., p. 433, 1780 (*non* Linné).

Vineyard Sound to Greenland; Spitzbergen; northern coasts of Europe. Vineyard Sound and Quick's Hole, 5 to 10 fathoms, on *Phyllophora*, etc., not uncommon.

CELLEPORA RAMULOSA Linné. (p. 312.)

Syst. Naturæ, ed. xii, p. 1285, 1767; Johnston, Brit. Zoöph., ed. ii, p. 296, Plate 52, figs. 4, 5; Smitt, op. cit., for 1867, Ap., p. 31, (separate copies, p. 31), Plate 28, figs. 198–210. *Cellepora verrucosa* Fabricius, Fauna Grœnl., p. 434 (variety) *Cellepora pumicosa* (*pars*) Linné, Syst. Nat., ed. xii, p. 1286; (?) Johnston, Brit. Zoöph., ed. ii, p. 295, Plate 52, figs. 1–3 (variety).

Long Island Sound to Greenland; Spitzbergen; northern coasts of Europe to Great Britain. Very common near New Haven, off South End, at Thimble Islands, and Faulkner's Island, in large tide-pools, low-water to 8 fathoms, chiefly on *Sertulariæ* and other hydroids, and slender red algæ, (mostly the variety *tuberosa*, or *verrucosa*); Watch Hill, Rhode Island, 4 to 5 fathoms; Buzzard's Bay and Vineyard Sound, 1 to 15 fathoms, on hydroids, common; abundant in Casco Bay; Bay of Fundy; and at Saint George's Bank; low-water to 145 fathoms.

RADIATA.

ECHINODERMATA.

HOLOTHURIOIDEA.

THYONE BRIAREUS Selenka. (p. 362.)

Zeitschrift für Wissenschaftliche Zoologie, vol. xvii, p. 353, 1867. *Holothuria Briareus* Lesueur, Journ. Acad. Nat. Sciences, Philadelphia, ser. i, vol. iv, p. 161, 1824. *Sclerodactyla Briareus* Ayres, Proc. Boston Soc. Nat. Hist., vol. iv, pp. 6, 7, 101–3, 1851; Verrill, Proc. Boston Soc. Nat. Hist., vol. x, p. 342, 1866. *Anaperus Bryareus* Pourtales, Proceedings American Assoc. for Adv. of Science, for 1851, p. 10, 1852. *Anaperus Carolinus* Troschel, Müller's Arch. für Anat., 1846, p. 62; Pourtales, op. cit., p. 10.

Texas to Cape Cod. Long Island Sound, at West Haven, Connecticut, Thimble Islands, etc., not common; Vineyard Sound and Buzzard's Bay, 1 to 10 fathoms, not uncommon; Gardiner's Bay, Long Island; Great Egg Harbor, New Jersey; Fort Macon, North Carolina, common (coll. Dr. Yarrow); West Florida (coll. E. Jewett).

STEREODERMA UNISEMITA Ayres. (p. 503.)

Proc. Boston Soc. Nat. Hist., vol. iv, p. 46, 1851; Selenka, op. cit., p. 344, Plate 19, figs. 96, 97. *Anaperus unisemita* Stimpson, Proc. Boston Soc. Nat. Hist., vol. iv, p. 8, 1851; Verrill, op. cit., vol. x, p. 357, 1866. *Cucumaria fusiformis* Desor, Proc. Boston Soc. Nat. Hist., vol. iii, p. 67 (*non* Forbes).

Off Martha's Vineyard, 22 fathoms, sand; Banks of Newfoundland (Stimpson). South Shoals of Nantucket, 22 fathoms, (Desor).

PENTAMERA PULCHERRIMA Ayres. (p. 420.)

Proc. Boston Soc. Nat. Hist., vol. iv, p. 207, 1852; Selenka, op. cit., p. 346.

South Carolina to Vineyard Sound. Off Holmes's Hole, 4 to 5 fathoms; Nobsca Beach, after storms, abundant; Fort Macon, North Carolina (coll. Dr. Yarrow). Fort Johnson, South Carolina (Stimpson).

? MOLPADIA OÖLITICA Selenka. (p. 510.)

Op. cit., p. 257 (in part), 1867. *Chirodota oölitica* Pourtales, Proc. Amer. Assoc. for 1851, p. 13, 1852. *Embolus pauper* Selenka, op. cit., p. 359, Plate 20, fig. 132 1867.

Off Block Island, 29 fathoms, sandy mud; off Boon Island, 95 fathoms, muddy, (A. S. Packard). Massachusetts Bay, in fish stomachs, (Pourtales). Selenka gives "Cape Palmas (?)" as the locality for his "*Embolus pauper*," which was based on specimens sent from the Museum of Comparative Zoölogy—perhaps the original ones described by Pourtales; the locality given is evidently erroneous.

The single specimen from off Block Island is small and imperfect, and may not be this species.

CAUDINA ARENATA Stimpson. (p. 362.)

Marine Invert. of Grand Manan, p. 17, 1853; Selenka, op. cit., p. 358, Plate 20, figs. 129–131; Clark, Mind in Nature, p. 187, figs. 114–116; A. and E. C. Agassiz.

Sea-Side Studies, p. 97, fig. 126. *Chirodota arenata* Gould, Invert. of Mass., ed. i, p. 346, (figure), 1841; Ayres, op. cit., p. 143; Pourtales, op. cit., p. 13. *Caudina* (*Molpadia*) *arenata* Verrill, Proc. Boston Soc. Nat. Hist., vol. x, p. 345, 1866.

Vineyard Sound to Chelsea, Massachusetts. Sometimes abundant on Chelsea Beach, after storms. Wood's Hole (H. E. Webster). Selenka gives "Grand Manan" (? from specimens in Mus. Comp. Zoöl.), but after very careful search during several excursions to that island, I have never been able to find it there, and believe this to be an error. Stimpson knew it only from Massachusetts Bay.

LEPTOSYNAPTA GIRARDII Verrill. Plate XXXV, figs. 265, 266. (p. 361.)

Synapta Girardii Pourtales, Proc. Amer. Assoc. Adv. Science, for 1851, p. 14. *Leptosynapta tenuis* Verrill, Trans. Conn. Acad., vol. i, p. 325. *Synapta tenuis* Ayres, op. cit., p. 11, 1851, (*non* Quoy and Gaimard); A. and E. C. Agassiz, Sea-Side Studies, p. 95, figs. 124, 125; Verrill, Proc. Boston Soc. Nat. Hist., vol. x, p. 342. *Synapta Ayresii* Selenka, op. cit., p. 362, 1867. (?) *Synapta gracilis* Selenka, op. cit., p. 363, Plate 20, figs. 123, 124.

New Jersey to Massachusetts Bay. Common in Long Island Sound, at Savin Rock, and other localities near New Haven, in sand at low-water; abundant in Vineyard Sound, on Naushon Island, etc.; Cape Cod; Chelsea Beach, Massachusetts. Sag Harbor, Long Island, (Ayres). Selenka erroneously gives "Cape Florida" as the locality for *S. Girardii*. It was based on Massachusetts specimens.

LEPTOSYNAPTA ROSEOLA Verrill, sp. nov. (p. 362.)

Body long, slender; integument translucent, filled with numerous minute, scattered, opaque, light-red spots, oval or sub-circular in form; perforated plates smaller than in the preceding species; anchors relatively much longer, with a very slender, elongated shank. General color, rosy or pale red, due to the minute red spots. Length 100^{mm} to 150^{mm}; diameter about 5^{mm} to 6^{mm}.

Long Island Sound, at Savin Rock, near New Haven; Vineyard Sound, at Naushon Island; in sand at low-water mark.

ECHINOIDEA.

STRONGYLOCENTROTUS DRÖBACHIENSIS A. Agassiz. Plate XXXV, figs. 368. (p. 406.)

Revision of the Echini, Parts I and II, pp. 162, 277, Plate 4^a, figs. 2–4, Plate 9, Plate 10, 1872. *Echinus Dröbachiensis* Müller, Zoöl. Dan. Prod., p. 235, 1776, *Toxopneustes Dröbachiensis* Agassiz, Catal. Rais., in Annal. des Sci. Nat., vol. vi. p. 367, 1846. *Euryechinus Dröbachiensis* Verrill, Proc. Boston Soc. Nat. Hist. vol. x, pp. 341, 352, 1866; Trans. Conn. Acad., vol. i, p. 304, 1867; American, Jour. Science, vol. xlix, p. 101. *Echinus neglectus* Lamarck, Anim. sans vert., p. 49, 1816. *Echinus granularis* Say, Journ. Acad. Nat. Sci., Philad., vol. v, p. 225, 1827 (*non* Lamarck). *Echinus granulatus* Gould, Invert., ed. i, p. 344, 1841. *Euryechinus granulatus* Verrill, Proc. Boston Soc., vol. x, pp. 340, 352. *Strongylocentrotus chlorocentrotus* Brandt, Prodr., p. 264, 1835.

Circumpolar: New Jersey to the Arctic Ocean; Spitzbergen to Great

Britain; Behring Straits to Gulf of Georgia; Northern Siberia to Okhotsk Sea and De Castrie's Bay. Very abundant in the Bay of Fundy, from low-water to 109 fathoms; Casco Bay; Massachusetts Bay; mouth of Vineyard Sound and off Gay Head, 10 to 20 fathoms, common; off Holmes's Hole; off Watch Hill, Rhode Island, 4 to 5 fathoms, not uncommon; off New London, Connecticut, plenty, (coll. Prudden); Faulkner's Island, Thimble Islands, and near New Haven, 4 to 8 fathoms, uncommon and small. Off New Jersey, on a bank, in 32 fathoms, (Captain Gedney). Off Saint George's Bank, 430 fathoms, (S. I. Smith).

Fossil in the Post-Pliocene of Portland, Maine; New Brunswick; Canada; and Labrador.

ARBACIA PUNCTULATA Gray. (p. 406.)

Proc. Zoöl. Soc. of London, 1835, p. 58; A. Agassiz, Revision of the Echini, Parts I and II, pp. 91, 263, Plate 2, fig. 4, Plate 5, figs. 1 to 18, 1872. *Echinus punctulatus* Lamarck, Anim. sans vert., p. 47, 1816. *Echinocidaris punctulata* Desmoulin, Syn., p. 306, 1837. *Echinocidaris Davisii* A. Agassiz, Bulletin Mus, Comp. Zoölogy, vol. i, p. 20, 1863; Verrill, Proc. Boston Soc. Nat. Hist., vol. x, p. 340, 1866.

Vineyard Sound to the West Indies and Gulf of Mexico. Common at Wood's Hole, and in Vineyard Sound and Buzzard's Bay, 1 to 12 fathoms; off Watch Hill, Rhode Island, 4 to 5 fathoms; Long Island Sound, near New Haven, and at Charles Island, not common; Fort Macon, North Carolina (coll. Dr. Yarrow). Off Tortugas, 13 to 125 fathoms, (Pourtales). West Florida (E. Jewett).

ECHINARACHNIUS PARMA Gray. Plate XXXV, fig. 267. (p. 362.)

Ann. Phil., p. 6, 1825; A. Agassiz, Revision of Echini, Parts I and II, pp. 107, 316, Plates 11[d], figs. 4, 5, 11[e], figs. 4, 5, 12, figs. 1–13, 1872. *Scutella parma* Lamarck, Anim. sans vert., p. 11, 1816.

New Jersey to Labrador. According to Mr. A. Agassiz, it occurs in the North Pacific, on the west coast of America, from the Aleutian Islands to Vancouver Island, and on the coast of Asia at Kamtchatka, 30 to 70 fathoms; and also at New Holland; India; Indian Ocean; Red Sea, etc. Common along the entire coast of New England and Long Island, from low-water to 100 fathoms, sand. Off New Jersey, on a distant bank, in 32 fathoms, (Captain Gedney). Very abundant at Saint George's Bank and vicinity, 15 to 430 fathoms, (S. I. Smith).

MELLITA PENTAPORA Lütken.

Bidrag til Kundskab om Echiniderne, p. 107, in Vidensk. Middelelser, 1864; Verrill, Trans. Connecticut Academy, vol. i, p. 345, 1867. *Echinus pentaporus* Gmelin, Syst. Nat., p. 3189, 1788. *Encope pentapora* Agassiz, Monog. Scut., Plate 3, 1841. *Scutella quinquefora* Lamarck, Anim. sans vert., p. 9, 1816. *Mellita quinquefora* Agassiz, Mon. Scut., p. 36, 1841; Catal. Rais., in Ann. Sci., vol. vii, p. 138, 1847. *Mellita testudinaria* Gray, Proc. Zöol. Soc., London, 1851, p. 36; Verrill, this Report, pp. 427, 429, (see errata). *Mellita testudinata* Agassiz, Mon. Scut., p. 40, Plate 4[a], figs. 7–9, 1841; A. Agassiz, Revision of the Echini, pp. 141, 322, Plate 11, figs. 13-22, Plate 12[a], Plate 12[c], figs. 1, 2, (name adopted from Klein, 1734, accidentally binomial).

New Jersey to Brazil; very abundant along the whole eastern coast of the United States, south of Cape Hatteras, and along the entire coast of the Gulf of Mexico; rare and local north of Cape Hatteras. Vineyard Sound, 5 to 8 fathoms, rare and dead; outer beach at Great Egg Harbor, New Jersey, dead. Nantucket (Agassiz).

ASTERIOIDEA.

ASTERIAS ARENICOLA Stimpson. Plate XXV, fig. 269. (p. 326.)

Proc. Boston Soc. Nat. Hist., vol. viii, p. 268, 1862; Verrill, vol. x, p. 339, 1866. *Asteracanthion berylinus* Ag. MSS., A. Agassiz, Embryology of Echinod., in Proc. Amer. Acad., 1863; Embryology of the Starfish, in Agassiz Contributions, vol. v, p. 3; Sea-Side Studies, p. 108, figs. 141-145, 1865 (t. Agassiz).

Massachusetts Bay to Northern Florida and the northern shores of the Gulf of Mexico; rare and local, in sheltered localities, north of Massachusetts, as at Quahog Bay, east of Portland, Maine; but not known from the eastern part of the coast of Maine, nor in the Bay of Fundy.

Very common in Long Island Sound; Buzzard's Bay; Vineyard Sound; and along the shores of Long Island, from low-water to 15 fathoms. Not uncommon in Massachusetts Bay, at Nahant, Beverly, &c.

ASTERIAS FORBESII Verrill.

Proc. Boston Soc. Nat. Hist., vol. x, p. 345, 1866. *Asteracanthion Forbesii* Desor, Proc. Boston Soc. N. H., vol. iii, p. 67, 1848.

Buzzard's Bay to Beverly, Massachusetts. Vineyard Sound and off Gay Head, 6 to 14 fathoms; Buzzard's Bay, 6 fathoms; Chelsea and Beverly, Massachusetts, low-water. Vineyard Sound, 8 fathoms, (Desor).

This is probably identical with the preceding species, the differences being, perhaps, chiefly sexual, but I have not yet had opportunities to satisfy myself fully in regard to this point, and, therefore, leave them, for the present, under separate names. Should they be united, the name *Forbesii* has the precedence over all others.

ASTERIAS VULGARIS Stimpson, MSS. (p. 496.)

Packard, in Canadian Naturalist and Geologist, Dec., 1863 (no description); Verrill, Proc. Boston Soc. Nat. Hist., vol. x, p. 347, 1866 (description). *Asteracanthion pallidus* Ag. MSS.; A. Agassiz, Embryology, in Proc. Amer. Acad., 1863 (no description); Embryology of the Starfish, in Agassiz' Contributions. vol. v, p. 3. *Asterias rubens* Gould, Invert., ed. i, p. 345 (*non* Linné).

Long Island Sound to Labrador, and (?) Greenland. Very abundant in Massachusetts Bay, Casco Bay, Bay of Fundy, from above low-water mark to 40 fathoms; in the deeper parts of Vineyard Sound and off Gay Head, in 6 to 25 fathoms, not uncommon; off Watch Hill, Rhode Island, 4 to 5 fathoms, common; Faulkner's Island, Connecticut, low-water, very rare.

LEPTASTERIAS COMPTA Verrill.

Proc. Boston Soc., vol. x, p. 350, 1866. *Asterias compta* Stimpson, Proc. Boston Soc. Nat. Hist., vol. viii, p. 270, 1862; Verrill, op. cit., p. 340.

Off New Jersey, 32 fathoms, (Captain Gedney). Off Martha's Vineyard, 20 to 25 fathoms, rare; off Casco Bay, 30 to 50 fathoms.

CRIBRELLA SANGUINOLENTA Lütken. (p. 407.)

Grœnl. Echinod., p. 31, 1859; Verrill, Proc. Boston Soc. Nat Hist., vol. x, p. 345, 1866. *Asterias sanguinolenta* Müller, Zoöl. Dan. Prod., 2836, 1776. *Asterias oculata* Pennant, Brit. Zoöl., vol. iv, p. 61, Plate 30, fig. 56, 1777. *Asterias spongiosa* Fabricius, Fauna Grœnl., p. 368, 1780. *Linkia oculata* Forbes, Wern. Mem., vol. viii, p. 120, 1839. *Cribella oculata* Forbes, British Starfishes, p. 100, (figure), 1841. *Echinaster oculatus* Müller and Troschel, Syst. Asterid., p. 24, 1842. *Linkia oculata* Stimpson, Invert. of Grand Manan, p. 14, 1853. *Linkia pertusa* Stimpson, op. cit., p. 14. *Echinaster sanguinolentus* Sars, Fauna Litt. Norveg., i, p. 47, Plate 8, figs. 3-6; Oversigt af Norges Echinodermer, p. 84, 1861.

Connecticut to the Arctic Ocean; northern coasts of Europe to Great Britain and France. Very common in the Bay of Fundy, Casco Bay, and on the entire coast of Maine, from low-water to 100 fathoms; Massachusetts Bay; Vineyard Sound, 5 to 20 fathoms, not uncommon; off Watch Hill, Rhode Island, 3 to 5 fathoms; off New London, Connecticut (coll. T. H. Prudden).

OPHIUROIDEA.

OPHIURA OLIVACEA Lyman. (p. 363.)

Ill. Catal. Mus. Comp. Zoölogy, No. 1, Ophiuridæ and Astrophytidæ, p. 23, 1865; Verrill, Proc. Boston Soc. N. H., vol. x, p. 339. *Ophioderma olivaceum* Ayres, Proc. Boston Soc. Nat. Hist., vol. iv, p. 134, 1852.

Cape Cod to North Carolina. Wood's Hole, Buzzard's Bay, and Vineyard Sound, not common; shores of Long Island, frequent; Fort Macon, North Carolina, common, (Dr. Yarrow).

OPHIOPHOLIS ACULEATA Gray. Plate XXXV, fig. 270. (p. 496.)

List of British Animals in Coll. of Brit. Mus., Part I, Rad. Anim., p. 25, 1848; Lütken Additamenta ad Hist. Ophiuridarum, p. 60, Plate 2, figs. 15, a. b, 16, a, b, 1858; Verrill, op. cit., p. 344, 1866. *Asterias aculeata* Linné (*pars*), Syst. Nat., p. 1101; Retzius Vetersk.-Akad., vol. iv, p. 240, 1783; Müller, Prod., 2841, 1776; Zoöl. Dan., vol. iii, p. 29, Plate 99, 1789. *Ophiura bellis* Fleming, Brit. Anim., p. 488, 1828. *Ophiocoma bellis* Forbes, Wern. Mem., vol. viii, p. 226; Brit. Starfishes, p. 53, figure. *Ophiopholis bellis* Lyman, op. cit., p. 96, Plate 1, figs. 4-6. *Ophiolepis scolopendrica* Müller and Troschel, Syst. Aster., p. 96, 1842. *Ophiopholis scolopendrica* Stimpson, Invert. of Grand Manan, p. 13, 1853.

Rhode Island and New Jersey to the Arctic Ocean; Iceland; Spitzbergen; northern coasts of Europe, to the English Channel, Ireland, etc. Very abundant in the Bay of Fundy, Casco Bay, and along the whole coast of Maine, from low-water to 100 fathoms; Massachusetts Bay; off Gay Head, 6 to 8 fathoms, rare; off Watch Hill, Rhode Island, in 4 to 5 fathoms, rocky. Off New Jersey, 30 to 38 fathoms, N. lat. 39° 54′; W. long. 73° 15′, (Josephine Exp., t. Ljungmann). A similar species, perhaps identical, occurs on the northwestern coasts of America.

AMPHIPHOLIS ELEGANS Ljungmann. (p. 420.)

Ophiuroidea viventia huc usque cognita, Öfvers. Kongl. Vet.-Akad. Förh., 1866, p. 312. *Ophiura elegans* Leach, Zoöl. Miscell., iii, p. 57, 1815. *Amphiura elegans* Norman, Ann. and Mag. Nat. Hist., vol. xv, p. 109, 1865. *Ophiocoma neglecta* Forbes, Brit. Starfishes, p. 30, 1841. *Ophiolepis tenuis* Ayres, Proc. Boston Soc. Nat. Hist., vol. iv, p. 133, 1852. *Amphiura tenuis* Lyman, Proc. B. S. N. H., vol. vii, p. 194, 1860. *Amphipholis tenuis* Ljungmann, Öfvers. af Kongl. Vet.-Akad. Förh., 1871, p. 635. *Amphiura squamata* Lyman, Catalogue Ophiur. and Astroph., p. 121, 1865 (*non* Delle Chiage, t. Ljungmann).

Off New Jersey to the Arctic Ocean; northern coasts of Europe to the English Channel. Common in Vineyard Sound, 4 to 15 fathoms; Massachusetts Bay; Casco Bay; Bay of Fundy, low-water to 60 fathoms. Greenland, 15 fathoms, (Lütken, as *A. neglecta*). Off New Jersey, 36 to 38 fathoms, N. lat. 39° 54′, W. long. 73° 15′, (Josephine Exp., t. Ljungmann).

Mr. Ljungmann, in his latest paper, regards this species as distinct both from the Mediterranean species (*Amphiura squamata*), and the English and Norwegian species (*Amphipholis elegans*). The former I have here regarded as distinct, but consider the latter identical with the American form, the differences mentioned being slight and apparently inconstant.

AMPHIURA ABDITA Verrill. (p. 433.)

Amphipholis abdita Verrill, Amer. Jour. of Science, ser. iii, vol. ii, p. 132, 1871; this Report, p. 433. (See errata).

Body plump, pentagonal; the interradial margins concave, and the angles, at base of arms, incised; margin thick, rounded; upper surface of disk covered with very numerous, minute, crowded scales, which encroach more or less upon the radial shields and run up between them in a wedge-like area; lower surface thickly covered with still more minute, granule-like scales. Radial shields elongated, three or more times longer than wide, curved; the outer end geniculate or bent downward, forming a prominent angle above; they are divergent, and separate for their whole length, or barely touch at the outer ends, and are more or less concealed laterally and proximally by the encroachment of the small scales. Arms or rays, 16 times as long as the diameter of the body, or even more, slender, flexible, gradually attenuated to the tips.

Six mouth-papillæ in each angle of the mouth, and two to four additional small rounded papillæ, or tentacle-scales, near the extreme outer angle. Two of the mouth-papillæ, on each side, are placed close together, at about the middle of the edge of the jaw; the outer of these, which is about twice as wide as the inner, is flat, scarcely longer than wide, with the end obtusely rounded or truncate; the inner one is scarcely wider than thick, oblong, rounded at the end; in one case these two papillæ are united together. The third mouth-papilla is stout and rounded, obtuse, larger and longer than either of the others, separated from them by a considerable interval, and brought close to the tooth at the end of the jaw, beyond which it projects inwardly and downwardly.

The mouth-shields are long-oval, or somewhat hexagonal, narrowed outwardly, the outer part of the lateral edges being nearly straight, the outer end rounded or sub-truncate, the inner end broadly rounded. Side mouth-shields triangular with the three edges concave, the inner ends not united, the surface finely granulated. The lower arm-plates are separated by the side plates; the first two are longer than broad, pentagonal, the inner end forming an obtuse angle, the outer edge straight; the next two are about as wide as long, squarish, with the corners rounded or truncate; the following ones are broader than long, somewhat octagonal, the outer and inner edges longest and nearly straight; beyond the middle of the arm they are again pentagonal, with an inner angle. On the first five joints of one specimen there is only a single pair of tentacle-scales, which are small and rounded; on the succeeding joints there are generally two pairs, one of them being considerably smaller than the other; the largest specimen has two pairs of tentacle-scales on all the joints.

Arm-spines three, on each side of all the joints, except the first, which has but two; they are thickened at base, gradually tapering, blunt at tip, sub-equal; the lower one a little curved downward; the upper one stoutest, flattened, scarcely tapering, obtuse; the middle one a little longer than the others, the length about equal to width of lower arm-plates. The upper arm-plates are transversely sub-elliptical, with the outer edge well rounded, the inner edge slightly prominent or angular in the middle, and a little concave to either side, so that the lateral portions are somewhat narrowed; the plates generally touch each other.

Color, when living, brown above, the central area dark brown, a radiating band of the same extending to each interradial margin, and bordered like the central area with pale gray; opposite the base of each arm is a squarish area or radial band of olive-brown; radial plates yellowish brown, the space between them bright blue. In the center of the disk is a small darker brown spot, and five similar ones, corresponding to the bases of the arms, form a circle around the center; five others, more distant, correspond to the interradial spaces; other more minute dark spots are scattered over the disk. Upper arm-plates are mostly dark brown, edged with pale brown or whitish; some of the plates are partially or wholly lighter, yellowish brown, and thus form transverse light bands, or mottlings, consisting of one or more plates; toward the tips these light bands become more numerous, and wider; spines bright brown. Lower side of disk yellowish brown, with a tinge of greenish; plates around the mouth whitish; each of the jaws with two brown spots; mouth-tentacles orange-yellow. Under arm-plates yellowish brown, with the edges paler, and with a distal median spot of whitish; lower arm-spines yellowish brown. In some specimens the arms are dull greenish above, instead of brown.

Diameter of the disk, of the largest specimen, 11^{mm}; length of arms, 180^{mm}.

Long Island Sound; off New Haven, in 4 to 6 fathoms, mud; off Thimble Islands, 3 to 8 fathoms, soft mud, rare.

This species is, in some respects, intermediate between *Amphipholis* and *Amphiura*. With the former it agrees best in the number of the arm-spines and general appearance; but in the structure of the mouth-parts it agrees better with the latter. It will, however, not go into any of the sections or sub-sections established by Ljungmann. It appears to be more nearly allied to *A. Eugeniæ* Ljung., from La Plata, than to any other species hitherto described; the latter has, however, four arm-spines instead of three.

ASTROPHYTON AGASSIZII Stimpson.

Invertebrata of Grand Manan, p. 12, 1853; Lyman, Catalogue, p. 186.

This species was first described from a specimen obtained "not far from the shoals of Nantucket," by Governor John Winthrop, in 1670 and 1671 (Philosophical Transactions), under the name of "Basket-fish" or "Net-fish." Crab Ledge, off Chatham, Massachusetts, (V. N. Edwards.) It occurs on the banks east and north of Cape Cod, and on Saint George's Bank, and is very common in the Bay of Fundy, low-water to 110 fathoms; and is especially abundant in Eastport Harbor, in 10 to 20 fathoms. According to Dr. Lütken it is also found at Greenland and Finmark.

CRINOIDEA.

Antedon dentatus Verrill.

Proc. Boston Soc. Nat. Hist., vol. x, p. 339, 1866. *Alecto dentata* Say, Journ. Acad. Nat. Sci., Philadelphia, vol. v, p. 153, 1825.

This species was described by Say, from a specimen obtained at Great Egg Harbor, New Jersey. It may possibly occur on the southern coast of New England, but I am not aware that it has actually been found so far north.

ACALEPHÆ.

CTENOPHORÆ.

MNEMIOPSIS LEIDYI A. Agassiz. (p. 449.)

Illustr. Catal. Mus. Comp. Zoölogy, North American Acalephæ, p. 20, figs. 22–24, 1865.

Buzzard's Bay and Vineyard Sound; Long Island Sound, off New Haven.

LESUEURIA HYBOPTERA A. Agassiz. (p. 454.)

Catal. North American Acalephæ, p. 23, figs. 25–28.

Newport, Rhode Island, to Massachusetts Bay (A. Agassiz).

PLEUROBRACHIA RHODODACTYLA Agassiz. (p. 448.)

Memoirs Amer. Academy, vol. iv, p. 314, Plates 1 to 5, 1849; Contributions to Nat. Hist. U. S., vol. iii, pp. 203, 294, Plate 2[a], 1860; A. Agassiz, Catalogue, p. 30, figs. 38–51, 1865.

Southern side of Long Island, to Greenland. Not uncommon in Long

Island Sound, near New Haven; common in Vineyard Sound and Massachusetts Bay; very abundant in Casco Bay, Bay of Fundy, and Gulf of Saint Lawrence. Off Saint George's Bank (S. I. Smith). Fire Island, Long Island (S. I. Smith).

IDYIA ROSEOLA Agassiz. (p. 451.)

Contributions to Nat. Hist. U. S., vol. iii, pp. 270–296, Plates 1, 2, 1860; A. Agassiz, Catalogue, p. 36, figs. 52–62, 1865.

Vineyard Sound to Labrador. Off Gay Head, not common; common in Massachusetts Bay and Casco Bay; very abundant in Bay of Fundy and Gulf of Saint Lawrence. Labrador (Packard).

? *Cestum Veneris* Lesueur.

Nouv. Bull. Soc. Phil., 1813, p. 281, Plate 5, fig. 1; Lesson, Zoöphytes Acalephes, p. 70, Plate 1, fig. 1.

Mr. S. I. Smith observed a species, apparently identical with this, at Saint George's Banks, and Mr. A. Agassiz has observed fragments of a similar species near Newport, Rhode Island. This is properly a more southern species, found in the warmer parts of the Atlantic and in the Mediterranean Sea.

DISCOPHORÆ.

AURELIA FLAVIDULA Péron and Lesueur. Plate XXXVI, fig. 271. (p. 449.)

Ann. Mus. Hist. Nat., vol. xiv, p. 47, 1809; Lesson, op. cit., p. 376, 1843; Agassiz, Contributions to Nat. Hist. U. S., vol. iii, Plates 6–11[b]; vol. iv, pp. 10, 160; A. Agassiz, Catalogue, p. 42, figs. 65, 66. *Aurelia aurita* Stimpson, Invert., of Grand Manan, p. 11, 1853.

Buzzard's Bay to Greenland. Common in the upper part of Buzzard's Bay, in spring; off Gay Head and in Vineyard Sound, in August; abundant in Massachusetts Bay; Casco Bay; Frenchman's Bay; Bay of Fundy; and Gulf of Saint Lawrence.

CYANEA ARCTICA Péron and Lesueur. (p. 449.)

Ann. Mus., vol. xiv, p. 51, 1809; Agassiz, Contributions, vol. iii, Plates 3, 4, 5, 5[a], 10, 10[a]; vol. iv, pp. 87, 162; A. Agassiz, Catalogue, p. 44, fig. 67. *Cyanea Postelsii* Gould, Invert., ed. i, p. 347; Stimpson, op. cit., p. 11 (*non* Brandt).

Long Island Sound to Greenland. Common near New Haven; in Buzzard's Bay; Vineyard Sound; very abundant in Massachusetts Bay; Casco Bay; Bay of Fundy; and Gulf of Saint Lawrence. Fire Island, Long Island (S. I. Smith).

Cyanea fulva Agassiz.

Contributions, vol. iv, pp. 119, 162, 1862; A. Agassiz, Catalogue, p. 46 (no description).

Long Island Sound (L. Agassiz). Vineyard Sound (A. Agassiz).

I have been unable to distinguish more than one species among the *Cyaneæ* of our waters, although they vary considerably in color, just as they do farther north, as in the Bay of Fundy. This is probably only a color-variety of *C. arctica.*

DACTYLOMETRA QUINQUECIRRA Agassiz. Plate XXXVI, fig. 272. (p. 449.)

Contributions, vol. iv, pp. 125, 166, 1862; A. Agassiz, Catalogue, p. 48, fig. 69.

Pelagia quinquecirrha Desor, Proc. Boston Soc. Nat. History, vol. iii, p. 76, 1848.

Bermudas to Cape Cod. Long Island Sound, near New Haven; common in Buzzard's Bay and Vineyard Sound.

Pelagia cyanella Péron and Lesueur.

Ann. du Mus. Hist. Nat., vol. xiv, p. 37, 1809; Agassiz, Contributions, vol. iii, Plates 12, 13, 13[a]; vol. iv, pp. 128, 164; A. Agassiz, Catalogue, p. 47, fig. 68.

Off Saint George's Bank (S. I. Smith). This species inhabits the Gulf of Mexico; Caribbean Sea; and coasts of Florida and North Carolina. It is carried northward by the Gulf Stream to the vicinity of Saint George's Bank, and is, therefore, like the two following, likely to occur occasionally at Nantucket and Martha's Vineyard.

Stomolophus meleagris Agassiz.

Contributions, vol. iii, Plate 14, 1860; vol. iv, pp. 138, 151, 1862; A. Agassiz, Catalogue, p. 40.

Coast of Georgia (Agassiz). Off Saint George's Bank (S. I. Smith).

? *Charybdea periphylla* Péron and Lesueur.

Ann. du Mus. Hist. Nat., vol. xiv, p. 332, 1809; Edwards in Cuvier, Règne Anim., Pl. 55, fig. 2 (from Lesueur); Lesson, op. cit., p. 265, 1843; Agassiz, Contributions, vol. iv, p. 173.

This species was originally described and figured from mutilated specimens taken under the equator in the Atlantic Ocean, and seems not to have been seen by later writers. Mr. S. I. Smith has apparently rediscovered this interesting species off Saint George's Bank.

The specimen obtained by him, while on the United States Coast-Survey steamer Bache, in 1872, is not quite perfect, but agrees pretty nearly with the descriptions and figure cited.

The body in the alcoholic specimen is elevated, bell-shaped, rounded above, with a marked constriction toward the border; transparent, the inner cavity showing through as a large, conical, dark reddish brown spot, with the apex slightly truncated. Border deeply divided into sixteen long, flat lobes, which are of nearly uniform breadth throughout, and slightly rounded, or sub-truncate, at the end; the edges and end thin and more or less frilled; the inner side with two sub-marginal carinæ. Eyes inconspicuous, but small bright red specks are scattered over the marginal lobes. The intervals between the lobes are narrow and generally smoothly rounded, without distinct evidence of the existence of tentacles, except that, in one of these intervals, there is a small and short papilliform process, with brown pigment at the base. The ovaries are mostly wanting, but portions are to be seen as slightly convoluted organs in the marginal region, opposite the intervals between the lobes.

TRACHYNEMA DIGITALE A. Agassiz. (p. 454.)

Catalogue, p. 57, figs. 81–86, 1865. *Medusa digitale* Fabricius, Fauna Grœnl., p. 366, 1780.

Vineyard Sound to Greenland. Wood's Hole, July 1, young specimens. Massachusetts Bay (A. Agassiz).

HYDROIDEA.

Sertularina.

TIAROPSIS DIADEMATA Agassiz. (p. 454.)

Memoirs Amer. Acad., vol. iv, p. 289, Plate 6, 1849; Contributions, vol. iii, p. 354, Plate 31, figs. 9–15; vol. iv, pp. 308, 311, figs. 45–48; A. Agassiz, Catalogue, p. 69, figs. 91–93.

Vineyard Sound to Bay of Fundy. Massachusetts Bay (A. Agassiz). Greenland (Mörch). Wood's Hole, April, 1873.

OCEANIA LANGUIDA A. Agassiz. (p. 454.)

In Agassiz, Contributions, vol. iv, p. 353, 1862; Catalogue, p. 70, figs. 94–102, 1865.

Buzzard's Bay to Bay of Fundy. Common in Vineyard Sound; not uncommon in Eastport Harbor.

EUCHEILOTA VENTRICULARIS McCready. (p. 454.)

Gymnophthalmata of Charleston Harbor, in Proc. of Elliott Society of Nat History, vol. i, p. 187, Plates 11, figs. 1–3, 12, figs. 1, 2, 1857; Agassiz, Contr butions, vol. iv, p. 353, 1862; A. Agassiz, Catalogue, p. 74, figs. 104, 105, 1865.

Charleston, South Carolina, to Vineyard Sound.

EUCHEILOTA DUODECIMALIS A. Agassiz. (p. 454.)

In Agassiz, Contributions, vol. iv, p. 353, 1862; Catalogue, p. 75, figs. 106–107[a].

Buzzard's Bay, Naushon Island (A. Agassiz).

CLYTIA JOHNSTONI Hincks. (p. 408.)

Hist. British Hydroid Zoöphytes, p. 143, Plate 24, fig. 1, 1868. *Campanularia Johnstoni* Alder, Northum. and Dur. Catal., in Trans. Tynes. F. C., vol. v, p. 126, Plate 4, fig. 8 (t. Hincks). *Sertularia uniflora* (*pars*) Pallas, Elench. Zoöph., p. 121, 1766. *Campanularia volubilis* Johnston, Brit. Zoöph., ed. ii, pp. 107, 108, fig. 18 (*not* of Linné and Pallas). *Clytia volubilis* Lamouroux, Expos. Meth., p. 15, Plate 4, figs. E, f, F, 1821. *Clytia bicophora* Agassiz, Contributions, vol. iv, pp. 304, 354, Plate 27, figs. 8, 9; Plate 29, figs. 6–9, 1862; A. Agassiz, Catalogue, p. 78, figs. 108–111.

Long Island Sound to the Arctic Ocean; northern coasts of Europe to Great Britain and France. Common near New Haven and at Thimble Islands, in tide-pools and 2 to 6 fathoms; Watch Hill, Rhode

Island, 3 to 5 fathoms; Buzzard's Bay; Vineyard Sound, 1 to 14 fathoms, common; off Block Island, 29 fathoms; abundant in Casco Bay and Bay of Fundy, low-water to 40 fathoms. Saint George's Bank (S. I. Smith).

This species is undoubtedly the one described by Pallas, and according to the strict rules of priority it should be called *Clytia uniflora*.

CLYTIA INTERMEDIA Agassiz. (p. 408.)

Contributions, vol. iv, p. 305, Plate 29, figs. 10, 11, 1862; A. Agassiz, Catalogue, p. 77 (no description).

Vineyard Sound, 6 to 8 fathoms, on *Phyllophora*. Massachusetts Bay (Agassiz).

PLATYPYXIS CYLINDRICA Agassiz. (p. 408.)

Clytia (Platypyxis) cylindrica Agassiz, Contributions, vol. iv, pp. 306, 354, figs. 42–44 (*not* 41, *nor* Plate 27, figs. 8, 9), 1862. *Platypyxis cylindrica* A. Agassiz, Catalogue, p. 80, figs. 112–114. *Campanularia volubilis* Leidy, Jour. Phil. Acad. Nat. Sciences, ser. ii, vol. iii, p. 138, 1855 (*not* Linné, sp.).

Long Island Sound to Massachusetts Bay. Near New Haven, 4 to 6 fathoms, on *Halecium*; Thimble Islands; Watch Hill, Rhode Island; Vineyard Sound; off Buzzard's Bay, 25 fathoms.

ORTHOPYXIS CALICULATA Verrill. (p. 408.)

Campanularia caliculata Hincks, in Annals and Mag. Nat. Hist., ser. ii, vol. xi, p. 178, Plate 5, B, 1853; Brit. Hydroid Zoöph., p. 164, Plate 31, figs. 2–2[d] *Clytia (Orthopyxis) poterium* Agassiz, Contributions, vol. iv, pp. 297, 302, fig. 40 Plate 28, Plate 29, figs. 1–5, 1862. *Orthopyxis poterium* A. Agassiz, Catalogue, p. 81, 1865.

Vineyard Sound to Labrador; northern coasts of Europe to Great Britain. Off Gay Head and in Vineyard Sound, 4 to 15 fathoms; common in Massachusetts Bay; Casco Bay; and Bay of Fundy, low water to 30 fathoms. Mingan Islands, Labrador, 6 fathoms, (A. E. V). Henley Harbor, Labrador, 20 to 30 fathoms (A. S. Packard, as *Clytia volubilis*).

CAMPANULARIA VOLUBILIS Alder. (p. 408.)

Catal. Zoöph. Northumb. and Durham, in Trans. Tynes. F. C., vol. iii, p. 125, Plate 4, fig. 7, 1857 (*not* of Johnston); Hincks, Brit. Hyd. Zoöph., p. 160, Plate 24, fig. 2. *Sertularia volubilis* Linné (*pars*), Syst. Nat., ed. x, sp. 19; ed. xii, p. 1311; Pallas, Elench. Zoöph., p. 122, 1766. *Clytia volubilis* A. Agassiz, Catalogue, p. 77 (*not* of Lamouroux).

Vineyard Sound to Greenland and Iceland; northern coasts of Europe to Great Britain; low-water to 100 fathoms. Common in the Bay of Fundy, low-water to 60 fathoms.

CAMPANULARIA FLEXUOSA Hincks. (p. 327.)

Brit. Hyd. Zoöph., p. 168, Plate 33. *Laomedea flexuosa* Hincks, Devon. and Cornwall Catalogue, in Ann. and Mag. Nat. Hist., ser. iii, vol. viii, p. 260, 1861.

Laomedea amphora Agassiz, Contributions, vol. iv, pp. 311, 314, fig. 50, p. 352, Plate 30, Plate 31, figs. 1–8, 1862; A. Agassiz, Catalogue, p. 93.

Long Island Sound to Gulf of Saint Lawrence; northern coasts of Europe, Isle of Man. New Haven, on piles of Long Wharf; Thimble Islands, near New Haven; Vineyard Sound, off Gay Head; abundant on the timbers of the wharves at Eastport, Maine.

OBELIA DIAPHANA Verrill. (p. 327.)

Thaumantias diaphana Agassiz, Mem. Amer. Acad., vol. iv, p. 300, figs. 1, 2, 1849 (? *non* Mörch). *Eucope diaphana* (*pars*) Agassiz, Contributions, vol. iv, Plate 33, fig. 2, 1862; A. Agassiz, Catalogue, p. 83, figs. 115–125.

Long Island Sound to Massachusetts Bay. Abundant in New Haven Harbor and Vineyard Sound, on *Zostera*, *Fucus*, etc.

OBELIA GENICULATA Allman. (p. 407.)

Annals and Mag. Nat. Hist., vol. xiii, May, 1864 (t. Hincks); Hincks, Brit. Hyd. Zoöphytes, p. 149, Plate 25, fig. 1, 1868. *Sertularia geniculata* Linné, Syst. Nat., ed. x, sp. 23; ed. xii, sp. 21, p. 1312; Pallas, Elench. Zooph., p. 117, 1766. *Laomedea geniculata* Lamouroux, Pol. Flex., p. 208; Johnston, Brit. Zoöph., ed. ii, p. 103, Plate 25, figs. 1, 2. *Eucope diaphana* (*pars*) Agassiz, Contributions, vol. iv, p. 322, Plate 34, figs. 1–9, 1862. *Eucope alternata* A. Agassiz, Catalogue, p. 86, 1865.

Long Island Sound to Labrador. Northern Europe, from North Cape to Great Britain. Common near New Haven; at Thimble Islands; Watch Hill, Rhode Island; Vineyard Sound, 4 to 15 fathoms; Massachusetts Bay; Casco Bay; Bay of Fundy, and northward, low-water to 40 fathoms, on *Laminaria*, *Rhodymenia*, etc.

OBELIA POLYGENA Verrill.

Eucope polygena A. Agassiz, Catalogue, p. 86, fig. 126, 1865.

Off Gay Head, 4 to 5 fathoms, not common. Nahant, Massachusetts (A. Agassiz).

OBELIA DIVARICATA Verrill.

Laomedea divaricata McCready, op. cit., p. 195, 1859. *Eucope? divaricata* A. Agassiz, Catalogue, p. 91, 1865.

Charleston, South Carolina (McCready, Agassiz). A few specimens were found on floating algæ in Vineyard Sound, which appear to belong to this species. It is closely allied to *O. fusiformis* (A. Agassiz, sp.).

OBELIA PYRIFORMIS Verrill. (p. 390.)

Catalogue, p. 88, figs. 127–129, 1865. *Laomedea gelatinosa* Leidy, Journ. Acad. Nat. Sci., Philad., ser. ii, vol. iii, p. 138, 1855 (*not* Pallas, sp.).

Long Island Sound to Bay of Fundy. Very abundant on piles of wharves, etc., at Wood's Hole.

This species is closely allied to the following; in the latter the young medusæ have sixteen tentacles when set free, and the reproductive capsules differ slightly in form.

OBELIA DICHOTOMA Hincks. (p. 407.)

Brit. Hydroid Zoöphytes, p. 156, Plate 28, fig. 1, 1868. *Sertularia dichotoma* Linné, Syst. Nat., ed. x, sp. 24; ed. xii, sp. 22, p. 1312. *Laomedea dichotoma*, var. *a*, Johnston, Brit. Zoöph., ed. ii, p. 102, Plate 26, figs. 1, 2.

Vineyard Sound, northward; northern coasts of Europe to Great Britain. Off Gay Head, 8 to 10 fathoms, on ascidians; Eastport, Maine.

OBELIA LONGISSIMA Hincks.

Brit. Hydroid Zoöph., p. 154, Plate 27, 1868. *Sertularia longissima* Pallas, Elench. Zoöph., p. 119, 1766 (excl. synonymy). *Laomedea longissima* Alder, Trans. Tynes. F. C., vol. iii, p. 121 (t. Hincks). *Laomedea dichotoma*, var. *b*, Johnston, Brit. Zoöph., ed. ii, p. 102. *Campanularia gelatinosa* Van Beneden, Mém. sur le Campan., p. 33, Plates 1, 2 (t. Hincks).

Gay Head; Cape Ann, Massachusetts; Bay of Fundy. Coasts of Belgium and Great Britain.

OBELIA FLABELLATA Hincks. (p. 390.)

Brit. Hydroid Zoöph., p. 157, Plate 29, 1868. *Campanularia flabellata* Hincks, Ann. and Mag. Nat. Hist., ser. iii, vol. xviii, p. 297.

Off Thimble Islands, 4 to 5 fathoms, on *Astrangia;* Watch Hill, Rhode Island, on *Laminaria;* Wood's Hole, on old wreck, in the passage. Coasts of Great Britain.

The hydrarium of this species very closely resembles the *Obelia commissuralis* of Agassiz, and may prove to be identical with it. But the original *O. commissuralis* of McCready, from Charleston, South Carolina, is, perhaps, distinct from that described by Agassiz.

OBELIA COMMISSURALIS McCready. Plate XXXVII, fig. 281. (p. 327.)

Proc. Elliott Soc., vol. i, p. 197, Plate 11, figs. 5–7, 1859; (?) Agassiz, Contributions, vol. iv, pp. 315, 351, Plate 33 (except fig. 2), Plate 34, figs. 10–21, 1862; (?) A. Agassiz, Catalogue, p. 91, fig. 134. *Laomedea dichotoma* Leidy, op. cit., p. 138, Plate 11, fig. 36 (*not* Linné, sp.). ? *Laomedea gelatinosa* Stimpson, Invert. of Grand Manan, p. 8, 1853 (*not* Pallas, sp.).

Charleston, South Carolina (McCready). New Jersey (Leidy). Newport, Rhode Island, and Nahant, Massachusetts (A. Agassiz). New Haven Harbor, on piles; Vineyard Sound, on floating algæ. Grand Manan (Mills, t. A. Agassiz).

The northern specimens possibly belong to the preceding species.

OBELIA GELATINOSA Hincks. (p. 391.)

British Hydroid Zoöphytes, p. 151, Plate 26, fig. 1, 1868. *Sertularia gelatinosa* Pallas, Elench. Zooph., p. 116, 1766. *Laomedea gelatinosa* Lamouroux, Polyp Flex., p. 92; Johnston, Brit. Zoöph., ed. ii, p. 104, Plate 27, fig. 1 (var. *b*). *Campanularia gelatinosa* Lamarck, Anim. sans Vert., ed. ii, p. 134 (t. Hincks). *Laomedea gigantea* A. Agassiz, Catalogue, p. 86, 1865.

New Jersey to Massachusetts Bay; northern coasts of Europe, from North Cape to Belgium and Great Britain; low-water to 20 fathoms. Great Egg Harbor, New Jersey, on oysters; New Haven, on piles of Long Wharf, abundant. Mouth of Charles River, near Boston (H. J. Clark, t. A. Agassiz).

RHEGMATODES TENUIS A. Agassiz. (p. 454.)

In Agassiz, Contributions, vol. iv, p. 361, 1862; Catalogue, p. 95, figs. 136–138.

Buzzard's Bay and Vineyard Sound.

ZYGODACTYLA GRŒNLANDICA Agassiz. Plate XXXVII, fig. 275. (p. 449.)

Contributions, vol. iv, p. 360, 1862; A. Agassiz, Catalogue, p. 103, figs. 153–156. *Æquorea Grœnlandica* Péron and Lesueur, Ann. du Mus., vol. xiv, p. 27, 1809 (t. A. Agassiz).

Buzzard's Bay to Greenland. Common in Vineyard Sound, in June and July.

ÆQUOREA ALBIDA A. Agassiz. (p. 454.)

In Agassiz, Contributions, vol. iv, p. 359, 1862; Catalogue, p. 110, figs. 160–162.

Buzzard's Bay (A. Agassiz).

TIMA FORMOSA Agassiz. (p. 449.)

Contributions, vol. iv, p. 362, 1862; A. Agassiz, Catalogue, p. 113, figs. 164–172.

Vineyard Sound, February and April. Massachusetts Bay (A. Agassiz).

EUTIMA LIMPIDA A. Agassiz. (p. 454.)

In Agassiz, Contributions, vol. iv, p. 363, 1862; Catalogue, p. 116, figs. 173–178.

Buzzard's Bay, Naushon (A. Agassiz).

LAFOËA CALCARATA A. Agassiz. (p. 408.)

Catalogue, p. 122, figs. 184–194. *Lafœa cornuta* Agassiz, Contr., vol. iv, p. 351 (*not* of Lamouroux). *Laodicea calcarata* A. Agassiz, in Agassiz, Contributions, vol. iv, p. 350, 1862. *Campanularia dumosa* Leidy, op. cit., p. 138, 1855 (*not* of Fleming).

South Carolina to Vineyard Sound; Buzzard's Bay and Vineyard Sound. The hydrarium was abundant on floating *Zostera* and algæ in Vineyard Sound, creeping over *Sertularia cornicina;* also at low-water, and in 6 to 8 fathoms on *Phyllophora;* Thimble Islands, in tide-pool, on *Vesicularia.* Charleston, South Carolina (McCready, described as a constituent part of his *Dynamena cornicina*).

HALECIUM GRACILE Verrill, sp. nov. (p. 328.)

Stems slender, flexible, clustered, compound, consisting of many very slender, united tubes, light brown or yellowish, pinnately much branched; branches alternate, ascending, long, slender, tapering, similar to the main stem, and usually similarly subdivided; the branches and branchlets mostly arise from opposite sides of the stem, so that they stand nearly in one plane; ends of branches and the branchlets simple, very slender, translucent, whitish, divided into rather long segments; the articulations not very conspicuous, somewhat oblique; each segment usually with a prominent cylindrical process, arising from near the upper end, which, on the older branches, bears the hydroid cell, but on the young branchlets are themselves hydroid cells, furnished with a thin, slightly expanded border, having a circle of dots near the edge; the older or secondary cells, arising from these, are rather elongated, narrow, cylindrical, with slightly expanded rim, more or less bent and crooked or geniculate at base, and usually with one or two irregular constrictions. Many of the older cells are much elongated, and have two or three old rims below, separated by distances equal to two or three times the diameter. The hydroids are long, slender, with numerous long tentacles, much exsert from the cells. The branchlets and gonothecæ (reproductive capsules) arise in the axils of the hydroid cells, and, like the latter, the gonothecæ are often secund on the branchlets. The male and female capsules are different in form. The male gonothecæ are oblong, subfusiform, about three times as long as broad, obtusely rounded at the end, more gradually tapered to the base; the female gonothecæ are broader, somewhat flattened, usually a little shorter, gradually expanding from the narrow base to near the distal end, which is emarginate; the outer angle broadly rounded and slightly produced; the inner angle prolonged into a short cylindrical hydroid cell, with the edge slightly everted, from which two hydroids usually protrude. Height, 75^{mm} to 150^{mm}; diameter of stems, seldom more than 1^{mm}; length of female gonothecæ, about 1^{mm}; breadth, 0.40^{mm} to 0.45^{mm}; length of male gonothecæ, 1^{mm} to 1.10^{mm}; breadth, 0.30^{mm} to 0.40^{mm}; diameter of hydrothecæ, about 0.12^{mm}.

Great Egg Harbor, New Jersey, on oysters, just below low-water mark; Long Island Sound, near New Haven, in 2 to 6 fathoms, abundant, and also in brackish water on floating timber; Thimble Islands, 2 to 6 fathoms; Buzzard's Bay and Vineyard Sound.

This species is more nearly allied to *H. halecinum* of Europe and Northern New England than to any other described species. It is a much more slender and delicate species, with longer joints, and narrower and more elongated hydrothecæ and polyps. The female gonothecæ, although similar, differ in having the distal ends decidedly emarginate, with the outer angle somewhat produced, though much less so than in those of *H. Beanii*.

ANTENNULARIA ANTENNINA Fleming. (p. 497.)

Brit. Anim., p. 546; Johnston, Brit. Zoöph., ed. ii, p. 86, Plate 19, figs. 1–3; Hincks, Brit. Hydr. Zoöph., p. 280, Plate 61. *Sertularia antennina* Linné, Syst. Nat., ed. x, 1758; ed. xii, p. 1310. *Antennularia indivisa* Lamarck, Anim. sans Vert., ed. ii, vol. ii, p. 156.

Martha's Vineyard to Bay of Fundy; northern coasts of Europe to Great Britain and France. Off Gay Head, 8 fathoms; Casco Bay, 6 to 30 fathoms; Bay of Fundy, 10 to 60 fathoms, not uncommon.

AGLAOPHENIA ARBOREA Verrill.

Plumularia arborea Desor, Proc. Boston Soc. Nat. Hist., vol. iii, p. 65, 1848; A. Agassiz, Catalogue, p. 140.

The original specimen of this species is still preserved in the collection of the Boston Society. It consists of a large number of long, mostly simple, but occasionally forked stems, forming a dense plume-like cluster, united at base by an intricate mass of creeping stolons, which cover what looks like the dead axis of a *Gorgonia*, but is most probably a dried-up black alga, and is certainly not, as Desor supposed, a part of the hydroid. The stems are mostly 4 to 6 inches long, more or less recurved, composed of short joints, and densely covered with the secund pinnæ, which increase in length from the base toward the tips; the pinnæ arise from every joint, and form two close alternating rows along the inner side of the stems; they are directed upward, and more or less curved inward, toward each other, near the tips, and mostly 5^{mm} to 8^{mm} in length, composed of short, stout, oblique joints, not twice as long as broad. Hydra-cells deep, slightly flaring, rising at an angle of about 45°, attached only at base, the upper side less than half as high as the lower, border strongly dentate; one slender median denticle on the upper edge; four lateral ones on each side, of which three are subequal, triangular, rather wide, obtuse, with rounded intervals; the lower or outer lateral one is twice as long, rather acute; the single odd median one, on the outer margin, is equally long and more slender, and usually bent upward. A single large tubular median nematophore is attached to the outer side of the cell, along most of its length, but separated at the end, which is obliquely truncate, with the aperture on the inner side, its tip nor extending beyond the long lateral denticles of the hydra-cell. Lateral nematophores small, sessile, not so long as the upper or inner side of the cells. The large, closed, oblong corbulæ are irregularly scattered among the other pinnæ; they occupy the terminal part of the modified pinnæ, but there are usually three or four unaltered hydra-cells on the basal portion, below the corbula; the pinnæ bearing corbulæ are somewhat shorter than the others.

Shoals of Nantucket, ten miles east of Sancati Head, 14 fathoms, (Desor).

PLUMULARIA TENELLA Verrill, sp. nov. (p. 407.)

Stems clustered, simple, slender, 1 to 2 inches high, horn-colored; branches alternate, very slender, not very long, mostly unbranched, placed toward one face of the stem, inclining forward, and ascending at an angle of about 45°, and originating from the alternate joints of the stem, the internodes being longer than the joints that bear branches; at one side of the base of each branch there is a hydrotheca and accompanying nematophores; the internodes of the stem also bear one or two nematophores. The basal segment of each branch is short; the rest are of three kinds; every third one is usually stouter, and bears a hydrotheca; just in front of each hydrotheca there is usually a very short segment, scarcely longer than broad, and sometimes indistinct, destitute of nematophores; then follows a much longer, slender segment, five or six times as long as broad, articulated by a very oblique joint at its distal end with the thicker and shorter polypiferous segment, and bearing one or two nematophores on the median line, which may be either near the middle or toward the proximal end. Hydrothecæ broad, subcylindrical, a little longer than broad, with a slightly flaring, even rim; the axis forms an angle of about 45° with the branches; the free part of the distal side is about half the length of the proximal side. Nematophores relatively large, usually three with each hydrotheca: one on each side, shorter than the hydrotheca, trumpet-shaped, with a round, cup-like opening, narrowed below, nearly sessile; another, similar in form, placed toward the proximal end of the segment, inclined forward, and nearly reaching the base of the hydrotheca. Gonothecæ not observed.

Off Gay Head, 8 to 10 fathoms, among ascidians; Vineyard Sound, 8 fathoms.

This species is related to *P. Catharinæ* Johnston and *P cornucopiæ* Hincks, from the English coast. The former differs in having opposite branches, smaller and more elongated nematophores, etc.; the latter agrees in having alternate branches, but the nematophores are smaller, longer, and more slender, and the joints of the branches are different.

This is the first genuine species of *Plumularia* that has been discovered on the New England coast.

SERTULARIA ARGENTEA Ellis and Solander. Plate XXXVII, fig. 280. (p. 408.)

Zoöphytes, p. 38; Johnston, Brit. Zoöph., ed. ii, p. 79, Plate 14, fig. 3, Plate 15, figs. 1–3; Hincks, Brit. Hydr. Zoöph., p. 268, Plate 56; A. Agassiz, Catalogue, p. 144.

New Jersey to the Arctic Ocean; northern shores of Europe to Great Britain and France; low-water to 110 fathoms. Great Egg Harbor, New Jersey, in April; common and of large size in Long Island Sound, near New Haven, Thimble Islands, and at Faulkner's Island, 1 to 8 fathoms; Watch Hill, Rhode Island; Vineyard Sound, 1 to 15 fathoms, very common; abundant in Casco Bay; Bay of Fundy; Nova Scotia coast; and Gulf of Saint Lawrence, low-water to 110 fathoms. Saint George's Bank (S. I. Smith).

SERTULARIA CUPRESSINA Linné. (p. 408.)

Syst. Naturæ, ed. x, 1758; ed. xii, p. 1308; Pallas, Elench. Zooph., p. 142, 1766; Johnston, op. cit., p. 80, Plate 16, figs. 1, 2; Hincks, op. cit., p. 270, Plate 57; A. Agassiz, Catalogue, p. 143.

New Jersey to the Arctic Ocean; northern coasts of Europe to Great Britain and France. Great Egg Harbor, New Jersey, with reproductive capsules, in April; Vineyard Sound, not common; Massachusetts Bay; Casco Bay; Bay of Fundy, in tide-pools and from 1 to 110 fathoms, common. Saint George's Bank (S. I. Smith). Absecom Beach, New Jersey (Leidy).

SERTULARIA PUMILA Linné. Plate XXXVII, fig. 279. (p. 327.)

Syst. Naturæ, ed. x, 1758; ed. xii, p. 1306; Pallas, Elench. Zooph., p. 130; Johnston, op. cit., p. 66, Plate 11, figs. 3, 4; Hincks, Brit. Hydr. Zoöph., p. 260, Plate 53, fig. 1. *Dynamena pumila* Lamouroux, Bulletin Soc. Phil., vol. iii, p. 184, 1812; Agassiz, Contributions, vol. iv, pp. 326, 355, Plate 32, 1862; A. Agassiz, Catalogue, p. 141, figs. 225, 226.

New Jersey to the Arctic Ocean; Finmark to Great Britain and France. Great Egg Harbor, New Jersey, on *Fucus;* abundant on the shores of Long Island Sound, Vineyard Sound, and northward, between tides.

SERTULARIA CORNICINA Verrill. (p. 408.)

Dynamena cornicina (*pars*) McCready, op. cit., p. 204, 1859; A. Agassiz, Catalogue, p. 142, 1865.

Charleston, South Carolina, to Vineyard Sound. Not uncommon in Vineyard Sound, 1 to 8 fathoms, often on *Halecium gracile;* also on floating *Zostera*, etc., and covered with *Lafoëa calcarata*.

This species somewhat resembles the preceding, but the hydra-cells are more distant, longer, more prominent, and freer, while the end is distinctly bent outward, making the lower side concave in the middle; aperture strongly bilabiate, often appearing tridentate.

HYDRALLMANIA FALCATA Hincks. (p. 408.)

Brit. Hyd. Zoöph., p. 273, Plate 58, 1868. *Sertularia falcata* Linné, Syst. Nat., ed. x, 1758; ed. xii, p. 1309; *Plumularia falcata* Lamarck, Anim. sans Vert., ed. ii, p. 160; Johnston, Brit. Zoöph., p. 90, Plate 21, figs. 1, 2. *Sertularia tenerissima* Stimpson, Mar. Invert. Grand Manan, p. 8, 1853.

Long Island Sound to the Arctic Ocean; northern shores of Europe to the British Channel. Common near New Haven, and off Thimble Islands, 4 to 8 fathoms; Watch Hill, Rhode Island; Vineyard Sound, and off Gay Head, 6 to 20 fathoms; Massachusetts Bay, abundant; very abundant in Casco Bay and Bay of Fundy, low-water to 110 fathoms; Mingan Islands, Labrador. Saint George's Bank, very abundant, 20 to 150 fathoms, (S. I. Smith, A. S. Packard).

Tubularina.

NEMOPSIS BACHEI Agassiz. (p. 454.)

Mem. Amer. Acad., vol. iv, p. 289, figure, 1849; Contributions, vol. iv, p. 345; A. Agassiz, Catalogue, p. 149, figs. 227–231. *Nemopsis Gibbesi* McCready, op. cit., p. 58, Plate 10, figs. 1-7, 1859.

Charleston, South Carolina, to Nantucket.

BOUGAINVILLIA SUPERCILIARIS Aggasiz. Plate XXXVII, fig. 276. (p. 328.)

Contributions, vol. iv, pp. 289, 291, figs. 37–39, Plate 27, figs. 1–7, 1862; A. Agassiz, Catalogue, p. 153, figs. 232–240. *Hippocrene superciliaris* Agassiz, Mem. Amer. Acad., vol. iv, p. 250, Plates 1–3, 1849.

Newport, Rhode Island, to Bay of Fundy; ? Greenland.

MARGELIS CAROLINENSIS Agassiz. (p. 450.)

Contributions, vol. iv, p. 344, 1862; A. Agassiz, Catalogue, p. 156, figs. 241–248. *Hippocrene Carolinensis* McCready, op. cit., p. 164 (separate copies, p. 62), Plate 10, figs. 8–10.

Charleston, South Carolina, to Vineyard Sound. Wood's Hole, at surface, evening.

EUDENDRIUM DISPAR Agassiz. (p. 408.)

Contributions, vol. iv, pp. 285, 289, 342, fig. 36, Plate 27, figs. 10–21, 1862; A Agassiz, Catalogue, p. 159, fig. 249.

Vineyard Sound to Bay of Fundy; 1 to 20 fathoms.

EUDENDRIUM TENUE A. Agassiz.

Catalogue, p. 160, fig. 250, 1865.

Buzzard's Bay to Bay of Fundy, low-water to 15 fathoms. This is closely allied to the English *E. capillare* Alder, but the latter seems to be a smaller and more delicate species.

EUDENDRIUM RAMOSUM Ehrenberg. (p. 408.)

Corall. roth. Meer, p. 72, 1834; Johnston, Brit. Zoöph., ed. ii, p. 46, Plate 6, figs. 1–3; Hincks, Brit. Hydr. Zoöph., p. 82, Plate 13; ? A. Agassiz, Catalogue, p. 160. *Tubularia ramosa* Linné, Syst. Nat., ed. xii, p. 1302.

Martha's Vineyard to Labrador; northern coasts of Europe to Great Britain. Off Gay Head, 8 to 20 fathoms; Casco Bay, 10 to 60 fathoms; Bay of Fundy, 6 to 100 fathoms. Off Saint George's Bank, 430 fathoms, (S. I. Smith).

DYSMORPHOSA FULGURANS A. Agassiz. (p. 448.)

Catalogue, p. 163, figs. 259, 260, 1865.

Buzzard's Bay, Naushon, and Massachusetts Bay (A. Agassiz).

TURRITOPSIS NUTRICULA McCready. (p. 454.)

Op. cit., pp. 55, 86, 127, Plates 4, 5, 8, fig. 1, 1857–9; Agassiz, Contributions, vol. iv, p. 347; A. Agassiz, Catalogue, p. 167, figs. 269, 270.

Charleston, South Carolina, to Vineyard Sound.

STOMOTOCA APICATA Agassiz. (p. 455.)

Contributions, vol. iv, p. 347, 1862; A. Agassiz, Catalogue, p. 168. *Saphenia apicata* McCready, op. cit., p. 129, Plate 8, figs. 2, 3, 1859.

Charleston, South Carolina (McCready); Newport, Rhode Island (A. Agassiz).

CLAVA LEPTOSTYLA Agassiz. (p. 328.)

Contributions, vol. iv, pp. 218, 222, fig. 32, Plate 20, figs. 11–16a, Plate 21, figs. 1–10a, 1862; A. Agassiz, Catalogue, p. 170, fig. 274; Hincks, op. cit., p. 6, Plate 2, fig. 1, 1868. *Clava multicornis* Stimpson, Invert. Grand Manan, p. 11, 1853; Leidy, Journ. Acad. Nat. Sciences, Philad., vol. iii, p. 135, Plate 11, figs. 33, 34, 1855 (*not* of Johnston).

Long Island Sound to Labrador; coasts of Great Britain. Near New Haven Light; Thimble Islands, in tide-pools; Beverly, Massachusetts; Casco Bay, on rocks and *Fucus*, abundant; Eastport, Maine, on piles. Point Judith, Rhode Island (Leidy). Nahant, Massachusetts (Agassiz). Morecombe Bay (Hincks).

CORDYLOPHORA, species undetermined.

Syncoryna, sp., Agassiz, Contributions, vol. iv, p. 339 (no description).

Newport Harbor, Rhode Island (Leidy, t. Agassiz). In 1860 I obtained a species of this genus from the vicinity of Cambridge, Massachusetts, in water that was fresh, or nearly so. It grew to the height of two inches or more, with long slender branches.

WILLIA ORNATA McCready. (p. 455.)

Op. cit., p. 149 (separate copies, p. 47), Plate 9, figs. 9–11, 1859 (Willsia); Agassiz, Contributions, vol. iv, p. 346, 1862; A. Agassiz, Catalogue, p. 171, figs. 274[a], 275.

Charleston, South Carolina (McCready). Buzzard's Bay (A. Agassiz).

CORYNE MIRABILIS Agassiz.

Contributions, vol. iii, Plate 11[c], figs. 14, 15, Plates 17–19; vol. iv, pp. 185–217, figs. 9–31, Plate 20, figs. 1–9, Plate 23[a], fig. 12; A. Agassiz, Catalogue, p. 175, figs. 283–287. *Sarsia mirabilis* Agassiz, Mem. Amer. Acad., vol. iv, p. 224, Plates 4, 5, 1849. ? *Tubularia stellifera* Couthouy, Boston Jour. Nat. Hist., vol. ii, p. 56, 1839. *Coryne gravata* Wright, Edinb. New Phil. Jour., Apr., 1858, Plate 7, fig. 5 (t. Hincks). *Syncoryne gravata* Hincks, Brit. Hydr. Zoöph., p. 53, Plate 10, fig. 1.

The species described by Couthouy may, possibly, have been this; but his species was described as unbranched, and as if it had two distinct circles of tentacles. Martha's Vineyard to Greenland. Common in Massachusetts Bay; Casco Bay; and Bay of Fundy. Scotland (Hincks).

DIPURENA CONICA A. Agassiz. (p. 455.)

In Agassiz, Contributions, vol. iv, p. 341, 1862; A. Agassiz, Catalogue, p. 181, figs. 301–305.

Buzzard's Bay, Naushon (A. Agassiz).

GEMMARIA GEMMOSA McCready. (p. 455.)

Op. cit., p. 151, Plate 8, figs. 4, 5, 1859; A. Agassiz, Catalogue, p. 184, fig. 306. *Zanclea gemmosa* McCready, op. cit., p. 151, 1849; Agassiz, Contributions, vol. iv, p. 344.

Charleston, South Carolina (McCready). Buzzard's Bay (A. Agassiz).

PENNARIA TIARELLA McCready. Plate XXXVII, figs. 277, 278. (p. 327.)

Op. cit., p. 153, 1859; A. Agassiz, Catalogue, p. 187, figs. 311–315. *Globiceps tiarella* Ayres, Proc. Boston Soc. Nat. Hist., vol. iv, p. 193, 1852. *Eucoryne elegans* Leidy, op. cit., p. 136, Plate 10, figs. 1–5, 1855. *Globiceps tiarella* Agassiz, Contributions, vol. iv, p. 344, 1862.

Charleston, South Carolina, to Massachusetts Bay. Great Egg Harbor, New Jersey; near New Haven; Vineyard Sound, common, low-water to 10 fathoms, and on floating algæ.

ECTOPLEURA OCHRACEA Agassiz. (p. 455.)

In Agassiz, Contributions, vol. iv, p. 343, 1862; Catalogue, p. 191, figs. 320–323.

Buzzard's Bay, Naushon (A. Agassiz).

CORYMORPHA PENDULA Agassiz. Plate XXXVI, fig. 273. (p. 510.)

Contributions, vol. iv, pp. 276, 343, Plate 26, figs. 7–17, 1862; A. Agassiz, Catalogue, p. 192, fig. 324. *Corymorpha nutans* Stimpson, Invert. of Grand Manan, p. 9, 1853.

Block Island to Gulf of Saint Lawrence. Common in Casco Bay and Bay of Fundy, 8 to 30 fathoms; off Block Island, 29 fathoms. Off Cape Cod (A. S. Bickmore).

HYBOCODON PROLIFER Agassiz. Plate XXXVIII, fig. 282. (p. 328.)

Contributions, vol. iv, pp. 243, 343, Plate 23[a], figs. 10, 11, Plate 25, figs. 1–15, 1862; A. Agassiz, Catalogue, p. 193, figs. 325–328.

Vineyard Sound to Massachusetts Bay.

PARYPHA CROCEA Agassiz. Plate XXXVI, fig. 274. (p. 390.)

Contributions, vol. iv, pp. 249, 342, Plates 23, 23[a], figs. 1–7, 1862; A. Agassiz, Catalogue, p. 195. ? *Tubularia cristata* McCready, op. cit., p. 156, 1859=*Parypha cristata* Ag., op. cit., p. 342.

Brooklyn, New York, to Boston, Massachusetts. Very abundant near New Haven, on piles in harbor, and in 2 to 6 fathoms, off Thimble Islands; Wood's Hole, on piles, abundant. Warren Bridge, Boston (Agassiz).

This is probably not distinct from *P. cristata*, which is abundant at Charleston, South Carolina, and Fort Macon, North Carolina.

THAMNOCNIDIA TENELLA Agassiz. (p. 407.)

Contributions, vol. iv, pp. 275, 342, Plate 22, figs. 21–30, 1862; A. Agassiz, Catalogue, p. 195.

Rhode Island to Bay of Fundy. Off Watch Hill, 4 to 5 fathoms; Vineyard Sound, 6 to 10 fathoms; common in Casco Bay and Bay of Fundy, low-water to 40 fathoms.

HYDRACTINIA POLYCLINA Agassiz. (p. 407.)

Contributions, vol. iii, Plate 16; vol. iv, pp. 227, 339, figs. 33–35, Plate 26, fig. 18, 1862; A. Agassiz, Catalogue, p. 198, figs. 329, 330. *Hydractinia echinata* Leidy, op. cit., p. 135, Plate xi, fig. 35, 1855 (? *not* of Johnston).

New Jersey to Labrador. Very abundant in Long Island Sound, Vineyard Sound, Casco Bay, and Bay of Fundy, low-water to 60 fathoms. Saint George's Bank (S. I. Smith). Labrador (Packard). Greenland (Mörch). ? Charleston, South Carolina (McCready).

The identity of this with the European species is somewhat doubtful, though united by Hincks and others. The latter extends southward on the European coasts to Great Britain and France.

Physophoræ.

NANOMIA CARA A. Agassiz. (p. 455.)

Proc. Boston Soc. Nat. Hist., vol. ix, p. 181, 1863; Catalogue, p. 200, figs. 332–350.

Newport, Rhode Island; Massachusetts Bay; Nahant (A. Agassiz).

Porpitæ.

PHYSALIA PELAGICA Lamarck. (p. 450.)

Syst. des Anim. sans Vert., p. 356, 1801; Lesson, Acalèphes, p. 545, 1843. *Physalis pelagica* Osbeck, Itin., p. 284, Plate 12, fig. 1, 1757 (t. Lesson). *Holothuria physalis* Linné, Syst. Nat., ed. xii, p. 1090, 1767. *Medusa caravella* Müller, Besch. der Berl. Naturf., vol. ii, p. 190, Plate 9, fig. 2 (t. Lesson); Gmelin, Syst. Nat., p. 3139, 1789. *Physalia caravella* Eschscholtz; Lesson, Hist. Nat. des Zooph. Acalèphes, Plate 11 (explanation). *Physalia arethusa* Tilesius, in Krusensterns Reise, vol. iii, p. 91, Plate 23, figs. 1–6, 1813 (t. Lesson); Agassiz, Contributions, vol. iv, pp. 335, 367, Plate 35, 1862; A. Agassiz, Catalogue, p. 214, figs. 351–354; this Report, p. 450. *Physalia aurigera* McCready, op. cit., p. 176, 1859.

Warmer parts of the Atlantic Ocean and Gulf of Mexico, coming northward in the Gulf Stream to the southern coast of New England and Long Island; and off Saint George's Bank and Nova Scotia. Not uncommon, in good condition, in Vineyard Sound and Buzzard's Bay. Watch Hill, Rhode Island (D. C. Eaton). East of Saint George's Bank (S. I. Smith). Fort Macon, North Carolina (coll. Dr. Yarrow).

VELELLA MUTICA Lamarck. (p. 455.)

Syst. des Anim. sans Vert., p. 355, 1801; Bosc, Hist. Nat. des Vers., vol. ii, p. 158; Lesson, Voy. de la Coquille, Zool., vol. ii, pp. 2, 52, Plate 6, figs. 1, 2; Acalèphes, p. 571, Plate 12, figs. 1, 2; A. Agassiz, Catalogue, p. 216, figs. 355–357. *Medusa velella* Linné, Syst. Nat., ed. xii, p. 1098.

Tropical parts of the Atlantic and Gulf of Mexico, coming northward in the Gulf Stream as far as Nantucket and off Saint George's Bank. Aspinwall (coll. F. H. Bradley); coasts of Florida (Agassiz); Long Island Sound (A. Agassiz).

POLYPI or ANTHOZOA.

ALCYONARIA.

ALCYONIUM CARNEUM Agassiz. Plate XXXVIII, fig. 283. (p. 497.)

Proc. American Association for Adv. of Science, 1850, p. 209; Verrill, Revision of Polyps of Eastern Coast U. S., in Memoirs Boston Soc. Nat. Hist., vol. i, p. 4, 1864; Verrill, Proc. Boston Soc. Nat. Hist., vol. x, p. 343, 1866. *Halcyonium carneum* A. and E. C. Agassiz, Sea-Side Studies, p. 19, figs. 21–23, 1865.

Rhode Island to Gulf of Saint Lawrence. Off Watch Hill, Rhode Island, 4 to 5 fathoms; off Cuttyhunk Island, 10 to 15 fathoms; off Gay Head, 8 to 10 fathoms; common in Massachusetts Bay, Casco Bay, Bay of Fundy, and coast of Nova Scotia, low-water to 80 fathoms. Gulf of Saint Lawrence (Whiteaves). Saint George's Bank (S. I. Smith).

Leptogorgia tenuis Verrill.

Memoirs Boston Soc. Nat. Hist., vol. i, p. 8, 1864. *Gorgonia tenuis* Verrill, Proc. Boston Soc. N. H., vol. x, p. 339, 1866. *Leptogorgia teres* (error typ.) Verrill, Amer. Jour. Science, vol. xlviii, p. 420, 1869.

"Bay of New York." Specimens in the museum of Yale College are supposed to have come from Long Island Sound, but the exact locality is not known.

ACTINARIA.

METRIDIUM MARGINATUM Milne-Edwards. (p. 329.)

Hist. Nat. des Coralliaires, vol. i, p. 254, 1857; Verrill, Revision of Polyps., in Mem. Boston Soc. Nat. Hist., vol. i, p. 22, 1864; Proc. Boston Soc. Nat. Hist., vol. x, p. 337, 1866; American Naturalist, vol. ii, p. 252; Tenney, Natural History, p. 523, figs. 515–517, 1865; A. and Mrs. E. C. Agassiz, Sea-Side Studies, p. 7, figs. 2–7, 1865. *Actinia marginata* Lesueur, Journal Acad. Nat. Sciences, Philad., vol. i, p. 172, 1817; Gould, Invert. Mass., ed. i, p. 349, 1841; Leidy, Journ. Acad. N. S., Philad., ser. ii, vol. iii, p. 140, 1855 Agassiz, Contributions, vol. iii, p. 39, fig. 8, 1860. *Actinia dianthus* Dawson, Canadian Naturalist and Geologist, vol. iii, p. 402, figs. 1, 2, 1858.

New Jersey to Labrador. Common in Long Island Sound, Buzzard's Bay, and Vineyard Sound, but mostly smaller than farther north; abundant in Massachusetts Bay, Casco Bay, and Bay of Fundy, low-water to 90 fathoms.

SAGARTIA LEUCOLENA Verrill. Plate XXXVIII, fig. 284. (p. 329.)

Proc. Boston Soc. Nat. Hist., vol. x, p. 336, 1866; American Naturalist, vol. ii, p. 261.

North Carolina to Cape Cod. Common in Long Island Sound, Buzzard's Bay, and Vineyard Sound; Great Egg Harbor, New Jersey. Fort Macon, North Carolina (coll. Dr. Yarrow).

SAGARTIA MODESTA Verrill. (p. 330.)

Proc. Boston Soc. Nat. Hist., vol. x, p. 337, 1866.

Long Island Sound to Vineyard Sound. Savin Rock, near New Haven; Goose Island; Stony Creek; Naushon Island; low-water, buried in sand or gravel.

PARACTIS RAPIFORMIS Milne-Edwards. (p. 363.)

Hist. Nat. des Coralliaires, vol. i, p. 249, 1857; Verrill, American Journal of Science, vol. iii, p. 436, 1872; Dana, Corals and Coral Islands, p. 23, figure, (in ed. i, as *Sagartia modesta* V.). *Actinia rapiformis* Lesueur, Journ. Acad. Nat. Sciences, Philad., vol. i, p. 171, 1817; Verrill, Memoirs Boston Soc. Nat. Hist., vol. i, p. 35, 1864; Proc. Boston Soc. N. H., vol. x, p. 338.

North Carolina to Long Island Sound. Fort Macon (coll. Dr. Yarrow); New Jersey (Lesueur); near New Haven (Dana).

HALOCAMPA PRODUCTA Stimpson, MSS. Plate XXXVIII, fig. 285. (p. 330.)

Verrill, Revision, in Memoirs Boston Soc. Nat. Hist., vol. i, p. 30, Plate 1, figs, 10, 11, 1864. *Actinia producta* Stimpson, Proc. Boston Soc. Nat. Hist., vol. v, p. 110, 1856. *Corynactis albida* Agassiz, Proc. Bost. Soc. Nat. Hist., vol. vii, p. 24, 1859. *Halcampa albida* Verrill, Memoirs Boston Soc. Nat. Hist., vol. i, p. 29, 1864; A. and E. C. Agassiz, Sea-Side Studies, p. 16, fig. 15, 1865; Verrill, Proc. Bost. Soc. Nat. Hist., vol. x, p. 338, 1870 (*Halocampa*).

South Carolina to Cape Cod. Shores of Long Island Sound, at Stony Creek, etc.; Naushon Island; Martha's Vineyard; Nantucket; Cape Cod. Charleston, South Carolina (Stimpson).

EDWARDSIA FARINACEA Verrill. (p. 510.)

American Journal of Science, vol. xlii, p. 118, 1866.

Off Gay Head, 19 fathoms; Casco Bay, 10 to 70 fathoms; Bay of Fundy, 8 to 90 fathoms.

EDWARDSIA LINEATA Verrill, sp. nov. (p. 497.)

Body cylindrical, elongated, covered over the base and sides with a dirty, brownish, slightly rough and wrinkled epidermis, except anteriorly, below the tentacles, where it is smooth, translucent, and usually with eight impressed, longitudinal, flake-white lines, showing through. Tentacles, 24 to 30, or more, in the larger specimens, slender, tapering, obtuse, white or pale flesh-color, each with a flake-white, longitudinal line along the inner side. Disk, with a white circle around the mouth, and often with 8, or more, radiating, white lines, extending to the base of the inner tentacles; border of the mouth sometimes pale-red; naked part of column pale flesh-color, often with a circle of white below the bases of the tentacles, and usually with eight oblong or fusiform flake-white spots between the longitudinal impressed lines.

Length, 25^{mm} to 35^{mm}; diameter, 2.5^{mm} to 3^{mm}. A very young specimen had 18 slender, equal, long tentacles, each with a median longitudinal line of white on the inside; disk with 6 radiating lines of white; naked part of the column with 6 impressed white lines, and with 6 oblong, flake-white spots between them. Breadth across the expanded tentacles, 3^{mm}.

This species is remarkable for not having, in any of the specimens found, a naked basal area, nor any true disk for attachment, thus differing both from *Phellia* and the other species of *Edwardsia*. This may be due to its peculiar habit of nestling in the crevices and interstices between rocks, ascidians, worm-tubes, etc.

Off Watch Hill, Rhode Island, 4 to 5 fathoms, in cavities in and beneath *Astrangia*, etc.; Vineyard Sound and off Gay Head, 6 to 12 fathoms, among ascidians, annelid-tubes, etc., abundant.

Arachnactis brachiolata A. Agassiz. (p. 451.)

Proc. Boston Soc. Nat. Hist., vol. ix, p. 159, 1862; Boston Journal of Nat. Hist., vol. vii, p. 525, 1863; Verrill, Memoirs Boston Soc. N. H., p. 33; Proceedings, vol. x, p. 343.

Mr. A. Agassiz has recently ascertained that this is only a larval form of some species of *Edwardsia*. As it had already developed 16 tentacles, it must belong to one of the species having numerous tentacles when adult.

Peachia parasitica Verrill.

Proc. Boston Soc. Nat. Hist., vol. x, p. 338, 1866; *Bicidium parasiticum* Agassiz, Proc. Boston S. N. H., vol. vii, p. 24, 1859; Verrill, Revision of Polyps, in Memoirs Boston S. N. H., vol. i, p. 31, Plate 1, figs. 14, 15, 1864; A. and Mrs. E. C. Agassiz, Sea-Side Studies, p. 15, fig. 14, 1865.

Cape Cod to Bay of Fundy, on *Cyanea arctica*; Eastport, Maine, buried in gravel at low-water mark (two specimens, of very large size). I am not aware that this species has been found south of Cape Cod, but it will probably be found hereafter, since the *Cyanea* is common.

EPIZOANTHUS AMERICANUS Verrill. Plate XXXVIII, figs. 286, 287. (p. 510.)

American Journal of Science, vol. ii, p. 361, 1871; Dana, Corals and Coral Islands, ed. i, p. 62, figs 1, 2, 1872. *Zoanthus parasiticus* Verrill, Revision of Polyps, in Mem. Boston Soc. N. H., vol. i, p. 34, 1864, (*not* of Duch. and Mich., 1860.) *Zoanthus Americanus* Verrill, op. cit., p. 45; Proc. Boston Soc. Nat. Hist., vol. x, p. 335, 1866. *Gemmaria Americana* Verrill, American Naturalist, vol. ii, p. 9, fig. 42.

Off New Jersey to Gulf of Saint Lawrence, in deep water. Off Block Island, 29 fathoms, on shells occupied by *Eupagurus;* off Grand Manan, in 40 to 50 fathoms, on shells covering *Eupagurus*, and in 109 fathoms, on rocks; off Saint George's Bank, 430 fathoms, on rocks, (S. I. Smith and O. Harger); Saint George's Bank, 60 fathoms, on shells occupied by *Eupagurus* (Smith and Harger); Gulf of Saint Lawrence, on rocks, (Whiteaves); Massachusetts Bay (J. E. Gray). Off New Jersey, N. lat. 40°, W. long. 73°, 32 fathoms, on shells inhabited by *Eupagurus pubescens*, (coll. Captain Gedney).

MADREPORARIA.

ASTRANGIA DANÆ Agassiz. (p. 408.)

Proc. American Assoc., vol. ii, p. 68, 1849 (*not* of Edw. and Haime, 1850); Verrill, Revision Polyps, p. 40, 1864; A. and Mrs. E. C. Agassiz, Sea-Side Studies, p. 16, figs. 16–20, 1865; Verrill, Proc. Boston Soc. Nat. Hist., vol. x, p. 335, 1866; Dana, Corals and Coral Islands, p. 68, figures, 1872. *Astrangia astræiformis* Edw. and Haime, Ann. des. Sci. Nat., vol. xii, p. 181, 1850; Coralliaires, vol. ii, p. 614, 1857; Leidy, Journ. Acad. Nat. Sciences, Philad., vol. iii, p. 139, Plate x, figs. 9–16, 1855; Verrill, Revision of Polyps, p. 39, 1864.

North Florida and west Florida to Cape Cod. Common in Long Island Sound, near New Haven, at Savin Rock, off Thimble Islands, etc., 1 to 6 fathoms, rocks; Watch Hill, Rhode Island, 4 to 5 fathoms; Vineyard Sound and Buzzard's Bay, 2 to 15 fathoms; Fort Macon, North Carolina (coll. Dr. Yarrow). Charleston, South Carolina (Agassiz). West Florida (E. Jewett).

PROTOZOA.

PORIFERA or SPONGIÆ.

CALCAREA.

GRANTIA CILIATA Fleming. (p. 330.)

British Anim., p, 325; Johnston, Brit. Sponges and Lithophytes, p. 176, Plate 20, figs. 4, 5, Plate 21, figs. 6, 7, 1842; Bowerbank, Monog. British Spongiadæ, vol. i, Plate 26, figs. 345, 346[a]; vol. ii, p. 19, 1866. *Spongia ciliata* Fabricius, Fauna Grœnlandica, p. 448, 1780. *Sycandra ciliata* Hæckel, Die Kalkschwämme, vol. ii, p. 296, Plate 51, figs. 1a–1t, Plate 58, fig. 9, 1872. *Spongia coronata* Ellis and Solander, Zoöphytes, p. 190, Plate 58, figs. 8, 9. *Grantia coronata* Hassall, Ann. and Mag. Nat. Hist., vol. vi, p. 174.

Rhode Island to Greenland; northern coasts of Europe. Common in Casco Bay and Bay of Fundy, low-water to 60 fathoms; Vineyard Sound, not uncommon. Point Judith, Rhode Island (Leidy).

? LEUCOSOLENIA BOTRYOIDES Bowerbank. (p. 500.)

Brit. Spong., vol. ii, p. 28, 1866. *Spongia botryoides* Ellis and Solander, Zoöph., p. 190, Plate 58, figs. 1–4, 1786. *Grantia botryoides* Fleming, Brit. Anim., p. 525; Johnston, op. cit., p. 178, Plate 21, figs. 1–5. *Ascaltis botryoides* Hæckel, op. cit., vol. ii, p. 65, Plate 9, fig. 10, Plate 10, figs. 7a–7e.

Martha's Vineyard to Gulf of Saint Lawrence; northern coasts of Europe to England and France.

I refer some of our larger specimens to this species with considerable doubt. They appear to be distinct from the following species, with which they have formerly been confounded.

ASCORTIS FRAGILIS Hæckel.

Op. cit., vol. ii, p. 74, Plate 11, figs. 5–9, Plate 12, figs. 5a–5i, 1872. *Leucosolenia thamnoides* Hæckel, Prodrom., p. 243, spec. 70. *Leucosolenia botryoides* H. J. Clark, Mem. Boston Soc. Nat. Hist., vol. i, part 3, p. 323, (sep. copies, p. 19), Plate 9, figs. 40–44, Plate 10, fig. 64, 1866 (*not* of Bowerbank); this Report, pp. 334, 391. *Grantia botryoides* Leidy, op. cit., p. 135, 1855.

Long Island Sound to Gulf of Saint Lawrence. Western coast of Norway, at Bergen, etc. (Hæckel). Common in Long Island Sound, near New Haven, at Thimble Islands, etc.; Watch Hill, Rhode Island; Vineyard Sound; Casco Bay, etc. Massachusetts Bay (H. J. Clark).

Hæckel names the form figured by Clark var. *bifida*.

SILICEA.

MICROCIONA PROLIFERA Verrill.

Spongia prolifera Ellis and Solander, Zoöphytes, p. 189, Plate 58, fig. 5, 1786; Lamouroux, Expos. Méthodique, p. 31, Plate 58, fig. 5. Red sponge, this Report, pp. 330, 409, 476.

This species, when young, forms broad, thin, bright red incrustations over the surfaces of stones and shells. In this stage it agrees well with the British species of *Microciona* described by Bowerbank, all of which are said to be incrusting forms. Our species, at a later period, rises up into irregular lobes and tubercular prominences, which eventually become elongated and subdivided into slender branches, until they often form a profusely and intricately branched sponge, frequently six inches high and as much in diameter. The branches are repeatedly dichotomous, more or less flattened, and often digitate or palmate at the ends They also frequently anastomose irregularly. The branches, when dry, are brittle and hispid. They consist of stout, horny fibers, which radiate outward and upward from the axis to the periphery, terminating in more or less irregular, slender, blunt papillæ, each of which bears a tuft of numerous slender, acute, more or less bent spicules, arising from its lateral and terminal surfaces. At the tips of the branches the papillæ are more slender and divergent, and the texture is more open and loose. During life these papillæ are connected together by a thin dermal membrane, through which the spicules project but little. The oscules are small and scattered over the surface. Color, when living, dark red to orange-red; when dried, generally dark grayish brown or umber-colored, fading to dull yellowish brown and gray. Diameter of branches mostly 2^{mm} to 5^{mm}.

South Carolina to Cape Cod. Very abundant in Long Island Sound and Vineyard Sound, low-water to 10 fathoms, on oysters and other shells, stones, etc.; Great Egg Harbor, New Jersey; Fort Macon, North Carolina (coll. Dr. Yarrow).

ISODICTYA, species undetermined.

Watch Hill, Rhode Island; Vineyard Sound and Nantucket, washed ashore after storms in winter; Casco Bay; Bay of Fundy.

The specimens from Watch Hill have few broad, thick, palmate branches, with large oscules and an open texture, with multispiculose fibers. They resemble *Isodictya palmata* Bowerbank.

CHALINA OCULATA Bowerbank. (p. 497.)

British Spongiadæ, vol. i, p. 208, Plate 13, fig. 262; vol. ii, p. 361. *Spongia oculata* Linné, Syst. Nat., ed. x, sp. 2; ed. xii, p. 1299; Pallas, Elench. Zooph., p. 390, 1766. *Halichondria oculata* Johnston, op. cit., p. 94, Plate 3.

Rhode Island to Labrador; northern coast of Europe to Great Britain. Off Watch Hill, Rhode Island, 4 to 5 fathoms; off Gay Head, 4 to 15 fathoms; very common in Massachusetts Bay, Casco Bay, and Bay of Fundy; low-water to 80 fathoms.

CHALINA ARBUSCULA Verrill, sp. nov. (p. 409.)

Sponge profusely branched, from close to the thick base; branches repeatedly dichotomous, slender, round or somewhat compressed, seldom broad or palmate. Oscules small, round, irregularly scattered. Texture of the surface finely reticulated when dry, with very delicate fibers, which usually have but a single row of very slender fusiform spicules, covered by a thin layer of horny matter; the reticulations do not usually exceed the length of a single spicule. Primary longitudinal fibers of the larger branches strong, horny, with several lines of spicules; secondary fibers at right angles to the primary ones, much smaller, with fewer spicules. The spicules are slender, fusiform ("acerate"), much smaller and more slender than in the preceding species. Color, when living, dull gray; when dried, brownish, yellowish, or white. The largest specimens are about one foot high; more commonly 6 to 8 inches (150^{mm} to 200^{mm}); breadth often nearly as much; diameter of branches,

4^{mm} to 10^{mm}, mostly about 5^{mm} to 6^{mm}; diameter of the oscules, in dry specimens, about 1^{mm}.

North Carolina to Cape Cod. Very common in Long Island Sound and Vineyard Sound, 1 to 8 fathoms; Watch Hill, Rhode Island; Great Egg Harbor, New Jersey.

This species has a much finer and more delicate texture than *C. oculata*, due to the smaller fibers and spicules, as well as to the smaller meshes of the skeleton. The branches are also smaller and much more numerous than they usually are in that species.

HALICHONDRIA PANICEA Johnston.

Brit. Sponges, p. 114, Plate 10, Plate 11, fig. 5, 1842; Bowerbank, British Spongiadæ, vol. i, p. 195, Plate 19, figs. 300, 303; vol. ii, p. 229, 1866. *Spongia panicea* Pallas, Elench. Zooph., p. 388, 1766. *Tedania* (?), this Report, p. 498.

Rhode Island to the Arctic Ocean; northern coasts of Europe to Great Britain. Abundant at Watch Hill, Rhode Island, on algæ, in 4 to 8 fathoms; off Gay Head; Casco Bay; Bay of Fundy.

HALICHONDRIA, species undetermined, *a*.

Watch Hill, Rhode Island, associated with the preceding.

Grows in large tuberous masses, on algæ, like the last, but has a smoother surface and finer and firmer texture. (See p. 498.)

HALICHONDRIA ?, species undetermined, *b*. (p. 334.)

Long Island Sound near New Haven; Vineyard Sound.

Forms broad, uneven incrustations on the under side of stones, at low-water mark. Color when living, bright yellow. Oscules rather large, conspicuous.

HALICHONDRIA ?, species undetermined, *c*.

Vineyard Sound, on the under side of overhanging banks, on the salt marshes near Waquoit; on the piles of wharves at Wood's Hole.

Forms large, irregular, thick masses, often containing much foreign matter; surface uneven, rising into irregular prominences. Soft and brittle.

This is, perhaps, a species of *Reniera* Schmidt (*Hymeniacidon* Bowerbank).*

RENIERA ?, species undetermined, *a*. (p. 334.)

Vineyard Sound, 1 to 10 fathoms. Forms large, irregular, soft masses, 3 to 5 inches in diameter, of a light yellow color when living.

RENIERA ?, species undetermined, *b*.

Vineyard Sound, 3 to 10 fathoms. Forms large, irregular, thick masses, with numerous acute, irregular, often ragged, conical prominences, rising from its upper surface.

* It was not studied carefully when recent; and I have no specimens of this and several of the other species at hand, for most of the sponges were sent elsewhere for comparison with named types, and have not yet been returned.

HALISARCA ?, Species undetermined, *a*.

Watch Hill, Rhode Island, 4 to 5 fathoms. Forms small, soft, somewhat gelatinous masses, on red algæ. (See p. 498.)

SUBERITES COMPACTA Verrill, sp. nov.

This species is remarkable for the compactness of its tissues and the smallness of the canals and pores permeating its substance, as well as for the large size of the plates and crest-like lobes in which it grows. A transverse section of the dried sponge shows very numerous irregular canals, most of them not larger than pin-holes (or less than 0.15^{mm} in diameter). The tissue is very compact throughout, but is more dense close to the surface, which is nearly smooth, the oscules being small and inconspicuous. The spicules are very abundant, crowded, very slender, mostly pin-shaped (spinulate), with the point very acute and the "head" but little enlarged, and often largest a slight distance from the end, so as to give the head a slightly ovate form. Color, when living, bright yellow.

Off Martha's Vineyard, 10 fathoms, sand; Nantucket; Eastern Shore of Virginia.

This is the species described as a "firm siliceous sponge," on page 503. In general appearance it somewhat resembles *Suberites suberea* Gray (*Hymeniacidon suberea* Bowerbank).

CLIONA SULPHUREA Verrill. (p. 421.)

Spongia sulphurea Desor, Proc. Boston Soc. Nat. Hist., vol. iii, p. 68, 1848.

South Carolina to Cape Cod; local farther north. Great Egg Harbor, New Jersey; very abundant in Long Island Sound and Vineyard Sound, on oysters and various other shells, 1 to 15 fathoms. Portland Harbor, Maine, in sheltered localities (C. B. Fuller).

? POLYMASTIA ROBUSTA Bowerbank. (p. 497.)

British Spongiadæ, vol. i, p. 178, Plate 29, fig. 358; vol. ii, p. 62, 1866.

Off Gay Head, 18 to 20 fathoms; common in Casco Bay and Bay of Fundy, 8 to 70 fathoms. Coast of Great Britain (Bowerbank).

The American specimens do not agree in all respects with the description, and may prove to be distinct when a direct comparison can be made. In our specimens the surface is finely hispid; the dermal tissue is firm, and filled with small, slender, often curved, needle-shaped ("acuate"), and pin-shaped ("spinulate") spicules, which project from the surface. The latter form is the predominant one, but the "head" is very small, and they pass gradually into the former kind, in which the "head" is obsolete, or not larger than the shaft. The spicules of the large, radiating fascicles in the body of the sponge are long and large, needle-shaped, with the central portion thickest ("fusiformi-acuate"). The large spicules in the longitudinal fascicles of the cloacal fistulæ are of the same form; the secondary fascicles of the body and the transverse secondary spicules of the fistulæ also have the same form, though much smaller. The "cloacal fistulæ" are numerous, and, when living, are round and tapering, but when dry become flat and bent, or curved to one side. They are mostly 20^{mm} to 40^{mm} long, and 4^{mm} to 6^{mm} in diameter near the base.

Several other species of sponges were collected, which have not been examined.

I have been unable to identify any of our specimens with the *Spongia urceolata* of Desor (Proceedings Boston Soc. Nat. History, vol. iii, p. 67). Possibly it was based on a peculiarly-shaped young specimen of *Microciona prolifera*.

FORAMINIFERA.

Numerous species were collected, especially in the deeper parts of Vineyard Sound and off Martha's Vineyard, but they have not been identified.

ADDENDA.

Crustacea.

CANCER BOREALIS Stimpson. (p. 546.)

A small specimen of this species was dredged off Watch Hill, Rhode Island, in 4 to 5 fathoms, among rocks and algæ, in April. It was found in abundance, and of large size, at Peak's Island and Pumkin Knob, in Casco Bay, Maine, in August, clinging to the sea-weeds, and in tide-pools, above low-water mark.

OCYPODA ARENARIA Say. (Megalops stage.) (p. 337.)

The megalops of this species was found in large numbers, swimming at the surface of Vineyard Sound in September, by Mr. Vinal N. Edwards.

HOMARUS AMERICANUS Edw. (Lobster.) (p. 492.)

Subsequent observations have shown that the breeding-season of the lobster extends over a large part of the year. In Casco Bay female lobsters were found carrying eggs in August and September. Mr. Vinal N. Edwards has forwarded two living females, of medium size, taken in Vineyard Sound, December 12th, both carying an abundance of freshly laid eggs. He states that he finds about "one in twenty" carrying eggs at that season.

THEMISTO, species undetermined.

A species of this genus was taken in large quantities in Vineyard Sound, in September, by Mr. Vinal N. Edwards. It occurred swimming at the surface in vast numbers, and was thrown up by the waves in windrows, extending several miles along the shores of Martha's Vineyard.

CONILERA CONCHARUM Harger. (p. 572.)

This species, previously quite rare, was taken this year in large numbers, in Vineyard Sound, both in spring and autumn, by Mr. Vinal N. Edwards.

Annelida.

PROCERÆA ORNATA Verrill, sp. nov.

Autolytus (?), banded species, this Report, p. 398.

Head short and broad, bluntly rounded or subtruncate above, slightly bilobed or emarginate below. Eyes moderately large; the anterior pair wider apart. Median antenna white, very long, slender, variously curled, reaching to about the twelfth body-segment; posterior tentacles also very long and slender, reaching to about the ninth segment, white at the tips; inner antennæ about one-fourth as long as the median one; the other two pairs of antennæ and tentacles about one-fourth as long as the median one; tentacular cirri of the second (post-buccal) segment short, about equal to the diameter of the body. Dorsal cirri short, about one-third as long as the breadth of the body; setigerous lobe short and broadly rounded; setæ short. Gizzard small, short, elliptical, situated at about the eighth segment. Caudal cirri two, slender, tapering, their length about equal to the diameter of the body. Color of the body white or pale yellowish, annulated with bands of bright red at unequal distances. Length, about 15^{mm}; breadth, 0.5^{mm}.

Long Island Sound, off New Haven; and at Thimble Islands, 1 to 5 fathoms, among hydroids and bryozoa.

ETEONE ROBUSTA Verrill. (p. 588.)

This species, previously known only from a single specimen, was taken at Wood's Hole, in abundance, and of large size, in November, by Mr. Vinal N. Edwards.

Turbellaria.

RHYNCHOSCOLEX PAPILLOSUS Diesing.

Revision der Turbellarien, op. cit., vol. xlv., p. 245, 1862. *Rhynchoprobolus papillosus* Schmarda, Neue wirbell. Thiere, i, p. 1, 11, Plate 2, fig. 25 (t. Diesing). Hoboken, New Jersey, in brackish water, (Schmarda).

POLYCELIS MUTABILIS Verrill, sp. nov.

Body much depressed, thin, changeable in form, often elliptical or oval, frequently broad and emarginate in front, and tapered posteriorly. Marginal ocelli minute, black, forming several rows along the front border, but only one row laterally. Dorsal ocelli larger, forming three pairs of rather ill-defined clusters; the outer clusters are largest, convergent backward; a pair of smaller clusters are situated a little in advance, and nearer together; the third pair is a little farther forward and closer together, often more or less confused with those next behind them. Color, yellowish brown, darker centrally; or pale yellowish, thickly specked with yellowish brown. Length, about 7^{mm} to 9^{mm}, breadth, 5^{mm} to 6^{mm}.

Thimble Islands, 1 to 2 fathoms, among algæ.

Bryozoa.

GEMELLARIA LORICATA Busk.

Catal. Mar. Polyzoa, Brit. Mus., part i, p. 34; Smitt, op, cit., p. 286, Plate 17, fig. 54. *Sertularia loricata* Linné, Syst. Nat., ed. x, p. 285 (t. Smitt). *Gemellaria loriculata* Johnston, Brit. Zoöph., ed. ii, pp. 293, 477, Plate 47, figs. 12, 13.

Nantucket to the Arctic Ocean; northern coasts of Europe to Great Britain. Very common in Casco Bay and Bay of Fundy, low-water to 110 fathoms.

The specimens from Nantucket differ somewhat from the ordinary form. They consist of rather dense tufts of stout stems, two or three inches high, and rather sparingly branched. The cells are larger than usual, elongated obovate, five or six times as long as broad; those of the same pair are not exactly opposite. Aperture deeply crescent-shaped, facing a little outward. Many of the cells, toward the base of the stems, give rise to one or more curious processes from near the base of the cell; these are, at first, slender tubes, rising from a thin roundish spot on the cell, but soon they divide at the tip into two, three, or four forks, which are at first regularly recurved; later these become much elongated, and are converted into slender rootlets or stolons.

ERRATA.

Page 307, line 23, for cavaluted, read convoluted.
Page 310, line 8, page 401, line 12, and elsewhere, for *Ostræa*, read *Ostrea*.
Page 383, line 23, for *Æolidia*, read *Montagua*.
Page 383, line 26, for *Cavolina*, read *Coryphella*.
Page 392, line 23, for micropthalma, read microphthalma.
Page 393, last line, for *Sargatia*, read *Sagartia*.
Page 399, line 21, for *Leptochiton*, read *Chætopleura*.
Page 399, line 32, for *Leptochiton*, read *Trachydermon*.
Page 405, line 27, for *Eucrate*, read *Eucratea*.
Page 407, line 38, for reproducsive, read reproductive.
Page 415 line 25, for *Unicola*, read *Unciola*.
Page 427, line 15, and page 429, line 28, for *Melitta testudinaria*, read *Mellita pentapora*
Page 433, line 34, for *Amphipholis*, read *Amphiura*.
Page 444, line 12, for *tidentata*, read *tridentata*.
Page 457, line 39, for *Pandaru*, read *Pandarus*.
Page 459, line 36, for *Echthrogalus*, read *Echthrogaleus*.
Page 487, line 10, for A. *planaria*, read A *Planaria*.
Page 488, line 4, for *cantenula*, read *catenula*.
Page 496, line 28, for *A. ternata*, read *C. ternata*.
Page 498, line 5, for *Tedania*, read *Halichondria panicea*.
Page 498, line 30, for Augustus, read angustus.
Page 504, line 41, for page 433, read 432.
Page 508, line 5, for *Acutum*, read *A. acutum*.
Page 509, line 18, for *lævigata*, read *discors*.
Page 509, line 32, for *thraci-formis*, read *thraciformis*.
Page 509, line 33, for Simpson, read Stimpson.
Page 547, line 15, for *Panopius*, read *Panopeus*.
Page 561, line 43, for *pingus*, read *pinguis*.
Page 619, line 16, for Cosco, read Casco.
Page 619, last line, for Cisco, read Casco.
Page 640, first line, for fig. 127, read fig. 124.
Page 666, line 15, after Montagua pilata, insert Plate XXV, fig. 124.
Page 680, line 18, for 185, B., read 184, B.
Page 695, line 34, for fig. 238, read 243.
Page 716, line 35, for fig. 368, read 268.

ALPHABETICAL INDEX TO THE REPORT ON THE INVERTEBRATA OF SOUTHERN NEW ENGLAND.

[In the following index the first reference, for the names of genera and species, is to the systematic catalogue, where the synonymy, descriptions, and references to plates may be found. In many cases references to the nominal lists have been omitted. The figures refer to the inside paging of the report.]

EXPLANATION OF PLATE I.

FIGURE 1.—Pinnixa cylindrica Say, (p. 546;) male, enlarged four diameters.
2.—Pinnotheres ostreum Say, (p. 546;) male, enlarged four diameters.
3.—Panopeus depressus Smith, (p. 547;) male, natural size.
4.—Platyonichus ocellatus Latreille, (p. 547;) male, slightly reduced in size.

(All the figures were drawn by J. H. Emerton.)

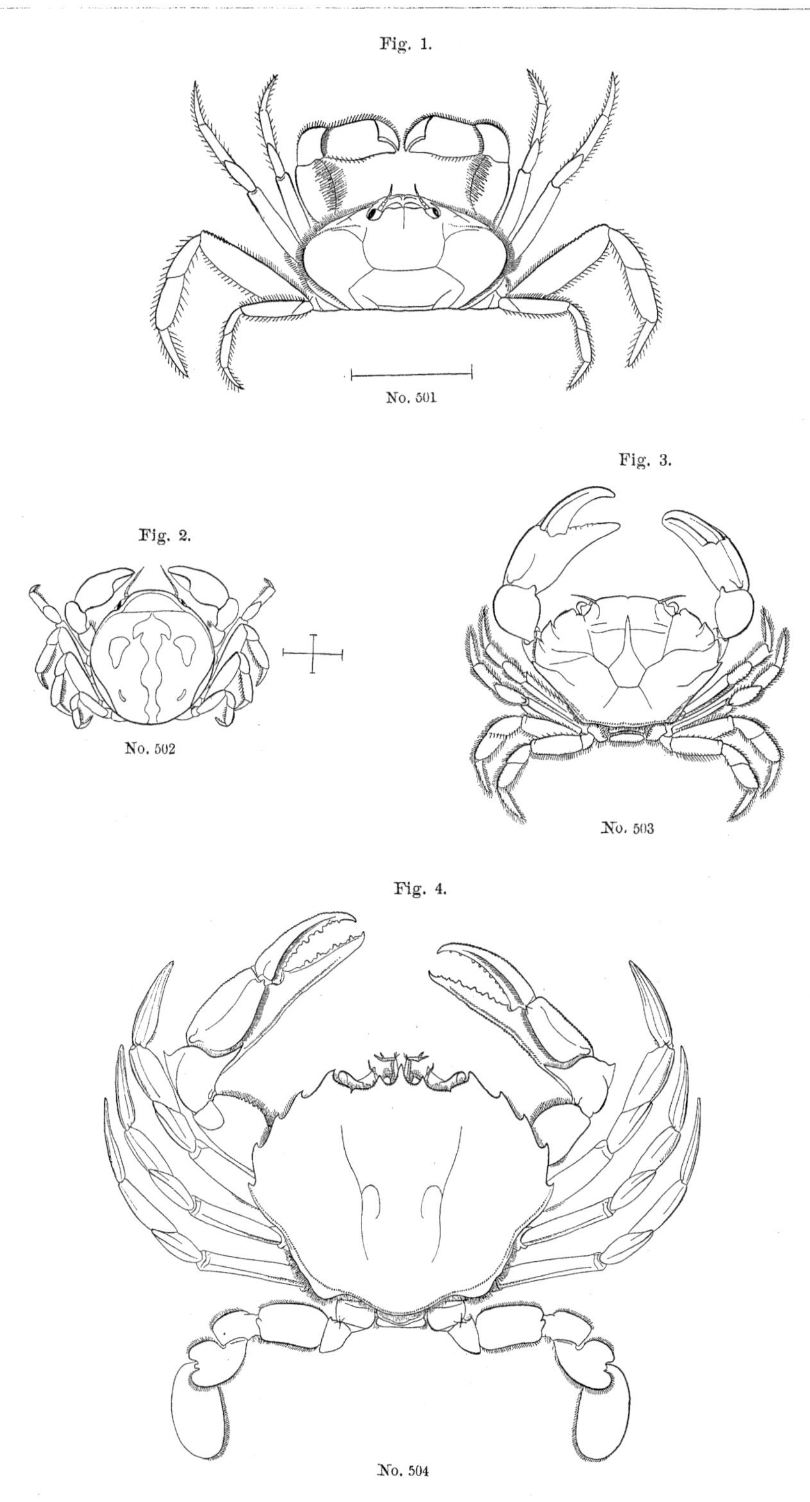
Fig. 1.
No. 501
Fig. 2.
No. 502
Fig. 3.
No. 503
Fig. 4.
No. 504

EXPLANATION OF PLATE II.

FIGURE 5.—Hippa talpoida Say, (p. 548;) dorsal view, enlarged about two diameters.

6.—Pandalus annulicornis Leach, (p. 550;) dorsal view, slightly reduced in size.

7.—Gebia affinis Say, (p. 549;) female; lateral view, slightly enlarged.

8.—Callianassa Stimpsoni Smith, (p. 549;) larger cheliped; outside, natural size.

9.—Palæmonetes vulgaris Stimpson, (p. 550;) male; lateral view, enlarged one and one-half diameters.

(All the figures were drawn by J. H. Emerton.)

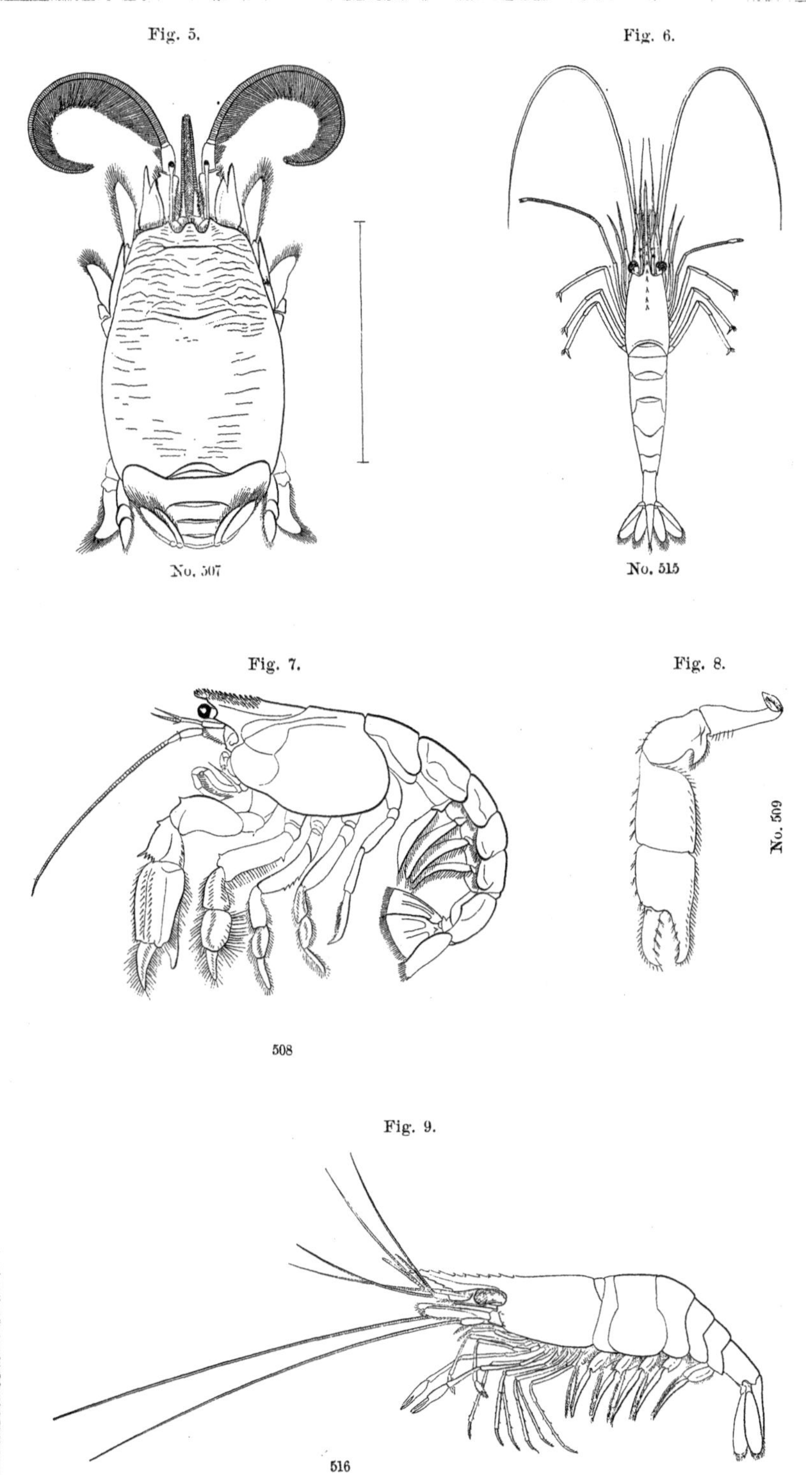
Fig. 5.
No. 507
Fig. 6.
No. 515
Fig. 7.
508
Fig. 8.
No. 509
Fig. 9.
516

EXPLANATION OF PLATE III.

FIGURE 10.—Crangon vulgaris Fabr., (p. 550;) male; dorsal view, natural size.

11.—Virbius Zostericola Smith, (p. 550;) female; lateral view, slightly enlarged.

12.—Mysis stenolepis Smith, (p. 551;) young female; lateral view, enlarged four diameters. The anterior margin of the carapax is not well represented in this figure; see description.

13.—Diastylis quadrispinosa G. O. Sars, (p. 554;) lateral view, enlarged seven diameters.

(All the figures were drawn by J. H. Emerton.)

Fig. 10.

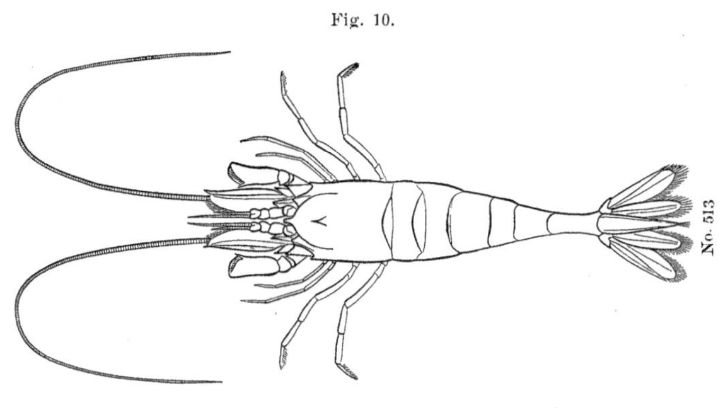

Fig. 11.

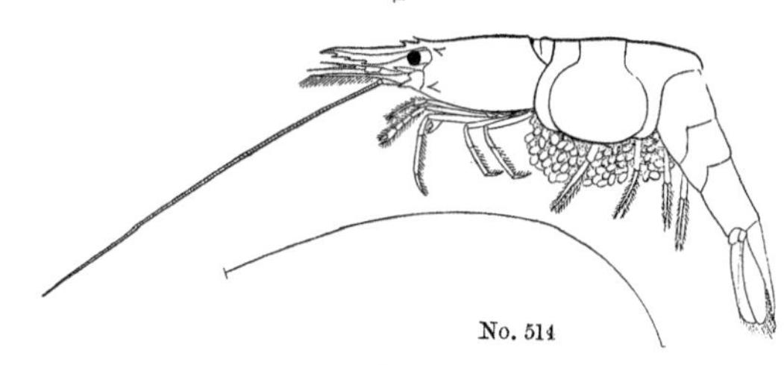

Fig. 12.

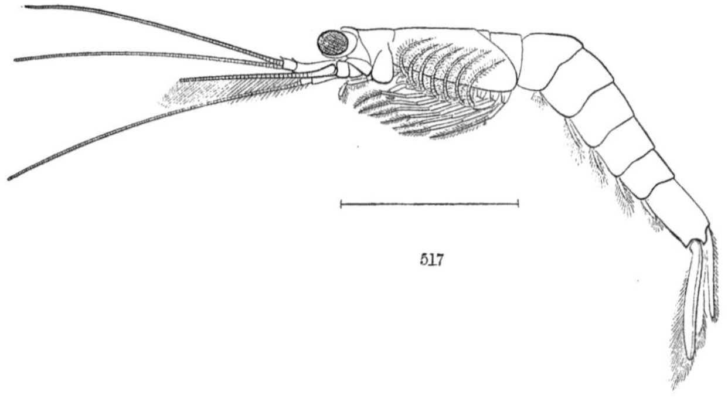

Fig. 13.

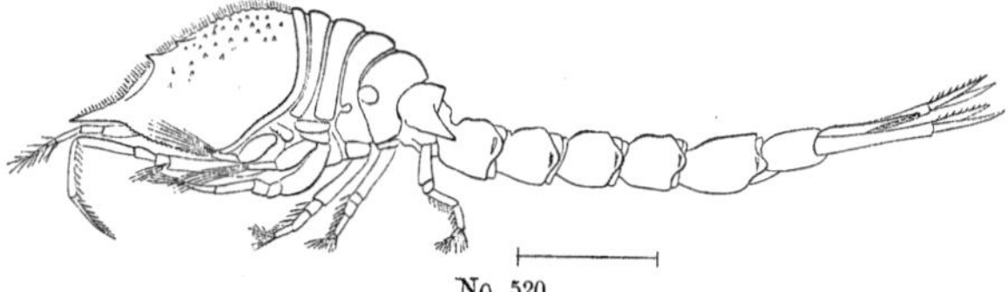

EXPLANATION OF PLATE IV.

FIGURE 14.—Orchestia agilis Smith, (p. 555;) male; lateral view, enlarged five diameters.

15.—Gammarus ornatus Edwards, (p. 557;) male; lateral view, enlarged two diameters.

16.—Amphithoë maculata Stimpson, (p. 563;) male; lateral view, enlarged two diameters.

17.—Ampelisca sp., (p. 561;) lateral view, enlarged five diameters.

18.—Cerapus rubricornis Stimpson, (p. 565;) female; lateral view, enlarged five diameters; and hand of the second pair of legs of the male, enlarged the same amount.

19.—Unciola irrorata Say, (p. 567;) male; dorsal view, enlarged six diameters.

(All the figures were drawn by J. H. Emerton and S. I. Smith.)

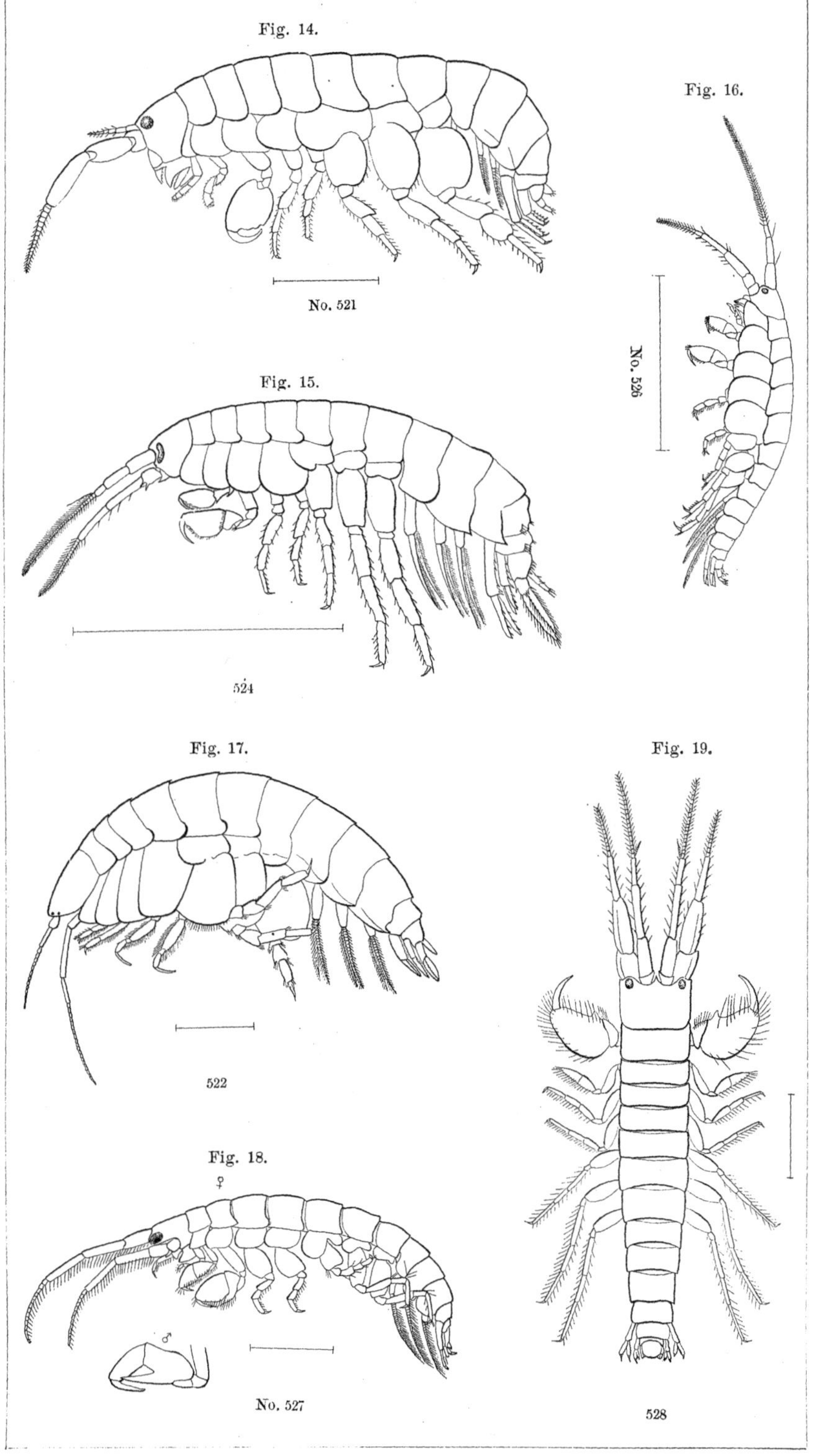
Fig. 14.
No. 521
Fig. 15.
524
Fig. 16.
No. 526
Fig. 17.
522
Fig. 18.
♀
♂
No. 527
Fig. 19.
528

EXPLANATION OF PLATE V.

FIGURE 20.—Caprella geometrica Say, (p. 567;) lateral view, enlarged about three diameters.

21.—Sphæroma quadridentata Say, (p. 569;) dorsal view, enlarged five diameters.

22.—Idotea cæca Say, (p. 569;) male; dorsal view, enlarged three diameters.

23.—Idotea irrorata Edwards, (p. 569;) male; dorsal view, enlarged two diameters.

24.—Idotea robusta Kroyer, (p. 569;) male; dorsal view, enlarged two diameters.

(Figures 20, 21, 23, and 24, were drawn by J. H. Emerton; figure 22 by O. Harger.)

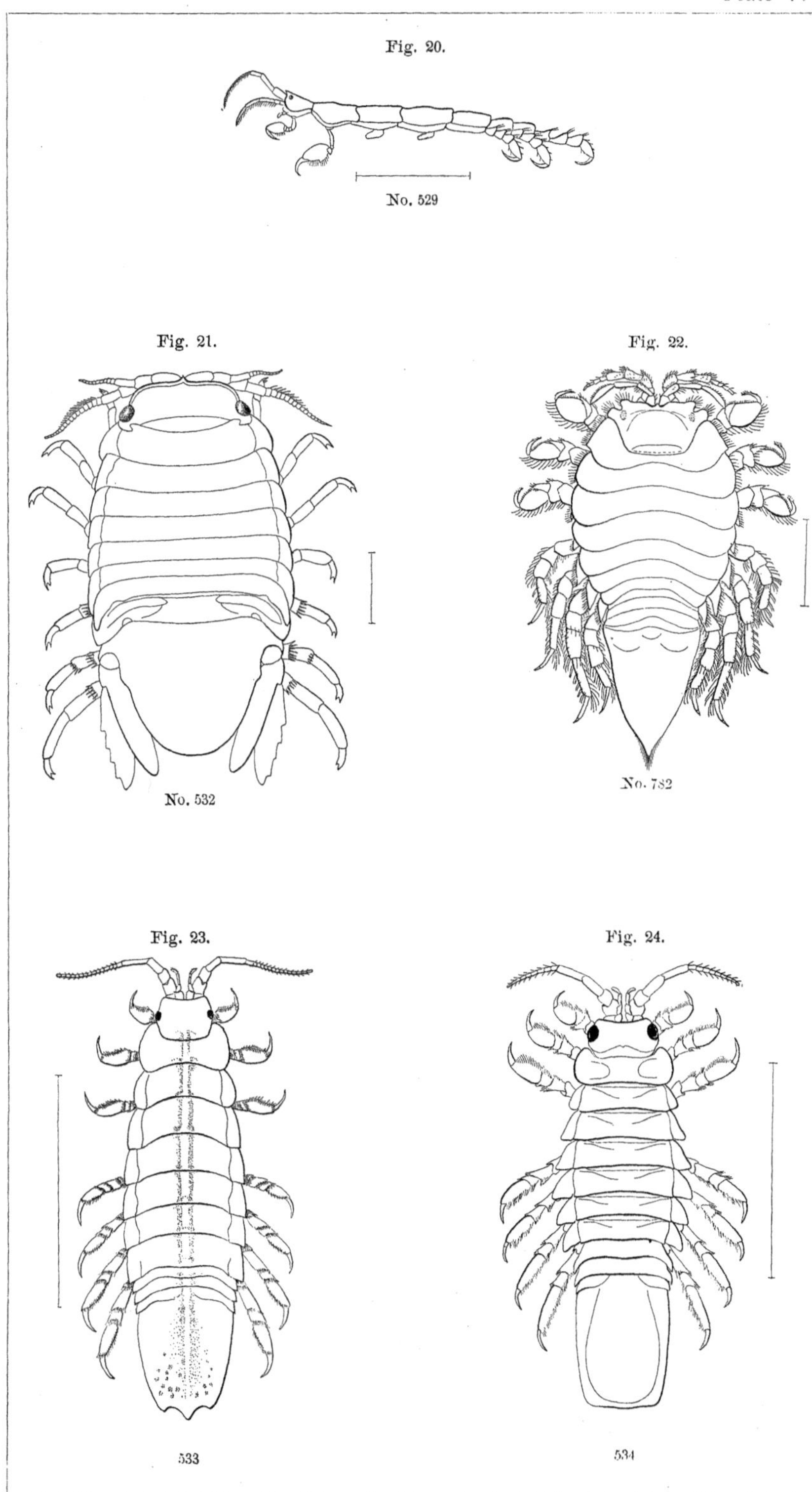
Fig. 20.
No. 529
Fig. 21.
No. 532
Fig. 22.
No. 782
Fig. 23.
533
Fig. 24.
534

EXPLANATION OF PLATE VI.

FIGURE 25.—Limnoria lignorum White, (p. 571;) dorsal view, enlarged ten diameters.

26.—Erichsonia filiformis Harger, (p. 570 ;) dorsal view, enlarged five diameters.

27.—Erichsonia attenuata Harger, (p. 570;) dorsal view, enlarged three diameters.

28.—Epelys trilobus Smith, (p. 571;) dorsal view, enlarged ten diameters.

29.—Livoneca ovalis Harger, (p. 572 ;) dorsal view, enlarged three diameters.

(Figure 25 was drawn by S. I. Smith; 26 and 28 by O. Harger; 27 and 29 by J. H. Emerton.)

Fig. 25.

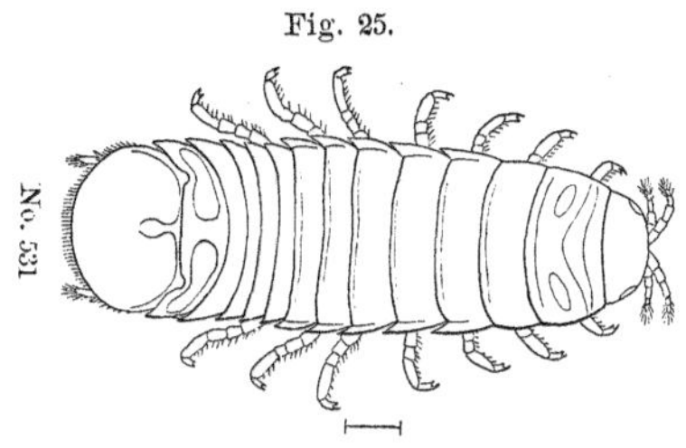
No. 531

Fig. 26.

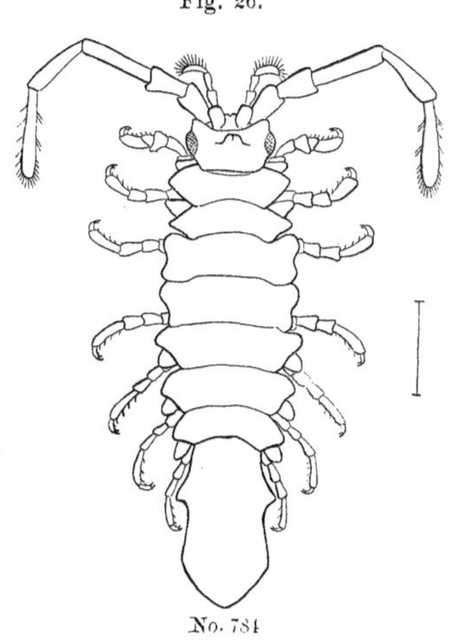
No. 784

Fig. 27

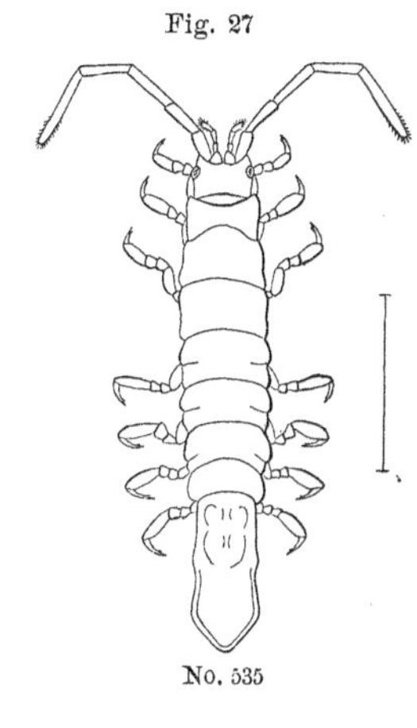
No. 535

Fig. 28.

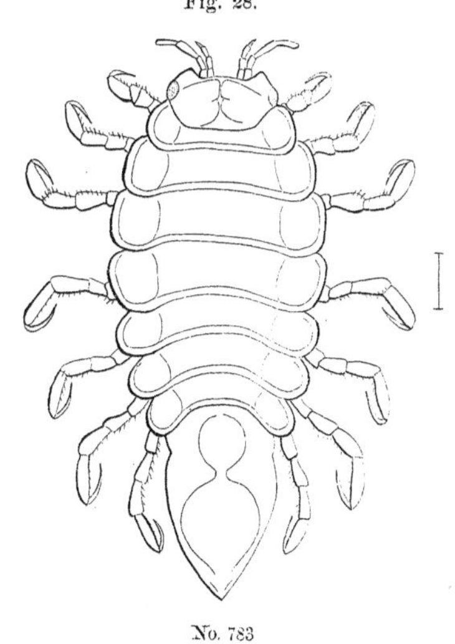
No. 783

Fig. 29.

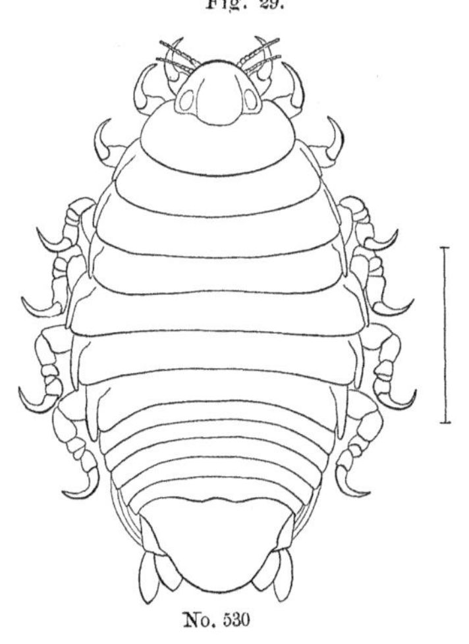
No. 530

EXPLANATION OF PLATE VII.

FIGURE 30.—Lerneonema radiata Steenstrup and Lütken, (p. 578;) female, enlarged two diameters.

31.—Pandarus, (p. 576;) female; dorsal view, enlarged five diameters.

32.—Nogagus Latreillii, (p. 576;) male; dorsal view, enlarged five diameters

33.—Sapphirina, (p. 573;) male; dorsal view, enlarged ten diameters.

34.—Lepas fascicularis Ellis and Solander, (p. 579;) lateral view of a single animal from a large cluster, slightly enlarged.

35.—Phoxichilidium maxillare Stimpson, (p. 544;) male; dorsal view, enlarged two diameters.

(Figure 33 was drawn by S. I. Smith; all the others by J. H. Emerton.)

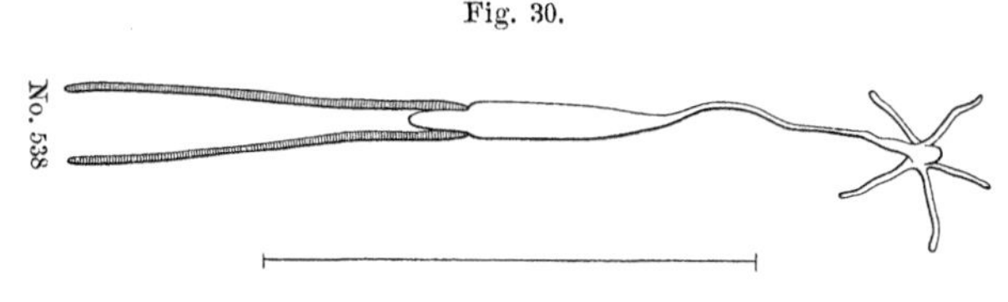
Fig. 30.
No. 538

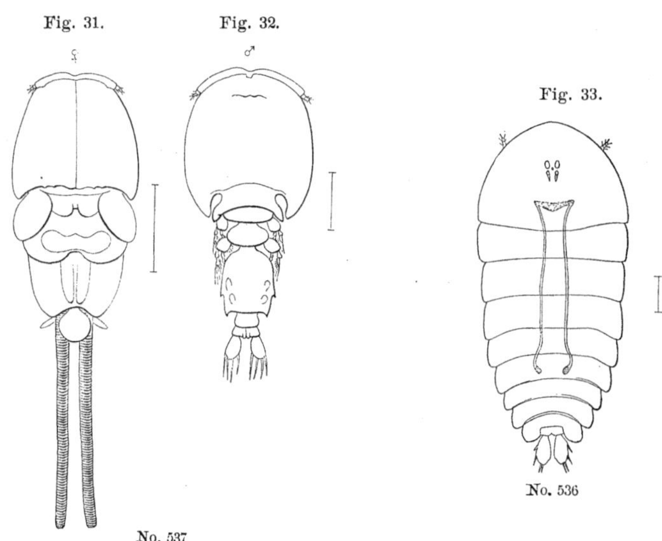
Fig. 31.
♀
No. 537
Fig. 32.
♂
Fig. 33.
No. 536

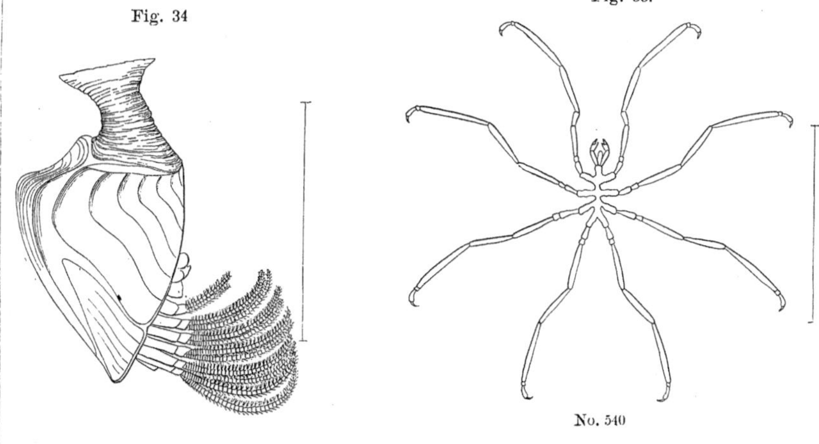
Fig. 34
Fig. 35.
No. 540

EXPLANATION OF PLATE VIII.

FIGURE 36.—Squilla empusa Say, (p. 536;) lateral view of the free-swimming larvæ in one of its later stages, enlarged ten diameters.

37.—Zoëa of the common crab, *Cancer irroratus*, (p. 530;) in the last stage just before it changes to the megalops condition; lateral view, enlarged seventeen diameters.

38.—Megalops stage of the same, just after the change from the zoëa condition; dorsal view, enlarged thirteen diameters.

(All the figures were drawn by J. H. Emerton.)

Plate VIII.

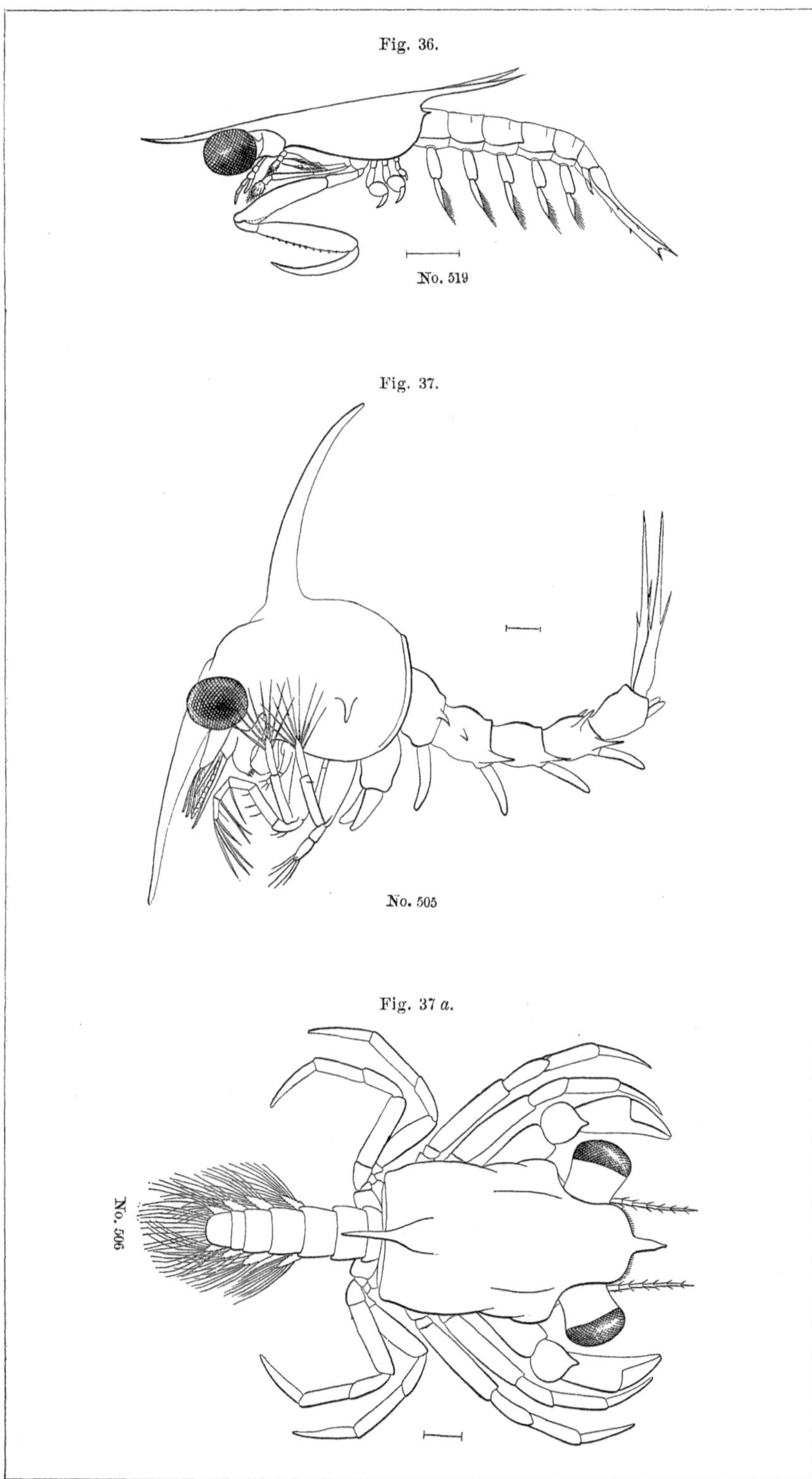

EXPLANATION OF PLATE IX.

Larval young of the Lobster, *Homarus Americanus* Edwards, (p. 522.)

FIGURE 38.—*A*. Lateral view of the larval young in the first stage observed, enlarged seven diameters.

B. The same in a dorsal view, the abdomen held horizontally.

C. Antennula, enlarged fourteen diameters.

D. One of the thoracic legs of the second pair, enlarged fourteen diameters; *a*, exopodus; *b*, epipodus; *c*, branchiæ.

39.—*E*. Lateral view of the larval young in the third stage, enlarged five and one-half diameters.

F. Terminal portion of the abdomen seen from above, enlarged ten diameters; *a*, one of the small spines of the posterior margin of the terminal segment, enlarged fifty diameters.

G. Basal portion of one of the legs of the second pair, showing the epipodus and branchiæ, enlarged fourteen diameters.

(All the figures were drawn from alcoholic specimens, by S. I. Smith.)

Fig. 38.

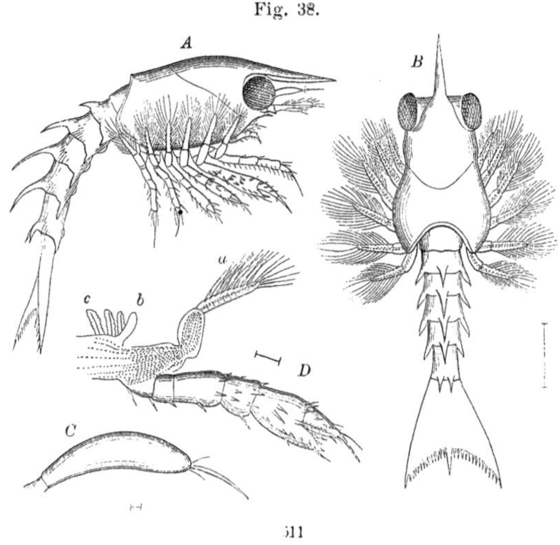

511

Fig. 39.

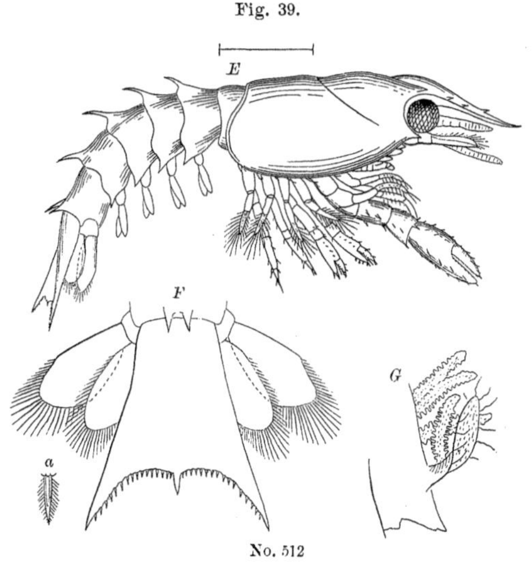

No. 512

EXPLANATION OF PLATE X.

FIGURE 40.—Lepidonotus squamatus, (p. 581;) anterior part of the body, head, and proboscis; dorsal view.

41.—The same; end of the proboscis; front view, showing the jaws and papillæ.

42.—Lepidonotus sublevis, (p. 581;) dorsal view.

43.—Rhynchobolus dibranchiatus, (p. 596;) anterior part of body, mouth and head; lower side.

44.—The same; lateral appendage, showing the dorsal cirrus, the upper and lower branchiæ and the setigerous lobes between them.

45.—Rhynchobolus Americanus, (p. 596;) anterior part of the body and extended proboscis; dorsal view.

46.—The same; lateral appendages, showing the dorsal cirrus, the branched gill, the setigerous lobes, and the ventral cirrus.

(Figures 40, 41, 42, 45, were drawn from nature by J. H. Emerton; 44 by A. E. Verrill; 43 and 46 were copied from Ehlers.)

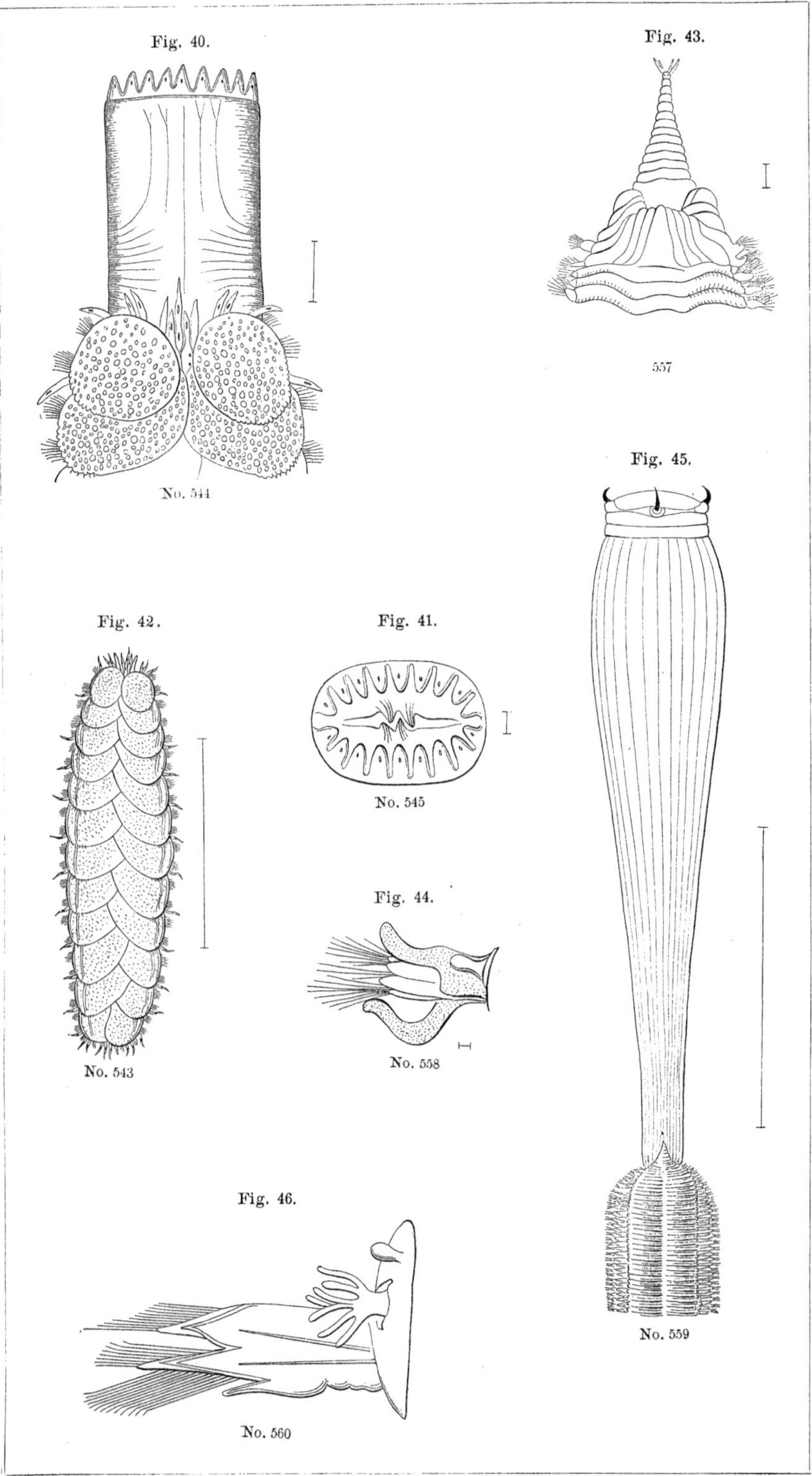
Fig. 40.
No. 544
Fig. 43.
557
Fig. 45.
No. 559
Fig. 42.
No. 543
Fig. 41.
No. 545
Fig. 44.
No. 558
Fig. 46.
No. 560

EXPLANATION OF PLATE XI.

FIGURE 47.—Nereis virens, (p. 590;) head little more than natural size; dorsal view.

48.—The same; extended proboscis; dorsal view.

49.—The same; probosci; sventral view.

50.—The same; lateral appendage.

51.—Nereis limbata, male, (p. 590;) a few segments of the middle region of the body, anterior region, head and extended proboscis; dorsal view.

52.—Nereis pelagica, female, (p. 591;) natural size; dorsal view.

53.—The same; male, natural size; dorsal view.

54.—The same; head more enlarged; dorsal view.

55.—The same; proboscis; ventral view.

56.—Phyllodoce gracilis?, (p. 586;) head; dorsal view.

(Figure 51 was drawn from nature by J. H. Emerton; 47, 48, 49, 50, 52, 53, were copied from Ehlers; 54, 55, from Malmgren; 56, from A. Agassiz.)

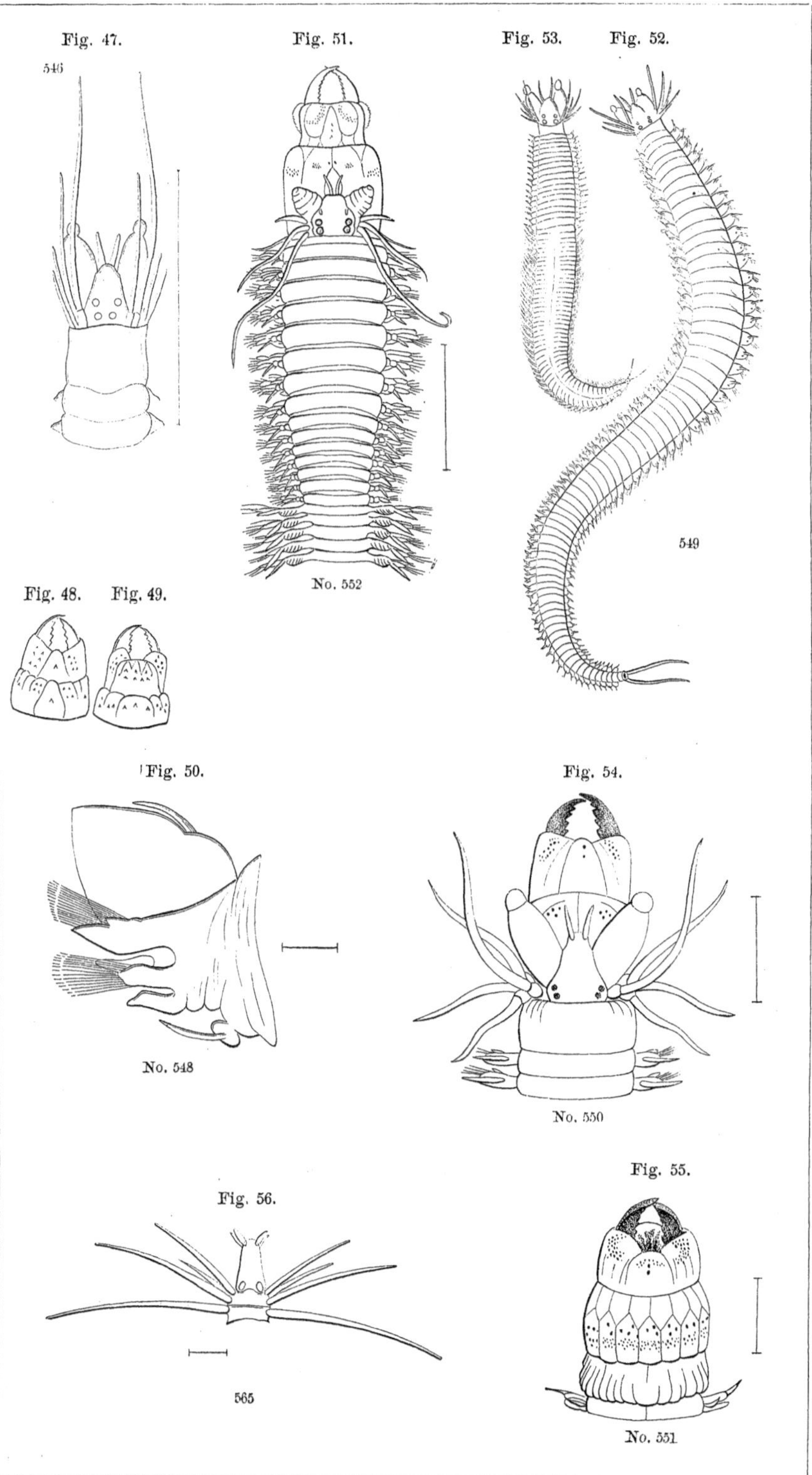
Fig. 47.
546
Fig. 51.
No. 552
Fig. 53.
Fig. 52.
549
Fig. 48.
Fig. 49.
Fig. 50.
No. 548
Fig. 54.
No. 550
Fig. 55.
No. 551
Fig. 56.
565

EXPLANATION OF PLATE XII.

FIGURE 57.—Nephthys picta, (p. 583;) anterior part of body and head, much enlarged; dorsal view.

58.—Nephthys bucera, (p. 583;) anterior part of body and head, enlarged; ventral view.

59.—Nephthys ingens, (p. 583;) anterior part of body and extended proboscis; ventral view.

60.—The same; dorsal view.

61.—Podarke obscura, (p. 589;) dorsal view, from a specimen preserved in alchohol and much contracted in length.

62.—Nectonereis megalops, (p. 592;) ventral view.

63.—The same; anterior region of body and head; dorsal view.

64.—Marphysa Leidyi, (p. 593;) anterior part of body and head, enlarged about three diameters; dorsal view.

(Figures 57 and 58 were copied from Ehlers; all the rest were drawn from nature by J. H. Emerton)

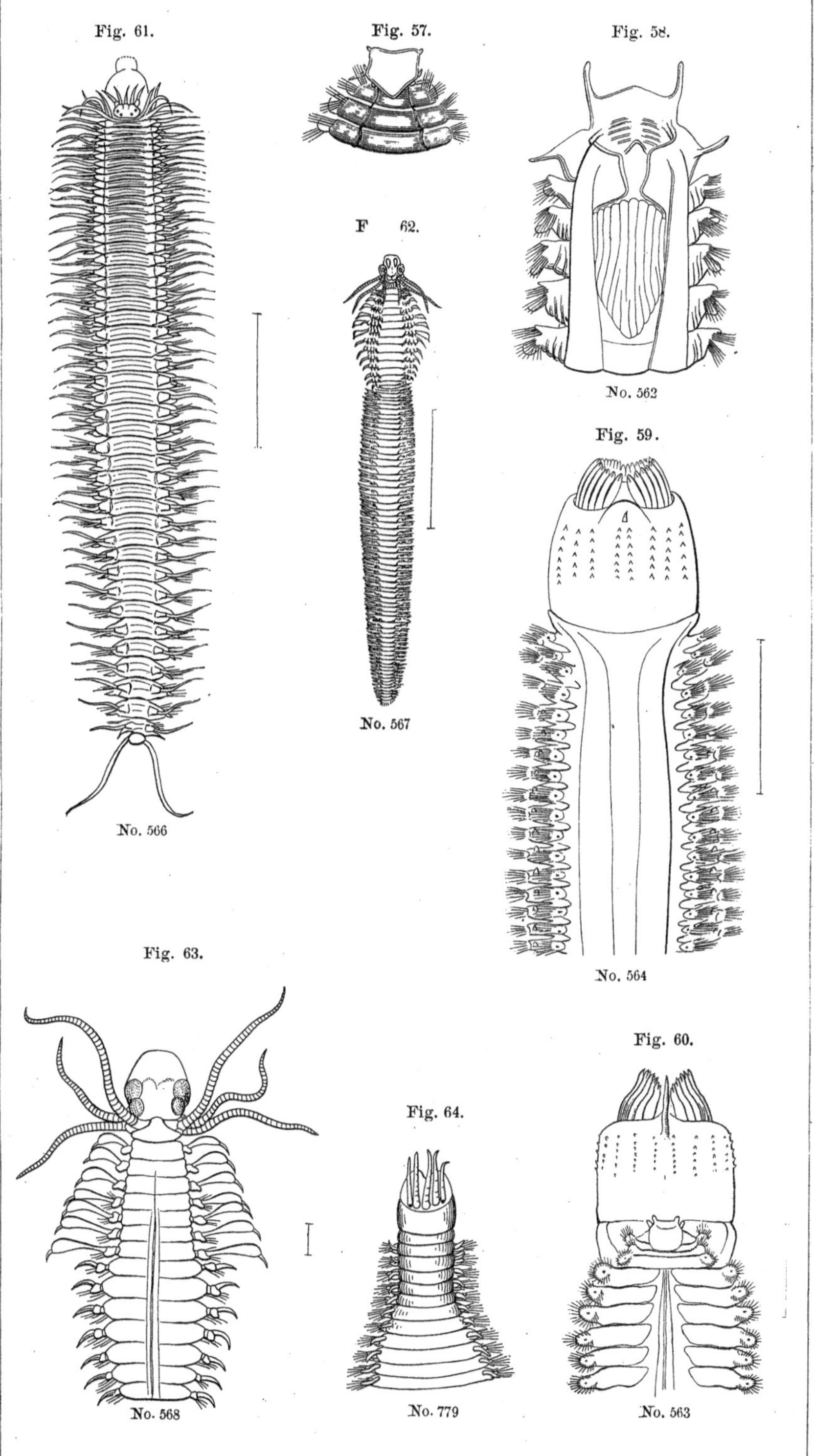

Fig. 61.
Fig. 57.
Fig. 58.
F 62.
No. 562
Fig. 59.
No. 567
No. 566
Fig. 63.
No. 564
Fig. 60.
Fig. 64.
No. 568
No. 779
No. 563

EXPLANATION OF PLATE XIII.

FIGURE 65.—Autolytus cornutus, (p. 590;) an asexual individual, from which a male is about to separate; dorsal view, enlarged about six diameters; A, A, A, antennæ of the former; C, C, C, C, two tentacles and one tentacular cirrus on each side, followed by the dorsal cirri; F, the intestine; *d*, the long setæ and dorsal cirri of the male.

66.—The same; anterior part of a female, more enlarged; the letters as before; *b*, the eyes; *e*, the eggs; *f*, the intestine; 3, one of the appendages of the anterior region of the body; *c*, the dorsal cirrus; *h*, the setigerous tubercle, supporting hooked setæ.

67.—Diopatra cuprea, (p. 593;) head and anterior part of body, showing part of the branchiæ; side view.

68.—The same; ventral view, showing the mouth open and jaws thrown back.

69.—Lumbriconereis opalina, (p. 594;) anterior part of body; dorsal view.

70.—The same; lateral appendage and setæ.

(Figures 65 and 66 were copied from A. Agassiz; 67, 68, 69 were drawn from nature by J. H. Emerton; 70, by A. E. Verrill.)

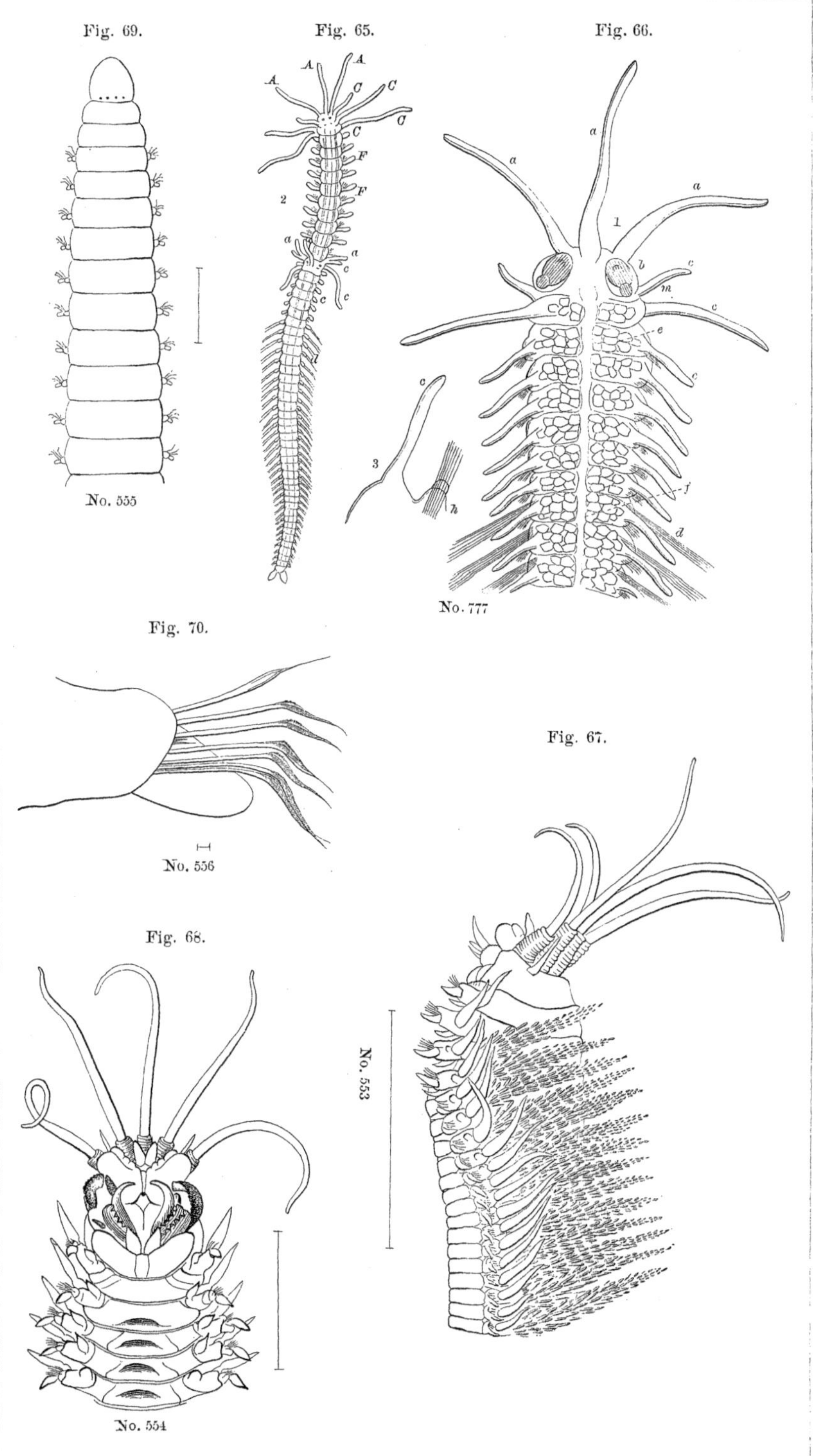
Fig. 69.
No. 555
Fig. 65.
A
A
A
C
C
C
C
F
F
2
a
a
c
c
c
d
Fig. 66.
a
a
a
1
b
c
m
c
e
c
c
3
h
f
d
No. 777
Fig. 70.
No. 556
Fig. 67.
No. 553
Fig. 68.
No. 554

EXPLANATION OF PLATE XIV.

FIGURE 71.—Clymenella torquata, (p. 608;) natural size; lateral view.

72.—The same; head and extended proboscis; front view.

73.—The same; posterior and caudal segments; dorsal view.

74.—Sternaspis fossor, (p. 606;) dorsal view.

75.—Trophonia affinis, (p. 605;) anterior portion; dorsal view.

76.—Anthostoma robustum, (p. 597;) anterior portion of body, head, and extended proboscis; dorsal view, natural size.

77.—Spio setosa, (p. 602;) anterior segments and head; side view; only one of the two large tentacles is represented.

78.—Polydora ciliatum, (p. 603;) anterior and posterior parts; dorsal view.

(Figures 71, 72, 73, 75, 76, were drawn from nature by J. H. Emerton; 74, by A. E. Verrill; 77, 78, were copied from A. Agassiz.)

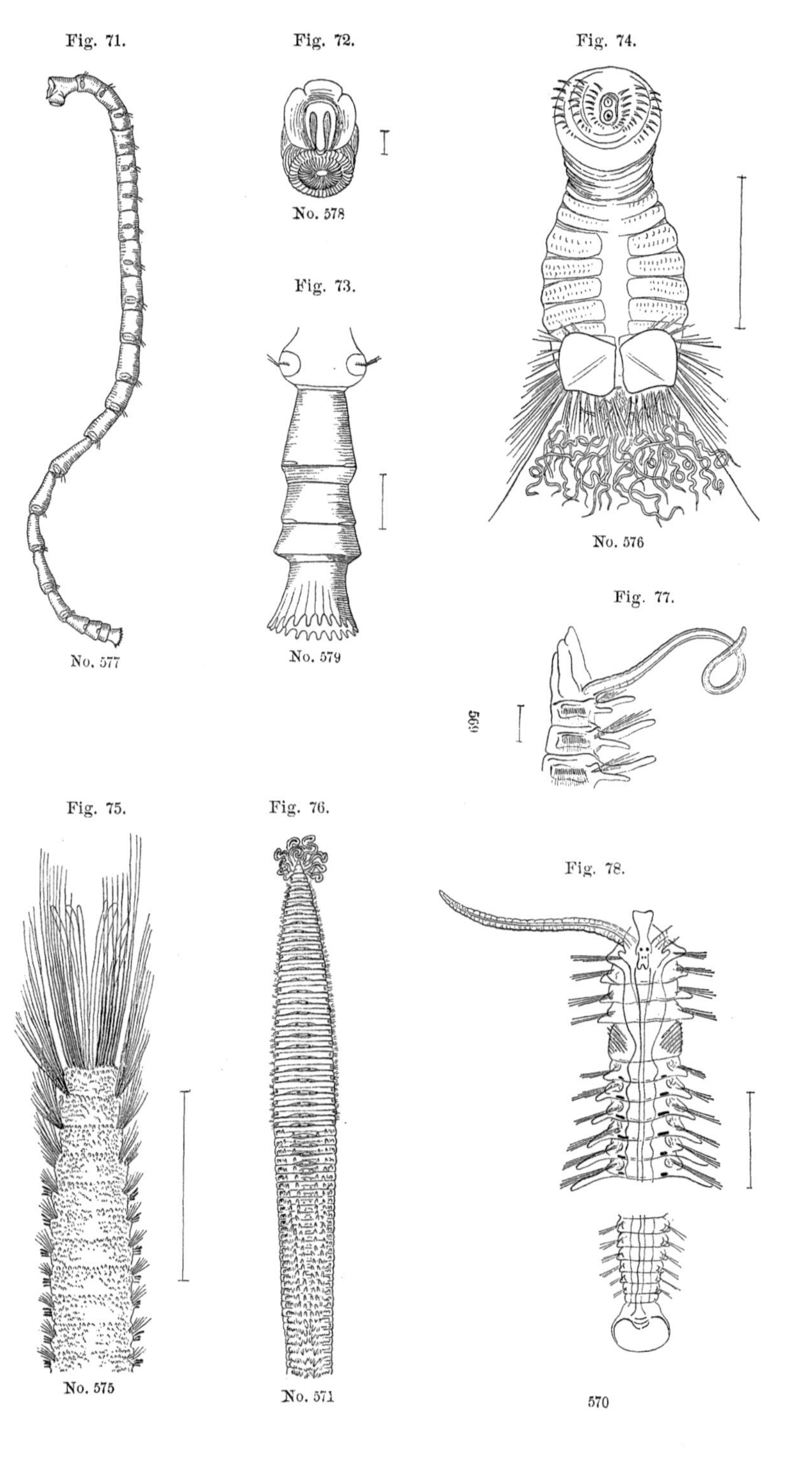
Fig. 71.
No. 577
Fig. 72.
No. 578
Fig. 73.
No. 579
Fig. 74.
No. 576
Fig. 77.
569
Fig. 75.
No. 575
Fig. 76.
No. 571
Fig. 78.
570

EXPLANATION OF PLATE XV.

FIGURE 79.– Ammotrypane fimbriata, (p. 604;) ventral view.

80.—Cirratulus grandis, (p. 606;) natural size, from a living specimen; lateral view.

81.—The same; natural size, from a preserved specimen; dorsal view.

(Figures 79 and 81 were drawn from nature by J. H. Emerton; figure 80, by A. E. Verrill.)

Fig. 79.

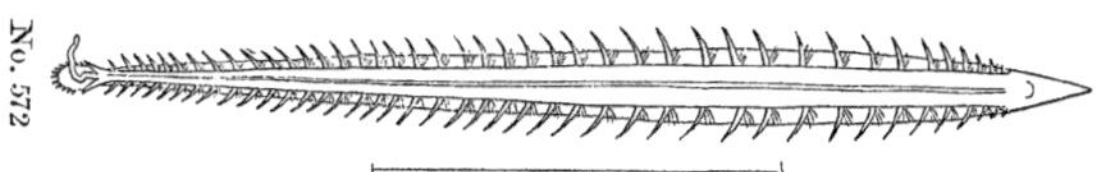

Fig. 80.

No. 574

Fig. 81.

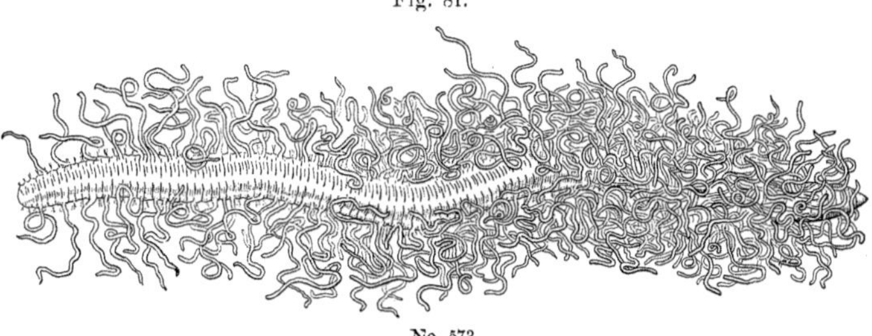

No. 573

EXPLANATION OF PLATE XVI.

FIGURE 82.—Amphitrite ornata, (p. 613;) lateral view, somewhat reduced, from a living specimen.

83.—Ampharete gracilis, (p. 612;) lateral view.

84.—Euchone elegans, (p. 618;) lateral view.

85.—Polycirrus eximius, (p. 616;) dorsal view of a living specimen creeping by means of its tentacles; natural size.

(Figures 82, 84, 85, were drawn from nature by A. E. Verrill; 83, by J. H. Emerton.)

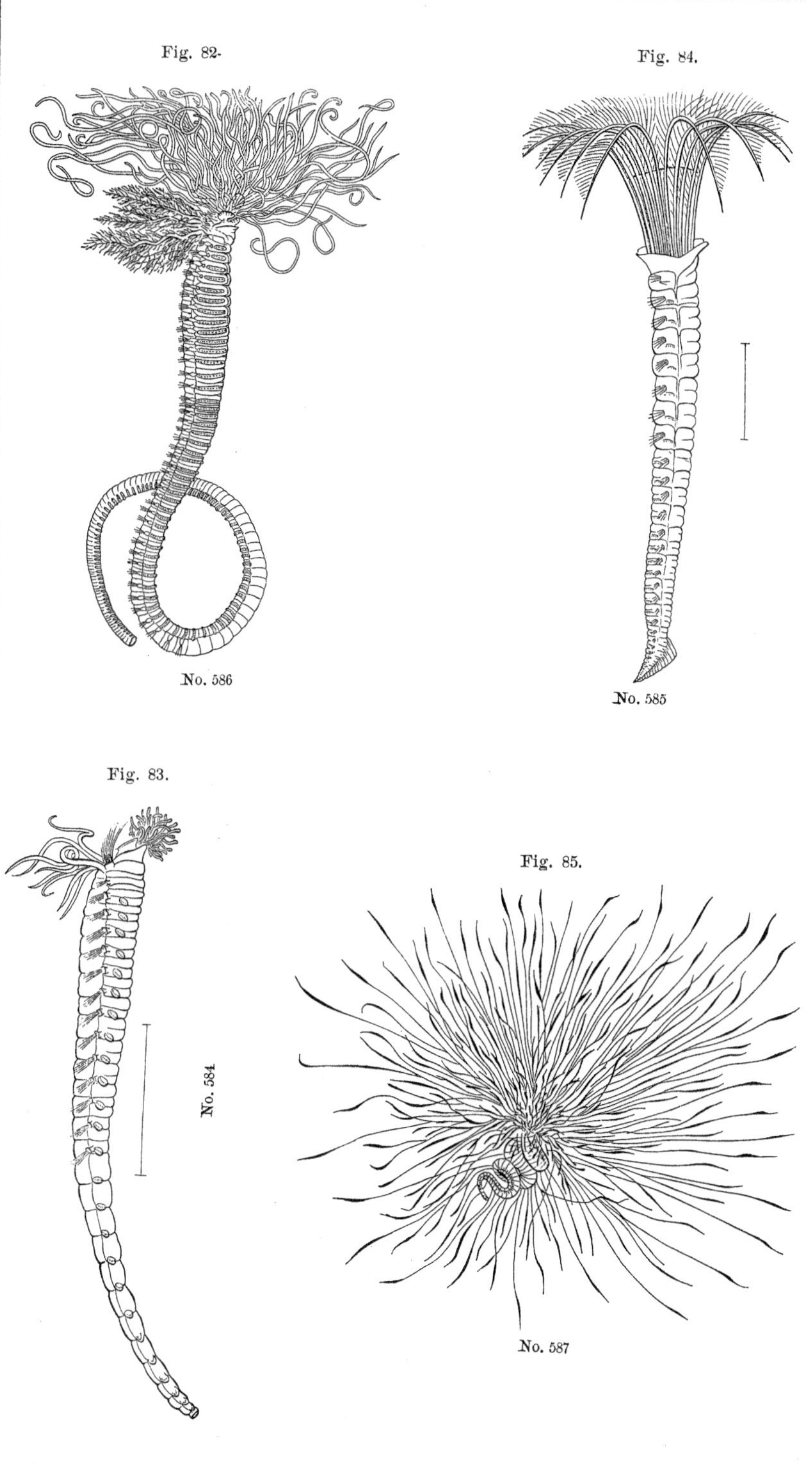
Fig. 82.
No. 586
Fig. 84.
No. 585
Fig. 83.
No. 584
Fig. 85.
No. 587

EXPLANATION OF PLATE XVII.

FIGURE 86.—Potamilla oculifera, (p. 617;) in its tube, with branchiæ fully expanded, from a living specimen, found at Eastport, Maine.

87.—Cistenides Gouldii, (p. 612;) lateral view.

87*a*.—The same; head and branchiæ, dorsal view.

88.—Sabellaria vulgaris, (p. 611;) lateral view.

88*a*.—The same; view of the operculum and tentacles, from above.

(Figures 84, 88, 88*a* were drawn from nature, by J. H. Emerton; 87, 87*a* by A. E. Verrill.)

Fig. 86.

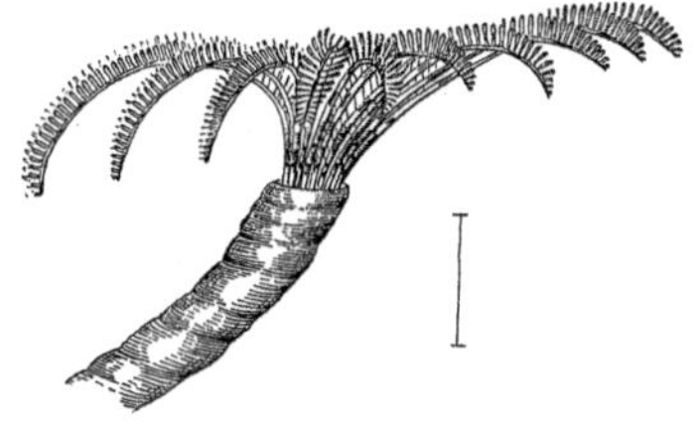

No. 778

Fig. 87.

No. 580

Fig. 87a.

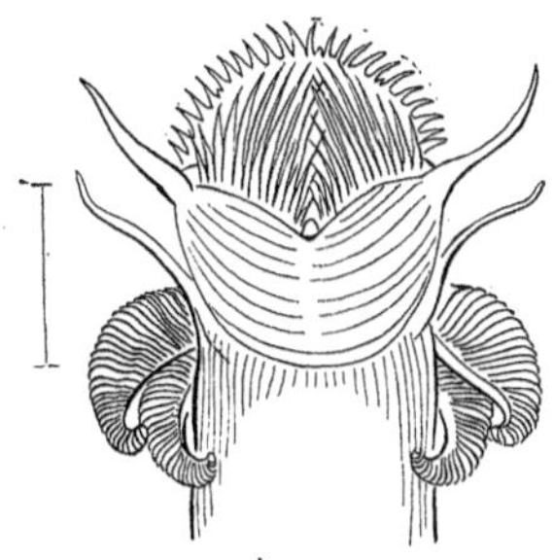

No. 581

Fig. 88.

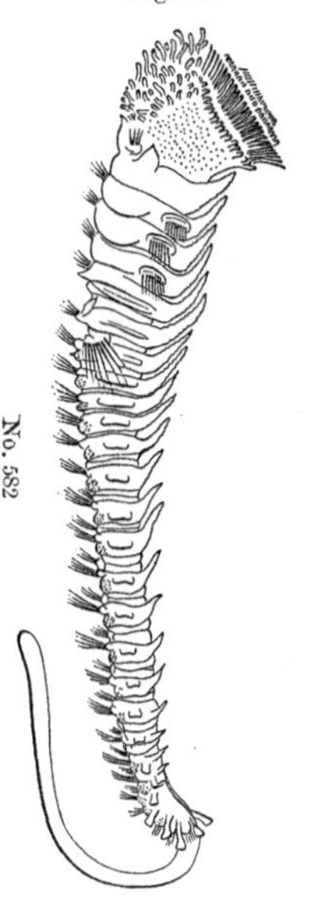

No. 582

Fig. 88a.

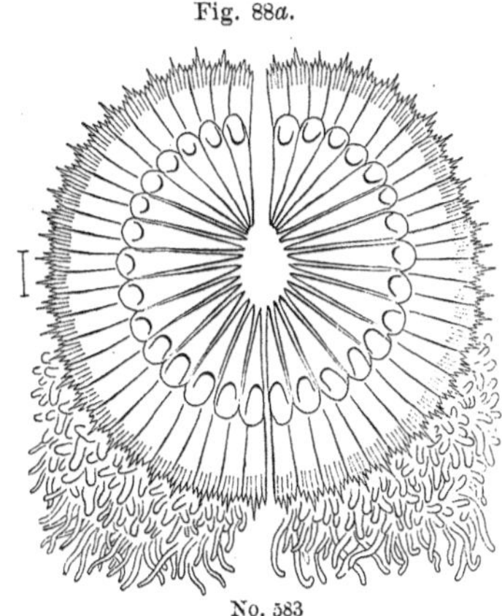

No. 583

EXPLANATION OF PLATE XVIII.

FIGURE 89.—Branchiobdella Ravenelii, (p. 624;) dorsal view, natural size.
90.—Malacobdella obesa, (p. 625;) dorsal view.
91.—Pontobdella rapax, (p. 625;) dorsal view.
92.—Phascolosoma cæmentarium, (p. 627;) lateral view.
93.—P. Gouldii, (p. 627;) lateral view, reduced one-half.
94.—Pontonema marinum, (p. 634;) female, lateral view, enlarged 15 diameters; *o*, eggs; *v*, genital orifice.

(Figure 94 was drawn from a living specimen, by A. E. Verrill; all the others were drawn from preserved specimens, by J. H. Emerton.)

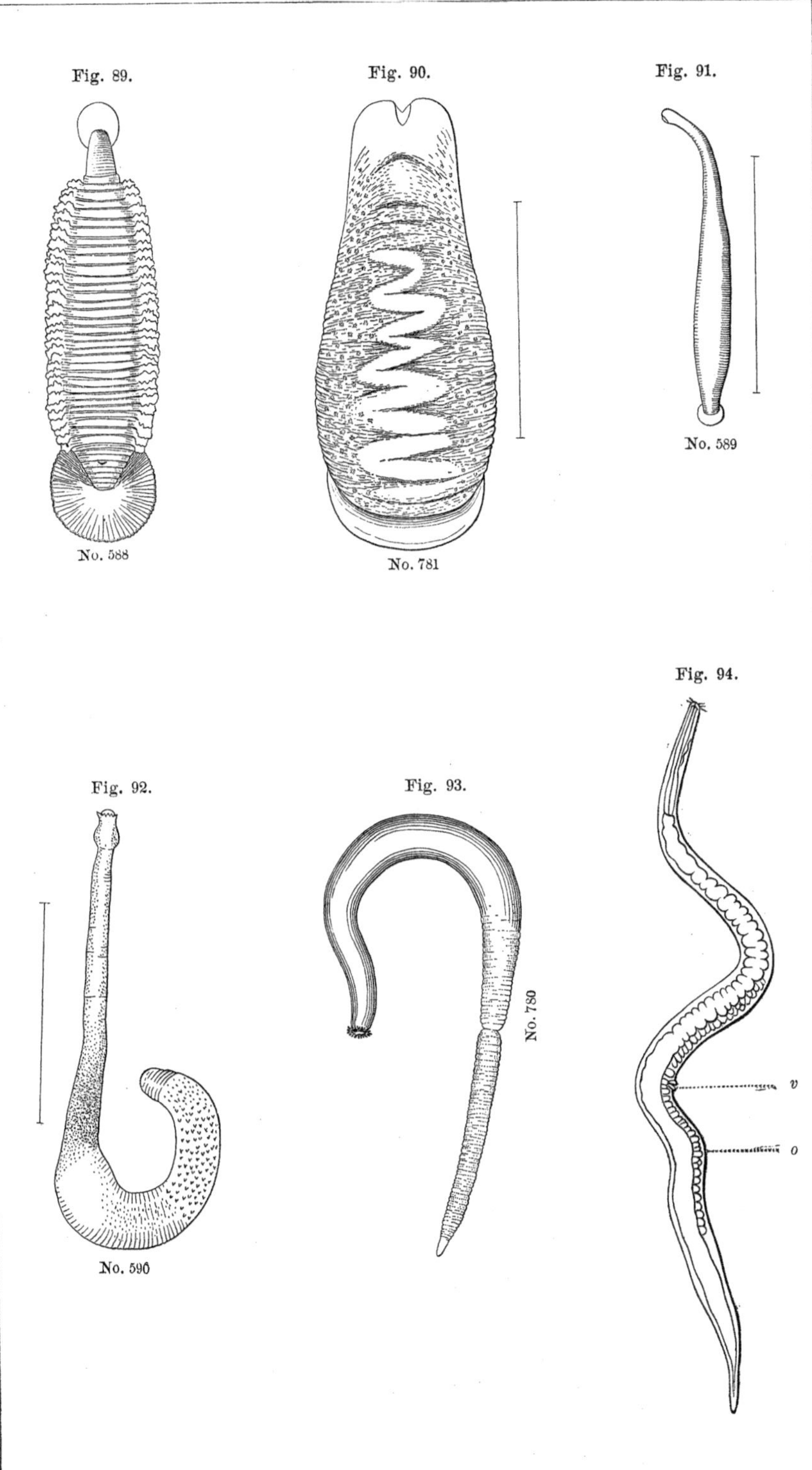
Fig. 89.
No. 588
Fig. 90.
No. 781
Fig. 91.
No. 589
Fig. 92.
No. 590
Fig. 93.
No. 780
Fig. 94.
v
o

EXPLANATION OF PLATE XIX.

FIGURE 95.—Cosmocephala ochracea, (p. 630 ;) anterior portion, enlarged nearly three diameters, dorsal view.

95*a*.—The same ; ventral view.

96.—Meckelia ingens, (p. 630 ;) anterior portion of a specimen not full grown, natural size.

96*a*.—The same; ventral view of the anterior portion and head of a larger specimen, in a different state of contraction, natural size.

97.—Polinia glutinosa, (p. 631 ;) dorsal view, enlarged two diameters.

98.—Tetrastemma arenicola, (p. 629 ;) dorsal view.

99.—Stylochopsis littoralis, (p. 632 ;) dorsal view.

100.—Planocera nebulosa, (p. 632 ;) dorsal view.

(All the figures were drawn from living specimens, by A. E. Verrill.)

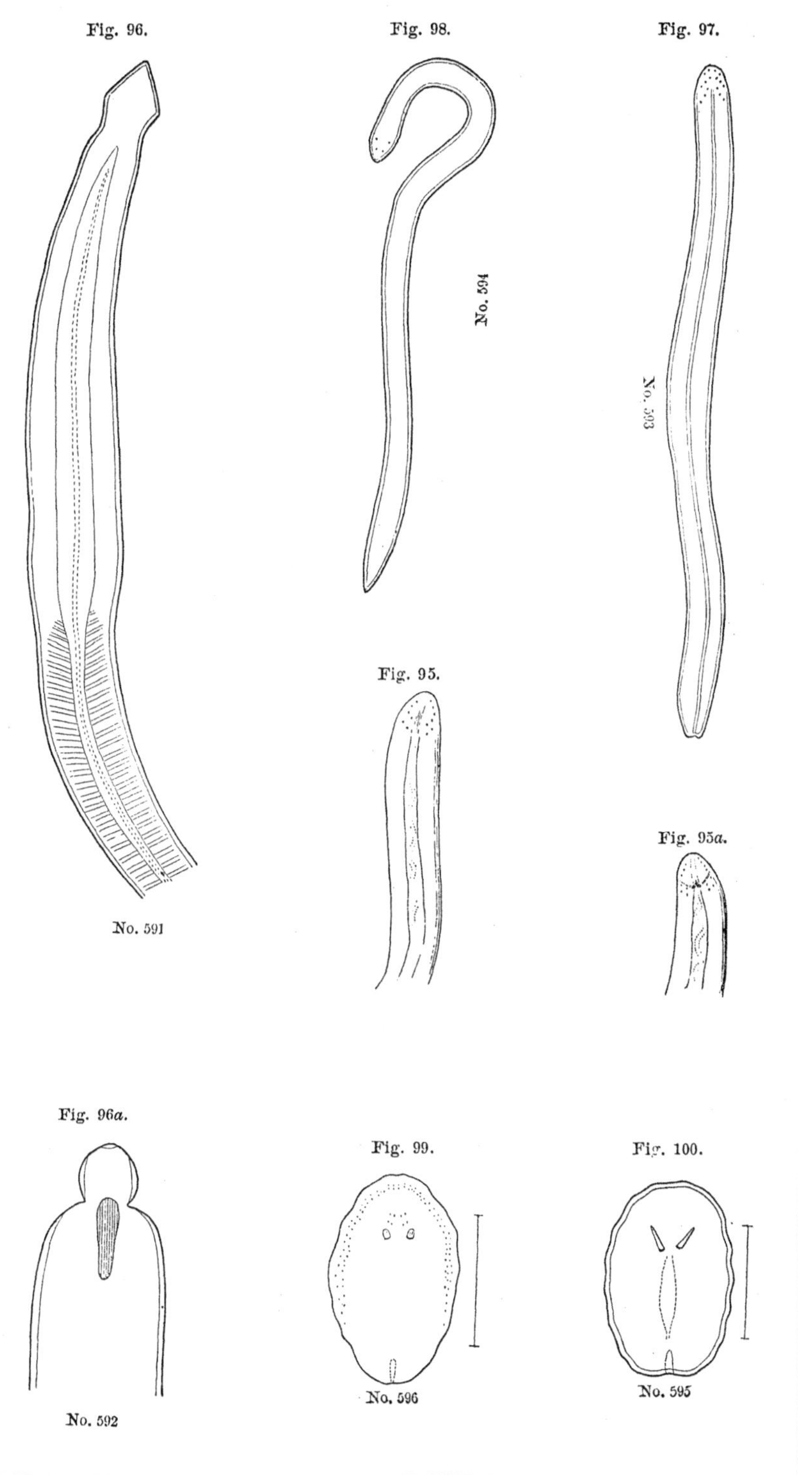
Fig. 96.
Fig. 98.
Fig. 97.
No. 594
No. 593
Fig. 95.
Fig. 95a.
No. 591
Fig. 96a.
Fig. 99.
Fig. 100.
No. 596
No. 595
No. 592

EXPLANATION OF PLATE XX.

FIGURE 101.—Loligo pallida, (p. 635;) dorsal view, about one-third natural size.

101*a*.—The same; the "pen" dorsal side.

102.—Loligo Pealii ?, (p. 635;) a cluster of the eggs.

103.—The same; an embryo just before hatching, much enlarged; *a'*, *a''*, *a'''*, *a''''*, the right "arms" belonging to four pairs; *c*, the side of the head; *e*, the eye; *f*, the caudal fins; *h*, the heart; *n*, the mantle in which color-vesicles are already developed and capable of changing their colors; *o*, the internal cavity of the ears; *s*, the siphon; *y*, the portion of the yolk not yet absorbed.

104.—The same; an embryo in an earlier stage of development, more highly magnified; the letters are the same as before.

105.—The same; a young specimen, recently hatched, found swimming at the surface, dorsal view.

(Figures 103, 104 are camera-lucida drawings made from the living specimens, by A. E. Verrill; all the others were drawn from preserved specimens, by J. H. Emerton.)

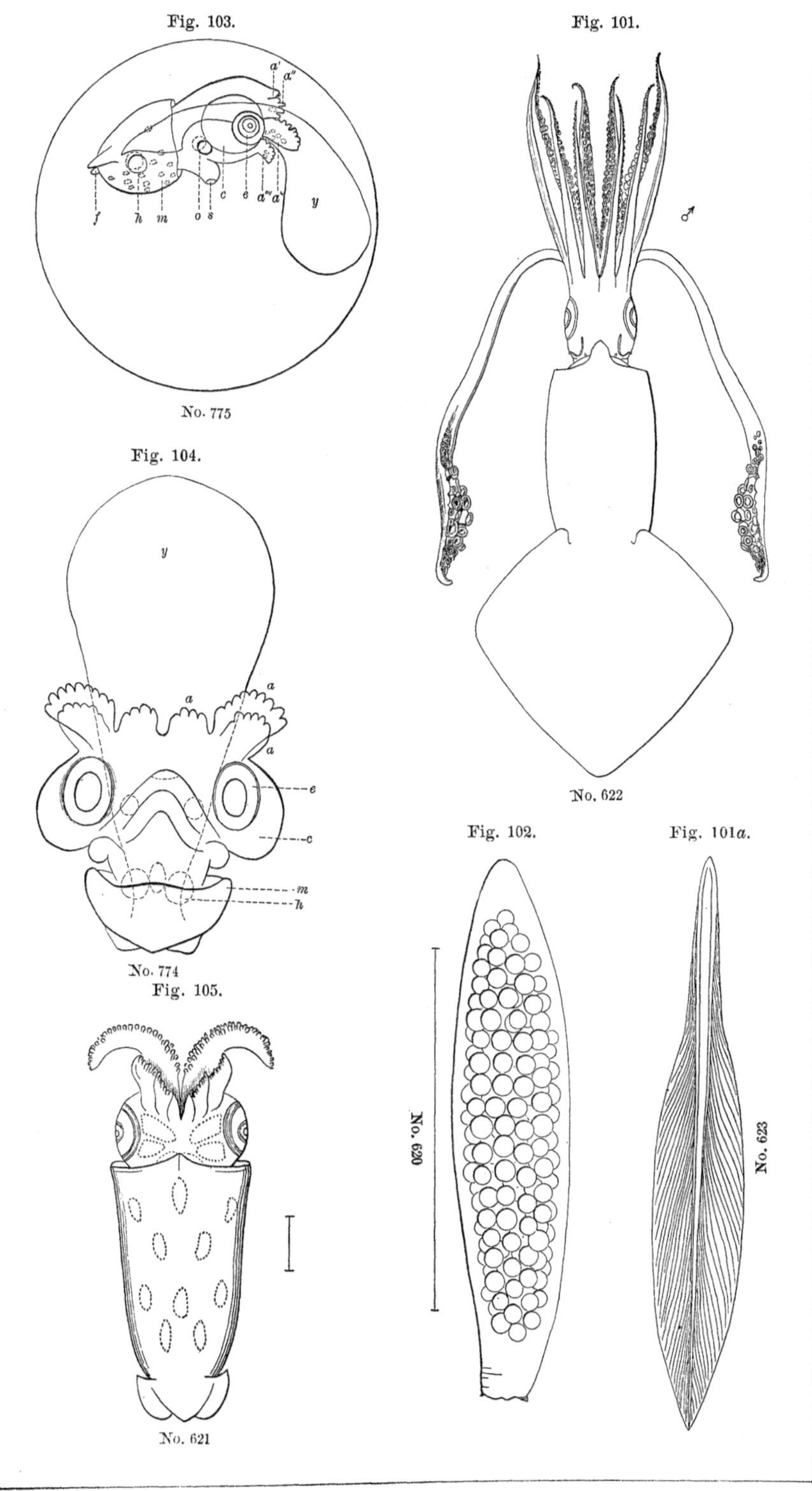
Fig. 103.
a'
a''
f
h
m
o
s
c
e
a'''
a'
y
No. 775
Fig. 101.
♂
No. 622
Fig. 104.
y
a
a
a
e
c
m
h
No. 774
Fig. 105.
No. 621
Fig. 102.
No. 620
Fig. 101a.
No. 623

EXPLANATION OF PLATE XXI.

FIGURE 106.—Pleurotoma bicarinatum, (p. 638;) natural size.
107.—Bela plicata, (p. 637;) natural size.
108.—Bela harpularia, (p. 636;) natural size.
109.—Anachis similis, (p. 644;) natural size.
110.—Astyris lunata, (p. 645;) enlarged.
111.—Astyris zonalis, (p. 645;) enlarged.
112.—Tritia trivittata, (p. 641;) natural size.
113.—Ilyanassa obsoleta, (p. 641;) natural size.
114.—Nassa vibex, (p. 640;) natural size.
115.—Neptunea pygmæa, (p. 639;) natural size.
116.—Urosalpinx cinerea, (p. 641;) natural size.
117.—Eupleura caudata, (p. 642;) natural size.
118.—Purpura lapillus, (p. 642;) natural size.
119.—The same; banded variety.
120.—The same; egg-capsules, enlarged one-third.
121.—Buccinum undatum, (p. 638;) natural size.
122.—Scalaria multistriata, (p. 660;) enlarged.
123.—Scalaria lineata, (p. 660;) enlarged.

(Figure 120 was drawn from nature by J. H. Emerton; the rest are from Binney's Gould, drawn by E. S. Morse.)

Fig. 107.

Fig. 106.

Fig. 109.

Fig. 111.

Fig. 110.

Fig. 108.

Fig. 112.

Fig. 114.

Fig. 113.

Fig. 118.

Fig. 119.

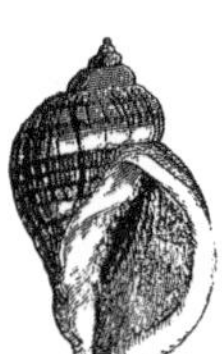

Fig. 120.

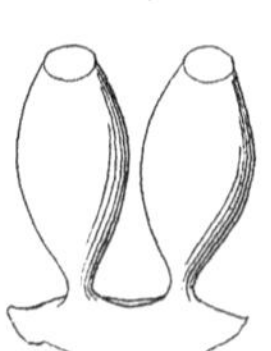

No. 785

Fig. 115.

Fig. 117.

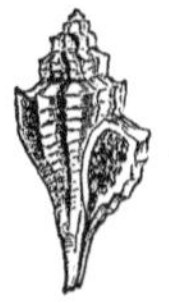

Fig. 116.

Fig. 121.

Fig. 122.

Fig. 123.

EXPLANATION OF PLATE XXII.

FIGURE 124.—Fulgur carica, (p. 640;) natural size.
(From Binney's Gould, drawn by E. S. Morse.)

Fig. 124.

EXPLANATION OF PLATE XXIII.

FIGURE 125.—Crucibulum striatum, (p. 651;) natural size.
126.—The same; side view.
127.—Crepidula plana, (p. 650;) natural size.
128.—C. convexa, (p. 650;) natural size.
129.—C. fornicata, (p. 649;) natural size.
129*a*.—The same; young specimen.
130.—Neverita duplicata, (p. 646;) natural size.
131.—Lunatia immaculata, (p. 646;) natural size.
132.—Natica pusilla, (p. 647;) slightly enlarged.
133.—Lunatia heros, (p. 646;) natural size.
134.—The same; with the animal extended, as in crawling; dorsal view.
135.—The same, variety triseriata, (p. 354;) young, natural size.
136.—The same variety; natural size, lower side.

(From Binney's Gould, drawn by E. S. Morse.)

Fig. 125.

Fig. 126.

Fig. 127.

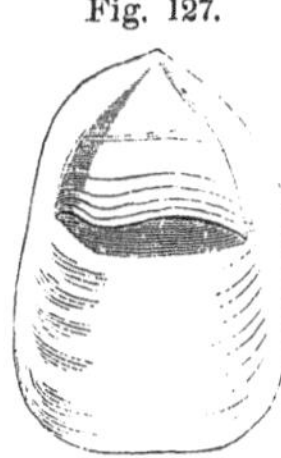

Fig. 128.

Fig. 129a.

Fig. 129.

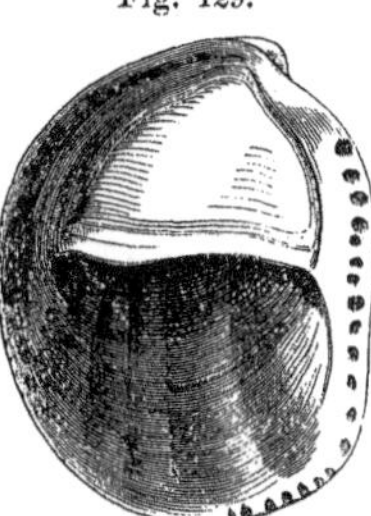

Fig. 130.

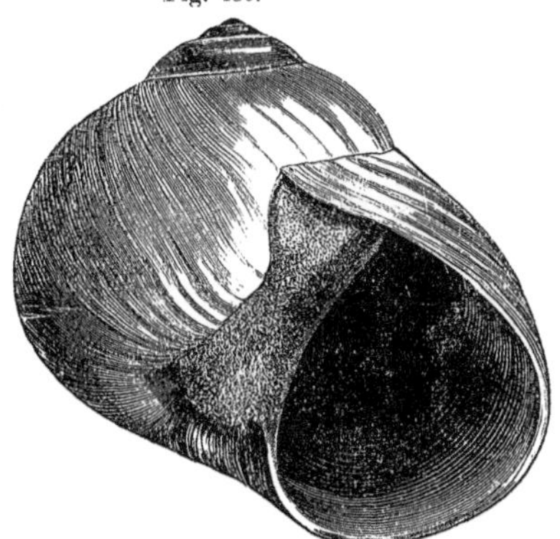

Fig. 131.

Fig. 132.

Fig. 135. Fig. 136.

Fig. 134.

Fig. 133.

EXPLANATION OF PLATE XXIV.

FIGURE 137.—Littorina rudis, (p. 651;) natural size.
138.—Littorina palliata, (p. 652;) natural size.
139.—Lacuna vincta, (p. 652;) enlarged.
140.—Littorinella minuta, (p. 653;) enlarged.
141.—Rissoa aculeus, (p. 654;) enlarged.
142.—Skenea planorbis, (p. 655;) enlarged.
143.—Odostomia producta, (p. 656;) enlarged.
144.—O. fusca, (p. 656;) enlarged.
145.—O. trifida, (p. 656;) enlarged.
146.—O. trifida, var., (p. 656;) enlarged.
147.—O. impressa, (p. 656;) enlarged.
148.—O. seminuda, (p. 657;) enlarged.
149.—Eulima oleacea, (p. 655;) natural size.
150.—Cerithiopsis terebralis, (p. 648;) enlarged.
151.—C. Emersonii, (p. 648;) enlarged.
152.—Triforis nigrocinctus, (p. 648;) enlarged.
153.—Cerithiopsis Greenii, (p. 647;) enlarged.
154.—Bittium nigrum, (p. 648;) enlarged.
155.—Turbonilla elegans, (p. 657;) much enlarged.
156.—Margarita obscura, (p. 661;) natural size.
157.—Vermetus radicula, (p. 649;) natural size.
158.—Cæcum pulchellum, (p. 649;) natural size and enlarged.
159.—Acmæa testudinalis, (p. 661;) natural size.
159*a*.—The same; lower side,
159*b*.—The same, variety alveus; natural size.

(Figure 155 was drawn from nature, by A. E. Verrill; the others are from Binney's Gould, mostly drawn by E. S. Morse.)

Fig. 137. Fig. 138.  Fig. 139.  Fig. 140. 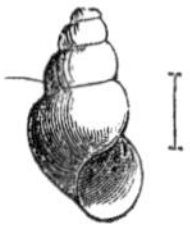 Fig. 141.  Fig. 142.

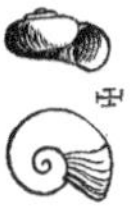

Fig. 143. 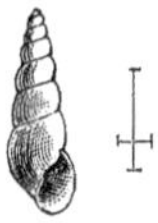 Fig. 144.  Fig. 145.  Fig. 146.  Fig. 147. 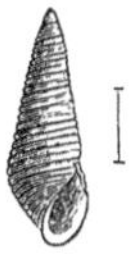 Fig. 148.  Fig. 149.

Fig. 150. 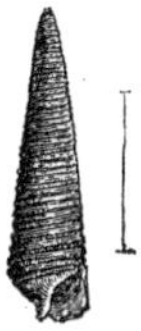 Fig. 151.  Fig. 152.  Fig. 153.  Fig. 154.  Fig. 155.

Fig. 156.

Fig. 157. 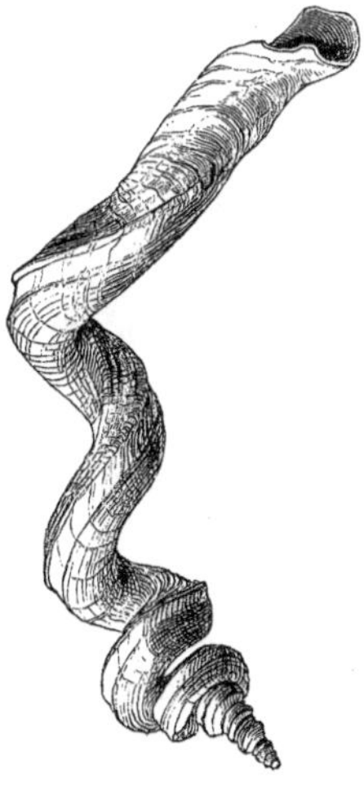 Fig. 158. 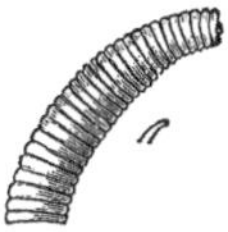 Fig. 159.

Fig. 159*b*.

EXPLANATION OF PLATE XXV.

FIGURE 160.—Utriculus canaliculatus, (p. 663;) enlarged.
161.—Bulla solitaria, (p. 662;) natural size.
162.—Amphisphyra debilis, (p. 663;) enlarged.
163.—Cylichna alba, (p. 664;) natural size.
164.—Cylichna oryza, (p. 664;) enlarged.
165.—Actæon puncto-striata, (p. 664;) enlarged.
166.—Trachydermon ruber, (p. 662;) natural size.
167.—Chætopleura apiculata, (p. 661;) natural size.
168.—Alexia myosotis, (p. 662;) natural size.
169.—Melampus bidentatus, (p. 662;) natural size.
169*a*.—The same; banded variety, (p. 662;) natural size.
170.—Doto coronata, (p. 665;) *a*, dorsal view, enlarged; *b*, head, from above; *c*, one of the branchiæ.
171.—Elysiella catulus, (p. 668;) enlarged three diameters.
172.—Elysia chlorotica, (p. 667;) enlarged two diameters.
173.—Doridella obscura, (p. 664;) *a*, dorsal view; *b*, ventral view, enlarged.
174.—Montagua pilata, (p. 666;) natural size.
175.—Hermæa cruciata, (p. 667;) enlarged.
176.—Doris bifida, (p. 664;) enlarged three diameters.
177.—Cavolina tridentata, (p. 669;) natural size.
178.—Styliola vitrea, (p. 668;) enlarged three diameters.

(Figures 171, 172, 173, 174, 178 were drawn from nature, by A. E. Verrill; 169*a*, 170 by E. S. Morse; 175 by A. Agassiz; 176, by J. H. Emerton; 177 was copied from Cuvier, (last ill. ed.). The rest are from Binney's Gould, mostly by E. S. Morse.)

Plate XXV.

Fig. 160.
Fig. 161.
Fig. 162.
Fig. 163.
Fig. 164.
Fig. 165.
Fig. 166.
Fig. 170.
q
p
Fig. 168.
ig. 169.
Fig. 169a.
Fig. 167.
Fig. 177.
Fig. 178.
Fig. 172.
Fig. 171.
a
Fig. 173.
b
Fig. 176.
a
Fig. 174.
Fig. 175.
No. 766
No. 770

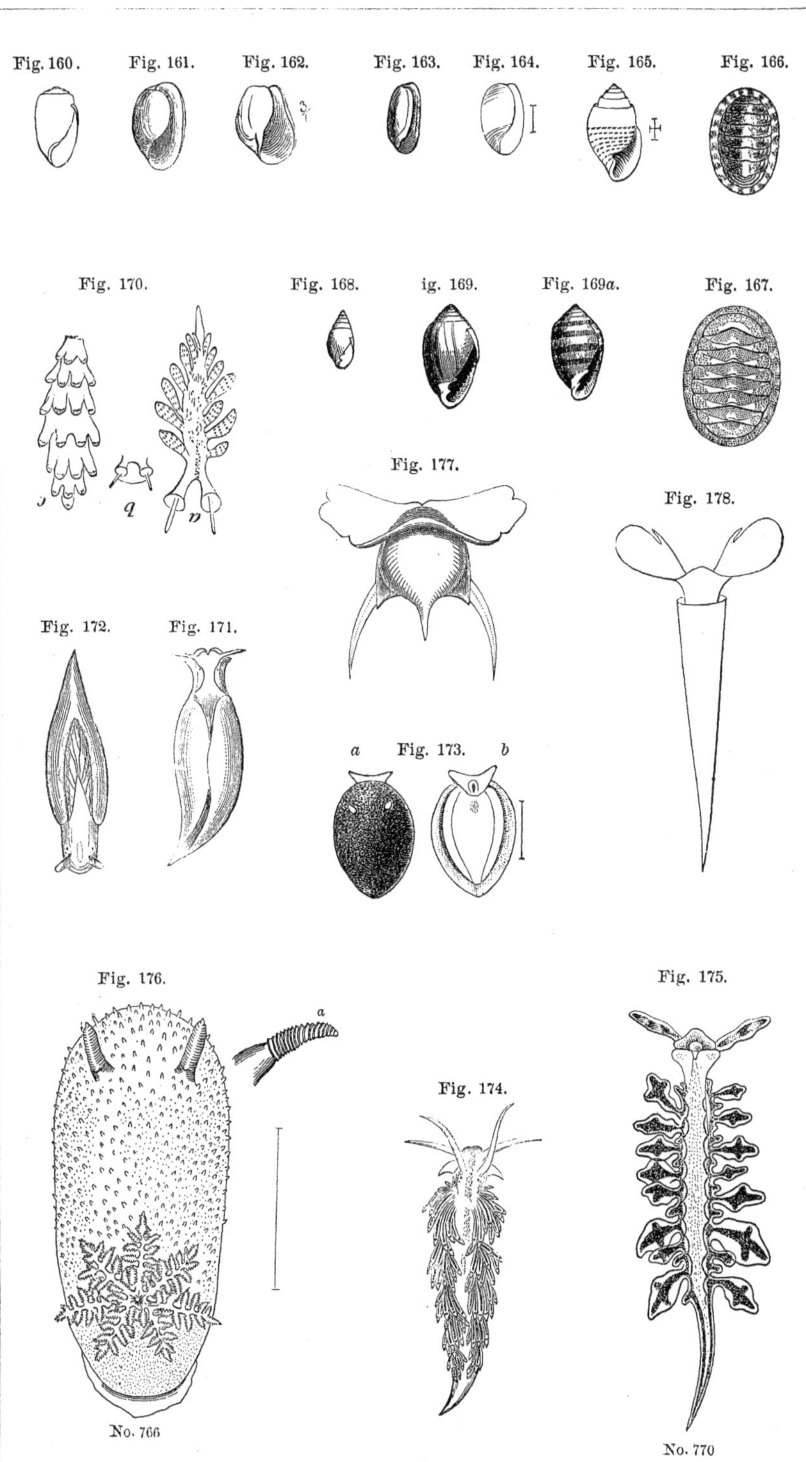

EXPLANATION OF PLATE XXVI.

FIGURE 179.—Mya arenaria, (p. 672;) with animal in extension, reduced to one-half the natural size.

180.—Angulus tener, (p. 677;) animal reduced one-half.

181.—Tagelus gibbus, (p. 675;) with animal, the siphons not fully extended, one-half natural size.

182.—Ensatella Americana, (p. 674;) with animal extended, one-half natural size. The figure at the right shows some of the terminal papillæ enlarged.

183.—Teredo navalis, (p. 669;) enlarged two diameters.

184, A.—Venus mercenaria, (p. 681;) natural size.

184, B.—Mulinia lateralis, (p. 680;) natural size.

(The figures were all drawn from nature, by A. E. Verrill.)

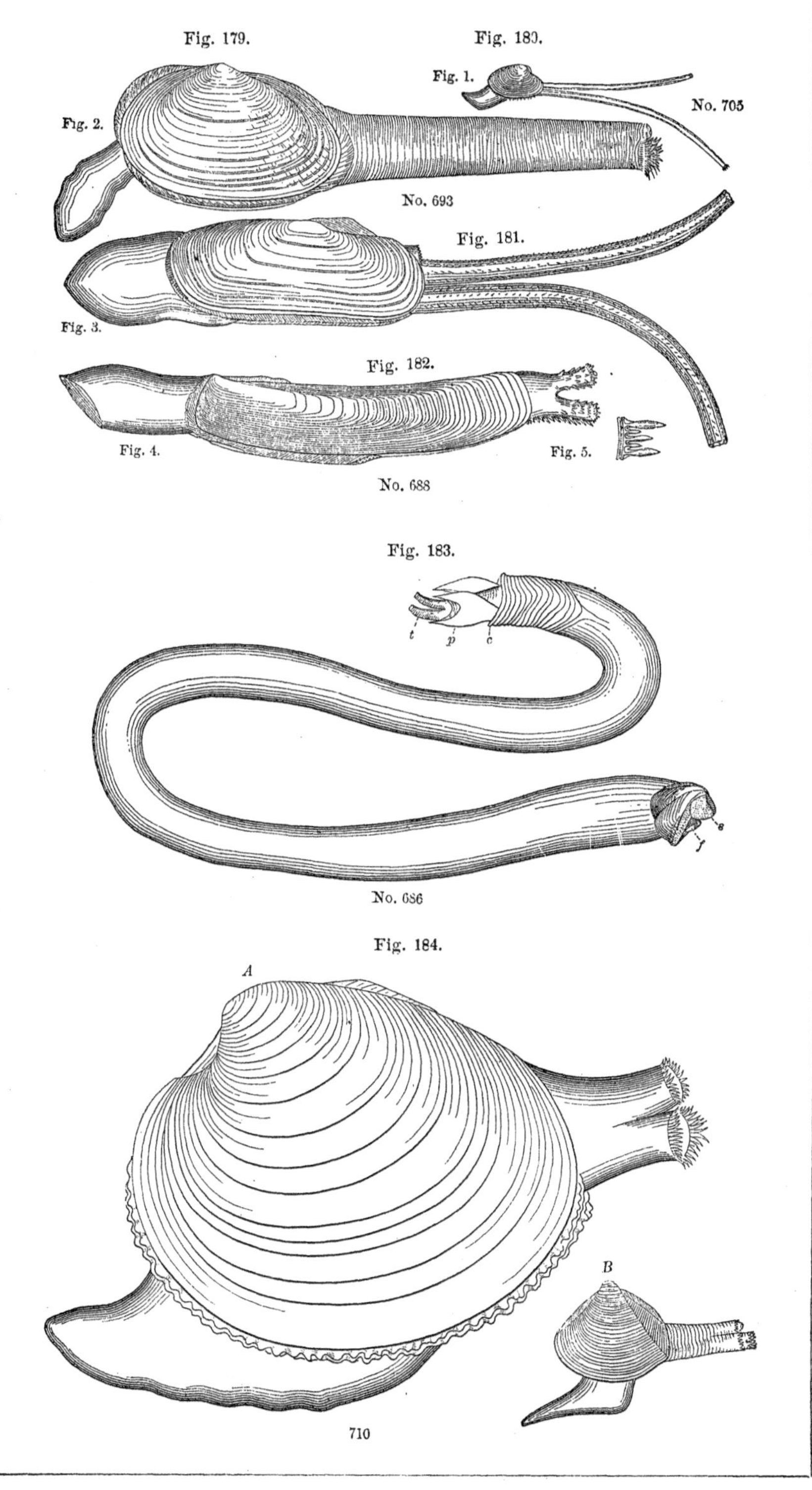
Fig. 179.
Fig. 180.
Fig. 1.
No. 705
Fig. 2.
No. 693
Fig. 181.
Fig. 3.
Fig. 182.
Fig. 4.
Fig. 5.
No. 688
Fig. 183.
t
p
c
s
f
No. 686
Fig. 184.
A
B

EXPLANATION OF PLATE XXVII.

FIGURE 186.—Teredo navalis, (p. 669;) shell and pallets.
187.—Teredo Thomsoni, (p. 670;) shell and pallets.
188.—Teredo megotara, (p. 670;) shell and pallets.
189.—Xylotrya fimbriata, (p. 670;) shell and pallets.
190.—Gastranella tumida, (p. 678;) shell, enlarged six diameters.
191.—Corbula contracta, (p. 672;) natural size.
192.—Saxicava arctica, (p. 671;) natural size.
193.—Clidiophora trilineata, (p. 673;) natural size, with animal.
194.—Lyonsia hyalina, (p. 672;) natural size.
195.—Thracia truncata, (p. 674;) natural size.
196.—Thracia myopsis, (p. 673;) natural size.
197.—Periploma papyracea, (p. 673;) natural size.
198.—Cochlodesma Leanum, (p. 673;) natural size.
199.—Petricola pholadiformis, (p. 680;) natural size.
200.—Pholas truncata, (p. 670;) natural size.

(Figure 190 was drawn by A. E. Verrill; all the rest are from Binney's Gould, mostly drawn by E. S. Morse.)

Plate XXVII.

Fig. 186.
Fig. 187.
Fig. 189.
Fig. 190.
Fig. 188.
Fig. 192.
Fig. 191.
Fig. 195.
Fig. 193.
Fig. 194.
Fig. 196.
Fig. 199.
Fig. 197.
Fig. 200.
Fig. 198.

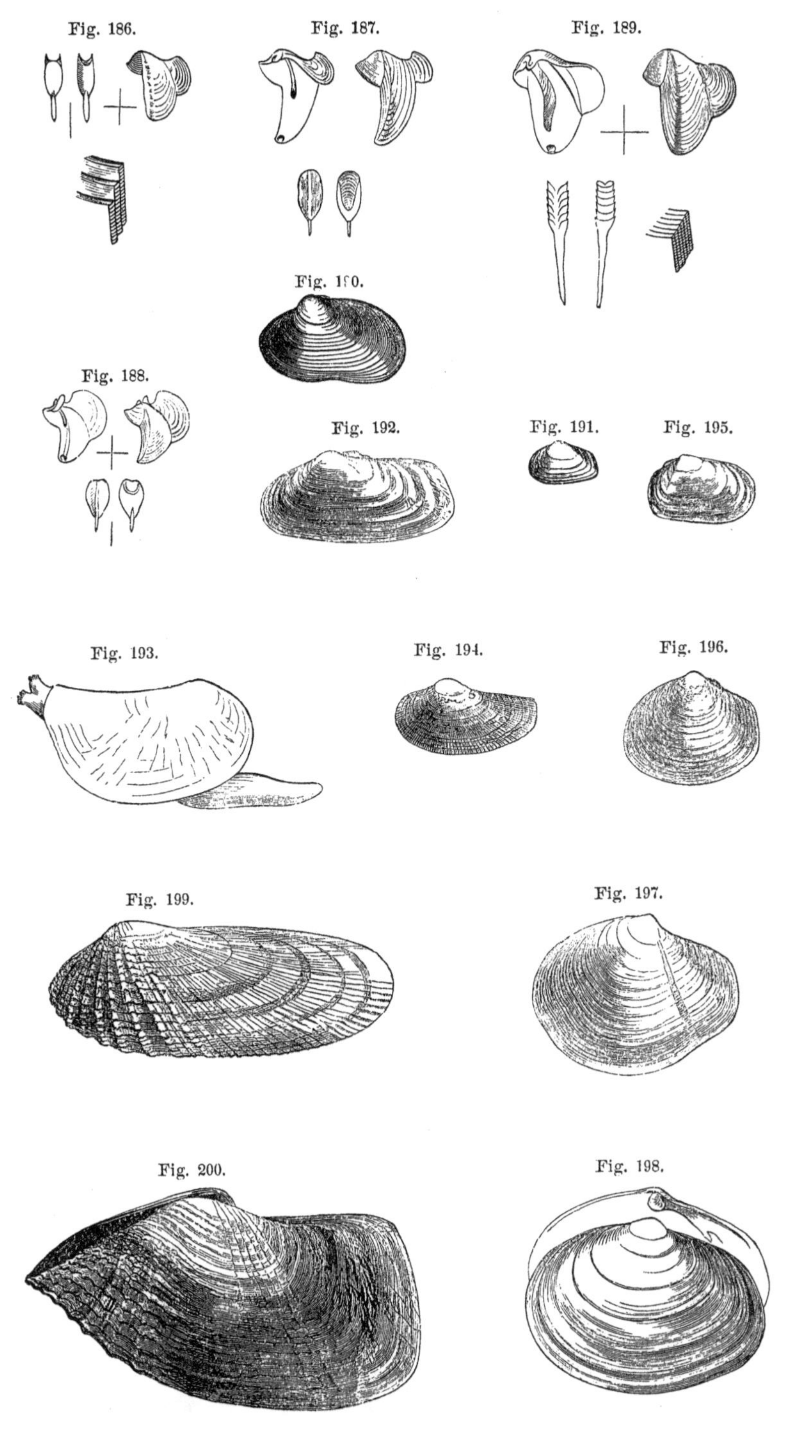

EXPLANATION OF PLATE XXVIII.

FIGURE 201.—Cyprina Islandica, (p. 683;) natural size.
202.—Mactra solidissima, (p. 680;) natural size.

(The figures are both from Binney's Gould, drawn by E. S. Morse.)

Fig 201.

Fig. 202

EXPLANATION OF PLATE XXIX.

FIGURE 203.—Astarte undata, (p. 684;) somewhat reduced.
204.—Astarte castanea, (p. 685;) natural size.
205.—Astarte quadrans, (p. 685;) natural size.
206.—Gouldia mactracea, (p. 685;) natural size.
207.—The same, inside of one valve, enlarged.
208.—Lævicardium Mortoni, (p. 683;) natural size, with animal.
209.—Cardium pinnulatum, (p. 683;) natural size.
210.—Solenomya velum, (p. 688;) natural size.
211.—Cyclas dentata, (p. 686;) natural size.
212.—Lucina filosa, (p. 686;) natural size.
213.—Cryptodon Gouldii, (p. 686;) enlarged two diameters.
214.—Cryptodon obesus, (p. 687;) enlarged three diameters.
215.—Cyclocardia Novangliæ, (p. 684;) natural size.
216.—Cyclocardia borealis, (p. 683;) natural size.

(Figures 203, 207, 214 were drawn by A. E. Verrill; 215 by E. S. Morse; the rest from Binney's Gould, and mostly drawn by E. S. Morse.)

Fig. 203.

Fig. 208.

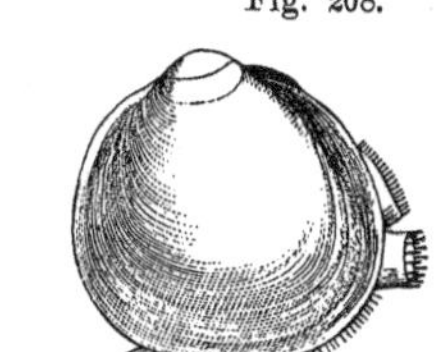

Fig. 210.

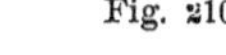

Fig. 204.

Fig. 205.

Fig. 209.

Fig. 211.

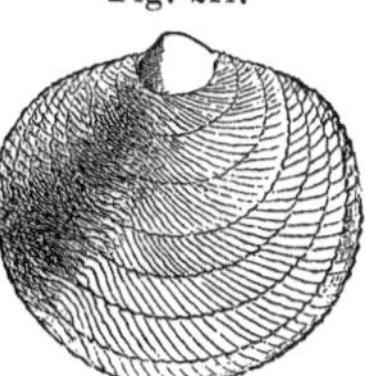

Fig. 207.

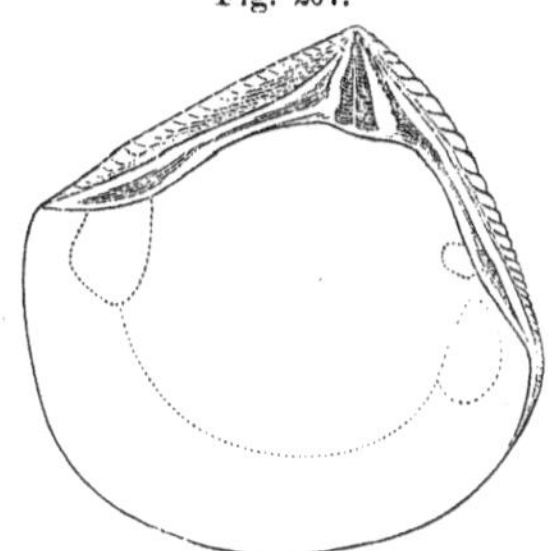

Fig. 206.

Fig. 212.

Fig. 215.

Fig. 213.

Fig. 214.

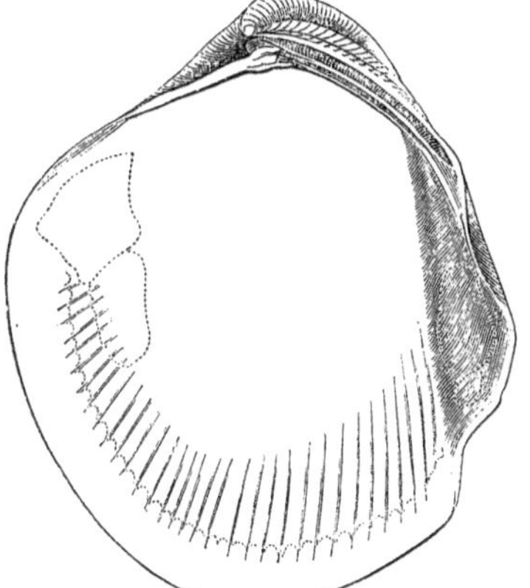

Fig. 216.

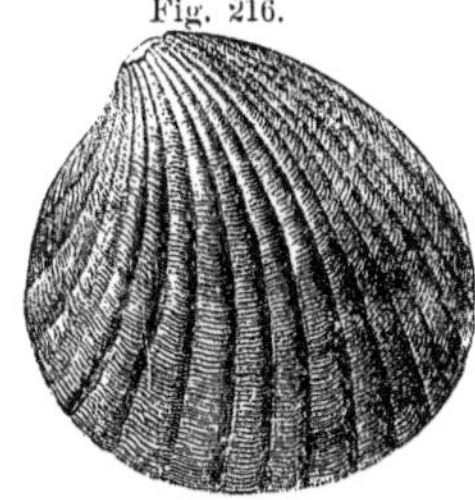

EXPLANATION OF PLATE XXX.

FIGURE 217.—Tagelus gibbus, (p. 675;) natural size.
218.—Tagelus divisus, (p. 676;) natural size.
219.—Callista convexa, (p. 681;) natural size.
220.—Tottenia gemma, (p. 682;) enlarged.
221.—Cumingia tellinoides, (p. 679;) natural size.
222.—Macoma fragilis, var. fusca, (p. 676;) natural size.
223.—Angulus tener, (p. 677;) natural size.
224.—Angulus tenellus, (p. 677;) natural size.
225.—Tellina tenta, (p. 678;) natural size.
226.—Kellia planulata, (p. 688;) enlarged.
227.—Argina pexata, (p. 692;) natural size.
228.—Scapharca transversa, (p. 691;) natural size.
229.—Nucula delphinodonta, (p. 691;) enlarged.
230.—Nucula proxima, (p. 691;) natural size.
231.—Yoldia sapotilla, (p. 689;) natural size.
232.—Yoldia limatula, (p. 689;) natural size.

(Figure 224 was drawn by A. E. Verrill; the rest are from Binney's Gould, by E. S. Morse.)

Fig 217.

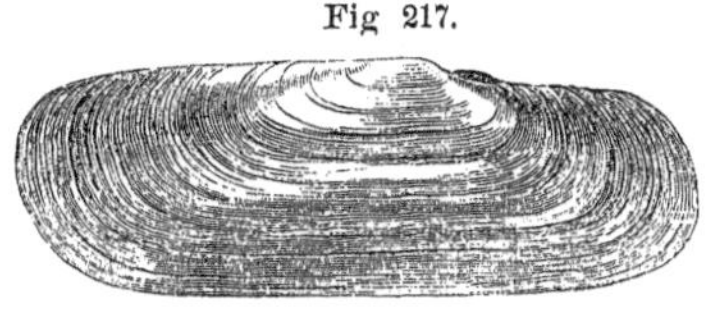

Fig. 218.

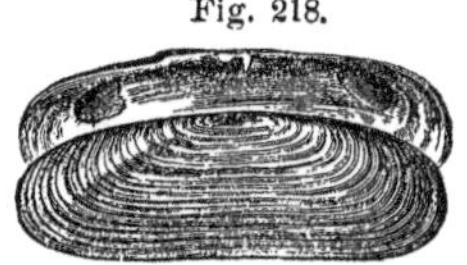

Fig. 219.

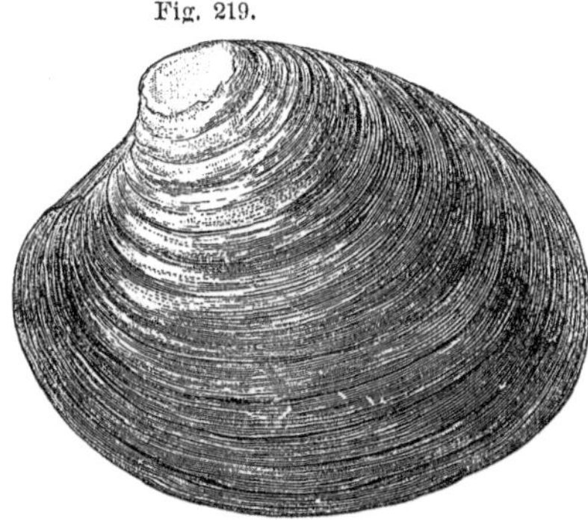

Fig. 220.

Fig. 221

Fig. 222.

Fig. 227.

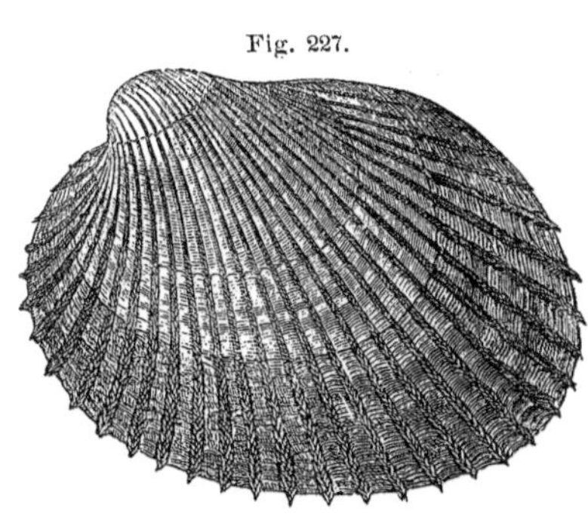

Fig. 224.

Fig. 223.

Fig. 229.

Fig. 230.

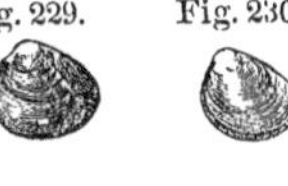

Fig. 225.

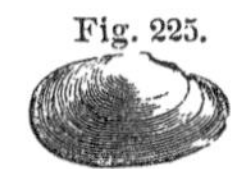

Fig. 231.

Fig. 226.

Fig. 228.

Fig. 232.

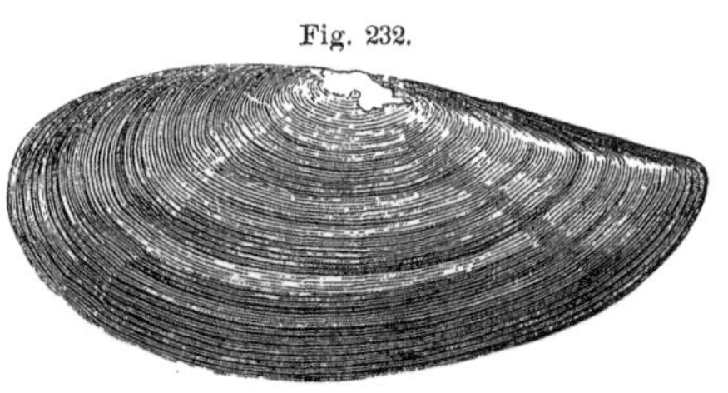

EXPLANATION OF PLATE XXXI.

FIGURE 233.—Crenella glandula, (p. 695.)
234.—Mytilus edulis, (p. 692.)
235.—Modiolaria corrugata, (p. 694.)
236.—Modiolaria nigra, (p. 694.)
237.—Modiola modiolus, (p. 693.)
238.—Modiola plicatula, (p. 693.)

(All the figures are of natural size, and from Binney's Gould, drawn by E. S. Morse.)

Plate XXXI.

Fig. 233.

Fig 234.

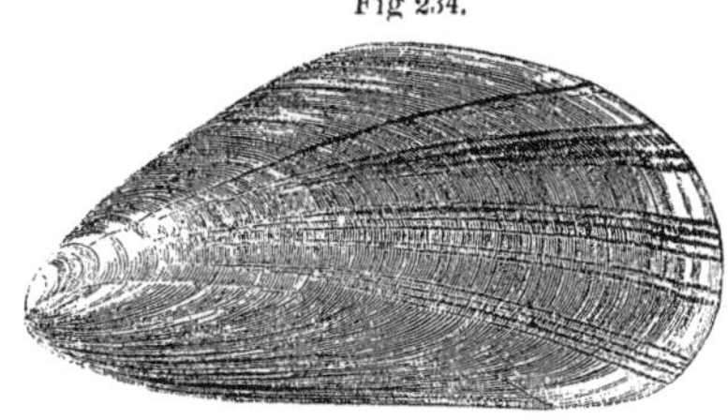

Fig. 235.

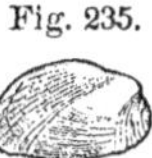

Fig. 236.

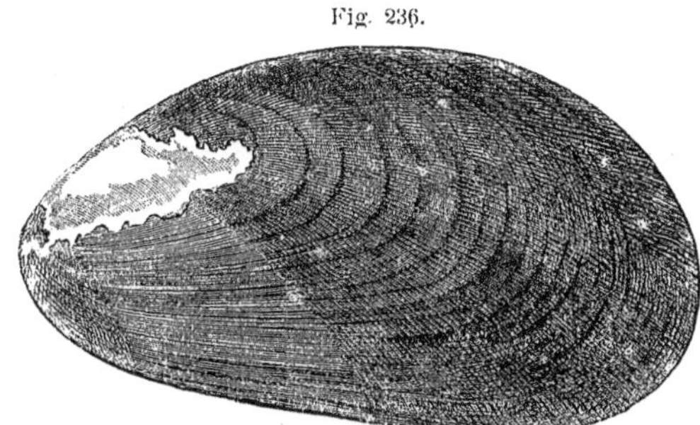

Fig. 237.

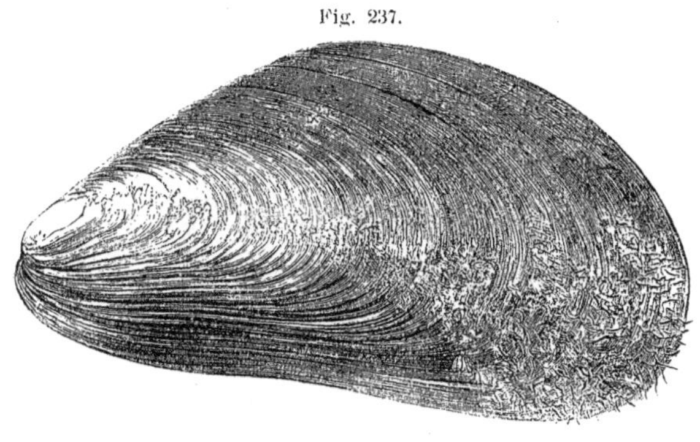

Fig. 238.

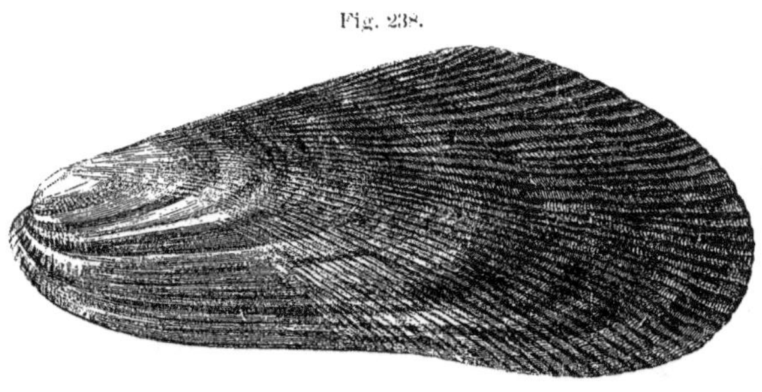

EXPLANATION OF PLATE XXXII.

FIGURE 239.—Anomia aculeata, (p. 697;) lower side, natural size.
240.—The same, upper side.
240*a*.—The same, portions of the upper side magnified.
241.—Anomia glabra, (p. 696;) profile view, natural size.
242.—The same, (p. 696;) lower side.
242*a*.—The same, (p. 696;) young, natural size.
243.—Pecten irradians, (p. 695;) natural size.
244.—Siliqua costata, (p. 675;) natural size.
245.—Ensatella Americana, (p. 674;) natural size.

(The figures are from Binney's Gould, drawn by E. S. Morse.)

Plate XXXII.

Fig. 239.

Fig. 240.

Fig. 244.

Fig. 241.

Fig. 242*a*.

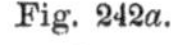

Fig. 240*a*.

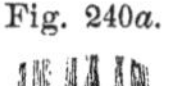

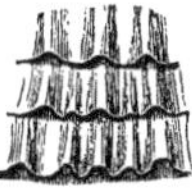

Fig. 242.

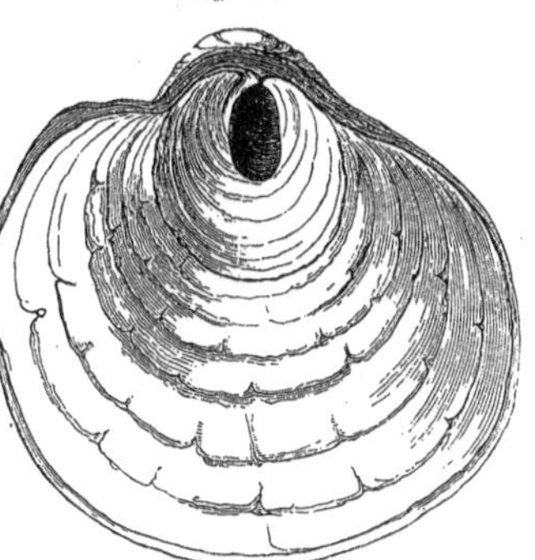

Fig. 245.

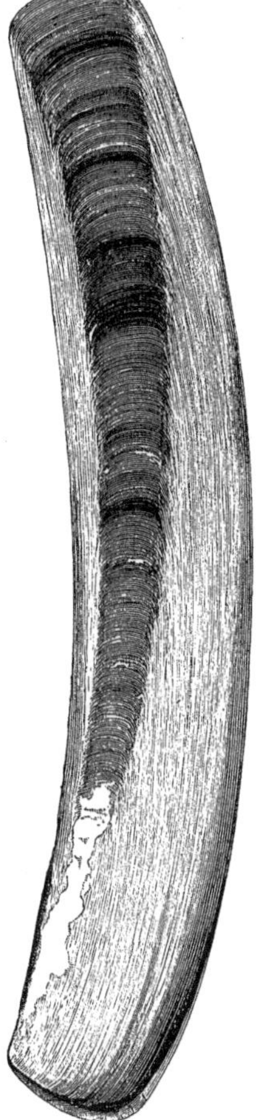

Fig. 243.

EXPLANATION OF PLATE XXXIII.

FIGURE 246.—Cynthia partita, variety stellifera, (p. 701;) natural size.

247.—Cynthia carnea, (p. 701;) natural size.

248.—The same, (p. 701;) younger specimens, natural size.

249.—Eugyra pilularis, (p. 700;) natural size.

250.—Molgula Manhattensis, (p. 699;) smooth variety, natural size.

251.—Molgula arenata, (p. 699;) natural size.

252.—Botryllus Gouldii, (p. 702;) colony incrusting the stem of Tubularia, somewhat enlarged.

253.—The same; one of the zoöids, enlarged ten diameters; *a*, anal tube and orifice; *s*, somach; *g*, groove and vessels along the edge of the branchial sac, inside; *o*, left ovary; *b*, bud, attached by a slender stolon.

254.—Salpa Cabotti, (p. 706;) solitary individual, from the dorsal side, enlarged; *h*, heart; *s*, small chain of salpæ budding within the old one.

255.—The same; one of the individuals from a mature chain, three-quarter view enlarged; *a*, posterior or anal opening; *b*, anterior or branchial opening; *c*, processes by which the individuals of the chain were united; *h*, heart; *n*, nervous ganglion; *o*, nucleus; *r*, gill.

256.—Escharella variabilis, (p. 713;) few of the cells, much enlarged.

(Figure 256 was drawn by A. Hyatt; 254 and 255 were copied from A. Agassiz; the others were drawn by A. E. Verrill.)

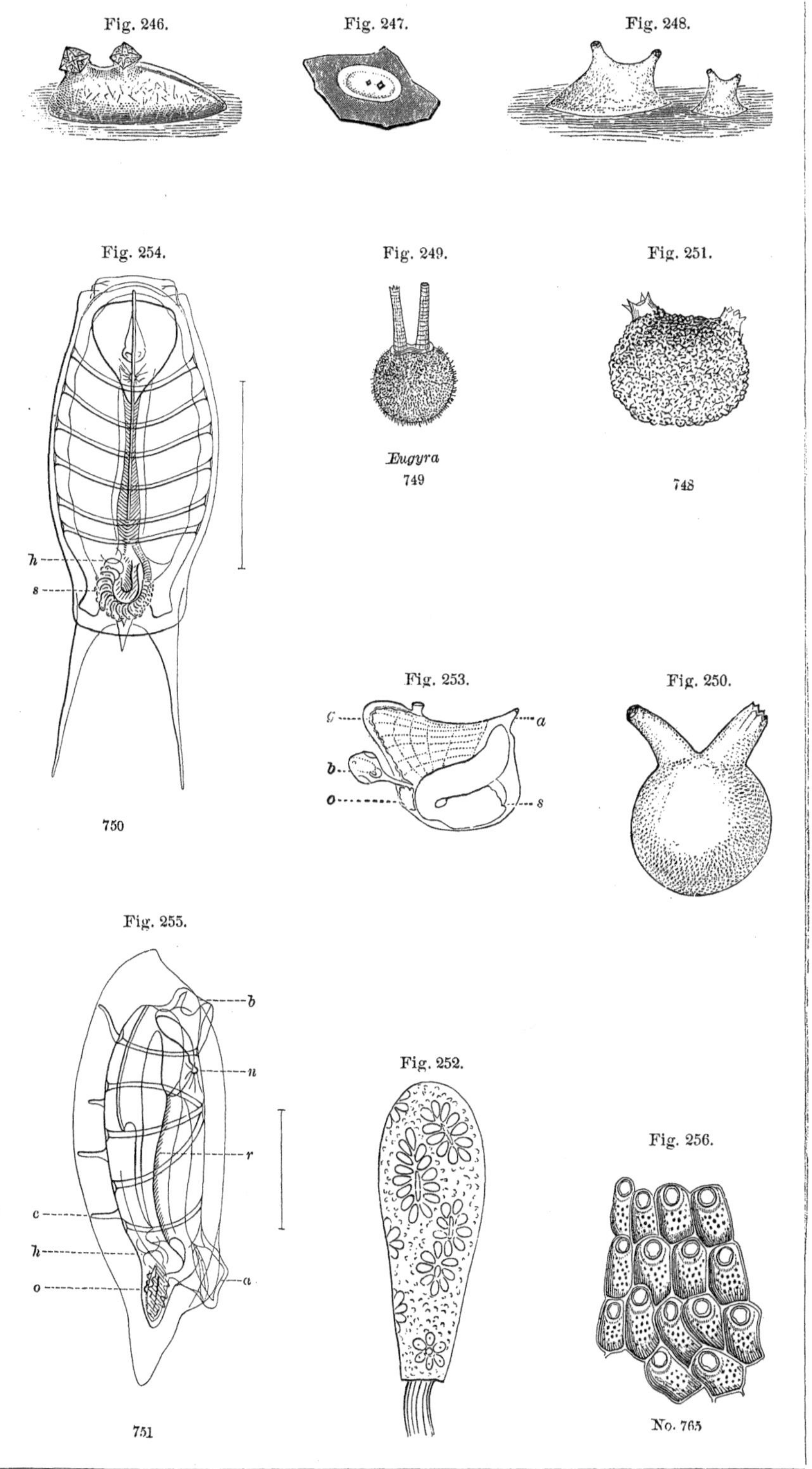
Fig. 246.
Fig. 247.
Fig. 248.
Fig. 254.
Fig. 249.
Fig. 251.
h
s
Eugyra
749
748
750
Fig. 253.
Fig. 250.
c
a
b
o
s
Fig. 255.
b
n
r
c
h
o
a
Fig. 252.
Fig. 256.
751
No. 765

EXPLANATION OF PLATE XXXIV.

FIGURE 257.—Alcyonidium ramosum, (p. 708;) a young unbranched specimen, enlarged two diameters.

258.—Bugula turrita, (p. 712;) extremity of a branch, enlarged.

259.—The same; a branchlet more highly magnified.

259*a*.—The same; a branchlet bearing ovicells.

260.—Crisia eburnea, (p. 707;) a cluster of branches, enlarged.

261.—The same; a branch bearing an ovicell, more highly magnified.

262.—Membranipora pilosa, (p. 712;) a few of the cells, seen from above, magnified.

262*a*.—The same; a single cell, seen in profile.

263.—The same; one of the zoöids expanded.

264.—Mollia hyalina, (p. 713;) one of the zoöids in expansion, highly magnified.

(Figures 257, 259, 259*a* were drawn by A. E. Verrill; the rest were furnished by A. Hyatt.)

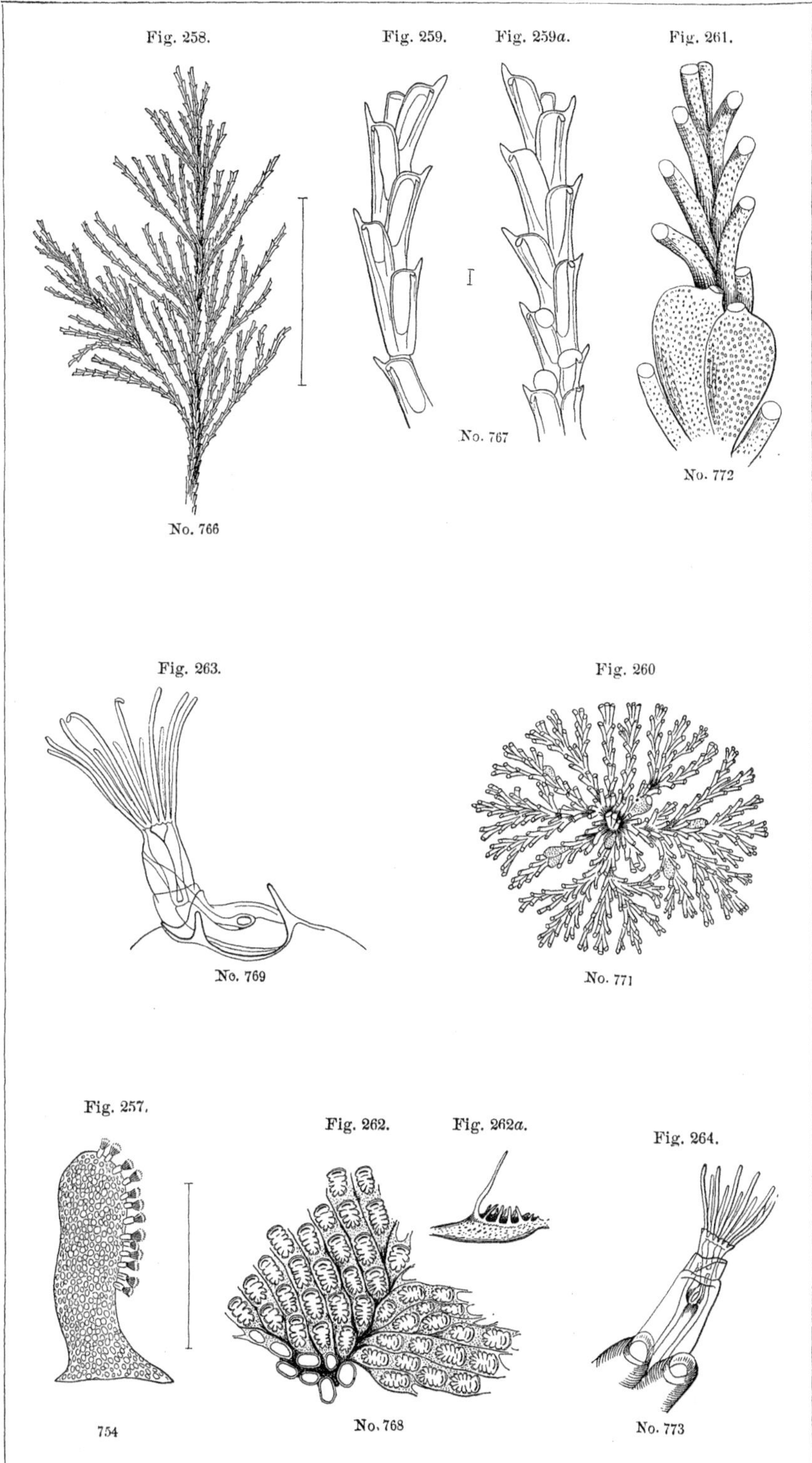
Fig. 258.
No. 766
Fig. 259.
Fig. 259a.
No. 767
Fig. 261.
No. 772
Fig. 263.
No. 769
Fig. 260
No. 771
Fig. 257.
754
Fig. 262.
Fig. 262a.
No. 768
Fig. 264.
No. 773

EXPLANATION OF PLATE XXXV.

FIGURE 265.—Leptosynapta Girardii, (p. 716;) anterior part of the body, enlarged one-half.

266.—The same; perforated plates from the skin, and the "anchors," highly magnified.

267.—Echinarachnius parma, (p. 717;) upper surface with the spines partly removed, natural size; *a*, ambulacral zones; *b*, interambulacral zones.

268.—Strongylocentrotus Dröbachiensis, (p. 716;) side view, natural size.

269.—Asterias arenicola, (p. 718;) dorsal view, somewhat reduced.

270.—Ophiopholis aculeata, (p. 719;) dorsal view, about one-half natural size

(Figures 265, 266 were drawn by A. E. Verrill; 267, 269 were copied from A. Agassiz; 268, 270 were drawn by E. S. Morse.)

Fig. 267.

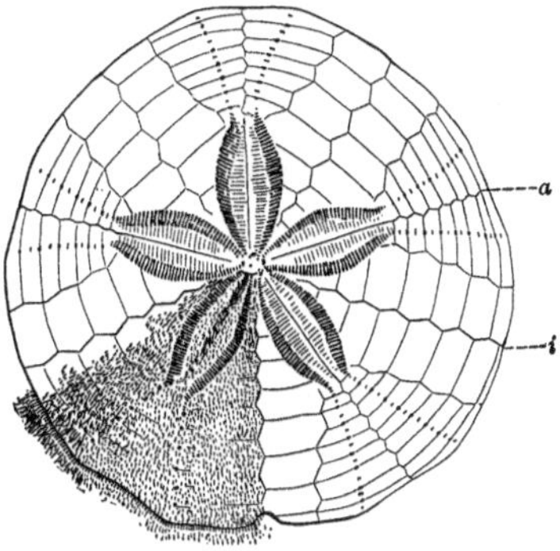

a

i

617

Fig. 270.

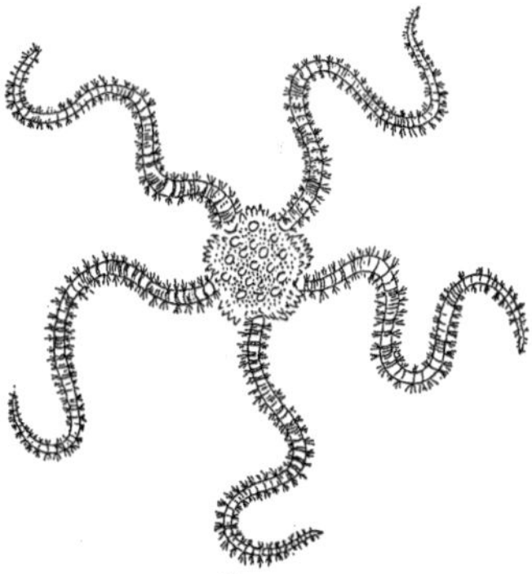

No. 615

Fig. 269.

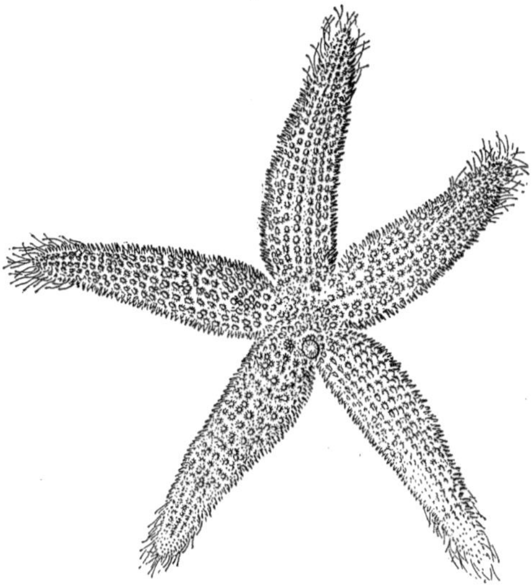

616

Fig. 265.

618

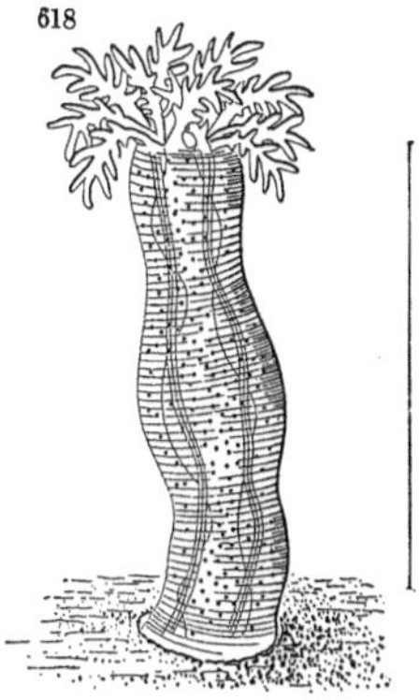

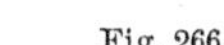

Fig. 266.

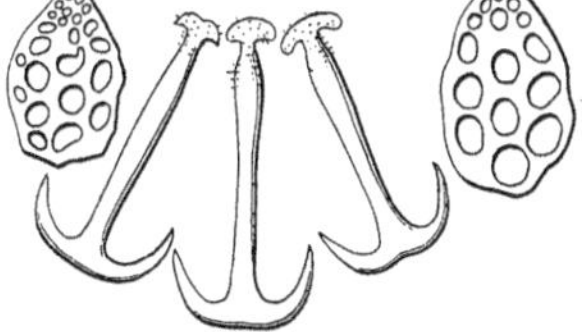

Fig. 268.

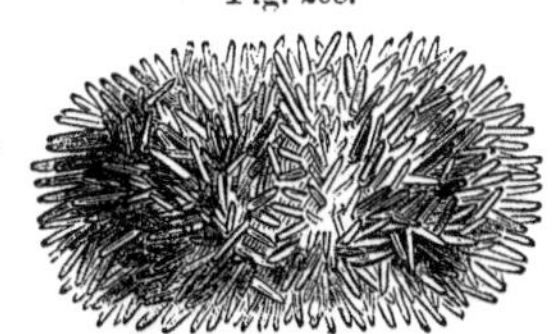

EXPLANATION OF PLATE XXXVI.

FIGURE 271.—Aurelia flavidula, (p. 723;) upper side, about one-fourth the natural size.

272.—Dactylometra quinquecirra, (p. 724;) lateral view, one-fourth the natural size.

273.—Corymorpha pendula, (p. 736;) natural size.

274.—Parypha crocea, (p. 736;) natural size.

(Figure 272 was copied from A. Agassiz, Catalogue Acalephs; the others were copied from L. Agassiz, Contributions to Natural History of United States.)

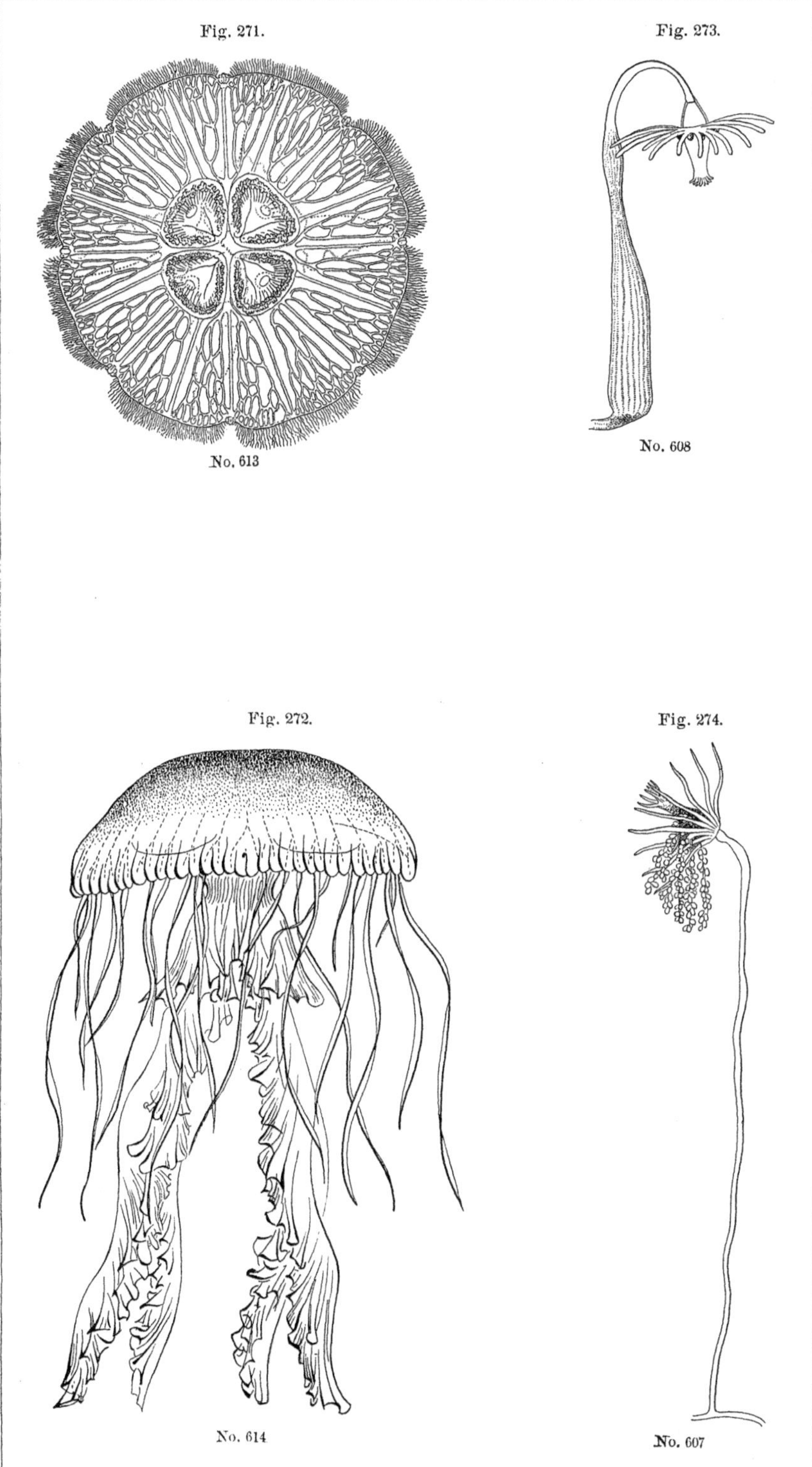
Fig. 271.
No. 613
Fig. 273.
No. 608
Fig. 272.
No. 614
Fig. 274.
No. 607